www.wadsworth.com

www.wadsworth.com is the World Wide Web site for Wadsworth and is your direct source to dozens of online resources.

At *www.wadsworth.com* you can find out about supplements, demonstration software, and student resources. You can also send email to many of our authors and preview new publications and exciting new technologies.

www.wadsworth.com
Changing the way the world learns[®]

UNDERSTANDING ARGUMENTS

An Introduction to Informal Logic

SEVENTH EDITION

ROBERT J. FOGELIN
Dartmouth College

WALTER SINNOTT-ARMSTRONG
Dartmouth College

THOMSON
™
WADSWORTH

Australia • Canada • Mexico • Singapore • Spain
United Kingdom • United States

THOMSON
WADSWORTH

PUBLISHER: Holly J. Allen
PHILOSOPHY EDITOR: Steve Wainwright
ASSISTANT EDITORS: Lee McCracken, Anna Lustig
EDITORIAL ASSISTANT: Barbara Hillaker
MARKETING MANAGER: Worth Hawes
MARKETING ASSISTANT: Andrew Keay
PROJECT MANAGER, EDITORIAL PRODUCTION: Rita Jaramillo
ART DIRECTOR: Robert Hugel

PRINT/MEDIA BUYER: Doreen Suruki
PERMISSIONS EDITOR: Sarah Harkrader
PRODUCTION: Mary Douglas, Rogue Valley Publications
COPY EDITOR: Susan Defossett
COVER DESIGNER: Yvo Riezebos
COVER PRINTER: Phoenix Color Corp.
COMPOSITOR: Better Graphics
PRINTER: Transcontinental

For more information about our products, contact us at:
Thomson Learning Academic Resource Center
1-800-423-0563

For permission to use material from this text or product, submit a request online at
http://www.thomsonrights.com.
Any additional questions about permissions can be submitted by email to
thomsonrights@thomson.com.

Library of Congress Control Number: 2004105766
ISBN-13: 978-0-534-62586-3
ISBN-10: 0-534-62586-X

Thomson Wadsworth
10 Davis Drive
Belmont, CA 94002-3098
USA

Asia
Thomson Learning
5 Shenton Way #01-01
UIC Building
Singapore 068808

Australia/New Zealand
Thomson Learning
102 Dodds Street
Southbank, Victoria 3006
Australia

Canada
Nelson
1120 Birchmount Road
Toronto, Ontario M1K 5G4
Canada

Europe/Middle East/Africa
Thomson Learning
High Holborn House
50/51 Bedford Row
London WC1R 4LR
United Kingdom

Latin America
Thomson Learning
Seneca, 53
Colonia Polanco
11560 Mexico D.F.
Mexico

Spain/Portugal
Paraninfo
Calle Magallanes, 25
28015 Madrid, Spain

To Eric, John, Lars, Miranda, and Nicholas
and the colleges of their choice

An argument isn't just contradiction.

Can be.

No it can't. An argument is a connected series of statements
intended to establish a proposition.

No it isn't.

Yes it is.

Argument Clinic, From MONTY PYTHON'S PREVIOUS RECORD

——————————■——————————

CONTENTS

CHAPTER 13
USES OF ARGUMENTS   405

PART II   AREAS OF ARGUMENTATION   433

CHAPTER 14
LEGAL REASONING   435

CHAPTER 15
MORAL REASONING   483

Traditionally, logic has been considered the most general science dealing with arguments. The task of logic is to discover the fundamental principles for distinguishing good arguments from bad ones.

For certain purposes, arguments are best studied as abstract patterns of reasoning. Logic can then focus on these general forms rather than on particular arguments, such as your attempt to prove to the bank that they, not you, made a mistake. The study of those general principles that make certain patterns of argument reasonable (or valid) and other patterns of argument unreasonable (or invalid) is called *formal logic*. Three chapters of this work are dedicated to formal logic.

A different but complementary way of viewing an argument is to treat it as a particular use of language: Presenting arguments is one of the important things we do with words. This approach stresses that arguing is a linguistic activity. Instead of studying arguments as abstract patterns, it examines them as they occur in concrete settings. It raises questions of the following kind:

What is the place of argument within language as a whole?

What words or phrases are characteristic of arguments?

How do these words function?

What task or tasks are arguments supposed to perform?

When an approach to argument has this emphasis, the study is called *informal logic*. Though it contains a substantial treatment of formal logic, *Understanding Arguments*, as its subtitle indicates, is primarily a textbook in informal logic.

The seventh edition of *Understanding Arguments* differs from the sixth edition in a number of significant ways. The examination of rhetorical devices and evaluative language is presented in a more systematic form in a new Chapter 2. Many arguments, perhaps most arguments, are concerned with questions of value—whether actions are right or wrong, things are good or bad, and so on. It is important, then, to understand how evaluative judgments function and how arguments can be used to establish or reject them. It is also important to recognize that rhetorical devices often play a central role in the presentation of arguments. Relying on the notion of conversational implication presented in Chapter 1, Chapter 2 explains the functions of such devices as rhetorical questions, understatement, overstatement, irony, and, most importantly, metaphors. This lays the foundation for distinguishing between proper and improper uses of such devices.

This edition also contains a new chapter, Chapter 17, on religious reasoning. The readings in this chapter focus on the main arguments for and against the existence of God. They illustrate the variety of religious arguments as well as their importance.

This edition includes a large-scale updating of examples, exercises, and discussion questions throughout the text. Most notable are new selections from the recent Michigan affirmative action cases in Chapter 14 on legal reasoning, new readings on evolution and creationism in Chapter 16 on scientific reasoning, and new mysteries for deep analysis in Chapter 5.

On more technical issues, we include a new and more accessible discussion of necessary and sufficient conditions in Chapter 6 on propositional logic. New diagrams clarify concepts for deep analysis in Chapter 5, for statistical syllogisms in Chapter 9 on induction, and for Bayes's theorem in Chapter 10 on probability. These class-tested diagrams have proved successful in getting across these difficult notions.

This new edition has been influenced by our teaching of this material with various colleagues, including visitors, at Dartmouth College. In this regard, we would especially like to thank Jillian Craigie, Catherine Driscoll, Jon Ellis, Jack Hanson, Sam Levey, and Christie Thomas, in addition to the many others who helped us on previous editions. We are also indebted to the following reviewers: Matthew W. McKeon, Michigan State University; Sharon Bishop, California State University, Los Angeles; Thomas C. Carroll, Jr., Saddleback College; and Greg Tropea, California State University, Chico. At Thomson Higher Education, we received expert advice and assistance from Lee McCracken, Rita Jaramillo, Mary Douglas, and Susan Defosset. Finally, we owe a great debt of thanks to Bill Fontaine (librarian), Kier Olsen DeVries (research assistant and editor), Andrew Verstein (student research assistant), and Florence Fogelin. Without all of these people, this book would contain many more mistakes than it undoubtedly does.

Robert J. Fogelin
Walter Sinnott-Armstrong

The Analysis of Argument

The Web of Language

Because presenting an argument is something that we do using language, this chapter will examine some of the basic features of language. In doing so, it will stress three main ideas. First, language is conventional. *Words acquire meaning within a rich system of linguistic conventions or rules. Second, the uses of language are* diverse. *We use language to communicate information, but we also use it to ask questions, issue orders, write poetry, keep score, formulate arguments, and perform an almost endless number of other tasks. Third, meaning is often conveyed* indirectly. *To understand the significance of many utterances, we must go beyond what is literally said to examine what is conversationally implied by saying it.*

LANGUAGE AND ARGUMENT

Logic is the general science of argument: Its goal is to lay down principles for distinguishing good arguments from bad arguments. The word "argument" may suggest quarrels or squabbles, but here it is used in the broader, logician's sense of *giving reasons* for or against some claim. Viewing arguments this way, we see that they are a common feature of daily life, for we are often involved in giving reasons for things we believe or in evaluating reasons given by others for things they want us to believe. Trying to decide which way to vote in an election, what play to use on third down and long, where to go to college, whether to support or oppose capital punishment—all involve weighing and evaluating reasons.

Arguing is also an activity—in particular, a *linguistic* activity. Arguing is one of the many things we can do with words. In fact, unlike things that we can accomplish both with words and without words (like making people happy, angry, and so forth), arguing is something we can *only* do with words. To understand how arguments work, it is thus important to understand how language works. Unfortunately, our understanding of human language is far from complete, and linguistics is a young science in which disagreement exists on many important issues. Still, certain facts about language are beyond dispute, and recognizing them will provide a background for understanding how arguments work.

4

LANGUAGE AND CONVENTION

As everyone who has bothered to think about it knows, language is conventional. There seems to be no reason why we, as English speakers, use the word "dog" to refer to a dog rather than to a cat, a tree, or anything else. It seems that any word might have been used to stand for anything. Beyond this, there seems to be no reason why we put words together the way we do. In English, we put adjectives before the nouns they modify. We thus speak of a "green salad." In French, adjectives usually follow the noun, and so instead of saying "verte salade," the French say "salade verte." The conventions of our own language are so much with us that it strikes us as odd when we discover that other languages have different conventions. A French diplomat once praised his own language because, as he said, it followed the natural order of thought. This strikes English speakers as silly, but in seeing why it is silly, we see that the word order in our own language is conventional as well.

Although it is important to realize that our language is conventional, it is also important not to misunderstand this fact and draw false conclusions from it. From the idea that language is conventional, it is easy to conclude that language is totally arbitrary. If language is totally arbitrary, then it might seem that it really does not matter which words we use or how we put them together. It takes only a little thought to see that this view, however daring it might seem, misrepresents the role of conventions in language. If we wish to communicate with others, we must follow the system of conventions that others use. Communication can only take place from within a shared system of conventions. Conventions do not destroy meaning by making it arbitrary; conventions bring meaning into existence.

A misunderstanding of the conventional nature of language can lead to pointless disputes. Sometimes, in the middle of a discussion, someone will declare that "the whole thing is just a matter of definition" or "what you say is true by your definition, false by mine." There are times when definitions are important and the truth of what is said turns on them, but usually this is not the case. Suppose someone has fallen off a cliff and is heading toward certain death on the rocks below. Of course, it is a matter of convention that we use the word "death" to describe the result of the sudden, sharp stop at the end of the fall. We might have used some other word—perhaps "birth"—instead. But it certainly will not help a person who is falling to his certain death to shout out, "By 'birth' I mean death." It will not help even if *everyone* agrees to use these words in this new way. If we all decided to adopt this new convention, we would then say, "He is falling from the cliff to his certain birth" instead of "He is falling from the cliff to his certain death." But speaking in this way will not change the facts. It will not save him from perishing. It will not make those who care for him feel better.

The upshot of this simple example is that the truth of what we say is rarely just a matter of definition. Whether what we have said is true or not will depend, for the most part, on how things stand in the world. For example, if Germans wish to say that snow is black, they will use the words, "Der

Schnee ist schwartz." Other Germans will *understand* these words, but unless snow is different in Germany than everywhere else, they will also think that what is being said is false. In general, then, though the *meaning of* what we say is dependent on convention, the *truth* of what we say is not.

In the last sentence we used the qualifying phrase, "in general." To say that a claim holds *in general* indicates that there may be exceptions. This qualification is needed because sometimes the truth of what we say *is* simply a matter of definition. Take a simple example: The claim that a triangle has three sides is true by definition, because a triangle is defined as "a closed figure having three sides." Again, if someone says that sin is wrong, he or she has said something that is true by definition, for a sin is defined as, among other things, "something that is wrong."

In sum, people are able to communicate with each other because they share certain linguistic conventions. These conventions could have been different, and in this sense they are arbitrary. But it does not follow from this that the truth of what we say is always just a matter of convention. Sometimes things are true just as a matter of convention; however, in general, the truth of what we say is settled not by definition but by looking at the facts.

LINGUISTIC ACTS

In the previous section we saw that a language is a system of shared conventions that allows us to communicate with one another. If we examine language, we will see that it contains many different kinds of conventions. These conventions govern what we will call linguistic acts, speech acts, and conversational acts. We will discuss linguistic acts first.

We have seen that words have meanings conventionally attached to them. The word "dog" is used conventionally to talk about dogs. Proper names are also conventionally assigned, for Harry Jones could have been named Wilbur Jones. Other conventions concern the ways words can be put together to form sentences; these are often called *grammatical* rules. Using the three words "John," "hit," and "Harry," we can formulate sentences with very different meanings. For example, "John hit Harry" and "Harry hit John." We recognize that these sentences have different meanings because we understand the grammar of our language. This grammatical understanding also allows us to see that the sentence "Hit John Harry" has no determinate meaning, even though the individual words do. (Notice that "Hit John, Harry!" *does* mean something: it is a way of telling Harry to hit John.) Grammatical rules are important, for they play a part in giving a meaning to combinations of words such as sentences.

Some of our grammatical rules play only a small role in this important task of giving meaning to combinations of words. It is bad grammar to say, "If I was you, I wouldn't do that," but it is still clear what information the person is trying to convey. It is also bad grammar to say, "Everyone took their seats" as a way of saying, "Everyone took his or her seat," but the former way of speaking is now often used as a way of being gender neutral. What might be called stylistic rules of grammar are of relatively little importance for logic, but grammatical rules that affect the meaning or content of what is said are essential to logical analysis. Grammatical rules of this kind can determine whether we have said one thing rather than another, or perhaps failed to say anything at all and have merely spoken nonsense.

Thus, at least two kinds of conventions give meaning to what we say. The ones that assign meanings to individual words are commonly called *semantic* conventions. The conventions that lay down rules for combining words into meaningful wholes are called *grammatical* or *syntactical* conventions. When essential semantic and syntactic conventions are satisfied, we will say that we have performed a *linguistic act*: we have said something meaningful in a language.[1] The ability to perform linguistic acts shows a command of a language. What the person says may be false, irrelevant, boring, and so on, but if in saying it linguistic rules are not seriously violated, that person can be credited with performing a linguistic act.

DISCUSSION QUESTIONS

1. When someone hums the *Star Spangled Banner*, does she perform a linguistic act? Why or why not?

2. Can a speaker mispronounce a word in a sentence without performing a linguistic act? Why or why not?

3. Lewis Carroll's poem "Jabberwocky" begins with this stanza:

   `Twas brillig, and the slithy toves
   Did gyre and gimble in the wabe:
   All mimsy were the borogoves,
   And the mome raths outgrabe.

   If someone recites this poem out loud, has the person performed a linguistic act? (As a start, you might run a spell-check on the passage.)

4. When an actor on a stage says lines such as "To be or not to be, that is the question," does the actor perform a linguistic act?

Later, in Chapter 11, we will look more closely at semantic and syntactic conventions, for at times they are sources of fallacies and other confusions. In particular, we shall see how these conventions can generate fallacies of ambiguity and fallacies of vagueness. But before examining the defects of

---

[1]J. L. Austin used the phrase "locutionary act" to refer to a level of language closely related to what we refer to as a "linguistic act." See J. L. Austin, *How to Do Things with Words*, 2d ed. (Cambridge: Harvard University Press, 1975), 94–109.

THE FAR SIDE® By GARY LARSON

**Understanding only German, Fritz was unaware
that the clouds were becoming threatening.**

our language, we should first appreciate that language is a powerful and subtle tool that allows us to perform a wide variety of jobs important for living in the world.

SPEECH ACTS

When we are asked about the function of language, it is natural to reply that we use language to communicate ideas. But this is only one of the purposes for which we use language. This becomes obvious as soon as we look at the ways in which our language actually works. Adding up a column of figures is a linguistic activity—though it is rarely looked at in this way—but it does not communicate any ideas to others. When I add the figures, I am not even communicating anything to myself: I am trying to figure something out. A look at our everyday conversations produces a host of other examples of language being used for different purposes. Grammarians, for example, have divided sentences into various moods, among which are:

Indicative	Imperative
Interrogative	Expressive

For example:

> Barry Bonds hit a home run.
>
> Did Barry Bonds hit a home run?
>
> Get in there and hit a home run, Barry!
>
> Hurray for Barry Bonds!!

The first sentence states a fact; we can use it to communicate information about something that Barry Bonds did. If we use it in this way, what we say will be either true or false. Notice that none of the other sentences can be called either true or false even though they are all meaningful.

PERFORMATIVES

The different types of sentences recognized by traditional grammarians indicate that we use language to do more than convey information. But this traditional classification of sentences gives only a small idea of the wide variety of things that we can accomplish using language. Sometimes, for example, in using language we actually *do* things in the sense of bringing something about. In one familiar setting, if one person says, "I do," and another person says, "I do," and finally a third person says, "I now pronounce you husband and wife," the relationship between the first two people changes in a fundamental way: They are thereby married. With luck, they begin a life of wedded bliss, but they also alter their legal relationship. For example, they may now file joint income tax returns and may not legally marry other people without first getting divorced.

In uttering sentences of this kind, the speaker thereby *does* something rather than merely *states* something. The philosopher J. L. Austin labeled such utterances *performatives*.[2] He called them performatives to contrast performing an action with simply describing something. For example, if an umpire shouts, "You're out!" then the batter is out. The umpire is not merely describing the situation but *declaring* the batter out. By way of contrast, if someone in the stands shouts, "He's out!" the batter is not *thereby* out, although the person who shouts this may be encouraging the umpire to call the batter out or complaining because he didn't.

Performatives come in a wide variety of forms. They are often in the first person, but not always. "You're all invited to my house after the game" is in the second person. One person can speak for another person or even for an institution. At political conventions, heads of delegations say things like this: "The delegates from Kentucky, the Bluegrass State and the home of the Kentucky Derby, cast their votes for the next President of the United States, Joe W. Blodgett." In saying this, Kentucky's votes get cast in favor of Blodgett. There are other oddities as well. Sometimes silence can amount to a performative act. When the chairperson of a meeting asks if there are any

---

[2]See, for example, J. L. Austin's *How to Do Things with Words*, cited previously.

objections to a ruling and none are voiced, then the voters, through their silence, have accepted the ruling.

Because of this diversity of forms that performatives can take, it is not easy to formulate a definition that covers them all. To avoid this difficulty, we will concentrate on one particularly clear type of performative, what J. L. Austin called *explicit performatives*. A singular first person utterance of the form "I . . . " expresses an explicit performative if it yields a true statement when plugged into the following pattern:

In saying " I _____," I thereby _____.

For example, "I congratulate you" expresses an explicit performative, because in saying "I congratulate you," I thereby congratulate you. Here a quoted expression occurs on the left side of the word "thereby," but not on the right side. This reflects the fact that the *saying*, which is referred to on the left side of the pattern, amounts to the *doing* referred to on the right side of the word "thereby." We will call this the *thereby test* for explicit performatives. It provides a convenient way of identifying explicit performatives.

The thereby test has to be qualified in an important way: *the context of the utterance must be appropriate.* You have not congratulated anyone if you say, "I congratulate you" when no one is around, unless, that is, you are congratulating yourself. Congratulations said by an actor in a play are not real congratulations, and so on. Later in this chapter we will try to clarify what makes a context appropriate.

Assuming an appropriate context, all of the following utterances meet the thereby test:

I promise to meet you tomorrow.

I bid sixty-six dollars. (Said at an auction.)

I bid one club. (Said in a bridge game.)

I resign from this club.

I apologize for being late.·

Notice that it doesn't make sense to *deny* any of these performatives. If someone says, "I bid sixty-six dollars," it is not appropriate for someone to reply "No, you don't" or "That's false." It could, however, be appropriate for someone to reply, "You can't bid sixty-six dollars, because the bidding is already up to seventy dollars." In this case, the person tried to make a bid, but failed to do so.

Some explicit performatives play important roles in constructing arguments. These include sentences of the following kind:

I conclude that this bill should be voted down.

I grant that there is much to be said on both sides of this issue.

We will call this kind of performative an *argumentative performative*. These performatives will be examined more closely in Chapter 3.

In contrast to the above sentences, which pass the thereby test, none of the following sentences does:

I'll meet you tomorrow. (This may simply be a prediction that, unlike a performative, can turn out to be false.)

Yesterday I bid sixty dollars. (This is a statement about a past activity and may be false.)

I am sorry for being late. (This is a statement about one's feelings and may be false.)

Questions, imperatives, and exclamations are not explicit performatives because they cannot sensibly be plugged into the pattern at all. In general, to pass the thereby test, a sentence must be first person singular indicative non-continuous present.[3]

EXERCISE I

Using the thereby test as described above, indicate which of the following sentences express explicit performatives (EP) and which do not express explicit performatives (N):

1. I pledge allegiance to the flag.
2. He pledged allegiance to the flag.
3. I always pledge allegiance at the beginning of a game.
4. Pierre is the capital of South Dakota.
5. I order you to leave.
6. Bummer!
7. I claim this land for Queen Victoria. (Said by an explorer.)
8. I'm out of gas.
9. Get lost!
10. I bring you official greetings from her Royal Highness, Queen Elizabeth.
11. Ask not what your country can do for you, but what you can do for your country.
12. I feel devastated.

KINDS OF SPEECH ACTS

Studying explicit performatives not only helps break the spell of the idea that language functions only to transmit information, it also introduces us to a kind of act distinct from linguistic acts. We will call them *speech acts*, and

[3]An example of the continuous present is "I bet ten dollars every week in the lottery." Since this sentence is not used to make a bet, this sentence and others with the continuous present do not pass the thereby test or express explicit performatives.

the rules that govern them *speech-act rules*. We will call such acts as stating, promising, swearing, and refusing *speech acts*. A speech act is the *conventional move* that a remark makes in a language exchange. It is what is done *in* saying something.[4]

It is difficult to give a precise definition of a speech act, but we can begin by contrasting speech acts with linguistic acts. A linguistic act, we said, is the act of saying something meaningful in a language. It is important to see that the same linguistic act can play different roles as it occurs in different contexts. This is shown by the following brief conversations.

1. A: Is there any pizza left?
   B: Yes.
2. A: Do you promise to pay me back by Friday?
   B: Yes.
3. A: Do you swear to tell the truth?
   B: Yes.
4. A: Do you refuse to leave?
   B: Yes.

Here the same linguistic act, uttering the word "yes," is used to do four different things: to state something, to make a promise, to take an oath, and to refuse to do something.

We can make this idea of a speech act clear by using the notion of an explicit performative. Explicit performatives provide a systematic way of identifying different kinds of speech acts. The basic idea is that different speech acts are named by the different verbs that occur in explicit performatives. We can thus use the thereby test to search for different kinds of speech acts. For example:

If I say, "I promise," I thereby promise.

So *promising* is a kind of speech act.

If I say, "I resign," I thereby resign.

So *resigning* is a kind of speech act.

If I say, "I apologize," I thereby apologize.

So *apologizing* is a kind of speech act.

If I say, "I question his honesty," I thereby question his honesty.

So *questioning* is a kind of speech act.

If I say, "I conclude that she is guilty," I thereby conclude that she is guilty.

So *concluding* is a kind of speech act.

---

[4]Austin calls this an "illocutionary act." See *How to Do Things with Words*, 98–132.

We will call the main verbs that appear in such explicit performatives *performative verbs*. Performative verbs name kinds of speech acts.[5]

Thus far, we have emphasized that we do a great deal more with language than make statements, assert facts, and describe things. That is, we do more with language than put forward claims that are either true or false. But we also use language to do these things; so stating, asserting, and describing are themselves kinds of speech acts. This can be shown by using the thereby test:

> If I say, "I state that I am a U.S. citizen," I thereby state that I am a U.S. citizen.
>
> If I say, "I assert that the defendant was in Detroit at the time of the crime," I thereby assert that the defendant was in Detroit at that time.
>
> If I say, "I describe him as being dark haired and just over six feet tall," I thereby describe him as being dark haired and just over six feet tall.

We now have a more accurate conception of the way in which language functions than the common conception that the function of language is to convey ideas. Making claims that are either true or false is one important kind of speech act, but we perform a great many other kinds of speech acts that are also important. In this brief survey we have identified the following kinds of speech acts:

promising	resigning	swearing	apologizing	refusing
stating	asserting	describing	questioning	concluding

EXERCISE II

Using a dictionary, add to the list above by finding ten verbs that can be used to construct explicit performatives.

SPEECH-ACT RULES

The distinctive feature of a performative utterance is that, in a sense we have tried to make clear, the saying constitutes a doing of something. In saying, "I pronounce you husband and wife," a minister is not simply describing a marriage ceremony, she is performing it. Here, however, an objection might arise. Suppose someone who is a supporter of family values goes about the streets pronouncing random couples husband and wife. First of all, unless this person is a member of the clergy, a justice of the peace, a ship's captain, or the like, that person will have no right to make such pronouncements.

---

[5]Although performative verbs name kinds of speech acts, not every kind of speech act has a corresponding performative verb. For example, insulting seems to be a kind of speech act, but "insult" is not a performative verb because you cannot insult someone simply by saying, "I insult you." We might have had a convention that enabled us to insult people just by saying, "I insult you." In English, however, we do not.

Furthermore, even if this person is, say, a crazed member of the clergy, the pronouncement will still not come off. The parties addressed have to say, "I do," they must have a proper license, and so on. This example shows that a speech act will *not come off* or will be *void* unless certain rules or conventions are satisfied. These rules or conventions that must be satisfied for a speech act to come off and not be void we will call *speech-act rules*. We will look briefly at some of the main types of speech-act rules by considering the following questions:

1. Must the speaker use any special words or formulas to perform the speech act?

Sometimes a speech act will come off only if certain *words* or *formulas* are used. In baseball the umpire must say, "Strike two," or something very close to this, in order to call a second strike. In a pickup game it might be all right to say instead, "Hey, that's two bad ones on you, baby!" but that way of calling strikes is not permitted in serious play. Certain legal documents are not valid if they are not properly signed, endorsed, notarized, and so forth.

2. Must the (a) speaker or (b) audience hold any special position for the speaker to perform the speech act?

Sometimes a speech act will come off only if it is performed by someone with an *official position*. We have already seen that, for someone to make two people husband and wife by pronouncing them husband and wife, that person must hold a certain official position. In the same way, although a shortstop can perform the linguistic act of *shouting*, "You're out," a shortstop cannot perform the speech act of *calling* someone out. Only an umpire can do that. A janitor cannot pronounce a body dead on arrival, even if the body is plainly dead when it arrives at the hospital. That is the job of a doctor or a coroner.

3. Are any other special circumstances required for the speech act?

Most speech acts also involve assumptions or presuppositions that certain *facts* obtain. A father cannot bequeath an antique car to his son if he does not own such a car. You cannot resign from the American Civil Liberties Union or the Veterans of Foreign Wars if you are not a member. These special circumstances might sometimes include the audience's desires. In promising someone to do something, for example, we usually do so in the belief that the person *wants* us to do it. For example, I will promise to drive someone to the airport only if I believe that person wants to go the airport and would like me to drive her there. Sometimes, however, we do promise to do things a person does not want done. I can promise to throw someone out if he doesn't behave himself. Here, however, I am making a threat, not a promise.

4. Is any response or uptake needed to complete the speech act?

Sometimes a speech act will come off only if there is an *uptake* by another person. A person can *offer* a bet by saying, "I bet you ten dollars that the Angels will win today," but this person will have *made* a bet only if the other person says, "Done" or "You're on," shakes hands, or in some other way accepts the bet. A marriage ceremony is completely flawed if one of the parties does not say, "I do," but instead says, "Well, maybe I should think about this for a while."

Thus far, we have considered conventions that must be satisfied for the speech act to come off (for it not to be void). Speech acts can, however, be flawed in another way: they can be *insincere*. If we apologize for something, we are expected to feel sorry for what we have done. Of course, the person who says, "I apologize" has apologized even if he or she does not feel sorry, but the apology will not be sincere. If we congratulate someone, we are usually supposed to be pleased with that person's success. If we state something, we are expected to believe what we say. In all these cases—in apologizing, congratulating, and stating—we do succeed in performing a speech act, but are subject to criticism when our feelings or beliefs were not appropriate for the kind of speech act we performed. We can, therefore, add a fifth question to our list concerning the sincerity of a speech act.

5. What feelings, desires, or beliefs is the speaker expected to have?

Finally, we can ask why a certain kind of speech act exists at all. Why, for example, is there the speech act of promising? That is rather a complicated question, but the primary reason for the institution of promising is that it helps people coordinate their activities. People who make promises place themselves under an obligation to do something. When promises are contractual, this obligation is a legal obligation. Promise-making, then, increases the reliance we can have that someone will do what they said they will do, and, for legal promises at least, provides remedies when they do not. So we can add a sixth, broad question to the list:

6. What general purpose or purposes are served by this kind of speech act?

To cite another example of the purpose of a speech act, apologizing expresses regret for harming or insulting someone. One of its purposes is to normalize relations between the speaker and the person harmed or insulted.

Answering the six questions listed above for a particular kind of speech act is called giving a *speech-act analysis*. For example, here is a brief speech-act analysis of "to appoint," as in, "I appoint you to the judiciary committee":

1. Appointments are usually made by using the word "appoint," but other words can be used as well; for example, "name" and "designate" can also be used to do this job. You cannot, however, say, "I wish you were on the judiciary committee."

2. Normally, someone who appoints a person to something must have the *power* to make such appointments. For example, Queen Elizabeth II does not have the power to appoint the commissioner of baseball.

3. A wide variety of facts is presupposed in this speech act, for example, that a position exists, that the person appointed to it is eligible for this appointment, and so on.

4. Sometimes further actions by others are necessary for an appointment to come off. Perhaps ratification is needed. Before ratification, the word "nominate" is often used. In such cases, only after the nomination is ratified has the appointment been made. Usually the appointment does not come off if the person declines the appointment.

5. Appointments are often made with the belief that the person appointed will do a good job. This is not always the case, however, as appointments are made for all sorts of different reasons—rewarding an important supporter, for example.

6. An important purpose of an appointment is to explicitly designate someone to play a particular role. For example, it is often important to know who is in charge. It can also be important that the person who gains this role does so through regular, authorized procedures.

EXERCISE III

Give a similar speech-act analysis of the five verbs below.

1. to thank
2. to deny
3. to promise
4. to vote
5. to give up (in a fight)

Do the same for five of the ten verbs that you found as answers to Exercise II.

DISCUSSION QUESTIONS

1. Imagine that an actor on stage during a modern play screams, "Fire! No, I really mean it. *Fire!*" The audience realizes that he is just acting, so they laugh. Then the actor sees a real fire behind the stage out of view of the audience. The actor again screams, "Fire! No, I really mean it. *Fire!*" Which speech act, if any, does the actor perform in uttering these words the second time? Why? What does this show about speech acts?

2. *Do* the speech acts in which people get married presuppose that the people who are getting married have different sexes? *Should* these speech acts presuppose this fact? Why?

3. The importance of deciding what kind of speech act has been performed is illustrated by a classic case from the law of contracts, *Hawkins v. McGee.*[6] McGee performed an operation on Hawkins that proved unsuccessful, and

[6]Supreme Court of New Hampshire, 1929, 84 N.H. 114, A. 641.

(continued)

Hawkins sued for damages. He did not sue on the basis of malpractice, however, but on the basis of breach of contract. His attorney argued that the doctor initiated a contractual relationship in that he tried to persuade Hawkins to have the operation by saying such things as "I will guarantee to make the hand a hundred percent perfect hand." He made statements of this kind a number of times, and finally Hawkins agreed to undergo the operation on the basis of these remarks. Hawkins's attorney maintained that these exchanges, which took place in the doctor's office on a number of occasions, constituted an offer of a contract that Hawkins explicitly accepted. The attorney for the surgeon replied that these words, even if uttered, would not constitute an offer of a contract, but merely expressed a *strong belief.*

It is important to remember that contracts do not have to be written and signed to be binding. A proper verbal offer and acceptance are usually sufficient to constitute a contract. The case, then, turned on two questions: (1) Did McGee utter the words attributed to him? In other words, did McGee perform the *linguistic act* attributed to him? The jury decided that he did. (2) The second, more interesting question was whether these words, when uttered in this particular context, amounted to an offer of a contract, as Hawkins's attorney maintained, or merely were an expression of strong belief, as McGee's attorney held. In other words, the fundamental question in this case was what kind of *speech act* McGee performed when trying to convince Hawkins to have the operation.

Explain how you would settle this case. (The court actually ruled in favor of Hawkins, but you are free to disagree.)

CONVERSATIONAL ACTS[7]

In examining linguistic acts (saying something meaningful in a language) and then speech acts (doing something in using words), we have largely ignored one of the central features of language: it is primarily a practical activity that takes place among people. It is usually—though not always—a social activity. We use language in order to inform people of things, get them to do things, amuse them, calm them down, and so on. We can capture this aspect of language by introducing the notion of a *conversational exchange*, that is, a situation where various speakers use speech acts in order bring about some effects in each other. We will call this act of using a speech act to cause a standard effect in another a *conversational act*.

---

[7]With some variation, this discussion of conversational rules and conversational implication is based on Paul Grice's important essay, "Logic and Conversation," which appears as the second chapter of his *Studies in the Way of Words* (Cambridge: Harvard University Press, 1989). To avoid British references that an American reader might find perplexing, we have sometimes altered Grice's wording.

Suppose, for example, *A* says to *B*, "Someone is following us." In this case, *A* has performed a linguistic act, that is, he has uttered a meaningful sentence in the English language. *A* has also performed a speech act—specifically, he has *stated* that they are being followed. The point of performing this speech act is to produce in *B* a particular belief, namely that they are being followed. If *A* is successful in this, then *A* has successfully performed the conversational act of producing this belief in *B. A*, of course, might fail in his attempt to do this. *A*'s linguistic act could be successful and his speech act successful as well, yet, for whatever reason, *B* might not accept as true what *A* is telling her. Perhaps *B* thinks that *A* is paranoid or just trying to frighten her.

Here are some other examples of the difference between performing a speech act and performing a conversational act.

> We can *urge* people to do things in order to *persuade* them to do these things. Here urging is the speech act; persuading is the intended conversational act.

> We can *warn* people about something in order to *put them on guard* concerning it. Here warning is the speech act; putting them on guard is the intended conversational act.

> We can *assure* people concerning something in order to *instill confidence in them*. Here assuring is the speech act; instilling confidence is the intended conversational act.

In each of these cases, our speech act may not succeed in having its intended conversational effect. Our urging, warning, and assuring may, respectively, fail to persuade, put on guard, or instill confidence. So we can perform a speech act without performing the intended conversational act.

EXERCISE IV

Indicate whether the verbs in the following sentences name a speech act, a conversational act, or neither. Assume a standard context. Explain your answers. (Be particularly careful with the last four sentences.)

1. He *denied* doing it.
2. She *told* him to get lost.
3. He *praised* her lavishly.
4. She *convinced* him he was wrong.
5. He *handed* in his resignation.
6. Her news *frightened* him half to death.
7. He *advised* her to go into another line of work.
8. She *blamed* him for her troubles.
9. His lecture *enlightened* her.

(continued)

10. She *challenged* his integrity.

11. He *amused* her with his jokes.

12. She *condemned* him in front of everyone.

13. She *embarrassed* him in front of everyone.

14. He *whistled* for a taxi.

15. He *whistled down* a taxi.

CONVERSATIONAL RULES

Just as there are rules that govern linguistic acts and other rules that govern speech acts, so there are rules that govern conversational acts. This should not be surprising, because conversations can be complicated interpersonal activities in need of rules to make them effective in attaining their goals. These underlying rules are implicitly understood by users of the language, but the philosopher Paul Grice was the first person to examine them in careful detail.

We can start by examining standard or normal conversational exchanges where conversation is a cooperative venture, that is, where the people involved in the conversation have some common goal they are trying to achieve in talking with one another. (A prisoner being interrogated and a shop owner being robbed are *not* in such cooperative situations.) According to Grice, such exchanges are governed by what he calls the *Cooperative Principle*. This principle states that the parties involved should use language in a way that contributes toward achieving their common goal. It tells them to cooperate.[8]

This general principle gains more content when we consider how people can cooperate to achieve a common goal. Compare people in conversation to carpenters who want to build a house. They need enough nails and wood, but not too much. They need the right kinds of nails and wood. They also need to put the nails and wood together in the relevant way, that is, according to their plans. And of course, they also want to perform their tasks quickly and in the right order.

Rational people who want to achieve common goals must follow similar general restrictions in other practical activities. Because cooperative conversations are one such practical activity, speakers who want to cooperate with one another must follow rules analogous to those for carpenters. Grice spells out four such rules.

---

[8]Grice states the Cooperative Principle in these words: "Make your conversational contribution such as is required, at the stage at which it occurs, by the accepted purpose or direction of the talk exchange in which you are engaged."

The first he calls the rule of *Quantity*. It tells us to give the right amount of information. More specifically:

1. Make your contribution as informative as is required (for the current purposes of the exchange).

and possibly:

2. Do not make your contribution more informative than is required.

Here is an application of this rule: A person rushes up to you and asks, "Where is a fire extinguisher?" You know that there is a fire extinguisher five floors away in the basement, and you also know that there is a fire extinguisher just down the hall. Suppose you say that there is a fire extinguisher in the basement. Here you have said something true, but you have violated the first part of the rule of Quantity. You have failed to reveal an important piece of information that, under the rule of Quantity, you should have produced. A violation of the second version of the rule would look like this: As smoke billows down the hall, you say where a fire extinguisher is located on each floor, starting with the basement. Eventually you will get around to saying that there is a fire extinguisher just down the hall, but you bury the point in a mass of unnecessary information.

Another of Grice's rules is called the rule of *Quality*. In general: Try to make your contribution one that is true. More specifically:

1. Do not say what you believe to be false.
2. Do not say that for which you lack adequate evidence.

In a cooperative activity, you are not supposed to tell lies. Beyond this, you are expected not to talk off the top of your head either. When we make a statement, we can be challenged in the following ways:

Do you really believe that?

Why do you believe that?

That a person has the right to ask such questions shows that statement making is governed by the rule of Quality. In a court of law, witnesses promise to tell the whole truth and nothing but the truth. The demand for *nothing but the truth* reflects the rule of Quality. The demand for *the whole truth* roughly reflects the rule of Quantity. Obviously, nobody really tells every truth he or she knows. Here the *whole* truth concerns all the known truths that are relevant in the context.

This brings us to our next rule, the rule of *Relevance*. Simply stated, the rule of Relevance says: Be relevant! Though easy to state, the rule is not easy to explain, because relevance itself is a difficult notion. It is, however, easy to illustrate. If someone asks me where he can find a doctor, I might reply that there is a hospital in the next block. Though not a direct answer to the question, it does not violate the rule of Relevance because it provides a piece of useful information. If, however, in response I tell the person that I like his haircut, then I have violated the rule of Relevance. Clear-cut violations of this principle often involve *changing the subject*.

Another rule concerns the manner of our conversation. We are expected to be clear in what we say. Under the general rule of *Manner* come various special rules:

1. Avoid obscurity of expression.
2. Avoid ambiguity.
3. Be brief.
4. Be orderly.

As an example of the fourth part of this rule, when describing a series of events it is usually important to state them in the order in which they occurred. It would certainly be misleading to say that two people had a child and got married when, in fact, they had a child after they were married.

There are probably many other rules that govern our conversations. *Be polite!* might be one of them. *Be charitable!* is another. That is, we should put the best interpretation on what others say, and our replies should reflect this. We should avoid quibbling and being picky. For the most part, however, we will not worry about these other rules.

EXERCISE V

Indicate which, if any, of Grice's conversational rules are violated by the italicized sentence of each of the following conversations. Assume a standard context. More than one rule might be violated.

1. "What did you get on the last test?" *"A grade."*
2. "Did you like her singing?" *"Her costume was beautiful."*
3. *"The governor has the brains of a three-year-old."*
4. *"The Lone Ranger rode into the sunset and jumped on his horse."*
5. *"Without her help, we'd be up a creek without a paddle."*
6. "Where is Palo Alto?" *"On the surface of the Earth."*
7. *"It will rain tomorrow."* "How do you know?" *"I just guessed."*
8. *"Does the dog need to go out for a W-A-L-K [spelled out]?"*
9. "Why did the chicken cross the road?" *"To get to the other side."*
10. Psychiatrist: "You're crazy." Patient: "I want a second opinion." Psychiatrist: "Okay. *You're ugly,* too."

CONVERSATIONAL IMPLICATION

We have seen that conversational exchanges are governed by a system of rules that help those involved in the exchange to achieve their goals. Of course, people do not always follow these rules when they make statements. People withhold information, they lie, they say the first thing that pops into

THE FAR SIDE® By GARY LARSON

When dumb animals attempt murder

their heads, they wander off the subject, they talk vaguely and obscurely. Yet in a normal setting where people are cooperating toward reaching a shared goal, they often conform quite closely to these rules. If, on the whole, people did not do this, we could not have the linguistic practices we do. If we thought, for example, that people very often lied (even about the most trivial matters), the business of exchanging information would be badly damaged.

But not only do we follow these conventions, we also (1) implicitly realize that we are following them, and (2) expect others to assume that we are following them. This mutual understanding of the commitments involved in a conversational act has the following important consequence: *people are able to convey a great deal of information without actually saying it.*

A simple example will illustrate this. Again suppose that a person, with smoke billowing behind him, comes running up to you and asks:

Where is a fire extinguisher?

And you reply:

There is one in the lobby.

Through a combination of conversational rules, notably relevance, quantity, and manner, this commits you to the claim that this is the closest, or at least the most accessible, fire extinguisher. Furthermore, the person you are speaking to assumes that you are committed to this. Of course, you have not actually *said* that it is the closest fire extinguisher, but you have, we might say, *implied* this. When we do not actually say something but imply it by virtue of a mutually understood conversational rule, the implication is called a *conversational implication*.

It is important to realize that conversational implication is a pervasive feature of human communication. It is not something we employ only occasionally for special effect. In fact, virtually every conversation relies on these implications, and most conversations would fall apart if people refused to go beyond literal meanings to take into account the implications of saying things. In the following conversation, B is literal-minded in just this way:

A: Do you know what time it is?

B: Not without looking at my watch.

B has answered A's question, but it is hard to imagine that A has received the information she was looking for. Presumably she wanted to know what time it was, not merely whether B, at that very moment, knew the time. Finding B rather obtuse, A tries again:

A: Can you tell me what time it is?

B: Oh, yes, all I have to do is look at my watch.

Undaunted, A gives it another try:

A: Will you tell me what time it is?

B: I suppose I will as soon as you ask me.

Finally:

A: What time is it?

B: Two o'clock. Why didn't you ask me that in the first place?

Notice that in each of these exchanges B gives a direct and accurate answer to A's question; yet, in all but the last answer, he does not provide A with what she wants. Here we might say that B is taking A's questions too literally, but we might better say that the problem is that B does nothing *more* than take A's remarks literally. In a conversational exchange, we expect others to take our remarks in the light of the obvious purpose we have in making them. We expect them to share our commonsense understanding of why people ask questions. At the very least, we expect people to respond to us in ways that are *relevant* to our purposes. Except at the end, B seems totally oblivious to the point of A's questions and, like a computer in a science-fiction movie, gives nothing more than the literally correct answer to each question as it is asked.

Though all the conversational rules we have examined can be the basis of conversational implication, the rule of Relevance is particularly powerful in this respect. Normal conversations are dense with conversational implications that depend on the rule of Relevance. Someone says, "Dinner's ready," and that is immediately taken to be a way of asking people to come to the table. Why? Because dinner's being ready is a transparent *reason* to come to the table to eat. This is an ordinary context that most people are familiar with. Change the context, however, and the conversational implications can be entirely different. Suppose the same words, "Dinner's ready," are uttered when guests have failed to arrive on time. In this context, the conversational implication, which will probably be reflected in an annoyed tone of voice, will be quite different.

To cite another example of context dependence, if someone says, "I broke a finger," people will naturally assume that it is the speaker's own finger that was broken. Why? Because when people break fingers, it is almost always their own fingers that they break. That is the standard context in which this remark is made. If, however, we shift the context, that conversational implication can be lost and another take its place. Suppose the speaker is a mobster in an extortion racket, that is, someone who physically harms people who do not pay protection money. Among his fellow extortionists, the conversational implication of "I broke a finger" is likely to be that it was someone who refused to pay up that had his finger broken. (We can imagine the extortionist canceling this implication by saying, "No, no, it was *my* finger that got broken when I slugged the guy.")

EXERCISE VI

Assuming a natural conversational setting, what might a person intend to conversationally imply by making the following remarks? Briefly explain why each of these conversational implications holds; that is, explain the relationship between what the speaker *literally* says and what the speaker intends to convey through conversational implication. For two of these examples, find a context where the standard conversational implication would fail and another arise instead.

1. It's getting chilly in here.
2. Do you mind if I borrow your pen?
3. We are out of soda.
4. I got here before he did. (Said in a ticket line.)
5. Don't blame me if you get in trouble.
6. Has this seat been taken?
7. These sweet potatoes are very filling.
8. Don't ask me.

VIOLATING CONVERSATIONAL RULES

If we look at basic conversational rules, we notice that these rules sometimes clash, or at least push us in different directions. The rule of Quantity encourages us to give as much information as possible, but this is constrained by the rule of Quality, which restricts our claims to things we believe to be true and can back up with good reasons. The demands of the rule of Quantity can also conflict with the demand for brevity. In order to be brief, we must sometimes simplify and even falsify, and this can come into conflict with the rule of Quality, which demands that we say only what we believe to be true. Sometimes it is not important to get things *exactly* right; sometimes it is. An ongoing conversation can be a constant series of adjustments to this background system of rules.

Because conversational rules can come into conflict with one another, speakers can sometimes *seem* to be violating the Cooperative Principle by violating one of its maxims. This can happen when one conversational rule is overridden by another. Grasping the resolution of such a conflict can generate interesting conversational implications. This may sound complicated, but an example from Grice should make it clear. Suppose *A* tells *B* that she wants to visit a friend, *C*, and the following conversation takes place:

> A: I'm planning to visit C; where does he live?
>
> B: Somewhere in the south of France.

If *A* is interested in visiting *C*, then *B*'s reply really does not give her the information she needs and thus seems to violate the first part of the rule of Quantity. We can explain this departure on the assumption that *B* does not know *exactly* where *C* lives and would thus violate the rule of Quality if he said anything more specific. In this case, *B*'s reply conversationally implies that he does not know exactly where *C* lives.

In a more extreme case, a person may even *flout* one of these conventions, that is, may openly violate a conversational rule without, as in the previous example, there being any other conversational rule that overrides it. Here is an adaptation of one of Grice's examples and his explanation of it:

> *A* is writing a letter of recommendation about one of his students who is applying to law school, and the letter reads as follows: "Dear Sir: Mr. *X*'s command of English is excellent, and his attendance in class has been regular. Yours, etc."
> (Gloss: *A* cannot be opting out, since if he wished to be uncooperative, why write at all? He cannot be unable, through ignorance, to say more, since the person is his student; moreover, he knows that more information is wanted. He must, therefore, be wishing to impart information he is reluctant to write down. This supposition is only tenable on the assumption that he thinks that Mr. *X* is not a good student. This, then, is what he is implicating.)

This is a case of *damning with faint praise*. Faint praise can be damning because, under the first part of the rule of Quantity, it conversationally implies that no stronger praise is warranted.

We can intentionally violate the rule of Relevance by pointedly changing the subject. Here is variation on another one of Grice's examples:

> Standing outside a classroom, *A* says, "Professor X is a moron." There is a moment of shocked silence; then *B* says, "Nice day, isn't it?"

A would have to be fairly dim not to realize that Professor *X*, whom he has just called a moron, may be somewhere nearby. Why else would *B* reply in such an irrelevant manner? So in saying, "Nice day, isn't it?" *B* conversationally implies that Professor *X* is nearby.

Winston Churchill provided a famous example of intentionally violating the rule of Manner. When criticized for ending a sentence with a preposition, he replied, "That is the type of criticism up with which I will not put."

There are also many examples of speakers generating conversational implication through flouting the rule of Quality, that is, through stating something that both the speaker and the audience mutually know to be false. Irony is a clear example of this; for instance, calling something "awesome" when both the speaker and the audience think it is pathetic. Since irony and other rhetorical devices often play an important role in presenting arguments, we will give a them separate treatment in the next chapter.

EXERCISE VII

These sentences appeared in Exercise V. For each, again identify the conversational rule being violated, but further, give a plausible account of what the speaker might be conversationally implying through violating the conversational rule.

1. "What did you get on the last test?" *"A grade."*
2. "Did you like her singing?" *"Her costume was beautiful."*
3. *"The governor has the brains of a three-year-old."*
4. *"Does the dog need to go out for a W-A-L-K* [spelled out]?"

EXERCISE VIII

Below are a set of paired questions and answers. What, in a normal context, do the replies conversationally imply? Explain why these conversational implications hold. (Try to rely on the content of what is said, rather than on the tone of voice in which it is uttered. In particular, don't think of these remarks being uttered with heavy sarcasm.)

1. Are you going to vote for a Republican? I just might.
2. Are you going to vote for a Republican? You can bet on it.
3. Are you going to vote for a Republican? Not unless hell freezes over.
4. Are you going to vote for a Republican? Don't be silly.
5. Are you going to vote for a Republican? I am voting for an independent.
6. Are you going to vote for a Republican? There is no other choice.
7. Did you vote for a Republican? Maybe yes, maybe no.
8. Did you vote for a Republican? I voted for the winner.

DECEPTION

In the examples we have just examined, a speaker intentionally violates a conversational rule to achieve some special effect, for example, damning with faint praise. It is important in these cases that the listeners *recognize* that a rule is being intentionally broken, for otherwise they may simply be misled. At other times, however, speakers intentionally break conversational rules because they are trying to mislead their listeners. A speaker may violate the first part of Grice's rule of Quality by uttering something she knows to be false with the intention of producing a false belief in her listeners. That is called *lying*. Notice that lying depends on the general acceptance of the Cooperative Principle. Because audiences generally assume that speakers are telling the truth, successful lying is sometimes possible.

Flat-out lying is not the only way (and often not the most effective way) of intentionally misleading people. We can say something literally true that, at the same time, conversationally implies something false. This is sometimes called making a *false suggestion*. If a son tells his parents that he "has had some trouble with the car," that could be true, but deeply misleading if, in fact, he had totaled it. It would be misleading because it would violate the rule of Quantity. In saying only that he has had some trouble with the car, he conversationally implies that nothing very serious happened. He conversationally implies this because, in this context, he is expected to come clean and reveal *all* that actually happened.

A more complex example of false suggestion arose in a lawsuit that reached the United States Supreme Court.

BRONSTON V. UNITED STATES
———————■———————
(409 U.S. 352, 1973)

MR. CHIEF JUSTICE BURGER delivered the opinion of the Court:

Petitioner's perjury conviction was founded on the answers given by him as a witness at that bankruptcy hearing, and in particular on the following colloquy with a lawyer for a creditor of Bronston Productions:

> Q. Do you have any bank accounts in Swiss banks, Mr. Bronston?
> A. No, sir.
> Q. Have you ever?
> A. The company had an account there for about six months, in Zurich.
> Q. Have you any nominees who have bank accounts in Swiss banks?
> A. No, sir.
> Q. Have you ever?
> A. No, sir.

It is undisputed that for a period of nearly five years, between October 1959 and June 1964, petitioner had a personal bank account at the International Credit Bank in Geneva, Switzerland, into which he made deposits and upon which he drew checks totaling more than $180,000. It is likewise undisputed that petitioner's answers were literally truthful. (i) Petitioner did not at the time of questioning have a Swiss bank account. (ii) Bronston Productions, Inc., did have the account in Zurich described by petitioner. (iii) Neither at the time of questioning nor before did petitioner have nominees who had Swiss accounts. The government's prosecution for perjury went forward on the theory that in order to mislead his questioner, petitioner answered the second question with literal truthfulness but unresponsively addressed his answer to the company's assets and not to his own—thereby implying that he had no personal Swiss bank account at the relevant time.

It is hard to read the witness's response to the second question in any other way than as a deliberate attempt to mislead the Court, for his response plainly implies that he did not have a personal account in a Swiss bank, when, in fact, he did. But the issue before the Court was not whether he intentionally misled the Court, but whether in doing so he committed perjury. The relevant statute reads as follows:

> Whoever, having taken an oath before a competent tribunal . . . that he will testify . . . truly, . . . willfully and contrary to such oath states or subscribes to any material matter which he does not believe to be true, is guilty of perjury.
> (18 U.S.C. 1621)

The lower courts ruled that Bronston violated this statute and thus had committed perjury. The Supreme Court reversed this decision, in part for the following reasons:

> It should come as no surprise that a participant in a bankruptcy proceeding may have something to conceal and consciously tries to do so, or that a debtor may be embarrassed at his plight and yield information reluctantly. It is the responsibility of the lawyer to probe; testimonial interrogation, and cross-examination in particular, is a probing, prying, pressing form of inquiry. If a witness evades, it is the lawyer's responsibility to recognize the evasion and to bring the witness back to the mark, to flush out the whole truth with the tools of adversary examination.
> (409 U.S. 352 at 358–359 [1973])

In other words, in a courtroom, where the relationship is typically adversarial rather than cooperative, not all the standard conversational rules are in force or fully in force. In particular, it would be unrealistic to assume that the rule of Quantity will be consistently honored in a courtroom clash; therefore, it becomes the task of the cross-examiner to force the witness to produce all the relevant facts.

DISCUSSION QUESTIONS

Refer back to the dialogue quoted in *Bronston v. United States*. Because it is difficult to read the witness's second response as anything but a willful attempt to deceive, why should this case be treated differently from lying? Alternatively, why not even drop the demand that witnesses tell the truth and make it the responsibility of the lawyers to get at the truth itself (rather than just the whole truth) through probing, prying, pressing inquiry?

AN OVERVIEW

In this chapter we have developed a rather complex picture of the way our language functions. In the process we have distinguished three kinds or levels of acts that are performed when we employ language. We have also examined the rules associated with each kind or level of act. The following table summarizes this discussion:

THREE LEVELS OF LANGUAGE

Kinds of Acts	Governing Rules
A LINGUISTIC ACT is an act of saying something meaningful in a language. It is the basic act that is needed to make anything part of language.	Semantic rules (such as definitions) and syntactic rules (as in grammar).
A SPEECH ACT concerns the move a person makes in saying something. Different kinds of speech acts are indicated by the various verbs found in explicit performatives.	Speech-act rules about special agents, formulas, circumstances, responses, and feelings appropriate to different kinds of speech acts.
A CONVERSATIONAL ACT is a speaker's act of causing a standard kind of effect in the listener. It is what I do by saying something—for example, I persuade someone to do something.	Conversational rules (the Cooperative Principle; Quantity, Quality, Relevance, and Manner).

EXERCISE IX

1. It is late, and *A* is very hungry. *A* asks *B*, "When will dinner be ready?" Describe the linguistic act, the speech act, and some of the conversational acts this person may be performing in this context.

2. Someone is trying to solve the following puzzle: One of thirteen balls is heavier than the others, which are of equal weight. In no more than three weighings on a balance scale, determine which ball is the heavier one. The person is stumped, so someone says to her: "Begin by putting four balls in each pan of the scale." Describe the linguistic act, the speech act, and the conversational act of the person who makes this suggestion.

RHETORIC AND EVALUATION

This chapter will extend ideas developed in Chapter 1 to two further areas: (1) figurative as opposed to literal uses of language and (2) evaluative as opposed to merely descriptive uses of language. The examination of figurative language is important because the arguments we encounter in everyday life often employ figurative language in an effort to achieve an argumentative or rhetorical advantage. These rhetorical devices include rhetorical questions, overstatement, understatement, irony, similes, and metaphors. It is also important to understand how evaluative statements function, because a great many arguments are not simply intended to establish what is the case, but what ought to be the case. We want to know what such claims mean and how they are established.

CONVERSATIONAL IMPLICATION AND RHETORICAL DEVICES

Conversational implication is so much a part of our everyday use of language that we hardly notice when we are employing it. Many rhetorical devices depend on conversational implication.

RHETORICAL QUESTIONS

Consider how *rhetorical questions* work. Normally when we ask a question, we are requesting information; but not always. If you ask someone, "Could you hurry up?" you certainly know that this person *could* hurry up if she chose to. It is not likely that you are asking this question to find out whether the person is suffering from some physical disability, such as a leg cramp. On most occasions, this question has the conversational force of telling someone to hurry up. But if the point of the question is to tell (or ask) someone to hurry up, why not just say, "Hurry up!" or, if you are being polite, "Please hurry up!"? For that matter, why do we employ rhetorical questions at all? Where do they get their force?

To make headway on these matters, we have to recognize that the activity of asking questions is governed by conversational rules—rules that in many ways parallel the rules for making statements: You should not ask stupid questions, for example, those based on false assumptions (Quality). You should not ask unclear or muddled questions (Manner). You should not ask irrelevant questions (Relevance). You should not ask questions when the information asked for is obvious and more than needs to be said for the purposes of the conversational exchange (Quantity).

Rhetorical questions often gain their force through flouting the Quantity rule for questions. For example, suppose *A* steps on *B*'s toes and *B* asks, "Can't you be more careful?" This is a peculiar thing to say as a request for information, for both *A* and *B* believe that *A* could have been more careful. Taken literally as a request for information, it would be dismissed by saying something like, "Of course, I can be more careful." That, however, is just the response that *B* wants to get from *A*. It gets *A* to acknowledge (at least inwardly) the very thing that *B* is accusing *A* of, that is, responsibility for causing harm to *B*.

It is important to see that the same question can be rhetorical in one context and not rhetorical in another. If you are visiting a friend and hear (or think you hear) someone in the basement, you might ask your friend, "Do you want me to call the police?" Here you are genuinely interested in someone's opinion, for calling the police might be unnecessary or even dangerous. On the other hand, if you are trying to get someone to move her car from your driveway, these same words will have the force of a rhetorical question. Your question, "Do you want me to call the police?" has the expected answer, "No," and because of this it conversationally implies the threat, "If you don't move your car, I will call the police." Because of this, identifying rhetorical questions, like identifying any rhetorical device, is a two-step process. First, we have to decide whether the question should be taken literally as a request for information or, instead, taken as a rhetorical maneuver. If the latter, then we have to figure out what the rhetorical force of the question is.

EXERCISE I

For each of the following questions, describe one context in which it is used nonrhetorically (that is, to request information), and another context in which it is used rhetorically (that is, not to request information but to make some rhetorical move).

Example: Are you looking for trouble?

It would normally be a nonrhetorical question if addressed to someone checking out fuses.

It would normally be a rhetorical question if addressed to someone acting obnoxiously.

1. Is that the last piece of pizza?
2. How can you say that to me?
3. Is that all you can say for yourself?

4. Could you just wait a minute?
5. Did I hear you correctly?
6. Do you know who I am?
7. Who do you think you are?
8. Can I say what I think?
9. Didn't I tell you not to do that?
10. What do you take me for, a moron?

OVERSTATEMENT AND UNDERSTATEMENT

With rhetorical questions, we do not expect our questions to be taken in a standard (information-seeking) way. At other times, we do not expect our listeners to take what we assert at face value. We sometimes exaggerate. When someone claims to be hungry enough to eat a horse, it does not dawn on us to treat this as a literal claim about how much she can eat. To do so would be to attribute to the speaker a blatant violation of Grice's first rule of Quality, namely, do not say what you believe to be false. Furthermore, the person who utters these words is not attempting to convince her listeners that she can in fact eat a horse. Because of all this, her audience will naturally interpret her remark figuratively, rather than literally. They will assume that she is exaggerating the amount she can eat in order to conversationally imply that she is very hungry. This rhetorical device is called *overstatement* or *hyperbole*. It is commonly employed, often in heavy-handed ways.

We sometimes use the opposite ploy and attempt to achieve rhetorical effect by *understating* things. We say that something is pretty good or not too bad when, as all can see, it is terrific. In these cases the speaker is violating something akin to the rule of Quantity. He is not saying just how good something really is. He expects his audience to recognize this and say (inwardly, at least) something like this: "Oh, it is much better than that." Understatement is often used as a way of fishing for compliments.

IRONY AND SARCASM

Sometimes, then, we do not intend to have others take our words at face value. Even beyond this, we sometimes expect our listeners to interpret us as claiming just the *opposite* of what we assert. This occurs, for example, with *irony* and *sarcasm*. Suppose at a crucial point in a game, the second baseman fires the ball ten feet over the first baseman's head, and someone shouts, "Great throw." Literally, it was not a great throw; it was the opposite of a great throw, and this is just what the person who says "Great throw" is indicating. How do the listeners know they are supposed to interpret it in this way? Sometimes this is indicated by tone of voice. A sarcastic tone of voice usually indicates that the person means the opposite of what he or she is say-ing. Even without the tone of sarcasm, the remark "Great throw" is not likely to be taken literally. The person who shouts this knows that it was not a great throw, as do the people who hear it. Rather than attributing an obviously false belief to the shouter, we assume that the person is blatantly violating the rule of Quality to draw our attention to just how bad the throw really was.

METAPHORS AND SIMILES

Metaphors and *similes* are perhaps the most common form of figurative lan-guage. With a metaphor, we speak of something by using a vocabulary that, at a literal level, is not appropriate to it. George Washington was not literally the father of his country. Taken literally, it hardly makes sense to speak of someone fathering a country. But the metaphor is so natural (or so familiar) that it does not cross our minds to treat the remark literally, asking, perhaps, who the mother was. With similes, we draw a comparison, but in a way that, taken literally, is inappropriate. To say that the home team fought like tigers does not mean that they clawed the opposing team and took large bites out of them. Taken literally, metaphors are usually obviously false and thus vio-late Grice's rule of Quality. Again, as with irony, when someone says some-thing obviously false, we have to decide what to make of that person's utterance. Perhaps the person is very stupid or a very bad liar, but often nei-ther suggestion is plausible. In such a situation sometimes the best supposi-tion is that the person is speaking metaphorically rather than literally.

Not all metaphors, however, are literally false. For example, "No man is an island" is literally true. We treat this remark as a metaphor because, taken literally, it is so obviously and boringly true that we cannot imagine why anyone would want to say it. Taken literally, it would make no greater con-tribution to the conversation than any other irrelevant, obvious truth—for example, that no man is a socket wrench. Taken literally, this metaphor vio-lates the rule of Relevance and, perhaps, the second part of the rule of Quan-tity. Taken figuratively, it is an apt, if somewhat overworked, way of indicating that no one is isolated and self-contained.

How do metaphors work? This is a difficult and disputed question, but many metaphors have the force of an implicit analogy. A metaphor leads us to view something in terms of striking or salient features of something else.

For example, supporters of welfare often describe it as a safety net; its opponents sometimes describe it as a hammock. The underlying structure of both metaphors has the following form:

A is to B as C is to D.

A safety net (A) is a good thing for an aerialist (B) to have when the aerialist falls. Analogously, welfare benefits (C) are a good thing for people (D) to have when they lose their jobs. In contrast, hammocks are places where people loaf, so comparing welfare benefits to hammocks suggests that welfare benefits encourage loafing. Through using these metaphors, people are being induced to look at welfare programs in ways that will shape their attitudes toward them. In this way, metaphors often function as vivid, highly condensed arguments.

Metaphors not only appear in statements, they also appear in imperatives. For example:

1. Don't rock the boat.

Maxims of commonsense are often formulated as metaphorical imperatives:

2. Keep your eye on the ball.
3. Don't put all your eggs in one basket.
4. Look before you leap.
5. Make hay while the sun shines.
6. Don't count your chickens before they hatch.
7. Don't change horses in the middle of the stream.

EXERCISE II

For 2–7 above, find a context where the imperative can be used in its literal way and another context where it is used metaphorically. For example, the first imperative (1) can be employed literally in a context where someone is moving around in a canoe in a way that could tip it. It can also be used metaphorically to tell someone not to do something that will cause a fuss.

A metaphor can lose its metaphorical force from constant use. It can become what is known as a *dead metaphor*. Example 4 above, "Look before you leap," will strike most people as simply a way of telling people to check things out before doing something that could have bad results. It doesn't *say* this, however. It tells you to use your eyes prior to making a big jump over or onto something. Similarly, most people who use the expression "He has something up his sleeve" are not thinking about magicians or cardsharks, who literally fool or exploit people by hiding things up their sleeves. It has simply become a way of saying that someone is about to do something sneaky and unexpected.

Metaphors can be powerful, but they can also be dull, lame, forced, mixed, trite, and so on. Aristotle thought that good metaphors present the hearer or reader with a kind of puzzle that has to be worked out. This is particularly true of metaphors that present an implicit analogy. In the process of working out this analogy, we can come to see things in a new and perhaps more fundamental way. We can come to recognize and appreciate connections that we have failed to recognize and appreciate before. Because metaphors can be powerful, they can also be dangerous. A metaphor can be vivid, clever, deep, and perhaps entertaining, but still deeply unfair, biased, and misleading. The light it casts can be a false light. Because metaphors often appear in arguments—especially political and moral arguments—we will have to develop ways of evaluating their argumentative force.

EXERCISE III

Identify each of the following sentences as overstatement, understatement, irony, metaphor, or simile. For each sentence, write another expressing its literal meaning.

1. He missed the ball by a mile.
2. A midair collision can ruin your whole day.
3. "Religion is the opiate of the masses." (Karl Marx)
4. It was a real team effort. (Said by a coach after his team loses by 40 points.)
5. He had to eat his words.
6. The concert was totally awesome.
7. This is a case of the tail wagging the dog.
8. They are throwing the baby out with the bathwater.
9. He acted like a bull in a china shop.
10. The exam blew me away.

EXERCISE IV

Unpack the following political metaphors by giving their literal content.

1. We can't afford a President who needs on-the-job training.
2. It's time for people on the welfare wagon to get off and help pull.
3. If you can't stand the heat, get out of the kitchen.
4. We need to restore a level playing field.
5. The special interests have him in their pockets.
6. The bill was passed through typical horse-trading.
7. He's a lame duck.

DISCUSSION QUESTION

At the start of the U.S. war with Iraq in 2003, some described Iraq as another Vietnam, while others described Saddam Hussein (Iraq's president) as another Hitler. Which metaphor was used by supporters of the war? Which was used by opponents? How can you tell? How do these metaphors work?

EVALUATIVE LANGUAGE

Many words in our language are used not just to describe things but to *evaluate* them positively or negatively. The clearest cases of evaluative language occur when we say that something is *good* or *bad*, that some course of action is *right* or *wrong*, or that something *should* or *should not* (or *ought to* or *ought not to*) be done.

The meaning of such evaluative terms as "good," "bad," and so on is very controversial, but one thing worth noting is that evaluative terms come into play any time one is faced with a choice or decision. To take an uncomplicated example, suppose that we need something to hold the door open so that the wind cannot blow it closed. Immediately, evaluative language becomes appropriate, as illustrated by remarks like "That rock is no good; it is too light," "That rock is no good; it's too heavy to lift," "This rock is just fine," "This one is even better," and so on. In all these cases, evaluative language is used to direct or guide action. This comes out when we notice the oddity of the following conversations:

1. A. This rock is good enough for the job.

   B. Granted, but is that any reason to use it?

2. A. This rock is better for the job than that one.

   B. Granted, but now tell me which one to use?

3. A. This rock is the best of the lot for doing the job.

   B. Granted, but still: Which rock should I use?

In these conversations, *B* seems to miss the point of *A*'s remarks, for in each case, *B*'s question has already been answered by *A*. It was the point of *A*'s remarks to answer them.

This shows that in some important contexts, evaluative statements are *action guiding—prescriptive* and not merely *descriptive*. Roughly, evaluative remarks have prescriptive force—that is, they direct someone to do or refrain from doing something—when evaluations concern a present choice open to someone engaged in the conversational exchange. They do not have prescriptive force when directed toward things that are remote in time or place. Saying that it was wrong for Brutus to betray Caesar does not tell Brutus not to betray him, for it is idle to address imperatives to people in the past.

Someone who says that it would be wrong for the president to pursue a particular policy is not telling the president not to pursue it, unless, that is, she is speaking or writing to the president.

We also evaluate things that are under no one's control. For example, a major earthquake on the San Andreas fault would be a very bad thing, but in saying this we are not telling anyone to prevent it from happening. Nevertheless, even in cases where evaluations lack direct prescriptive force, sometimes they can have prescriptive force indirectly. Calling a past action wrong may, through analogy, be a way of telling someone that what he or she is now planning on doing is wrong as well. When evaluative statements have prescriptive force, either directly or indirectly, their conversational force can change the audience's behavior or feelings.

In our example of evaluating rocks as door stops, we dealt with a problem of choice that, in all likelihood, can be resolved with little difficulty. Our lives, however, consist of a constant stream of choices of varying kinds and of various levels of importance. Because we often have to make these choices or decisions under time pressure, it is not always possible to make all of them on a case-by-case basis. It is for this reason, among others, that we come to rely on *standards* in making evaluations. In most cases, we call something good because we believe that it meets or satisfies relevant standards. Thus, calling something good or bad by itself can be fairly empty of content. Such remarks gain content—sometimes a very rich content—by virtue of the standards they invoke. This explains why the word "good" can be applied to so many different kinds of things. When we say that Hondas are good cars, we are probably applying standards that involve reliability, efficiency, comfort, and so on. We call someone a good firefighter because we think the person is skilled at the tasks of a firefighter, is motivated to do those tasks, works well with other firefighters, and so on. Our standards for calling someone an ethically good person concern honesty, generosity, fairness, and so on. The standards we have for calling something a good car, a good firefighter, and an (ethically) good person have little in common, but, even so, the word "good" functions in the same way in all three cases: It invokes the standards that are relevant in a given context and indicates that something adequately satisfies these standards. Though the *reasons* we give for calling something good can vary widely from context to context, this does not show that the *meaning* of the word "good" changes from context to context. If the *meaning* of "good" did change for each kind of thing it was applied to, then the dictionary entry for "good" would be vastly larger than it is now.

As these examples show, different kinds of standards govern different areas. We speak of aesthetic values, economic values, personal values, religious values, and, of course, moral values. All these kinds of values have associated standards for evaluation. These different standards of evaluation relate to one another in complex ways: They sometimes support each other, but they sometimes conflict. Religious values and moral values often support each other. On the other hand, consider an extreme example of a possible conflict between standards: Given the huge amount of pollution that humans produce, it might be a good thing, from an ecological standpoint, to wipe out half of the world's human population. Yet virtually everyone would agree that from a moral perspective this would be a profoundly wrong thing to do.

Because evaluative statements invoke standards, they stand in contrast to utterances that *merely express* personal feelings. If I say that I like a particular singer, then I am expressing a personal taste, one that I might realize others do not share. Unless I were being accused of lying or being self-deceived, it would normally be very odd for someone to reply, "No, you don't like that singer." Generally, people have a good idea about what they like or dislike. On the other hand, if I call someone a good singer (or a great singer or the best singer in years), then I am going beyond expressing my personal tastes. I am saying something that others may accept or reject. Of course, the standards for judging singers may be imprecise, and they may shift from culture to culture. Still, to call someone a good singer is to evaluate that person as a singer, which involves invoking standards and indicating that the person in question meets them.

The words "good" and "bad" are perfectly general evaluative terms. Other evaluative terms are more restrictive in their range of application. The word "delicious" is usually used for evaluating the taste of foods; it means "good tasting." A *sin* is a kind of wrong action, but, more specifically, it is an action that is wrong according to religious standards. A *bargain* has a good price. An *illegal* action is one that is legally wrong. Words of this kind indicate that things are good or bad, right or wrong, and so forth in specific ways. Our language contains a great many such specific terms of evaluation. Here are some other examples:

beautiful	dangerous	cute
wasteful	sneaky	murderous
deceitful	prudent	nosy
sloppy	honest	skuzzy

Each of these words expresses either a positive or a negative evaluation of a quite specific kind.

Positive and negative evaluations can be subtle. Consider a word like "clever." It presents a positive evaluation in terms of quick mental ability. In contrast, "cunning" often presents a negative evaluation of someone for misusing mental abilities. It thus makes a difference which one of these words we choose. It also makes a difference where we apply them. When something is supposed to be profound and serious, it is insulting to call it merely clever. Prayers, for example, should not be clever.

Sometimes seemingly innocuous words can shift evaluative force. The word "too" is the perfect example of this. This word introduces a negative evaluation, sometimes turning a positive quality into a negative one. Compare the following sentences:

John is smart.	John is too smart.
John is honest.	John is too honest.
John is ambitious.	John is too ambitious.
John is nice.	John is too nice.
John is friendly.	John is too friendly.

The word "too" indicates an excess, and thereby contains a criticism. If you look at the items in the second column, you will see that the criticism is sometimes rather brutal—for example, calling someone "too friendly."

When analyzing arguments it is important to identify evaluative terms, for the strength of an argument often depends on whether these terms are used legitimately. This, however, can be a subtle task because the difference between an evaluative term and a descriptive term is not always obvious. To see this, consider the terms "homicide" and "murder." The words are closely related but do not mean the same thing. "Homicide" is a descriptive term meaning "the killing of a human being." "Murder" is an evaluative term meaning, in part at least, "the *wrongful* killing of a human being." It takes more to show that something is a murder than it does to show that something is a homicide. The test for an evaluative term is this: Does the word mean that something is good or bad (right or wrong) in a particular way?

Just as it is easy to miss evaluative terms because we fail to recognize the evaluative component built into their meanings, it is also possible to interpret words as evaluative when they are not because of positive or negative associations that the term might evoke. The word "nuclear," for example, has bad connotations because of its association with bombs and wars, but the word itself is purely descriptive. To call people nuclear scientists is not to say that they are bad in a certain way. Similarly, although most people think that biological warfare would be a very bad thing, this does not mean that the term "biological" is an evaluative term.

Words such as "good," "bad," "right," and "wrong" commonly occur in *moral* or *ethical* judgments. Not all uses of these words are moral, for we can speak about a good pipe wrench or a wrong turn, and in such cases we are not making moral judgments. Moral judgments are, however, a centrally important kind of evaluative judgment. They are used often in daily life, and a great many arguments concern them. In fact, arguments over moral questions may be both the most common and the most important kind of argument in which human beings engage. What, then, makes a judgment a moral judgment? Moral judgments are judgments that invoke moral standards. Saying this does not take us very far, however, for we now want to know what moral standards are and what determines which moral standards are correct. These are all difficult issues. We will return to them in Chapter 15, where we examine specifically moral arguments. What we want to emphasize here is that in making an evaluative judgment of any kind, we are invoking standards. Thus, in general, if you make an evaluative claim (a value judgment), others have a right to ask you to specify the relevant standards and show that they apply.

EXERCISE V

Indicate whether the following italicized terms are positively evaluative (E+), negatively evaluative (E−), or simply descriptive (D). Remember, the evaluations need not be moral evaluations.

1. Janet is an *excellent* golfer.
2. The group was playing very *loudly*.
3. The group was playing *too* loudly.
4. William was *rude* to his parents.
5. William *shouted* at his parents.
6. They mistakenly turned *right* at the intersection.
7. *Fascists* ruled Italy for almost twenty years.
8. That's a *no-no*.
9. *Bummer*.
10. Debbie *lied*.
11. Debbie *said something false*.
12. Joe *copped out*.
13. Jake is a *bully*.
14. Mary Lou was a *gold medalist*.
15. She is *sick*.
16. He suffers from a hormonal *imbalance*.

EXERCISE VI

For each of the following sentences, construct two others—one that reverses the evaluative force, and one that is as neutral as possible. The symbol "0" stands for neutral, "+" for positive evaluative force, and "−" for negative evaluative force. Try not to make substantial changes in the descriptive content of the sentence.

Example: − Professor Conrad is rude.

   + Professor Conrad is uncompromisingly honest in his criticisms.

   0 Professor Conrad often upsets people with his criticisms.

1. − Larry is a lazy lout.
2. + Brenda is brave.
3. − Sally is a snob.
4. + Bartlett is a blast.
5. − George is a goody-goody.
6. − Walter is a weenie.
7. + Carol is a caring person.
8. − Bill is bossy.
9. − Oprah is opinionated.
10. − This is a Mickey Mouse exercise.

Farcus

by David Waisglass
Gordon Coulthart

© 1996 Farcus Cartoons   WAISGLASS/COULTHART

Reprinted by permission of LaughingStock Licensing, Inc.

**"Let's hope corporate communications
can put a positive spin on this."**

EUPHEMISM AND SPIN DOCTORING

There are many ways in which language can be used to gain argumentative advantage through either associating something with or disassociating something from other things that are evaluated either positively or negatively. With *euphemism*, for example, we attempt to substitute a delicate, inoffensive, or even positive term for one that in some way carries negative connotations. The standard example is the use of such words as "bathroom," "restroom," "lavatory," and "Gents" as euphemisms for the word "toilet"; "toilet" itself was at one time an elegant, French-sounding euphemism. Euphemisms tend to get replaced by other euphemisms. Countries that were at one time called "primitive" or "backward" were then called "underdeveloped," then "developing," then "newly emerging" nations. People who at one time were called "crippled" were referred to as "handicapped," then as "physically challenged."

Euphemisms are often used simply to be polite or considerate. Saying that someone "has passed away" or "is no longer with us" is certainly gentler than the alternative of bluntly saying the person "has died" or, worse, "has croaked." An avalanche of ways of saying that something is dead—some euphemistic, some not—appears in the "Parrot Sketch" from Monty Python's Flying Circus: After discovering that the parrot he just bought is dead, a customer (played by John Cleese) returns to the pet store and complains. The shop owner insists that the parrot is "just resting" or "just pining," so the customer responds:

That parrot is definitely deceased. . . . It's bleeding demised. It's not pining; it's passed on. This parrot is no more. It has ceased to be. It's expired and gone to meet its maker. This is a late parrot. It's a stiff. Bereft of life, it rests in peace. If you hadn't nailed it to the perch, it would be pushing up the daisies. It dropped down the curtain and joined the choir invisible. This is an ex-parrot.

You can decide for yourself which of these descriptions are euphemistic and which of them are not.

Euphemism can also be used to cover things up—such as, for example, when concealment and evasion are referred to as "damage control." The expression "spin doctor" seems to combine two metaphors. The first concerns putting the right spin on things—that is, presenting things in ways that make them look good or bad, depending on how one wants them to be perceived. The second concerns doctoring things up to accomplish this. Spin doctoring often involves trying to find the right way of describing or labeling something. To take a fictitious example, suppose Congress was considering sharp cuts in Social Security benefits for the elderly. Supporters of such a measure might refer to it as the "Senior Citizen's Self-Reliance Act." To cite an actual example, when discussing a measure that would repeal a large number of environmental regulations, President Clinton sarcastically referred to it as the "Polluter's Bill of Rights"—not exactly a generous way of describing a bill based on the belief that environmental regulations had gone too far. Referring to the Iraq war, those who favored it spoke of the "liberation" of Iraq; those who were against it called it an "invasion." One person's freedom fighter is another person's terrorist, or so it is said. Of course, these words *can* have definite meanings, but they are often used to mislead and avoid real issues.

Slogans often come in pairs, reflecting opposing sides of an issue. Here are four contrasting pairs in wide use today:

Pro-Choice versus Pro-Life

Progressive Education versus Back to Fundamentals

Liberal versus Conservative

Alternative Lifestyles versus Family Values

The task of critical analysis is to see through such sloganeering to the important issues that lie behind it.

EXERCISE VII

Be a spin doctor yourself by writing upbeat, good-sounding titles or descriptions for the following proposals. Remember, as a professional spin doctor you should be able to make things you personally hate sound good.

1. Imposing a $1,000 fee on graduating seniors
2. Requiring all students to participate in a twenty-one-meal-per-week food plan

3. Abolishing coed dormitories

4. Abolishing fraternities

5. Requiring women students to return to their dormitories by midnight (such rules were once quite common)

6. Abolishing failing grades

7. Restoring failing grades

8. Requiring four years of physical education

9. Abolishing intercollegiate football

10. Introducing a core curriculum in Western civilization

11. Abolishing such a curriculum

12. Abolishing faculty tenure

EXERCISE VIII

Listen to a talk show and collect at least five examples of people using rhetorical devices in ways that are either utterly unfair or just plain stupid. (This will take less time than you think.)

DISCUSSION QUESTION

It is sometimes not clear whether certain terms are evaluative or have any negative connotations. One controversial area is the language used in talking about women. To take just one example, Robin Lakoff discusses the term "lady":[1]

> If in a particular sentence, both *woman* and *lady* might be used, the use of the latter tends to trivialize the subject matter under discussion, often subtly ridiculing the woman involved. Thus, for example, a mention in the *San Francisco Chronicle* of January 31, 1972, of Madalyn Murray O'Hair as the "lady atheist" reduces her position to that of a scatterbrained eccentric, or at any rate, one who need not be taken seriously. Even *woman atheist* is scarcely defensible: first, because her sex is irrelevant to her philosophical position, and second, because her name makes it clear in any event. But *lady* makes matters still worse. Similarly a reference to a *woman sculptor* is only mildly annoying (since there is no term **male sculptor*, the discrepancy suggests that such activity is normal for a man but not for a woman), but still it could be used with reference to a serious artist. *Lady sculptor*, on the other hand, strikes me as a slur against the artist, deliberate or not, implying that the woman's art is frivolous, something she does to fend off the boredom of suburban housewifery, or at any rate, nothing of moment in the art world. Serious artists have shows, not *dilettantes*. So we hear of *one-woman shows*, but never *one-lady shows*.

[1]Robin Lakoff, *Language and Woman's Place* (New York: Harper & Row, 1975), 23–25. Lakoff follows a common practice in linguistics of putting an asterisk before any expression that is linguistically anomalous.

Another realm of usage in which *lady* contrasts with *woman* is in titles of organizations. It seems that organizations of women who have a serious purpose (not merely that of spending time with one another) cannot use the word *lady* in their titles, but less serious ones may. Compare the *Ladies' Auxiliary* of a men's group, or the *Thursday Evening Ladies Browning and Garden Society*, with *Ladies' Lib or *Ladies Strike for Peace.* . . .

Besides or possibly because of being explicitly devoid of sexual connotation, *lady* carries with it overtones recalling the age of chivalry: the exalted stature of the person so referred to, her existence above the common sphere. This makes the term seem polite at first, but we must also remember that these implications are perilous: they suggest that a "lady" is helpless, and cannot do things for herself. In this respect the use of a word like *lady* is parallel to the act of opening doors for women—or ladies. At first blush it is flattering: the object of the flattery feels honored, cherished, and so forth; but by the same token, she is also considered helpless and not in control of her own destiny. Women who protest that they *like* receiving these little courtesies, and object to being liberated from them, should reflect a bit on their deeper meaning and see how much they like *that*.

Do you agree with Lakoff's claims about the connotations of the term "lady"? Why or why not? In your opinion, which other terms used to refer to women reflect a sexist bias in our society? Lakoff also discusses "mistress," "girl," "widow," "spinster," and, of course, "Mrs." (as opposed to "Ms."). You should also consider terms like "broad" and "chick."

Finally, you might want to collect a series of articles concerning women and see if they reveal a sexist bias. One way to bring this matter into sharper focus is to compare the language used about a woman with the language used about a man in a similar context, for example, in a description of the individual's appointment to some high position. Pay attention not only to what is mentioned but also to what is left out, such as when a woman's spouse is mentioned but a man's spouse is not.

THE LANGUAGE OF ARGUMENT

Using the techniques developed in Chapters 1 and 2, this chapter will examine the use of language to formulate arguments and will provide methods to analyze genuine arguments in their richness and complexity. The first stage in analyzing an argument is the discovery of its basic structure. *To do this, we will examine the words, phrases, and special constructions that indicate the premises and conclusions of an argument. The second stage is the study of techniques used to* protect *an argument. These include* guarding *premises so that they are less subject to criticism,* offering *assurances* concerning debatable claims, and discounting *possible criticisms in advance.*

THE BASIC STRUCTURE OF ARGUMENTS

In Chapters 1 and 2 we saw that language is used for a great many different purposes. One important thing that we do with language is construct arguments. Arguments are constructed out of statements, but arguments are not just lists of statements. Here is a simple list of statements:

> Socrates is a man.
>
> All men are mortal.
>
> Socrates is mortal.

This list is not an argument, because none of these statements is presented as a reason for any other statement. It is, however, simple to turn this list into an argument. All we have to do is to add the single word "therefore":

> Socrates is a man.
>
> All men are mortal.
>
> Therefore, Socrates is mortal.

Now we have an argument. The word "therefore" converts these sentences into an argument by signaling that the statement following it is a *conclusion*, and that the statement or statements that come before it are offered as *reasons* in behalf of this conclusion. The argument we have produced in this way is a good one, because the conclusion follows from the reasons stated in its behalf.

There are other ways of linking these sentences to form an argument. Here is one:

Since Socrates is a man,

and all men are mortal,

Socrates is mortal.

Notice that the word "since" works in roughly the opposite way that "therefore" does. The word "therefore" is a *conclusion marker*, because it indicates that the statement that follows it is a conclusion. In contrast, the word "since" is a *reason marker*, because it indicates that the statement or statements that follow it are reasons. In our example, the conclusion comes at the end, but there is a variation on this. Sometimes the conclusion is given at the start:

Socrates is mortal, since all men are mortal and Socrates is a man.

"Since" flags reasons; the remaining connected statement is then taken to be the conclusion, whether it appears at the beginning or at the end of the sentence.

Many other terms are used to introduce an argumentative structure into language by marking either reasons or conclusions. Here is a partial list:

Reason Markers	Conclusion Markers	
since	therefore	so
because	hence	ergo
far	then	accordingly
as	thus	

We shall call such terms "argument markers" because each presents one or more statements as part of an argument or backing for some other statement.

It is important to realize that these words are not always used as argument markers. The words "since" and "then" are often used as indicators of time, as in, "He's been an American citizen since 1973" and "He ate a hot dog, then a hamburger." The word "for" is often used as a preposition; for example, "John works for IBM." Because some of these terms have a variety of meanings, it is not possible to identify argument markers in a mechanical way just by looking at words. It is necessary to examine the function of words in the context in which they occur. One test of whether a word is functioning as an argument marker in a particular sentence is whether you can substitute another argument marker without changing the meaning of the sentence. In the last example, it makes no sense to say, "John works since IBM."

There are also many *phrases* available to signal that an argument is being presented. Here is just a small sample:

from which it follows that . . .

from which we may conclude that . . .

from which we see that . . .

which goes to show that . . .

which establishes that . . .

We can also indicate conclusions and reasons by using *argumentative performatives,* which we examined briefly in Chapter 1. If someone says, "I conclude that . . . ," the words that follow are given the status of a conclusion. More pretentiously, if someone says, "Here I base my argument on the claim that . . . ," what comes next has the status of a reason.

Examination of actual arguments will show that we have a great many ways of introducing an argumentative structure into our language by using the two forms of argument markers: reason markers and conclusion markers. The first, and in many ways the most important, step in analyzing an argument is to identify the conclusion and the reasons given in its behalf. We do this by paying close attention to these argument markers.

IF . . . THEN . . .

If-then sentences, which are also called *conditionals,* often occur in arguments—but they do not present arguments. To see this, consider the following conditional:

If the Dodgers get better hitting, then they will win the Western Division.

The sentence between the "if" and the "then" is called the *antecedent* of the conditional. The sentence after the "then" is called its *consequent.* In uttering such a conditional, we are not asserting the truth of its antecedent, and we are not asserting the truth of its consequent either. Thus, the person who makes the above remark is not claiming that the Dodgers will win the Western Division. All she is saying is that *if* they get better hitting, *then* they will win. Furthermore, she is not saying that they will get better hitting. Because the speaker is not committing herself to either of these claims, she is not presenting an argument. This becomes clear when we contrast this conditional with a statement that does formulate an argument:

CONDITIONAL: *If* the Dodgers get better hitting, *then* they will win the Western Division.

ARGUMENT: *Since* the Dodgers will get better hitting, they will win the Western Division.

The sentence that follows the word "since" is asserted. That is why "since" is an argument marker, whereas the connective "if . . . then . . ." is not an argument marker.

Even though conditionals by themselves do not mark arguments, there is a close relationship between conditionals and arguments: indicative conditionals provide *patterns* that can be converted into an argument whenever the antecedent is taken to be true.[1] Thus, we often hear people argue in the following way:

---

[1]We also get an argument when the consequent is said to be *false.* This will be discussed in Chapter 6.

> If international terrorism continues to grow, there will be a worldwide crisis.

> But international terrorism will certainly continue to grow, so a world crisis is on the way.

The first sentence is an indicative conditional. It makes no claims *one way or the other* whether terrorism will continue or whether a world crisis will occur. The next sentence asserts the antecedent of this conditional and then draws a conclusion signaled by the argument marker "so." We might say that when the antecedent of an indicative conditional is found to be true, the conditional can be *cashed in* for an argument.

Often the antecedent of a conditional is not asserted explicitly but is conversationally implied. When asked which player should be recruited for a team, the coach might just say, "If Deon is as good as our scouts say he is, then we ought to go for Deon." This conditional does not actually assert that Deon is as good as the scouts report. Nonetheless, it would be irrelevant and pointless for the coach to utter this conditional alone if he thought that the scouts were way off the mark. The coach might immediately add that he disagrees with the scouting reports. But unless the coach cancels the conversational implication in some way, it is natural to interpret him as giving an argument that we ought to pick Deon. In such circumstances, then, an indicative conditional can conversationally imply an argument, even though it does not state the argument explicitly.

This makes it easy to see why indicative conditionals are a useful feature of our language. By providing patterns for arguments, they prepare us to draw conclusions when the circumstances are right. Much of our knowledge of the world about us is contained in such conditionals. Here is an example: If your computer does not start, the plug might be loose. This is a useful piece of practical information, for when your computer does not start, you can immediately infer that the plug might be loose, then check it out.

Other words function in similar ways. When your computer fails to start, a friend might say, "Either the plug is loose or you are in deep trouble." Now, if you check the plug, and it is not loose, then you can conclude that you are in deep trouble. "Either . . . or . . ." sentences thus provide patterns for arguments, just as conditionals do. However, neither if-then sentences nor either-or sentences by themselves explicitly present an argument, so they should not be labeled as argument markers.

ARGUMENTS IN STANDARD FORM

Because arguments come in all shapes and forms, it will help to have a standard way of presenting arguments. For centuries, logicians have used a format of the following kind:

All men are mortal.
Socrates is a man.
_____

∴ Socrates is mortal.

The reasons (or premises) are listed above the line, the conclusion is listed below the line, and the symbol "∴" is read "therefore." Arguments presented in this way are said to be in *standard form*.

The notion of a standard form is useful because it helps us see that the same argument can be expressed in different ways. For example, the following two sentences formulate the argument that was stated in standard form above.

Socrates is mortal, since all men are mortal, and Socrates is a man.

All men are mortal, so Socrates is mortal, because he is a man.

More important, by putting arguments into standard form, we perform the most obvious, and in some ways most important, step in the analysis of an argument: the identification of premises and conclusion.

EXERCISE I

Identify which of the following sentences expresses an argument. For each that does, (1) circle the argument marker (or markers), and (2) restate the argument in standard form.

1. Since Chicago is north of Boston, and Boston is north of Charleston, Chicago is north of Charleston.
2. Toward evening, clouds formed and the sky grew darker; then the storm broke.
3. Texas has a greater area than Topeka, and Topeka has a greater area than the Bronx Zoo, so Texas has a greater area than the Bronx Zoo.
4. Both houses of Congress may pass a bill, but the president may still veto it.
5. Other airlines will carry more passengers because United Airlines is on strike.
6. Since Jesse James left town, taking his gang with him, things have been a lot quieter.
7. Things are a lot quieter because Jesse James left town, taking his gang with him.
8. Witches float because witches are made of wood, and wood floats.
9. The hour is up, so you must hand in your exams.
10. Joe quit because his boss was giving him so much grief.

VALIDITY, TRUTH, AND SOUNDNESS

Not all arguments are good arguments; so, having identified an argument, the next task is to *evaluate* it. Evaluating arguments is a complex business. In fact, this entire book is aimed primarily at developing procedures for doing so. There are, however, certain fundamental terms used in evaluating arguments that should be introduced from the start. They are validity, truth, and soundness. Here they will be introduced informally. Later (in Chapters 6–8) they will be examined with more rigor.

VALIDITY

In some good arguments, the conclusion is said to follow from the premises. But this commonsense notion of *following from* is hard to pin down precisely. For that reason, most logicians instead discuss whether an argument is *valid*. Calling something valid can mean a variety of things, but in this context, validity is a technical notion. This will be our definition of validity:

> An argument is *valid* if and only if it is not possible for all of its premises to be true and its conclusion false.

Alternatively, one could say that its conclusion must be true if its premises are all true. The following argument passes this test for validity:

> All senators are paid.
> Sam is a senator.
> ─────────────
> ∴ Sam is paid.

Clearly, if the two premises are true, then the conclusion has to be true as well. Contrast this with a different argument:

> All senators are paid.
> Sam is paid.
> ─────────────
> ∴ Sam is a senator.

Here the premises and the conclusion are all in fact true, but that is not enough to make the argument valid because validity concerns what is possible. This conclusion *could* be false even when the premises are true, as Sam *could* leave the Senate but still be paid for some other job.

An argument, then, is said to be *valid* if and only if there is no possible situation in which its premises are true and its conclusion is false. This definition shows why validity is a valuable feature for an argument to possess: There can be no valid argument that leads one from true premises to a false conclusion. This should square with your commonsense ideas about reasoning. If you reason well, you should not be led from truth into error.

What are known as *deductive* arguments are put forward as meeting this standard of validity, so validity is one criterion for a good deductive argument. Other arguments—so-called *inductive* arguments—are not presented as meeting this standard. Roughly, an inductive argument is presented as providing strong support for its conclusion. The standards for evaluating inductive arguments will be examined in Chapter 9. For now we will concentrate on deductive arguments.

TRUTH

Although a deductive argument must be valid to be a good argument, validity is not enough. One reason is that an argument can be valid even when some (or all) of the statements it contains are false. For example:

> All clowns are from Tennessee.
> Sam is a clown.
> ───────────────
> ∴ Sam is from Tennessee.

This is a bad argument because at least one of its premises is false. Nonetheless, this argument does satisfy our definition of validity: If all of the premises were true, then the conclusion could not be false. This makes it obvious that validity is not the same as truth. It also makes it obvious that another requirement of a good argument is that *all of its premises must be true*.

SOUNDNESS

We thus make at least two demands of a deductive argument that we will accept as proving its conclusion:

1. The argument must be valid.
2. The premises must be true.

When an argument meets both of these standards, it is said to be *sound*. If it fails to meet either one, it is *unsound*. Thus, an argument is unsound if it is invalid, and it is also unsound if at least one of its premises is false.

	All Premises True	At Least One False Premise
Valid	Sound	Unsound
Invalid	Unsound	Unsound

Soundness has one great benefit: A sound argument must have a true conclusion. We know this because its premises are true and, because it is valid, it is not possible that its premises are true and its conclusion is false. This is why people who seek truth want sound arguments, not merely valid arguments.

EXERCISE II

Indicate whether each of the following statements is an argument and, if so, whether it is valid and whether it is sound. Explain your answers where necessary.

1. Charles went bald, and most men go bald.
2. Charles went bald because most men go bald.
3. Most professors agree that they are paid too little, so they are.
4. Republicans agree that tax breaks will stimulate the economy, and they will.
5. If this school were at the South Pole, I'd be at the South Pole. But I'm not at the South Pole. Therefore, this school is not at the South Pole.
6. There can't be a largest six-digit number, because six-digit numbers are numbers, and there is no largest number.
7. Lee can't run a company right, since he can't do anything right.
8. David Letterman is over five feet tall, so he is over two feet tall.
9. Since Clinton was president, he must have won an election.

EXERCISE III

Assume that the following sentences are either true (T) or false (F) as indicated.

All my children are teenagers. (T)
All teenagers are students. (T)
All teenagers are my children. (F)
All my children are students. (T)

Using these assigned values, label each of the following arguments as (a) either valid or invalid, and (b) either sound or unsound.

1. All my children are teenagers.
   All teenagers are students.
   ∴ All my children are students.

2. All my children are students.
   All teenagers are students.
   ∴ All my children are teenagers.

3. All teenagers are my children.
   All my children are students.
   ∴ All teenagers are students.

4. All teenagers are students.
   All my children are students.
   ∴ All my children are students.

EXERCISE IV

Indicate whether each of the following sentences is true. For those that are true, explain why they are true. For those that are false, show why they are false by giving an example.

1. Every argument with a false conclusion is invalid.
2. Every argument with a false premise is invalid.
3. Every argument with a false premise and a false conclusion is invalid.
4. Every argument with a false premise and a true conclusion is invalid.
5. Every argument with true premises and a false conclusion is invalid.
6. Every argument with a true conclusion is sound.
7. Every argument with a false conclusion is unsound.

A PROBLEM AND SOME SOLUTIONS

Although soundness guarantees a true conclusion, we usually expect even more from an argument than soundness. In the first place, an argument can be sound, but trivially uninteresting:

Nigeria is in Africa.

∴ Nigeria is in Africa.

Here the premise is true. The argument is also valid, because the premise cannot be true without the conclusion (which repeats it) being true as well. Yet the argument is completely worthless as a proof that Nigeria is in Africa. The reason is that this argument is *circular*. We will examine circular arguments in detail in Chapter 12, but it is obvious why such arguments are useless. If *A* is trying to prove something to *B* that *B* has doubts about, then citing the very matter in question will not do any good. In general, for *A* to convince *B*, *A* must marshal facts that *B* accepts and then show that they justify the claim at issue. In circular arguments, the doubt about the conclusion immediately turns into a doubt about the premise as well.

Now, however, *A* seems to run into a problem. *A* cannot cite a proposition as a reason for *itself*, for that would be circular reasoning. If, however, *A* cites some *other* propositions as premises leading to the conclusion *A* is trying to establish, the question naturally arises why these premises should be accepted. Does *A* not have to present arguments for them as well? Yet if *A* does that, *A* will introduce further premises that are also in need of proof, and so on indefinitely. It now looks as if every argument, to be successful, will have to be infinitely long.

This potential regress causes deep problems in theoretical philosophy. In everyday life, however, we try to avoid these problems by relying on shared beliefs—beliefs, that is, that we believe will not be challenged. Beyond this, we expect people to believe us when we cite information that only we possess. But there are limits to this, for people sometimes believe things that are false and sometimes lie about what they know to be true. This presents a practical problem: How can we present our reasons in a way that does not produce just another demand for an argument—a demand for more reasons? Here we use three main strategies:

1. *Assuring*: Indicating that there are backup reasons even though we are not fully giving them right now.
2. *Guarding*: Weakening our claims so that they are less subject to attack.
3. *Discounting*: Anticipating criticisms and dismissing them.

In these ways we build a defensive perimeter around our premises. Each of these defenses is useful, but each can also be abused.

ASSURING

When will we want to give assurances about some statement we have made? If we state something that we know everyone believes, assurances are not necessary. For that matter, if everyone believes something, we may not even state it at all; we let others fill in this step in the argument. We offer assurances when we think that someone might doubt or challenge what we say.

There are many ways to give assurances. Sometimes we cite authorities:

Doctors agree . . .

Recent studies have shown . . .

An unimpeachable source close to the White House says . . .

It has been established that . . .

Here we indicate that authorities have these reasons without specifying what their reasons are. We merely indicate that good reasons exist, even if we ourselves cannot—or choose not to—spell them out. When the authority cited can be trusted, this is often sufficient, but authorities often can and should be questioned. This topic will be discussed more fully in Chapter 12. Another way to give assurances is to comment on the strength of our own belief:

I'm certain that . . .

I'm sure that . . .

I can assure you that . . .

I'm not kidding. . . .

Over the years, I have become more and more convinced that . . .

Again, when we use these expressions, we do not actually present reasons, but we conversationally imply that there are reasons that back our assertions.

A third kind of assurance abuses the audience:

Everyone with any sense agrees that . . .

Of course, no one will deny that . . .

It is just common sense that . . .

There is no question that . . .

Nobody but a fool would deny that . . .

These assurances not only do not give any reason, they also suggest that there is something wrong with you if you ask for a reason. We call this the *trick of abusive assurances.*

Just as we can give assurances that something is true, we can also give assurances that something is false. For example:

It is no longer held that . . .

It is wholly implausible to suppose that . . .

No one seriously maintains that . . .

You would have to be pretty dumb to think that . . .

The last two examples clearly involve abusive assurances.

Although many assurances are legitimate, we as critics should always view assurances with some suspicion. Following the conversational rule of Quality, we should expect people to give assurances only when they have good reasons to do so. Yet assuring remarks often mark the weakest parts of the argument, not the strongest. If someone says "I hardly need argue that . . . ," it is often useful to ask why she has gone to the trouble of saying it. In particular, when we distrust an argument—as we sometimes do—this is precisely the place to look for weakness. If assurances are used, they are used for some reason. Sometimes the reason is a good one. Sometimes, however, it is a bad one. In honest argumentation, assurances save time and simplify discussion. In a dishonest argument, they are used to paper over cracks.

GUARDING

Guarding represents a different strategy for protecting premises from attack. We reduce our claim to something less strong. Thus, instead of saying "all," we say "many." Instead of saying something straight out, we use a qualifying phrase, such as "it is likely that" or "it is very possible that." Law school professors like the phrase "it is arguable that." This is wonderfully noncommittal, for it does not indicate how strong the argument is, yet it does get the statement into the discussion.

Broadly speaking, there are three ways of guarding what we say:

1. Weakening the *extent* of what has been said: retreating from "all" to "most" to "a few" to "some," and so on.

2. Using *probability* phrases such as "it is virtually certain that," "it is likely that," "might," and so on.

3. Describing our *level of commitment*: moving from "I know that" to "I believe that" to "I suspect that," and so on.

These guarding phrases are often legitimate and useful. If you want to argue that a friend needs fire insurance for her house, you do not need to claim that her house *will* burn down. All you need to claim is that there is a significant *chance* that her house will burn down. Your argument is better if you start with this weaker premise, because it is easier to defend and it is enough to support your conclusion.

If we weaken a claim sufficiently, we can make it completely immune to criticism. What can be said against a remark of the following kind: "There is some small chance that perhaps a few politicians are honest on at least some occasions"? You would have to have a *very* low opinion of politicians to deny this statement. On the other hand, if we weaken a premise too much, we pay a price. The premise no longer gives strong support to the conclusion.

The goal in using guarding terms is to find a *middle way*: We should weaken our premises sufficiently to avoid criticism, but not weaken them so much that they no longer provide strong enough evidence for the conclusion. Balancing these factors is one of the most important strategies in making and criticizing arguments.

Just as it was useful to zero in on assuring terms, it is useful to keep track of guarding terms. Guarding terms are easily corrupted. One common trick is to use guarding terms to *insinuate* things that cannot be stated explicitly in a conversation. Consider the effect of the following remark: "Perhaps the secretary of state has not been candid with the Congress." This does not actually say that the secretary of state has been less than candid with the Congress, but, by the rule of Relevance, clearly suggests it. Furthermore, it suggests it in a way that is hard to combat.

A more subtle device for corrupting guarding terms is to introduce a statement in a guarded form and then go on to speak as if it were not guarded at all.

> Perhaps the secretary of state has not been candid with the Congress. Of course, he has a right to his own views, but this is a democracy where officials are accountable to Congress. It is time for him to level with us.

The force of the guarding term "perhaps" that begins this passage disappears at the end, where it is taken for granted that the secretary of state has not been candid.

What is commonly called *hedging* is a sly device that operates in the opposite direction from our last example. With hedging, one shifts ground from a strong commitment to something weaker. Things, as they say, get "watered down" or "taken back." Strong statements made at one stage of an argument are later weakened without any acknowledgment that the position has thereby been changed in a significant way. A promise to *pass* a piece of legislation is later whittled down to a promise to *bring it to a vote*.

DISCOUNTING

The general pattern of discounting is to cite a possible criticism in order to reject it or counter it. Notice how different the following statements sound:

The ring is beautiful, but expensive.

The ring is expensive, but beautiful.

Both statements assert the same facts—that the ring is beautiful and that the ring is expensive. Both statements also suggest that there is some opposition between these facts. Yet these statements operate in different ways. We might use the first as a reason for *not* buying the ring; we can use the second as a reason *for* buying it. The first sentence acknowledges that the ring is beautiful, but overrides this by pointing out that it is expensive. In reverse fashion, the second statement acknowledges that the ring is expensive, but overrides this by pointing out that it is beautiful. Such assertions of the form "*A* but *B*" thus have four components:

1. The assertion of *A*
2. The assertion of *B*
3. The suggestion of some opposition between *A* and *B*
4. The indication that the truth of *B* is more important than the truth of *A*

The word "but" thus discounts the statement that comes before it in favor of the statement that follows it.

"Although" is also a discounting connective, but it operates in reverse fashion from the word "but." We can see this, using the same example:

Although the ring is beautiful, it is expensive.

Although the ring is expensive, it is beautiful.

Here the statement following the word "although" is discounted in favor of the connected statement. A partial list of terms that function as discounting connectives includes the following conjunctions:

although	but
though	however
while	nonetheless
whereas	nevertheless
even if	yet
still	

The clearest cases of discounting occur when we are dealing with facts that point in different directions. We discount the facts that go against the position we wish to take. But discounting is often more subtle than this. We sometimes use discounting to block certain conversational implications of what we have said. This comes out in examples of the following kind:

Jones is an aggressive player, but he is not dirty.

The situation is difficult, but not hopeless.

The Republicans have the upper hand in Congress, but only for the time being.

A truce has been declared, but who knows for how long?

Take the first example. There is no opposition between Jones being aggressive and his not being dirty. Both would be reasons to pick Jones for our team. However, the assertion that Jones is aggressive might *suggest* that he is dirty. The "but" clause discounts this suggestion without, of course, denying that Jones is aggressive.

The nuances of discounting terms can be subtle, and a correct analysis is not always easy. All the same, the role of discounting terms is often important. It can be effective in an argument to beat your opponents to the punch by anticipating and discounting criticisms before your opponents can raise them. The proper use of discounting can also help you avoid side issues and tangents.

Still, discounting terms, like the other argumentative terms we have examined, can be abused. People often spend time discounting *weak* objections to their views in order to avoid other objections that they know are harder to counter. Another common trick is to discount objections no one would raise. This is called attacking *straw men*. Consider the following remark: "A new building would be great, but it won't be free." This does not actually say that the speaker's opponents think we can build a new building for free, but it does conversationally imply that they think this, because otherwise it would be irrelevant to discount that objection. The speaker is thus trying to make the opponents look bad by putting words in their mouths that they would never say themselves. To counter tricks like this, we need to ask whether a discounted criticism is one that really would be raised, and whether there are stronger criticisms that should be raised.

ARGUMENTATIVE PERFORMATIVES

We have looked at many acts that are performed in arguments. Speakers can draw conclusions, give reasons, assure, guard, and discount. Because these are speech acts, it should come as no surprise that many of these acts can also be done by explicit performatives that pass the thereby test introduced in Chapter 1:

If I say, "I conclude that such and such," I thereby conclude that such and such.

If I say, "I base my argument on the claim that such and such," I thereby base my argument on that claim.

If I say, "I assure you that he will meet you," I thereby assure you that he will meet you.[2]

If I say, "I give my unqualified support to this measure," I thereby give my unqualified support to this measure.

[2]This is a tricky case, because, even though I assured you, you still might not *feel* assured.

There are, in fact, a great many examples of performatives used for argumentative purposes. Here are a few more:

If I say, "I deny such and such," I thereby deny such and such.

If I say, "I reply that such and such," I thereby reply that such and such.

If I say, "I concede the point," I thereby concede the point.

If I say, "I stipulate that such and such," I thereby stipulate that such and such.

When a performative is used to make a move in an argument, we call it an *argumentative performative*. As with other performatives, it is inappropriate to deny such utterances. If a lawyer finishes his speech to the jury by saying, "I conclude that the evidence merits acquittal," it would be ridiculous for someone to say, "No you don't!" We may disagree that the evidence merits acquittal, but we cannot disagree that the lawyer has drawn this conclusion.

We can also make these argumentative moves in other ways. Instead of saying, "I deny that," we can say, "That's not so," "No way," or "Oh, yeah?" Since there are so many ways to make each move, why do we have argumentative performatives at all? Part of the answer is that argumentative performatives make our argumentative moves explicit. If I want to make it perfectly clear *that* I am disagreeing and also exactly which *part* of my opponent's argument I am disagreeing with, I can do this by saying, "I deny that . . ." We usually reserve argumentative performatives for the *important* parts of opposing arguments.

Performatives also allow *subtle* moves to be made in the course of an argument. Sometimes an arguer will say, "I grant the point for the sake of argument" (thereby granting the point for the sake of argument). This is a powerful move if it can be carried off, for nothing is better than refuting an opponent on his own grounds. This device also contains an escape hatch, for if our efforts go badly, we can still challenge the statement previously granted just for the sake of argument.

Somewhat differently, we can say, "I reserve comment" (thereby reserving comment). Here we neither reject nor accept a claim (even for the sake of argument). We let it pass until we see what is made of it. This is a useful tactical device. By reserving comment we can avoid being drawn into irrelevant discussions that will cloud the issue. At other times we do not know what we want to say in response to a particular point, or we are not quite sure what the person is going to make of it. Reserving comment is a way of not sticking our necks out prematurely. We can also question something just by saying, "I question that." Questioning something is different from denying it. When we deny something, we take a definite stance on it. We do not do this when we call something into question. Calling something into question is not an entirely safe argumentative mood. It is a bad idea to question things that have straightforward, satisfactory answers. Still, questioning, along with granting things for the sake of argument and reserving comment, can be powerful and subtle tools for making different kinds of moves in an argument. They are often made by using argumentative performative and should be watched carefully.

For each of the numbered words or expressions in the following sentences, indicate whether it is an argument marker, an assuring term, a guarding term, a discounting term, an argumentative performative, or none of these. For each argument marker, specify what the conclusion and the reasons are, and for each discounting term, specify what criticism is being discounted and what the response to this criticism is.

1. *Although* [1] no mechanism has been discovered, *most* [2] *researchers in the field agree* [3] that smoking *greatly increases the chances* [4] of heart disease.
2. *Since* [5] *historically* [6] public debt leads to inflation, *I maintain* [7] that, *despite* [8] recent trends, inflation will return.
3. *Take it from me* [9], there hasn't been a decent center fielder *since* [10] Joe DiMaggio.
4. *Whatever anyone tells you* [11], there is *little* [12] to the rumor that Queen Elizabeth II will step down *for* [13] her son, Prince Charles.
5. The early deaths of Janis Joplin and Jimi Hendrix *show* [14] *how really* [15] dangerous drugs are.
6. I *think* [16] he is out back somewhere.
7. I *think* [17], *therefore* [18] I am.
8. I *concede* [19] that the evidence is *hopelessly* [20] weak, *but* [21] I still think he is guilty.
9. I *deny* [22] that I had *anything* [23] to do with it.
10. The wind has shifted to the northeast, *which means* [24] that snow is *likely* [25].

1. Construct three new and interesting examples of statements containing assuring terms.
2. Do the same for guarding terms.
3. Do the same for argumentative performatives.
4. Do the same for discounting terms, and indicate which statement is being discounted in favor of the other.
5. Do the same for argument markers, and indicate what is presented as a reason for what.

The Art of Close Analysis

*T*his chapter will largely be dedicated to a single purpose: the close and careful analysis of a speech drawn from the Congressional Record, *using argumentative devices introduced in Chapter 3. We will also illustrate a global analysis of the overall purpose, audience, and standpoint of an argument. The point of this chapter is to show in detail how these methods of analysis can be applied to an actual argument of some richness and complexity.*

AN EXTENDED EXAMPLE

It is now time to apply all of our previously discussed notions to a genuine argument. Our example will be a debate that occurred in the House of Representatives on the question of whether there should be an increase in the allowance given to members of the House for clerical help—the so-called clerk hire allowance. The argument against the increase presented by Representative Kyl (Republican, Iowa) will be examined in detail. We will put it under an analytic microscope.

The choice of this example may seem odd, for the question of clerk hire allowance is not one of the burning issues of our time. This, in fact, is one reason for choosing it. It will be useful to begin with an example about which feelings do not run high to learn the habit of objective analysis. Later on we shall examine arguments about which almost everyone has strong feelings and try to maintain an objective standpoint even there. The example is good for two other reasons: (1) it contains most of the argumentative devices we have listed, and (2) relatively speaking, it is quite a strong argument. This last remark may seem ironic after we seemingly tear the argument to shreds, but in comparison to other arguments we shall examine, it stands up well.

We can begin by reading through a section of the *Congressional Record*[1] without comment:

---

[1]*Congressional Record*, vol. 107, part 3 (March 15, 1961), 4059–60.

CLERK HIRE ALLOWANCE,
HOUSE OF REPRESENTATIVES
——————————■——————————

Mr. FRIEDEL. Mr. Speaker, by direction of the Committee on House Administration, I call up the resolution (H. Res. 219) to increase the basic clerk hire
allowance of each Member of the House, and for other purposes, and ask for
its immediate consideration.

The Clerk read the resolution as follows:

> *Resolved,* That effective April 1, 1961, there shall be paid out of the contingent
> fund of the House, until otherwise provided by law, such sums as may be neces-
> sary to increase the basic clerk hire allowance of each Member and the Resident
> Commissioner from Puerto Rico by an additional $3,000 per annum, and each
> such Member and Resident Commissioner shall be entitled to one clerk in addi-
> tion to those to which he is otherwise entitled by law.

Mr. FRIEDEL. Mr. Speaker, this resolution allows an additional $3,000 per
annum for clerk hire and an additional clerk for each Member of the House
and the Resident Commissioner from Puerto Rico. Our subcommittee heard
the testimony, and we were convinced of the need for this provision to be
made. A few Members are paying out of their own pockets for additional
clerk hire. This $3,000 is the minimum amount we felt was necessary to help
Members pay the expenses of running their offices. Of course, we know that
the mail is not as heavy in some of the districts as it is in others, and, of
course, if the Member does not use the money, it remains in the contingent
fund.

Mr. KYL. Mr. Speaker, will the gentleman yield?

Mr. FRIEDEL. I yield to the gentleman from Iowa [Mr. Kyl.] for a statement.

Mr. KYL. Mr. Speaker, I oppose this measure. I oppose it first because it is
expensive. I further oppose it because it is untimely.

I do not intend to belabor this first contention. We have been presented a
budget of about $82 billion. We have had recommended to us a whole series
of additional programs or extensions of programs for priming the pump, for
depressed areas, for the needy, for unemployed, for river pollution projects,
and recreation projects, aid to education, and many more. All are listed as
"must" activities. These extensions are not within the budget. Furthermore,
if business conditions are as deplorable as the newspapers indicate, the Government's income will not be as high as anticipated. It is not enough to say
we are spending so much now, a little more will not hurt. What we spend,
we will either have to recover in taxes, or add to the staggering national
debt.

The amount of increase does not appear large. I trust, however, there is no
one among us who would suggest that the addition of a clerk would not
entail allowances for another desk, another typewriter, more materials, and
it is not beyond the realm of possibility that the next step would then be a
request for additional office space, and ultimately new buildings. Some will
say, "All the Members will not use their maximum, so the cost will not be
great." And this is true. If the exceptions are sufficient in number to consti-

tute a valid argument, then there is no broad general need for this measure. Furthermore, some Members will use these additional funds to raise salaries. Competition will force all salaries upward in all offices and then on committee staffs, and so on. We may even find ourselves in a position of paying more money for fewer clerks and in a tighter bind on per person workload.

This measure proposes to increase the allowance from $17,500 base clerical allowance to $20,500 base salary allowance. No member of this House can tell us what this means in gross salary. That computation is almost impossible. Such a completely absurd system has developed through the years on salary computations for clerical hire that we have under discussion a mathematical monstrosity. We are usually told that the gross allowed is approximately $35,000. This is inaccurate. In one office the total might be less than $35,000 and in another, in complete compliance with the law and without any conscious padding, the amount may be in excess of $42,000. This is possible because of a weird set of formulae which determines that three clerks at $5,000 cost less than five clerks at $3,000. Five times three might total the same as three times five everywhere else in the world—but not in figuring clerk hire in the House.

This is an application of an absurdity. It is a violation of bookkeeping principles, accounting principles, business principles and a violation of commonsense. Listen to the formula:

First, 20 percent increase of first $1,200; 10 percent additional from $1,200 to $4,600; 5 percent further additional from $4,600 to $7,000.

Second, after applying the increases provided in paragraph 1, add an additional 14 percent or a flat $250 whichever is the greater, but this increase must not exceed 25 percent.

Third, after applying the increases provided in both paragraphs 1 and 2, add an additional increase of 10 percent in lieu of overtime.

Fourth, after applying the increases provided in paragraphs 1, 2, and 3, add an additional increase of $330.

Fifth, after applying the increases provided in paragraphs 1, 2, 3, and 4, add an additional increase of 5 percent.

Sixth, after applying the increases provided in paragraphs 1, 2, 3, 4, and 5, add an additional increase of 10 percent but not more than $800 nor less than $300 a year.

Seventh, after applying the increases provided in paragraphs, 1, 2, 3, 4, 5, and 6, add an additional increase of $7\frac{1}{2}$ percent.

Eighth, after applying the increases provided in paragraphs, 1, 2, 3, 4, 5, 6, and 7, add an additional increase of 10 percent.

Ninth, after applying the increases provided in paragraphs 1, 2, 3, 4, 5, 6, 7, and 8, add an additional increase of $7\frac{1}{2}$ percent.

The Disbursing Office has a set of tables to figure House salaries for office staffs and for about 900 other employees. It contains 45 sheets with 40 entries per sheet. In the Senate, at least, they have simplified the process some by figuring their base in multiples of 60, thus eliminating 11 categories. Committee staffers, incidentally, have an $8,880 base in comparison to the House $7,000 base limitation.

Now, Mr. Speaker, I have planned to introduce an amendment or a substitute which would grant additional clerk hire where there is a demonstrable need based on heavier than average population or "election at large" and possible other factors. But after becoming involved in this mathematical maze, I realize the folly of proceeding one step until we have corrected this situation. We can offer all kinds of excuses for avoiding a solution. We cannot offer reasonable arguments that it should not be done or that it cannot be done.

Someone has suggested that the Members of this great body prefer to keep the present program because someone back in the home district might object to the gross figures. I know this is not so. When a Representative is busy on minimum wage, or aid to education, or civil rights, such matters of housekeeping seem too picayune to merit attention. The Member simply checks the table and hires what he can hire under the provisions and then forgets the whole business. But I know the Members also want the people back home to realize that what we do here is open and frank and accurate, and that we set an example in businesslike procedures. The more we can demonstrate responsibility the greater will be the faith in Congress.

May I summarize. It is obvious that some Members need more clerical help because of large population and large land area. I have been working for some time with the best help we can get, on a measure which would take these items into consideration. Those Members who are really in need of assistance should realize that this temporary, hastily conceived proposition we debate today will probably obviate their getting a satisfactory total solution.

First, we should await redistricting of the Nation.

Second, we should consider appropriate allowance for oversize districts considering both population and total geographic area.

Finally, I hope we can develop a sound and sensible formula for computing salaries of office clerks and other statutory employees in the same category.

Before going any further, it will be useful to record your general reactions to this speech. Perhaps you think that on the whole Kyl gives a well-reasoned argument on behalf of his position. Alternatively, you might think that he is making a big fuss over nothing, trying to confuse people with numbers, and just generally being obnoxious. When you are finished examining this argument in detail, you can look back and ask yourself why you formed this original impression and how, if at all, you have changed your mind.

The first step in the close analysis of an argument is to go through the text, labeling the various argumentative devices we have examined. Here some abbreviations will be useful:

argument marker	AM
assuring term	A
guarding term	G

discounting term	D
argumentative performative	AP
evaluative term	E $(+ \ or \ -)$
rhetorical device	R

The last label is a catchall for the various rhetorical devices discussed in Chapter 2, such as rhetorical questions, irony, metaphor, and so on. Even this simple process of labeling brings out features of an argument that could pass by unnoticed. It also directs us to ask sharp critical questions. To see this, we can look at each part of the argument in detail.

> Mr. KYL. Mr. Speaker, (I oppose) this measure. I (oppose) it — AP
>
> AM ——— first (because) it is expensive. I further (oppose) it (because) it — AP
> — AM
> is untimely.

This is a model of clarity. By the use of a performative utterance in the opening sentence, Kyl makes it clear that he opposes the measure. Then by twice using the argument marker "because," he gives his two main reasons for opposing it: *it is expensive* and *it is untimely*. We must now see if he makes good on each of these claims.

The next paragraph begins the argument for the claim that the measure is expensive:

> (I do not intend to belabor this first contention.) We have been — A
>
> presented a budget of about $82 billion. We have had recommended to us a whole series of additional programs or extensions of programs for priming the pump, for depressed areas, for the needy, for unemployed, for river pollution projects, and recreation projects, aid to education, and many more. All are listed as ⊘ must ⊘ activities. These extensions — R
>
> are not within the budget. (Furthermore), if business condi- — AM
> tions are as deplorable as the newspapers indicate, the Government's income will not be as high as anticipated. (It is not — D
> enough to say) we are spending so much now, a little more will not hurt. What we spend, we will either have to recover in taxes, or add to the staggering national debt.

(a) "I do not intend to belabor this first contention." This is an example of *assuring*. The conversational implication is that the point is so obvious that little has to be said in its support. Yet there is something strange going on here. Having said that he will *not* belabor the claim that the bill is expensive, Kyl actually goes on to say quite a bit on the subject. It is a good idea to look closely when someone says that he or she is not going to do something, for often just the opposite is happening. For example, saying, "I am not suggesting that Smith is dishonest" is one way of suggesting that Smith *is* dishonest. If no such suggestion is being made, why raise the issue at all?

(b) Kyl now proceeds in a rather flat way, stating that the proposed budget comes to $82 billion and that it contains many new programs and extensions of former programs. Because these are matters of public record and nobody is likely to deny them, there is no need for guarding or assuring. Kyl also claims, without qualification, that these extensions are not within the budget. This recital of facts does, however, carry an important conversational implication: Since the budget is already out of balance, any further extensions should be viewed with suspicion.

(c) Putting the word "must" in quotation marks, or saying it in a sarcastic tone of voice, is a common device for denying something. The plain suggestion is that some of these measures are *not* must activities at all. We see the same device in a more dramatic fashion when Marc Antony, in Shakespeare's *Julius Caesar* (III, ii), ironically repeats, "Brutus is an honorable man." Anyway, Kyl here suggests that some of the items already in the budget are not necessary. He does this, of course, without defending this suggestion.

(d) "Furthermore, if business conditions are as deplorable as the newspapers indicate, the Government's income will not be as high as anticipated." The word "furthermore" suggests that an argument is about to come. However, the following sentence as a whole is an *indicative conditional* (with the word "then" dropped out). As such, the sentence does not produce an argument, but instead provides a pattern for an argument. To get an argument from this pattern, one would have to assert the antecedent of the conditional. The argument would then come to this:

(1) If business conditions are as deplorable as the newspapers indicate, then the government's income will not be as high as anticipated.

(2) Business conditions are as deplorable as the newspapers indicate.

(3) Therefore, the government's income will not be as high as anticipated.

The first premise seems like a perfectly reasonable conditional, so, if Kyl could establish the second premise, he would have moved the argument along in an important way. Yet he does not explicitly state that business conditions are so deplorable; all he says is that "the newspapers *indicate*" this. Still, he never questions what the newspapers claim, and it would be misleading to bring up these newspaper reports without questioning them if he thought they were way off the mark. So Kyl does seem to have in mind something like the argument (1)–(3).[2]

(e) "It is not enough to say we are spending so much now, a little more will not hurt." The opening phrase is, of course, used to deny what follows it. Kyl is plainly rejecting the argument that we are spending so much now, a little more will not hurt. Yet his argument has a peculiar twist, for who

[2]This passage also contains a vague *appeal to authority*, because no specific newspaper is cited. We will discuss appeals to authority in Chaper 12.

would come right out and make such an argument? If you stop to think for a minute, it should be clear that nobody would want to put it that way. An opponent, for example, would use quite different phrasing. He might say something like this: "Considering the large benefits that will flow from this measure, it is more than worth the small costs." What Kyl has done is attribute a bad argument to his opponents and then reject it in an indignant tone. This is a common device, and when it is used, it is often useful to ask whether anyone would actually argue or speak in the way suggested. When the answer to this question is no, as it often is, we have what was called "the trick of discounting straw men" in Chapter 3. In such cases, it is useful to ask what the speaker's opponent would have said instead. This leads to a further question: has the arguer even addressed himself to the *real* arguments of his opponents?

So far, Kyl has not addressed himself to the first main point of his argument: that the measure is *expensive*. This is not a criticism, because he is really making the preliminary point that the matter of expense is significant. Here he has stated some incontestable facts—for example, that the budget is already out of balance. Beyond this he has indicated, with varying degrees of strength, that the financial situation is grave. It is against this background that the detailed argument concerning the cost of the measure is actually presented in the next paragraph.

> The amount of increase does not appear large. (I trust,) (however,) (there is no one among us who would suggest that) the addition of a clerk would not entail allowances for another desk, another typewriter, more materials, (and it is not beyond the realm of possibility that) the next step would then be a request for additional office space, and ultimately new buildings. (Some will say), "All the Members will not use their maximum, so the cost will not be great." And this is true. If the exceptions are sufficient in number to constitute a valid argument, then there is no broad general need for this measure. (Furthermore,) (some) Members will use these additional funds to raise salaries. Competition will force all salaries upward in all offices and then on committee staffs, and so on. We (may) even find ourselves in a position of paying more money for fewer clerks and in a tighter bind on per person workload.

D · A · G · D · AM · G · G

(a) "The amount of increase does not appear large." Words like "appear" and "seem" are sometimes used for guarding, but we must be careful not to apply labels in an unthinking way. The above sentence is the beginning of a discounting argument. As soon as you hear this sentence, you can feel that a word like "but" or "however" is about to appear. Sure enough, it does.

(b) "I trust, however, there is no one among us who would suggest that the addition of a clerk would not entail allowances for another desk, another typewriter, more materials, . . ." This is the beginning of Kyl's argument that is intended to rebut the argument that the increase in expenses will not be large. Appearances to the contrary, he is saying, the increase *will* be large. He then ticks off some additional expenses that are entailed by hiring new clerks. Notice that the whole sentence is covered by the assuring phrase "I trust . . . there is no one among us who would suggest . . ." This implies that anyone who would make such a suggestion is merely stupid. But the trouble with Kyl's argument so far is this: He has pointed out genuine additional expenses, but they are not, after all, very large. It is important for him to get some genuinely large sums of money into his argument. This is the point of his next remark.

(c) ". . . and it is not beyond the realm of possibility that the next step would then be a request for additional office space, and ultimately new buildings." Here, at last, we have some genuinely large sums of money in the picture, but the difficulty is that the entire claim is totally guarded by the phrase "it is not beyond the realm of possibility." There are very few things that *are* beyond the realm of possibility. Kyl's problem, then, is this: There are certain additional expenses that he can point to without qualification, but these tend to be small. On the other hand, when he points out genuinely large expenses, he can only do so in a guarded way. So we are still waiting for a proof that the expense will be large. (Parenthetically, it should be pointed out that Kyl's prediction of new buildings actually came true.)

(d) "Some will say, 'All the Members will not use their maximum, so the cost will not be great.' And this is true. If the exceptions are sufficient in number to constitute a valid argument, then there is no broad general need for this measure." This looks like a "tricky" argument, and for this reason alone it demands close attention. The phrase "some will say" is a standard way of beginning a discounting argument. This *is*, in fact, a discounting argument, but its form is rather subtle. Kyl cites what some will say, and then adds, somewhat surprisingly: "And this is true." To understand what is going on here, we must have a good feel for conversational implication. Kyl imagines someone reasoning in the following way:

All the Members will not use their maximum.

So the cost will not be great.

Therefore, we should adopt the measure.

Given the same starting point, Kyl tries to derive just the *opposite* conclusion along the following lines:

All the Members will not use their maximum.

If the exceptions are not sufficient, then the cost will be too great.

But if the exceptions are sufficient, then there is no broad general need for this measure.

Therefore, whether it is expensive or not, we should reject this measure.

In order to get clear about this argument, we can put it into schematic form:

Kyl's argument

If (1) expensive, then   → Reject

If (2) inexpensive, then, because that demonstrates
    no general need,   → Reject

The opposite argument

If (1) inexpensive, then   → Accept

If (2) expensive, then, because that demonstrates
    a general need,   → Accept

When the arguments are spread out in this fashion, it should be clear that they have equal strength. Both are no good. The question that must be settled is this: Does a genuine need exist that can be met in an economically sound manner? If there is no need for the measure, then it should be rejected, however inexpensive. Again, if there is a need, then some expense is worth paying. The real problem is to balance need against expense and then decide on this basis whether the measure as a whole is worth adopting. Kyl's argument is a sophistry because it has no tendency to answer the real question at hand. A *sophistry* is a clever but fallacious argument intended to establish a point through trickery. Incidentally, it is one of the marks of a sophistical argument that, though it may baffle, it almost never convinces. We think that few readers will have found this argument persuasive even if they cannot say exactly what is wrong with it. The appearance of a sophistical argument (or even a complex and tangled argument) is a sign that the argument is weak. Remember, when a case is strong, people usually argue in a straightforward way.

(e) "Furthermore, some Members will use these additional funds to raise salaries. Competition will force all salaries upward in all offices and then on committee staffs, and so on." The word "furthermore" signals that further reasons are forthcoming. Here Kyl returns to the argument that the measure is more expensive than it might at first sight appear. Although Kyl's first sentence is guarded by the term "some," he quickly drops his guard and speaks in an unqualified way about *all* salaries in *all* offices. Yet the critic is bound to ask whether Kyl has any right to make these projections. Beyond this, Kyl here projects a *parade of horrors.* He pictures this measure leading by gradual steps to quite disastrous consequences. Here the little phrase "and so on" carries a great burden in the argument. Once more, we must simply ask ourselves whether these projections seem reasonable.

(f) "We may even find ourselves in a position of paying more money for fewer clerks and in a tighter bind on per person workload." Once more, the use of a strong guarding expression takes back most of the force of the argument. Notice that if Kyl could have said straight out that the measure *will* put us in a position of paying more money for fewer clerks and in a tighter bind on per-person workload, that would have counted as a very strong objection. You can hardly do better in criticizing a position than showing that it will have just the opposite result from what is intended. In fact, however, Kyl has not established this; he has only said that this is something that we "may even find."

Before we turn to the second half of Kyl's argument, which we shall see in a moment is much stronger, we should point out that our analysis has not been entirely fair. Speaking before the House of Representatives, Kyl is in an *adversarial* situation. He is not trying to prove things for all time; rather, he is responding to a position held by others. Part of what he is doing is *raising objections,* and a sensitive evaluation of the argument demands a detailed understanding of the nuances of the debate. But even granting this, it should be remembered that objections themselves must be made for good reasons. The problem so far in Kyl's argument is that the major reasons behind his objections have constantly been guarded in a very strong way.

Turning now to the second part of Kyl's argument—that the measure is untimely—we see that he moves along in a clear and direct way with little guarding.

> This measure proposes to increase the allowance from $17,500 base clerical allowance to $20,500 base salary allowance. No member of this House can tell us what this means in gross salary. That computation is (almost) impossi-   G
> ble. Such a (completely absurd) system has developed   E–
> through the years on salary computations for clerical hire
> that we have under discussion a (mathematical monstrosity.)   E–
> We are usually told that the gross allowed is approximately
> $35,000. This is inaccurate. In one office the total might be
> less than $35,000 and in another, in complete compliance
> with the law and without any conscious padding, the
> amount may be in excess of $42,000. This is possible because
> of a (weird) set of formulae which determines that three   E–
> clerks at $5,000 cost less than five clerks at $3,000. (Five times   R
> three might total the same as three times five everywhere
> else in the world—but not in figuring clerk hire in the House.)
>   This is an application of (an absurdity.) It is a violation of   E–
> bookkeeping principles, accounting principles, business
> principles and a (violation of commonsense.) Listen to the   E–
> formula.

The main point of the argument is clear enough: Kyl is saying that the present system of clerk salary allowance is utterly confusing, and this matter should be straightened out before *any* other measures in this area are adopted. There is a great deal of negative evaluation in this passage. Notice the words and phrases that Kyl uses:

a completely absurd system

weird set of formulae

violation of commonsense

mathematical monstrosity

an absurdity

There is also a dash of irony in the remark that five times three might total the same as three times five everywhere else in the world, but not in figuring clerk hire in the House. Remember, there is nothing wrong with using negative evaluative and expressive terms if they are deserved. Looking at the nine-step formula in Kyl's speech, you can decide for yourself whether he is on strong grounds in using this negative language.

> Now, Mr. Speaker, I have planned to introduce an amend-
> ment or a substitute which would grant additional clerk hire
> where there is a demonstrable need based on heavier than
> average population or "election at large" and possible other
> factors.

(a) This passage discounts any suggestion that Kyl is unaware that a genuine problem does exist in some districts. It also indicates that he is willing to do something about it.

(b) The phrase "and possible other factors" is not very important, but it seems to be included to anticipate other reasons for clerk hire that should at least be considered.

D   (But) after becoming involved in this (mathematical maze,) I   E–

A   (realize) the (folly) of proceeding one step until we have cor-   E–

rected this situation.

(a) Here Kyl clearly states his reason for saying that the measure is untimely. Notice that the reason offered has been well documented and is not hedged in by qualifications.

(b) The phrases "mathematical maze" and "folly" are again negatively evaluative.

> We can offer all kinds of (excuses) for avoiding a solution.   E–
>
> (We cannot offer reasonable arguments that) it should not be   A
> done or that it cannot be done.

(a) Notice that the first sentence ridicules the opponents' arguments by calling them *excuses*, a term with negative connotations. The second sentence gives assurances that such a solution can be found.

Someone has suggested that the Members of this great body prefer to keep the present program because someone back in the home district might object to the gross figures. (I know) A this is not so. When a Representative is busy on minimum wage, or aid to education, or civil rights, such matters of housekeeping seem too picayune to merit attention. The Member simply checks the table and hires what he can hire under the provisions and then forgets the whole business.

D (But) (I know) the Members also want the people back home A to realize that what we do here is (open and frank and accu- E+ rate,) and that we set an example in businesslike procedures. The more we can demonstrate responsibility the greater will be the faith in Congress.

(a) Once more the seas of rhetoric run high. Someone (though not Kyl himself) has suggested that the members of the House wish to conceal information. He disavows the very thought that he would make such a suggestion by the sentence "I know this is not so." All the same, he has gotten this suggestion into the argument.

(b) Kyl then suggests another reason why the members of the House will not be concerned with this measure: It is "too picayune." The last two sentences rebut the suggestion that it is too small to merit close attention. Even on small matters, the more the House is "open and frank and accurate," the more it will "set an example in businesslike procedures" and thus "demonstrate responsibility" that will increase "the faith in Congress." This is actually an important part of Kyl's argument, for presumably his main problem is to get the other members of the House to take the matter seriously.

May I summarize. (It is obvious that) some Members need A AM more clerical help (because) of large population and large land area. (I have been working for some time with the best A help we can get,) on a measure which would take these items into consideration. Those Members who are really in need of A assistance should (realize) that this (temporary, hastily con- E− ceived) proposition we debate today will (probably) obviate G their getting a satisfactory total solution.

(a) This is a concise summary. Kyl once more assures the House that he is aware that a genuine problem exists. He also indicates that he is working on it.

(b) The phrase "temporary, hastily conceived proposition we debate today" refers back to his arguments concerning untimeliness.

(c) The claim that "it will probably obviate their getting a satisfactory total solution" refers back to the economic argument. Notice, however, that, as before, the economic claim is guarded by the word "probably."

E+   First, we (should) await redistricting of the Nation.

E+   Second, we (should) consider appropriate allowance for oversize districts considering both population and total geographic area.

     Finally, I hope we can develop a (sound and sensible) formula for computing salaries of office clerks and other statutory employees in the same category.   E+

This is straightforward except that a new factor is introduced: We should await redistricting of the nation. This was not mentioned earlier in the argument, and so seems a bit out of place in a summary. Perhaps the point is so obvious that it did not need any argument to support it. On the other hand, it is often useful to keep track of things that are smuggled into the argument at the very end. If redistricting was about to occur in the *near* future, this would give a strong reason for delaying action on the measure. Because the point is potentially so strong, we might wonder why Kyl has made so little of it. Here, perhaps, we are getting too subtle.

GLOBAL ANALYSIS

Now that we have looked at Representative Kyl's argument in close detail, we can step back and notice some important features of the argument as a whole. Global analysis involves an examination of *purpose, audience,* and *standpoint.*

First, Kyl's overall *purpose* is clear. As his opening sentence indicates, he is presenting an argument intended to justify his opposition to an increase in the clerk hire allowance. Virtually everything he says is directed toward this single goal. In other cases, arguers pursue multiple goals, and sorting things out can be a complex matter. Sometimes it is hard to tell what an argument is even intended to establish. This is usually a sign that the person presenting the argument is confused or, perhaps, trying to confuse his audience.

Second, Kyl's argument is addressed to a specific *audience.* He is not speaking to an enemy of the United States who would love to see our government waste its money. Nor is he speaking to clerks or to those U.S. citizens who might be hired as clerks if the clerk hire allowance were raised. He is presenting his argument to other representatives in Congress. He is trying to show this group that they and he have reasons to oppose this increase in the clerk hire allowance. His task, then, is to present reasons that *they* accept—or should accept—for rejecting an increase in the clerk hire allowance.

Third, Kyl not only addresses his argument to a particular audience, he also adopts a particular *standpoint* to it. Good arguments are usually presented not only *to* specific audiences but also *from* particular standpoints. Kyl's standpoint is clear and powerful. He puts himself across as a tough-minded, thoroughly honest person who is willing to stand up against majority opinion. This, in fact, may be an accurate representation of his character, but by adopting this standpoint he gains an important argumentative advantage: He suggests that those who disagree with him are a bit soft-minded, not altogether candid, and, anyway, mere tools of the Democratic majority that runs the Congress. By adopting this stance, Kyl casts his opponents in a light that is hardly flattering.

This tactic of adopting a standpoint that puts one's opponent at a disadvantage is a common argumentative device that deserves close attention. A standard ploy is to claim a *middle ground* between two extreme positions. This strategy is used by the distinguished economist Paul A. Samuelson in the opening paragraphs of an article published in *Newsweek* under the title "New York Dilemma." At the time (1975), New York City was faced with a financial crisis that threatened bankruptcy.

> This is a hard column to write. How easy it would be if one were simpleminded and could baldly assert: "Let New York go down the drain. It couldn't happen to a nicer bunch of fellows anyway. Bankruptcy not only will teach a lesson, punish the guilty and deter those tempted in the future, but it will also be the first step on the road back to fiscal probity."
>
> Likewise, it would be an easy position to hold if one could believe with conviction: "The Federal government should take responsibility for the city's present plight. After all, *the crisis has national not local causes. . . .* "
>
> Neither of these positions is tenable for an intelligent person of goodwill. But where in the wide middle ground between them is the feasible optimum for policy to be found? Here are some tentative economic considerations that may help set bounds on possible policy alternatives.[3]

We thus find Samuelson dismissing two extreme positions and defining himself as an "intelligent person of goodwill" occupying a reasonable middle ground. He concludes the passage using guarding terms that show his modesty.

Another device is to seize an extreme position and accuse those who occupy a middle position of being cowardly, indecisive, or lukewarm. William Lloyd Garrison made brilliant use of this strategy in the first issue of his abolitionist newspaper *The Liberator* in 1831. Part of the opening editorial read as follows:

> Assenting to the "self evident truth" maintained in the American Declaration of Independence, "that all men are created equal, and endowed by their Creator with certain inalienable rights—among which are life, liberty and the pursuit of happiness," I shall strenuously contend for the immediate enfranchisement of our slave population. In Park Street Church, on the Fourth of July, 1829, in an address on slavery, I unreflectingly assented to the popular but pernicious doctrine of *gradual* abolition. I seize this opportunity to make a full and unequivocal recantation, and thus publicly to ask pardon of my God, of my country, and of my brethren the poor slaves, for having uttered a sentiment so full of timidity,

[3]*Newsweek* (November 10, 1975), 102.

injustice and absurdity. A similar recantation, from my pen, was published in the *Genius of Universal Emancipation* at Baltimore, in September, 1829. My conscience is now satisfied.

I am aware that many object to the severity of my language; but is there not cause for severity? I *will be* as harsh as truth, and as uncompromising as justice. On this subject, I do not wish to think, or speak, or write, with moderation. No! No! Tell a man whose house is on fire, to give a moderate alarm; tell him to moderately rescue his wife from the hands of the ravisher; tell the mother to gradually extricate her babe from the fire into which it has fallen;—but urge me not to use moderation in a cause like the present. I am in earnest—I will not equivocate—I will not excuse—I will not retreat a single inch—*AND I WILL BE HEARD.*[4]

Notice that, although calling for immediate radical change, Garrison is careful at the start to emphasize that he is applying a doctrine of a traditionally revered document, the Declaration of Independence. In that way, Garrison presents himself as traditional and also radical. Quite a trick!

It is important to recognize that the people Garrison is addressing are not anti-abolitionists, but moderate abolitionists—those who favor the gradual emancipation of slaves. He begins by apologizing to God, to his fellow countrymen, and to the slaves themselves for his having once been a moderate abolitionist himself. The conversational implication of this maneuver is clear: The moderate abolitionists he is addressing owe a similar apology to God, their fellow countrymen, and the slaves. Through adopting this standpoint, he discounts and dismisses out of hand the arguments in behalf of gradual abolition.

Speakers can use a great many devices to establish an argumentative standpoint that puts them at an advantage or the opponent at a disadvantage. Here are just a few:

The disinterested party: Although I have no personal stake in this matter . . .

The reasonable person: By now it should be obvious to everyone . . .

The voice in the wilderness: I don't suppose that it will help much to point out that . . .

The world-weary cynic: Are we really going to go through all this again?

Moral indignation: It is high time that . . .

The mature person: When I was a child I spoke as a child . . .

The modest person: I don't claim to know all the answers . . .

The plain person: I may not have gone to Harvard but . . .

The expert: Things are not as simple as they might seem.

The agonizer: I've worried about this problem for a long, long time, and . . .

[4]Richard Heffner, ed., *A Documentary History of the United States* (New York: Mentor Books, 1952), 106–07.

Sometimes these argumentative moves hit their mark, and sometimes they do not. Fair or foul, however, being addressed from a standpoint can infuriate those against whom it is directed. If the Expert tells you that things are not as simple as they seem, this plainly suggests that you are not knowledgeable enough to enter into the discussion. You have to dig your way out of this hole before you can even get into the argument. This is a kind of abusive assurance.

Two additional ploys are worth mentioning: These are used by the *Uplifter* and the *Debaser*. Uplifters appeal to your better instincts, claiming that in your conscience or in your heart you really agree with them. Uplifters strike the pose of bringing you up to their level, a particularly obnoxious move when you hold that you *do* disagree with them, and for perfectly sound and moral reasons. Debasers are even slimier. Their strategy is to acknowledge all sorts of base motives and low qualities in themselves, and then go on to say that everyone else is in the same boat. Whereas Uplifters lift you up to their preferred heights, Debasers drag you down to their acknowledged depths. Debasers often use the phrase "Let's face it":

> "Let's face it, everyone is out to get what he can get for himself."

> "Let's face it, you would do the same thing if you thought you could get away with it."

If you disagree, you are accused not only of being naive but also of being dishonest or hypocritical. Debasing, then, is a way of discounting an opponent's position as insincere or hypocritical. Uplifting, on the other hand, is a form of assuring. In essence, the Uplifter says that the person addressed already agrees (in his or her heart) with what the Uplifter is saying. It often turns out that Debasers are not so bad as they pretend to be, and Uplifters are almost never as righteous as they assume they are. However this may be, both of these standpoints can produce strong—even violent—responses in those targeted with them.

EXERCISE I

Read the following passage. Then, for each of the numbered expressions, either answer the corresponding question or label the main argumentative move, if any, using these abbreviations:

AM = argument marker
A = assuring term
G = guarding term
D = discounting term
E− = negative evaluative term
E+ = positive evaluative term
R = rhetorical device
N = none of the above

This letter to the editor appeared in the *Dartmouth* on September 23, 1992, although references to a specific college have been removed. The author was president of the student assembly and a member of a single-sex fraternity at the time.

GREEKS SHOULD BE CO-ED

■

by Andrew Beebe

For some time now, people have been asking the question "Why should the Greek [fraternity and sorority] system go co-ed?" To them, *I pose an answer* [1] in a question, *"Why not?"* [2]

    Learning in college extends beyond the classrooms, onto the athletic fields, into the art studios, and into our social environs. [3] *In fact* [4], some [5] say that *most* [6] of what we learn at college comes from interaction with people and ideas during time spent outside of the lecture halls. The concept of segregating students in their social and residential environments by gender directly contradicts the *ideals* [7] of a college experience. This is *exactly* [8] what the fraternity and sorority system does.

    With all the *benefits* [9] of a small, closely-bonded group, the potential for strong social education would seem *obvious* [10]. *But* [11] is it *fair* [12] for us to remove the other half of our community from that education? [13] In many colleges, this voluntary segregation exists in fraternities and sororities.

    From the planning of a party or involvement in student activities to the sharing of living and recreational space, the fraternity and sorority system is a social environment *ripe* [14] with *educational potential* [15]. The idea that women and men would receive as complete an experience from these environments while *virtually* [16] separated is *implausible* [17].

    But [18] *what do women and men learn from one another that they don't already know*? [19] Problems in gender relations between all ages *prove* [20] that our society is *plagued by gender-based prejudice* [21]. *Since* [22] *prejudice is the ignorance of one group by another* [23], it will best be addressed by education. The question *then* [24] becomes: Which way is best to educate one another?

    Sexism, homophobia, date rape, eating disorders, and other social *problems* [25] are *often* [26] connected to gender-relation issues. As campus experience *shows* [27], we have a long way to go in combating these problems. Defenders of fraternities and sororities *may* [28] argue that they do not, solely by nature of being single sex, promote sexism or other prejudices. *But* [29], if we can recognize that these problems exist in our society, it is not important to find the blame, *but* [30] rather to offer a solution. It is *clear* [31] that separating people by gender is not the *right* [32] way to promote *better* [33] understanding between the sexes. To the contrary, bringing different people together is the only way prejudice, *no matter what the cause (or result) may be* [34], can be overcome.

    Acknowledging that breaking down walls of separation *may* [35] help foster better understanding, it is important to look at what *might* [36] change for the

worse. There would be *some* [37] *obvious* [38] logistical changes in rush, pledg-
ing, relationships with national organization, and house leadership. *But* [39]
where are the real consequences? [40] Men *could* [41] still cultivate strong
bonds with other men. Women *could* [42] still bond with other women. The difference is that there would be a *well-defined* [43] environment where men and
women *could* [44] create strong, lasting bonds and friendships between one
another.

There are many more *benefits* [45] to a coed system than there are *sacrifices*
[46]. Men and women could share the responsibilities of running what is now
a *predominantly* [47] male-controlled social structure. First-year men and
women could interact with older students in a social environment beyond the
classroom or the dining halls. People in a co-ed system could find a strong support group that extends beyond their own sex. With these *advantages* [48] and
more, it is *clear* [49] that the all-co-ed system offers everything found in a single-sex organization and more. *Although* [50] there are *some* [51] minor sacrifices to be made, they are insignificant in comparison to the *gain* [52] for all.

College is the last place we want to isolate ourselves. The entire idea of the
"holistic education" is *based on* [53] expanding our knowledge, not separating
ourselves from one another. Our fraternity and sorority system includes *many*
[54] different types of students. *So* [55] why should some houses refuse women
simply *because* [56] they are women? Why do some houses refuse men solely
because [57] they are men? The only solution is desegregation of the fraternity
and sorority system. *After all* [58], when it comes to challenging one another to
learn, *what are we afraid of*? [59]

QUESTIONS:

    [1]: Is this sentence an explicit performative?
    [2]: Explain the difference between asking "Why?" and asking "Why
        not?" in this context.
    [3]: Why does the author begin with this point?
 [4]–[12]: Write labels.
   [13]: What is the expected answer to this rhetorical question?
   [14]: What kind of rhetorical device is this? What is its point?
[15]–[18]: Write labels.
   [19]: Who is supposed to be asking this question?
[20]–[22]: Write labels.
   [23]: What is the point of this definition?
[24]–[33]: Write labels.
   [34]: Why does this author add this dependent clause?
[35]–[39]: Write labels.
   [40]: What does this question imply in this context?
[41]–[58]: Write labels.
   [59]: What is the expected answer to this rhetorical question?

The following passages argue for opposing views on the religious duties of elected officials. In each case, read the whole passage; then, for each of the numbered expressions, either answer the corresponding question or label the main argumentative move, if any, using the abbreviations listed in Exercise I.

PASSAGE 1

The first passage is excerpted from a speech given by Mario Cuomo at the University of Notre Dame, a Catholic institution, in September 1984, and published in the *Notre Dame Journal of Law, Ethics, and Public Policy* (vol. 1, 1984, pp. 13–31). The speech was given while Cuomo was governor of New York.

RELIGIOUS BELIEF AND PUBLIC MORALITY: A CATHOLIC GOVERNOR'S PERSPECTIVE

■

by Mario Cuomo

In addition to all the *weaknesses, dilemmas, and temptations* [1] that impede every pilgrim's progress, the Catholic who holds political office in a pluralistic democracy—who is elected to serve Jews and Muslims, atheists and Protestants, as well as Catholics—bears special responsibility. He or she undertakes to help create conditions under which *all* can live with a maximum of *dignity* [2] and with a *reasonable* [3] degree of freedom; where everyone who chooses may hold beliefs different from specifically Catholic ones—*sometimes* [4] contradictory to them; where the laws protect people's right to divorce, to use birth control and even to choose abortion.

In fact [5], Catholic public officials take an oath to preserve the Constitution that guarantees this freedom. And they do so gladly. Not *because* [6] they love what others do with their freedom, *but* [7] *because* [8] they realize that in guaranteeing freedom for all, they guarantee our right to be Catholics: our right to pray, to use the sacraments, to refuse birth control devices, to reject abortion, not to divorce and remarry if we believe it to be wrong. . . .

But [9] insistence on freedom is easier to accept as a general proposition than in its applications to specific situations. There are other *valid* [10] general principles firmly embedded in our Constitution, which, operating at the same time, create interesting and *occasionally* [11] troubling problems. *Thus* [12], the same amendment of the Constitution that forbids the establishment of a State Church affirms my legal right to argue that my religious belief would serve *well* [13] as an article of our universal public morality. I *may* [14] use the prescribed processes of government—the legislative and executive and judicial processes—to convince my fellow citizens—Jews and Protestants and Buddhists and nonbelievers—that what I propose is as *beneficial* [15] for them as I believe it is for me: that it is not just parochial or narrowly sectarian *but* [16] fulfills a human desire for *order, peace, justice, kindness, love* [17], any of the values *most* [18] of us agree are desirable *even* [19] apart from their specific religious base or context.

I am free to argue for a governmental policy for a nuclear freeze not just to avoid sin *but* [20] *because* [21] I think my democracy should regard it as a *desirable* [22] goal.

I can, if I wish, argue that the State should not fund the use of contraceptive devices not *because* [23] the Pope demands it *but* [24] *because* [25] I think that the whole community—*for* [26] the *good* [27] of the whole community—should not sever sex from an openness to the creation of life.

And *surely* [28], I can, if so inclined, demand some kind of law against abortion not *because* [29] my bishops say it is wrong *but* [30] *because* [31] I think that the whole community, regardless of its religious beliefs, should agree on the importance of protecting life—including life in the womb, which is *at the very least* [32] potentially human and should not be extinguished casually. [33]

No law prevents us from advocating any of these things: I am free to do so. *So* [34] are the bishops. And so is Reverend Falwell. *In fact* [35], the Constitution guarantees my right to try. And theirs. And his. *But* [36] *should* [37] I? Is it *helpful* [38]? Is it essential to human *dignity* [39]? Does it promote *harmony and understanding* [40]? Or does it divide us so fundamentally that it *threatens* [41] our ability to function as a pluralistic community? . . .

Today there are a *number* [42] of issues involving life and death that raise questions of public morality. . . . Abortion is one of these issues, and *while* [43] it is one issue among many, it is one of the most controversial and affects me in a special way as a Catholic public official. *So* [44] let me spend some time considering it.

I should start, I believe, by noting that the Catholic Church's actions with respect to the interplay of religious values and public policy make *clear* [45] that there is no inflexible moral principle which determines what our *political* conduct should be. For example, on divorce and birth control, *without changing its moral teaching* [46], the Church abides the civil law as it now stands, *thereby* [47] accepting—without making much of a point of it—that in our pluralistic society we are not required to insist that *all* our religious values be the law of the land.

Abortion is treated differently.

Of course [48] there are differences both in degree and quality between abortion and *some* [49] of the other religious positions the Church takes: abortion is a "matter of life and death," and degree counts. *But* [50] the differences in approach reveal a truth, *I think* [51], that is not well enough perceived by Catholics and *therefore* [52] still further complicates the process for us. That is, *while* [53] we always owe our bishops' words respectful attention and careful consideration, the question whether to engage the political system in a struggle to have it adopt certain articles of our belief as part of public morality, is not a matter of doctrine: it is a matter of prudential political judgment. . . .

As [54] Catholics, my wife and I were enjoined never to use abortion to destroy the life we created, and we never have. We thought Church doctrine was *clear* [55] on this, and—more than that—both of us felt it in full agreement with what our hearts and our consciences told us. For me, life or fetal life in the womb *should* [56] be protected, *even if* [57] five of nine Justices of the Supreme

Court and my neighbor disagree with me. A fetus is different from an appendix or a set of tonsils. *At the very least* [58], *even if* [59] the argument is made by *some* [60] scientists or some theologians that in the early stages of fetal development we can't discern human life, the full potential of human life is *indisputably* [61] there. That—to my less subtle mind—by itself *should demand respect, caution, indeed . . . reverence* [62].

But [63] *not everyone* [64] in our society agrees with me and Matilda. *And those who don't—those who endorse legalized abortions—aren't a ruthless, callous alliance of anti-Christians determined to overthrow our moral standards* [65]. In many cases, the proponents of legal abortion are the very people who have worked with Catholics to realize the goals of social justice set out in papal encyclicals: *the American Lutheran Church, the Central Conference of American Rabbis, the Presbyterian Church in the United States, B'nai B'rith Women, the Women of the Episcopal Church* [66]. These are just a few of the religious organizations that don't share the Church's position on abortion.

Certainly [67], we should not be forced to mold Catholic morality to conform to disagreement by non-Catholics *however* [68] sincere or severe their disagreement. Our bishops *should* [69] be teachers, not pollsters. They *should not* [70] change what we Catholics believe in order to ease our consciences or please our friends or protect the Church from criticism.

But [71] if the breadth, intensity, and sincerity of opposition to church teaching shouldn't be allowed to shape our Catholic morality, it *can't help but* [72] determine our ability—our realistic, political ability—to translate our Catholic morality into civil law, a law not for the believers who don't need it *but* [73] for the disbelievers who reject it.

And it is here, in our attempt to find a political answer to abortion—an answer beyond our private observance of Catholic morality—that we encounter controversy within and without the Church over how and in what degree to press *the case that our morality should be everybody else's* [74], and to what effect. . . .

Respectfully, and after careful consideration [75] of the position and arguments of the bishops, *I have concluded that* [76] the approach of a constitutional amendment is not the *best* [77] way for us to seek to deal with abortion.

I believe that legal interdicting of abortion by either the federal government or the individual states is not a *plausible* [78] possibility, and, *even* [79] if it could be obtained, it wouldn't work. *Given* [80] present attitudes, it would be "Prohibition" revisited *legislating what couldn't be enforced and in the process creating a disrespect for law in general* [81]. And as much as I admire the bishops' hope that a constitutional amendment against abortion would be the basis for a full, new bill of rights for mothers and children, I disagree that this would be the result.

I believe that, *more likely* [82], a constitutional prohibition would allow people to ignore the causes of many abortions instead of addressing them, *much* [83] the way the death penalty is used to escape dealing more fundamentally and more *rationally* [84] with the problem of violent crime. Other legal options that have been proposed are, *in my view* [85], equally ineffective. . . .

I am not implying that we should stand by and pretend indifference to whether a woman takes a pregnancy to its conclusion or aborts it [86]. I believe we should in all cases try to teach a respect for life. And I believe with regard to abortion that, *despite* [87] *Roe v. Wade*, we can, in practical ways. Here, *in fact* [88], *it seems to me* [89] that *all of us can agree* [90].

Without lessening their insistence on a woman's right to an abortion [91], the people who call themselves "pro-choice" can support the development of government programs that present an impoverished mother with the full range of support she needs to bear and raise her children, to have a *real* [92] choice.

Without dropping their campaign to ban abortion [93], those who gather under the banner of "pro-life" can join in developing and enacting a legislative bill of rights for mothers and children, as the bishops have already proposed.

While [94] we argue over abortion, the United States' infant mortality rate places us sixteenth among the nations of the world. Thousands of infants die each year because of inadequate medical care. Some are born with birth defects that, *with proper treatment, could* [95] be prevented. Some are stunted in their physical and mental growth because of *improper* [96] nutrition.

If we want to prove our regard for life in the womb, for the helpless infant— if we care about women having real choices in their lives and not being driven to abortions by a sense of helplessness and despair about the future of their child—then there is work *enough* [97] for all of us. Lifetimes of it.

QUESTIONS:

[1]–[32]: Write labels.

    [33]: Explain the point of this paragraph.

[34]–[45]: Write labels.

    [46]: Why does Cuomo add this clause?

[47]–[64]: Write labels.

    [65]: Explain the point of this sentence.

    [66]: Why does Cuomo list these groups?

[67]–[73]: Write labels.

    [74]: Is this a fair description of the controversy? Who wants to press *this* case?

[75]–[80]: Write labels.

    [81]: Explain the point of this clause.

[82]–[85]: Write labels.

    [86]: Explain the point of this sentence.

[87]–[89]: Write labels.

    [90]: Why is it important to Cuomo that "all of us can agree"?

    [91]: Explain the point of this clause.

    [92]: Write a label.

    [93]: Explain the point of this clause.

[94]–[96]: Write labels.

    [97]: Explain the point of this word.

PASSAGE 2

The following response to Cuomo's speech is from the *New Republic* (May 6, 1991, pp. 16–18). Using the same abbreviations as in Exercise I, indicate the primary function of each numbered expression.

DEAD END—CUOMO'S ABORTION CONTORTION

■

by Andrew Sullivan

Mario Cuomo's September 1984 speech on abortion at Notre Dame University is second only to his convention keynote address of the same year in the lore surrounding the philosophical *prowess* [1] of the governor of New York. *Some* [2] likened the Notre Dame speech to John F. Kennedy's 1960 address to Protestant ministers in Houston on the role of Catholics in American public life. The *New Republic* said it contained a *"seriousness and depth* [3] rarely seen in the American political arena." A *National Review* writer called it *"brilliant* [4]." *Although* [5] criticisms were made at the time, they failed to stick. The *tour de force* [6] *largely* [7] ended the abortion issue as a *major problem* [8] in Mario Cuomo's career.

It shouldn't have. *In fact* [9], the speech is a work of *evasion* [10], and so *muddled* [11] on *so* [12] pressing a moral matter that it *casts doubt* [13] on Cuomo's seriousness both as an intellectual and as a politician. It *glosses over* [14] its own central contradiction, finds a solution where there is only an impasse. Cuomo's singular *achievement* [15] *may* [16] *in fact* [17] have been to have staked out the only *truly* [18] *incoherent* [19] position imaginable for a Catholic politician on abortion.

Cuomo argues in his speech that, *though* [20] as a Catholic he accepts the Church's teaching that abortion is *wrong* [21], as a politician in a pluralist society he upholds the right of others to abort. He argues that, *although* [22] he is bound as a Catholic to believe the Church's teaching, he can differ from the Church on the practical response to such a teaching, which is a matter of prudential political judgment, and not of *ecclesiastical obedience* [23].

The problem with the position is *simple* [24]: its private-Catholic/public-pluralist position makes *some* [25] sense for *almost* [26] any other moral issue for Catholics *except* abortion. It's *possible* [27], for example, for a Catholic to hold that, say, divorce is *wrong* [28] *but* [29] not wish to make it illegal, out of a respect for the right of others to choose differently. The upshot of such a stance, *after all* [30], is not so *bad* [31]: at worst a *lowering of public morals* [32], at best an affirmation of the good of *free moral choice* [33].

With abortion, *however* [34], this balance between public and private goes *awry* [35]. To accept the Church's position on abortion is to believe that abortion is the taking of human life, a *somewhat* [36] more drastic event than the breakup of a *marriage* [37]. In his Notre Dame speech, Cuomo states that he accepts this position in the *clearest* [38] terms:

As [39] Catholics, my wife and I were enjoined never to use abortion to destroy the life we created, and we never have. We thought Church doctrine was *clear* [40] on this, and—more than that—both of us felt it in full agreement with what our hearts and our consciences told us. For me, life or fetal life in the womb *should* [41] be protected. . . . *At the very least* [42] . . . the full potential of human life is there. That . . . by itself *should demand respect, caution, indeed . . . reverence* [43].

For a Catholic holding this belief, merely enforcing the public laws as a public servant, *while* [44] arguing for their reversal, is hard enough. *But* [45] actually favoring legal abortion, and the provision of public funds for it, *must mean* [46] consciously tolerating the taking of millions of human lives as a normal occurrence in American society. And this is Cuomo's position. *At times* [47] he has gone even further than this. He recently joined eight governors in an amicus brief to the Supreme Court that *implicitly* [48] asked the Court not to overturn *Roe v. Wade*. He *ducked* [49], in a recent interchange with the editors of the liberal Catholic journal *Commonweal*, an invitation to support a ban on third trimester abortions, preferring to say that the ethical and legal implications of medical data "be explored." And he has made statements, subsequently qualified, that, *as* [50] a man, he has no right to discuss abortion at all.

Cuomo recognizes that he is free to act otherwise, to argue democratically against abortion according to his own convictions. *But* [51] in the Notre Dame speech, he adds: "But should I? Is it *helpful* [52]? Is it *essential to human dignity* [53]? Does it promote *harmony and understanding* [54]? Or does it *divide us* [55] so fundamentally that it *threatens* [56] our ability to function as a pluralistic community?" There is a virtue, *to be sure* [57], in harmony—and a Catholic virtue at that. *But* [58] could it possibly outweigh what Cuomo himself *must* [59] believe is legal homicide? Cuomo, in short, says he'd never "destroy life" himself (his words) but actively supports the right of others to do so, *in order to* [60] avoid public *discord* [61]. Compare this with the clarity of his opposition to the death penalty, where he has vetoed, to public uproar, capital punishment laws passed by majorities in both houses of the New York legislature, and favored by a majority of New York voters.

None of this *contortion* [62], *of course* [63], is necessary. Cuomo could, for example, say he doesn't believe abortion *is* the taking of life. He could say he doesn't believe it's homicide; or that "life" is at stake, *but* [64] a "person" does not exist until a certain number of weeks of pregnancy. Or he could simply say he's so deeply troubled by the issue *that* [65] he's prepared to give others the benefit of the doubt. All of these views *might* [66] fit with his pro-choice position. *For this* [67], he would *doubtless* [68] receive sympathy from his fellow Catholics. Instead, he chooses to affirm the Church's view that abortion is life-taking and *yet* [69] be in favor of laws that permit it.

A college student raised this *problem* [70] in an interview in the Catholic Columbia undergraduate magazine, *Newman Journal*, in the spring of 1988. At one point in the dialogue, Cuomo claims the bishops don't mandate the same obedience to the teaching on birth control as they do on abortion, which prompts the reply:

NEWMAN JOURNAL: It's not the same.

MARIO CUOMO: Well, why is it not the same?

NJ: Well, one is murder.

MC: No, murder is a word that doesn't count. Murder is a civil word, and the Supreme Court says it's not murder. *So* [71] you can't do it with the word "murder."

NC: Well, the Church teaches that it's a taking of a life and *therefore* [72] the *violation of the natural law* [73].

MC: Well, that's what you teach about birth control. You don't teach that there is a different order of seriousness. Then they get all upset on that point. Now, I *may* [74] have my theology wrong *but* [75] I don't think so.

. . .

The truth is, *of course* [76], that Cuomo does have his theology wrong. The Church does teach that there is an order of seriousness in breaches of natural law, homicide being far *graver* [77] than the use of condoms.

How did the governor manage to avoid confronting this issue in his Notre Dame speech? By two *rhetorical sleights of hand* [78]. First, he plays down his belief in the public doctrine of the Church on abortion. *Rather than* [79] saying that he actually "believes" in the teaching of the Church on abortion, he uses the term "accept." His "belief" in the sin of abortion is reserved entirely for himself, in a firmly private context.

Second, Cuomo faces up to the *central dilemma* [80] of legal killing once—and rebuts it with an *irrelevance* [81]. He admits *at one point* [82] that "abortion is treated differently" by the Church than other social evils:

> Abortion is a "matter of life and death," and degree counts. *But* [83] the differences in approach reveal a truth, *I think* [84], that is not well enough perceived by Catholics and *therefore* [85] still further complicates the process for us. That is, *while* [86] we always owe our bishops' words respectful attention and careful consideration, the question whether to engage the political system in a struggle to have it adopt certain articles of our belief as public morality, is not a matter of doctrine: it is a matter of prudential political argument.

This is a *decent* [87] point. The Church defers to lay people in matters of prudential political judgment. *The trouble* [88] is, Cuomo's argument doesn't actually tackle the question raised. The issue is whether the fact that Catholics believe abortion is homicide short-circuits much political judgment on what to do about it. And *surely* [89] it does. There cannot be *much* [90] debate among Catholics over whether killing should be legal or not. There may be differences over tactics, *to be sure* [91]: making abortion illegal, for example, could be the last part of a broad social, educational economic, and spiritual strategy to end it. *But* [92] the *goal* is *unmistakable* [93]. *Yet* [94] it is precisely on this goal—of ultimately banning abortion—that Cuomo is silent. And on making it illegal now, he's actively opposed.

No one's pretending, *of course* [95], that this is an easy problem for a Catholic politician to grapple with, and Cuomo *deserves respect* [96] for engaging with it in public. What he shouldn't *get away with* [97], *however* [98], is the impression of having made a *definitive contribution* [99] to the subject, when in *reality* [100] he hasn't confronted the central issue at all.

EXERCISE III

Advertisements also often contain arguments. Provide a close analysis of each of the following advertisements by circling and labeling each of the key argumentative terms. Then state what you take to be the central conclusions and premises. What criticisms, if any, do you have of each argument?

ADVERTISEMENT 1

This advertisement for Equal Exchange Coffee ran in a number of nationally distributed monthly magazines in 1997, 1998, and 1999.[4]

It may be a little early in the morning to bring this up, but if you buy coffee from large corporations, you are inadvertently maintaining the system which keeps small farmers poor while lining the pockets of rich corporations. By choosing Equal Exchange Coffee, you can help to make a change. We believe in trading directly with small farming cooperatives at mutually agreed-upon prices with a fixed minimum rate. Then, should the coffee market decline, the farmers are still guaranteed a fair price. So have a cup of Equal Exchange Coffee and make a small farmer happy. Of course, your decision to buy Equal Exchange need not be completely altruistic. For we take as much pride in refining the taste of our gourmet coffees as we do in helping the farmers who produce them. For more information about Equal Exchange or to order our line of gourmet, organic, and shade-grown coffee directly, call 1-800-406-8289.

*"Excuse me waiter, there's the blood and misery
of a thousand small farmers in my coffee."*

[4]From *Equal Exchange*. Advertisement. Copyright 1997, 1998, 1999.

ADVERTISEMENT 2

This advertisement appeared in various national magazines in 1999.

It looks like now, but it's built like then.

Ring spun yarn. *Cotton fibers are stretched during spinning, to produce stronger, more lustrous yarn. A time-tested technique (dates back to the 1840's).*

Full-fashioned. *Each piece is knit to size, not just cut-and-sewn. Produces a better fit, no lumpy seams. First done by home knitters. (Found only in finer sweaters, now.)*

Yarn is two-ply. *Each ply twists in opposite direction. So, one balances the other. A method used since Queen Victoria's day, for a smoother, loftier feel.*

Lands' End®
Drifter Sweater

100% combed cotton. *Tiny steel fingers comb out shorter fibers, dirt and such. Leaves cotton softer, stronger than merely carding it – a traditional, extra step often omitted today.*

Think fine craftwork is a thing of the past? Well, our Drifter™ just may change your mind. Oh, it's *contemporary,* all right – a smart, classically styled cotton sweater that belongs in anybody's wardrobe, man or woman.

But like most things in our catalog, it's full of details and construction features you don't find most places anymore.

For that matter, you don't get our kind of *service* most places, either. Which you discover on your very first call.

You get a neighborly greeting. From someone who gladly answers your questions, and treats you like you're our only customer.

And the biggest surprise is – our prices. They're always honest and fair.

Our Drifter, for example, starts at only $34.50.

And *that,* after all, may really be the most old-fashioned thing about it. © *1999 Lands' End, Inc.*

Guaranteed. Period.®

If you'd like a free catalog call

1-800-814-1387

Or visit us at

www.landsend.com

Provide a close analysis of the following passages by circling and labeling each of the key argumentative terms. Then state what you take to be the central conclusions and premises. What criticisms, if any, do you have of each argument?

PASSAGE 1

The following encomium was written by an art critic for the *New York Times*, in which this review appeared (June 6, 1992, pp. 1, 31). If you are not familiar with Eakins's work, looking at some reproductions might help you appreciate this argument. You might also look up the rest of the essay, as only a small part is reproduced here.

IS EAKINS OUR GREATEST PAINTER?

by John Russell

There never was a painter like Thomas Eakins, who was born in 1844, died in 1916, and is the subject of a great exhibition that has just opened in the Philadelphia Museum of Art. It is not simply that in his hands painting became an exact science, so that if he paints two men rowing on a river, we can tell the month, day, and the hour that they passed under a certain bridge. We admire Eakins for that, but we prize him above all for the new dimension of moral awareness that he brought to American painting.

The question that he asks is not "What do we look like?" It is "What have we done to one another?" And it is because he gives that question so full and so convincing an answer that we ask ourselves whether Thomas Eakins was not the greatest American painter who ever lived. Even if the question strikes us as meaningless, we find it difficult after an exhibition such as this to think of a convincing rival. . . .

PASSAGE 2

This article was published in the *Washington Post* (November 25, 1997, p. A19).

A PIECE OF "GOD'S HANDIWORK"

by Robert Redford

Just over a year ago, President Clinton created the Grand Staircase-Escalante National Monument to protect once and for all some of Utah's extraordinary red rock canyon country. In response to plans of the Dutch company Andalex to mine coal on the Kaiparowits Plateau, President Clinton used his authority under the Antiquities Act to establish the new monument, setting aside for protection what he described as "some of the most remarkable land in the world." I couldn't agree more. For over two decades, many have fought battle after battle to keep mining conglomerates from despoiling the unique treasures of this stunning red rock canyon country. Now, we thought at least some of it was safe.

Not so. Shocking as it sounds, Clinton's Bureau of Land Management (BLM) has approved oil drilling within the monument. BLM has given Conoco Inc., a subsidiary of the corporate giant DuPont, permission to drill for oil and gas in the heart of the new monument. You may wonder, as I do, how can this happen? Wasn't the whole purpose of creating the monument to preserve its colorful cliffs, sweeping arches and other extraordinary resources from large-scale mineral development? Didn't the president say he was saving these lands from mining companies for our children and grandchildren?

The BLM says its hands are tied. Why? Because these lands were set aside subject to "valid existing rights," and Conoco has a lease that gives it the right to drill. Sure Conoco has a lease—more than one, in fact—but those leases were originally issued without sufficient environmental study or public input. As a result, none of them conveyed a valid right to drill. What's more, in deciding to issue a permit to drill now, the BLM did not conduct a full analysis of the environmental impacts of drilling in these incomparable lands, but instead determined there would be no significant environmental harm on the basis of an abbreviated review that didn't even look at drilling on the other federal leases.

Sounds like Washington double-speak to me. I've spent considerable time on these extraordinary lands for years, and I know that an oil rig in their midst would have a major impact. What's more, Conoco wants to drill a well to find oil. Inevitably, more rigs, more roads, new pipelines, toxic wastes and bright lights would follow to get the oil out. The BLM couldn't see this, but the U.S. Fish and Wildlife Service and the Environmental Protection Agency did. Both of those agencies recognized the devastating effects extensive oil drilling would have on this area and urged the BLM to refuse to allow it, in order to protect the monument.

Maybe the problem comes from giving management responsibility for this monument to the BLM. This is the BLM's first national monument; almost all the others are managed by the National Park Service. The Park Service's mission is to protect the resources under its care while the bureau has always sought to accommodate economic uses of those under its. Even so, the BLM seemed to be getting off to a good start by enlisting broad public involvement in developing a management plan for the area. Yet the agency's decision to allow oil drilling in the monument completely undercuts this process just as it is beginning.

What we're talking about is, in the words of President Clinton, a small piece of "God's handiwork." Almost 4$\frac{1}{2}$ million acres of irreplaceable red rock wilderness remain outside the monument. Let us at least protect what is within it. The many roadless areas within the monument should remain so—protected as wilderness. The monument's designation means little if a pattern of exploitation is allowed to continue.

Environmentalists—including the Southern Utah Wilderness Alliance, the Natural Resources Defense Council, and the Wilderness Society—appealed BLM's decision to the Interior Department's Board of Land Appeals. This appeal, however, was rejected earlier this month. This is a terrible mistake. We shouldn't be drilling in our national monuments. Period. As President Clinton said when dedicating the new monument, "Sometimes progress is measured in mastering frontiers, but sometimes we must measure progress in protecting frontiers for our children and children to come."

Allowing drilling to go forward in the Grand Staircase-Escalante Monument would permanently stain what might otherwise have been a defining legacy of the Clinton presidency.

PASSAGE 3

The following passage is an excerpt from an essay that appeared in the *Boston Review* (vol. 7, no. 5 [October 1982], pp. 13–19), which is funded by the National Endowment for the Humanities, a government agency that supports scholarship and the arts. Its author is professor emeritus of drama at Stanford University.

BEYOND THE WASTELAND: WHAT AMERICAN TV CAN LEARN FROM THE BBC

■

by Martin Esslin

What are the advantages and disadvantages of a public TV service as compared to a completely commercial system? One of the dangers inherent in a public service system is paternalism: Some authority decides what the viewers should see and hear simply on the basis of what it arbitrarily feels would be good for them. Yet in countries where a highly developed public system exists alongside a commercial one, that danger is minimized because of the market pressure on the commercial system to give its audience what it wants. Indeed, in a dual system the danger is often that the public service may be tempted to ignore its stated purpose to serve the public interest and instead pander to mass preferences because of a sense of competition with the commercial networks.

Another problem that plagues public TV service is that it may run short of money, which in turn can increase its dependence on the government. The extent of government dependence is intimately connected to how the public broadcasting service is financed. In West Germany and Italy, for example, the public broadcasting service takes advertising, but it is usually confined to a clearly delimited area of the network's programming. In Britain the BBC . . . relies entirely on its annual license fee, which guarantees it a steady income and allows long-term planning. In periods of severe inflation, the license-fee system leaves the BBC in a dangerous position vis-a-vis the government, and the network's income may decline in real terms. In countries where the public broadcasting service is financed by an annual allocation in the national budget, long-term planning becomes more difficult and the dependence on the government is far greater. Nevertheless, public TV services financed on that pattern, such as the ABC in Australia and the CBC in Canada, provide programs of high quality that are genuine alternatives to the fare on the numerous popular and prosperous commercial networks. In Canada, this includes programs from the three commercial American networks.

One of the most important positive features of services under public control is their ability to provide planned, high-quality viewing alternatives. The BBC, for example, has two television channels, BBC 1 and BBC 2. The program planning on these two networks is closely coordinated so that highly popular material on one channel is regularly paired with more specialized or demanding fare on the other. And though the percentage of the audience that tunes in to the challenging programming may be small, the scale of magnitude operative in the mass media is such that even a small percentage of the viewing audience represents a very large number of people indeed. A popular dramatic series on BBC 1, for instance, may reach an audience of 20 percent of the adult population of Britain—about ten million people. A play by Shakespeare on BBC 2 that may attract an audience of only 5 percent nonetheless reaches about two-and-a-half million people—a substantial audience for a work of art. It would take a theater with a seating capacity of 1,000 about seven years, or 2,500 performances, to reach an equivalent number of people! Nor should it be overlooked that this audience will include people whose influence may be greater in the long run than that of the ten million who watched the entertainment program. In this system, no segment of the viewing public is forced to compromise with any other. In our example, not only did BBC 1 provide a popular entertainment program as an alternative to the Shakespeare, but, in addition, the commercial network offered still another popular program. By careful—perhaps paternalistic—planning the general audience satisfaction was substantially increased.

One of the difficulties of the American situation is that the size of the United States favors decentralization and the fragmentation of initiatives for the more ambitious programming of the public service network. A revitalized PBS would need a strong central governing body that could allocate to local producing stations the substantial sums of money they require for ambitious projects—projects that could compete with the best offerings of the rich commercial competitors.

Using existing satellite technology, such a truly national network of public service television could be made available to the entire country. If a public service television organization was able to provide simultaneous, alternative programming along the lines of BBC 1 and BBC 2, the cultural role of television in the United States could be radically improved, and the most powerful communication medium in history could realize its positive potential to inform, educate, and provide exposure to diverse cultural ideas.

PASSAGE 4

This article was published in the *New York Times* (January 15, 2004, p. A33).

LIFE (AND DEATH) ON MARS

■

by Paul Davies

SYDNEY, Australia—President Bush's announcement yesterday that the United States will soon be pointing its rockets toward Mars will doubtless be greeted with delight by space scientists. . . . And yet the scientific community's enthusiasm will surely be tempered by skepticism. Scientists, it's worth remembering, rejoiced when President George H. W. Bush unveiled a Mars project in 1989. The same scientists then despaired when the plan quickly evaporated amid spiraling projected costs and shifting priorities. . . .

Why is going to Mars so expensive? Mainly it's the distance from Earth. At its closest point in orbit, Mars lies 35 million miles away from us, necessitating a journey of many months, whereas reaching the Moon requires just a few days' flight. On top of this, Mars has a surface gravity that, though only 38 percent of Earth's, is much greater than the Moon's. It takes a lot of fuel to blast off Mars and get back home. If the propellant has to be transported there from Earth, costs of a launching soar. . . .

There is, however, an obvious way to slash the costs and bring Mars within reach of early manned exploration. The answer lies with a one-way mission.

Most people react with instinctive horror at the suggestion. I recall my own sense of discomfort when I met an aging American scientist who claimed to have trained for a one-way mission to the Moon in the pre-Apollo days. And in the case of the barren Moon, that reaction is largely justified. There is little on the Moon to sustain human life. Mars, however, is a different story. Because of the planet's relatively benign environment, it is theoretically able to support a permanent human presence. If provided with the right equipment, astronauts would have a chance of living there for years. A one-way trip to Mars need not mean a quick demise.

Every two years the orbit of Mars creates a window of opportunity to send fresh supplies at a reasonable cost. An initial colony of four astronauts, equipped with a small nuclear reactor and a couple of rover vehicles, could make their own oxygen, grow some food and even initiate building projects using local raw materials. Supplemented by food shipments, medical supplies and replacement gadgets from home, the colony could be sustained indefinitely. To be sure, the living conditions would be uncomfortable, but the colonists would have the opportunity to do ground-breaking scientific work and blaze a trail that would ensure them a permanent place in the annals of discovery.

Obviously this strategy carries significant risks in addition to those faced by a conventional Mars mission. Major equipment failure could leave the colony without enough power, oxygen or food. An accident might kill or disable an astronaut who provided some vital expertise. A supply drop might fail, condemning the colonists to starve in a very public way. Even if nothing went wrong, the astronauts' lives would certainly be shortened by the harsh conditions. . . .

Would it be right to ask people to accept such conditions for the sake of science, or even humanity? The answer has to be yes. We already expect certain people to take significant risks on our behalf, such as special forces operatives or test pilots. Some people gleefully dice with death in the name of sport or adventure. Dangerous occupations that reduce life expectancy through exposure to hazardous conditions or substances are commonplace. . . .

Who would put their hand up for a one-way ticket to Mars? I work among people who study astrobiology and planetary science, and there is no lack of eager young scientists who would sign up right now, given half a chance. But it would make more sense to pick mature, older scientists with reduced life expectancy. Other considerations, like weight, emotional stability and scientific credentials, would of course have to be factored in.

The early outpost wouldn't be left to wither and die. Rather, it would form the basis for a much more ambitious colonization program. Over the years new equipment and additional astronauts would be sent to join the original crew. In time, the colony would grow to the point of being self-sustaining.

When this stage was reached, humanity would have a precious insurance policy against catastrophe at home. During the next millennium there is a significant chance that civilization on Earth will be destroyed by an asteroid, a killer plague or a global war. A Martian colony could keep the flame of civilization and culture alive until Earth could be reverse-colonized from Mars.

Would NASA entertain a one-way policy for human Mars exploration? Probably not. But other, more adventurous space agencies in Europe or Asia might. The next giant leap for mankind won't come without risk.

PASSAGE 5

The following extract comes from *Compulsory Mis-Education and the Community of Scholars* (New York: Vintage Books, 1966).

A PROPOSAL TO ABOLISH GRADING[5]

◼

by Paul Goodman

Let half a dozen of the prestigious Universities—Chicago, Stanford, the Ivy League—abolish grading, and use testing only and entirely for pedagogic purposes as teachers see fit.

Anyone who knows the frantic temper of the present schools will understand the transvaluation of values that would be effected by this modest innovation. For most of the students, the competitive grade has come to be the essence. The naïve teacher points to the beauty of the subject and the ingenuity of the research; the shrewd student asks if he is responsible for that on the final exam.

Let me at once dispose of an objection whose unanimity is quite fascinating. I think that the great majority of professors agree that grading hinders teaching and creates a bad spirit, going as far as cheating and plagiarizing. I have before me the collection of essays, *Examining in Harvard College*, and this is the consensus. It is uniformly asserted, however, that the grading is inevitable; for how else will the graduate schools, the foundations, the corporations *know* whom to accept, reward, hire? How will the talent scouts know whom to tap? By testing the applicants, of course, according to the specific task-requirements of the inducting institution, just as applicants for the Civil Service or for licenses in medicine, law, and architecture are tested. Why should Harvard professors do the testing *for* corporations and graduate-schools? . . .

There are several good reasons for testing, and kinds of test. But if the aim is to discover weakness, what is the point of down-grading and punishing, and thereby inviting the student to conceal his weakness, by faking and bulling, if not cheating? The natural conclusion of [education] is the insight itself, not a grade for having had it. For the important purpose of placement, if one can establish in the student the belief that one is testing *not* to grade and making invidious comparisons but for his own advantage, the student should normally seek his own level, where he is challenged and yet capable, rather than trying to get by. If the student dares to accept himself as he is, a teacher's grade is a crude instrument compared with a student's self-awareness. But it is rare in our universities that students are encouraged to notice objectively their vast confusion. Unlike Socrates, our teachers rely on power-drives rather than shame and ingenuous idealism.

Many students are lazy, so teachers try to goad or threaten them by grading. In the long run this must do more harm than good. Laziness is a character-defense. It may be a way of avoiding learning, in order to protect the conceit that one is already perfect. . . . It may be a way of avoiding just the risk of failing and being down-graded. Sometimes it is a way of politely saying, "I won't." But since it is the authoritarian grown-up demands that have created such attitudes in the first place, why repeat the trauma? There comes a time when we must treat people as adults, laziness and all. It is one thing courageously to fire a do-nothing out of your class; it is quite another thing to evaluate him with a lordly F.

Most important of all, it is often obvious that balking in doing the work, especially among bright young people who get to great universities, means exactly what it says: The work does not suit me, not this subject, or not at this time, or not in this school, or not in school altogether. The student might not be bookish; he might be school-tired; perhaps his development ought now to take another direction. Yet unfortunately, if such a student is intelligent and is not sure of himself, he *can* be bullied into passing, and this obscures everything. My hunch is that I am describing a common situation. What a grim waste of young life and teacherly effort! Such a student will retain nothing of what he has "passed" in. Sometimes he must get mononucleosis to tell his story and be believed.

And ironically, the converse is also probably commonly true. A student flunks and is mechanically weeded out, who is really ready and eager to learn in a scholastic setting, but he has not quite caught on. A good teacher can recognize the situation, but the computer wreaks its will.

PASSAGE 6

The following letter to the editor was written by Charlie Buttrey, a lawyer, and published in the White River Junction, Vermont *Valley News* on Wednesday, August 29, 2001.

THREE FALLACIES ABOUT GUN RIGHTS

by Charlie Buttrey

In the never-ending debate on these pages over gun ownership, those who favor expansive gun rights appear to have adopted one (or more) of three lines of argument:

The Constitution protects the individual right to gun ownership.

The crime rate in Great Britain (where gun ownership is strictly controlled) is "skyrocketing."

In colonial days, the vast majority of people owned guns.

Each premise, however, is erroneous.

In our constitutional system, the ultimate arbiter of what the Constitution says is the Supreme Court. One may not agree with its rulings (for example, many people do not approve of its ruling extending First Amendment protections to flag burning or Fourth Amendment protections to the decision to terminate a pregnancy), but, under our system of government, once the Supreme Court has ruled a certain way, that ruling stands as the law of the land. On the issue of whether the Second Amendment encompasses an individual's right to possess firearms, the Supreme Court has spoken. And the answer is that it does not. Like it or not, that is the law of the land. It is true that the state constitutions in both Vermont and New Hampshire provide for the protection of individual gun ownership. In neither instance, however, is such a right absolute. For example, the New Hampshire Supreme Court has ruled that a law prohibiting felons from possessing firearms is not unconstitutional. Similarly, a Vermont law prohibiting people from carrying loaded firearms in their vehicles was held to be permissible.

The notion that Great Britain's crime rate is skyrocketing is belied by the facts. British government statistics reveal a steady increase in most crime categories between 1980 and 1995 and a gradual leveling off in the last five years. Of course, gun-related crimes are minuscule when compared with those in the United States. Guns are used in robberies in Great Britain less than 5 percent of the time. And from 1980 to 1999, annual gun-related homicides in Britain ranged from a low of 7 to a high of 42. In comparison, according to U.S. Bureau of Justice statistics, an average of 10,000 gun-related homicides occurred each year in this country during the same period.

Finally, the suggestion that our colonial forebears were almost universally armed has been thoroughly repudiated. In his recent book, *Arming America*, Emory University historian Michael Bellesiles reveals that the average colonial citizen had virtually no access to or training in the use of firearms, and that the few guns that did exist were kept under strict control. The fewer than 10 percent of Americans who did possess guns in the years prior to the Civil War were generally neglectful of the weapons and those guns were expensive, clumsy, unreliable, and hard to maintain.

There may be sound policy grounds that can be advanced in favor of relatively unrestricted gun ownership. Those arguments should be made, however, from a perspective of historical truth and legal accuracy.

EXERCISE V

Practice close analysis some more by doing close analyses of: (1) an editorial or advertisement from your local paper, or (2) one of the articles in Part II of this book, or (3) something that you read for another course, or (4) a lecture by your professor in another course (or this course!), or (5) a paper by you or a friend in another course.

EXERCISE VI

Describe the purpose, audience, and standpoint in each of the arguments in Exercises I–IV. In describing the standpoint of the person giving the argument, you may use the categories listed on page 75 or, even better, some of your own.

EXERCISE VII

For each of the ten argumentative standpoints listed on page 75, try to decide whether it is primarily assuring, discounting, or guarding in orientation. For some of the standpoints, you might want to say more than one of these orientations. If so, explain why.

EXERCISE VIII

Sometimes a writer shifts standpoint, speaking first in one role then in another. In the statement below, circle each occurrence of "I," "we," and "us" and identify the standpoint from which the word is written.

STATEMENT ON TUITION INCREASE

Fully mindful of the central educational and intellectual role that the residential colleges play in the life of Yale College and of the University and of how overcrowding in the colleges undermines the achievement of the educational mission, I have recommended and the Corporation has voted to reduce the total number of students in Yale College next year. . . . Clearly, there are costs associated with reduction of college and class size, and clearly the term bill level—including room, board, and tuition—must be seen as part of the whole issue of the size of Yale College. Last year, the Consumer Price Index indicated that inflation rose at 9 percent. Yale, like everyone else, must live in that world. On the other hand, we must also be aware of the difficulties imposed on us— parents, friends, students—by the inflationary spiral. In order, therefore, to assist us in meeting the real costs of an education at Yale, while never forgetting the burdens on all of us, I have recommended and the Corporation has voted an increase in the term bill in Yale College of 8.5 percent. This means an increase of $640. . . .

DISCUSSION QUESTIONS

1. If, as some social critics have maintained, the pervasive nature of television has created generation upon generation of intellectually passive automatons, why study close analysis?
2. Television commercials are often arguments in miniature. Recount several recent television commercials and identify the argumentative devices at work.

DEEP ANALYSIS

Arguments in everyday life rarely occur in isolation. They usually come in the middle of much verbiage that is not essential to the argument itself. Everyday arguments are also rarely complete. Essential premises are often omitted. Many such omissions are tolerable because we are able to convey a great deal of information indirectly by conversational implication. Nevertheless, to give a critical evaluation of an argument, it is necessary to isolate the argument from extraneous surroundings, to make explicit unstated parts of the argument, and to arrange them in a systematic order. This puts us in a better position to decide on the soundness or unsoundness of the argument in question. This chapter will develop methods for reconstructing arguments so that they may be understood and evaluated in a fair and systematic fashion. These methods will then be illustrated by applying them to a disagreement that depends on fundamental principles.

GETTING DOWN TO BASICS

To understand an argument, it is useful to put it into standard form. As we saw in Chapter 3, this is done by writing down the premises, drawing a line, adding the symbol "∴", and finishing with the conclusion. That is all we write down. But there is often a lot more in the passage that includes the argument. It is not uncommon for the stated argument to stretch over several pages, whereas the basic argument has only a few premises and a single conclusion.

One reason for this is that people often go off on *tangents*. They start to argue for one claim, but that reminds them of something else, so they talk about that for a while; then they finally return to their original topic. Such tangents can be completely irrelevant or unnecessary, but they often make it hard to follow the argument. Some people even go off on tangents on purpose to confuse their opponents and hide gaping holes in their arguments. This might be called the trick of *excess verbiage*. It violates the conversational rules of Quantity, Relevance, or Manner, which were discussed in Chapter 1.

To focus on the argument itself, we need to look carefully at each sentence to determine whether that particular sentence affects the validity of the argument or the truth of its premises.[1] If we decide that a sentence is not necessary for the argument, then we should not add it when we list the premises and conclusion in standard form. Of course, we have to be careful not to omit anything that would improve the argument, but including irrelevant material simply makes it more difficult to analyze and evaluate the argument.

Another source of extra material is *repetition*. People often repeat their main points to remind their audience of what was said earlier. Repetition is more subtle when it is used to explain something. A point can often be clarified by restating it in a new way. Repetition can also function as a kind of assurance, as an expression of confidence, or as an indication of how important a point is. Some writers seem to think that if they say something often enough, people will come to believe it. Whether or not this trick works, if two sentences say equivalent things, there is no need to list both sentences when the argument is put into standard form. Listing the same premise twice will not make the argument any better from a logical point of view.

Sometimes *guarding* terms can also be dropped. If I say, "I think Miranda is at home, so we can meet her there," this argument might be represented in standard form thus:

I think Miranda is at home.
_____

∴ We can meet her there.

This is misleading. My *thoughts* are not what make us able to meet Miranda at home. It is the *fact* that Miranda is at home that provides a reason for the conclusion. Thus, it is clearer to drop the guarding phrase ("I think") when putting the argument into standard form. But you have to be careful. Not all guarding phrases can be dropped. If a friend says that you ought to buckle your seat belt because you could have an accident, it would distort her argument to drop the guarding term ("could"), because she is not claiming that you definitely will have an accident, or even that you probably will have one. The *chance* of an accident is significant enough to show that you ought to buckle your seat belt, so this guarding term should be kept when the argument is put into standard form.

It is also possible to drop *assuring* terms in some cases. Suppose someone says, "You obviously cannot play golf in Alaska in January, so there's no point in bringing your clubs." There is no need to keep the assuring term ("obviously") in the premise. It might even be misleading, because the issue

---

[1]Other factors are important in inductive arguments. We will discuss inductive arguments in Chapter 9. The present chapter will focus on deductive arguments.

is whether the premise is true, not whether it is obvious. The argument cannot be refuted by showing that, even though you in fact cannot play golf in Alaska in January, this is not obvious, since there might be indoor golf courses. In contrast, assuring terms *cannot* be dropped in some other cases. For example, if someone argues, "We know that poverty causes crime, because many studies have shown that it does," then the assuring terms ("We know that . . ." and "studies have shown that . . .") cannot be dropped without turning the argument into an empty shell: "Poverty causes crime, because it does." The point of this argument is to cite the sources of our knowledge ("studies") and to show that we have knowledge instead of just a hunch. That point is lost if we drop the assuring terms.

Unfortunately, there is no mechanical method for determining when guarding or assuring terms and phrases can be dropped, or whether certain sentences are unnecessary tangents. We simply have to look closely at what is being said and think hard about what is needed to support the conclusion. It takes skill, care, and insight to pare an argument down to its essential core without omitting anything that would make it better.

EXERCISE I

Put the following arguments into standard form and omit anything that does not affect the validity of the argument or the truth of its premises.

1. Philadelphia is rich in history, but it is not now the capital of the United States, so the U.S. Congress must meet somewhere else.

2. Not everybody whom you invited is going to come to your party. Some of them won't come. So this room should be big enough.

3. I know that my wife is at home, since I just called her there and spoke to her. We talked about our dinner plans.

4. I'm not sure, but Joseph is probably Jewish. Hence, he is a rabbi if he is a member of the clergy.

5. Some students could not concentrate on the lecture because they did not eat lunch before class, although I did.

6. The most surprising news of all is that Johnson dropped out of the race because he thought his opponent was better qualified than he was for the office.

7. The Democrat is likely to win, since experts agree that more women support him.

8. It seems to me that married people are happier, so marriage must be a good thing, or at least I think so.

During the Democratic presidential candidates' debate in New Hampshire on January 22, 2004, Peter Jennings and Senator John Edwards had the following exchange. Remove its excess verbiage and put Edwards's essential argument in standard form:

> **MR. JENNINGS:** Senator Kerry was one of only fourteen senators who voted against [the Defense of Marriage Act]. I would like to know from you whether or not you think he was right or wrong, and why.

> **SEN. EDWARDS:** I think he was right. I think he was right, because what happened with the Defense of Marriage Act is it took away the power of states, like Vermont, to be able to do what they chose to do about civil unions, about these kinds of marriage issues. These are issues that should be left—Massachusetts, for example, has just made a decision— the Supreme Court at least has made a decision—that embraces the notion of gay marriage. I think these are decisions the states should have the power to make. And the Defense of Marriage Act, as I understand it—you're right, I wasn't there when it was passed—but as I understand it, would have taken away that power. And I think that's wrong—that power should not be taken away from the states. . . .

CLARIFYING CRUCIAL TERMS

After the essential premises and conclusion are isolated, we often need to clarify these claims before we can begin our logical analysis. The goal here is not perfect clarity, for there probably is no such thing. It is, however, often necessary to eliminate ambiguity and reduce vagueness before we can give an argument a fair assessment. In particular, it is often helpful to specify the referents of pronouns, because such references can depend on a context that is changed when the argument is put into standard form. We also often need to specify whether a claim is about all, most, many, or just some of its subject matter.

Another common problem arises when someone argues like this:

You should just say "No" to drugs, because drugs are dangerous.

What counts as a drug? What about penicillin or aspirin? The speaker might seem to mean "drugs like cocaine," but "like" them in which respects? Maybe what is meant is "addictive drugs," but what about alcohol and nicotine (which are often addictive)? You might think that the speaker means "dangerous drugs," but then the premise becomes empty: "Dangerous drugs are dangerous." Or maybe the idea is "illegal drugs," but that seems to assume that the law is correct about what is dangerous. In any case, we cannot begin to evaluate this argument if we do not know the extent of what it claims.

Of course, we should not try to clarify every term in the argument. Even if this were possible, it would make the argument extremely long and boring. Instead, our goal is to clarify anything that seems likely to produce confusion later if it is not cleared up now. As our analysis continues, we can always return and clarify more if the need arises, but it is better to get the most obvious problems out of the way at the start.

DISSECTING THE ARGUMENT

A single sentence often includes several clauses that make separate claims. When this happens, it is usually useful to dissect the sentence into its smallest parts, so that we can investigate each part separately. Because simpler steps are easier to follow than complex ones, we can understand the argument better when it is broken down. Dissection makes us more likely to notice any flaws in the argument. It also enables us to pinpoint exactly where the argument fails, if it does.

The process of dissecting an argument is a skill that can be learned only by practice. Let's start with a simple example:

> Joe won his bet, because all he had to do was eat five pounds of oysters, and he ate nine dozen, which weigh more than five pounds.

The simplest unpacking of this argument yields the following restatement in standard form:

> All Joe had to do was eat five pounds of oysters, and he ate nine
>   dozen, which weigh more than five pounds.
> ──
> ∴ Joe won his bet.

If we think about the premise of this argument, we see that it actually contains three claims. The argument will be clearer if we separate these claims into independent premises and add a few words for the sake of clarity. The following, then, is a better representation of this argument:

> (1) All Joe had to do (to win his bet) was eat five pounds of oysters.
> (2) Joe ate nine dozen (oysters).
> (3) Nine dozen oysters weigh more than five pounds.
> ──
> ∴ (4) Joe won his bet.

With the premise split up in this way, it becomes obvious that there are three separate ways in which the argument could fail. One possibility is that Joe had to do more than just eat five pounds of oysters to win his bet: Maybe what he bet was that he could eat five pounds in five minutes. Another possibility is that Joe did not really eat nine dozen oysters: Maybe he really ate one dozen oysters cut into nine dozen pieces. A final way in which the argument could fail is if nine dozen oysters do not weigh more than five pounds: Maybe the oysters that Joe ate were very small, or maybe nine dozen oysters weigh more than five pounds only when they are still in their shells, but Joe did not eat the shells. In any case, breaking down complex premises into simpler ones makes it easier to see exactly where the argument goes wrong, if it does. Consequently, we can be more confident that an argument does not go wrong if we do not see any problem in it even after we have broken it down completely.

Although it is a good idea to break down the premises of an argument when this is possible, we have to be careful not to do this in a way that changes the logical structure of the argument. Suppose someone argues like this:

> Socialism is doomed to failure because it does not provide the incentives that are needed for a prosperous economy.

The simplest representation of this argument yields the following standard form:

> Socialism does not provide the incentives that are needed for a
>   prosperous economy.
> ∴ Socialism is doomed to failure.

It is tempting to break up the first premise into two parts:

> Socialism does not provide incentives.
> Incentives are needed for a prosperous economy.
> ∴ Socialism is doomed to failure.

In this form, the argument is open to a fatal objection: Socialism *does* provide *some* incentives. Workers often get public recognition and special privileges when they produce a great deal in socialist economies. But this does not refute the original argument. The point of the original argument was not that socialism does not provide any incentives at all, but only that socialism does not provide enough incentives or the right kind of incentives to create a prosperous economy. This point is lost if we break up the premise in the way suggested. A better attempt is this:

> (1) Socialism does not provide adequate incentives.
> (2) Adequate incentives are needed for a prosperous economy.
> ∴ (3) Socialism is doomed to failure.

The problem now is to specify when incentives are *adequate*. What kinds of incentives are needed? How much of these incentives? The answer seems to be "enough for a prosperous economy." But then premise (2) reduces to "Enough incentives for a prosperous economy are needed for a prosperous economy." This is too empty to be useful. Thus, we are led back to something like the original premise:

> Socialism does not provide enough incentives for a prosperous
>   economy.
> ∴ Socialism is doomed to failure.

In this case, we cannot break the premise into parts without distorting the point.

ARRANGING SUBARGUMENTS

When the premises of an argument are dissected, it often becomes clear that some of these premises are intended as reasons for others. The premises then form a chain of simpler arguments that culminate in the ultimate conclusion, but only after some intermediate steps. Consider this argument:

> There's no way I can finish my paper before the 9 o'clock show, since I have to do the reading first, so I won't even start writing until at least 9 o'clock.

It might seem tempting to put this argument into standard form as:

> I have to do the reading first.
> I won't even start writing until at least 9 o'clock.
> ∴ I can't finish my paper before the 9 o'clock show.

This reformulation does include all three parts of the original argument, but it fails to indicate the correct role for each part. The two argument markers in the original argument indicate that there are really *two* conclusions. The word "since" indicates that what precedes it is a conclusion, and the word "so" indicates that what follows it is also a conclusion. We cannot represent this as a single argument in standard form, because each argument in standard form can have only one conclusion. Thus, the original sentence must have included two arguments. The relationship between these arguments should be clear: The conclusion of the first argument functions as a premise or reason in the second argument. To represent this, we let the two arguments form a chain. This is the first argument:

> I have to do the reading first.
> ∴ I won't even start writing until at least 9 o'clock.

This is the second argument:

> I won't even start writing until at least 9 o'clock.
> ∴ I can't finish my paper before the 9 o'clock show.

If we want to, we can then write these two arguments in a chain like this:

> (1) I have to do the reading first.
> ∴ (2) I won't even start writing until at least 9 o'clock.
> ∴ (3) I can't finish my paper before the 9 o'clock show.

This chain of reasoning can also be diagrammed like this:

(1)

↓

(2)

↓

(3)

The arrow indicates which claims are supposed to provide reasons for which other claims.

Although it is often illuminating to break an argument into stages, this can be misleading if done incorrectly. For example, the first sentences of Kyl's speech cited in Chapter 4 read as follows:

> Mr. Speaker, I oppose this measure. I oppose it first because it is expensive. I further oppose it because it is untimely.

If we try to force this into a simple chain, we might get this:

> (1) This measure is expensive.
>
> ∴ (2) This measure is untimely.
>
> ∴ (3) I oppose this measure.

This reconstruction suggests that the measure's expense is what makes it untimely. That might be true (say, during a temporary budget crisis), but it is not what Kyl actually says. Instead, Kyl is giving two separate reasons for the same conclusion. First,

> (1) This measure is expensive.
>
> ∴ (2) I oppose this measure.

Second,

> (1*) This measure is untimely.
>
> ∴ (2) I oppose this measure.

The structure of this argument can now be diagrammed as a branching tree:

The two arrows indicate that there are two separate reasons for the conclusion. We have to be careful not to confuse branching arguments like this with chains of arguments that do not branch.

We also need to distinguish this branching structure from cases where several premises work together to support a single conclusion. Consider this:

My keys must be either at home or at the office. They can't be at the office, because I looked for them there. So they must be at home.

With some clarifications, we can put this argument in standard form:

> (1) My keys are either at my home or at my office.
> (2) My keys are not at my office.
> ∴ (3) My keys are at my home.

Although this argument has two premises, it does not give two separate reasons for its conclusion. Neither premise by itself, without the other, is enough to give us any reason to believe the conclusion. Thus, it would be misleading to diagram this argument in the same way as Kyl's argument. Instead, we need to indicate that the premises work together. Here's a simple way:

(1) + (2)
↓
(3)

The symbol "+" with a single arrow indicates that the two premises together provide a single reason for the conclusion. If three or more premises provided a single reason, then we could simply add to the list: (1) + (2) + (3), and so on. If you wanted to be really careful, you could draw a single line under the premises to show which ones are grouped together.

The argument that we are diagramming included one part that we have not incorporated yet:

They can't be at the office, because I looked for them there.

The standard form is this:

> (2*) I looked for my keys at my office.
> ∴ (2) My keys can't be at my office.

By itself, this argument has this diagram:

(2*)
↓
(2)

Since the conclusion of this background argument is a premise in the other part of the argument, we can put the diagrams together like this:

(2*)
↓
(1) + (2)
↓
(3)

The fact that the arrow goes from (2*) to (2) but not to (1) indicates that this background argument supports premise (2), but not the other premise. In cases like this, you need to be careful where you draw your arrows.

Argument structures can get very complex, but we can diagram most arguments by connecting the simple forms that we illustrated. Begin by identifying the premises and conclusions. Give each different claim a different number. When two premises work together to support a single conclusion, put a "+" between the premises and a single arrow to the conclusion. When two or more premises (or sets of premises) provide separate reasons for a conclusion, draw separate arrows from each reason to the conclusion. When a conclusion of one argument is a premise in another, put it in the middle of a chain. The whole diagram together will then show how the parts of the argument fit together.

EXERCISE III

Put the following arguments into standard form. Break up the premises and form chains of arguments wherever this can be done without distorting the argument. Then diagram the argument.

1. I know Pat can't be a father, because she is not a male. So she can't be a grandfather either.

2. Either Jack is a fool or Mary is a crook, because she ended up with all of his money.

3. Our team can't win this Saturday, both because they are not going to play, and because they are no good, so they wouldn't win even if they did play.

4. Mercury is known to be the only metal that is liquid at room temperature, so a pound of mercury would be liquid in this room, which is at room temperature, and it would also conduct electricity, since all metals do. Therefore, some liquids do conduct electricity.

5. Since he won the lottery, he's rich and lucky, so he'll probably do well in the stock market, too, unless his luck runs out.

6. Joe is not a freshman, since he lives in a fraternity, and freshmen are not allowed to live in fraternities. He also can't be a senior, since he has not declared a major, and every senior has declared a major. And he can't be a junior, because I never met him before today, and I would have met him before now if he were a junior. So Joe must be a sophomore.

7. Since many newly emerging nations do not have the capital resources necessary for sustained growth, they will continue to need help from industrial nations to avoid mass starvation.

In "A Piece of 'God's Handiwork'" (Passage 2 in Exercise IV in Chapter 4), Robert Redford argues that the Bureau of Land Management (BLM) should not allow Conoco to drill for oil in Utah's Grand Staircase-Escalante National Monument. The following passage is a crucial part where Redford answers an objection. Arrange its subarguments so as to reveal the structure of his argument. Then diagram the overall argument.

> The BLM says its hands are tied. Why? Because these lands were set aside subject to "valid existing rights," and Conoco has a lease that gives it the right to drill. Sure Conoco has a lease—more than one, in fact—but those leases were originally issued without sufficient environmental study or public input. As a result, none of them conveyed a valid right to drill. What's more, in deciding to issue a permit to drill now, the BLM did not conduct a full analysis of the environmental impacts of drilling in these incomparable lands, but instead determined there would be no significant environmental harm on the basis of an abbreviated review that didn't even look at drilling on the other federal leases. Sounds like Washington double-speak to me.

SUPPRESSED PREMISES

SHARED FACTS

Arguments in everyday life are rarely completely explicit. They usually depend on unstated facts understood by those involved in the conversation. Thus, if we are told that Chester Arthur was a president of the United States, we have a right to conclude a great many things about him—for example, that at the time he was president, he was a live human being. Appeals to facts of this kind lie behind the following argument:

Benjamin Franklin could not have been our second president, because he died before the second election was held.

This argument obviously turns on a question of fact: Did Franklin die before the second presidential election was held? (He did.) The argument would not be sound if this explicit premise were not true. But the argument also depends on a more general principle that ties the premise and conclusion together:

The dead cannot be president.

This new premise is needed to make the argument valid (and thus sound).

Traditionally, logicians have called premises that are needed but are not stated *suppressed premises*. An argument depending on suppressed premises is called an *enthymeme* and is said to be *enthymematic*. If we look at arguments that occur in daily life, we discover that they are, almost without exception, enthymematic. Therefore, to trace the pathway between premises and conclusion, it is usually necessary to fill in these suppressed premises that serve as links between the stated premises and the conclusion.

Suppressed premises often concern rules or conventions that might have been otherwise. Our example assumed that the dead are not eligible for the presidency, but we can imagine a society in which the deceased are elected to public office as an honor (something like posthumous induction into the Baseball Hall of Fame). Our national government is not like that, however, and this is something that most Americans know. This makes it odd to come right out and say that the deceased cannot hold public office. In most settings, this would involve a violation of the conversational rule of Quantity, because it says more than needs to be said.

But even if it would be odd to state it, this fact plays a central role in the argument. To assert the conclusion without believing the suppressed premise would involve a violation of the conversational rule of Quality, because the speaker would not have adequate reasons for the conclusion. Furthermore, if this suppressed premise were not believed to be true, then to give the explicit premise as a reason for the conclusion would violate the conversational rule of Relevance (just as it would be irrelevant to point out that Babe Ruth is dead when someone asks whether he is in the Baseball Hall of Fame). For these reasons, anyone who gives the original argument conversationally implies a commitment to the suppressed premise.

Suppressed premises are not always so obvious. A somewhat more complicated example is this:

> Arnold Schwarzenegger cannot become president of the United States, because he was born in Austria.

Why should being from Austria disqualify someone from being president? It seems odd that the founding fathers should have something against that particular part of the world. The answer is that the argument depends on a more general suppressed premise:

> Only a natural-born U.S. citizen may become president of the United States.

It is this provision of the U.S. Constitution that lies at the heart of the argument. Knowing this provision is, of course, a more specialized piece of knowledge than knowing that you have to be alive to be president. For this reason, more people will see the force of the first argument (about Franklin) than the second (about Schwarzenegger). The second argument assumes an audience with more specialized knowledge.

The argument still has to draw a connection between being born in Austria and being a natural-born United States citizen. So it turns out that the argument has three stages:

(1) Schwarzenegger was born in Austria.

(2) Austria has never been part of the United States.

∴ (3) Schwarzenegger was born outside the United States. (from 1–2)

(4) Anyone who was born outside the United States is not a natural-born U.S. citizen.

∴ (5) Schwarzenegger is not a natural-born U.S. citizen. (from 3–4)

(6) Only a natural-born U.S. citizen may become president of the United States.

∴ (7) Schwarzenegger cannot become president of the United States. (from 5–6)

With the addition of suppressed premises (2), (4), and (6), the argument is now valid.

The argument is still not sound, however, because some of the suppressed premises that were added are not true. In particular, there is an exception to the suppressed premise about who is a natural-born U.S. citizen. This exception is well known to U.S. citizens who live overseas. People who were born in Austria are U.S. citizens if their parents were U.S. citizens. They also seem to count as natural-born citizens, since they are not naturalized. This is not completely settled, but it does not matter here, as Arnold Schwarzenegger's parents were not U.S. citizens when he was born. Thus, the second stage of the above argument can be reformulated as follows:

(3) Schwarzenegger was born outside the United States.

(4*) Schwarzenegger's parents were not U.S. citizens when he was born.

(4**) Anyone who was born outside the United States and whose parents were not U.S. citizens at the time is not a natural-born U.S. citizen.

∴ (5) Schwarzenegger is not a natural-born U.S. citizen.

This much of the argument is now sound.

EXERCISE V

There is a less well-known exception to the premise that only a natural-born citizen may become president of the United States. The Constitution does allow a person who is not a natural-born citizen to become president if he or she was "a citizen of the United States at the time of the adoption of this Constitution." This exception is said to have been added to allow Alexander Hamilton to run for president, but it obviously does not apply to Schwarzenegger or to anyone else alive today. Nonetheless, this exception keeps the argument from being sound in its present form. Reformulate the final stage of the argument to make it sound.

An argument with a single premise has grown to include three stages with at least four suppressed premises. Some of the added premises are obvious, but others are less well known, so we cannot assume that the person who gave the original argument had the more complete argument in mind. Many people would be convinced by the original argument even without all these added complexities. Nonetheless, the many suppressed premises are necessary to make the argument sound. Seeing this brings out the assumptions that must be true for the conclusion to follow from the premises. This process of making everything explicit enables us to assess these background assumptions directly.

LINGUISTIC PRINCIPLES

Often an argument is valid, but it is not clear *why* it is valid. It is not clear *how* the conclusion follows from the premises. Arguments are like pathways between premises and conclusions, and some of these pathways are more complicated than others. Yet even the simplest arguments reveal hidden complexities when examined closely. For example, there is no question that the following argument is valid:

> Harriet is in New York with her son.
> ∴ Harriet's son is in New York.

It is not possible for the premise to be true and the conclusion false. If asked why this conclusion follows from the premise, it would be natural to reply that you cannot be someplace with somebody unless that person is there, too. This is not something we usually spell out, but it is the principle that takes us from the premise to the conclusion.

One thing to notice about this principle is that it is quite general—that is, it does not depend on any special features of the people or places involved. It is also true that if Benjamin is in St. Louis with his daughter, then Benjamin's daughter is in St. Louis. Although the references have changed, the general pattern that lies behind this inference will seem obvious to anyone who understands the words used to formulate it. For this reason we shall say that principles of this kind are basically *linguistic* in character.

If we look at arguments as they occur in everyday life, we will discover that almost all of them turn on unstated linguistic principles. To cite just one more example: If a wife is taller than her husband, then there is at least one woman who is taller than at least one man. This inference relies on the principles that husbands are men and wives are women. We do not usually state these linguistic principles, for to do so will often violate the rule of Quantity. (Try to imagine a context in which you would come right out and say, "Husbands, you know, are men." Unless you were speaking to someone just learning the language, this would be a peculiar remark.) But even if, in most cases, it would be peculiar to come right out and state such linguistic principles, our arguments typically presuppose them. This observation reveals yet another way in which our daily use of language moves within a rich, though largely unnoticed, framework of rules, as we emphasized in Chapter 1.

OTHER KINDS OF SUPPRESSED PREMISES

We have examined two kinds of suppressed premises, factual and linguistic. Many arguments also contain unstated *moral* premises. Consider the following argument as a case in point:

> You shouldn't buy pornography, because it leads to violence toward women.

This argument clearly relies on the moral principle that you should not buy anything that leads to violence toward women. A different example contains *religious* premises:

> You shouldn't take the name of the Lord in vain, because this shows disrespect.

The suppressed premise here is that you should not do anything that shows disrespect (to the Lord). More examples could be given, but the point should be clear. Most arguments depend on unstated assumptions, and these assumptions come in many different varieties.

THE USE AND ABUSE OF SUPPRESSED PREMISES

Talk about *suppressed* premises may bring to mind suppressing a rebellion or an ugly thought, and using *hidden* premises may sound somewhat sneaky. But the way we are using them, these expressions do not carry such negative connotations. A suppressed or hidden premise is simply an *unstated* premise. It is often legitimate to leave premises unstated. It is legitimate if (1) those who are given the argument can easily supply these unstated premises for themselves, and (2) the unstated premises are not themselves controversial. If done properly, the suppression of premises can add greatly to the efficiency of language. Indeed, without the judicious suppression of obvious premises, many arguments would become too cumbersome to be effective.

On the other hand, suppressed premises can also be used improperly. People sometimes suppress questionable assumptions so that their opponents will not notice where an argument goes astray. For example, when election debates turn to the topic of crime, we often hear arguments like this:

> My opponent is opposed to the death penalty, so he must be soft on crime.

The response sometimes sounds like this:

> Since my opponent continues to support the death penalty, he must not have read the most recent studies, which show that the death penalty does not deter crime.

The first argument assumes that anyone who is opposed to the death penalty is soft on crime, and the second argument assumes that anyone who read the studies in question would be convinced by them and would turn against the death penalty. Both of these assumptions are questionable, and the questions they raise are central to the debate. If we want to understand these issues and address them directly, we have to bring out these suppressed premises explicitly.

EXERCISE VI

The following arguments depend for their validity on suppressed premises of various kinds. For each of them, list enough suppressed premises to make the argument valid and to show why it is valid. This might require several suppressed premises of various kinds.

Example: Carol has no sisters, because all her siblings are brothers.

Suppressed Premises: A sister would be a sibling.
                                    A brother is not a sister.

1. Britney Spears is under age thirty-five. Therefore, she cannot run for president of the United States.
2. Nixon couldn't have been president in 1950 because he was still in the Senate.
3. 81 is not a prime number, because 81 is divisible by 3.
4. There's no one named Rupert here; we have only female patients.
5. Columbus did not discover the New World because the Vikings explored Newfoundland centuries earlier.
6. There must not be any survivors, since they would have been found by now.
7. Lincoln could not have met Washington, because Washington was dead before Lincoln was born.
8. Philadelphia cannot play Los Angeles in the World Series, since they are both in the National League.
9. Mildred must be over forty-three, since she has a daughter who is thirty-six years old.
10. He cannot be a grandfather because he never had children.
11. That's not acid rock; you can understand the lyrics.
12. Harold can't play in the Super Bowl, because he broke his leg.
13. Shaquille must be a basketball player, since he is so tall.
14. Dan is either stupid or very cunning, so he must be stupid.
15. Susan refuses to work on Sundays, which shows that she is lazy and inflexible.
16. Jim told me that Mary is a professor, so she can't be a student, since professors must already have degrees.
17. This burglar alarm won't work unless we are lucky or the burglar uses the front door, so we can't count on it.
18. His natural talents were not enough; he still lost the match because he had not practiced sufficiently.

THE METHOD OF RECONSTRUCTION

We can summarize the discussion so far by listing the steps to be taken in reconstructing an argument. The first two steps were discussed in Chapters 4 and 3, respectively.

1. Do a *close analysis* of the passage containing the argument.
2. List all explicit premises and the conclusion in *standard form*.
3. *Clarify* the premises and the conclusion where necessary.
4. *Break up* the premises and the conclusion into smaller parts where this is possible.
5. *Arrange* the parts of the argument into a chain or tree of subarguments where this is possible.
6. Assess each argument and subargument for *validity*.[2]
7. If any argument or subargument is not valid, or if it is not clear why it is valid, add *suppressed premises* that will show how to get from the premises to the conclusion.
8. Assess the *truth* of the premises.

After reconstructing the argument, it is often helpful to add some indication of its structure. This can be done by numbering the premises and then, after each conclusion, listing the premises from which that conclusion follows. (We did this in our examples.) The argument's structure can also be shown by a diagram like those discussed above. Either way, we need to make it clear exactly how the separate parts of the argument are supposed to fit together.

This method is not intended to be mechanical. Each step requires care and intelligence. As a result, a given argument can be reconstructed in various ways with varying degrees of illumination and insight. The goal of this method is to reveal as much of the structure of an argument as possible and to learn from it as much as you can. Different reconstructions approach this goal more or less closely.

The whole process is more complex than our discussion thus far has suggested. This is especially clear in the last three steps of reconstruction, which must be carried out simultaneously. In deciding whether an argument is acceptable, we try to find a set of true suppressed premises that, if added to the stated premises, yields a sound argument for the conclusion. Two problems typically arise when we make this effort:

1. We find a set of premises strong enough to support the conclusion, but at least one of these premises is false.
2. We modify the premises to avoid falsehood, but the conclusion no longer follows from them.

---

[2]With inductive arguments, we assess the argument for *strength* instead of validity. Inductive arguments will be examined in Chapter 9.

The reconstruction of an argument typically involves shifting back and forth between the demand for a valid argument and the demand for true premises. Eventually, we either show the argument to be sound or we abandon the effort. In the latter case, we conclude that the argument in question has no sound reconstruction. It is still possible that *we* were at fault in not finding a reconstruction that showed the argument to be sound. Perhaps we did not show enough ingenuity in searching for a suppressed premise that would do the trick. There is, in fact, no purely formal or mechanical way of dealing with this problem. A person presenting an argument may reasonably leave out steps, provided that they can easily be filled in by those to whom the argument is addressed. So in analyzing an argument, we should be charitable—but our charity has limits. After a reasonable search for those suppressed premises that would show the argument to be sound, we should not blame ourselves if we fail to find them. Rather, the blame shifts to the person who formulated the argument for not doing so clearly.

EXERCISE VII

During the Democratic presidential candidates' debate in New Hampshire on January 22, 2004, Senator Joseph Lieberman from Connecticut explained why he supported the war against Iraq in 2003. Reconstruct and diagram his arguments in the following passage:

> Well, very briefly, we made the right decision. I didn't need George Bush to convince me that Saddam Hussein was a threat to the United States of America. John McCain and I wrote the law that made it national policy to change the regime in Baghdad. This man was a homicidal maniac—killed hundreds of thousands of people, did have weapons of mass destruction in the '90s—used them against the Kurdish Iraqis and Iranians—admitted to the United Nations he had enough chemical and biological weapons to kill millions of people, supported terrorism, tried to assassinate former President Bush. I repeat: We are safer with Saddam Hussein in prison than in power. . . .
>
> I have criticized the president for overstating some of the arguments about why we went to war. I've said I was shocked that the administration wasn't better prepared to take advantage of the military victory. But I repeat again: This was a just war. Look, when I voted for the resolution in the fall of 2002, I had no illusions—I knew it would be an unpopular vote in parts of the Democratic Party in my race for the presidency. But I did it because I put my hand on the Bible and took an oath to protect the security of the United States, and I believed that Saddam Hussein was a clear and present danger and threat to the security of the United States, the people of Iraq, and the stability of the world. I've said before that at times in its policy the Bush administration has given a bad name to a just war. But a just war it was, and again we are safer as a people with Saddam Hussein in prison, not in power. Now we have an extraordinary opportunity in the war against terrorism to build an Iraq, a democraticizing, modernizing country in the middle of the Arab and Islamic worlds, which will send a message to the majority in the Islamic world that there is a better way than the hatred and death that al Qaeda presents to them. It is, if you'll forgive me, the American, the democratic way.

EXERCISE VIII

Reconstruct and diagram Andrew Beebe's argument in "Greeks Should Be Co-ed" (Exercise I in Chapter 4).

EXERCISE IX

Practice the method of reconstruction on one or more of the following:

1. One of the other passages at the end of Chapter 4.
2. An editorial from your local paper.
3. Your last term paper or a friend's last term paper.
4. Part of one of the readings in Part II.

DIGGING DEEPER

After we have reconstructed an argument as well as we can, doubts still might arise about its premises. If we agree with its premises, others might deny them or ask why they are true. If we disagree with its premises, we might be able to understand the source of our disagreement better if we determine why it is believed by other people—including the person who gave the argument. Either way, it is useful to try to construct supporting arguments for the premises that may be questioned. These supporting arguments are not parts of the explicit argument or even of its reconstruction, but are arguments further back in a chain of arguments.

When we look for further arguments to support the premises in an argument, we might then wonder whether the premises of each new argument can be accepted without supporting arguments as well. We seem faced with the unpleasant task of producing endless chains of argument. (A similar problem was mentioned in Chapter 3.) When pressed in this way to give reasons for our reasons, and reasons for our reasons for our reasons, we eventually come upon *fundamental principles*—principles for which we cannot give any more basic argument. These fundamental principles can concern morality, religion, politics, and our general views concerning the nature of the world. We often argue within a framework of such principles without actually stating them, because we assume (sometimes incorrectly) that others accept them as well. When someone argues that environmental destruction should be stopped because it will lead to the annihilation of the human race, he or she will not feel called on to say explicitly, "And the annihilation of the human race would be a very bad thing." That, after all, is something that most people take for granted.

Though fundamental principles are often obvious and generally accepted, at times it is not clear what principles are being assumed and just how acceptable they really are. Then we need to make our assumptions explicit and look for deeper arguments, continuing the process as far as we can. There is a limit to how far we can go, but the deeper we go, the better we will understand our own views and, in addition, the views of our opponents.

EXERCISE X

The following arguments depend on suppressed premises for their validity. (1) State what these underlying premises might be. In some cases, there might be more than one. (2) Indicate whether these premises are fundamental principles in the sense just described. (3) For each premise that is not fundamental, give a supporting argument that is as plausible as you can make it. Remember, you do not have to accept an argument to detect its underlying principles and to understand the kind of argument that could be used to support it.

Example:	General Snork has no right to rule, because he came to power by a military coup.
Suppressed Premise:	Someone who came to power by a military coup has no right to rule.
Supporting Argument:	Someone has a right to rule only if he or she has been elected by the people.
	Someone who comes to power by a military coup has not been elected by the people.
∴	Someone who came to power by a military coup has no right to rule.

(Further support for the first premise might be provided by some general theory of democracy, such as that all rights to use power come from the people, and the only legitimate way for the people to delegate these rights is in elections.)

1. You shouldn't call Kirk guilty, because he has not even been tried yet.
2. Cows cannot live in a desert, because they eat grass.
3. The liquid in this glass must not be water, since the sugar I put in it isn't dissolving.
4. People can vote and be drafted at age eighteen, so they should also be allowed to drink at eighteen.
5. We have no right to attack Muslim dictatorships if we support Christian dictatorships. So we should not attack Muslim dictatorships.
6. That chair won't hold you, since it almost broke a few minutes ago when your little sister sat in it.
7. Bringing down our deficits should be a high priority, because, if high deficits continue, inflation will return.
8. The thought of eating ostrich meat will seem strange to most people, so your ostrich farm is bound to go broke.
9. Getting good grades must be hard, since, if getting good grades were easy, more people would do it.

10. Morris does not deserve his wealth, for he merely inherited it.

11. Frank should not be punished, because it is wrong to punish someone just to make an example of him.

12. There can't be UFOs (unidentified flying objects), because there is no life on other planets.

13. The sky is red tonight, so it isn't going to rain tomorrow.

14. Parents take care of their children when they are young, so their children should take care of them when they get old.

DISCUSSION QUESTION

How can you tell when you have reached a fundamental principle? Must every argument start with some basic claim for which no further argument can be given or for which you can give no argument?

ADVANCED SECTION: CAPITAL PUNISHMENT

We can illustrate these methods of deep analysis by examining the difficult question of the constitutionality of capital punishment. It has been argued that the Supreme Court should declare the death penalty unconstitutional because it is a cruel and unusual punishment. The explicitly stated argument has the following basic form:

The death penalty is a cruel and unusual punishment.

∴ The death penalty should be declared unconstitutional.

The argument plainly depends on two suppressed premises:

SP1: The Constitution prohibits cruel and unusual punishments.

SP2: Anything that the Constitution prohibits should be declared unconstitutional.

So the argument, more fully spelled out, looks like this:

(1) The death penalty is a cruel and unusual punishment.
(2) SP: The Constitution prohibits cruel and unusual punishments.

∴ (3) The Constitution prohibits the death penalty. (from 1–2)

(4) SP: Anything that the Constitution prohibits should be declared unconstitutional.

∴ (5) The death penalty should be declared unconstitutional. (from 3–4)

This reconstruction seems to be a fair representation of the intent of the original argument.

We can now turn to an assessment of this argument. First, the argument is valid: Given the premises, the conclusion does follow. All that remains is to determine the truth of the premises one by one.

Premise (4) seems uncontroversial. Indeed, it might sound like a truism to say that anything that violates a constitutional provision should be declared unconstitutional. But in fact, this notion was once controversial, for nothing in the Constitution explicitly gives the courts the right to declare acts of legislators unconstitutional and hence void. The courts have acquired and consolidated this right in the years since 1789, and it is still sometimes challenged by those who think that it gives the courts too much power. But even if the judiciary's power to declare laws unconstitutional is not itself a constitutionally stated power, it is so much an accepted part of our system that no one would challenge it in a courtroom procedure today.

The second premise is clearly true, for the Constitution does, in fact, prohibit cruel and unusual punishments. Its Eighth Amendment reads, "Excessive bail shall not be required, nor excessive fines imposed, nor cruel and unusual punishments inflicted." It is not clear, however, just what this prohibition amounts to. In particular, does the punishment have to be *both* cruel *and* unusual to be prohibited, or is it sufficient for it to be *either* cruel *or* unusual? This would make a big difference if cruel punishments were usual, or if some unusual punishments were not cruel. For the moment, let us interpret the language as meaning "both cruel and unusual."

The first premise—"The death penalty is a cruel and unusual punishment"—obviously forms the heart of the argument. What we would expect, then, is a good supporting argument to be put forward in its behalf. Consider the following argument by Supreme Court Justice Potter Stewart, intended to support this claim in particular cases in which the death penalty was imposed for rape and murder:

> In the first place, it is clear that these sentences are "cruel" in the sense that they excessively go beyond, not in degree but in kind, the punishments that the state legislatures have determined to be necessary. . . . In the second place, it is equally clear that these sentences are "unusual" in the sense that the penalty of death is infrequently imposed for murder, and that its imposition for rape is extraordinarily rare. But I do not rest my conclusion upon these two propositions alone. These death sentences are cruel and unusual in the same way that being struck by lightning is cruel and unusual. For, of all the people convicted of rapes and murders in 1967 and 1968, many just as reprehensible as these, the petitioners are among a capriciously selected random handful upon whom the sentence of death has in fact been imposed. My concurring brothers [the Justices who agree with Stewart] have demonstrated that, if any basis can be discerned for the selection of these few to be sentenced to die, it is the constitutionally impermissible basis of race.[3]

[3]From Justice Stewart's concurring opinion in *Furman v. Georgia*, 408 U.S. 239 at 309–310 (1972). Stewart provided one of the crucial swing votes in this important case.

The first sentence argues that the death penalty is *cruel*. The basic idea is that punishments are cruel if they inflict harms that are much worse than what is necessary for any legitimate and worthwhile purpose. Stewart then seems to accept the state legislatures' view that the death penalty does go far beyond what is necessary. This makes it cruel.

Now let us concentrate on the part of this argument intended to show that the death penalty is an *unusual* punishment. Of course, in civilized nations, the death penalty is reserved for a small range of crimes, but this is hardly the point at issue. The point of the argument is that the death penalty is unusual even for those crimes that are punishable by death, including first-degree murder. Moreover, Stewart claims that, among those convicted of crimes punishable by death, who actually receives a death sentence is determined either capriciously or on the basis of race. The point seems to be that whether a person who is convicted of a capital crime will be given the death penalty depends on the kind of legal aid he or she receives, the prosecutor's willingness to offer a plea bargain, the judge's personality, the beliefs and attitudes of the jury, and many other considerations. At many points in the process, choices that affect the outcome could be based on mere whim or caprice, or even on the race of the defendant or the victim. Why are these factors mentioned? Because, as Stewart says, it is unconstitutional for sentencing to be based on caprice or race.

We can then restate this supporting argument more carefully as follows:

> Very few criminals who were found guilty of crimes that are
> punishable by death are actually sentenced to death.
> Among those found guilty of crimes punishable by death, who is
> sentenced to death depends on caprice or race.
> It is unconstitutional for sentencing to depend on caprice or race.
> A punishment is unusual if it is imposed infrequently and on an
> unconstitutional basis.

∴ The death penalty is an unusual punishment.

This conclusion is part of the first premise in our original argument. Now we can spread the entire argument out before us:

(1) An act is cruel if it inflicts harms that are much worse than what is necessary for any legitimate and worthwhile purpose.
(2) The death penalty inflicts harms that are much worse than what is necessary for any legitimate and worthwhile purpose.

∴ (3) The death penalty is cruel. (from 1–2)

(4) Very few criminals who were found guilty of crimes that are punishable by death are sentenced to death.
(5) Among those found guilty of crimes punishable by death, who is sentenced to death depends on caprice or race.
(6) It is unconstitutional for sentencing to depend on caprice or race.
(7) A punishment is unusual if it is imposed infrequently and on an unconstitutional basis.

∴ (8) The death penalty is an unusual punishment. (from 4–7)

∴ (9) The death penalty is both cruel and unusual. (from 3 and 8)

(10) The Constitution prohibits cruel and unusual punishments.

∴ (11) The Constitution prohibits the death penalty. (from 9–10)

(12) Anything that the Constitution prohibits should be declared unconstitutional.

∴ (13) The death penalty should be declared unconstitutional. (from 11–12)

These propositions provide at least the skeleton of an argument with some force. The conclusion does seem to follow from the premises, and the premises themselves seem plausible. We have produced a charitable reconstruction of the argument.

We can now see how an opponent might respond to it. One particularly probing objection goes like this:

> It is sadly true that caprice and race sometimes determine who, among those found guilty of crimes punishable by death, is given the death sentence. However, this fact reflects badly not on the law but on its administration. If judges and juries met their obligations, these factors would not affect who receives the death penalty, and this punishment would no longer be unusual in any relevant sense. What is needed, then, is judicial reform and not the removal of the death penalty on constitutional grounds.

This response is probing because it insists on a distinction between a law itself and the effects of its application—or, more pointedly, its misapplication. Because this distinction was not drawn in the argument above, it is not clear which premise is denied in this response. Probably the best interpretation is that this response denies premise (7), because it is not the death penalty itself that is unusual in the relevant sense when the conditions in premise (7) are met. Instead, it is the present administration of the death penalty that is problematic.

To meet this objection, the original argument could be strengthened in the following way:

> A law should not be judged in isolation from the likely effects of implementing it. Because of the very nature of our system of criminal justice, for the foreseeable future, the death penalty will almost certainly continue to be applied in a capricious and racially discriminatory manner, and those who receive it will be determined partly by factors that the Constitution forbids as a basis for sentencing. The death penalty will therefore remain an unusual punishment, so it should be declared unconstitutional.

This argument suggests ways to avoid the above objection by strengthening premises (5)–(7) of the above argument. The new versions of these premises can be spelled out in the following way:

(5*) It is very likely in the foreseeable future that, among those found guilty of crimes punishable by death, who is given the death sentence will continue to depend on either caprice or race.

(6) It is unconstitutional for sentencing to depend on caprice or race.

(7*) A punishment is unusual if it is very likely in the foreseeable future that it will continue to be imposed infrequently and on an unconstitutional basis.

∴ (8) The death penalty is an unusual punishment. (from 5*–7*)

Of course, an opponent can still respond that these premises are false if he or she can show that there is some way to avoid the problems that are raised by premise (5*). This will not be easy to show, however, if the argument is right about "the very nature of our system of criminal justice."

Another kind of question is raised by premise (7*). Should a law be declared unconstitutional whenever there is a good chance that it will be abused in ways that infringe on constitutional rights? Many laws have this potential—for example, all laws involving police power. This is why certain police powers have been limited by court rulings. Strict rules governing interrogations and wiretaps are two results. But only an extremist would suggest that we should abolish all police powers because of the inevitable risk of unconstitutional abuse. Accordingly, those who argue in favor of the death penalty might try to show that the problems in the application of the death penalty are not sufficiently important to be constitutionally intolerable.

The supporter of the death penalty also might take a very different tack:

> Those who argue against the constitutionality of the death penalty on the grounds that it is a cruel and unusual punishment use the expression "cruel and unusual" in a way wholly different from that intended by the framers of the Eighth Amendment. By "cruel" they had in mind punishments that involved torture. By "unusual" they meant bizarre or ghoulish punishments of the kind that often formed part of public spectacles in barbaric times. Modern methods of execution are neither cruel nor unusual in the constitutionally relevant senses of these words. Therefore, laws demanding the death penalty cannot be declared unconstitutional on the grounds that they either directly or indirectly involve a punishment that is cruel and unusual.

The core of this counterargument can be expressed as follows:

(1) In appeals to the Constitution, its words should be taken as they were originally intended.

(2) Modern methods of carrying out a death penalty are neither "cruel" nor "unusual" if these words are interpreted as they were originally intended.

∴ (3) The death penalty should not be declared unconstitutional on the ground that it violates the prohibition against cruel and unusual punishments.

The second premise of this argument states a matter of historical fact that might not be altogether easy to verify. The chances are, however, that it comes close to the truth, because the Constitution refers to the death penalty without criticism, and the death penalty was rarely questioned at the time. Given this, the opponent of the death penalty must either attack the first premise or find some other grounds for holding that the death penalty should be declared unconstitutional.

The first premise might seem like a truism, for how can a document guide conduct if anyone can reinterpret its words regardless of what was intended? Isn't the literal meaning of the document simply what was meant at the time, with everything else being interpretation? Of course, there are times when it is not easy to discover what its meaning was. (In the present case, for example, it is not clear whether the Eighth Amendment prohibits punishments that are either cruel or unusual or only those that are both cruel and unusual.) It seems unlikely, however, that those who drafted the Eighth Amendment used either the word "cruel" or the word "unusual" in the ways in which they are employed in the argument against the death penalty.

Does this last concession end the debate in favor of those who reject the anti-capital punishment argument that we have been examining? The argument certainly seems to be weakened, but there are those who would take a bold course by simply denying the first premise of the argument used to refute them. They would deny, that is, that we are bound to read the Constitution in the way intended by its framers. An argument in favor of this position might look something like this:

> The great bulk of the Constitution was written in an age almost wholly different from our own. To cite just two examples: Women were denied fundamental rights of full citizenship, and slavery was a constitutionally accepted feature of national life. The Constitution has remained a live and relevant document just because it has undergone constant reinterpretation. So, even if it is true that the expression "cruel and unusual" meant something quite special to those who framed the Eighth Amendment, plainly a humane desire to make punishment more civilized lay behind it. The present reading of this amendment is in the spirit of its original intention and simply makes it applicable to our own times.

The argument has now moved to an entirely new level, one concerning whether the Constitution should be read strictly in accord with the original intentions of those who wrote it or more freely to accommodate modern realities.

We shall not pursue the discussion further into these complex areas. Instead, we should consider how we were led into them. Recall that our original argument did not concern the general question of whether capital punishment is morally right or wrong. The argument turned on a much more specific point: Does the death penalty violate the prohibition against cruel and unusual punishments in the Eighth Amendment to the Constitution? The argument with which we began seemed to be a straightforward proof that it does. Yet as we explored principles that lay in back of this deceptively simple argument, the issue became broader and more complex. We finally reached a point at which the force of the original argument was seen to depend on what we consider the proper way to interpret the Constitution—strictly or more freely. If we now go on to ask which method of interpretation is best, we will have to look at the role of the courts and, more generally, the purpose of government. Eventually we will come to fundamental principles for which we can give no further argument.

In examining the question of the constitutionality of capital punishment, we have had to compress a complicated discussion into a few pages. We have only begun to show how the issues involved in this complex debate can be sorted out and then addressed intelligently. There is, however, no guarantee that these procedures, however far they are carried out, will eventually settle this or any other fundamental dispute. It is entirely possible that the parties to a dispute may reach a point where they encounter a fundamental or rock-bottom disagreement that they cannot resolve. They simply disagree and cannot conceive of any deeper principles that could resolve their disagreement. But even if this happens, they will at least understand the source of their disagreement. They will not be arguing at cross-purposes, as so often happens in the discussion of important issues. Finally, even if they continue to disagree, they may come to appreciate that others may view things quite differently from the way they do. This may in turn help them deal with their basic disagreements in an intelligent, humane, and civilized way.

EXERCISE XI

What is the best argument that Justice Stewart could give in support of the premise that the death penalty "excessively go[es] beyond" what is necessary for any legitimate and worthwhile purpose? Is this argument adequate to justify this premise?[4]

[4]For one such argument, see Justice Brennan's opinion in *Furman v. Georgia*.

EXERCISE XII

How could one best argue in support of premise (5*), that it is very likely in the foreseeable future that, among those found guilty of crimes punishable by death, who is given the death sentence will continue to depend on either caprice or race? How could defenders of the death penalty try to refute this argument?[5]

[5]For an excellent discussion of this issue, see Charles L. Black, Jr., *Capital Punishment: The Inevitability of Caprice and Mistake* (New York: Norton, 1974).

Formulate the best argument you can in support of the premise that in appeals to the Constitution, its words should be taken as they were originally intended. Is this argument adequate to justify this premise? Why or why not?[6]

[6]For further discussion of this issue, see Susan Brison and Walter Sinnott-Armstrong, eds., *Contemporary Perspectives on Constitutional Interpretation* (Boulder: Westview, 1993), especially the Introduction.

The final argument in our examination of whether or not the death penalty violates the Constitution attempts to show that the Constitution must be read in a free or liberal way that makes it relevant to present society. Filling in suppressed premises where necessary, restate this argument as a sequence of explicit steps. After you have given the argument the strongest restatement you can, evaluate it for soundness.

To solve a mystery, you need to determine which facts are crucial and then argue from those facts to a solution. Solve the following mysteries and reconstruct your own argument for your solution. These stories come from *Five-Minute Whodunits*, by Stan Smith (New York: Sterling, 1997). The first passage introduces our hero:

> Even those acquainted with Thomas P. Stanwick are often struck by his appearance. A lean and lanky young man, he stands six feet two inches tall. His long, thin face is complemented by a full head of brown hair and a droopy mustache. Though not husky in build, he is surprisingly strong and enjoys ruggedly good health.
>
> His origins and early life are obscure. He is undeniably well educated, however, for he graduated with high honors from Dartmouth College as a philosophy major. . . .

MYSTERY 1: A MERE MATTER OF DEDUCTION

Thomas P. Stanwick, the amateur logician, removed a pile of papers from the extra chair and sat down. His friend Inspector Matthew Walker had just returned to his office from the interrogation room, and Stanwick thought he looked unusually weary.

"I'm glad you dropped by, Tom," said Walker. "We have a difficult case on hand. Several thousand dollars' worth of jewelry was stolen from Hoffman's

Jewel Palace yesterday morning. From some clues at the scene and a few handy tips, we have it narrowed down to three suspects: Addington, Burke, and Chatham. We know that at least one of them was involved, and possibly more than one."

"Burke has been suspected in several other cases, hasn't he?" asked Stanwick as he filled his pipe.

"Yes, he has," Walker replied, "but we haven't been able to nail him yet. The other two are small potatoes, so what we really want to know is whether Burke was involved in this one."

"What have you learned about the three of them?"

"Not too much. Addington and Burke were definitely here in the city yesterday. Chatham may not have been. Addington never works alone, and carries a snub-nosed revolver. Chatham always uses an accomplice, and he was seen lurking in the area last week. He also refuses to work with Addington, who he says once set him up."

"Quite a ragamuffin crew!" Stanwick laughed. "Based on what you've said, it's not too hard to deduce whether Burke was involved."

Was Burke involved or not?

MYSTERY 2: MURDER IN A LONDON FLAT

Lord Calinore was gunned down in his London flat by a robber, who then ransacked the flat. The case was placed in the capable hands of Inspector Gilbert Bodwin of Scotland Yard. Bodwin's investigation revealed that one man had planned the crime, another had carried it out, and a third had acted as lookout.

Bodwin discussed the case at length one evening over dinner at his club with an old friend, Thomas P. Stanwick, the amateur logician, visiting from America.

"It's quite a case," Stanwick remarked. "Have you any suspects?"

Bodwin sliced his roast beef with relish. "Yes, indeed. Four. We have conclusive evidence that three of those four were responsible for the crime."

"Really! That's remarkable progress. What about the fourth?"

"He had no prior knowledge of the crime and is completely innocent. The problem is that we're not sure which of the four are the planner, the gunman, the lookout, and the innocent bystander."

"I see." Stanwick took more Yorkshire pudding. "What do you know about them at this point?"

"Well, the names of the four are Merrick, Cross, Llewellyn, and Halifax. Halifax and Cross play golf together every Saturday. They're an odd pair! Halifax can't drive, and Cross has been out of Dartmoor Prison for only a year."

"What was he in for?"

"Forgery. We know that Merrick and Halifax kept the flat under surveillance for several days just before the day the crime was committed, the 17th. Llewellyn and Merrick, with their wives, had dinner together on the Strand on the 12th."

"An interesting compilation," said Stanwick, "but hardly conclusive. Is that all of it?"

"Not quite. We know that the gunman spent the week before the crime in Edinburgh, and that the innocent bystander was acquainted with the planner and the gunman, but not with the lookout."

"That is very helpful," said Stanwick with a smile. He raised his wine glass. "Bodwin, old fellow, your case is complete."

Who are the planner, the gunman, and the lookout?

MYSTERY 3: A THEFT AT THE ART MUSEUM

The theft of several valuable paintings from the Royston Art Museum created a sensation throughout New England. Two days after Stanwick's return from a visit to Scotland, he was visited by Inspector Matt Walker, who was in charge of the case. As Stanwick poured tea, Walker quickly brought his friend up to date on the case.

"We've identified the gang of five thieves who must have done this job," Walker reported. "Archie McOrr, who never finished high school, is married to another one of the five, Charlayne Trumbull. The other three are Beverly Cuttle, Ed Browning, and Douglas Stephens."

"I thought you told me earlier that only four people were involved in the robbery," said Stanwick.

"That's right. One stayed in the car as the driver, another waited outside and acted as lookout, and two others entered the museum and carried out the actual theft. One of the five gang members was not involved in this particular job at all."

"And the question, I hope," said Stanwick with a smile, "is who played what part, if any, in the theft."

"Exactly." Walker flipped open his notebook. "Though I'm glad to say that our investigation is already bearing some fruit. For example, we have good reason to believe that the lookout has a Ph.D. in art history, and that the driver was first arrested less than two years ago."

"A remarkable combination," Stanwick chuckled.

"Yes, indeed. We know that Douglas was on the scene during the robbery. One of the actual thieves (who entered the museum) is the sister of Ed Browning. The other thief is either Archie or his wife."

"What else do you have on Douglas?" asked Stanwick.

"Not much. Although he's never learned to drive, he used to be a security guard at the Metropolitan Museum of Art in New York."

"Interesting. Please go on."

"The rest is mainly odds and ends." Walker thumbed through a few more pages of notes. "Charlayne, an only child, is very talented on the saxophone. Beverly and Ed both have criminal records stretching back a decade or more. We've also learned that the driver has a brother who is not a member of the gang."

"Most interesting indeed," remarked Stanwick. He handed Walker a mug of tea and sat down with his own. "Your investigation has made excellent progress. So much, in fact, that you already have enough to tell who the thieves, the lookout, and the driver are."

Who are they?

MYSTERY 4: TRIVIA AND SIGNIFICA

■

"For April, this is starting out to be a pretty quiet month," remarked Inspector Walker as he rummaged in his desk drawer for a cigar.

Thomas P. Stanwick, the amateur logician, finished lighting his pipe and leaned back in his chair, stretching his long legs forward.

"That is indeed unusual," he said. "Spring usually makes some young fancies turn to crime. The change is welcome."

"Not that we police have nothing to do." Walker lit his cigar. "A couple of the youth gangs, the Hawks and the Owls, have been screeching at each other lately. In fact, we heard a rumor that they were planning to fight each other this Wednesday or Thursday, and we're scrambling around trying to find out whether it's true."

"The Hawks all go to Royston North High, don't they?" asked Stanwick.

"That's right. The Owls are the street-smart dropouts who hang out at Joe's Lunch Cafe on Lindhurst. You know that only those who eat at Joe's collect green matchbooks?"

Stanwick blinked and smiled. "I beg your pardon?"

"That's right." Walker picked up a few papers from his desk. "That's the sort of trivia I'm being fed in my reports. Not only that, but everyone at Royston North High wears monogrammed jackets. What else have I got here? Only kids who hang out on Laraby Street fight on weekdays. Laraby is three blocks from Lindhurst. The Hawks go out for pizza three times a week."

"Keep going," chuckled Stanwick. "It's wonderful."

"A hog for useless facts, eh? No one who eats at Joe's wears a monogrammed jacket. The Owls elect a new leader every six months, the Hawks every year. Elections! Furthermore, everyone who hangs out on Laraby Street collects green matchbooks. Finally, the older (but not wiser) Owls buy beer at Johnny's Package Store."

Stanwick laughed heartily. "Lewis Carroll," he said, "the author of *Symbolic Logic* and the 'Alice in Wonderland' books, taught logic at Oxford, and he used to construct soriteses, or polysyllogisms,[7] out of material like that. In fact, his were longer and much wilder and more intricate, but of course they were fiction.

"As it is, the information you've cited should ease your worries. Those gangs won't get together to fight until at least Saturday."

How does he know?

---

[7] A sorites is a chain of categorical syllogisms of the type we will examine in Chapter 7.

THE FORMAL ANALYSIS OF ARGUMENTS: PROPOSITIONAL LOGIC

This chapter will examine some more technical procedures for analyzing and evaluating arguments. In particular, it will consider the notion of validity, for this is a central concept of logic. The first part of the chapter will show how the notion of validity introduced in Chapter 3 can be developed rigorously in one area—what is called propositional logic. This branch of logic deals with connectives such as "and" and "or," which allow us to build up compound propositions from simpler ones. Throughout most of the chapter, the focus will be theoretical rather than immediately practical. It is intended to provide insight into the concept of validity by examining it in an ideal setting. The chapter will close with a discussion of the relationship between the ideal language of symbolic logic and the language we ordinarily speak.

VALIDITY AND THE FORMAL ANALYSIS OF ARGUMENTS

When we carry out an informal analysis of an argument, we pay close attention to the key terms used to present the argument and then ask ourselves whether these key terms have been used properly. So far, we have no exact techniques for answering the question of whether a term is used correctly. We rely, instead, on logical instincts that, on the whole, are fairly good. In a great many cases, people can tell whether an argument marker is used correctly in indicating that one claim follows from another. But if we ask the average intelligent person *why* one claim follows from the other, he or she will probably have little to say except, perhaps, that it is just obvious. That is, it is often easy to see *that* one claim follows from another, but to explain *why* can turn out to be difficult. The purpose of this chapter is to provide such an explanation for some arguments.

This quality of "following from" is elusive, but it is related to the technical notion of validity, which was introduced in Chapter 3. The focus of our attention will be largely on the *concept* of validity. We are not, for the time being at least, interested in whether this or that argument is valid; we want to understand validity itself. To this end, the arguments we will examine are so simple that you will not be able to imagine anyone not understanding them at a glance. Who needs logic to deal with arguments of this kind? There is, however, good reason for dealing with simple—trivially simple—arguments at the start. The analytic approach to a complex issue is first to break it down into subissues, repeating the process until we reach problems simple enough to be solved. After these simpler problems are solved, we can reverse the process and construct solutions to larger and more complex problems. When done correctly, the *result* of such an analytic process may seem dull and obvious—and it often is. The *discovery* of such a process, in contrast, often demands the insight of genius.

PROPOSITIONAL LOGIC

CONJUNCTION

The first system of arguments we will examine concerns propositional (or sentential) connectives. *Propositional connectives* are terms that allow us to build new propositions from old ones, usually combining two or more propositions into a single proposition. For example, given the propositions "John is tall" and "Harry is short," we can use the term "and" to *conjoin* them, forming a single compound proposition: "John is tall and Harry is short."

Let us look carefully at the simple word "and" and ask how it functions. "And," in fact, is a curious word, for it does not seem to stand for anything, at least in the way in which a proper name ("Churchill") and a common noun ("dog") seem to stand for things. Instead of asking what this word stands for, we can ask a different question: What *truth conditions* govern this connective? That is, under what conditions are propositions containing this connective true? To answer this question, we imagine every possible way in which the component propositions can be true or false. Then, for each combination, we decide what truth value to assign to the entire proposition. This may sound complicated, but an example will make it clear:

John is tall.	Harry is short.	John is tall and Harry is short.
T	T	T
T	F	F
F	T	F
F	F	F

Here the first two columns cover every possibility for the component propositions to be either true or false. The third column states the truth value of the whole proposition for each combination. Clearly, the conjunction of two propositions is true if both of the component propositions are true; otherwise, it is false. It should also be obvious that our reflections have not depended on the particular propositions we have selected. We could have been talking about dinosaurs instead of people, and we still would have come to the conclusion that the conjunction of two propositions is true if both propositions are true, but false otherwise. This neglect of the particular content of propositions is what makes our account *formal*. To reflect the generality of our concerns, we can drop the reference to particular sentences altogether and use variables instead. Just as the letters "x," "y," and "z" can be replaced by any numbers in mathematics, so we can use the letters "p," "q," "r," "s," . . . as variables that can be replaced by any propositions in logic. We will also use the symbol "&" (called an *ampersand*) for "and."

Consider the expression "*p* & *q*." Is it true or false? There is obviously no answer to this question. This is not because we do not know what "*p*" and "*q*" stand for, for in fact, "*p*" and "*q*" do not stand for any proposition. Thus, "*p* & *q*" is not a proposition, but rather a pattern for a whole series of propositions. To reflect this, we will say that "*p* & *q*" is a *propositional form*. It is a pattern, or form, for a whole series of propositions, including "John is tall and Harry is short."

To repeat the central idea, we can pass from a proposition to a propositional form by replacing propositions with propositional variables.

Proposition	Propositional Form
John is tall and Harry is short.	*p* & *q*

When we proceed in the opposite direction by uniformly substituting propositions for propositional variables, we get what we will call a *substitution instance* of that propositional form.

Propositional Form	Substitution Instance
p & *q*	Roses are red and violets are blue.

Thus, "John is tall and Harry is short" and "Roses are red and violets are blue" are both substitution instances of the propositional form "*p* & *q*."

These ideas are perfectly simple, but to be clear about them, it is important to notice that "*p*" is also a propositional form, with *every* proposition, including "Roses are red and violets are blue," among its substitution instances. There is no rule against substituting compound propositions for propositional variables. Perhaps a bit more surprisingly, our definitions allow "Roses are red and roses are red" to be a substitution instance of "*p* & *q*." We get a substitution instance of a propositional form by uniformly replacing the same variable with the same proposition throughout. We have not said that different variables must be replaced with different propositions throughout. The rule is this:

Different variables may be replaced with the same proposition, but different propositions may not be replaced with the same variable.

To summarize the discussion thus far:

"Roses are red and violets are blue" is a substitution instance of "*p* & *q*."

"Roses are red and violets are blue" is also a substitution instance of "*p*."

"Roses are red and roses are red" is a substitution instance of "*p* & *q*."

"Roses are red and roses are red" is a substitution instance of "*p* & *p*."

"Roses are red and violets are blue" is *not* a substitution instance of "*p* & *p*."

"Roses are red" is *not* a substitution instance of "*p* & *p*."

We are now in a position to give a perfectly general definition of conjunction with the following truth table, using propositional variables where previously we used specific propositions.

p	*q*	*p* & *q*
T	T	T
T	F	F
F	T	F
F	F	F

There is no limit to the number of propositions we can conjoin to form a new proposition. "Roses are red and violets are blue; sugar is sweet and so are you" is a substitution instance of "*p* & *q* & *r* & *s*." We can also use parentheses to group propositions. This last example could be treated as a substitution instance of "(*p* & *q*) & (*r* & *s*)"—that is, as a conjunction of two conjunctions. Later we will see that, just as in mathematics, parentheses can make an important difference to the meaning of a total proposition.

One cautionary note: The word "and" is not always used to connect two distinct sentences. Sometimes a sentence has to be rewritten for us to see that it is equivalent to a sentence of this form. For example,

Serena and Venus are tennis players

is simply a short way of saying

Serena is a tennis player, and Venus is a tennis player.

At other times, the word "and" is *not* used to produce a conjunction of propositions. For example,

Serena and Venus are playing each other

does *not* mean that

Serena is playing each other, and Venus is playing each other.

That does not even make sense. The original sentence does not express a conjunction of two propositions. Instead, it expresses a single proposition about two people taken as a group. At other times, it is unclear whether a sentence expresses a conjunction of propositions or a single proposition about a group. The sentence

Serena and Venus are playing tennis

could be taken either way. When a sentence containing the word "and" expresses the conjunction of two propositions, we will say that it expresses a *propositional conjunction*. When a sentence containing "and" does not express the conjunction of two propositions, we will say that it expresses a *nonpropositional conjunction*. In this chapter we are concerned only with sentences that express propositional conjunctions. A sentence should be translated into the symbolic form "*p & q*" only if it expresses a propositional conjunction. There is no mechanical procedure that can be followed to determine whether a certain sentence expresses a conjunction of two propositions. You must think carefully about what the sentence means and about the context in which that sentence is used. This takes practice.

EXERCISE I

The proposition "The night is young, and you're so beautiful" is a substitution instance of which of the following propositional forms?

1. *p*
2. *q*
3. *p & q*
4. *p & r*
5. *p & q & r*
6. *p & p*
7. *p* or *q*

EXERCISE II

Which of the following propositions is a substitution instance of "*p & q & q*"?

1. The night is young, and you're so beautiful, and my flight leaves in thirty minutes.
2. The night is young, and you're so beautiful, and my flight leaves in thirty minutes, and my flight leaves in thirty minutes.
3. You're so beautiful, and you're so beautiful, and you're so beautiful.

EXERCISE III

For each of the following propositions, give three different propositional forms of which that proposition is a substitution instance.

1. The night is young, and you're so beautiful, and my flight leaves in thirty minutes.
2. The night is young, and you're so beautiful, and you're so beautiful.

Indicate whether each of the following sentences expresses a propositional conjunction or a nonpropositional conjunction—that is, whether or not it expresses a conjunction of two propositions. If the sentence could be either, then specify a context in which it would naturally be used to express a propositional conjunction and a different context in which it would naturally be used to express a nonpropositional conjunction.

1. A Catholic priest married John and Mary.
2. Fred had pie and ice cream for dessert.
3. The presidential candidate who wins the election usually carries New York and California.
4. Susan got married and had a child.
5. Jane speaks both French and English.
6. Someone who speaks both French and English is bilingual.
7. Ken and Naomi are two of my best friends.
8. Miranda and Nick cooked dinner.
9. I doubt that John is poor and happy.

VALIDITY FOR CONJUNCTION. Now we can look at an argument involving conjunction. Here is one that is ridiculously simple:

> Harry is short and John is tall.
> _____
> ∴ Harry is short.

This argument is obviously valid. But why is it valid? Why does the conclusion follow from the premise? The answer in this case seems obvious, but we will spell it out in detail as a guide for more difficult cases. Suppose we replace these particular propositions with propositional forms, using a different variable for each distinct proposition throughout the argument. This yields what we will call an *argument form*. For example:

> $p \& q$
> _____
> ∴ p

This is a pattern for endlessly many arguments, each of which is called a substitution instance of this argument form. Every argument that has this general form will also be valid. It really does not matter which propositions we put into this schema; the resulting argument will be valid—so long as we are careful to substitute the same proposition for the same variable throughout.

Let's pursue this matter further. If an argument has true premises and a false conclusion, then we know at once that it is invalid. But in saying that an argument is *valid*, we are not only saying that it does not have true premises and a false conclusion; we are saying that the argument *cannot* have a false conclusion when the premises are true. Sometimes this is true because the argument has a structure or form that rules out the very possibility of true premises and a false conclusion. We can appeal to the notion of an argument form to make sense of this idea. A somewhat more complicated truth table will make this clear:

		PREMISE	CONCLUSION
p	*q*	*p & q*	*p*
T	T	T	T
T	F	F	T
F	T	F	F
F	F	F	F

The first two columns give all the combinations for the truth values of the propositions that we might substitute for "*p*" and "*q*." The third column gives the truth value of the premise for each of these combinations. (This column is the same as the definition for "&" given above.) Finally, the fourth column gives the truth value for the conclusion for each combination. (Here, of course, this merely involves repeating the first column. Later on, things will become more complicated and interesting.) If we look at this truth table, we see that no matter how we make substitutions for the variables, we never have a case in which the premise is true and the conclusion is false. In the first line, the premise is true and the conclusion is also true. In the remaining three lines, the premise is not true, so the possibility of the premise being true and the conclusion false does not arise. Here it is important to remember that a valid argument can have false premises, for one proposition can follow from another proposition that is false. Of course, an argument that is sound cannot have a false premise, because a sound argument is defined as a valid argument with true premises. But our subject here is validity, not soundness.

Let's summarize this discussion. In the case we have examined, validity depends on the form of an argument and not on its particular content. A first principle, then, is this:

An *argument* is valid if it is an instance of a valid argument form.

So the argument "Harry is short and John is tall; therefore, Harry is short" is valid because it is an instance of the valid argument form "*p & q; ∴ p.*"

Next we must ask what makes an argument form valid. The answer to this is given in this principle:

An argument *form* is valid if and only if it has no substitution instances in which the premises are true and the conclusion is false.

We have just seen that the argument form "*p & q; ∴ p*" meets this test. The truth table analysis showed that. Incidentally, we can use the same truth table to show that the following argument is valid:

John is tall.	p
Harry is short.	q
∴ John is tall and Harry is short.	∴ p & q

The argument on the left is a substitution instance of the argument form on the right, and a glance at the truth table will show that there can be no cases for which all the premises could be true and the conclusion false. This pretty well covers the logical properties of conjunction.

Notice that we have not said that *every* argument that is valid is so in virtue of its form. There may be arguments in which the conclusion follows from the premises but we cannot show that the argument's validity is a matter of logical form. There are, in fact, some obviously valid arguments that have yet to be shown to be valid in terms of their form. Explaining validity by means of logical form has long been an ideal of logical theory, but there are arguments—many of them quite common—where this ideal has yet to be adequately fulfilled. Many arguments in mathematics fall into this category. At present, however, we will only consider arguments in which the strategy we used for analyzing conjunction continues to work.

EXERCISE V

Are the following arguments valid by virtue of their propositional form? Why or why not?

1. Donald owns a tower in New York and a palace in Atlantic City. Therefore, Donald owns a palace in Atlantic City.

2. Tom owns a house. Therefore, Tom owns a house and a piece of land.

3. Ilsa is tall. Therefore, Ilsa is tall, and Ilsa is tall.

4. Bernie has a son and a daughter. Bernie has a father and a mother. Therefore, Bernie has a son and a mother.

5. Mary got married and had a child. Therefore, Mary had a child and got married.

6. Bess and Katie tied for MVP. Therefore, Bess tied for MVP.

EXERCISE VI

For each of the following claims, determine whether it is true or false. Defend your answers.

1. An argument that is a substitution instance of a valid argument form is always valid.

2. An argument that is a substitution instance of an invalid argument form is always invalid.

3. An invalid argument is always a substitution instance of an invalid argument form.

DISJUNCTION

Just as we can form a conjunction of two propositions by using the connective "and," we can form a *disjunction* of two propositions by using the connective "or," as in the following compound sentence:

John will win or Harry will win.

Again, it is easy to see that the truth of this whole compound proposition depends on the truth of the component propositions. If they are both false, then the compound proposition is false. If just one of them is true, then the compound proposition is true. But suppose they are both true. What shall we say then?

Sometimes when we say "either-or," we seem to rule out the possibility of both. When a waiter approaches your table and tells you, "Tonight's dinner will be chicken or steak," this suggests that you cannot have both. In other cases, however, it does not seem that the possibility of both is ruled out—for example, when we say to someone, "If you want to see tall mountains, go to California or Colorado."

One way to deal with this problem is to say that the English word "or" has two meanings: one *exclusive*, which rules out both, and one *inclusive*, which does not rule out both. Another way to deal with this problem is to claim that the English word "or" always has the inclusive sense, but utterances with "or" sometimes conversationally imply the exclusion of both because of special features of certain contexts. It is, for example, our familiarity with common restaurant practices that leads us to infer that we cannot have both when the waiter says, "Tonight's dinner will be chicken or steak." If we may have both, then the waiter's utterance would not be as informative as is required for the purpose of revealing our options, so it would violate Grice's conversational rule of Quantity (as discussed in Chapter 1). That explains why the waiter's utterance seems to exclude both.

Because such explanations are plausible, and because it is simpler as well as traditional to develop propositional logic with the inclusive sense of "or," we will adopt that inclusive sense. Where necessary, we will define the exclusive sense using the inclusive sense as a starting point. Logicians symbolize disjunctions using the connective "∨" (called a *wedge*). The truth table for this connective has the following form:

p	q	$p \vee q$
T	T	T
T	F	T
F	T	T
F	F	F

We will look at some arguments involving this connective in a moment.

NEGATION

With conjunction and disjunction, we begin with two propositions and construct a new proposition from them. There is another way in which we can construct a new proposition from another one—by *negating* it. Given the proposition "John is clever," we can get a new proposition, "John is not clever," simply by inserting the word "not" in the correct place in the sentence.

What, exactly, does the word "not" mean? This can be a difficult question to answer. Does it mean "nothing" or, maybe, "nothingness"? Although some respectable philosophers have sometimes spoken in this way, it is important to see that the word "not" does not stand for anything at all. It has an altogether different function in the language. To see this, think about how conjunction and disjunction work. Given two propositions, the word "and" allows us to construct another proposition that is true only when both original propositions are true, and is false otherwise. With disjunction, given two propositions, the word "or" allows us to construct another proposition that is false only when both of the original propositions are false, and true otherwise. (Our truth table definitions reflect these facts.) Using these definitions as models, how should we define *negation*? A parallel answer is that the negation of a proposition is true just in the cases in which the original proposition is false, and it is false just in the cases in which original proposition is true. Using the symbol "~" (called a *tilde*) to stand for negation, this gives us the following truth table definition:

p	$\sim p$
T	F
F	T

Negation might seem as simple as can be, but people quite often get confused by negations. If Diana says, "I could not breathe for a whole minute," she might mean that something made her unable to breathe for a whole minute (maybe she was choking), or she might mean that she was able to hold her breath for a whole minute (if she had to, say, to win a bet). If "A" symbolizes "Diana could breathe some time during this minute," then "$\sim A$" symbolizes the former claim (that Diana was unable to breathe for this minute). Consequently, the latter claim (that Diana could hold her breath for this minute) should not also be symbolized by "$\sim A$." Indeed, this interpretation of the original sentence is not a negation, even though the original sentence did include the word "not." Moreover, some sentences are negations even though they do not include the word "not." For example, "Nobody owns Mars" is the negation of "Somebody owns Mars." If the latter is symbolized as "A," the former can be symbolized as "$\sim A$," even though the former does not include the word "not."

There is no mechanical procedure for determining whether an English sentence can be symbolized as a negation. All you can do is think carefully about the sentence's meaning and context. The best way to get good at this is to practice.

Put each of the following sentences in symbolic form. Be sure to specify exactly which sentence is represented by each capital letter, and pay special attention to the placement of the negation. If the sentence could be interpreted in more than one way, symbolize each interpretation and describe a context in which it would be natural to interpret it in each way.

1. It won't rain tomorrow.
2. It might not rain tomorrow.
3. There is no chance that it will rain tomorrow.
4. I believe that it won't rain tomorrow.
5. Joe is not too smart, or else he's very clever.
6. Kristin is not smart or rich.
7. Sometimes you feel like a nut; sometimes you don't.

DISJUNCTIVE SYLLOGISM

Using only negation and disjunction, we can analyze the form of one common pattern of reasoning, which is called *disjunctive syllogism* or, more popularly, *process of elimination*. As an example, consider this argument:

> Her phone line is busy, so she must either be talking on the phone or using her modem. She is not using her modem, since I just tried to e-mail her and she did not respond. So she must be talking on the phone.

After trimming off assurances and subarguments that support the premises, the core of this argument can be put in standard form:

> She is either using her modem or talking on the phone.
> She is not using her modem.
> ∴ She is talking on the phone.

This core argument is then an instance of this argument form:

1. $p \vee q$
   $\sim p$
   ∴ q

It does not matter if we change the order of the disjuncts, so that the first premise is "She must be either talking on the phone or using her modem." Then the argument takes this form:

2. $p \vee q$
   $\sim q$
   ∴ p

Both of these argument forms are valid, so the core of the original argument is also valid.

Explain why argument forms 1–2 are valid. Use common language that would be understandable to someone who has not read this chapter.

Disjunctive syllogism is sometimes confused with a similar but crucially different pattern of reasoning, which can be called *affirming a disjunct*. This pattern includes both of these forms:

3. $p \vee q$

$\quad p$

∴ $\sim q$

4. $p \vee q$

$\quad q$

∴ $\sim p$

These forms of argument are invalid. This can be shown by the following single instance:

> She is either using her modem or talking on the phone.
> She is using her modem.

∴ She is not talking on the phone.

This argument might seem valid if one assumes that she cannot talk on the phone while using her modem. The premises, however, do not specify that she has only one phone line. If she talks on one phone line while using her modem on a different phone line, then the premises are true and the conclusion is false. Because this is possible, the argument is invalid, and so is its form, (3). Moreover, this argument would remain invalid if the disjuncts were listed in a different order, so that the argument took the form of (4). Thus, affirming a disjunct is a fallacy.

Give other instances of argument forms (3)–(4) that are not valid. Explain why these instances are invalid and why they show that the general argument form is invalid.

HOW TRUTH-FUNCTIONAL CONNECTIVES WORK

We have now defined conjunction, disjunction, and negation. That, all by itself, is sufficient to complete the branch of modern logic called propositional logic. The definitions themselves may seem peculiar. They do not look like the definitions we find in a dictionary. But the form of these definitions is important, for it tells us something interesting about the character of such words as "and," "or," and "not." Two things are worth noting: (1) These expressions are used to construct a new proposition from old ones; (2) the newly constructed proposition is always a *truth function* of the original propositions—that is, the truth value of the new proposition is always determined by the truth value of the original propositions. For this reason these connectives are called *truth-functional connectives*. (Of course, with negation, we start with a *single* proposition.) For example, suppose that "*A*" and "*B*" are two true propositions and "*G*" and "*H*" are two false propositions. We can then determine the truth values of more complex propositions built from them using conjunction, disjunction, and negation. Sometimes the correct assignment is obvious at a glance:

A & B	True
A & G	False
~A	False
~G	True
$A \vee H$	True
$G \vee H$	False
~A & G	False

As noted earlier, parentheses can be used to distinguish groupings. Sometimes the placement of parentheses can make an important difference, as in the following two expressions:

~A & G

~(A & G)

Notice that in one expression the negation symbol applies only to the proposition "*A*," whereas in the other expression it applies to the entire proposition "*A* & *G*." Thus, the first expression above is false, and the second expression is true. Only the second expression can be translated as "Not both *A* and *G*." Both of these expressions are different from "~*A* & ~*G*," which means "Neither *A* nor *G*."

As expressions become more complex, we reach a point where it is no longer obvious how the truth values of the component propositions determine the truth value of the entire proposition. Here a regular procedure is helpful. The easiest method is to fill in the truth values of the basic propositions and then, step-by-step, make assignments progressively wider, going from the inside out. For example:

~(($A \vee G$) & ~(~H & B))

~(($T \vee F$) & ~(~F & T))

~(($T \vee F$) & ~(T & T))

~(T & ~(T))

~(T & F)

~(F)

T

With a little practice, you can master this technique in dealing with other very complex examples.

EXERCISE X

Given that "A," "B," and "C" are true propositions and "X," "Y," and "Z" are false propositions, determine the truth values of the following compound propositions:

1. ~X ∨ Y
2. ~(X ∨ Y)
3. ~(Z ∨ Z)
4. ~(Z ∨ ~Z)
5. ~ ~(A ∨ B)
6. (A ∨ Z) & B
7. (A ∨ X) & (B ∨ Z)
8. (A & Z) ∨ (B & Z)
9. ~(A ∨ (Z ∨ X))
10. ~(A ∨ ~(Z ∨ X))
11. ~A ∨ ~(Z ∨ X)
12. ~Z ∨ (Z & A)
13. ~(Z ∨ (Z & A))
14. ~((Z ∨ Z) & A)
15. A ∨ ((~B & C) ∨ ~(~B ∨ ~(Z ∨ B)))
16. A & ((~B & C) ∨ ~(~B ∨ ~(Z ∨ B)))

TESTING FOR VALIDITY

What is the point of all this? In everyday life, we rarely run into an expression as complicated as the one in our example at the end of the previous section. Our purpose here is to sharpen our sensitivity to how truth-functional connectives work and then to express our insights in clear ways. This is important because the validity of many arguments depends on the logical features of these truth-functional connectives. We can now turn directly to this subject.

Earlier we saw that every argument with the form "p & q; ∴ p" will be valid. This is obvious in itself, but we saw that this claim could be justified by an appeal to truth tables. A truth table analysis shows us that an argument with this form can never have an instance in which the premise is true and the conclusion is false. We can now apply this same technique to arguments that are more complex. In the beginning, we will examine arguments that are still easy to follow without the use of technical help. In the end, we will consider some arguments that most people cannot follow without guidance.

Consider the following argument:

Valerie is either a doctor or a lawyer.
Valerie is neither a doctor nor a stockbroker.

∴ Valerie is a lawyer.

We can use the following abbreviations:

D = Valerie is a doctor.
L = Valerie is a lawyer.
S = Valerie is a stockbroker.

Using these abbreviations, the argument and its counterpart argument form look like this:

$D \vee L$ $p \vee q$
$\sim(D \vee S)$ $\sim(p \vee r)$

∴ L ∴ q

The expression on the right gives the argument form of the argument presented on the left. To test the argument for validity, we ask whether the argument form is valid. The procedure is cumbersome, but perfectly mechanical:

			PREMISE		PREMISE	CONCLUSION	
p	q	r	$(p \vee q)$	$(p \vee r)$	$\sim(p \vee r)$	q	
T	T	T	T	T	F	T	
T	T	F	T	T	F	T	
T	F	T	T	T	F	F	
T	F	F	T	T	F	F	
F	T	T	T	T	F	T	
F	T	F	T	F	T	T	O.K.
F	F	T	F	T	F	F	
F	F	F	F	F	T	F	

Notice that there is only one combination of truth values for which both premises are true, and in that case the conclusion is true as well. So the original argument is valid because it is an instance of a valid argument form—that is, an argument form with no substitution instances for which true premises are combined with a false conclusion.

This last truth table may need some explaining. First, why do we get eight rows in this truth table where before we got only four? The answer to this is that we need to test the argument form for *every possible combination of truth values* for the component propositions. With two variables, there are four possible combinations: (TT), (TF), (FT), and (FF). With three variables, there are eight possible combinations: (TTT), (TTF), (TFT), (TFF), (FTT), (FTF), (FFT), and (FFF). The general rule is this: If an argument form has n variables, the truth table used in its analysis must have 2^n rows. For four variables there will be sixteen rows; for five variables, thirty-two rows; for six variables, sixty-four rows; and so on. You can be sure that you capture all possible combinations of truth values by using the following pattern in constructing the columns of your truth table under each individual variable:

FIRST COLUMN	SECOND COLUMN	THIRD COLUMN . . .
First half Ts,	First quarter Ts,	First eighth Ts,
second half Fs.	second quarter Fs,	second eighth Fs,
	and so on.	and so on.

A glance at the earlier examples in this chapter will show that we have been using this pattern, and it is the standard way of listing the possibilities. Of course, as soon as an argument becomes at all complex, these truth tables become very large indeed. But there is no need to worry about this, because we will not consider arguments with many variables. Those who do so turn to a computer for help.

The style of the truth table above is also significant. The premises are plainly labeled, and so is the conclusion. A line is drawn under every row in which the premises are all true. (In this case, there is only one such row— row 6.) If the conclusion on this line is also true, it is marked "O.K." If every line in which the premises are all true is O.K., then the argument form is valid. Marking all this may seem rather childish, but it is worth doing. First, it helps guard against mistakes. More important, it draws one's attention to the purpose of the procedure being used. Cranking out truth tables without understanding what they are about—or even why they might be helpful— does not enlighten the mind or elevate the spirit.

For the sake of contrast, we can next consider an invalid argument:

> Valerie is either a doctor or a lawyer.
> Valerie is not both a lawyer and a stockbroker.
> ───────────────
> ∴ Therefore, Valerie is a doctor.

Using the same abbreviations used earlier, this becomes:

$$D \lor L$$
$$\sim(L \mathbin{\&} S)$$
$$\therefore D$$

$$p \lor q$$
$$\sim(q \mathbin{\&} r)$$
$$\therefore p$$

The truth table for this argument form looks like this:

			PREMISE		PREMISE	CONCLUSION	
p	q	r	$(p \lor q)$	$(q \ \& \ r)$	$\sim(q \ \& \ r)$	p	
T	T	T	T	T	F	T	
T	T	F	T	F	T	T	O.K.
T	F	T	T	F	T	T	O.K.
T	F	F	T	F	T	T	O.K.
F	T	T	T	T	F	F	
F	T	F	T	F	T	F	Invalid
F	F	T	F	F	T	F	
F	F	F	F	F	T	F	

This time, we find four rows in which all the premises are true. In three cases the conclusion is true as well, but in one of these cases (row 6), the conclusion is false. This line is marked "Invalid." Notice that every line in which all of the premises are true is marked either as "O.K." or as "Invalid." If even one row is marked "Invalid," then the argument form as a whole is invalid. The argument form under consideration is thus invalid, because it is possible for it to have a substitution instance in which all the premises are true and the conclusion is false.

The labeling not only shows *that* the argument form is invalid, it also shows *why* it is invalid. Each line that is marked "Invalid" shows a combination of truth values that makes the premises true and the conclusion false. Row 6 presents the combination in which Valerie is not a doctor, is a lawyer, and is not a stockbroker. With these assignments, it will be true that she is either a doctor or a lawyer (premise 1), and also true that she is not both a lawyer and a stockbroker (premise 2), yet false that she is a doctor (the conclusion). It is this possibility that shows why the argument form is not valid.

EXERCISE XI

Using the truth table technique outlined above, show that argument forms 1–2 in the above section on disjunctive syllogism are valid and that argument forms 3–4 in the same section are invalid.

Using the truth table technique outlined above, test the following argument forms for validity:

1. $\sim p \vee q$
   p
   $\therefore \sim q$

2. $\sim (p \vee q)$
   $\therefore \sim q$

3. $\sim (p \vee q)$
   p
   $\therefore q$

4. $\sim (p \vee q)$
   p
   $\therefore r$

5. $\sim (p \& q)$
   q
   $\therefore \sim p$

6. $\sim (p \& q)$
   $\sim q$
   $\therefore p$

7. $(p \& q) \vee (p \& r)$
   $\therefore p \& (q \vee r)$

8. $(p \vee q) \& (p \vee r)$
   $\therefore p \& (q \vee r)$

9. $p \& q$
   $\therefore (p \vee r) \& (q \vee r)$

10. $p \vee q$
    $\therefore (p \& r) \vee (q \& r)$

SOME FURTHER CONNECTIVES

We have developed the logic of propositions using only three basic notions corresponding (perhaps roughly) to the English words "and," "or," and "not." Now let us go back to the question of the two possible senses of the word "or": one exclusive and the other inclusive. Sometimes "or" seems to rule out the possibility that both alternatives are true; at other times "or" seems to allow this possibility. This is the difference between exclusive and inclusive disjunction.

Suppose we use the symbol "$\veebar$" to stand for exclusive disjunction. This is the same as the symbol for inclusive disjunction except that it is underlined. (After this discussion, we will not use it again.) We could then give two truth table definitions, one for each of these symbols:

		INCLUSIVE	EXCLUSIVE
p	q	$p \vee q$	$p \veebar q$
T	T	T	F
T	F	T	T
F	T	T	T
F	F	F	F

We could also define this new connective in the following way:

$(p \veebar q) =$ (by definition) $((p \vee q) \& \sim(p \& q))$

It is not hard to see that the expression on the right side of this definition captures the force of exclusive disjunction. Because we can always define exclusive disjunction when we want it, there is no need to introduce it into our system of basic notions.

EXERCISE XIII

Construct a truth table analysis of the expression on the right side of the preceding definition, and compare it with the truth table definition of exclusive disjunction.

EXERCISE XIV

Use truth tables to test the following argument forms for validity:

1. p _____

∴ $p \veebar q$

2. $p \veebar q$

p _____

∴ $\sim q$

3. $p \& q$ _____

∴ $\sim(p \veebar q)$

4. $\sim(p \& q)$ _____

∴ $p \veebar q$

5. $p \veebar q$ _____

∴ $p \vee q$

6. $p \vee q$ _____

∴ $p \veebar q$

Actually, in analyzing arguments we have been defining new logical connectives without thinking about it much. For example, "not both p and q" was symbolized as "$\sim(p \& q)$." "Neither p nor q" was symbolized as "$\sim(p \vee q)$." Let us look more closely at the example "$\sim(p \vee q)$." Perhaps we should have symbolized it as "$\sim p \& \sim q$." In fact, we could have used this symbolization, because the two expressions amount to the same thing. Again, this may be obvious, but we can prove it by using a truth table in yet another way. Compare the truth table analysis of these two expressions:

p	q	$\sim p$	$\sim q$	$\sim p \& \sim q$	$(p \vee q)$	$\sim(p \vee q)$
T	T	F	F	F	T	F
T	F	F	T	F	T	F
F	T	T	F	F	T	F
F	F	T	T	T	F	T

Under "$\sim p \& \sim q$" we find the column (FFFT), and we find the same sequence under "$\sim(p \vee q)$." This shows that, for every possible substitution we make, these two expressions will yield propositions with the same truth value. We will say that these propositional forms are *truth-functionally equivalent*. The above table also shows that the expressions "~q" and "~p & ~q" are *not* truth-functionally equivalent, because the columns underneath these two expressions differ in the second row, so some substitutions into these expressions will not yield propositions with the same truth value.

Given the notion of truth-functional equivalence, the problem of more than one translation can often be solved. If two translations of a sentence are truth-functionally equivalent, then it does not matter which one we use in testing for validity. Of course, some translations will seem more natural than others. For example, "p ∨ q" is truth-functionally equivalent to

~((~p & ~p) & (~q ∨ ~q))

Despite this equivalence, the first form of expression is obviously more natural than the second when translating sentences, such as "It is either cloudy or sunny."

EXERCISE XV

Use truth tables to test which of the following propositional forms are truth-functionally equivalent to each other:

1. ~(p ∨ q)
2. ~(~p ∨ ~q)
3. ~p & ~q
4. p & q

EXERCISE XVI

Use truth tables to determine whether the expressions in each of the following pairs are truth-functionally equivalent:

1. "p" and "p & p"
2. "p" and "p ∨ p"
3. "p ∨ ~p" and "~(p & ~p)"
4. "p" and "p & (q ∨ ~q)"
5. "p" and "p & (q & ~q)"
6. "p" and "p ∨ (q & ~q)"
7. "p & (q ∨ r)" and "p ∨ (q & r)"
8. "p & (q & r)" and "(p & q) & r"
9. "~(p ∨ q)" and "~p ∨ q"
10. "~(p ∨ q)" and "~p & ~q"

11. "~~($p \lor q$)" and "~~p & ~~q"
12. "~(p & q)" and "~$p \lor q$"
13. "~~(p & q)" and "~~$p \lor$ ~~q"
14. "~~$p \lor$ ~~q" and "~(~p & ~q)"
15. "~~p & ~~q" and "~(~$p \lor$ ~q)"
16. "p & ~~q" and "~~p & q"

SUMMARY

So far in this chapter we have seen that by using conjunction, disjunction, and negation, it is possible to construct compound propositions out of simple propositions. A distinctive feature of compound propositions constructed in these three ways is that the truth of the compound proposition is always a function of the truth of its component propositions. Thus, these three notions allow us to construct truth-functionally compound propositions. Some arguments depend for their validity simply on these truth-functional connectives. When this is so, it is possible to test for validity in a purely mechanical way. This can be done through the use of truth tables. Thus, in this area at least, we are able to give a clear account of validity and to specify exact procedures for testing for validity.

CONDITIONALS

This approach might seem problematic in another area: *conditionals*. We will argue that an important group of conditionals can be handled in much the same way as negation, conjunction, and disjunction. We separate conditionals from the other connectives only because a truth-functional treatment of conditionals is more controversial and faces problems that are instructive.

Conditionals have the form "If _____, then _____." What goes in the first blank of this pattern is called the *antecedent* of the conditional; what goes in the second blank is called its *consequent*. Sometimes conditionals appear in the indicative mood:

If it rains, then the crop will be saved.

Sometimes they occur in the subjunctive mood:

If it had rained, then the crop would have been saved.

There are also conditional imperatives:

If a fire breaks out, then call the fire department first!

There are conditional promises:

If you get into trouble, then I promise to help you.

Indeed, conditionals get a great deal of use in our language, often in arguments. It is important, therefore, to understand them.

Unfortunately, there is no general agreement among experts concerning the correct way to analyze conditionals. We will simplify matters and avoid some of these controversies by considering only indicative conditionals. We will not examine conditional imperatives, conditional promises, or subjunctive conditionals. Furthermore, at the start, we will examine only what we will call *propositional conditionals*. We get a propositional conditional by substituting indicative sentences that express propositions—something either true or false—into the schema "If _____, then _____." Or, to use technical language already introduced, a propositional conditional is a substitution instance of "If *p*, then *q*" in which "*p*" and "*q*" are propositional variables. Of the four conditional sentences listed above, only the first is clearly a propositional conditional.

Even if we restrict our attention to propositional conditionals, this will not avoid all controversy. Several competing theories claim to provide the correct analysis of propositional conditionals, and no consensus has been reached concerning which is right. It may seem surprising that theorists disagree about such a simple and fundamental notion as the if-then construction, but they do. In what follows, we will first describe the most standard treatment of propositional conditionals, and then consider alternatives to it.

TRUTH TABLES FOR CONDITIONALS

For conjunction, disjunction, and negation, the truth table method provides an approach that is at once plausible and effective. A propositional conditional is also compounded from two simpler propositions, and this suggests that we might be able to offer a truth table definition for these conditionals as well. What should the truth table look like? When we try to answer this question, we get stuck almost at once, for it is unclear how we should fill in the table in three out of four cases.

p	*q*	If *p*, then *q*
T	T	?
T	F	F
F	T	?
F	F	?

It seems obvious that a conditional cannot be true if the antecedent is true and the consequent is false. We record this by putting an F in the second row. But suppose "*p*" and "*q*" are replaced by two arbitrary true propositions— say, "Two plus two equals four" and "Chile is in South America." Consider what we shall say about the conditional:

If two plus two equals four, then Chile is in South America.

This is a *very* strange statement, because the arithmetical remark in the antecedent does not seem to have anything to do with the geographical remark in the consequent. So this conditional is odd—indeed, extremely odd—but is it true or false? At this point, a reasonable response is bafflement.

Consider the following argument, which is intended to solve all these problems by providing reasons for assigning truth values in each row of the truth table. First, it seems obvious that, if "If *p*, then *q*" is true, then it is not the case that both "*p*" is true and "*q*" is false. That in turn means that "~(*p* & ~*q*)" must be true. The following, then, seems to be a valid argument form:

If *p*, then *q*.
∴ ~(*p* & ~*q*)

Second, we can also reason in the opposite direction. Suppose we know that "~(*p* & ~*q*)" is true. For this to be true, "*p* & ~*q*" must be false. We know this from the truth table definition of negation. Next let us suppose that "*p*" is true. Then "~*q*" must be false. We know this from the truth table definition of conjunction. Finally, if "~*q*" is false, then "*q*" itself must be true. This line of reasoning is supposed to show that the following argument form is valid:

~(*p* & ~*q*)
∴ If *p*, then *q*.

The first step in the argument was intended to show that we can validly derive "~(*p* & ~*q*)" from "If *p*, then *q*." The second step was intended to show that the derivation can be run in the other direction as well. But if each of these expressions is derivable from the other, this suggests that they are equivalent. We use this background argument as a justification for the following definition:

If *p*, then *q* = (by definition) not both *p* and not *q*.

We can put this into symbolic notation using "⊃" (called a *horseshoe*) to symbolize the conditional connective:

p ⊃ *q* = (by definition) ~(*p* & ~*q*)

Given this definition, we can now construct the truth table for propositional conditionals. It is simply the truth table for "~(*p* & ~*q*)":

p	*q*	~(*p* & ~*q*)	*p* ⊃ *q*	~*p* ∨ *q*
T	T	T	T	T
T	F	F	F	F
F	T	T	T	T
F	F	T	T	T

Notice that "~(p & ~q)" is also truth-functionally equivalent to the expression "~p ∨ q." We have cited it here because "~p ∨ q" has traditionally been used to define "p ⊃ q." For reasons that are now obscure, when a conditional is defined in this truth-functional way, it is called a *material conditional*.

Let's suppose, for the moment, that the notion of a material conditional corresponds exactly with our idea of a propositional conditional. What would follow from this? The answer is that we could treat conditionals in the same way in which we have treated conjunction, disjunction, and negation. A propositional conditional would be just one more kind of truth-functionally compound proposition capable of definition by truth tables. Furthermore, the validity of arguments that depend on this notion (together with conjunction, disjunction, and negation) could be settled by appeal to truth table techniques. Let us pause for a moment to examine this.

One of the most common patterns of reasoning is called *modus ponens*. It looks like this:

If p, then q.   p ⊃ q
p   p
_____   _____
∴ q   ∴ q

The truth table definition of a material conditional shows at once that this pattern of argument is valid:

PREMISE		PREMISE	CONCLUSION	
p	q	p ⊃ q	q	
T	T	T	T	O.K.
T	F	F	F	
F	T	T	T	
F	F	T	F	

EXERCISE XVII

The argument form called *modus tollens* looks like this:

p ⊃ q

~q
_____
∴ ~p

Use truth tables to show that this argument form is valid.

These same techniques allow us to show that one of the traditional fallacies is, indeed, a fallacy. It is called the fallacy of *denying the antecedent*, and it has this form:

Farcus

by David Waisglass
Gordon Coulthart

WAISGLASS/COULTHART

**"So, I say if it's not worth doing well,
it's not worth doing at all."**

$$p \supset q$$
$$\sim p$$
$$\therefore \sim q$$

The truth table showing the invalidity of this argument form looks like this:

		PREMISE	PREMISE	CONCLUSION	
p	q	$p \supset q$	$\sim p$	$\sim q$	
T	T	T	F	F	
T	F	F	F	T	
F	T	T	T	F	Invalid
F	F	T	T	T	O.K.

EXERCISE XVIII

A second standard fallacy is called *affirming the consequent*. It looks like this:

$$p \supset q$$
$$q$$
$$\therefore p$$

Use truth tables to show that this argument form is invalid.

In his radio address to the nation on April 17, 1982, President Ronald Reagan argued that the United States should not accept a treaty with the Soviet Union that would mutually freeze nuclear weapons at current levels, because he believed that the United States had fallen behind. Here is a central part of his argument:

> It would be wonderful if we could restore the balance of power with the Soviet Union without increasing our military power. And, ideally, it would be a long step towards assuring peace if we could have significant and verifiable reductions of arms on both sides. But let's not fool ourselves. The Soviet Union will not come to any conference table bearing gifts. Soviet negotiators will not make unilateral concessions. To achieve parity, we must make it plain that we have the will to achieve parity by our own effort.

Put Reagan's central argument into standard form. Then symbolize it and its form. Does his argument commit any fallacy? If so, identify it.

We can examine one last argument form that has been historically significant. It is called a *hypothetical syllogism* and has the following form:

$$p \supset q$$
$$q \supset r$$
$$\therefore p \supset r$$

Because we are dealing with an argument form containing three variables, we must perform the boring task of constructing a truth table with eight rows:

p	q	r	PREMISE $p \supset q$	PREMISE $q \supset r$	CONCLUSION $p \supset r$	
T	T	T	T	T	T	O.K.
T	T	F	T	F	F	
T	F	T	F	T	T	
T	F	F	F	T	F	
F	T	T	T	T	T	O.K.
F	T	F	T	F	T	
F	F	T	T	T	T	O.K.
F	F	F	T	T	T	O.K.

This is fit work for a computer, not for a human being, but it is important to see that it actually works.

Why is it important to see that these techniques work? Most people, after all, could see that hypothetical syllogisms are valid without going through all of this tedious business. We seem only to be piling boredom on top of triviality. This protest deserves an answer. Suppose we ask someone *why* he or she thinks that the conclusion follows from the premises in a hypothetical syllogism. The person might answer that anyone can see that—which, by the way, is false. Beyond this, he or she might say that it all depends on the meanings of the words or that it is all a matter of definition. But if we go on to ask *which words* and *what definitions*, most people will fall silent. We have discovered that the validity of some arguments depends on the meanings of such words as "and," "or," "not," and "if-then." We have then gone on to give explicit definitions of these terms—definitions, by the way, that help us see how these terms function in an argument. Finally, by getting all these *simple* things right, we have produced what is called a *decision procedure* for determining the validity of every argument depending only on conjunctions, disjunctions, negations, and propositional conditionals. Our truth table techniques give us a mechanical procedure for settling questions of validity in this area. In fact, truth table techniques have practical applications, for example, in computer programming. But the important point here is that, through an understanding of how these techniques work, we can gain a deeper insight into the notion of validity.

EXERCISE XX

Using the truth table techniques employed above, test the following argument forms for validity. (For your own entertainment, guess whether the argument form is valid or invalid before working it out.)

1. $p \supset q$
   $\therefore\ q \supset p$

2. $p \supset q$
   $\therefore\ \lnot q \supset \lnot p$

3. $\lnot q \supset \lnot p$
   $\therefore\ p \supset q$

4. $p \supset q$
   $q \supset r$
   $\therefore\ p \supset (q\ \&\ r)$

5. $p \supset q$
   $q \supset r$
   $\lnot r$
   $\therefore\ \lnot p$

6. $p \supset q$
   $q \supset r$
   $\therefore\ \lnot r \supset \lnot p$

7. $p \lor q$
   $p \supset r$
   $q \supset r$
   $\therefore\ r$

8. $p \supset (q \lor r)$
   $\lnot q$
   $\lnot r$
   $\therefore\ \lnot p$

9. $(p \lor q) \supset r$
   $\therefore\ p \supset r$

10. $(p\ \&\ q) \supset r$
    $\therefore\ p \supset r$

11. $p \supset (q \supset r)$
    $\therefore\ (p\ \&\ q) \supset r$

12. $(p\ \&\ q) \supset r$
    $\therefore\ p \supset (q \supset r)$

13. $p \supset (q \supset r)$
    q
    $\sim r$

    $\therefore \sim p$

14. $p \supset (q \supset r)$
    $p \supset q$

    $\therefore r$

15. $(p \lor q) \& (p \lor r)$
    $\sim r$

    $\therefore \sim q$

16. $(p \supset q) \& (p \supset \sim r)$
    $q \& r$

    $\therefore \sim p$

17. $(p \lor q) \supset p$

    $\therefore \sim q$

18. $(p \lor q) \supset (p \& q)$

    $\therefore (p \supset q) \& (q \supset p)$

19. $(p \& q) \supset (p \lor q)$

    $\therefore (p \supset q) \lor (q \supset p)$

20. r

    $\therefore (p \supset q) \lor (q \supset p)$

LOGICAL LANGUAGE AND EVERYDAY LANGUAGE

Early in this chapter we started out by talking about such common words as "and" and "or," and then we slipped over to talking about *conjunction* and *disjunction*. The transition was a bit sneaky, but intentional. To understand what is going on here, we can ask how closely these logical notions we have defined match their everyday counterparts. We will start with conjunction, and then come back to the more difficult question of conditionals.

At first sight, the match between conjunction as we have defined it and the everyday use of the word "and" may seem fairly bad. To begin with, in everyday discourse, we do not go about conjoining random bits of information. We do not say, for example, that two plus two equals four and Chile is in South America. We already know why we do not say such things, for unless the context is quite extraordinary, this is bound to violate the rule of Relevance. But if we are interested in validity, the rule of Relevance—like all other conversational (or pragmatic) rules—is simply beside the point. When dealing with validity, we are interested in only one question: If the premises of an argument are true, must the conclusion be true as well? Conversational rules, as we saw in Chapter 1, do not affect truth.

The truth-functional notion of conjunction is also insensitive to another important feature of our everyday discourse: By reducing all conjunctions to their bare truth-functional content, the truth-functional notion often misses the argumentative point of a conjunction. We have already seen that each of the following remarks has a very different force in the context of an argument:

The ring is beautiful, but expensive.

The ring is expensive, but beautiful.

These two remarks point in opposite directions in the context of an actual argument, but from a purely truth-functional point of view, we treat them as equivalent. We translate the first sentence as "*B & E*" and the second as "*E & B*." Their truth-functional equivalence is too obvious to need proof. Similar oddities arise for all discounting terms, such as "although," "whereas," and "however."

It might seem that if formal analysis cannot distinguish an "and" from a "but," then it can hardly be of any use at all. This is not true. A formal analysis of an argument will tell us just one thing: whether the argument is valid or not. If we expect the analysis to tell us more than this, we will be disappointed. It is important to remember two things: (1) We expect deductive arguments to be valid, and (2) usually we expect much more than this from an argument. To elaborate on the second point, we usually expect an argument to be sound as well as valid; we expect the premises to be true. Beyond this, we expect the argument to be informative, intelligible, convincing, and so forth. Validity, then, is an important aspect of an argument, and formal analysis helps us evaluate it. But validity is not the only aspect of an argument that concerns us. In many contexts, it is not even our chief concern.

We can now look at our analysis of conditionals, for here we find some striking differences between the logician's analysis and everyday use. The following argument forms are both valid:

1. p
$\therefore q \supset p$

2. $\sim p$
$\therefore p \supset q$

EXERCISE XXI

Check the validity of the argument forms above using truth tables.

Though valid, both argument forms seem odd—so odd that they have actually been called *paradoxical*. The first argument form seems to say this: If a proposition is true, then it is *implied by* any proposition whatsoever. Here is an example of an argument that satisfies this argument form and is therefore valid:

Lincoln was president.

$\therefore$ If the moon is made of cheese, Lincoln was president.

This is a peculiar argument to call valid. First, we want to know what the moon has to do with Lincoln's having been president. Beyond this, how can his having been president depend on a blatant falsehood? We can give these questions even more force by noticing that even the following argument is valid:

Lincoln was president.

$\therefore$ If Lincoln was not president, then Lincoln was president.

Both arguments are instances of the valid argument form "p; ∴ $q \supset p$."

The other argument form is also paradoxical. It seems to say that a false proposition implies any proposition whatsoever. The following is an instance of this argument form:

Columbus was not president.

∴ If Columbus was president, then the moon is made of cheese.

Here it is hard to see what the falsehood that Columbus was president has to do with the composition of the moon.

At this point, non-philosophers become impatient, whereas philosophers become worried. We started out with principles that seemed to be both obvious and simple. Now, quite suddenly, we are being overwhelmed with a whole series of peculiar results. What in the world has happened, and what should be done about it? Philosophers remain divided in the answers they give to these questions. The responses fall into two main categories: (1) Simply give up the idea that conditionals can be defined by truth-functional techniques and search for a different and better analysis of conditionals that avoids the difficulties involved in truth-functional analysis; or (2) take the difficult line and argue that there is nothing wrong with calling the aforementioned argument forms valid.

The first approach is highly technical and cannot be pursued in detail in this book, but the general idea is this: Instead of identifying "If p, then q" with "Not both p and not q," identify it with "Not *possibly* both p and not q." This provides a stronger notion of a conditional and avoids some—though not all—of the problems concerning conditionals. This theory is given a systematic development by offering a logical analysis of the notion of possibility. This branch of logic is called *modal* logic, and it has shown remarkable development in recent decades.

The second line has been taken by Paul Grice, whose theories played a prominent part in Chapter 1. He acknowledges—as anyone must—that the two argument forms above are decidedly odd. He denies, however, that this oddness has anything to do with *validity*. Validity concerns one thing and one thing only: a relationship between premises and conclusion. An argument is valid if the premises cannot be true without the conclusion being true as well. The above arguments are valid by this definition of "validity."

Of course, arguments can be defective in all sorts of other ways. Look at the first argument form: (1) p; ∴ $q \supset p$. Because "q" can be replaced by any proposition (true or false), the rule of Relevance will often be violated. It is worth pointing out violations of the rule of Relevance, but, according to Grice, this issue has nothing to do with validity. Beyond this, arguments having this form can also involve violations of the rule of Quantity. A conditional will be true whenever the consequent is true. Given this, it does not matter to the truth of the whole conditional whether the antecedent is true or false. Yet it can be misleading to use a conditional on the basis of this logical feature. For example, it would be misleading for a museum guard to say, "If you give me five dollars, then I will let you into the exhibition," when, in fact, he will admit you in any case. For Grice, this is misleading because it violates the rule of Quantity. Yet strictly speaking, it is not false. Strictly speaking, it is true.

The Grice line is attractive because, among other things, it allows us to accept the truth-functional account of conditionals, with all its simplicity. Yet sometimes it is difficult to swallow. Consider the following remark:

If God exists, then there is evil in the world.

If Grice's analysis is correct, even the most pious person will have to admit that this conditional is true provided only that he or she is willing to admit that there is evil in the world. Yet this conditional plainly suggests that there is some connection between God's existence and the evil in the world—presumably, that is the point of connecting them in a conditional. The pious will wish to deny this suggestion. All the same, this connection is something that is conversationally implied, not asserted. So, once more, this conditional could be misleading—and therefore is in need of criticism and correction—but it is still, strictly speaking, true.

Philosophers and logicians have had various responses to Grice's position. No consensus has emerged on this issue. The authors of this book find it adequate, at least in most normal cases, and therefore have adopted it. This has two advantages: (1) The appeal to conversational rules fits in well with our previous discussions, and (2) it provides a way of keeping the logic simple and within the range of a beginning student. Other philosophers and logicians continue to work toward a definition superior to the truth table definition for indicative conditionals.

OTHER CONDITIONALS IN ORDINARY LANGUAGE

So far we have considered only one form in which propositional conditionals appear in everyday language: the conditional "If p, then q." But propositional conditionals come in a variety of forms, and some of them demand careful treatment.

We can first consider the contrast between constructions using "if" and those using "only if":

1. I'll clean the barn if Hazel will help me.
2. I'll clean the barn only if Hazel will help me.

Adopting the following abbreviations:

B = I'll clean the barn

H = Hazel will help me

the first sentence is translated as follows:

$H \supset B$

Notice that in the prose version of (1), the antecedent and consequent appear in reverse order; "q if p" means the same thing as "If p, then q."

How shall we translate the second sentence? Here we should move slowly and first notice what seems incontestable: If Hazel does not help me, then I will not clean the barn. This is translated in the following way:

$\sim H \supset \sim B$

And that is equivalent to:

$B \supset H$

If this equivalence is not obvious, it can quickly be established using a truth table.

A more difficult question arises when we ask whether an implication runs the other way. When I say that I will clean the barn only if Hazel will help me, am I committing myself to cleaning the barn if she does help me? There is a strong temptation to answer the question "yes" and then give a fuller translation of (2) in the following way:

$(B \supset H) \;\&\; (H \supset B)$

Logicians call such two-way implications *biconditionals,* and we will discuss them in a moment. But adding this second conjunct is almost surely a mistake, for we can think of parallel cases where we would not be tempted to include it. A government regulation might read as follows:

> A student may receive a New York State Scholarship only if the student attends a New York State school.

From this it does not follow that anyone who attends a New York State school may receive a New York State Scholarship. There may be other requirements as well—for example, being a New York State resident.

Why were we tempted to use a biconditional in translating sentences containing the connective "only if"? Why, that is, are we tempted to think that the statement "I'll clean the barn only if Hazel will help me" implies "If Hazel helps me, then I will clean the barn"? The answer turns on the notion of conversational implication first discussed in Chapter 1. If I am *not* going to clean the barn whether Hazel helps me or not, then it will be misleading—a violation of the rule of Quantity—to say that I will clean the barn only if Hazel helps me. For this reason, in many contexts, the *use* of a sentence of the form "*p* only if *q*" will conversationally imply a commitment to "*p* if and only if *q*."

We can next look at sentences of the form "*p* if and only if *q*"—so-called biconditionals. If I say that I will clean the barn if and only if Hazel will help me, then I am saying that I will clean it if she helps and I will not clean it if she does not. Translated, this becomes:

$(H \supset B) \;\&\; (\sim H \supset \sim B)$

This is equivalent to:

$(H \supset B) \;\&\; (B \supset H)$

We thus have an implication going both ways—the characteristic form of a biconditional. In fact, constructions containing the expression "if and only if" do not often appear in everyday speech. They appear almost exclusively in technical or legal writing. In ordinary conversation, we capture the force of a biconditional by saying something like this:

I will clean the barn, but only if Hazel helps me.

The decision whether to translate a remark of everyday conversation into a conditional or a biconditional is often subtle and difficult. We have already noticed that the use of sentences of the form "*p* only if *q*" will often conversationally imply a commitment to the biconditional "*p* if and only if *q*." In the same way, the *use* of the conditional "*p* if *q*" will carry this same implication. If I plan to clean the barn whether Hazel helps me or not, it will certainly be misleading—again, a violation of the rule of Quantity—to say that I will clean the barn *if* Hazel helps me.

We can close this discussion by considering one further, rather difficult case. What is the force of saying "*p unless q*"? Is this a biconditional, or just a conditional? If it is just a conditional, which way does the implication go? There is a strong temptation to treat this as a biconditional, but the following example shows this to be wrong:

Bush will lose the election unless he carries the South.

This sentence clearly indicates that Bush will lose the election if he does not carry the South. Using abbreviations, we get the following:

N = Bush will carry the South.

L = Bush will lose the election.

$\sim N \supset L$

The original statement does not imply—even conversationally—that Bush will win the election if he does carry the South. Thus,

p unless $q = \sim q \supset p$

In short, "unless" means "if not." We can also note that "$\sim p$ unless q" means the same thing as "*p* only if *q*," and they both are translated thus:

$p \supset q$

Our results can be diagrammed as follows:

	Translates As	Often Conversationally Implies
p if *q*	$q \supset p$	$(p \supset q) \,\&\, (q \supset p)$
p only if *q*	$p \supset q$	$(p \supset q) \,\&\, (q \supset p)$
p unless *q*	$\sim q \supset p$	$(p \supset \sim q) \,\&\, (\sim q \supset p)$

Translate each of the following sentences into symbolic notation, using the suggested symbols as abbreviations.

1. The Reds will win only if the Dodgers collapse. (*R, D*)
2. The Steelers will win if their defense holds up. (*S, D*)
3. If it rains or snows, the game will be called off. (*R, S, O*)
4. If she came home with a trophy and a prize, she must have won the tournament. (*T, P, W*)
5. If you order the dinner special, you get dessert and coffee. (*S, D, C*)
6. If you order the dinner special, you get dessert; but you can have coffee whether or not you order the dinner special. (*S, D, C*)
7. If the house comes up for sale, and if I have the money in hand, I will bid on it. (*S, M, B*)
8. If you come to dinner, I will cook you a lobster, if you want me to. (*D, L, W*)
9. You can be a success if only you try. (*S, T*)
10. You can be a success only if you try. (*S, T*)
11. Only if you try can you be a success. (*S, T*)
12. You can be a success if you are the only one who tries. (*S, O*)
13. Unless there is a panic, stock prices will continue to rise. (*P, R*)
14. I won't scratch your back unless you scratch mine. (*I, Y*)
15. You will get a good bargain provided you get there early. (*B, E*)
16. You cannot lead a happy life without friends. (Let *H* = You can lead a happy life, and let *F* = You have friends.)
17. The only way that horse will win the race is if every other horse drops out. (Let *W* = That horse will win the race, and let *D* = Every other horse drops out.)
18. You should take prescription drugs if, but only if, they are prescribed for you. (*T, P*)
19. The grass will die without rain. (*D, R* = It rains.)
20. Given rain, the grass won't die. (*R, D* = The grass will die.)
21. Unless it doesn't rain, the grass won't die. (*R, D* = The grass will die.)

(a) Translate each of the following arguments into symbolic notation. Then (b) test each argument for truth-functional validity using truth table techniques, and (c) comment on any violations of conversational rules.

Example: Harold is clever; so, if Harold isn't clever, then Anna isn't clever either. (*H, A*)

(a) H p

$\therefore \sim H \supset \sim A$ $\therefore \sim p \supset \sim q$

(b)

PREMISE				CONCLUSION	
p	q	$\sim p$	$\sim q$	$\sim p \supset \sim q$	
T	T	F	F	T	O.K.
T	F	F	T	T	O.K.
F	T	T	F	F	
F	F	T	T	T	

(c) The argument violates the rule of Relevance, because Anna's cleverness is irrelevant to Harold's cleverness.

1. Jones is brave, so Jones is brave or Jones is brave. (J)

2. The Republicans will carry either New Mexico or Arizona; but, since they will carry Arizona, they will not carry New Mexico. (A, N)

3. The Democrats will win the election whether they win Idaho or not. Therefore, they will win the election. (D, I)

4. The Democrats will win the election. Therefore, they will win the election whether they win Idaho or not. (D, I)

5. The Democrats will win the election. Therefore, they will win the election whether they win a majority or not. (D, M)

6. If Bobby moves his queen there, he will lose her. Bobby will not lose his queen. Therefore, Bobby will not move his queen there. (M, L)

7. John will play only if the situation is hopeless. But the situation is hopeless. So John will play. (P, H)

8. Although Brown will pitch, the Rams will lose. If the Rams lose, their manager will get fired. So their manager will get fired. (B, L, F)

9. America will win the Olympics unless Russia does. Russia will win the Olympics unless East Germany does. So America will win the Olympics unless East Germany does. (A, R, E)

10. If you dial 0, you will get the operator. So, if you dial 0 and do not get the operator, then there is something wrong with the telephone. (D, O, W)

11. The Democrats will run either Jones or Borg. If Borg runs, they will lose the South. If Jones runs, they will lose the North. So the Democrats will lose either the North or the South. (J, B, S, N)

12. I am going to order either the fish special or the meat special. Either way, I will get soup. So I'll get soup. (F, M, S)

13. The grass will die if it rains too much or it does not rain enough. If it does not rain enough, it won't rain too much. If it rains too much, then it won't not rain enough. So the grass will die. (D = The grass will die, M = It rains too much, E = It rains enough.)

14. If you flip the switch, then the light will go on. But if the light goes on, then the generator is working. So if you flip the switch, then the generator is working. (F, L, G) (This example is due to Charles L. Stevenson.)

NECESSARY AND SUFFICIENT CONDITIONS

Our discussion of conditionals can help us understand two important notions used in the analysis of many forms of argumentation: that of a *sufficient condition* and that of a *necessary condition*. Later we will introduce a more general definition of both these notions, but we will begin here by defining when the truth of one proposition is necessary or sufficient for the truth of another proposition.

The definitions are simple. First,

A is a *sufficient condition* for *B* = if *A* is true, then *B* is true.

Thus, the antecedent of a propositional conditional always lays down a sufficient condition for its consequent:

Sufficient condition

$$\downarrow$$

$$A \supset B$$

For example, if we say, "If Joan is a mother, then Joan is female," we are indicating that Joan's being a mother is sufficient for her being female.

As an initial definition of a necessary condition, we will say that

B is a *necessary condition* for *A* = *A* is true *only if B* is true.

We know that this is equivalent to "$A \supset B$." Thus, the consequent of any propositional conditional lays down a necessary condition for its antecedent:

$$A \supset B$$

$$\uparrow$$

Necessary condition

For example, if we say, "If Joan is a mother, then Joan is female," we are indicating that Joan's being female is a necessary condition for her being a mother.

It is important not to confuse sufficient conditions and necessary conditions. Something can be a sufficient condition without being a necessary condition. For example, Joan's being a mother is a sufficient condition for Joan's being female, but it is not a necessary condition for her being female. Furthermore, something can be a necessary condition without being a sufficient condition. Although Joan's being a female is a necessary condition for Joan's being a mother, it is not a sufficient condition for her being a mother. Of course, some necessary conditions are also sufficient conditions. Joan's being a female parent is both necessary and sufficient for her being a mother. Nonetheless, because many necessary conditions are not sufficient conditions, and many sufficient conditions are not necessary conditions, we need to distinguish the two kinds of conditions.

Despite their distinctness, necessary conditions and sufficient conditions are related in interesting ways. The above definitions clearly imply the following:

PRINCIPLE I: A is a sufficient condition for B if and only if B is a necessary condition for A.

More principles can be formulated by introducing negative conditions. For example, we can say that a car's being out of gas is *sufficient* to guarantee that it will *not* be able to run. Alternatively, we can say that a car's having gasoline is *necessary* for its being able to run. We can express these ideas symbolically in the following way:

Let G = The car has gas.

Let R = The car can run.

We can then state that not having gas is a sufficient condition for a car's not being able to run as follows:

1. $\sim G \supset \sim R$

This means that, if a car does not have gas, the car cannot run. The claim that having gas is a necessary condition for a car's running can be stated this way:

2. $R \supset G$

This means that a car can run only if it has gas. But we know from the earlier discussion of conditionals that (1) and (2) are logically equivalent. This allows us to introduce two further principles relating necessary conditions and sufficient conditions:

PRINCIPLE II: If A is a sufficient condition for B, then $\sim A$ is a necessary condition for $\sim B$.

PRINCIPLE III: If A is a necessary condition for B, then $\sim A$ is a sufficient condition for $\sim B$.

These principles are guaranteed by the equivalence of "$A \supset B$" and "$\sim B \supset \sim A$."

Although the original definitions of necessary conditions and sufficient conditions are simple, the picture gets complicated by the introduction of negative conditions and of principles relating necessary conditions to sufficient conditions. These complications might explain part of the widespread tendency to confuse necessary conditions with sufficient conditions. We have also seen another reason for this common confusion: Conditionals often conversationally imply biconditionals. For example, recall the following statement:

1. I'll clean the barn only if Hazel will help me.

Does this logically commit me to cleaning the barn if Hazel will help? As we saw, the answer to this question is "No." The statement says that Hazel's helping is a necessary condition for my cleaning the barn, but it does not explicitly state that Hazel's helping is a sufficient condition of anything. Yet in many contexts, saying (1) conversationally implies that I will clean the barn if Hazel will help and, thereby, that Hazel's helping is a sufficient condition for my cleaning the barn.

Confusing sufficient conditions and necessary conditions is especially easy when conditionals lay down complex conditions that include conjunctions or disjunctions. Suppose, for example, that you are caught speeding while under the influence of alcohol, and your insurance agent tells you:

2. If you get one more ticket for speeding and one more ticket for DWI (driving while intoxicated), then you will lose your automobile insurance.

This conditional has a conjunction for an antecedent and, thus, lays down a conjunctive sufficient condition for losing one's insurance. Now suppose that, in fact, getting one more speeding ticket is *alone* sufficient for the loss of one's insurance, and so is getting one more ticket for DWI. Then what will we say about (2)? One temptation is to say that it is false, but that is wrong. To see this, suppose that you did get one more ticket for speeding *and* one more ticket for DWI. This will certainly be sufficient—we might want to say, more than sufficient—for you to lose your insurance. So, strictly speaking, (2) is true.

Yet in this context, (2) seems misleading. We can explain why it is misleading by appealing to the rule of Quantity discussed in Chapter 1. Generally, people are interested in sufficient conditions because they are interested in what is needed in order to guarantee that something will happen. Given these practical concerns, what they want is a *minimal* sufficient condition. For this reason, (2) is misleading because it does not state the minimum conditions that are sufficient for you to lose your insurance. For it to do so, (2) would have to be replaced by the following statement:

2*. If you get one more ticket for speeding *or* one more ticket for DWI, then you will lose your automobile insurance.

This statement, like (2), is true; but unlike (2), it is not misleading, because (2*) does state a minimal sufficient condition.

Misunderstandings can run in the other direction as well. We are sometimes inclined to treat necessary conditions as sufficient conditions. Suppose a student wants to take an advanced seminar, but she lacks the prerequisites, so she asks the professor what she needs to do in order to get into the seminar. The professor looks over the student's record and says,

3. I will let you into my seminar only if you read this book and write a five-page paper about it before next Monday.

The student reads the book and writes the paper before Monday, but on that day the professor says, "You must also read this second book and write a paper about it." The student would feel cheated. Why? It might be true that the professor would not have let this student into the seminar if she had not read the first book and written the first paper in time. If so, (3) is literally true: It specifies conditions that are necessary for getting into the seminar.

Nonetheless, it was misleading for the professor to say what he did. The reason is that he violated the rule of Quantity as it concerns statements of necessary conditions. In stating necessary conditions, we are expected to specify *all* of the necessary conditions that are relevant in the given context, except, perhaps, those that are so obvious that they can be taken for granted. The professor failed to satisfy this expectation.

In addition, we often, though perhaps not always, assume that doing *everything necessary* to accomplish something is *sufficient* to accomplish it. If two parties do everything necessary to enter into a contract, then that is sufficient for them to have entered into a contract. If someone mixes all the ingredients necessary to make brownies, then that person has mixed ingredients sufficient to make brownies. And so on. We usually assume that, by doing everything necessary, we have done enough. Stated more carefully, we often assume that the total set of necessary conditions is also a sufficient condition.[1]

If we grant these points, then it is easy to see how we can naturally treat a statement of necessary conditions as a statement of sufficient conditions:

1. A statement that certain conditions are necessary often conversationally implies that these are all of the necessary conditions (except perhaps those that can be taken for granted).

2. In many contexts, we assume that all necessary conditions taken together will be a sufficient condition.

3. Therefore, in many contexts, the statement of necessary conditions will often be taken as the statement of a sufficient condition.

Seeing how it is natural for us to confuse sufficient conditions and necessary conditions can help us guard against doing so. It is important to keep these concepts straight, for as we have seen, the rules concerning them are fundamentally different.

EXERCISE XXIV

Using the above definitions, state whether the underlined words express a necessary condition or a sufficient condition of the italicized words.

Example: If you work hard, then *you will succeed*.

Solution: Your working hard is a sufficient condition for your success.

1. *This piece of litmus paper will turn red* if it is put in acid.
2. *This piece of litmus paper will turn red* only if it is put in acid.
3. *This piece of litmus paper will not turn red* unless it is put in acid.

---

[1]This principle might seem obviously true, but it might be false if there are genuinely indeterministic events at the subatomic level or genuinely spontaneous acts of free will at the human level. In both cases, it seems that everything necessary for an event to take place is present, yet the event need not take place.

4. *This piece of litmus paper will not turn red* provided that it is not put in acid.
5. This piece of litmus paper will turn red if *it is put in acid.*
6. This piece of litmus paper will not turn red if *it is not put in acid.*
7. You have to rewrite your paper in order to *pass the course.*
8. Rewriting your paper is all you have to do in order to *pass the course.*
9. If you don't rewrite your paper, you can't *pass the course.*
10. If you rewrite your paper, you can't fail to *pass the course.*
11. You can't *pass this course* unless you rewrite your paper.
12. You can't pass this course unless you *rewrite your paper.*

EXERCISE XXV

Indicate whether each of the following sentences is true or false.

1. If ~A is a sufficient condition of X, then A is a necessary condition of ~X.
2. If $A \lor B$ is a sufficient condition of X, then A is a sufficient condition of X.
3. If A & B is a sufficient condition of X, then A is a sufficient condition of X.
4. If A & B is a sufficient condition of X, then A is a necessary condition of X.
5. If $A \lor B$ is a sufficient condition of X, then A is a necessary condition of X.
6. If ~(A & B) is a sufficient condition of X, then ~A is a sufficient condition of X.
7. If ~A is a necessary condition of X, then ~($A \lor B$) is a necessary condition of X.
8. If $A \lor B$ is a sufficient condition of X, then ~A is a necessary condition of ~X.

1. If "~p unless q" is translated as "p ⊃ q," then "p unless q" can be translated as "p ∨ q." Why?

2. Is a valid argument always a substitution instance of a valid argument form? Why or why not?

3. Whatever its conclusion, any argument with inconsistent premises will always be valid. First of all, why is this true? Second, why does this not allow us to prove anything we please?

4. Are arguments of the form "p; ∴ p" valid? Are they ever sound? Does this show that they are good and useful arguments? Why or why not?

5. Symbolize the following argument and give its form. Does this example show that *modus ponens* is not always valid? Why or why not?

   Opinion polls taken just before the 1980 election showed the Republican Ronald Reagan decisively ahead of the Democrat Jimmy Carter, with the other Republican in the race, John Anderson, a distant third. Those apprised of the poll results believed, with good reason:

   1. If a Republican wins the election, then if it's not Reagan who wins it will be Anderson.
   2. A Republican will win the election.

   Yet they did not have reason to believe:

   3. If it's not Reagan who wins, it will be Anderson.[2]

6. Symbolize the following argument and give its form. Does this example show that *modus tollens* is not always valid? Why or why not?

   1. If it rained, it didn't rain hard.
   2. It rained hard.
   3. So, it didn't rain.[3]

---

[2]Vann McGee, "A Counterexample to *Modus Ponens*," *Journal of Philosophy* 82, 9 (September 1985), 462. See also Walter Sinnott-Armstrong, James Moor, and Robert Fogelin, "A Defense of *Modus Ponens*," *Journal of Philosophy* 83, 5 (May 1986), 296–300.

[3]Ernest Adams, "*Modus Tollens* Revisited," *Analysis* 48, 3 (1988), 122–28. See also Walter Sinnott-Armstrong, James Moor, and Robert Fogelin, "A Defense of *Modus Tollens*," *Analysis* 50, 1 (1990), 9–16.

The Formal Analysis of Arguments: Categorical Logic

In Chapter 6, we saw how validity can depend on the external connections among propositions. This chapter will demonstrate how validity can depend on the internal structure of propositions. In particular, we will examine two types of categorical arguments—immediate inferences and syllogisms—whose validity or invalidity depends on relations among terms in their premises and conclusions. Our interest in these kinds of arguments is mostly theoretical. Understanding the theory of the syllogism deepens our understanding of validity, even if this theory is, in some cases, difficult to apply directly to complex arguments in daily life.

BEYOND PROPOSITIONAL LOGIC

Armed with the techniques developed in Chapter 6, let's look at the following argument:

> All squares are rectangles.
> All rectangles have parallel sides.
>
> ∴ All squares have parallel sides.

It is obvious at a glance that the conclusion follows from the premises, so this argument is valid. Furthermore, it seems to be valid in virtue of its form. But it is not yet clear what the form of this argument is. To show the form of this argument, we might try something of the following kind:

$$p \supset q$$
$$q \supset r$$
$$\therefore p \supset r$$

But this is a mistake, and a bad mistake. We have been using the letters "p," "q," and "r" as *propositional variables*—they stand for arbitrary propositions. But the proposition "All squares are rectangles" is not itself composed of two propositions. Nor does it contain "if _____ , then _____ ," or any other propositional connective. In fact, if we attempt to translate the above argument into the language of propositional logic, we get the following result:

$$p$$
$$q$$
$$\therefore r$$

This, of course, is *not* a valid argument form. But if we look back at the original argument, we see that it is obviously valid. This shows that propositional logic—however adequate it is in its own area—is not capable of explaining the validity of all valid arguments. There is more to logic than propositional logic.

CATEGORICAL PROPOSITIONS

To broaden our understanding of the notion of validity, we will examine a modern version of a branch of logic first developed in ancient times—categorical logic. Categorical logic concerns immediate inferences and syllogisms that are composed of categorical propositions, so we need to begin by explaining what a categorical proposition is.

In the argument above, the first premise asserts some kind of relationship between squares and rectangles; the second premise asserts some kind of relationship between rectangles and things with parallel sides; finally, in virtue of these asserted relationships, the conclusion asserts a relationship between squares and things having parallel sides. Our task is to understand these relationships as clearly as possible so that we can discover the *basis* for the validity of this argument. Again, we shall adopt the strategy of starting from simple cases and then use the insights gained there for dealing with more complicated cases.

A natural way to represent the relationships expressed by the propositions in an argument is through diagrams. Suppose we draw one circle standing for all things that are squares and another circle standing for all things that are rectangles. The claim that all squares are rectangles may be represented by placing the circle representing squares completely inside the circle representing rectangles.

Another way of representing this relationship is to begin with overlapping circles.

We then shade out the portions of the circles in which nothing exists, according to the proposition we are diagramming. If all squares are rectangles, there is nothing that is a square that is not a rectangle—that is, there is nothing in region 1. So our diagram looks like this:

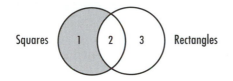

Either method of representation seems plausible. Perhaps the first seems more natural. We shall, however, use the system of overlapping circles, because they will work better when we get to more complex arguments. They are called *Venn diagrams*, after their inventor, John Venn, a nineteenth-century English logician.

Having examined one relationship that can exist between two classes, it is natural to wonder what other relationships might exist. Going to the opposite extreme from our first example, two classes may have *nothing* in common. This relationship could be expressed by saying, "All triangles are not squares," but it is more common and natural to say, "No triangles are squares." We diagram this claim by indicating that there is nothing in the overlapping region of things that are both triangles and squares:

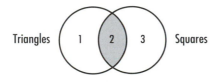

This is one of the relationships that could not be diagrammed by putting one circle inside another. (Just try it!)

In these first two extreme cases, we have indicated that one class is either completely included in another ("All squares are rectangles") or completely excluded from another ("No triangles are squares"). Sometimes, however, we claim only that two classes have at least *some* things in common. We might say, for example, "Some aliens are spies." How shall we indicate this relationship in the following diagram?

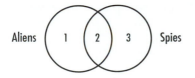

In this case, we do not want to cross out any whole region. We do not want to cross out region 1 because we are not saying that *all* aliens are spies. Plainly, we do not want to cross out region 2, for we are actually saying that some persons *are* both aliens and spies. Finally, we do not want to cross out region

3, for we are not saying that all spies are aliens. Saying that some aliens are spies does not rule out the possibility that some spies are homegrown. So we need some new device to represent claims that two classes have at least *some* members in common. We shall do this in the following way:

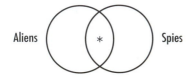

Here the asterisk indicates that there is at least one person who is both an alien and a spy. Notice, by the way, that we are departing a bit from an everyday way of speaking. "Some" is usually taken to mean "more than one"; here we let it mean "at least one." This makes things simpler and will cause no trouble, so long as we remember that this is what we are using "some" to mean.

Given this new method of diagramming class relationships, we can immediately think of other possibilities. The following diagram indicates that there is someone who is an alien but not a spy. In more natural language, it represents the claim that *some aliens are not spies*.

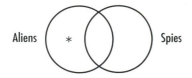

Next we can indicate that there is someone who is a spy but not an alien. More simply, the claim is that *some spies are not aliens*, and it is represented like this:

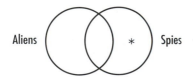

These last three claims are, of course, compatible, because there might be some aliens who are spies, some aliens who are not spies, and some spies who are not aliens.

THE FOUR BASIC CATEGORICAL FORMS

Although two classes can be related in a great many different ways, it is possible to examine many of these relationships in terms of four basic propositional forms:

A: All S is P.   E: No S is P.

I: Some S is P.   O: Some S is not P.

These forms are called *categorical forms,* and propositions with these forms are called *categorical propositions.*

As with the propositional forms discussed in the previous chapter, the A, E, I, and O forms for categorical propositions are not themselves propositions, so they are neither true nor false. Instead, they are patterns for whole groups of propositions. We get propositions from these forms by uniformly replacing the variables S and P with terms that refer to classes of things. For example, "Some spies are not aliens" is a substitution instance of the O propositional form. Nonetheless, we will refer to propositions with the A, E, I, or O form simply as A, E, I, or O propositions, except where this might cause confusion.

A and E propositions are said to be *universal* propositions (because they are about *all S*), and I and O propositions are called *particular* propositions (because they are about *some S*). A and I propositions are described as *affirmative* propositions (because they say what *is P*), and E and O propositions are referred to as *negative* propositions (because they say what is *not P*). Thus, these four basic propositional forms can be described this way:

A: Universal Affirmative   E: Universal Negative

I: Particular Affirmative   O: Particular Negative

These four forms fit into the following table:

	Affirmative	Negative
Universal	A: All S is P.	E: No S is P.
Particular	I: Some S is P.	O: Some S is not P.

Here are the Venn diagrams for the four basic categorical forms:

A: All S is P.

E: No S is P.

I: Some S is P.

O: Some S is not P.

These basic categorical forms, together with their labels, classifications, and diagrams, should be memorized, because they will be referred to often in the rest of this chapter.

EXERCISE I

Using just the four basic categorical forms, indicate what information is given in each of the following diagrams:

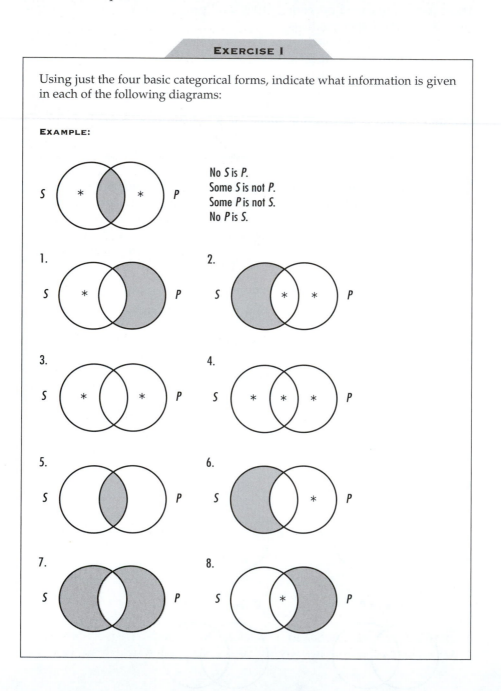

EXAMPLE:

No S is P.
Some S is not P.
Some P is not S.
No P is S.

TRANSLATION INTO THE BASIC CATEGORICAL FORMS

Propositions with the specific A, E, I, and O forms do not appear often in everyday conversations. Normal people rarely say things like "All whales are mammals. All mammals breathe air. Therefore, all whales breathe air." Most people talk more like this: "Whales breathe air, since they're mammals." Thus, if our logical apparatus could be applied only to propositions with the explicit forms of A, E, I, and O, then it would apply to few arguments in everyday life.

Fortunately, however, many common statements that are not explicitly in a categorical form can be translated into a categorical form. For example, when someone says, "Whales are mammals," the speaker presumably means to refer to *all* whales, so this statement can be translated into "All whales are mammals," which is an A proposition. We need to be careful, however. If someone says, "Whales are found in the North Atlantic," the speaker probably does *not* mean to refer to *all* whales, because there are many whales in the Pacific as well. Similarly, if someone says, "A whale is a mammal," this can usually be translated as "All whales are mammals," which is an A proposition, but this translation would be inappropriate for "A whale is stranded on the beach," which seems to mean "One whale is stranded on the beach." Thus, we can be misled badly if we look only at the surface structure of what people say. We also need to pay attention to the context when we translate everyday talk into the basic categorical forms.

Despite these complications, it is possible to give some rough-and-ready guides to help in translating many common forms of expression into propositions with the A, E, I, and O forms. Let's begin with one problem that arises for all these categorical forms: They all require a class of things as a predicate. Thus, "All whales are big" and "No whales live on land" should strictly be reformulated as "All whales are big things" and "No whales are things that live on land" or "No whales are land dwellers." This much is easy.

Things get more complicated when we look at the word "all" in A propositions. We have already seen that the word "all" is sometimes dropped in everyday conversation, as in "Whales are mammals." The word "all" can also be moved away from the start of a sentence. "Democrats are all liberal" usually means "All Democrats are liberal," which is an A proposition. Moreover, other words can be used in place of "all." Each of the following claims can, in standard contexts, be translated into an A proposition with the form "All S is P":

Every Republican is conservative.

Any investment is risky.

Anyone who is human is mortal.

Each ant is precious to its mother.

To translate such claims, we sometimes need to construct noun phrases out of adjectives and verbs. These transformations are often straightforward, but sometimes they require ingenuity, and even then they can seem somewhat contorted. For example, "Nobody but a fool would do that" can usually be translated into "All people who do that are fools." This translation might not seem so natural as the original, but, since it has the A form, it explicitly shows that this claim has the logical properties shared by other A propositions.

With some stretching, it is also possible to translate statements about individuals into categorical form. The standard method is to translate "Socrates is a man" as the A proposition "All things that are Socrates are men." Similarly, "The cannon is about to go off" in a typical context must not be translated as the I proposition "Some cannon is about to go off," because the original statement is about a particular cannon. Instead, the original statement should be translated as the A proposition "All things that are that cannon are about to go off." These translations might seem stilted, but they are necessary in order to apply syllogistic logic to everyday forms of expression.

Similar difficulties arise with the other basic propositional forms. If a woman says, "I am looking for a man who is not attached," and a friend responds, "All of the men in my church are not attached," then this response should probably be translated as "No men in my church are attached," which is an E proposition. In contrast, "All ocean dwellers are not fish" should usually be translated not as the E proposition "No ocean dwellers are fish" but rather as "Not all ocean dwellers are fish." This means "Some ocean dwellers are not fish," which is an O proposition. Thus, some statements with the form "All *S* are not *P*" should be translated as E propositions, but others should be translated as O propositions. (This ambiguity in the form "All *S* are not *P*" explains why it is standard to give E propositions in the less ambiguous form "No *S* is *P*.") Other sentences should also be translated as E propositions even though they do not explicitly contain the word "no." "Underground cables are not easy to repair" and "If a cable is underground, it is not easy to repair" and "There aren't any underground cables that are easy to repair" can all be translated as the E proposition "No underground cables are easy to repair."

Similar complications also arise for I and O propositions. We already saw that "Whales are found in the North Atlantic" should be translated as the I proposition "*Some* whales are found in the North Atlantic." In addition, some common forms of expression can be translated as O propositions even though they do not contain either the word "not" or the word "some." For example, "There are desserts without chocolate" can be translated as "Some desserts are not chocolate," which is an O proposition.

Because of such complications, there is no mechanical procedure for translating common English sentences into A, E, I, and O propositions. To find the correct translation, you need to think carefully about the sentence and its context.

EXERCISE II

Translate each of the following sentences into an A, E, I, or O proposition. Be sure that the subjects and predicates in your translations use nouns that refer to classes of things (rather than adjectives or verbs). If the sentence can be translated into different forms in different contexts, give each translation and specify a context in which it seems natural.

1. Real men eat ants.
2. Everything that is cheap is no good.
3. Some things that are expensive are no good.
4. My friends are the only people who understand me.
5. Somebody loves you.
6. Not all crabs live in water.
7. The hippo is a noble beast.
8. The hippo is charging.
9. Bats are not birds.
10. Only seniors may take this course.

CONTRADICTORIES

Once we understand A, E, I, and O propositions by themselves, the next step is to ask how they are related to each other. From their diagrams, some relationships are immediately evident. Consider the Venn diagrams for the E and I propositional forms:

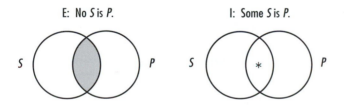

The first diagram has shading in the very same region that contains an asterisk in the second diagram. This makes it obvious that an E proposition and the corresponding I proposition (that is, the I proposition that has the same subject and predicate terms as the E proposition) cannot both be true. For an E proposition to be true, there must be *nothing* in the central region. But for the corresponding I proposition to be true, there must be *something* in the central region. Thus, they cannot both be true. They also cannot both be false. The only way for an E proposition to be false is for there to be something in the central region, but then the corresponding I proposition is not false but true. The only way for the I proposition to be false is if there is nothing in the central region, and then the E proposition is not false but true. Thus, they cannot both be true, and they cannot both be false. In other words, they always have opposite truth values. This relation is described by saying that these propositions are *contradictories.*

More generally, we can produce a diagram for the denial of a proposition by a simple procedure. The only information given in a Venn diagram is represented either by shading out some region, thereby indicating that nothing exists in it, or by putting an asterisk in a region, thereby indicating that something does exist in it. We are given no information about regions that are unmarked. To represent the denial of a proposition, we simply reverse the information in the diagram. That is, where there is an asterisk, we put in shading; where there is shading, we put in an asterisk. Everything else is left unchanged. Thus, we can see at once that corresponding E and I propositions are denials of one another, so they must always have opposite truth values. This makes them contradictories.

The same relation exists between an A proposition and its corresponding O proposition. Consider their forms:

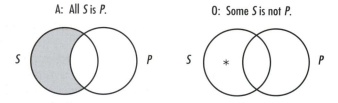

A: All *S* is *P*.   O: Some *S* is not *P*.

The diagram for an A proposition has shading exactly where the corresponding O proposition has an asterisk, and they contain no other information. Consequently, corresponding A and O propositions cannot both be false and cannot both be true, so they are contradictories.

EXERCISE III

1. Is an A proposition a contradictory of its corresponding E proposition? Why or why not?

2. Is an I proposition a contradictory of its corresponding O proposition? Why or why not?

3. If one proposition is the contradictory of another, is the latter always the contradictory of the former? Why or why not?

EXISTENTIAL COMMITMENT

It might also seem that an A proposition (with the form "All *S* is *P*") implies the corresponding I proposition (with the form "Some *S* is *P*"). This, however, raises a difficult problem that logicians have not fully settled. Usually when we make a statement, we are talking about certain specific things. If someone claims that all whales are mammals, that person is talking about whales and mammals and stating a relationship between them. In making this statement, the person seems to be taking the *existence* of whales and mammals for granted. The remark seems to involve what logicians call *existential commitment* to the things referred to in the subject and predicate terms. In the same way, stating an E proposition often seems to commit the speaker to the existence of things in the subject and predicate classes and, thus, to imply an O proposition. For example, someone who says, "No whales are fish" seems committed to "Some whales are not fish."

In other contexts, however, we seem to use universal (A and E) propositions without committing ourselves to the existence of the things referred to in the subject and predicate terms. For example, if we say, "All trespassers will be fined," we are not committing ourselves to the existence of any trespassers or to any actual fines for trespassing; we are only saying, "*If* there are trespassers, then they will be fined." Similarly, if we tell a sleepy child, "No ghosts are under your bed," we are not committing ourselves to the existence of ghosts or anything under the bed. Finally, when Newton said, "All bodies that are acted on by no forces are at rest," he did not commit himself to the existence of bodies that are acted on by no forces. Given these examples of A and E propositions that carry no commitment to the things referred to, it is easy to think of many others.

The question then arises whether we should include existential commitment in our treatment of universal propositions or not. Once more, we must make a decision. (Remember that we had to make decisions concerning the truth-table definitions of both disjunction and conditionals in Chapter 6.) *Classical* logic was developed on the assumption that universal (A and E) propositions carry existential commitment. *Modern* logic makes the opposite decision, treating the claim "All men are mortal" as equivalent to "If someone is a man, then that person is mortal," and the claim "No men are islands" as equivalent to "If someone is a man, then that person is not an island." This way of speaking carries no commitment to the existence of any men.

Which approach should we adopt? The modern approach is simpler and has proved more powerful in the long run. For these reasons, we will adopt the modern approach and *not* assign existential commitment to universal (A and E) propositions, so these propositions do not imply particular (I and O) propositions. All the same, there is something beautiful about the classical approach, and it does seem appropriate in some contexts to some people, so it is worth exploring in its own right. Appendix A in this chapter will show how to develop the classical theory by adding existential commitment to the modern theory.

EXERCISE IV

Give other examples of contexts in which:

1. Stating an A proposition does not seem to commit the speaker to the existence of the things to which the subject term refers.

2. Stating an A proposition does not seem to commit the speaker to the existence of the things to which the predicate term refers.

3. Stating an E proposition does not seem to commit the speaker to the existence of the things to which the subject term refers.

4. Stating an E proposition does not seem to commit the speaker to the existence of the things to which the predicate term refers.

VALIDITY FOR ARGUMENTS CONTAINING CATEGORICAL PROPOSITIONS

We have introduced Venn diagrams because they provide an efficient and illuminating way to test the validity of arguments made up of categorical (A, E, I, and O) propositions. The basic idea is simple: An argument made up of categorical propositions is valid if all the information contained in the Venn diagram for the conclusion is already contained in the Venn diagram for the premises. There are only two ways to put information into a Venn diagram: We can either shade out an area or put an asterisk in an area. Hence, to test the validity of an argument made up of categorical propositions, we need only examine the diagram of the conclusion for its information (its shading or asterisks) and then check to see if the diagram for the premises contains this information (the same shading or asterisks).

The following simple example will give a general idea of how this works:

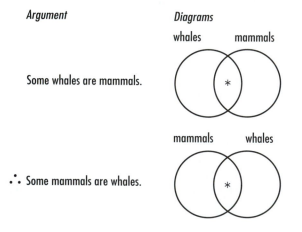

Argument

Some whales are mammals.

∴ Some mammals are whales.

Diagrams

Notice that the only information contained in the diagram for the conclusion is the asterisk in the overlap between the two circles, and that information is already included in the diagram for the premise. Thus, the argument is valid.

The same method can be used to test argument *forms* for validity. The form of the previous argument and the corresponding diagrams look like this:

Argument Form   Diagrams

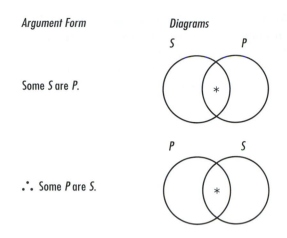

Some S are P.

∴ Some P are S.

This argument form is valid, because all the information contained in the Venn diagram for the conclusion is contained in the Venn diagram for the premise. And any argument that is a substitution instance of a valid argument form is valid.

Notice that we did not say that an argument is *invalid* if it fails these tests—that is, if some of the information in the Venn diagram for the conclusion (or its form) is not contained in the Venn diagram for the premises (or their forms). As with truth tables in propositional logic (see Chapter 6), Venn diagrams test whether arguments are valid by virtue of a certain form, but some arguments will be valid on a different basis, even though they are not valid by virtue of their categorical form. Here is one example:

Argument   Diagrams

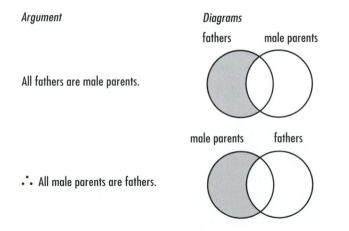

All fathers are male parents.

∴ All male parents are fathers.

The Venn diagram for the conclusion includes shading in a different circle than does the Venn diagram for the premise, so this *form* of argument is *not* valid, and some arguments of this form are not valid. Nonetheless, this particular argument *is* clearly valid, since it is not possible for the premise to be true when the conclusion is false, for the simple reason that the conclusion cannot be false. Because of such cases, Venn diagrams can show us that an argument is valid, but they cannot prove that an argument is invalid.

Despite this limitation, the method of Venn diagrams can be used to test many different kinds of arguments and argument forms for validity. We will show how this method works for two main kinds of argument: immediate inferences and syllogisms.

IMMEDIATE INFERENCES

An *immediate inference* is an argument with the following features:

1. It has a single premise. (That is why the inference is called immediate.)
2. It is constructed from A, E, I, and O propositions.

Of course, there are all sorts of other arguments involving just one premise, but those involving categorical propositions have been singled out for special attention. These arguments deserve such attention because they occur quite often in everyday reasoning.

We will focus on the simplest kind of immediate inference, which is *conversion*. We *convert* a proposition (and produce its *converse*) simply by reversing the subject term and the predicate term. By the *subject term,* we mean the term that occurs as the grammatical subject; by the *predicate term,* we mean the term that occurs as the grammatical predicate. In the A proposition "All spies are aliens," "spies" is the subject term and "aliens" is the predicate term; the converse is "All aliens are spies."

In this case, identifying the predicate term is straightforward because the grammatical predicate is a noun—a predicate nominative. Often, however, we have to change the grammatical predicate from an adjective to a noun phrase in order to get a noun that refers to a class of things. "All spies are dangerous" becomes "All spies are dangerous things." Here "spies" is the subject term and "dangerous things" is the predicate term. Although this change is a bit artificial, it is necessary because, when we convert a proposition (that is, reverse its subject and predicate terms), we need a noun phrase to take the place of the grammatical subject. In English we cannot say, "All dangerous are spies," but we can say, "All dangerous things are spies."

Having explained what conversion is, we now want to know when this operation yields a *valid* immediate inference. To answer this question, we use Venn diagrams to examine the relationship between each of the four basic categorical propositional forms and its converse. The immediate inference is valid if the information contained in the conclusion is also contained in the premise—that is, if any region that is shaded in the conclusion is shaded in the premise, and if any region that contains an asterisk in the conclusion contains an asterisk in the premise.

Two cases are obvious: Both I and E propositions validly convert. From an I proposition with the form "Some S is P," we may validly infer its converse, which has the form "Some P is S."

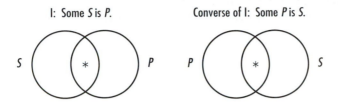

I: Some S is P.   Converse of I: Some P is S.

From an E proposition with the form "No S is P," we may validly infer its converse, which has the form "No P is S."

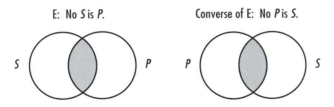

E: No S is P.   Converse of E: No P is S.

Notice that in both these cases, the information is in the center of the original diagram, and the diagram for the converse flips the original diagram. Thus, the two diagrams contain the same information, since the diagram for the converse has exactly the same markings in the same areas as does the diagram for the original propositional form. This shows that E and I propositions not only logically *imply* their converses but are also logically *implied by* them. Because the implication runs both ways, these propositions are said to be *logically equivalent* to their converses, and they always have the same truth values as their converses.

The use of a Venn diagram also shows that an O proposition cannot always be converted validly. From a proposition with the form "Some S is not P," we may not always infer its converse, which has the form "Some P is not S."

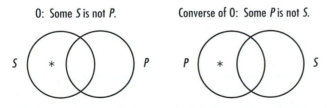

O: Some S is not P.   Converse of O: Some P is not S.

Notice that in this case the information is not in the center but is instead off to one side. As a result, the information changes when the diagram is flipped. The asterisk is in a different circle—it is in the circle for S in the diagram for an O proposition, but it is in the circle for P in the diagram for the converse of the O proposition. That shows that an argument from an O proposition to its converse is not always valid.[1]

Finally, we can see that A propositions also do not always validly convert. From a proposition with the form "All *S* is *P*," we may not always infer its converse, which has the form "All *P* is *S*."

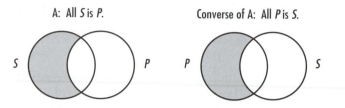

A: All *S* is *P*.   Converse of A: All *P* is *S*.

Since the diagram is not symmetrical, the information changes when the diagram is flipped; the shading ends up in a different circle. That shows why this form of argument is not always valid.

Traditionally, other immediate inferences have also been studied, but we will not run through them all here. (For those who are interested, a more complete theory of immediate inferences is presented in Appendix B.) The single example of conversion is enough to illustrate how Venn diagrams can be used to test some arguments for validity.

EXERCISE V

Use Venn diagrams to determine whether the following immediate inferences are valid:

1. All dinosaurs are animals. Therefore, all animals are dinosaurs.
2. Some pterodactyls can fly. Therefore, some flying things are pterodactyls.
3. Some eryopses are not meat eaters. Therefore, some things that eat meat are not eryopses.
4. No tyrannosaurus is a king. Therefore, no king is a tyrannosaurus.
5. Some dinosaurs are reptiles. Therefore, all dinosaurs are reptiles.
6. Some dinosaurs are not alive today. Therefore, no dinosaurs are alive today.
7. All dimetrodons eat meat. Therefore, some dimetrodons eat meat.
8. No dinosaurs are warm-blooded. Therefore, some dinosaurs are not warm-blooded.

---

[1]We say "not always" rather than simply "not," because there are some strange cases—logicians call them "degenerate cases"—for which inferences of this pattern are valid. For example, from "Some men are not men," we may validly infer "Some men are not men." Here, by making the subject term and the predicate term the same, we trivialize conversion. Keeping cases of this kind in mind, we must say that the inference from an O proposition to its converse is usually, but not always, invalid. In contrast, the set of valid arguments holds in all cases, including degenerate cases.

THE THEORY OF THE SYLLOGISM

In an immediate inference, we draw a conclusion directly from a single A, E, I, or O proposition. Moreover, when two categorical propositions are contradictories, the falsity of one can be validly inferred from the truth of the other, and the truth of one can be validly inferred from the falsity of the other. All these forms of argument contain only one premise. The next step in understanding categorical propositions is to consider arguments containing two premises.

An important group of such arguments is called *categorical syllogisms*. The basic idea behind these arguments is commonsensical. Suppose you wish to prove that all squares have four sides. A proof should present some *link* or *connection* between squares and four-sided figures. This link can be provided by some intermediate class, such as rectangles. You can then argue that, because the set of squares is a subset of the set of rectangles and rectangles are a subset of four-sided figures, squares must also be a subset of four-sided figures.

Of course, there are many other ways to link two terms by means of a third term. All such arguments with categorical propositions are called categorical syllogisms. More precisely, a categorical syllogism is any argument such that:

1. The argument has exactly two premises and one conclusion;
2. The argument contains only basic A, E, I, and O propositions;
3. Exactly one premise contains the predicate term;
4. Exactly one premise contains the subject term; and
5. Each premise contains the middle term.

The *predicate term* is simply the term in the predicate of the conclusion. It is also called the *major term*, and the premise that contains the predicate term is called the *major premise*. The *subject term* is the term in the subject of the conclusion. It is called the *minor term*, and the premise that contains the subject term is called the *minor premise*. It is traditional to state the major premise first, the minor premise second.

Our first example of a categorical syllogism then looks like this:

All rectangles are things with four sides.	(Major premise)
All squares are rectangles.	(Minor premise)
∴ All squares are things with four sides.	(Conclusion)

Subject term = "Squares"

Predicate term = "Things with four sides"

Middle term = "Rectangles"

To get the form of this syllogism, we replace the terms with variables:

All *M* is *P*.
All *S* is *M*.
_____

∴ All *S* is *P*.

Of course, many other arguments fit the definition of a categorical syllogism. Here is one with a negative premise:

No ellipses are things with sides.
All circles are ellipses.
_____

∴ No circles are things with sides.

The next categorical syllogism has a particular premise:

All squares are things with equal sides.
Some squares are rectangles.
_____

∴ Some rectangles are things with equal sides.

EXERCISE VI

In each of the last two syllogisms, what is the subject term? The predicate term? The middle term? The major premise? The minor premise? The form of the syllogism (using *S*, *P*, and *M*)? Is the syllogism valid? Why or why not?

HONORS EXERCISE

Given the restrictions in the definition of a categorical syllogism, there are exactly 256 possible forms of categorical syllogism. Explain why.

VENN DIAGRAMS FOR SYLLOGISMS. In a previous section, we used Venn diagrams to test the validity of immediate inferences. Immediate inferences contain only two terms or classes, so the corresponding Venn diagrams need only two overlapping circles. Categorical syllogisms contain three terms or classes. To reflect this, we will use diagrams with three overlapping circles. If we use a bar over a letter to indicate that things in the area are not in the class (so that *S̄* indicates that something is not in *S*), then our diagram looks like this:

This diagram has eight different areas, which can be listed in an order that resembles a truth table:

S	P	M
S	P	$\overline{M}$
S	$\overline{P}$	M
S	$\overline{P}$	$\overline{M}$
$\overline{S}$	P	M
$\overline{S}$	P	$\overline{M}$
$\overline{S}$	$\overline{P}$	M
$\overline{S}$	$\overline{P}$	$\overline{M}$

Notice that, if something is neither an S nor a P nor an M, then it falls completely outside the system of overlapping circles. In every other case, a thing is assigned to one of the seven compartments within the system of overlapping circles.

THE VALIDITY OF SYLLOGISMS.   To test the validity of a syllogism using a Venn diagram, we first fill in the diagram to indicate the information contained in the premises. Remember that the only information contained in a Venn diagram is indicated either by shading out an area or by putting an asterisk in it. The argument is valid if the information expressed by the conclusion is already contained in the diagram for the premises.[2] To see this, consider the diagrams for examples that we have already given:

> All rectangles have four sides.
> All squares are rectangles.
>
> ∴ All squares have four sides.

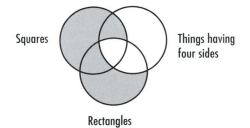

Squares · Things having four sides · Rectangles

Notice that all the things that are squares are corralled into the region of things that have four sides. That shows that this syllogism is valid.

---

[2]We cannot say "only if" here because of degenerate cases of categorical syllogisms that are valid, but not by virtue of their syllogistic form. Here is one example: "All numbers divisible by two are even. No prime number other than two is divisible by two. Therefore, no prime number other than two is even." This syllogism is valid because it is not possible that its premises are true and its conclusion is false, but other syllogisms with this same form are not valid.

Next, let's try a syllogism with a negative premise:

No ellipses have sides.
All circles are ellipses.
_____
∴ No circles have sides.

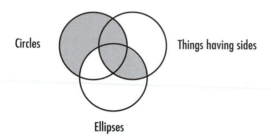

We diagram the conclusion "No circles have sides" as follows:

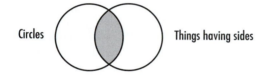

That information is already contained in the Venn diagram for the premises, so this syllogism is also valid.

Let us try a syllogism with a particular premise:

All squares have equal sides.
Some squares are rectangles.
_____
∴ Some rectangles have equal sides.

It is a good strategy to diagram a universal premise *before* diagramming a particular premise. The diagram for the above argument then looks like this:

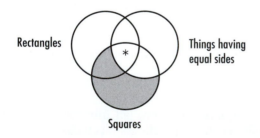

The conclusion—that there is something that is a rectangle that has equal sides—already appears in the diagram for the premises.

So far we have looked only at valid syllogisms. Let us see how this method applies to invalid syllogisms. Here is one:

All pediatricians are doctors.
All pediatricians like children.

∴ All doctors like children.

We can diagram the premises at the left and the conclusion at the right:

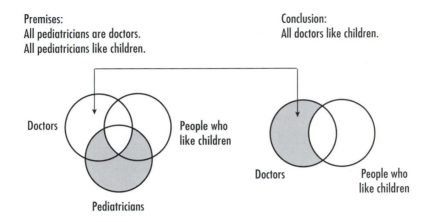

Premises:
All pediatricians are doctors.
All pediatricians like children.

Conclusion:
All doctors like children.

Doctors — People who like children

Pediatricians

Doctors — People who like children

It is evident that the information in the diagram for the conclusion is *not* already contained in the diagram for the premises. The arrow shows differences in informational content. Thus, this form of syllogism is not valid.

Notice that the difference between these diagrams not only tells us *that* this form of syllogism is invalid; it also tells us *why* it is invalid. In the diagram for the premises, there is no shading in the upper left-hand area, which includes people who are doctors but are not pediatricians and do not like children. This shows that the premises do not rule out the possibility that some people are doctors without being pediatricians or liking children. But if anyone is a doctor and not a person who likes children, then it is not true that all doctors like children. Because this is the conclusion of the syllogism, the premises do not rule out all of the ways in which the conclusion might be false. As a result, this conclusion does not follow.[3]

Here is an example of an invalid syllogism with particular premises:

Some doctors are golfers.
Some fathers are doctors.

∴ Some fathers are golfers.

_____

[3] Actually, all the diagram proves is that the syllogism is not valid *by virtue of its categorical form.* As we saw above, it still might be valid on some other basis. In this particular example, however, nothing else makes this argument valid.

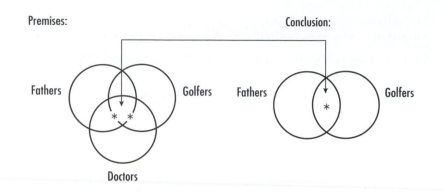

Examine this diagram closely. Notice that in diagramming "Some doctors are golfers," we had to put an asterisk *on the boundary* of the circle for fathers, because we were not given information saying whether anything falls into the category of fathers or not. For the same reason, we had to put an asterisk on the boundary of the circle for golfers when diagraming "Some fathers are doctors." The upshot was that we did not indicate that anything exists in the region of overlap between fathers and golfers. But this is what the conclusion demands, so the form of this syllogism is not valid.

Here is an invalid syllogism with negative premises:

No babies are golfers.
No fathers are babies.
─────────────────
∴ No fathers are golfers.

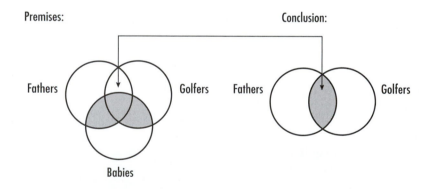

Again, we see that the form of this syllogism is not valid.

The method of Venn diagrams is adequate for deciding the validity or invalidity of all possible forms of categorical syllogism. For an alternative method using rules, see Appendix C.

EXERCISE VII

Using Venn diagrams, test the following syllogistic forms for validity:

1. All *M* is *P*.
   All *M* is *S*.
   ∴ All *S* is *P*.

2. All *P* is *M*.
   All *M* is *S*.
   ∴ All *S* is *P*.

3. All *M* is *P*.
   Some *M* is *S*.
   ∴ Some *S* is *P*.

4. All *P* is *M*.
   Some *M* is *S*.
   ∴ Some *S* is *P*.

5. All *P* is *M*.
   Some *S* is *M*.
   ∴ Some *S* is *P*.

6. All *P* is *M*.
   Some *S* is not *M*.
   ∴ Some *S* is not *P*.

7. All *M* is *P*.
   Some *S* is not *M*.
   ∴ Some *S* is not *P*.

8. All *M* is *P*.
   Some *M* is not *S*.
   ∴ Some *S* is not *P*.

9. No *M* is *P*.
   Some *S* is *M*.
   ∴ Some *S* is not *P*.

10. No *P* is *M*.
    Some *S* is *M*.
    ∴ Some *S* is not *P*.

11. No *P* is *M*.
    Some *S* is not *M*.
    ∴ Some *S* is not *P*.

12. No *M* is *P*.
    Some *S* is not *M*.
    ∴ Some *S* is not *P*

13. No *P* is *M*.
    Some *M* is not *S*.
    ∴ Some *S* is not *P*.

14. No *P* is *M*.
    No *M* is *S*.
    ∴ No *S* is *P*.

15. No *P* is *M*.
    All *M* is *S*.
    ∴ No *S* is *P*.

16. No *P* is *M*.
    All *S* is *M*.
    ∴ No *S* is *P*.

17. All *P* is *M*.
    No *S* is *M*.
    ∴ No *S* is *P*.

18. All *M* is *P*.
    No *S* is *M*.
    ∴ No *S* is *P*.

19. Some *M* is *P*.
    Some *M* is not *S*.
    ∴ Some *S* is not *P*.

20. Some *P* is *M*.
    Some *S* is not *M*.
    ∴ Some *S* is *P*.

Explain why it is a good strategy to diagram a universal premise before diagramming a particular premise.

PROBLEMS IN APPLYING THE THEORY OF THE SYLLOGISM.   After mastering the techniques for evaluating syllogisms, students naturally turn to arguments that arise in daily life and attempt to use these newly acquired skills. They are often disappointed with the results. The formal theory of the syllogism seems to bear little relationship to everyday arguments, and there does not seem to be any easy way to bridge the gap.

This gap between formal theory and its application occurs for a number of reasons. First, as we saw in Chapters 1 and 5, our everyday discourse leaves much unstated. Many things are conversationally implied rather than explicitly asserted. We do not feel called on to say many things that are matters of common agreement. Before we can apply the theory of the syllogism to everyday arguments, these things that are simply understood must be made explicit. This is often illuminating, and sometimes boring, but it usually involves a great deal of work. Second, the theory of the syllogism applies to statements only in a highly stylized form. Before we apply the theory of the syllogism to an argument, we must cast its premises and conclusion into the basic A, E, I, and O forms. As we saw earlier in this chapter, the needed translation is not always simple or obvious. It may not always be possible. For these and related reasons, modern logicians have largely abandoned the project of reducing all reasoning to syllogisms.

Why study the theory of the syllogism at all, if it is hard to apply in some circumstances and perhaps impossible to apply in others? The answer to this question was given at the beginning of Chapter 6. The study of formal logic is important because it deepens our insight into a central notion of logic: *validity.* Furthermore, the argument forms we have studied do underlie much of our everyday reasoning, but so much else is going on in a normal conversational setting that this dimension is often hidden. By examining arguments in idealized forms, we can study their validity in isolation from all the other factors at work in a rich conversational setting.

There is a difference, then, between the techniques developed in Chapters 1–5 and the techniques developed in Chapters 6–8. The first five chapters presented methods of informal analysis that may be applied directly to the rich and complex arguments that arise in everyday life. These methods of analysis are not wholly rigorous, but they do provide practical guides for the analysis and evaluation of actual arguments. The chapters concerning formal logic have the opposite tendency. In comparison with the first five chapters, the level of rigor is very high, but the range of application is correspondingly smaller. In general, the more rigor and precision you insist on, the less you can talk about.

DISCUSSION QUESTIONS

1. What are the chief differences between the logical procedures developed in this chapter and those developed in the chapter on propositional logic?
2. If we evaluate arguments as they occur in everyday life by using the exact standards developed in Chapters 6 and 7, we discover that our everyday arguments rarely satisfy these standards, at least explicity. Does this show that most of our ordinary arguments are illogical? What else might it show?

APPENDIX A: THE CLASSICAL THEORY

The difference between classical and modern logic is simply that the classical approach adds one more assumption—namely, that every categorical proposition is about something. More technically, the assumption is that A, E, I, and O propositions all carry commitment to the existence of something in the subject class and something in the predicate class. To draw Venn diagrams for categorical propositions on the classical interpretation, then, all we need to do is add existential commitment to the diagrams for their modern interpretations, which were discussed above.

But how should we add existential commitment to Venn diagrams? The answer might seem easy: Just put an asterisk wherever there is existential commitment. The story cannot be quite so simple, however, for the following reason. The Venn diagram for the E propositional form on the modern interpretation is this:

Modern E: No S is P.

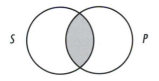

The classical interpretation adds existential commitment in both the subject and the predicate, so if we represent existential commitment with an asterisk, we get this diagram:

Classical E: No S is P. (???)

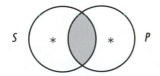

Although this diagram might seem to work, it breaks down when we perform operations on it. We are supposed to be able to diagram the contradictory of a proposition simply by substituting shading for asterisks and asterisks for shading. If we perform this operation on the previous diagram, we get this:

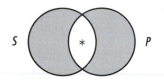

This diagram is very different from the Venn diagram for the I propositional form, which is the same on both classical and modern interpretations:

I: Some S is P.

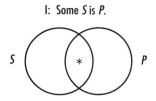

An I proposition, however, is supposed to be the contradictory of the corresponding E proposition even on the classical interpretation. So something has gone wrong. This problem shows that existential commitment cannot be treated exactly like explicit existential assertion, as in I and O propositions. As a result, we cannot use the same asterisk to represent existential commitment in Venn diagrams. Instead, we will use a plus sign: "+." With this new symbol, we can diagram the E propositional form on the classical interpretation this way:

Classical E: No S is P.

The plus sign indicates that an E proposition carries commitment to the existence of something in each class, even though it does not explicitly assert that something exists in either class.

From this new diagram, we can get the contradictory of a proposition by substituting shading for asterisks and asterisks for shading, as long as we also add plus signs to ensure that no class is empty, and drop plus signs that are no longer needed to indicate this existential commitment. When this procedure is applied to the previous diagram, the shading becomes an asterisk in the central area, and we can then drop the plus signs in the side areas because the central asterisk already assures us that something exists in both circles. Thus, we get the (modern and classical) diagram for the I propositional form. Moreover, when this procedure is applied to the diagram for the I propositional form, it yields the above diagram for the E propositional form on the classical interpretation.

It might not be so clear, however, that E and I propositions are contradictories on their classical interpretations; let us see why this is so. Two propositions are contradictories if and only if they cannot both be true and also cannot both be false. The diagram for an E proposition has shading in the same area in which the diagram for its corresponding I proposition has an asterisk, so they cannot both be true. It is harder to see why these propositions cannot both be false on the classical interpretation, but this can be shown by the following argument. Suppose that an I proposition is false. Then there is nothing in the central area, so that area should be shaded. The classical interpretation insists that the subject and predicate classes are not empty, so if there is nothing in the central area, there must be something in each side area, which is indicated by a plus sign in each side area. That gives us the diagram for the corresponding E proposition, so that proposition is true. Thus, if an I proposition is false, its corresponding E proposition is true. That means that they cannot both be false. We already saw that they cannot both be true. So they are contradictories.

The same procedure yields a classical O proposition when it is applied to a classical A proposition, and a classical A proposition when it is applied to a classical O proposition:

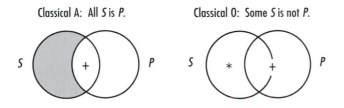

Classical A: All S is P.   Classical O: Some S is not P.

(The plus sign on the line indicates that the commitment is to something in the right-hand circle, but not to anything in either specific part of that circle.) Propositions of these forms on their classical interpretations cannot both be true and cannot both be false, so they are contradictories. Thus, this method of diagramming seems to capture the classical interpretation of the basic propositions.

EXERCISE IX

Explain why an A proposition and its corresponding O proposition are contradictories on their classical interpretations, using the diagrams above.

THE CLASSICAL SQUARE OF OPPOSITION

In addition to the contradictories, there is a more extensive and elegant set of logical relationships among categorical propositions on the classical interpretation. This system of relationships produces what has been called the *square of opposition.*

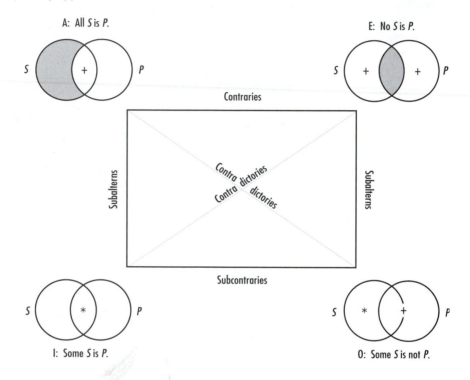

The lines in this diagram show the logical relationships each proposition has to the other three. These relationships are explained below. Throughout the discussion, it is important to remember that all of the basic propositions are interpreted as carrying existential commitment in both their subjects and their predicates.

CONTRADICTORIES.   Two propositions are *contradictories* of each other (and they contradict each other) when they are related in the following way:

1. They cannot both be true, and
2. They cannot both be false.

More simply, contradictory pairs of propositions always have opposite truth values. We have already seen that the E and I propositions are contradictories of one another, as are the A and O propositions. This relationship holds on both the modern interpretation and the classical interpretation.

CONTRARIES.   Two propositions are said to be *contraries* of one another if they are related in this way:

1. They cannot both be true, but
2. They can both be false.

On the classical interpretation (but not the modern interpretation), A and E propositions with the same subject and predicate are contraries of one another.

In common life, the relationship between such corresponding A and E propositions is captured by the notion that one claim is the *complete opposite* of another. The complete opposite of "Everyone is here" is "No one is here." Clearly, such complete opposites cannot both be true at once. We see this readily if we look at the diagrams for A and E propositions on the classical interpretation. The middle region of the diagram for an A proposition shows the existence of something that is both S and P, whereas the middle region of the diagram for the corresponding E proposition is shaded, showing that nothing is both S and P. It should also be clear that these A and E propositions can both be false. Suppose that there is some S that is P and also some S that is not P:

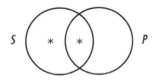

Going from left to right, the first asterisk shows that the A proposition of the form "All S is P" is false; the second asterisk shows that the corresponding E proposition of the form "No S is P" is also false. Thus, these propositions can both be false, but they cannot both be true. This makes them contraries.

SUBCONTRARIES.   Propositions are *subcontraries* of one another when

1. They can both be true, and
2. They cannot both be false.

On the classical approach (but not the modern approach), corresponding I and O propositions are subcontraries. To see how this works, compare the diagrams for I and O propositions:

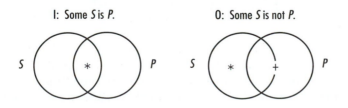

It should be clear that corresponding propositions with these forms can both be true, since there can be some *S* that is *P* and another *S* that is not *P*. But why can they not both be false? Consider the left-hand side of the following diagram:

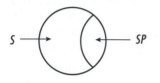

We know that, on the classical approach, there must be something in this circle somewhere. If there is something in the overlapping region *SP*, then the I proposition is true. If there is something in the nonoverlapping region of *S*, then there must be something else in the circle for *P*, because *P* cannot be empty on the classical approach; therefore, the O proposition is true. Thus, either the I proposition or the corresponding O proposition must be true, so they cannot both be false. We already saw that they can both be true. Consequently, corresponding I and O propositions are subcontraries.

SUBALTERNS.   *Subalternation* is the relationship that holds down the sides of the classical square of opposition. Quite simply, an A proposition implies the corresponding I proposition, and an E proposition implies the corresponding O proposition. This relationship depends on the existential commitment found on the classical approach and does not hold on the modern approach.
    The validity of subalternation is illustrated by the following diagrams:

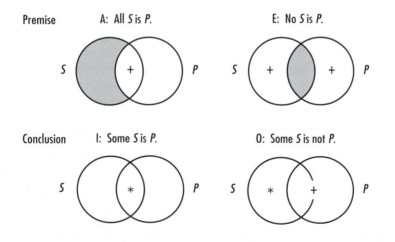

An A proposition includes a plus sign where the corresponding I proposition includes an asterisk, but both symbols indicate that something lies in the middle area. Thus, the information for the I proposition is already included in the diagram for the A proposition, which means that the A proposition implies the I proposition.

The same point applies to the implication on the right-hand side, because the diagram for an E proposition includes a plus sign in the same area as the asterisk in the diagram for the corresponding O proposition. The diagram for the E proposition also has a plus sign in the rightmost area. If something exists in that area, then something exists in either that area or the middle area, which is what is meant by the plus sign on the line in the diagram for the O proposition. Thus, an E proposition implies its corresponding O proposition.

The information given by the classical square of opposition can now be summarized in two charts. We shall ask two questions. First, for each propositional form, if we assume that a proposition with that form is *true*, what consequences follow for the truth or falsity of a corresponding proposition with a different form?

		A	E	I	O
	A	T	F	T	F
Assumed true	E	F	T	F	T
	I	?	F	T	?
	O	F	?	?	T

"T" indicates that the corresponding proposition in that column is true, "F" indicates that it is false, and "?" indicates that it might have either truth value, because neither consequence follows.

Second, for each propositional form, if we assume that a proposition with that form is *false*, what consequences follow for the truth or falsity of a corresponding proposition with a different form?

		A	E	I	O
	A	F	?	?	T
Assumed false	E	?	F	T	?
	I	F	T	F	T
	O	T	F	T	F

THE CLASSICAL THEORY OF IMMEDIATE INFERENCE

The difference between the modern and classical approaches is simply that the classical approach assigns more information—specifically, existential commitment—to the basic propositions than the modern interpretation does. Because of this additional information, certain immediate inferences hold on the classical approach that do not hold on the modern approach. In particular, though conversion of an A proposition fails on both approaches, what is known as *conversion by limitation* holds on the classical approach but not on the modern approach. That is, from a proposition with the form "All S is P," we may not validly infer the proposition with the form "All P is S," but on the classical approach, we may validly infer "*Some P is S.*" The reason is simple: From a proposition with the form "All S is P" on the classical interpretation, we may infer a proposition with the form "*Some S is P*," and then we may convert this to get a proposition with the form "*Some P is S*."

EXERCISE X

Using the Venn diagrams for the classical interpretation of the A propositional form given above, show that conversion by limitation is classically valid for an A proposition.

THE CLASSICAL THEORY OF SYLLOGISMS

As in the case of immediate inferences, the premises of syllogisms will contain more information—specifically, existential commitment—on the classical interpretation than they do on the modern interpretation. This will make some syllogisms valid on the classical approach that were not valid on the modern approach.

We begin our study of this matter with an example that has had a curious history:

> All rectangles are four-sided.
> All squares are rectangles.
>
> ∴ *Some* squares are four-sided.

The argument is peculiar because its conclusion is weaker than it needs to be. We could, after all, conclude that *all* squares are four-sided. The argument thus violates the conversational rule of Quantity. Perhaps for this reason, this syllogism was often not included in traditional lists of valid syllogisms. Yet the argument is valid on the classical interpretation of existential commitment, and our diagram should show this.

Step I: Diagram the first premise

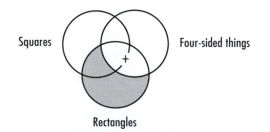

Notice that the plus sign is placed on the outer edge of the circle for squares, because we are not in a position to put it either inside or outside that circle. We now add the information for the second premise:

Step II: Add the second premise

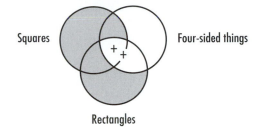

Squares   Four-sided things

Rectangles

As expected, the conclusion that some squares are four-sided is already dia-grammed, so the argument is valid—provided that we take A propositions to have existential commitment.

Because classical logicians tended to ignore the previous argument, their writings did not bring out the importance of existential commitment in eval-uating it. There is, however, an argument that did appear on the classical lists that makes clear the demand for existential commitment. These are syl-logisms with the following form:

All *M* is *P*.
All *M* is *S*.
∴ Some *S* is *P*.

This form of syllogism is diagrammed as follows:

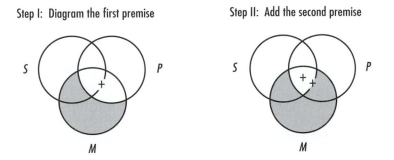

Step I: Diagram the first premise   Step II: Add the second premise

Again, we see that the conclusion follows, but only if we diagram A propo-sitions to indicate existential commitment. This, then, is an argument that was declared valid on the classical approach, but invalid on the modern approach.

EXERCISE XI

Use Venn diagrams to test the following syllogism forms for validity on the classical approach:

1. All *M* is *P.*
   No *M* is *S.*
   ∴ Some *S* is not *P.*

2. No *M* is *P.*
   All *M* is *S.*
   ∴ Some *S* is not *P.*

3. No *M* is *P.*
   All *S* is *M.*
   ∴ Some *S* is not *P.*

4. No *M* is *P.*
   No *M* is *S.*
   ∴ Some *S* is not *P.*

EXERCISE XII

Are the following claims true or false? Explain your answers.

1. Every syllogism that is valid on the modern approach is also valid on the classical approach.
2. Every syllogism that is valid on the classical approach but not on the modern approach has a particular conclusion that starts with "Some."

APPENDIX B: IMMEDIATE INFERENCES WITH COMPLEMENTARY CLASSES

The standard theory of immediate inference includes not only conversion but also obversion and contraposition. These other inferences are more complicated than conversion, because they employ complements of classes.

The complement of a class is simple enough to define. Given any class *C,* its *complement* or *complementary class* is the class that includes all those things that are not in *C.* A *complementary term* is a term that refers to the complement of the class in question. One standard way of referring to the complementary class is to use the prefix "non." Here are some examples:

Class	Complementary Class
Residents	Nonresidents
Combatants	Noncombatants
Republicans	Non-Republicans
Squares	Nonsquares

A bar over a letter indicates a complementary class. If R is the class of Republicans, then $\bar{R}$ is the class of non-Republicans. If we look at the class of non-Republicans, we see that it is a mixed bag, for we have defined it as everything that is not a Republican. This includes coyotes, subatomic particles, prime numbers, and the British royal family. In everyday life, we do not wish to include all these things in our notion of a non-Republican. When we speak about non-Republicans, the context will usually make it clear that we are referring to people, and even to a limited group of people, such as American voters. In other words, talk about non-Republicans normally *presupposes* that we are considering only persons or voting Americans.

We can capture this idea by using the notion of a *domain of discourse*. We might say that the domain of discourse here includes all Americans who can vote. A non-Republican is then someone in this domain of discourse who is not a Republican. To reflect this domain of discourse, we need to make our diagrams a bit more elaborate. We will enclose the circles with a box that indicates the *domain of discourse* (DD):

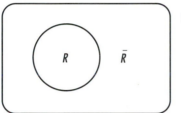

DD: Voting Americans

When two or more circles are used, we will assume that they share a domain of discourse, so we will enclose them all in the same box.

Deciding on a domain of discourse is somewhat arbitrary. It depends on good sense and present interests. In our example, we might have taken the domain of discourse to include only members of political parties, or perhaps only American politicians. Actually, it is not always useful to specify the domain of discourse precisely, although sometimes it is. In this discussion, we will be quite casual about specifying a domain of discourse, and will only do so when it serves some useful purpose.

OBVERSION

We can now define the immediate inference called *obversion*. To pass from a basic proposition to its obverse, we do the following:

1. Reverse the quality of the proposition (that is, change it from affirmative to negative or negative to affirmative, as the case may be).
2. Replace the predicate term with its complementary term.

Starting with "All men are mortal," this two-step process works as follows:

1. Reversing the quality yields: "No men are mortal."
2. Replacing the predicate term with its complement yields: "No men are nonmortal."

This final proposition is the obverse of "All men are mortal."

We now want to know when this operation of obversion is legitimate—that is, when obversion yields an immediate inference that is valid. The answer to this is that a proposition is always logically equivalent to its obverse.[4] To show this, we will run through the four basic propositional forms. Because all these equivalences hold between a proposition and its obverse, there is no need to draw a diagram twice. The reader should, however, check to see whether the diagram is accurate for both propositions.

> A: A proposition with the form "All S is P" is logically equivalent to its obverse, which has the form "No S is non-P."

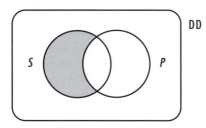

In this diagram, the class of things that are non-P includes all those things in the domain of discourse that are not in P. We can see that there is nothing in the class of things that are S that is also in the complementary class of P, because all the things in S are in the class P. This might sound a bit complicated, but with a little thought the validity of inferences through obversion becomes obvious.

> E: A proposition with the form "No S is P" is logically equivalent to its obverse, which has the form "All S is non-P."

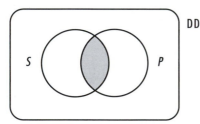

> I: A proposition with the form "Some S is P" is logically equivalent to its obverse, which has the form "Some S is not non-P."

[4]This equivalence also holds in the classical system, because the standard classical theory assumes that not only the subject and predicate classes but also the complements of these classes are not empty; they have something in them.

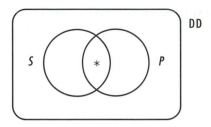

O: A proposition with the form "Some S is not P" is logically equivalent to its obverse, which has the form "Some S is non-P."

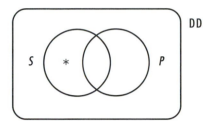

It is important to see that the final equivalence is a genuine equivalence and not a mere repetition. A proposition with the form "Some S is not P" is an O proposition, whereas a proposition with the form "Some S is non-P" is an I proposition. That is, the first proposition is negative, for it indicates that there is at least one thing that is *not* in a certain class. The second proposition is affirmative, for it indicates that something *is* in a given class—a complementary class.

CONTRAPOSITION

Contraposition is the final relationship we shall examine. We get the *contrapositive* of a proposition by using the following two-step process:

1. We convert the proposition.
2. We replace both terms with their complementary terms.

For example, starting with "All men are mortal," this two-step process works as follows:

1. We convert "All men are mortal" to get "All mortal things are men."
2. We replace each term with its complement to get "All nonmortal things are nonmen."

The final proposition is the contrapositive of "All men are mortal."

We must now ask when the contrapositive can be validly inferred from a given proposition. Here the situation is generally the reverse of what we discovered for conversion:

A: A proposition with the form "All *S* is *P*" is logically equivalent to its contrapositive, which has the form "All non-*P* is non-*S*."

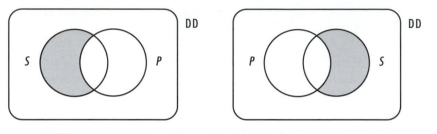

E: From a proposition with the form "No *S* is *P*" we may not always validly infer its contrapositive,[5] which has the form "No non-*P* is non-*S*."

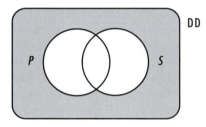

I: From a proposition with the form "Some *S* is *P*," we may not always validly infer its contrapositive, which has the form "Some non-*P* is non-*S*."

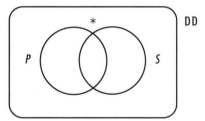

O: A proposition with the form "Some *S* is not *P*" is logically equivalent to its contrapositive, which has the form "Some non-*P* is not non-*S*."

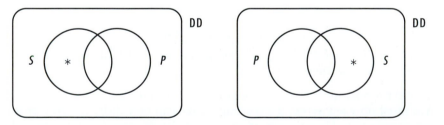

[5]The qualification is needed here and in the next case because of degenerate cases of immediate inferences with this form that are valid, but not by virtue of their categorical form.

The following table summarizes all these equivalence relationships:

Propositional Form	Obverse	Converse	Contrapositive
A: All S is P.	No S is non-P. (Equivalent)	All P is S. (does *not* follow)	All non-P is non-S. (Equivalent)
E: No S is P.	All S is non-P. (Equivalent)	No P is S. (Equivalent)	No non-P is non-S. (does *not* follow)
I: Some S is P.	Some S is not non-P. (Equivalent)	Some P is S. (Equivalent)	Some non-P is non-S. (does *not* follow)
O: Some S is not P.	Some S is non-P. (Equivalent)	Some P is not S. (does *not* follow)	Some non-P is not non-S. (Equivalent)

If we compare the propositions we have been studying with remarks that we make in everyday life, some of them, at least, will seem artificial. It is hard to imagine a case in which we would actually say, "Some nonspies are not nonaliens." It would certainly be easier to say, "Some aliens are not spies," which is its equivalent by contraposition.

In fact, we do use these complicated sentences in some contexts. Discussing the voting patterns of nonresidents, we might find ourselves saying that some nonresidents are not nonvoters. Given the context, this remark loses much of its oddness. Usually, however, we choose simple, clear formulations. The ability to do this depends on an implicit understanding of the logical relationships within this system of propositions. Here we are trying to bring this implicit understanding to the surface so that we can understand it better. That is, we are trying to give clear rules for inferences that we make routinely in everyday life.

EXERCISE XII

For each of the following propositions, use Venn diagrams to determine which of the above immediate inferences are valid.

Example: All ministers are noncombatants.

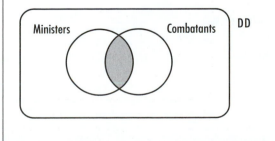

Obverse: No ministers are non-noncombatants.

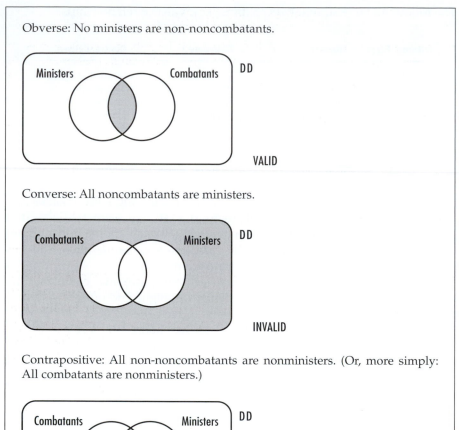

Converse: All noncombatants are ministers.

Contrapositive: All non-noncombatants are nonministers. (Or, more simply: All combatants are nonministers.)

1. Some dudes are not cowards.
2. All nonresidents are taxpayers.
3. Some nonaligned nations are wealthy (nations).
4. No daughters are sons.
5. No nonnegotiable stocks are safe (stocks).
6. All that glitters is not gold.
7. Some people cannot be bought.
8. There is no such thing as a bad boy.

EXERCISE XIV

Put the following sentences into plain, respectable English. Indicate the immediate inference or immediate inferences you have used to do so. (Be careful!)

1. No noncombatant is a minister.
2. Some nonresident is not a non-nonvoter.
3. Not all snakes are not dangerous (things).
4. No all-time losers are non-nonpersons.

APPENDIX C: A SYSTEM OF RULES FOR EVALUATING SYLLOGISMS

The method of Venn diagrams that we have used in this chapter is probably
the most natural technique for analyzing and evaluating syllogisms, because
the relationship between overlapping figures is a clear analogy for the relationship between classes. Another method for evaluating syllogisms employs
a system of rules. Although this system has less intuitive appeal than Venn
diagrams do, it is easier to apply. The procedure is to lay down a set of rules
such that any form of syllogism that satisfies all of the rules is valid, and any
form of syllogism that fails to satisfy any one of them is invalid.

QUALITY

The system of rules that we will present here starts with the idea of the *quality* of a proposition—whether it is affirmative or negative. Recall that A and I
propositions are said to be *affirmative* propositions, and E and O propositions
are said to be *negative* propositions.

QUANTITY

The next idea used in this system of rules concerns the *quantity* of a proposition—whether it is universal or particular. Recall that A and E propositions
are said to be *universal* propositions, and I and O propositions are said to be
particular propositions.

DISTRIBUTION

The final idea used in these rules is new. It is the notion of the *distribution* or
extension of a term. The basic idea is that a term is used distributively in a
proposition if it is used to refer to the whole of a class or to all the members
in it. We shall first simply state the distributional properties for A, E, I, and O
propositions and then try to make sense out of the notion.

Proposition	Subject	Predicate
A	Distributed	Undistributed
E	Distributed	Distributed
I	Undistributed	Undistributed
O	Undistributed	Distributed

The subject term is distributed in universal (A and E) propositions because they refer to *all* S. In contrast, particular (I and O) propositions are about *some* S, so the subject term is undistributed in these propositions.

The reasoning thus runs smoothly for the subject term, but the predicate term is not so easy to deal with. Notice that there is no word like "some" or "all" governing the predicate term. The reasoning for the predicate term usually proceeds along the following lines. Suppose we assert that no squares are circles.

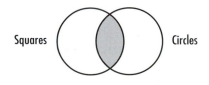

For this to be true, there can be no square that is identical with *any* circle. The appearance of the word "any" shows that the predicate term is distributed in this E proposition. Consider next the corresponding O proposition: Some square is not a circle. For this to be true, there must be some square that is not identical with *any* circle. Again, the appearance of the word "any" shows that the predicate term is distributed in this O proposition. In contrast, consider the I proposition that some closed figures are circles. This means that some closed figures are identical with some circles. The word "any" does not appear, so the predicate term is not distributed in this I proposition. Our test for the distribution of terms is then to compare the basic A, E, I, or O proposition with a counterpart statement involving identity as follows:

A:	All *S* is *P*.	For *any* S, there is *some* P that is identical with it.
E:	No *S* is *P*.	For *any* S, there is not *any* P that is identical with it.
I:	Some *S* is *P*.	For *some* S, there is *some* P that is identical with it.
O:	Some *S* is not *P*.	For *some* S, there is not *any* P that is identical with it.

This comparison gives the pattern for the distribution of terms noticed earlier.

THE RULES

Now, using the ideas of quality, quantity, and distribution, we can formulate a set of rules that are adequate for testing the validity of all forms of categorical syllogism on the modern approach.

Rules of Quality:

1. Nothing follows from two negative premises.
2. If one premise is negative, then the conclusion must also be negative.

Rules of Distribution:

3. The middle term must be distributed at least once.
4. The subject term may not be distributed in the conclusion if it is not distributed in the premises.
5. The predicate term may not be distributed in the conclusion if it is not distributed in the premises.

Rule of Quantity:

6. A particular conclusion cannot be derived from two universal premises.[6]

The fallacies that result from violating these rules are called by the following names:

1. The fallacy of *two negative premises*
2. The fallacy of *deriving an affirmative conclusion from a negative premise*
3. The fallacy of *undistributed middle*
4. The fallacy of *illicitly distributed subject*
5. The fallacy of *illicitly distributed predicate*
6. The fallacy of *deriving a particular conclusion from two universal premises*

The following devices facilitate the application of these rules. Mark each proposition in the syllogism with "+" or "−" to indicate its quality. Circle all terms that are distributed, leaving all undistributed terms uncircled. This makes it easy to see if the first five rules of the syllogism have been satisfied, and so whether the syllogism is valid or invalid. No special devices are necessary to check the sixth rule.

The following examples illustrate these methods:

(1) + All (M) is P.   Valid
    + All (S) is M.
    ∴ + All (S) is P.

(2) − No (M) is (P).   Valid
    + Some M is S.
    ∴ − Some S is not (P).

---

[6]The classical theory of the syllogism does not contain a rule of quantity of this kind. It does, however, contain an additional quality rule: 2*. If the conclusion is negative, then one premise must be negative. The fallacy that results from violating rule 2* can be called the fallacy of *deriving a negative conclusion from two affirmative premises*.

(3) + All Ⓜ is P.   Invalid[7]–
 + All Ⓜ is S.   Particular conclusion from universal premises
 ∴ + Some S is P.

(4) + All Ⓜ is P.   Invalid–
 + All Ⓜ is S.   Illicitly distributed subject
 ∴ + All Ⓢ is P.

(5) + All Ⓟ is M.   Invalid–
 + All Ⓢ is M.   Undistributed middle
 ∴ + All Ⓢ is P.

(6) – No Ⓟ is Ⓜ.   Invalid–
 – No Ⓢ is Ⓜ.   Two negative premises
 ∴ – No Ⓢ is Ⓟ.

EXERCISE XV

Using the rules in this appendix, test the syllogisms given in Exercise VII for validity. Where a fallacy occurs, give the name of that fallacy.

EXERCISE XVI

Using the rules in this appendix, test the syllogisms given in Exercise XI for validity. Where a fallacy occurs, give the name of that fallacy.

HONORS EXERCISE

To a person familiar with computer programming, this system of rules immediately suggests that a program can be written for the evaluation of syllogisms. In fact, such a program can be written and is only moderately difficult. The first problem is to find some method for encoding all possible syllogisms. After this, the notions of distribution and quality must be given mathematical analogues. In writing such a program, there is a good chance that the programmer will rediscover large portions of medieval logic. Try it.

[7]This form of syllogism is valid in the classical approach.

THE FORMAL ANALYSIS OF ARGUMENTS: QUANTIFICATIONAL LOGIC

Modern quantificational logic makes fundamental and far-reaching advances over previous logical theories. It not only introduces mathematical rigor into the study of logic but also presents a theory with a much wider range of application than any previous logical theory. It encompasses propositional logic, categorical logic, and much more that could not be dealt with in either of these two logical systems. Quantificational theory, when fully developed, becomes very complicated, so it is not possible to give a complete account of it here. This chapter is intended to do three things: explain the basic concepts of quantificational logic, show how sentences of everyday language can be translated into the notation of quantificational logic, and show how validity can be determined in one restricted area of quantificational logic.

COMBINING TWO BRANCHES OF LOGIC

In Chapter 6 we examined propositional logic, the logic concerned with truth-functional connections between propositions. In Chapter 7 we examined categorical logic, including the theory of immediate inference and the theory of the categorical syllogism—roughly, the logic concerned with relationships between classes of things.[1] We have presented these two branches of logic independently of one another. In fact, for centuries these two branches of logic were treated separately, and there was some debate concerning which was more important or more fundamental. A central achievement of modern symbolic logic was to combine these previously separate areas of logic into a single coherent system.[2] In this chapter we will examine some of the fundamental ideas involved in this important synthesis. Although we cannot present a fully developed system of quantificational logic, we can examine some of its basic ideas and show how they help us

---

[1]Although this chapter contains a number of references to Chapter 7, it is not necessary to have read that chapter to follow the present discussion, as the material referred to in Chapter 7 is explained again here. However, this chapter cannot be understood without a thorough grasp of the material discussed in Chapter 6.

[2]The pioneering work in this area was done by Gottlob Frege (1848–1925) and Bertrand Russell (1872–1970).

understand arguments in daily life that cannot be dealt with using the methods developed in the previous two chapters.

We will begin by presenting a new way of interpreting the four basic propositional forms discussed in Chapter 7—the A, E, I, and O categorical propositional forms:

A: All *S* is *P.*

E: No *S* is *P.*

I: Some *S* is *P.*

O: Some *S* is not *P.*

We will first show how these propositional forms are handled using modern logical techniques. We will then show how these modern techniques can be extended to deal with a vast number of other propositional forms (and hence argument forms) not addressed in traditional logic.

THE INTRODUCTION OF QUANTIFIERS

The following is an example of an A proposition:

1. All sisters are female.

There are various ways we might paraphrase this proposition to bring out its logical structure. The following sounds like a reasonable paraphrase:

2. Anyone who is a sister is also female.

That seems to say:

3. Take anything at all, if it is a sister, then it is female.

Thus, (3) suggests that (1) has an underlying conditional form. Modern logicians capture the meaning of (3) more formally by using the following translation:

4. For all *x*, if *x* is a sister, then *x* is female.

If we examine this formula, we see that it begins with the expression "For all *x*." Logicians call expressions of this kind *quantifiers* because they indicate the quantity or range of things being referred to. The expression "for all *x*" indicates that we are referring to *all* instances of *x* rather than, say, to *some* or *most* of them. The symbol "(*x*)" is used to express "for all *x*." Because this expression refers to all instances of *x*, it is called the *universal* quantifier. Propositions that begin with this quantifier are called *universally quantified propositions.* So we can begin our translation of (4) in the following way:

5. (*x*) (if *x* is a sister, then *x* is female).

In (5), the quantifier "For all *x*" is followed by the clause "if *x* is a sister, then *x* is female." This expression has a conditional form, but it is clearly not a propositional conditional, because neither "*x* is a sister" nor "*x* is female" expresses a proposition. Neither, that is, says anything either true or false.

Here the letter "*x*" functions as a variable, which means that it can be replaced by names, but "*x* is a sister" does not express a proposition *until* "*x*" is replaced by a name. Logicians symbolize expressions of the form "*x* is a sister" as "*Sx*," where "*S*" refers to the property of being a sister. Adopting this convention, we can symbolize "*x* is female" as "*Fx*," where "*F*" refers to the property of being female. Here, by tradition, properties are represented by capital letters; lowercase letters from the end of the alphabet are used to stand for variables. We can now symbolize the universally quantified proposition "For all *x*, if *x* is a sister, then *x* is female" as follows:

6. $(x) (Sx \supset Fx)$

Having translated an affirmative A proposition, we turn next to a negative E proposition. Just as we can say that *all* sisters are female, we can, in contrast, say that *no* brothers are female. We can express this second claim as follows:

7. For all *x*, if *x* is a brother, then it is not the case that *x* is female.

Symbolically:[3]

8. $(x) (Bx \supset \sim Fx)$

This, then, is the way to translate a traditional E proposition into quantificational notation.

Having translated A and E propositions into the notation of modern quantificational theory, is there a way of doing the same thing for I and O propositions? Although these translations can be made using the universal quantifier already introduced, this produces cumbersome translations that are hard to understand. For this reason a second quantifier, called the *existential quantifier*, is normally added to the notation. The intuitive idea is to analyze a proposition, such as "Some ferns are green," as saying:

9. There is at least one thing that is a fern and is green.

If we employ variables, (9) becomes:

10. There is at least one *x* such that *x* is F and *x* is G.

Here the leading phrase "There exists at least one *x*" expresses the existential quantifier. We will represent it using the symbol "$(\exists x)$." Because the remainder of (10) is a conjunction, it gets translated thus:

11. $(Fx \mathbin{\&} Gx)$

And (10) is fully translated thus:

12. $(\exists x) (Fx \mathbin{\&} Gx)$

---

[3]Where the context makes it clear, we will usually not offer an explicit interpretation of the symbols we use. In this example, it would be a waste of time to point out that "*Bx*" means "*x* is a brother."

All propositions with the form "Some Fs are Gs" can be translated in this way. Similarly, propositions of the form "Some Fs are not Gs" (such as "Some ferns are not green") can be translated thus:

13. $(\exists x)\,(Fx\ \&\ {\sim}Gx)$

There is something a bit odd about these translations, since "some" is usually taken to mean *more* than one rather than *at least* one. (It would be odd to say, "Some women are the queen of England" when only one is.) As it turns out, however, this shift from ordinary language is a great simplification. One reason is that "There is at least one thing that is *F*" means the same as "It is not the case that everything is not *F*." Symbolically, "$(\exists x)Fx$" can be defined as "${\sim}(x){\sim}Fx$." In any case, a fully developed theory provides ways of saying *more than one* if that needs to be said, so nothing is lost by interpreting the existential quantifier to mean "at least one."[4]

To summarize, the traditional A, E, I, and O propositions are translated into the notation of quantification theory as follows:

A:	All *Fs* are *Gs*	$(x)(Fx \supset Gx)$
E:	No *Fs* are *Gs*	$(x)(Fx \supset {\sim}Gx)$
I:	Some *Fs* are *Gs*	$(\exists x)(Fx\ \&\ Gx)$
O:	Some *Fs* are not *Gs*	$(\exists x)(Fx\ \&\ {\sim}Gx)$

EXERCISE I

Using the suggested symbols to the right of each sentence, translate it into the language of quantification theory, first in prose, then symbolically.

Example: No swans are green. (*S, G*)

        For any *x*, if *x* is a swan, then *x* is not green.

        $(x)(Sx \supset {\sim}Gx)$

Example: Some pigs eat turnips. (*P, T* = "is a turnip eater")

        There is at least one *x* such that *x* is a pig and *x* is a turnip eater.

        $(\exists x)(Px\ \&\ Tx)$

1. All whales are mammals. (*W, M*)
2. Every story has two sides. (*S, T*)
3. Some courses are not boring. (*C, B*)
4. Some students are boring. (*S, B*)
5. Elephants are mammals. (*E, M*)
6. Cobras are never good pets. (*C, P*)

---

[4]The decision here in some ways parallels our earlier decision to take inclusive disjunction as primary and define exclusive disjunction when the need arises.

7. Anyone who smokes is a fool. (*S, F*)
8. There aren't any Civil War veterans alive today. (*V, A*)
9. Some questions are hard to answer. (*Q, H*)
10. Some questions are not hard to answer. (*Q, H*)

LIMITED DOMAINS

If we let "*Hx*" mean "*x* is happy," then "(*x*)*Hx*" says that everything is happy. This is clearly false, because at least some people are not happy. But since the claim is literally about *everything*, it is also false because there are trees that are not happy, waves in the middle of the ocean that are not happy, numbers that are not happy, and so on. Generally, when we use words such as "everything," "all," or "some," we have in mind a more restricted domain than literally everything. Sometimes we use language that explicitly makes this clear. For example, when we use such words as "everybody," "somebody," "everyone," or "someone," we are indicating that we are referring to people. At other times we rely on context to fix the domain of things under consideration. Seeing an empty place at the dinner table, a person might remark, "Someone isn't here." To this the reply, "Of course someone isn't here; billions of people are not here" would clearly be out of order. As the context makes clear, in saying "Someone isn't here," the speaker does not have in mind all human beings, just those who were expected to attend the dinner. This example shows that a domain is assumed even when we use an existential quantifier.

It is, in fact, always possible to make clear what domain of things we are concerned with, and many logic texts insist that this always be done. This strikes us as excessively fussy. Except for cases in which confusion might arise, we will rely on context to determine the domain of things under consideration. There is, however, one restriction you need to remember in order to avoid confusion. If one sentence in an argument is about people, but another sentence in the same argument is about animals, then you should not limit the domain to people when translating the first sentence, because then you will need a different domain to translate the sentence about animals. The domain that you assume should always be big enough to be used consistently throughout the whole argument that you are translating.

ELABORATE A, E, I, AND O PROPOSITIONS

Because we have the resources of Chapter 6 at our command, we can easily construct complex propositions not normally considered in categorical logic. For example, the proposition "All males over age eighteen are eligible for the draft" is translated thus:

$(x)((Mx \mathbin{\&} Ox) \supset Ex)$

Here "Ox" symbolizes "x is over age eighteen." The interpretation of the other symbols is obvious. Here is another example: "All major-league teams are either in the National League or in the American League" is translated thus:

$$(x)(Mx \supset (Nx \vee Ax))$$

Existential generalizations can have complex contents as well. For example, the proposition "Someone here is either stupid or wicked" is translated thus:

$$(\exists x)(Hx \mathbin{\&} (Sx \vee Wx))$$

Thus, quantificational theory combines the resources of propositional logic with the resources of categorical logic in a way that allows us to symbolize many different kinds of propositions.

The examples we have given thus far are straightforward and present no special problems for translation. Sometimes, however, it is easy to go wrong. Consider the claim that both men and women may attend West Point. If you did not stop to think about it, you might be tempted to translate this as follows:

$$(x)((Mx \mathbin{\&} Wx) \supset Ax)$$

(Here, "Ax" means "x may attend West Point.") What that says is that any-one who is both a man and a woman may attend West Point—certainly not the point of the original statement. The correct translation is:

$$(x)((Mx \vee Wx) \supset Ax)$$

which means "Anyone who is either a man or a woman may attend West Point."

There is, in fact, no purely mechanical way of translating sentences from English into the symbolism of quantification theory. One problem, already mentioned in Chapter 7, is that the words used in a sentence do not always indicate whether all or only some things of a certain kind are being referred to. The following sentences illustrate this:

Dogs have fleas.
Dogs have a good sense of smell.

The first sentence is most naturally interpreted as "Some dogs have fleas." The second is most naturally interpreted as "All dogs, or at least all *normal* dogs, have a good sense of smell." The correct way to interpret a sentence often depends on its context.

Problems can also arise from the complexity of the sentence we are attempting to translate. Here, two rules of thumb for translating quantified propositions will prove helpful.

Universally quantified statements very often take the following form:

$$(x)(\quad \supset \quad)$$

This is the pattern for both A propositions and E propositions, and many propositions are simple or complex versions of A or E propositions.

Existentially quantified statements very often take the following form:

$(\exists x) (\quad \& \quad)$

This is the pattern for both I propositions and O propositions, and many propositions are simple or complex versions of I or O propositions.

Although a great many sentences can be translated into one of these two forms—including all the examples given in this section—other patterns of translation are possible. That is why we speak of a *rule of thumb* for translating quantified propositions. A simple example of a proposition that does not fit either pattern is "Everything is interesting," which is translated thus:

$(x)Ix$

EXERCISE II

Using the suggested letters, translate the following propositions into the language of quantification theory:

1. Nothing lasts forever. (L = lasts forever)
2. Everything is either good or bad. (G, B)
3. Some person either stole the book or took it by mistake. (P, S, M)
4. Oysters and clams are delicious. (O, C, D)
5. Anyone who is sick or injured will be evacuated first. (S, I, F)
6. No varsity football players are both slow and tiny. (V, S, T)
7. No decent human being will attend. (D, H, A)
8. Croats, Muslims, and Serbs are all human beings. (C, M, S, H)
9. The thing in the box is animal, vegetable, or mineral. (B, A, V, M)
10. Old soldiers never die; they just fade away. (O, S, D, F)

RELATIONS AND MULTIPLE QUANTIFIERS

Consider the following proposition:

1. Some cats are bigger than some dogs.

This proposition differs from propositions we have already discussed in two ways: (1) It contains the *relational* term "bigger than," and (2) it contains two occurrences of the quantifier "some." Both involve significant departures from what we have seen before. We will consider these new developments one at a time.

Until now, we have dealt only with *properties* that individual things possess. We have symbolized this using expressions of the form "Fx." But using a relational term, such as "bigger than," involves a reference to two things.

To capture this aspect of a relational claim, we need to employ two variables. It would seem natural, then, to symbolize "x is bigger than y" as "xBy." There is nothing wrong with this symbolization, and, in fact, it has been used at times. It does have this inconvenience: Sometimes relations involve more than two things being related to one another. Here are two examples:

2. Rx is between y and z.

3. u, v, w, and x play cards together.

The first relation is a three-term relation; the second is a four-term relation. A relation, such as "marched off to war together," can be a million-term relation. It proves convenient to have a uniform way of representing relations, no matter how many terms they involve. This is done by starting with the relational term and then putting the variables after it. Thus, (2) and (3) can be symbolized as follows:

2*. $Bxyz$

3*. $Puvwx$

Notice that the order of the variables makes a difference in (2*), but not in (3*).

The second feature of "Some cats are bigger than some dogs" worth noting is that it contains two occurrences of a quantifier—in particular, two occurrences of the quantifier "some." This forces us to do something we have not done before: introduce more than one quantifier into our translation of a single proposition. To see why we must do this, notice what happens if we try to translate (1) using only one existential quantifier. We would have to write something like this:

$(\exists x)(Cx \ \& \ Dx \ \& \ Bxx)$

What that says is that there is something that is both a cat and a dog and bigger than itself—certainly not what we were looking for. Furthermore, it will not be sufficient to use the same quantifier, "$(\exists x)$," twice in this translation. This becomes clear as soon as we try to decide where to place these two quantifiers. No placement will result in what we want. Because we cannot do what we want with a single variable, what we need is something we have not needed before—quantifiers containing *different* variables. Given two quantifiers containing different variables, the translation of "Some cats are bigger than some dogs" is actually quite simple:

$(\exists x)(\exists y)(Cx \ \& \ Dy \ \& \ Bxy)$

That says what we want: "There is at least one thing x and at least one thing y such that x is a cat, y is a dog, and x is bigger than y."

Propositions containing more than one quantifier are called *multiply quantified propositions*. The interaction between these quantifiers sometimes raises problems for translation. For example, it is true that every integer has an integer that is its immediate successor: 1 is followed by 2, 2 by 3, and so on. How can this claim be symbolized? We first notice that the remark is made about *every* integer. It is clearly a universal proposition. Using the first rule of thumb given above, we can begin our translation using the following general pattern:

$(x)(\quad \supset \quad)$

Since the proposition is plainly about all *integers,* we have no trouble filling in the antecedent of this conditional:

$(x)(Ix \supset \quad)$

This leaves only the expression "an integer that is its immediate successor" to deal with. What the sentence as a whole seems to be saying is this: For any integer, there is *some* integer that is its immediate successor. The term "some" indicates that we are dealing with an existential, rather than a universal, quantifier. Using the second rule of thumb, which tells us that existentially quantified statements with more than one predicate usually involve conjunction, we continue the translation as follows:

$(x)(Ix \supset (\exists y)(\quad \& \quad))$

The completed translation, then, looks like this:

$(x)(Ix \supset (\exists y)(Iy \ \& \ Syx))$

In words: "For any x, if x is an integer, then there exists a y such that y is an integer and y is the immediate successor of x." A little thought will show that this is precisely what we were saying when we said that every integer has an immediate successor.

Two cautions: Because parentheses determine the scope of a quantifier, it is important when translating quantified propositions to be careful in using them. One sure sign that something has gone wrong is that the translation does not have the same number of right-hand and left-hand parentheses. That, however, is not enough. It is also important that no variable fall outside the scope of an appropriate quantifier, as in the following case:

$(x)Ix \supset (\exists y)(Iy \ \& \ Syx)$

Here the last x is not in the scope of any quantifier. What this sentence says is this:

> If everything is an integer, then there exists an integer that is the immediate successor of x.

This hardly makes sense. To avoid such nonsense, it is important to make sure that every variable lies inside the scope of a quantifier.

Another pitfall to avoid is using two quantifiers that range over the same variable. If "Bxy" means "x is bigger than y," then it makes sense to say "$(x)(\exists y)Bxy$" (which means "Everything is bigger than something") and "$(y)(\exists x)Bxy$" (which means "For everything, there is something that is bigger than it"). But it does not make sense to say "$(x)(\exists x)Bxx$," as this formula does not tell us which quantifier refers to which place in the relation—the thing that is bigger or the thing it is bigger than. To avoid such confusions, each quantifier should use a different variable.

EXERCISE III

Translate the following propositions into quantificational notation. Let $Hx = x$ is a human being, and $Lxy = x$ loves y.

1. Every human being loves some human being.
2. Every human being loves himself.
3. There is a human being whom every human being loves.
4. Some human being loves every human being.
5. Every human being who loves a human being also loves himself.
6. No human being who does not love himself loves any human being.

EXERCISE IV

Translate the following propositions into quantificational notation. Let $Fx = x$ is a freshman, $Jx = x$ is a junior, $Sx = x$ is a senior, and $Oxy = x$ is older than y.

1. Every senior is older than some freshman.
2. Every senior is older than every freshman.
3. Some senior is older than every junior.
4. Some freshman is older than some junior.
5. All seniors and juniors are older than any freshman.
6. All seniors are older than any junior or freshman.
7. Not every senior is older than every junior.
8. Not every senior or junior is older than some freshman.

SCOPE FALLACIES

Propositions involving multiple quantifiers are complicated and hence easy to misunderstand. One problem is that it is easy to get confused about the scope of quantifiers because natural languages often fail to make this important logical feature of propositions clear. The standard example of such an ambiguity is the proposition:

Everything has a cause.

This can be read in two distinct ways, depending on how one orders the quantifiers.

$(y)(\exists x)Cxy$

$(\exists x)(y)Cxy$

The first proposition tells us that for any y there exists some x that is its cause. That, roughly, is the thesis of determinism. The second proposition says something much stronger: that there exists something that is the cause of everything. This claim is often used in proofs for the existence of God. Logic alone cannot determine whether either of these propositions is true or false. It can, however, show that the inference from the first proposition to the second is a fallacy—in particular, a *scope* fallacy. The argument depends on ignoring the difference the order of the quantifiers makes. We can see this at once by considering a parallel case. From the fact that every human being has a mother, it does not follow that there is someone who is the mother of all human beings. Or again, from the fact that every automobile has a steering wheel, it does not follow that there is a single steering wheel that every automobile has.

DISCUSSION QUESTIONS

1. Is it fallacious to reason as follows: If something is the cause of everything $(\exists x)(y)Cxy$, then everything has a cause $(y)(\exists x)Cxy$? Why or why not?

2. Above we said that it is a fallacy to argue from the claim that everything has some cause $(y)(\exists x)Cxy$ to the conclusion that there must be something that is the cause of everything $(\exists x)(y)Cxy$. Suppose someone replied in the following way: "When I speak of everything having a cause, I mean everything including the entire chain of causes itself. It is the cause of the entire chain of causes that I associate with God." Does this way of stating the argument avoid the fallacy? Is it a good argument?

VALIDITY FOR ARGUMENTS WITH QUANTIFIERS

In Chapters 6 and 7 we first gave a clear specification of two kinds of argument and then laid down principles for determining their validity. In each case we found a procedure for deciding whether or not arguments of the kind under consideration were valid: truth tables in one case, Venn diagrams in the other. It is not possible to proceed in the same way with quantificational theory because it has been shown that no such procedure exists for a fully developed quantificational logic. In other words, there is no purely mechanical procedure for deciding for every argument employing quantified propositions whether it is valid or not. Even though no general decision procedure exists for quantification theory, such procedures do exist for large and important segments of it. But even where such procedures do exist, they are often complicated and not particularly illuminating.

RUDIMENTARY QUANTIFICATIONAL LOGIC

Our goal in this section is to provide insight into validity as it is treated in quantificational logic without getting deeply involved in technical details. To do this, we will place the following simplifying restrictions on the arguments we will consider:

1. They contain at most two premises.
2. They contain no relational terms.
3. The propositions that make up these arguments come in only three forms:

    i. $(x)(\ldots x \ldots)$

    ii. $(\exists x)(\ldots x \ldots)$

    iii. $(\ldots a \ldots)$

The material within the scope of the two quantifiers in (i) and (ii) is made up only of such expressions as "Fx" and "Gx" and truth-functional combinations of them. The material contained in propositions of type (iii) is made up of expressions such as "Fa" and "Ga" and truth-functional combinations of them.[5] This third kind of proposition is explained below.

Here are some examples of the kinds of propositions we will allow into the arguments we consider:

    i*. $(x)(Fx \vee (Gx \ \& \ Hx))$

    ii*. $(\exists x)(Fx \ \& \ (Gx \vee Hx))$

    iii*. $Fa \supset (Ga \vee Ha)$

We will call the theory that operates under these restrictions Rudimentary Quantificational Logic (RQL).

The motivation behind developing RQL is to present a system of quantificational logic rich enough to show how the basic rules of quantificational logic work, but not so rich that the methods for testing the validity of arguments become overly time consuming and obscure. These restrictions do place severe limits on the range of arguments we can consider. Even with these restrictions in force, however, we still will be able to give a systematic account of a wide variety of arguments, including categorical syllogisms and many arguments that cannot be dealt with using syllogistic methods. RQL, though limited, is surprisingly powerful.

---

[5]These restrictions exclude propositions that contain more than one quantifier, more than one individual constant, or a quantifier in addition to an individual constant. (We will discuss constants in the next section.)

INSTANTIATIONS OF QUANTIFIED PROPOSITIONS

Our discussion thus far has peculiar limitations. In particular, we are not in a position to symbolize the following famous argument:

All humans are mortal.
Socrates is human.

∴ Socrates is mortal.

We have a way of saying that *all* humans are mortal and a way of saying that *some* humans are mortal, but not yet any way of naming a particular person (for example, Socrates) and saying of him that *he* is mortal. The situation is easily remedied. The standard way of doing this is to use lowercase letters from "*a*" through "*t*" as names for individual persons or things.[6] Logicians call such names *singular terms* or *individual constants.*[7] We will use the latter expression. If we assign to Socrates the individual constant "*s*," then we can symbolize "Socrates is human" thus:

Hs

The above argument can now be translated as follows:

$(x)(Hx \supset Mx)$
Hs

∴ Ms

This, however, still does not show us how "Socrates is mortal" follows from the stated premises.

One way to solve this problem is to look at the universal proposition

$(x)(Hx \supset Mx)$

as providing a pattern—or a recipe—for the propositional conditional

$Hs \supset Ms$

It also provides the pattern for indefinitely many other propositional conditionals, depending on which individual constant we substitute for the variable x. For example:

$Hb \supset Mb$

$Hc \supset Mc$

$Hd \supset Md$

We will say that all these propositions are *instantiations* of the universal proposition "$(x)(Hx \supset Mx)$." We get an instantiation of a universal proposition by dropping the universal quantifier and replacing each of its variables

---

[6] Lowercase letters from the very end of the alphabet are usually reserved for variables.

[7] They are called constants because their reference is fixed, in contrast with variables, which do not have a fixed reference.

with the same individual constant. In what follows, the notion of an instanti-ation will play a fundamental role in the analysis of arguments employing quantifiers.

UNIVERSAL INSTANTIATION

It should be clear that if a universal conditional is true, then all of its instan-tiations are also true. In fact, this is a feature of all universal propositions, whether they are conditionals or not. If something is true of everything, then it is true of each thing taken individually. (For example, what is true of all people is also true of Tom, Dick, and Hilary.) These thoughts are captured in the following principle:

> If a universal proposition is true, then all of its instantiations are true.

Corresponding to this, we may introduce the following rule, called *universal instantiation* (UI).

> UI: You may instantiate a universally quantified premise with any indi-vidual constant.[8]

Universal instantiation is one of the fundamental principles of modern quantification theory. Once you understand it, it should strike you as obvi-ously true.

We are now in a position to see why

1. $(x)(Hx \supset Mx)$
   Hs
   $\overline{}$
   $\therefore$ Ms

is valid. If the first premise is true, then so are all of its instantiations. By instantiating the first premise with respect to Socrates, (1) becomes:

2. $Hs \supset Ms$ UI
   Hs
   $\overline{}$
   $\therefore$ Ms PL valid

The result of this instantiation is that we are now dealing with propositions related in a way already examined in our study of propositional logic in Chapter 6. Thus, this argument can be tested for validity simply by using the machinery of propositional logic. That its propositional form is, in fact, valid is indicated by putting "PL valid" to the right of the conclusion.[9]

At this point, the symbolism may be a bit confusing. In propositional logic, we symbolized specific propositions using capital letters, such as "*A*,"

---

[8]We will see later why this rule is limited to premises and does not apply to conclusions.

[9]This argument will be given a more rigorous analysis later in this chapter.

"B," and "C." Propositional variables were symbolized using lowercase letters, such as "p," "q," and "r." The symbolism of quantification theory is more complex, because we are not simply dealing with whole propositions and the truth-functional connections among them; we are also interested in the inner structure of noncompound propositions. Thus, in propositional logic, we could have symbolized "Socrates is mortal" by the single letter "M"; this letter gives no indication of the inner structure of "Socrates is mortal." In the notation of quantificational logic, we symbolize it as "Ms," thus indicating that a particular individual (Socrates) has the specific property of being mortal. In this way, the notation of quantificational logic is more *fine-grained* than the notation of propositional logic.

But even so, the procedures of propositional logic apply to quantificational logic when we are dealing with truth-functional connections between whole propositions. Thus, (2) is a substitution instance of (3):

2. $Hs \supset Ms$
   Hs
   ─────────
   $\therefore\ Ms$ PL valid

3. $p \supset q$
   p
   ─────────
   $\therefore\ q$ PL valid

Because (3) is a valid argument form in propositional logic, (2), its substitution instance, is a valid argument. It is for this reason that the conclusion is marked "PL valid."

This example gives us a model for constructing a test for the validity of arguments in RQL. The basic strategy will be to develop a system of rules that tells us how we may or may not instantiate the propositions in an argument. An instantiation that obeys these rules will be called a *proper instantiation*. An argument in RQL will then be valid if and only if it has a proper instantiation whose form is valid in propositional logic. Argument (1) satisfies this test.

One way to think about what is going on here is that the proper instantiation provides intermediate steps that enable us to argue from the premises to the conclusion of the original argument. First we move to the right and derive the premises of the instantiation from the premises of the original argument. Next we move down and derive the conclusion of the instantiation from the premises of the instantiation, using propositional logic. Finally, we move back to the left and derive the conclusion of the original argument from the conclusion of the instantiation. In our example, the whole procedure looks like this:

1. $(x)\,(Hx \supset Mx)$ ⟶   2. $Hs \supset Ms$ UI
   Hs ⟶ Hs
   ─────────   ─────────
   $\therefore\ Ms$ ⟵ $\therefore\ Ms$ PL valid

The original argument is then valid if both (i) the instantiation is valid in propositional logic and (ii) we can get to the instantiation and back by following the rules. To fill out this picture, what we now need is a set of rules that tells us when we can properly move to and from an instantiation.

Use rule UI to check the following arguments for validity in RQL:

1. All humans are rational.
   Fido is not rational.

   ∴ Fido is not human.

2. All rational beings are human.
   Fido is not human.

   ∴ Fido is not rational.

3. No human is metallic.
   My clock is metallic.

   ∴ My clock is not human.

4. No human is metallic.
   My brother is human.

   ∴ My brother is not metallic.

5. No metallic object is human.
   My clock is metallic.

   ∴ My clock is not human.

6. No metallic object is human.
   My brother is human.

   ∴ My brother is not metallic.

EXISTENTIAL GENERALIZATION

Turning now to existentially quantified propositions, we can speak of their instantiations as well. For example,

$(\exists x) (Hx \,\&\, Mx)$ (that is, "Some humans are mortal")

has an instantiation:

$Hs \,\&\, Ms$ (that is, "Socrates is both human and mortal")

There is, however, an important difference between this instantiation and the instantiation of "All humans are mortal." If *all* humans are mortal, then, if Socrates is human, he is mortal. In contrast, that *some* humans are mortal does not guarantee that Socrates is mortal, even though he is human.

In fact, the relationship between existential propositions and their instantiations is roughly the reverse of the relationship between universal propositions and their instantiations:

If at least one of the instantiations of an existential proposition is true, then that existential proposition is true.

This allows us to introduce the following rule, called *existential generalization* (EG):

EG: You may instantiate an existentially quantified conclusion with any individual constant.

For example, if Socrates is mortal, then at least one person is mortal. Symbolically:

Argument	**Instantiation**	
Ms	*Ms*	
∴ (∃x)*Mx*	∴ *Ms*	EG, PL valid

Because this instantiation obeys the rules, it is a proper instantiation. Its form (*p*; ∴ *p*) is also valid in propositional logic. So the original argument is valid.

Rule EG allows us to derive a quantified or general conclusion (such as "(∃x)*Mx*"), and that is why the rule is called existential *generalization*. Recall that what rule EG does is allow us to move left from the conclusion of the instantiation back to the conclusion of the original argument:

Ms	⟶	*Ms*	
∴ (∃x)*Mx*	⟵	∴ *Ms*	EG, PL valid

When you think of it that way, it should be obvious why we want to be able to move from something like "*Ms*" in the conclusion of the instantiation to something like "(∃x)*Mx*" in the conclusion of the original argument. That is exactly what rule EG allows us to do.

EXERCISE VI

Use rule EG to check the following arguments for validity in RQL:

1. My dog is not human.
   ∴ Something is not human.

2. Spot is a dog that is frisky.
   ∴ Some dogs are frisky.

3. Ariel is a cat that is not frisky.
   ∴ Some cats are not frisky.

4. Everything is funny.

∴ Something is funny.

5. All jokes are funny.

∴ Some jokes are funny.

UNIVERSAL GENERALIZATION

Universal instantiation and existential generalization are both easy rules. They are easy to understand and easy to apply. The next two rules are more difficult. The first is called *universal generalization*. Whereas universal instantiation applies when a *premise* is universally quantified, universal generalization applies when a *conclusion* is universally quantified.

To understand this rule, we can first note that the following generalization principle is clearly invalid:

If some particular thing has a property, then everything does.

From the fact that Albert is fifty years old, we clearly cannot conclude that everything or everyone is fifty years old. But if we allowed a universally quantified conclusion to be instantiated with any individual constant, then the instantiation of this invalid argument would be PL valid. We will mark instantiations with the letter "i," so the symbolization of this argument and its instantiation look like this:

1. Fa 1i. Fa

∴ $(x)Fx$ ∴ Fa UG ???

This seems to settle the issue concerning universal generalization: The rule is not valid in general.

As it turns out, however, a *restricted* version of this rule is useful. To see why, we can consider the following simple argument: Everything is funny, so everything is either funny or grave. Symbolically,

2. $(x)Fx$

∴ $(x)(Fx \lor Gx)$

That is, if everything has some property F, then everything has either the property F or the property G. This, of course, looks much like the following argument form, which is valid in propositional logic:

p

∴ $p \lor q$

In fact, the argument involving quantifiers does rely on the validity of this argument form in propositional logic. Our problem, to put it crudely, is that we have to find some way of getting the quantifiers out of the way so that we can use this argument form from propositional logic to show the validity of the quantified argument.

This problem is solved by introducing a *controlled* version of universal generalization that does not lead to fallacious inferences. Returning to (2), suppose we instantiate the entire argument with respect to the letter "*a*." This yields:

2. $(x)Fx$	2i. Fa	UI
$\therefore (x)(Fx \lor Gx)$	$\therefore Fa \lor Ga$	UG, PL valid

Of course, (2i) is valid in propositional logic. It is still not clear, however, how the validity of (2i) bears on the validity of (2). But we should notice that the premise of (2i) is itself an instantiation of a *universal* proposition. That shows that this premise could have been instantiated with respect to *any* individual constant whatsoever, so that, in this case, what holds for one individual holds for *all* individuals. That is what makes it all right to instantiate the conclusion with respect to the same individual.

To reflect this idea, we can formulate the rule of universal generalization (UG) as follows:

UG: You may instantiate a universally quantified conclusion with an individual constant if, but only if, that individual constant does not appear anywhere else in the instantiation except where it was derived by UI.

This rule allows us to instantiate the conclusion of (2) as was done in (2i), because the premise in (2i) in which the individual constant "*a*" appears was derived by UI. But UG does not allow us to instantiate the conclusion of (1) as was done in (1i), because the premise in (1i) includes "*a*" but was not derived by UI. To apply UG properly to the conclusion of (1), we would have to use some individual constant other than "*a*," but then this proper instantiation would not be valid in propositional logic. Rule UG thus explains why (2) is valid but (1) is not. The rule works because its restrictions force us to use a different constant when instantiating invalid arguments, and using a different constant makes the instantiation invalid in propositional logic.

The examples so far have been simple, but the same method also works for more complex arguments with more than one premise. Consider the argument that all swimmers in the pool are members of the club, and all members of the club are politicians, so all swimmers in the pool are politicians. Here are its symbolization and an instantiation:

3. $(x)(Sx \supset Mx)$	3i. $Sa \supset Ma$	UI
$(x)(Mx \supset Px)$	$Ma \supset Pa$	UI
$\therefore (x)(Sx \supset Px)$	$\therefore Sa \supset Pa$	UG, PL valid

Because (3i) obeys our rules, it is a proper instantiation. Thus, because the form of (3i) is valid in propositional logic, (3) is valid.

We can next examine what happens when we apply this test to an invalid syllogism:

4. $(x)(Sx \supset Mx)$ 4i. $Sa \supset Ma$ UI
   $(x)(Px \supset Mx)$ $Pa \supset Ma$ UI
∴ $(x)(Sx \supset Px)$ ∴ $Sa \supset Pa$ UG, PL invalid

The form of (4i) is invalid in propositional logic. Nonetheless, it is important to remember that the invalidity of this one proper instantiation does not show that the original argument is invalid, since there still might be a different proper instantiation that is valid in propositional logic, and all it takes to show that an argument is valid in RQL is *one* proper instantiation that is valid in propositional logic. In this case, however, it is clear that no other proper instantiation will turn out valid in propositional logic. Instantiating one or more of the premises of (4) with respect to an individual constant other than "*a*," though legal, will not help here. It will only disconnect the premise from the conclusion, as the following example shows:

4i*. $Sa \supset Ma$ UI
     $Pb \supset Mb$ UI
∴ $Sa \supset Pa$ UG, PL invalid

It is also true that (4i*) is invalid in propositional logic. In fact, it is almost always obvious, just by looking, that instantiating universal premises with respect to an individual constant different from the individual constant used to instantiate the conclusion will weaken, not strengthen, the instantiated argument. Since there is no way to construct a proper instantiation of (4) that is valid in propositional logic, (4) is not valid in RQL, just as one would hope.

EXERCISE VII

Check the following arguments for validity in RQL:

1. $(x)(Mx \supset Sx)$ 4. $(x)(Sx \supset {\sim}Mx)$
   $(x)(Px \supset Mx)$ $(x)(Mx \supset {\sim}Px)$
∴ $(x)(Px \supset Sx)$ ∴ $(x)(Sx \supset {\sim}Px)$

2. $(x)(Mx \supset Sx)$ 5. $(x)(Mx \supset Sx)$
   $(x)(Mx \supset Px)$ $(x)Mx$
∴ $(x)(Px \supset Sx)$ ∴ $(x)Sx$

3. $(x)(Sx \supset {\sim}Mx)$ 6. $(x)(Mx \supset Sx)$
   $(x)(Px \supset Mx)$ $(x)Sx$
∴ $(x)(Px \supset {\sim}Sx)$ ∴ $(x)Mx$

7. $(x)(Mx \supset Sx)$	8. $(x)(Mx) \supset Sx)$
$(x)(\sim Sx)$	$(x)(\sim Mx)$
$\therefore (x)(\sim Mx)$	$\therefore (x)(\sim Sx)$

EXISTENTIAL INSTANTIATION

We can now turn to our final quantification rule, *existential instantiation.* We already saw that the rule of existential generalization (EG) tells us what we may do when a *conclusion* is existentially quantified, but now we need an instantiation rule that applies when a *premise* is existentially quantified. Clearly, the following argument is invalid:

1. $(\exists x)Fx$

$\therefore Fa$

From the premise that something or someone is fat, we may not conclude that Alan is fat. But if we allowed an existentially quantified premise to be instantiated with any individual constant, then the instantiation of this invalid argument would be PL valid:

1i. Fa

$\therefore Fa$

Our rules should not allow such instantiations.

There are, however, other arguments with existential quantifiers in their premises that *are* valid, and we must find ways of dealing with them. The following is an example of such an argument:

2. $(\exists x)(Fx \ \& \ Hx)$

$\therefore (\exists x)Hx$

From the premise that at least one thing is fat and happy, we may conclude that at least one thing is happy. Why is this argument valid? The reason is that it does not matter which thing is fat and happy. Whatever it is that is fat and happy, it will still be true that *something* is happy.

In contrast, it *does* matter that we used the constant "*a*" when we instantiated (1) to form (1i). If we had instantiated the premise with a different constant, say "*b*," the resulting instantiation would not have been valid in propositional logic. Less formally, because the premise of (1) says only that *someone* is fat, it does matter *who* it is that is fat, since the conclusion that Alan is fat is true only if Alan is one of the people who make the premise true.

The general idea, then, is that you may instantiate an existentially quantified premise with respect to a particular individual constant, provided that picking that individual constant rather than any other has no effect on the validity of the argument in question. To turn this vague idea into a precise rule, we need to determine when it matters which individual constant is used to instantiate an existentially quantified premise. We already saw that this does not matter in arguments like (2), in which the conclusion is existentially quantified, but it can matter in arguments like (1), in which the conclusion is not quantified. It also matters in arguments in which the conclusion is universally quantified, such as this:

3. $(\exists x)Fx$	3i. *Fa*	EI ???
$\therefore$ $(x)Fx$	$\therefore$ *Fa*	UG ???

From the premise that someone is fat, we cannot validly conclude that everyone is fat. Thus, the only case in which we can instantiate an existentially quantified premise with the same constant as in the conclusion is when the instantiation of the conclusion is derived by existential generalization, as in (2).

We also need to consider arguments with more than one premise. The following, for example, is clearly an invalid argument:

> Some *S* is *M*.
> Some *M* is *P*.
> ────────────
> $\therefore$ Some *S* is *P*.

Even if some Swedes are marathoners, and some marathoners are from Poland, it does not follow that some Swedes are from Poland. Symbolically, this argument and an instantiation of it take the following form:

4. $(\exists x)(Sx \ \& \ Mx)$	4i. $(Sa \ \& \ Ma)$	EI ???
$(\exists x)(Mx \ \& \ Px)$	$(Ma \ \& \ Pa)$	EI ???
$\therefore$ $(\exists x)(Sx \ \& \ Px)$	$\therefore$ $(Sa \ \& \ Pa)$	EG, PL valid

As it turns out, (4i) is a valid argument in propositional logic, so, if our rules did not declare this instantiation improper, our system would declare (4) valid when it is not. It should be clear what has gone wrong. By instantiating both premises with the same individual constant, we have introduced a relationship that was not found in the original argument. In the original, the *M* that is *S* need not be the same as the *M* that is *P*. To avoid mistakes of this kind, we need to prohibit the use of the same constant to instantiate two existentially quantified premises. If rule EI is restricted in this way, we can still construct a proper instantiation this way:

4. $(\exists x)(Sx \ \& \ Mx)$	4i*. $(Sa \ \& \ Ma)$	EI
$(\exists x)(Mx \ \& \ Px)$	$(Mb \ \& \ Pb)$	EI
$\therefore$ $(\exists x)(Sx \ \& \ Px)$	$\therefore$ $(Sa \ \& \ Pa)$	EG, PL invalid

This proper instantiation, however, is not valid in propositional logic. Moreover, it should be obvious that nothing would be gained by using a different pattern of instantiation. Using "*a*" in the second premise and "*b*" in the first would yield an argument that is invalid for the same reason. Instantiating one of the premises with some third individual constant would merely weaken the argument. This shows that argument (4) is not valid in RQL.

In contrast, consider an argument in which the other premise is universally quantified:

5. $(\exists x)(Sx \,\&\, Mx)$ 5i. $(Sa \,\&\, Ma)$ EI
     $(x)(Mx \supset Rx)$ $(Ma \supset Ra)$ UI
∴ $(\exists x)(Sx \,\&\, Rx)$ ∴ $(Sa \,\&\, Ra)$ UG, PL valid

Some Swedes are marathoners, and all marathoners are runners, so some Swedes are runners. This is valid, because the relationship between Swedish marathoners and runners is guaranteed if the second premise is true. Thus, we should allow existential instantiation in such cases.

Considering these and other cases, we can now formulate the rule of existential instantiation (EI) more precisely as follows:

> EI: You may instantiate an existentially quantified premise with an individual constant if, but only if, that individual constant does not appear anywhere else in the instantiation except in a premise that was derived by UI or in a conclusion that was derived by EG.

This rule shows why (2) is valid, because the conclusion can be instantiated using EG, and why (1) and (3) are not valid, since their conclusions are not instantiated by applying EG. EI also explains why (5) is valid, but (4) is not, since UI is used to instantiate the other premise in (5), but not in (4).

APPLICATION TO IMMEDIATE INFERENCES AND SYLLOGISMS

Though RQL is restricted in its range of application, it still has a number of important applications. For example, both the theory of immediate inference and the theory of the syllogism examined in Chapter 7 can be handled elegantly in RQL with only the rules that we have learned so far (UI, UG, EI, and EG).

The only immediate inference examined in the body of Chapter 7 was conversion, which is the inference that results from reversing the subject and predicate terms. There are four cases: the conversions of A, E, I, and O propositions. We will consider two of them: those of A and I propositions.

Categorical Form	Quantificational Form	Instantiation	
A: All S is P.	$(x)(Sx \supset Px)$	$Sa \supset Pa$	UI
∴ All P is S.	∴ $(x)(Px \supset Sx)$	∴ $Pa \supset Sa$	UG, PL invalid

Because the instantiated argument is not valid in propositional logic, the conversion of an A proposition is not valid in RQL.[10]

---

[10]When it is transparent that changing the pattern of instantiation will make no difference to the validity of the instantiated argument, we will not always bother to say so.

Categorical Form	Quantificational Form	Instantiation	
I: Some S is P.	$(\exists x)(Sx \ \& \ Px)$	$Sa \ \& \ Pa$	EI
∴ Some P is S.	∴ $(\exists x)(Px \ \& \ Sx)$	∴ $Pa \ \& \ Sa$	EG, PL valid

Since the instantiation of this argument is valid in propositional logic, the conversion of an I proposition is valid in RQL.

Examples of applying these methods to categorical syllogisms have already been given in the process of explaining quantification rules. See (4) and (5) in the previous section, as well as (3) and (4) in the section before that.

EXERCISE VIII

Test to see whether the conversions of E and O propositions are valid in RQL. In other words, test the validity of:

  1. No S is P.

  ∴ No P is S.

  2. Some S is not P.

  ∴ Some P is not S.

EXERCISE IX

Using the methods of RQL, determine the validity of the syllogisms in Exercise VII in Chapter 7. To do this, you must first translate these arguments into quantificational notation.

APPLICATION TO NONCATEGORICAL ARGUMENTS

Because of the limitations we have introduced, the methods developed cannot be applied to all arguments that can be formulated in the symbolism of quantificational logic. Nonetheless, these procedures still apply to many arguments that cannot be handled using only the methods of categorical logic. Here we will give some more examples of such arguments.

First: All sunsets are pretty, and there are some sunsets, so there are some pretty things. This argument can be symbolized and instantiated as follows:

  1. $(x)(Sx \supset (Px)$ 1i. $Sa \supset Pa$ UI
       $(\exists x)Sx$ Sa EI

  ∴ $(\exists x)Px$ ∴ Pa EG, PL valid

Because (1i) follows the rules, and its form is valid in propositional logic, (1) is valid.

Consider this argument: Since oysters and clams are delicious, clams are delicious. This gets translated thus:

2. $(x)((Ox \lor Cx) \supset Dx)$ 2i. $(Oa \lor Ca) \supset Da$ UI

∴ $(x)(Cx \supset Dx)$ ∴ $Ca \supset Da$ UG, PL valid

Again, because (2i) follows the rules and is valid in propositional logic, (2) is valid.

In the next example, a restriction in a rule blocks an invalid argument from being declared valid. Here is the argument and its symbolization:

Everything is either alive or dead.   3. $(x)(Ax \lor Dx)$

Some things are not alive. $(\exists x)(\sim Ax)$

∴ Everything is dead.   ∴ $(x)Dx$

One might instantiate this argument this way:

$Aa \lor Da$ UI

$\sim Aa$ EI ???

∴ Da UG ???

This instantiation is valid in propositional logic, but this is not a proper instantiation; it violates the restrictions in EI and UG, because the same constant appears in both the second premise and the conclusion. To avoid violating these restrictions, we must use a different individual constant in these two locations in the instantiation. Suppose, then, we use the constant "a" to instantiate the conclusion as "Da," but we use the constant "b" to instantiate the second premise as "$\sim Ab$." Now there are two ways to instantiate the first premise. Because it is universally quantified, the rules allow us to instantiate it with respect to either "a" or "b," but neither instantiation yields an argument that is valid in propositional logic:

3i. $Aa \lor Da$ 3i*. $Ab \lor Db$

    $\sim Ab$ $\sim Ab$

∴ Da ∴ Da

It would not help to instantiate the conclusion with respect to "b," because then the restrictions in EI and UG would require us to instantiate the second premise with a different individual constant, and the same problems would arise again. Thus, there is no way to construct a proper instantiation that is valid in propositional logic, so (3) is not valid in RQL.

Finally, we can look at a tricky example in which the order of instantiation makes a difference. The following is, in fact, a valid argument:

4. $(\exists x)(Fx \& Gx)$

    $(\exists x)(Hx \& Ix)$

∴ $(\exists x)Hx$

(Because some things are both flat and gray, and some things are both heavy and made of iron, some things are heavy.) Proceeding in a natural way leads us into trouble. Suppose, as we are allowed to, we instantiate both the conclusion and the first premise with respect to the letter "*a*," so that our instantiation has "*Fa & Ga*" as its first premise and "*Ha*" as its conclusion. Because of the restrictions in rule EI, we cannot now instantiate the second existential premise with respect to "*a*," so we have to shift to a new letter, yielding this result:

4i. *Fa & Ga*   EI
    Hb & Ib   EI
  ∴ *Ha*   EG, PL invalid

This is a proper instantiation, but it is not valid in propositional logic. The invalidity of this one instantiation, however, does not show that the original argument is invalid, because the original argument is still valid if it has another proper instantiation that is valid in propositional logic. In this case, it does have such an instantiation. If we had started out instead by instantiating the second premise with respect to "*a*," the result would have been different:

4i*. *Fb & Gb*   EI
    Ha & Ia   EI
  ∴ *Ha*   EG, PL valid

This argument is a proper instantiation, and it is also valid in propositional logic. Of course, it is odd because the first premise plays no role in supporting the conclusion. That, however, does not affect its validity. We have presented this argument because it shows that the order in which we instantiate premises can sometimes make a difference. That is why we must check *all* possible patterns of instantiation before we can conclude that an argument is invalid, because it is valid if *any* proper instantiation is valid in propositional logic.[11]

EXERCISE X

Test the following arguments for validity in RQL:

1. $(x)(Sx \supset Px)$
   $(\exists x)Sx$
  ∴ $(\exists x)Px$

2. $(x)(Sx \supset Px)$
   $(\exists x)Sx$
  ∴ $(\exists x)(Px \vee Mx)$

---

[11]One reason why we have limited RQL to arguments containing no more than two premises is that the number of ways in which the premises of an argument can be instantiated grows exponentially as the number of premises increases.

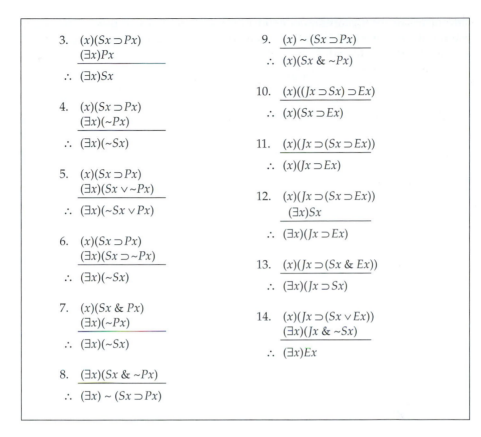

3. $(x)(Sx \supset Px)$
   $(\exists x)Px$
   ∴ $(\exists x)Sx$

4. $(x)(Sx \supset Px)$
   $(\exists x)(\sim Px)$
   ∴ $(\exists x)(\sim Sx)$

5. $(x)(Sx \supset Px)$
   $(\exists x)(Sx \vee \sim Px)$
   ∴ $(\exists x)(\sim Sx \vee Px)$

6. $(x)(Sx \supset Px)$
   $(\exists x)(Sx \supset \sim Px)$
   ∴ $(\exists x)(\sim Sx)$

7. $(x)(Sx \,\&\, Px)$
   $(\exists x)(\sim Px)$
   ∴ $(\exists x)(\sim Sx)$

8. $(\exists x)(Sx \,\&\, \sim Px)$
   ∴ $(\exists x) \sim (Sx \supset Px)$

9. $(x) \sim (Sx \supset Px)$
   ∴ $(x)(Sx \,\&\, \sim Px)$

10. $(x)((Jx \supset Sx) \supset Ex)$
    ∴ $(x)(Sx \supset Ex)$

11. $(x)(Jx \supset (Sx \supset Ex))$
    ∴ $(x)(Jx \supset Ex)$

12. $(x)(Jx \supset (Sx \supset Ex))$
    $(\exists x)Sx$
    ∴ $(\exists x)(Jx \supset Ex)$

13. $(x)(Jx \supset (Sx \,\&\, Ex))$
    ∴ $(\exists x)(Jx \supset Sx)$

14. $(x)(Jx \supset (Sx \vee Ex))$
    $(\exists x)(Jx \,\&\, \sim Sx)$
    ∴ $(\exists x)Ex$

ARGUMENTS CONTAINING INDIVIDUAL CONSTANTS

Throughout this chapter we have used *individual constants* in evaluating arguments for validity. We have not, however, laid down general rules for evaluating arguments that themselves contain individual constants. Thus, we still have no rigorous way of exhibiting the validity of this argument:

All humans are mortal.
Socrates is human.
∴ Socrates is mortal.

As we said early on, the solution is to symbolize and instantiate this argument as follows:

1. $(x)(Hx \supset Mx)$ 1i. $Hs \supset Ms$ UI
   Hs Hs
∴ Ms ∴ Ms PL valid

We do not yet have any explicit rule, however, that allows us to repeat the second premise of the argument on the second line of its instantiation. We simply took that for granted, because it seemed obvious that this move cannot make the instantiation valid in propositional logic unless the argument was already valid in RQL. Even so, we now need to state that rule of reiteration more formally:

REIT: You may reiterate any premise or conclusion with an individual constant.

In other words, the instantiation may contain the same premises or conclusion as the ones in the argument that contain an individual constant.

This simple rule might not seem so obvious in light of the restrictions that were needed in some other rules, but the rule REIT can be kept simple just because the restrictions in the other rules prevent problems from arising. To see how this works, let us apply REIT to some different kinds of examples.

We want this argument to turn out valid in RQL:

2. $(x)Wx$		2i. Wa	UI
∴ Wa		∴ Wa	REIT, PL valid

Because (2i) follows the rules, and its form is valid in propositional logic, (2) is valid, just as we wanted. If we could not use REIT in the conclusion, we could not have shown how this argument is valid.

In contrast, we want this argument to turn out invalid in RQL:

3. Wa		3i. Wa	REIT
∴ $(x)Wx$		∴ Wa	UG ???

This instantiation is, of course, valid in propositional logic, but it is not a proper instantiation because it violates one of the restrictions in UG: UG cannot be used to instantiate a universal conclusion with an individual constant if that individual constant appears anywhere else in the instantiation where it was not derived by UI. Here the constant "a" is used in UG, and "a" appears in the premise, where it was derived by REIT rather than by UI. Thus, this instantiation is not proper. There is clearly no other way to construct a proper instantiation that will be valid in propositional logic. Therefore, this argument is not valid in RQL, again as we expected.

We get similar results when we test arguments with existential quantifiers. The following argument should be valid, and its instantiation is both proper and valid in propositional logic:

4. Wa		4i. Wa	REIT
∴ $(\exists x)Wx$		∴ Wa	EG, PL valid

The following argument is not valid:

5. $(\exists x)Wx$		5i. Wa	EI ???
∴ Wa		∴ Wa	REIT, PL valid

In propositional logic, (5i) is valid. However, it is not a proper instantiation of (5); (5i) violates the restriction in EI against instantiating with an individual constant that appears in the conclusion of the instantiation without being derived by EG, because the conclusion of (5i) was derived by REIT rather than by EG.

Finally, let us consider arguments with two premises. We already saw in (1) that reiterating a premise maintains validity when the other premise is universal, so we can turn to an example in which the other premise is existential:

6. $(\exists x)(Wx \lor Hx)$ 6i. $Wa \lor Ha$ EI ???
    $\sim Wa$ $\sim Wa$ REIT

∴ $(\exists x)Hx$ ∴ Ha EG, PL valid

This argument is clearly invalid, but its instantiation is valid in propositional logic. However, this instantiation is not a proper instantiation because it violates the restriction in EI against using an individual constant that appears in another premise without being derived there by UI. Thus, REIT achieves the right results in all these cases. The reason why this simple rule works, as we said, is that the restrictions on UG and EI prevent any invalid arguments from being declared valid.

One tricky case might seem to create a problem. Consider the following valid argument: Albert is wise, so everyone who is wise is wise. This argument gets symbolized as follows:

7. Wa

∴ $(x)(Wx \supset Wx)$

Admittedly, this is a peculiar argument. Because the conclusion cannot be false, there is obviously no way for the premise to be true and the conclusion false. But even if the argument is peculiar, we want to declare it valid. We seem to run into a problem, however, if we begin by instantiating the conclusion with the letter "a":

....

∴ $Wa \supset Wa$ UG

Now we are stuck, because we cannot use REIT to instantiate the first premise without violating the restrictions in UG.

The solution to this problem is actually quite simple. We begin by instantiating the premise using REIT, and then we have to instantiate the conclusion with a different constant to avoid violating the restrictions in UG. We end up with this:

7. Wa 7i. Wa REIT

∴ $(x)(Wx \supset Wx)$ ∴ $Wb \supset Wb$ UG, PL valid

In propositional logic, (7i) is valid, and it is also a proper instantiation, because it violates none of the rules. Thus, (7) is valid. Things have worked out exactly as we wanted them to.

EXERCISE XI

Test the following arguments for validity in RQL.

1. $(x)(Sx \supset Px)$
   $\sim Pa$

   $\therefore \ \sim Sa$

2. $(x)(Sx \supset Px)$
   Sa

   $\therefore \ (\exists x)Px$

3. $(x)(Sx \supset Px)$

   $\therefore \ \sim Sa \vee Pa$

4. $(x)(Sx \supset Px)$
   $(Sa \supset \sim Pa)$

   $\therefore \ \sim Sa$

5. $(x)(Sx \supset (Px \vee Qx))$
   $Sa \ \& \sim Qa$

   $\therefore \ (\exists x)Px$

6. Fa
   $(\exists x)(\sim Fx \vee Gx)$

   $\therefore \ Ga$

7. $(\exists x)(Fx \ \& \ Gx)$
   Fa

   $\therefore \ Ga$

8. $(\exists x)(Fx \supset Gx)$
   $\sim Ga$

   $\therefore \ \sim Fa$

A GENERAL RULE FOR RQL

We are now in a position to state a general rule for the validity of arguments in RQL. As we have developed RQL, we have introduced five rules governing instantiation:

UI: You may instantiate a universally quantified premise with any individual constant.

EG: You may instantiate an existentially quantified conclusion with any individual constant.

UG: You may instantiate a universally quantified conclusion with an individual constant if, but only if, that individual constant does not appear anywhere else in the instantiation except where it was derived by UI.

EI: You may instantiate an existentially quantified premise with an individual constant if, but only if, that individual constant does not appear anywhere else in the instantiation except in a premise that was derived by UI or in a conclusion that was derived by EG.

REIT: You may reiterate any premise or conclusion with an individual constant.

These rules follow a pattern:

	Universal Quantifier	Existential Quantifier	Individual Constant
Premise	UI	EI	REIT
Conclusion	UG	EG	REIT

Thus, our rules allow instantiations for all of the propositions in arguments that meet the restrictions of RQL.

Any instantiation that obeys these rules is then called a *proper instantiation*. The notion of a proper instantiation allows us to lay down the following general rule for validity in RQL:

> **VALIDITY IN RQL:** An argument is valid in RQL if and only if it has a proper instantiation whose form is valid in propositional logic.

This sounds quite simple, but, of course, a great deal of complexity is packed into the notion of a proper instantiation.

Given this account, it is fairly easy to show that an argument is valid. Just give a proper instantiation whose form is valid in propositional logic. It is not so easy, however, to show that an argument is *not* valid in RQL. To show invalidity, you have to show that there does not exist *any* proper instantiation that is PL valid. But even if one proper instantiation is not PL valid, that does not show that no other proper instantiation is PL valid. To show that, you need a procedure that will always produce a proper instantiation that is PL valid whenever there is one. Luckily, because of the restrictions on arguments in RQL, there is such a procedure:[12]

> **STEP 1:** Reiterate all sentences that have individual constants (but no quantifiers).
>
> **STEP 2:** Instantiate each existential premise and universal conclusion. In each case, use a constant that does not yet appear in the instantiation you are constructing.
>
> **STEP 3:** Instantiate each universal premise and existential conclusion with each constant occurring in the instantiation after step 1 and step 2. (If no constant occurs, use a new constant. If two constants occur, construct one proper instantiation for each constant.)

If this procedure yields a proper instantiation whose form is valid in propositional logic, then the original argument is valid in RQL. Otherwise the original argument is invalid in RQL. Thus, we have a mechanical procedure that will tell us, for any argument that meets the restrictions of RQL, whether or not it is valid.

---

[12]We are indebted to Jim Moor for suggesting this procedure.

THE LIMITS OF RQL

In developing RQL we have placed strong limitations on its range of application. We have done this because our primary aim has been to explain the concepts and the basic rules of quantificational logic. Some of these restrictions are intended merely to keep matters clear and simple, and they could have been removed without having to alter RQL in fundamental ways. Limiting the number of premises to no more than two falls into this category. This just avoids complications. In contrast, extending RQL to include propositions with more than one quantifier would demand major revisions. But even if our procedures are not adequate for dealing with all arguments employing quantifiers, they are still applicable to a wide variety of important types of arguments—including syllogisms and many others. Seeing how RQL works in its area of application provides a good understanding of the basic notions of quantificational logic. In particular, it shows how developing a single system that encompasses both categorical logic and propositional logic sheds light on the basic structure of many arguments.

INDUCTIVE REASONING

In previous chapters, we have been concerned primarily with deductive arguments that aim at validity. Many arguments encountered in daily life, however, are not intended to meet the standard of validity. They are claimed only to provide reasons (perhaps very strong reasons) for their conclusions. Such arguments are called inductive. *This chapter will discuss five kinds of inductive reasoning. First, in* inferences to the best explanation, *explanatory power is said to provide evidence for certain hypotheses. Second, in* arguments from analogy, *the fact that two things have certain features in common is taken as evidence that they have further features in common. Third, we will develop tests for* necessary *conditions and for* sufficient *conditions, which apply to* causal reasoning. *Fourth, we will discuss* statistical generalizations, *where a claim is made about a population on the basis of features of a sample of that population. Finally, the chapter examines* statistical applications. *Here a claim is made about members of a population on the basis of features of the population.*

INDUCTION VERSUS DEDUCTION

The distinction between deductive arguments and inductive arguments can be drawn in a variety of ways, but the fundamental difference concerns the relationship that is claimed to hold between the premises and the conclusion for each type of argument. An argument is *deductive* insofar as it is intended or claimed to be *valid*. As we know from Chapter 3, an argument is valid if and only if it is impossible for the conclusion to be false when its premises are true. The following is a valid deductive argument:

All ravens are black.

∴ If there is a raven on top of Pikes Peak, then it is black.

Because the premise lays down a universal principle governing all ravens, if it's true, then it *must* be true of all ravens (if any) on top of Pikes Peak. This same relationship does not hold for invalid arguments. Nonetheless, arguments that are not valid can still be deductive if they are intended or claimed to be valid.

In contrast, inductive arguments are not intended to be valid, so they should not be criticized for being invalid. The following is an example of an inductive argument:

> All ravens that we have observed so far are black.
>
> ∴ All ravens are black.

Here we have drawn an inductive inference from the characteristics of *observed* ravens to the characteristics of *all* ravens, most of which we have not observed. Of course, the premise of this argument *could be* true, yet the conclusion turn out to be false. A raven that has not yet been observed might be albino. The obviousness of this possibility suggests that someone who gives this argument does not put it forth as valid, so it is not a deductive argument. Instead, the premise is put forth as a *reason* or *support* for the conclusion. When an argument is not claimed to be valid but is intended only to provide a reason for the conclusion, the argument is *inductive.*

Because inductive arguments are supposed to provide reasons, and reasons vary in strength, inductive arguments can be evaluated as *strong* or *weak,* depending on the strength of the reasons that they provide for their conclusions. If we have seen only ten ravens, and all of them were in our back yard, then the above argument gives at most a very weak reason to believe that all ravens are black. But, if we have traveled around the world and seen over half the ravens that exist, then the above argument gives a strong reason to believe that all ravens are black. Inductive arguments are usually intended to provide strong support for their conclusions, in which case they can be criticized if the support they provide is not strong enough for the purposes at hand.

The most basic distinction, then, is not between two kinds of argument but instead between two standards for evaluating arguments. The deductive standard is validity. The inductive standard is strength. Arguments themselves are classified as either deductive or inductive in accordance with the standard that they are intended or claimed to meet.

There are several important differences between deductive and inductive standards. One fundamental feature of the deductive standard of validity is that adding premises to a valid argument cannot make it invalid. The definition of validity guarantees this: In a valid argument, it is not possible for the premises to be true without the conclusion being true as well. If any further premises could change this, then it would be possible for this relationship not to hold, so the argument would not be valid after all. Additional information might, of course, lead us to question the truth of one of the premises, but that is another matter.

The situation is strikingly different when we deal with inductive arguments. To cite a famous example, before the time of Captain Cook's voyage to Australia, Europeans had observed a great many swans, and every one of them was white. Thus, up to that time Europeans had very strong inductive evidence to support the claim that all swans are white. Then Captain Cook discovered black swans in Australia. What happens if we add this new piece of information to the premises of the original inductive argument? Provided that we accept Cook's report, we now produce a sound *deductive* argument in behalf of the claim that *not* all swans are white; for, if some swans are black, then not all of them are white. This, then, is a feature of every inductive argument: No matter how strong an inductive argument is, the possibility remains open that further information can undercut, perhaps completely, the support that the premises give to the conclusion. Because all inductive arguments are able to be defeated in this way, they are described as *defeasible*. Valid deductive arguments do not face a similar peril, so they are *indefeasible*.[1]

A second important difference between inductive and deductive standards is that inductive strength comes in degrees, but deductive validity does not. An argument is either valid or invalid. There is no question of how much validity an argument has. In contrast, inductive arguments can be more or less strong. The more varied ravens or swans we observe, the stronger the inductive arguments above. Some inductive arguments are extremely strong and put their conclusions beyond any reasonable doubt. Other inductive arguments are much weaker, even though they still have some force.

Because of the necessary relationship between the premises and the conclusion of a valid deductive argument, it is often said that the premises of valid deductive arguments (if true) provide *conclusive* support for their conclusions, whereas true premises of strong inductive arguments provide only *partial* support for their conclusions. There is something to this. Because the premises of a valid deductive argument necessitate the truth of the conclusion, if those premises are known to be true, then they do supply conclusive reasons for the conclusion. The same cannot be said for inductive arguments.

It would be altogether misleading, however, to conclude from this that inductive arguments are inherently inferior to deductive arguments in supplying a justification or ground for a conclusion. In the first place, inductive arguments often place matters beyond any reasonable doubt. It is possible that the next pot of water will not boil at any temperature, however high, but this is not something we worry about. We do not take precautions against it, and we shouldn't.

More important, deductive arguments normally enjoy no advantages over their inductive counterparts. We can see this by comparing the two following arguments:

---

[1]This difference is sometimes described by saying that deductive standards are *monotonic*, whereas inductive standards are *non-monotonic*. These labels come from an analogy with mathematical curves. A (positive) monotonic curve rises, perhaps flattens out, but never changes direction. A non-monotonic curve can change direction; for example, rise, then fall. Similarly, the strength of an inductive argument can change up or down as further information is added, but the validity of a deductive argument is never lost by adding more premises.

DEDUCTIVE	INDUCTIVE
All ravens are black.	All observed ravens are black.
∴ If there is a raven on top of Pikes Peak, it is black.	∴ If there is a raven on top of Pikes Peak, it is black.

Of course, it is true for the deductive argument (and not true for the inductive argument) that if the premise is true, then the conclusion must be true. This may seem to give an advantage to the deductive argument over the inductive argument. But before we can decide how much support a deductive argument gives its conclusion, we must ask if its premises are, after all, true. That is not something we can just take for granted. If we examine the premises of these two arguments, we see that it is easier to establish the truth of the premise of the inductive argument than it is to establish the truth of the premise of the deductive argument. If we have observed carefully and kept good records, then we might be fully confident that all *observed* ravens have been black. On the other hand, how can we show that *all* ravens (observed and unobserved—past, present, and future) are black? The most obvious way (though there may be other ways) would be to observe ravens to see if they are black or not. This, of course, involves producing an inductive argument (called a statistical generalization) for the premise of the deductive argument. Here our confidence in the truth of the premise of the deductive argument should be no greater than our confidence in the strength of the inference in the statistical generalization. In this case—and it is not unusual—the deductive argument provides no stronger grounds in support of its conclusion than does its inductive counterpart, because any reservations we might have about the *strength* of the inductive inference will be paralleled by doubts concerning the *truth* of the premise of the deductive argument.

We will also avoid the common mistake of saying that deductive arguments always move from the general to the particular, whereas inductive arguments always move from the particular to the general. In fact, both sorts of arguments can move in either direction. There are inductive arguments intended to establish particular matters of fact, and there are deductive arguments that involve generalizations from particulars. For example, when scientists assemble empirical evidence to determine whether the extinction of the dinosaurs was caused by the impact of a meteor, their discussions are models of inductive reasoning. Yet they are not trying to establish a generalization or a scientific law. Instead, they are trying to determine whether a particular event occurred some 65 million years ago. Inductive reasoning concerning particular matters of fact occurs constantly in everyday life as well, for example, when we check to see whether our television reception is being messed up by someone using a computer. Deductive arguments from the particular to the general also exist, though they tend to be trivial, and hence boring. Here's one: Benjamin Franklin was the first postmaster general; therefore, anyone who is identical with Benjamin Franklin was the first postmaster general.

Of course, many deductive arguments do move from the general to the particular, and many inductive arguments do move from particular premises to a general conclusion. It is important to remember, however, that this is not the *definitive* difference between these two kinds of arguments. Indeed, the first kind of inductive reasoning that we will discuss often leads to conclusions about particular matters of fact.

EXERCISE I

Assuming a standard context, label each of the following arguments as deductive or inductive. Explain what it is about the words or form of argument that indicates whether or not each argument is intended or claimed to be valid. If it is not clear whether the argument is inductive or deductive, say why.

1. The sun is coming out, so the rain will probably stop soon.

2. It's going to rain tomorrow, so it will either rain or be clear tomorrow.

3. No woman has ever been elected president. Therefore, no woman will ever be elected president.

4. Diet cola never keeps me awake at night. I know because I drank it just last night without any problems.

5. The house is a mess, so Jeff must be home from college.

6. If Harold were innocent, he would not go into hiding. Since he is hiding, he must not be innocent.

7. Nobody in Paris seems to understand me, so either my French is rotten or Parisians are unfriendly.

8. Because both of our yards are near rivers in Tennessee, and my yard has lots of mosquitoes, there must also be lots of mosquitoes in your yard.

9. Most likely, her new husband speaks English with an accent, because he comes from Germany, and most Germans speak English with an accent.

10. There is no even number smaller than 2, so 1 is not an even number.

DISCUSSION QUESTIONS

1. The following arguments are not clearly inductive and also not clearly deductive. Explain why.
   a. All humans are mortal, and Socrates is a human, so Socrates is likely to be mortal also.
   b. We checked every continent there is, and evey raven in every continent was observed to be black, so every raven is black.
   c. If there's radon in your basement, this monitor will go off. The monitor is going off, so there must be radon in your basement. (Said by an engineer while running the monitor in your basement.)

2. In mathematics, proofs are sometimes employed using the method of *mathematical induction*. If you are familiar with this procedure, determine whether these proofs are deductive or inductive in character. Explain why.

INFERENCES TO THE BEST EXPLANATION

One of the most common forms of inductive argument is *inference to the best explanation*.[2] The general idea behind such inferences is that a hypothesis gains inductive support if, when added to our stock of previously accepted beliefs, it enables us to explain something that we observe or believe, and no competing explanation works nearly as well.

To see how inferences to the best explanation work, suppose you return to your home and discover that the lock on your front door is broken and some valuables are missing. In all likelihood, you will immediately conclude that you have been burglarized. Of course, other things *could* have produced the mess. Perhaps the police mistakenly busted into your house looking for drugs and took your valuables as evidence. Perhaps your friends are playing a strange joke on you. Perhaps a meteorite struck the door and then vaporized your valuables. In fact, all of these things *could* have happened (even the last), and further investigation could show that one of them did. Why, then, do we so quickly accept the burglary hypothesis without even considering these competing possibilities? The reason is that the hypothesis that your home was robbed is not highly improbable; and this hypothesis, together with other things we believe, provides the best—the strongest and the most natural—explanation of the phenomenon. The possibility that a meteorite struck your door is so wildly remote that it is not worth taking seriously. The possibility that your house was raided by mistake or that your friends are playing a strange practical joke on you is not wildly remote, but neither fits the overall facts very well. If it was a police raid, then you would expect to find a police officer there or at least a note. If it is a joke, then it is hard to see the point of it. By contrast, burglaries are not very unusual, and that hypothesis fits the facts extremely well. Logically, the situation looks like this:

(1) OBSERVATION: Your lock is broken, and your valuables are missing.

(2) EXPLANATION: The hypothesis that your house has been burglarized, combined with previously accepted facts and principles, provides a suitably strong explanation of observation 1.

(3) COMPARISON: No other hypothesis provides an explanation nearly as good as that in 2.

(4) CONCLUSION: Your house was burglarized.

The explanatory power of the conclusion gives us reason to believe it because doing so increases our ability to understand our observations and to make reliable predictions. Explanation is important because it makes sense out of things—makes them more intelligible—and we want to understand

[2]Gilbert Harman deserves much credit for calling attention to the importance of inferences to the best explanation; see, for example, his *Thought* (Princeton: Princeton University Press, 1973). A similar form of argument called abduction was analyzed long ago by Charles Saunders Peirce; see, for example, his *Collected Papers of Charles Saunders Peirce* (Cambridge: Harvard University Press, 1931), 5:189. A wonderful recent discussion is Peter Lipton, *Inference to the Best Explanation* (London: Routledge, 1991).

the world around us. Prediction is important because it tests our theories with new data and sometimes allows us to anticipate or even control future events. Inference to the best explanation enables us to achieve such goals.

Here it might help to compare inferences to the best explanation with other forms of argument. Prior to any belief about burglars, you were already *justified* in believing *that* your lock was broken and your valuables were missing. You could see that much. What you could not see was *why* your lock was broken. That question is what the explanation answers. Explanations help us understand why things happen, when we are already justified in believing those things did happen. (See Chapter 13.)

Explanations often take the form of arguments. In our example, we could argue:

> (1) Your house was burglarized.
> (2) When houses are burglarized, valuables are missing.
> ∴ (3) Your valuables are missing.

This explanatory argument starts with the hypothesis that was the conclusion of the inference to the best explanation, and it ends with the observation that was the first premise in that inference to the best explanation. The difference is that this new argument *explains* why its conclusion is true—why the valuables are missing—whereas the inference to the best explanation *justified* belief in its conclusion that your house was burglarized.

More generally, in an explanatory use of argument, we try to make sense of something by deriving it (sometimes deductively) from premises that are themselves well established. With an inference to the best explanation, we reason in the opposite direction: Instead of deriving an observation from its explanation, we derive the explanation from the observation. That a hypothesis provides the best explanation of something whose truth is already known provides evidence for the truth of that hypothesis.

Once we grasp the notion of an inference to the best explanation, we can see this pattern of reasoning everywhere. Solutions to murder mysteries almost always have the form of an inference to the best explanation. The facts of the case are laid out and then the clever detective argues that, given these facts, only one person could possibly have committed the crime. In the story "Silver Blaze," Sherlock Holmes concludes that the trainer must have been the dastardly fellow who stole Silver Blaze, the horse favored to win the Wessex Cup, which was to be run the following day. Holmes's reasoning, as usual, was very complex, but the key part of his argument was that the dog kept in the stable did not bark loudly when someone came and took away the horse.

> I had grasped the significance of the silence of the dog, for one true inference invariably suggests others. [I knew that] a dog was kept in the stables, and yet, though someone had been in and fetched out a horse, he had not barked enough to arouse the two lads in the loft. Obviously the midnight visitor was someone whom the dog knew well.[3]

[3]Sir Arthur Conan Doyle, "Silver Blaze," *The Complete Sherlock Holmes* (Garden City, NY: Doubleday, 1930), 1:349. The stories describe Holmes as a master of deduction, but his arguments are inductive as we define the terms.

Together with other facts, this was enough to identify the trainer, Straker, as the person who stole Silver Blaze. In this case, it is the fact that something *didn't* occur that provides the basis for an inference to the best explanation.

Of course, Holmes's inference is not absolutely airtight. It is possible that Straker is innocent and Martians with hypnotic powers over dogs committed the crime. But that only goes to show that this inference is neither valid nor deductive in our sense. It does not show anything wrong with Holmes's inference. Since his inference is inductive, it is enough for it to be strong.

Inferences to the best explanation are also defeasible. No matter how strong such an inference might be, it can always be overturned by future experience. Holmes might later find traces of a sedative in the dog's blood or someone else might confess or provide Straker with an alibi. Alternatively, Holmes (or you) might think up some better explanation. Still, unless and until such new evidence or hypothesis comes along, we have adequate reason to believe that Straker stole the horse, because that hypothesis provides the best available explanation of the information that we have now. The fact that future evidence or hypotheses always might defeat inferences to the best explanation does not show that such inferences are all bad.

We still need some way to determine which explanation is the *best*. There is, in fact, no simple rule for deciding this, but we can list some factors that go into the evaluation of an explanation.[4]

First, the hypothesis should really *explain the observations*. A good explanation makes sense out of that which it is intended to explain. In our original example, the broken lock can be explained by a burglary but not by the hypothesis that a friend came to see you (unless you have strange friends). Moreover, the hypothesis needs to explain *all* of the observations. The hypothesis of a mistaken police raid might explain the broken lock but not the missing valuables or the lack of any note or police officers when you return home.

The explanation should also be *deep*. An explanation is not deep but shallow when the explanation itself needs to be explained. It does not help to explain something that is obscure by citing something just as obscure. Why did the police raid your house? Because they had the wrong address. If they did not have the wrong address, then we would wonder why they suspected you. Without an explanation of *that*, the police raid hypothesis could not adequately explain even the broken lock.

Third, the explanation should be *powerful*. It is a mark of excellence in an explanation that the same kind of explanation can be used successfully over a wide range of cases. Many broken locks can be explained by burglaries. Explanatory range is especially important in science. One of the main reasons why Einstein's theory of relativity replaced Newtonian physics is that

---

[4]This discussion in many ways parallels and is indebted to the fifth chapter of W. V. Quine and J. S. Ullian, *The Web of Belief*, 2d ed. (New York: Random House, 1978).

Einstein could explain a wider range of phenomena, including very small particles at very high speeds.

Explanations go too far, however, when they could explain any possible event. Consider the hypothesis that each particle of matter has its own individual spirit that makes it do exactly what it does. This hypothesis might seem to explain some phenomena that even Einstein's theory cannot explain. But the spirit hypothesis really explains nothing, because it does not explain why any particle behaves one way as opposed to another. Either behavior is compatible with the hypothesis, so neither is explained. To succeed, therefore, explanations need to be incompatible with some possible outcome. In short, they need to be *falsifiable*. (See Chapter 12 on self-sealers.)

Moreover, explanations should be *modest* in the sense that they should not claim too much, that is, any more than is needed to explain the observations. When you find your lock broken and valuables gone, you should not jump to the conclusion that there is a conspiracy against you or that gangs have taken over your neighborhood. Without further information, there is no need to specify that there was more than one burglar in order to explain what you see. There is also no need to hypothesize that there was only one burglar. For this reason, the most modest explanation would not specify any number of burglars, so no inference to the best explanation could justify any claim about the number of burglars, at least until more evidence comes along.

Modesty is related to *simplicity.* One kind of simplicity is captured by the celebrated principle known as Occam's razor, which tells us not to multiply entities beyond necessity. Physicists, for example, should not postulate new kinds of subatomic particles or forces unless there is no other way to explain their experimental results. Similar standards apply in everyday life. We should not believe in ghosts unless they really are necessary to explain the noises in our attic or some other phenomenon. Simplicity is not always a matter of new kinds of entities. In comparison with earlier views, the theory that gases are composed of particles too small to see was simpler insofar as the particle theory allowed gas laws to be explained by the standard physical principles governing the motions of larger particles without having to add any new laws. Simplicity is a mark of excellence in an explanation partly because simple explanations are easier to understand and apply, but considerations of plausibility and aesthetics are also at work in judgments of which explanation is simplest.

The tests of modesty and simplicity might seem to be in tension with the test of power. This tension can be resolved only by finding the right balance. The best explanation will not claim any more than is necessary (so it will be modest), but it will claim enough to cover a wide range of phenomena (so it will be powerful). This is tricky, but the best explanations do it.

Finally, an explanation should be *conservative*. Explanations are better when they force us to give up fewer well-established beliefs. We have strong reasons to believe that cats cannot break metal locks. This rules out the hypothesis that your neighbor's cat broke your front-door lock. Explanations should also not contain claims that are themselves unlikely to be true. A meteorite would be strong enough to break your lock, but it is very unlikely that a meteorite struck your lock. That makes the burglary hypothesis better, at least until we find other evidence (such as meteorite fragments) that cannot be explained except by a meteorite.

In sum, a hypothesis provides the best explanation when it is more explanatory, powerful, falsifiable, modest, simple, and conservative than any competing hypothesis. Each of these standards can be met to varying degrees, and they can conflict. As we saw, the desire for simplicity might have to be sacrificed to gain a more powerful explanation. Conservatism also might have to give way to explain some unexpected observations, and so on. These standards are not always easy to apply, but they can often be used to determine whether a particular explanation is better than its competitors.

Once we determine that one explanation is the best, we still cannot yet infer that it is true. It might turn out that the best explanation out of a group of weak explanations isn't good enough. For centuries people were baffled by the floods that occurred in the Nile River each spring. The Nile, as far as anyone knew, flowed from an endless desert. Where, then, did the flood waters come from? Various wild explanations were suggested—mostly about deities of one kind or another—but none was any good. Looking for the best explanation among these weak explanations would be a waste of time. It was only after it was discovered that central Africa contains a high mountain range covered with snow in the winter that a reasonable explanation became possible. That, in fact, settled the matter. So it must be understood that the best explanation must also be a *good* explanation.

Even when an explanation is both good and best, what it explains might be illusory. Many people believe that shark cartilage prevents cancer, because the best explanation of why sharks do not get cancer lies in their cartilage. One serious problem for this inference is that sharks *do* get cancer. They even get cancer in their cartilage. So this inference to the best explanation fails.

When a particular explanation is both good and much better than any competitor, and when the explained observation is accurate, then an inference to the best explanation will provide *strong* inductive support. At other times, no clear winner or even reasonable contender emerges. In such cases, an inference to the best explanation will be correspondingly *weak*.

Whether an inference to the best explanation is strong *enough* depends on the context. As contexts shift, standards of rigor can change. Evidence that is strong enough to justify my belief that my spouse took our car might not be strong enough to convict our neighbor of stealing our car. Good judgment is often required to determine whether a certain degree of strength is adequate for the purposes at hand.

Context can also affect the rankings of various factors. Many explanations, for example, depend on universal premises. In such cases, compatibility with observation is usually the primary test. The universal principle should not be refuted by counterexamples (see Chapter 13). But sometimes explanatory power will take precedence: If a principle has strong explanatory power, we may accept it even in the face of clear disconfirming evidence. We do not give up good explanations lightly—nor should we. To understand why, notice that we do not test single propositions in isolation from other propositions in our system of beliefs. When faced with counterevidence to our beliefs, we often have a choice between what to give up and what to continue to hold onto. A simple example will illustrate this. Suppose that we believe the following things:

(1) Either John or Joan committed the crime.

(2) Whoever committed the crime must have had a motive for doing so.

(3) Joan had no motive to commit the crime.

From these three premises we can validly infer that John committed the crime. Suppose, however, that we discover that John could not have committed the crime. (Three bishops and two judges swear that John was somewhere else at the time.) Now, from the fact that John did not commit the crime, we could not immediately conclude that Joan committed it, for that would lead to an inconsistency. If she committed the crime, then, according to (3), she would have committed a motiveless crime, but that conflicts with (2), which says that motiveless crimes do not occur. So the discovery that John did not commit the crime entails that at least one of the premises in the argument must be abandoned, but it does not tell us which one or which ones.

This same phenomenon occurs when we are dealing with counterevidence to a complex system of beliefs. Counterevidence shows that there must be something wrong somewhere in the system, but it does not show exactly where the problem lies. One possibility is that the *supposed* counterevidence is itself in error. Imagine that a student carries out an experiment and gets the result that one of the fundamental laws of physics is false. This will not shake the scientific community even a little, for the best explanation of the student's result is that she messed things up. Given well-established principles, she could not have gotten the result she did if she had run the experiment correctly. Of course, if a great many reputable scientists find difficulties with a supposed law, then the situation is different. The hypothesis that all of these scientists, like the student, simply messed up is itself highly unlikely. But it is surprising how much contrary evidence will be tolerated when dealing with a strong explanatory theory. Scientists often continue to employ a theory in the face of counterevidence. Sometimes this perpetuates errors. For years, instruments reported that the levels of ozone above Antarctica were lower than before, but scientists attributed these measurements to bad equipment, until finally they announced an ozone hole there. Still, there is often good reason to hold on to a useful theory despite counterevidence, as long as its defects do not make serious trouble—that is, give bad results in areas that count. Good judgment is required to determine when it is finally time to shift to a different explanation.

Give two competing hypotheses that might be offered to explain each of the following phenomena. Which of these hypotheses is better? Why?

1. You follow a recipe carefully, but the bread never rises.
2. Your house begins to shake so violently that pictures fall off your walls.
3. Your key will not open the door of your house.
4. People start putting television cameras on your lawn, and a man with a big smile comes walking up your driveway.
5. Virtually all of the food in markets has suddenly sold out.
6. You put on a shirt and notice that there is no pocket on the front like there used to be.
7. A cave is found containing the bones of both prehistoric humans and now-extinct predators.
8. A cave is found containing the bones of both prehistoric humans and now-extinct herbivores.
9. After being visited by lobbyists for cigarette producers, your senator votes in favor of tobacco price supports, although he opposed them before.
10. Large, mysterious patterns of flattened wheat appear in the fields of Britain. (Some people attribute these patterns to visitors from another planet.)
11. A palm reader foretells that something wonderful will happen to you soon, and it does.
12. A neighbor sprinkles purple powder on his lawn to keep away tigers, and, sure enough, no tigers show up on his lawn.

Imagine that you offer an explanation, and a critic responds in the following way. Which virtue (explanatoriness, depth, power, falsifiability, modesty, simplicity, or conservativeness) is your critic claiming that your explanation lacks?

1. But that won't explain anything other than this particular case.
2. But that conflicts with everything we know about biology.
3. But you don't have to claim all of that in order to explain what we see.
4. But that just raises new questions that you need to answer.
5. But that explains only a small part of the story.
6. But that would apply whatever happened.

EXERCISE IV

For each of the following explanations, specify which standard of a good explanation, if any, it violates. The standards require that a good explanation be explanatory, deep, powerful, falsifiable, modest, simple, and conservative. A single explanation might violate more than one standard.

1. Although we usually have class at this time in this room, I don't see anybody in the classroom, because a wicked witch made them all invisible.

2. Although we usually have class at this time in this room, I don't see anybody in the classroom, because they all decided to skip class today.

3. Although we usually have class at this time in this room, I don't see anybody in the classrooom, because it's Columbus Day.

4. My house fell down, because it was painted red.

5. My house fell down, because of a powerful earthquake centered on my property that did not affect anything or anybody else.

6. My house fell down, because its boards were struck by a new kind of subatomic particle.

7. Although I fished here all day, I didn't catch any fish, because there are no fish in this whole river.

8. Although I fished here all day, I didn't catch any fish, because the river gods did not answer my prayers.

9. Although I fished here all day, I didn't catch any fish, because I was unlucky today.

10. That light far up in the night sky is moving quickly, because it is the daily United Airlines flight from Boston to Los Angeles.

11. That light far up in the night sky is moving quickly, because it is an alien space ship.

12. That light far up in the night sky looks like it is moving quickly, because there's something wrong with my eyes right now.

DISCUSSION QUESTIONS

1. Put the following inference to the best explanation in standard form, and then evaluate it as carefully as you can, using the tests discussed above.

[During the Archean Era, which extended from about 3.8 to 2.5 million years before the present,] the sun's luminosity was perhaps 25% less than that of today. . . . This faint young sun has led to a paradox. There is no evidence from the scant rock record of the Archean that the planetary surface was frozen. However, if Earth had no atmosphere or an atmosphere of composition like that of today, the amount of radiant energy received by Earth from the sun would not be enough to keep it from freezing. The way out of this dilemma is to have an atmosphere present during the early Archean that was diffrent in composition that that of today. . . . For a variety of reasons, it has been concluded, although still debated, that the most likely gases present in greater abundance in the Archean atmosphere were carbon dioxide, water vapor (the most important greenhouse gas) and perhaps methane. The presence of these greenhouse gases warmed the atmosphere and planetary surface and prevented the early Archean Earth from being frozen.[5]

2. Find three inferences to the best explanation in the readings on scientific reasoning in Chapter 16. This should be easy because scientists use this form of argument often. As in question 1, put those inferences in standard form, and then evaluate them as carefully as you can, using the tests discussed above.

3. Sherlock Holmes was lauded for his ability to infer a great deal of information about strangers from simple observations of their clothing and behavior. He displays this ability in the following exchange with his brother, Mycroft, in front of his friend Dr. Watson, who is the first-person narrator. Reconstruct and evaluate the inferences to the best explanation by Holmes and Mycroft in the closing paragraphs.

"THE GREEK INTERPRETER"

■

from *The Memoirs of Sherlock Holmes*

by Sir Arthur Conan Doyle

. . . The two sat down together in the bow-window of the club. "To anyone who wishes to study mankind this is the spot," said Mycroft. "Look at the magnificent types! Look at these two men who are coming towards us for example."

"The billiard-marker and the other?"

Precisely. What do you make of the other?

The two men had stopped opposite the window. Some chalk marks over the waistcoat pocket were the only signs of billiards which I could see in one of them. The other was a very small, dark fellow, with his hat pushed back and several packages under his arm.

"An old soldier, I perceive," said Sherlock.

"And very recently discharged," remarked the brother.

"Served in India, I see."

"And a non-commissioned officer."

"Royal Artillery, I fancy" said Sherlock.

"And a widower."

"But with a child."

"Children, my dear boy, children."

"Come," said I, laughing, "this is a little too much."

"Surely," answered Holmes, "it is not hard to say that a man with that bearing, expression of authority, and sun-baked skin, is a soldier, is more than a private, and is not long from India."

[5]From Fred T. Mackenzie, *Our Changing Planet* (Upper Saddle River, NJ: Prentice-Hall, 1998), 192.

"That he has not left the service long is shown by his still wearing his ammunition boots, as they are called," observed Mycroft.

"He had not the cavalry stride, yet he wore his hat on one side, as is shown by the lighter skin on that side of his brow. His weight is against his being a sapper [a soldier who builds and repairs fortifications]. He is in the artillery."

"Then, of course, his complete mourning shows that he has lost someone very dear. The fact that he is doing his own shopping looks as though it were his wife. He has been buying things for children, you perceive. There is a rattle, which shows that one of them is very young. The wife probably died in childbed. The fact that he has a picture-book under his arm shows that there is another child to be thought of."

ARGUMENTS FROM ANALOGY

Another common kind of inductive argument moves from a premise that two things are similar in some respects to a conclusion that they must also be analogous in a further respect. Such arguments from analogy can be found in many areas of everyday life. When we buy a new car, how can we tell whether it is going to be reliable? *Consumer Reports* might help if it is an old model; but if it is a brand-new model with no track record, then all we can go on is its similarities to earlier models. Our reasoning then seems to be that the new model is like the old model in various ways, and the old model was reliable, so the new model is probably reliable, too.

The same form of argument is used in science. Here's an example from geology:

> Meteorites composed predominantly of iron provide evidence that parts of other bodies in the solar system, presumably similar in origin to Earth, were composed of metallic iron. The evidence from meteorite compositions and origins lends support to the conclusion that Earth's core is metallic iron.[6]

The argument here is that Earth is analogous to certain meteors in their origins, and those meteors have a large percentage of iron, so the Earth as a whole probably contains about the same percentage of iron. Because a smaller amount of iron is present in the Earth's crust, the rest must lie in the Earth's core.

Similarly, archaeologists might argue that a certain knife was used in ritual sacrifices because it resembles other sacrificial knives in its size, shape, materials, carvings, and so on. The analogy in this case is between the newly discovered knife and the other knives. This analogy is supposed to support a conclusion about the function of the newly discovered knife.

[6]Mackenzie, *Our Changing Planet*, 42.

Although such arguments from analogy have diverse contents, they share a common form that can be represented like this:

    (1) Object A has properties P, Q, R, and so on.
    (2) Objects B, C, D, and so on also have properties P, Q, R, and so on.
    (3) Objects B, C, D, and so on have property X.

∴ (4) Object A probably also has property X.

In the archaeological example, object A is the newly discovered knife, and objects B, C, D, and so on are previously discovered knives that are known to have been used in sacrifices. Properties P, Q, R, and so on are the size, shape, materials, and carvings that make A analogous to B, C, D, and so on. X is the property of being used as a sacrificial knife. Premise (3) says that the previously discovered artifacts have this property. The conclusion, (4), says that the newly discovered artifact probably also has this property.

Since arguments from analogy are inductive, they normally aren't valid. It is possible that, even though this knife is analogous to other sacrificial knives, this knife was used to shave the king or just to cut bread. Such arguments are also defeasible. The argument about knives loses all of its strength if we find "Made in China" printed on the newly discovered knife. But none of this shows that arguments from analogy are no good. Despite being inductive, some arguments from analogy can still provide reasons—even strong reasons—for their conclusions.

How can we tell whether an argument from analogy is strong or weak? One obvious requirement is that the premises must be *true*. If the previously discovered knives were not really used in sacrifices, or if they do not really have the same carvings on their handles as the newly discovered knife, then this argument from analogy does not provide much, if any, support for its conclusion.

In addition, the cited similarities must be *relevant* and *important*. Suppose someone argues that his old car was red with a black interior and had four doors and a sunroof, and his new car also has these properties, so his new car is probably going to be as reliable as his old car. This argument is very weak because the cited similarities are obviously irrelevant to reliability. Such assessments of relevance depend on background beliefs, such as that reliability depends on the drive train and the engine rather than on the color or the sunroof.

Similarities are usually more important the more specific they are. Lots of cars with four tires and a motor are reliable, but this is not enough to infer that, because this particular car also has four tires and a motor, it will be reliable, too. The reason is obvious: There are also lots of unreliable cars with four tires and a motor. In general, if many objects have properties P, Q, and R, and many of those lack property X, then arguments from these analogies will be weak. In contrast, if a smaller percentage of objects that have properties P, Q, and R lack property X, then the argument from these analogies will be strong.

If we are not sure which respects *are* important, we still might have some idea of which respects *might* be important; and then we can try to cite objects that are analogous in as many as possible of those respects. By increasing the number of potentially relevant respects for which the analogy holds, we can increase the likelihood that the important respects will be on our list. That shows why arguments from analogy are usually stronger when they cite *more and closer analogies* between the objects.

Another factor that affects the strength of an argument from analogy is the presence of *relevant disanalogies*. Because arguments from analogy are defeasible, as we saw, a strong argument from analogy can become weak if we add a premise that states an important disanalogy. Suppose my new car is like my old cars in many ways, but there is one difference: The new car has an electric motor, whereas the old cars were powered by gas. This one difference is enough to remove much (if not all) of the strength from any argument to the conclusion that the new car will be reliable. Of course, other disanalogies, such as a different color, won't matter to reliability; and it will often require background knowledge to determine how important a disanalogy is.

We need to be careful here. Some disanalogies that are relevant do not undermine an argument from analogy. If a new engine design was introduced by top engineers to increase reliability, then this disanalogy might not undermine the argument from analogy. Differences that point to more reliability rather than less might even make the argument from analogy stronger.

Other disanalogies can increase the strength of an argument from analogy in a different way. If the same markings are found on very different kinds of sacrificial knives, then the presence of those markings on the newly discovered knife is even stronger evidence that this knife was also used in sacrifices. Differences among the cases cited only in the premises as analogies (that is, B, C, D, and so on) can strengthen an argument from analogy.

Finally, the strength of an argument from analogy depends on its conclusion. Analogies to other kinds of cars provide stronger evidence for a weak conclusion (such as that the new model will probably be pretty reliable) and weaker evidence for a strong conclusion (such as that the new model will definitely be just as reliable as the old model). As with other forms of argument, an argument from analogy becomes stronger as its conclusion becomes weaker and vice versa.

These standards can be summarized by saying that an argument from analogy is stronger when:

1. It cites more and closer analogies that are more important.
2. There are fewer or less important disanalogies between the object in the conclusion and the other objects.
3. The objects cited only in the premises are more diverse.
4. The conclusion is weaker.

After learning about arguments from analogy, it is natural to wonder how they are related to inferences to the best explanation. Although this is sometimes disputed, it seems to us that arguments from analogy are often—if not always—implicit and incomplete inferences to the best explanation. As we pointed out, analogies don't support any conclusion unless they are relevant, and whether they are relevant depends on how they fit into explanations. The color of a car is irrelevant to its reliability, because color plays no role in explaining its reliability. What explains its reliability is its drive train design, materials, care in manufacturing, and so on. That is why analogies in those respects can support a conclusion about reliability. Similarly, the markings on an artifact are relevant to whether it is a sacrificial knife *if* the best explanation of why it has those markings is that it was used in sacrifices. What makes that explanation best is that it also explains similar markings on other sacrificial knives. Thus, such arguments from analogy can be seen as involving an inference to the best explanation of why objects *B, C, D,* and so on have property *X* followed by an application of that explanation to the newly discovered object *A*.

Sometimes the explanation runs in the other direction. Whereas the conclusion about the knife's use (*X*) is supposed to explain its shared markings (*P, Q, R*), sometimes it is the shared features (*P, Q, R*) that are supposed to explain the feature claimed in the conclusion (*X*). Here is a classic example:

> We may observe a very great [similarity] between this earth which we inhabit, and the other planets, Saturn, Jupiter, Mars, Venus, and Mercury. They all revolve around the sun, as the earth does, although at different distances and in different periods. They borrow all their light from the sun, as the earth does. Several of them are known to revolve around their axis like the earth, and, by that means, must have a like succession of day and night. Some of them have moons that serve to give them light in the absence of the sun, as our moon does to us. They are all, in their motions, subject to the same law of gravitation, as the earth is. From all this similarity it is not unreasonable to think that those planets may, like our earth, be the habitation of various orders of living creatures. There is some probability in this conclusion from analogy.[7]

The argument here seems to be that some other planet probably supports life, because Earth does and other planets are similar to Earth in revolving around the sun and around an axis, getting light from the sun, and so on. What makes certain analogies relevant is not, of course, that the motion of Earth is explained by the presence of life here. Rather, certain features of Earth explain why Earth is habitable. The argument suggests that the best explanation of why there is life on our planet is that certain conditions make life possible. That generalization can then be used to support the conclusion that other planets with the same conditions probably support life as well.

In one way or another, arguments from analogy can be seen as inferences to the best explanation. But they are usually incomplete explanations. The argument for life on other planets did not have to commit itself to any particular theory about the origin of life or about which conditions are needed to support life. Nor did the car argument specify exactly what makes cars

---

[7]Thomas Reid, *Essays on the Intellectual Powers of Man* (Cambridge, MA: MIT Press, 1969), essay I, section 4, 48.

reliable. Such arguments from analogy merely list a number of similarities so that the list will be likely to include whatever factors are needed for life or for reliability. In this way, arguments from analogy can avoid depending on any complete theory about what is and what is not relevant.

This incompleteness makes arguments from analogy useful in situations where we do not yet know enough to formulate detailed theories or even to complete an inference to the best explanation. Yet the incompleteness of arguments from analogy also makes them more vulnerable to refutation, since the analogies that they list might fail to include a crucial respect. This does not mean that arguments from analogy are never any good. They can be strong. But it does suggest that their strength will increase as they approach or approximate more complete inferences to the best explanation.[8]

EXERCISE V

For each of the following arguments, state whether the indicated changes would make the argument weaker or stronger, and explain why. The strength of the argument might not be affected at all. If so, say why it is not affected.

1. My friend and I have seen many movies together, and we have always agreed on whether they are good or bad. My friend liked the movie trilogy *The Lord of the Rings*. So I probably will like it as well.

   Would this argument be weaker or stronger if:

   a. The only movies that my friend and I have watched together are come-dies, and *The Lord of the Rings* is not a comedy.

   b. My friend and I have seen very many, very different movies together.

   c. My friend and I always watched movies together on Wednesdays, but my friend watched *The Lord of the Rings* on a weekend.

   d. The conclusion claims that I definitely will like *The Lord of the Rings* a lot.

   e. The conclusion claims that I probably won't totally dislike *The Lord of the Rings*.

2. All the students from Joe's high school with high grades and high board scores did well in college. Joe also had high grades and board scores. So he will probably do well in college.

   Would this argument be weaker or stronger if:

   a. The other students worked hard, but Joe's good grades came easy to him, so he never learned to work hard.

   b. Joe is going to a different college than the students with whom he is being compared.

   c. Joe plans to major in some easy subject, but the other students were pre-med.

   d. Joe recently started taking drugs on a regular basis.

   e. Joe needs to work full-time to pay his college expenses, but the others had their expenses paid by their parents.

[8]For more on arguments from analogy, see "Precedents" in Chapter 14 and "Analogical Reason-ing in Ethics" in Chapter 15.

3. A new drug cures a serious disease in rats. Rats are similar to humans in many respects. Therefore, the drug will probably cure the same disease in humans.

   Would this argument be weaker or stronger if:

   a. The disease affects the liver, and rat livers are very similar to human livers.

   b. The drug does not cure this disease in cats.

   c. The drug has to be injected into the rat's tail to be effective.

   d. No drug of this general type has been used on humans before.

   e. The effects of the drug are enhanced by eating cooked foods.

EXERCISE VI

Using the criteria mentioned above, evaluate each of the following arguments as strong or weak. Explain your answers. Be sure to specify the properties on which the analogy is based, as well as any background beliefs on which your evaluation depends.

1. This landscape by Cézanne is beautiful. He did another painting of a similar scene around the same time. So it is probably beautiful, too.

2. My aunt had a Siamese cat that bit me, so this Siamese cat will probably bite me, too.

3. The students I know who took this course last year got grades of A. I am a lot like them, since I am also smart and hardworking; and the course this year covers very similar material. So I will probably get an A.

4. This politician was caught cheating in his marriage, and he will have to face similarly strong temptations in his public duties, so he will probably cheat in political life as well.

5. A very high minimum wage led to increased unemployment in one country. That country's economy is similar to the economy in a different country. So a very high minimum wage will probably lead to increased unemployment in the other country as well.

6. I feel pain when someone hits me hard on the head with a baseball bat. Your body is a lot like mine. So you would probably feel pain if I hit you hard on the head with a baseball bat. (This is related to the so-called "Problem of Other Minds.")

7. It is immoral for a doctor to lie to a patient about a test result, even if the doctor thinks that lying is in the patient's best interest. We know this because even doctors would agree that it would be morally wrong for a financial advisor to lie to them about a potential investment, even if the financial advisor thinks that this lie is in the doctor's best interests.

8. Chrysler was held legally liable for damages due to defects in the suspension of its Corvair. The defects in the Pinto gas tank caused injuries that were just as serious. Thus, Ford should also be held legally liable for damages due to those defects.

1. In Chapter 14, critics argue that affirmative action is unconstitutional because of analogies to other forms of racial discrimination that were found unconstitutional in precedents. Reconstruct these arguments in the form of arguments from analogy, then evaluate them by applying the criteria discussed above.

2. In Chapter 15, Thomson defends the morality of abortion by means of an analogy to a kidnapped violinist. Reconstruct this argument in the form of an argument from analogy, then evaluate it by applying the criteria discussed above.

3. In Chapter 17, Paley argues for the existence of God on the basis of an analogy to a watch. Reconstruct this argument in the form of an argument from analogy, then evaluate it by applying the criteria discussed above.

4. In Chapter 18, Searle argues that computers cannot think just by virtue of their formal structure, because of an analogy to a Chinese room with the same formal structure. Reconstruct this argument in the form of an argument from analogy, then evaluate it by applying the criteria discussed above.

5. The following excerpt comes from a newspaper report in the *Toronto Star,* October 10, 1999. Put the central argument from analogy, which is italicized, into standard form. Then reconstruct the argument as an inference to the best explanation. Which representation best captures the force of the argument, or are they equally good?

A GNAWING QUESTION IS ANSWERED

by Michael Downey

Tim White is worried that he may have helped to pin a bad rap on the Neanderthals, the prehistoric Europeans who died out 25,000 years ago. "There is a danger that everyone will think that all Neanderthals were cannibals and that's not necessarily true," he says. White was part of a French-American team of paleoanthropologists who recently found conclusive evidence that at least some Neanderthals ate others about 100,000 years ago. But that doesn't mean they were cannibalistic by nature, he stresses. Most people don't realize that cannibalism is widespread throughout nature, says White, a professor at the University of California at Berkeley and the author of a book on prehistoric cannibalism.

The question of whether the Neanderthals were cannibals had long been a hotly debated topic among anthropologists. No proof had ever been found. That debate ended, however, with the recent analysis by the team of stone tools and bones found in a cave at Moula-Guercy in southern France. The cave is about the size of a living room, perched about 80 metres above the Rhone River. "This one site has all of the evidence right together," says White. "It's as if somebody put a yellow tape around the cave for 100,000 years and kept the scene intact." The bones of deer and other fauna show the clear markings of the nearby stone tools, indicating the deer had been expertly butchered; they were skinned, their body parts cut off and the meat and tendons sliced from the bone. Long bones were bashed open "to get at the fatty marrow inside," says White.

So what does all this have to do with cannibalism? *The bones of the six (so far) humans in the same locations have precisely the same markings made by the same tools. That means these fairly modern humans were skinned and eaten in the same manner as the deer.*

And if you are thinking they were eaten after they just happened to die, they do represent all age groups. Two were children about 6 years old, two were teenagers and two were adults.

But maybe they were eaten at a time when food was unusually scarce, right? Not so. There is a large number of animal bones at the same dig, indicating that there were options to eating other Neanderthals.

Human bones with similar cut marks have been found throughout Europe, from Spain to Croatia, providing tantalizing hints of Neanderthal cannibalism activity over tens of thousands of years. But finding such clear evidence of the same preparation techniques being used on deer in the same cave site in France, will "necessitate reassessment of earlier finds," always attributed to ritual burial practices or some other explanation, says White.

It was not clear whether the Neanderthals ate human flesh of their own tribe or exclusively from an enemy tribe, White stresses. Nor was there any indication the purpose of the cannibalism involved nourishment. Eating human flesh could have had another purpose altogether, he says. Surprising to some, cannibalism has been found in 75 mammal species and in 15 primate groups. White says it has often been practiced for reasons not associated with normal hunger. White quotes an archeological maxim: "Actions fossilize, intentions don't." In other words, the reason for the cannibalism remains unknown. He notes that the flesh of other humans has sometimes been eaten to stave off starvation, to show contempt for an enemy or as part of a ritual of affection for the deceased. "Were the victims already dead or killed to be eaten?" he asks, "Were they enemies of the tribe or family members?" Learning these details is the "important and extremely difficult part."

This excavation represents a breakthrough in archeological practice. In a series of papers, White has long advocated the importance of treating a dig site like a crime scene, leaving every piece of evidence in place. In many earlier digs, animal bones were frequently pulled out and thrown away as being irrelevant and human bones were often coated with shellac. The human bones were all tossed into the same bag with no regard to their juxtaposition to each other or precise location. This is one of the first times that modern forensic techniques have been utilized in an archeological excavation, White says, and conclusions drawn have been much more precise than in previous digs that used cruder methods. The project team, which is headed by Alban Defleur of the Universite du Mediterrane at Marseilles, has been digging in the cave since 1991.

REASONING ABOUT CAUSES

Many explanations depend on causal generalizations. If our car goes dead in the middle of rush-hour traffic just after its 20,000-mile checkup, we assume that there must be some reason why this happened. Cars just don't stop for no reason at all. So we ask, "What caused our car to stop?" The answer might be that it ran out of gas. If we find, in fact, that it did run out of gas, then that will usually be the end of the matter. We will think that we have discovered why this particular car stopped running. This reasoning is about a particular car on a particular occasion, but it rests on certain *generalizations:* We are confident that *our* car stopped running when it ran out of gas, because we believe that *all* cars stop running when they run out of gas. We probably did not think about this, but our causal reasoning in this particular case appealed to a commonly accepted *causal generalization:* Cars will not run without gas.

Causal generalizations are also used to *predict* the consequences of particular actions or events. A race car driver might wonder, for example, what would happen if he added just a bit of nitroglycerin to his fuel mixture. Would it give him better acceleration, blow him up, do very little, or what? In fact, the driver may not be in a position to answer this question straight off, but his thinking will be guided by the causal generalization that igniting nitroglycerin can cause a dangerous explosion.

So a similar pattern arises for both causal explanation and causal prediction. These inferences contain two essential elements:

1. The facts in the particular case. (For example, the car stopped and the gas gauge reads empty; or I just put a pint of nitroglycerine in the gas tank of my Maserati, and I am about to turn the ignition key.)
2. Certain causal generalizations. (For example, cars do not run without gas, or nitroglycerin explodes when ignited.)

The basic idea is that causal inferences bring particular facts under causal generalizations.

This shows why causal generalizations are important, but what exactly are they? Although this issue remains controversial, here we will treat them as a kind of *general conditional*. A general conditional has the following form:

For all x, if x has the feature F, then x has the feature G.

We will say that, according to this conditional, x's having the feature F is a *sufficient condition* for its having the feature G; and x's having the feature G is a *necessary condition* for its having the feature F.

Some general conditionals are not *causal*. Neither of these two general conditionals expresses a causal relationship:

If something is a square, then it is a rectangle.

If you are eighteen years old, then you are eligible to vote.

The first conditional tells us that being a square is sufficient for being a rectangle, but this is a mathematical (or a priori) relationship, not a causal one. The second conditional tells us that being eighteen years old is a sufficient condition for being eligible to vote. The relationship here is legal, not causal.

Although many general conditionals are not causal, all causal conditionals are general, in our view. Consequently, if we are able to show that a causal conditional is false just by virtue of its being a general conditional, we will have refuted it. This will serve our purposes well, for in what follows we will be largely concerned with finding reasons for *rejecting* causal generalizations.

It is important to weed out false causal generalizations, because they can create lots of trouble. Doctors used to think that bloodletting would cure disease. They killed many people in the process of trying to heal them. Thus, although we need causal generalizations for getting along in the world, we also need to get them right. We will be more likely to succeed if we have proper principles for testing and applying such generalizations. It is one of the central tasks of inductive logic to supply these principles.

In the past, very elaborate procedures have been developed for this purpose. The most famous set of such procedures was developed by John Stuart Mill and has come to be known as Mill's methods.[9] Though inspired by Mill's methods, the procedures introduced here involve some fundamental simplifications; whereas Mill introduced five methods, we will introduce only three primary rules.

The first two rules are the Sufficient Condition Test (SCT) and the Necessary Condition Test (NCT). We will introduce these tests first at an abstract level. One advantage of formulating these tests abstractly is so that they can be applied to other kinds of sufficient and necessary conditions, for example, those that arise in legal and moral reasoning, the topics of Chapters 14 and 15. Once it is clear how these tests work in general, we will apply them specifically to causal reasoning.

SUFFICIENT CONDITIONS AND NECESSARY CONDITIONS

To keep our discussion as general as possible, we will adopt the following definitions of sufficient conditions and necessary conditions:

> Feature *F* is a *sufficient* condition for feature *G* if and only if anything that *has* feature *F* also *has* feature *G*.

> Feature *F* is a *necessary* condition for feature *G* if and only if anything that *lacks* feature *F* also *lacks* feature *G*.

[9]Mill's methods of experimental enquiry" are found in book 3, chap. 8 of his *A System of Logic* (London: John W. Parker, 1843). Mill's method of difference, method of agreement, and joint method parallel our SCT, NCT, and Joint Test, respectively. Our simplification of Mill's methods derives from Brian Skyrms, *Choice and Chance,* 3d ed. (Belmont, CA: Wadsworth, 1986), chap. 4.

These definitions are equivalent to those in the previous section, because, if anything that *lacks* feature F also *lacks* feature G, then anything that *has* feature G must also *have* feature F; and if anything that *has* feature G must also *have* feature F, then anything that *lacks* feature F also *lacks* feature G. It follows that feature F is a sufficient condition for feature G if and only if feature G is a necessary condition for feature F.[10]

When F is sufficient for G, the relation between these features can be diagrammed like this:

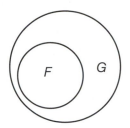

The inside circle represents the sufficient condition, because anything inside that inside circle must also be inside the outside circle. The outside circle represents the necessary condition, for anything outside the outside circle must also be outside the inside circle.

These diagrams, along with the preceding definitions, should make it clear that something can be a sufficient condition for a feature without being a necessary condition for that feature, and vice versa. For example, being the element mercury is a *sufficient* condition for being a metal, but it is not a *necessary* condition for being a metal, since there are other metals. Similarly, being a metal is a *necessary* condition for being mercury, but it is not a *sufficient* condition for being mercury. Of course, some necessary conditions are also sufficient conditions. Being mercury is both necessary and sufficient for being a metallic element that is liquid at twenty degrees Centigrade. Nonetheless, many necessary conditions are not sufficient conditions, and vice versa, so we need to be careful not to confuse the two kinds of conditions.

This distinction becomes complicated when conditions get complex. Our definitions and tests hold for all features, whether positive or negative (such as not having hair) and whether simple or conjunctive (such as having both a beard and a mustache) or disjunctive (such as having either a beard or a mustache). Thus, not having any hair (anywhere) on your head is a sufficient condition of not having a beard, so not having a beard is a necessary condition of not having any hair on your head. But not having any hair on your head is not necessary for not having a beard, because you can have some hair on the top of your head without having a beard. Negation can create confusion, so we need to think carefully about what is being claimed to be necessary or sufficient for what.

---

[10]Symbolization might make this clearer, because in quantificational logic, "$(x)(Fx \supset Gx)$" is equivalent to "$(x)(\sim Gx \supset \sim Fx)$" (see Chapter 8).

Even in simple cases, there is a widespread tendency to confuse necessary conditions with sufficient conditions, as we saw in Chapter 6, It is important to keep these concepts straight, for, as we will see, the tests concerning them are fundamentally different.

EXERCISE VII

Which of the following claims are true? Which are false?

1. Being a car is a sufficient condition for being a vehicle.
2. Being a car is a necessary condition for being a vehicle.
3. Being a vehicle is a sufficient condition for being a car.
4. Being a vehicle is a necessary condition for being a car.
5. Being an integer is a sufficient condition for being an even number.
6. Being an integer is a necessary condition for being an even number.
7. Being an integer is a sufficient condition for being either even or odd.
8. Being an integer is a necessary condition for being either even or odd.
9. Not being an integer is a sufficient condition for not being odd.
10. Not being an integer is a sufficient condition for not being even.
11. Being both an integer and divisible by 2 without remainder is a sufficient condition for being even.
12. Being both an integer and divisible by 2 without remainder is a necessary condition for being even.
13. Being divisible by 2 without remainder is a necessary condition for being even.
14. Driving seventy-five miles per hour (for fun) is a sufficient condition for violating a legal speed limit of sixty-five miles per hour.
15. Driving seventy-five miles per hour (for fun) is a necessary condition for violating a legal speed limit of sixty-five miles per hour.
16. Cutting off Joe's head is a sufficient condition for killing him.
17. Cutting off Joe's head is a necessary condition for killing him.
18. Cutting off Joe's head and then holding his head under water for ten minutes is a sufficient condition for killing him.

EXERCISE VIII

Indicate whether the following principles are true or false and why.

1. If having feature *F* is a *sufficient* condition for having feature *G*, then having feature *G* is a *necessary* condition for having feature *F*.
2. If having feature *F* is a *sufficient* condition for having feature *G*, then lacking feature *F* is a *necessary* condition for lacking feature *G*.

3. If lacking feature *F* is a *sufficient* condition for having feature *G*, then having feature *F* is a *necessary* condition for lacking feature *G*.

4. If having feature *F* is a *sufficient* condition for having feature *G*, then lacking feature *F* is a *necessary* condition for lacking feature *G*.

5. If having either feature *F* or feature *G* is a *sufficient* condition for having feature *H*, then having feature *F* is a *sufficient* condition for having feature *H*.

6. If having either feature *F* or feature *G* is a *sufficient* condition for having feature *H*, then having feature *G* is a *sufficient* condition for having feature *H*.

7. If having either feature *F* or feature *G* is a *sufficient* condition for having feature *H*, then not having feature *F* is a *necessary* condition for not having feature *H*.

8. If having both feature *F* and feature *G* is a *necessary* condition for having feature *H*, then lacking feature *F* is a *sufficient* condition for lacking feature *H*.

9. If not having both feature *F* and feature *G* is a *sufficient* condition for having feature *H*, then lacking feature *F* is a *sufficient* condition for having feature *H*.

10. If having either feature *F* or feature *G* is a *sufficient* condition for having feature *H*, then having both feature *F* and feature *G* is a *sufficient* condition for having feature *H*.

THE SUFFICIENT CONDITION TEST

We can now formulate tests to determine when something meets our definitions of sufficient conditions and necessary conditions. It will simplify matters if we first state these tests formally using letters. We will also begin with a simple case where we consider only four *candidates*—*A*, *B*, *C*, and *D*—for sufficient conditions for a *target* feature, *G*. *A* will indicate that the feature is present; ~*A* will indicate that this feature is absent. Using these conventions, suppose that we are trying to decide whether any of the four features—*A*, *B*, *C*, or *D*—could be a sufficient condition for *G*. To this end, we collect data of the following kind:

TABLE 1

Case 1:	*A*	*B*	*C*	*D*	*G*
Case 2:	~*A*	*B*	*C*	~*D*	~*G*
Case 3:	*A*	~*B*	~*C*	~*D*	~*G*

We know by definition that, for something to be a sufficient condition of something else, when the former is present, the latter must be present as well. Thus, to test whether a candidate really is a sufficient condition of *G*, we only have to examine cases in which the target feature, *G*, is absent, and then check to see whether any of the candidate features are present. The sufficient condition test (SCT) can be stated as follows:

SCT: Any candidate that is present when G is absent is eliminated as a possible sufficient condition of G.

The test applies to Table 1 as follows: Case 1 need not be examined because G is present, so there can be no violation of SCT in Case 1. Case 2 eliminates two of the candidates, B and C, for both are present in a situation in which G is absent. Finally, Case 3 eliminates A for the same reason. We are thus left with D as our only remaining candidate for a sufficient condition for G.

Now let's consider D. Having survived the application of the SCT, does it follow that D is a sufficient condition for G? No! On the basis of what we have been told so far, it remains entirely possible that the discovery of a further case will reveal an instance where D is present and G absent, thus showing that D is not a sufficient condition for G either.

Case 4: A B $\sim C$ D $\sim G$

In this way, it is always possible for new cases to refute any inference from a limited group of cases to the conclusion that a certain candidate is a sufficient condition. In contrast, no further case can change the fact that A, B, and C are not sufficient conditions, because they fail the SCT.

This shows that, when we apply the SCT to rule out a candidate as a sufficient condition, our argument is *deductive*. We simply find a counterexample to the universal claim that a certain feature is sufficient. However, when a candidate is not ruled out and we draw the positive conclusion that that candidate *is* a sufficient condition, then our argument is *inductive*. Inductive inferences, however well confirmed, are always defeasible. (Remember Captain Cook's discovery of black swans.) That is why our inductive inference to the conclusion that D is a sufficient condition could be refuted by the new case, 4.

THE NECESSARY CONDITION TEST

The necessary condition test (NCT) is like the SCT but works in the reverse fashion. With SCT we eliminated a candidate F from being the sufficient condition for G, if F was ever present when G was absent. With the necessary condition test, we eliminate a candidate F from being a necessary condition for G if we can find a case where G is present, but F is not. This makes sense, because if G can be present when F is not, then F cannot be necessary for the occurrence of G. Thus, in applying the necessary condition test, we only have to examine cases in which the target feature, G, is present, and then check to see whether any of the candidate features are absent.

NCT: Any candidate that is absent when G is present is eliminated as a possible necessary condition of G.

The following table gives an example of an application of this test:

TABLE 2:

Case 1:	A	B	C	D	~G
Case 2:	~A	B	C	D	G
Case 3:	A	~B	C	~D	G

Because Case 1 does not provide an instance where G is present, it cannot eliminate any candidate as a necessary condition. Case 2 eliminates A, since it shows that G can be present without A being present. Case 3 eliminates both B and D, leaving C as the only possible candidate for being a necessary condition for G. From this, of course, it does not follow that C *is* a necessary condition for G, for, as always, new cases might eliminate it as well. The situation is the same as with the SCT. An argument for a negative conclusion that a candidate is not a necessary condition, because that candidate fails the NCT, is a deductive argument that cannot be overturned by any further cases. In contrast, an argument for a positive conclusion that a candidate is a necessary condition, because that candidate passes the NCT, is an inductive argument that can be overturned by a further case where this candidate fails the NCT.

THE JOINT TEST

It is also possible to apply these rules simultaneously in the search for possible conditions that are both sufficient and necessary. Any candidate cannot be both sufficient and necessary if it fails either the SCT or the NCT. In Table 2, C is the only possible necessary condition for G, and it is not also a possible sufficient condition, since C fails the SCT in Case 1, where C is present and G is absent. In Table 1, however, D is a possible sufficient condition of G, because D is never present when G is absent; and D might also be a necessary condition for G, since G is never present when D is absent. Thus, none of the cases in Table 1 eliminates D as a candidate for a condition that is both sufficient and necessary. As before, this possibility still might be refuted by Case 4, so any inference to a positive conclusion that some candidate is a necessary and sufficient condition must be defeasible and, hence, inductive.

EXERCISE IX

For each of the following tables decide:

a. Which, if any, of the candidates—A, B, C, or D—is not eliminated by the sufficient condition test?

b. Which, if any, of the candidates—A, B, C, or D—is not eliminated by the necessary condition test?

c. Which, if any, of the candidates—A, B, C, or D—is not eliminated by either test?

EXAMPLE: Case 1: A B $\sim C$ D $\sim G$

                Case 2: $\sim A$ B C D G

                Case 3: A $\sim B$ C D G

a. Only C passes the SCT.
b. Only C and D pass the NCT.
c. Only C passes both tests.

1. Case 1: A B C D G
    Case 2: $\sim A$ B $\sim C$ D $\sim G$
    Case 3: A $\sim B$ C $\sim D$ G

2. Case 1: A B C $\sim D$ G
    Case 2: $\sim A$ B C D G
    Case 3: A $\sim B$ C $\sim D$ G

3. Case 1: A B C D $\sim G$
    Case 2: $\sim A$ B C D G
    Case 3: A $\sim B$ C $\sim D$ G

4. Case 1: A B $\sim C$ D G
    Case 2: $\sim A$ $\sim B$ C D G
    Case 3: A B $\sim C$ $\sim D$ $\sim G$

5. Case 1: A $\sim B$ C D $\sim G$
    Case 2: $\sim A$ B C $\sim D$ $\sim G$
    Case 3: A $\sim B$ $\sim C$ D G

6. Case 1: A B $\sim C$ D G
    Case 2: $\sim A$ $\sim B$ C D $\sim G$
    Case 3: A $\sim B$ C $\sim D$ $\sim G$

7. Case 1: A B $\sim C$ D $\sim G$
    Case 2: $\sim A$ B $\sim C$ D $\sim G$
    Case 3: A B $\sim C$ $\sim D$ $\sim G$

8. Case 1: A B C D $\sim G$
    Case 2: $\sim A$ $\sim B$ C D G

EXERCISE X

Imagine that your computer system won't work, and you want to find out
why. After checking to make sure that it is plugged in, you experiment with a
new CPU (central processing unit), a new external hard drive, a new monitor,
and new system software in the combinations on the table below.

	Plug	CPU	Hard Drive	Monitor	Software	Result
Case 1	In	Old CPU	Old HD	Old MO	Old SW	Works
Case 2	In	Old CPU	Old HD	Old MO	New SW	Works
Case 3	In	Old CPU	Old HD	New MO	Old SW	Fails
Case 4	In	Old CPU	Old HD	New MO	New SW	Works
Case 5	In	Old CPU	New HD	Old MO	Old SW	Works
Case 6	In	Old CPU	New HD	Old MO	New SW	Works
Case 7	In	Old CPU	New HD	New MO	Old SW	Fails
Case 8	In	Old CPU	New HD	New MO	New SW	Works
Case 9	In	New CPU	Old HD	Old MO	Old SW	Fails
Case 10	In	New CPU	Old HD	Old MO	New SW	Works
Case 11	In	New CPU	Old HD	New MO	Old SW	Fails
Case 12	In	New CPU	Old HD	New MO	New SW	Works

The candidates for necessary conditions and sufficient conditions of failure are the plug position, the CPU, the hard drive, the monitor, and the software. For each candidate, say (1) which cases, if any, eliminate it as a sufficient condition of your computer's failure and (2) which cases, if any, eliminate it as a necessary condition of your computer's failure. Which candidates, if any, are not eliminated as a sufficient condition of failure? As a necessary condition of failure? Does it follow that these candidates are necessary conditions or sufficient conditions of failure? Why or why not?

EXERCISE XI

After a banquet, several diners get sick and die. You suspect that something they ate or drank caused their deaths. The following table records their meals and fates:

Cases	Soup	Entrée	Wine	Dessert	Result
Ann	Tomato	Chicken	White	Pie	Alive
Barney	Tomato	Fish	Red	Cake	Dead
Cathy	Tomato	Beef	Red	Ice Cream	Alive
Doug	Tomato	Beef	Red	Cake	Alive
Emily	Tomato	Fish	Red	Pie	Dead
Fred	Tomato	Fish	Red	Cake	Dead
Gertrude	Leek	Fish	White	Pie	Alive
Harold	Tomato	Beef	White	Cake	Alive
Irma	Leek	Fish	Red	Pie	Dead
Jack	Leek	Beef	Red	Ice Cream	Alive
Ken	Leek	Chicken	Red	Ice Cream	Alive
Leslie	Tomato	Chicken	White	Cake	Alive

The target feature is death. The candidates for necessary conditions and sufficient conditions of death are the soup, entrée, wine, and dessert. For each candidate, say (1) which cases, if any, eliminate it as a sufficient condition of death and (2) which cases, if any, eliminate it as a necessary condition of death. Which candidates, if any, are not eliminated as a sufficient condition of death? As a necessary condition of death? Does it follow that these candidates are necessary conditions or sufficient conditions of death? Why or why not?

RIGOROUS TESTING

Going back to Table 1, it is easy to see that A, B, C, and D are not eliminated by NCT as necessary conditions of G, as G is present in only one case (Case 1) and A, B, C, and D are present there as well. So far, so good. But if we wanted to test these features more rigorously, it would be important to find more cases in which G was present and see if these candidates are also present and thus continue to survive the NCT.

The following table gives a more extreme example of nonrigorous testing:

TABLE 3

Case 1:	A	$\sim B$	C	D	G
Case 2:	A	$\sim B$	$\sim C$	$\sim D$	$\sim G$
Case 3:	A	$\sim B$	C	$\sim D$	$\sim G$
Case 4:	A	$\sim B$	$\sim C$	D	G

Here, A is eliminated by SCT (in Cases 2 and 3) but is not eliminated by NCT, so it is a possible necessary condition but not a possible sufficient condition. B is not eliminated by SCT but is eliminated by NCT (in Cases 1 and 4), so it is a possible sufficient condition but not a possible necessary condition. C is eliminated by both rules (in Cases 3 and 4). Only D is not eliminated by either test, so it is the only candidate for being both a necessary and a sufficient condition for G.

The peculiarity of this example is that A is always present whether G is present or not, and B is always absent whether G is absent or not. Now if something is always present, as A is, then it cannot possibly fail the NCT; for there cannot be a case where the target is present and the candidate is absent if the candidate is *always* present. If we want to test A rigorously under the NCT, then we should try to find cases in which A is absent and then check to see whether G is absent as well.

In reverse fashion, but for similar reasons, if we want to test B rigorously under the SCT, we should try to find cases in which B is present and then check to see if G is present as well. If we restrict our attention to cases where B is always absent, as in Table 3, then B cannot fail the SCT, but passing that test will be trivial for B and so will not even begin to show that B is a sufficient condition.

Now consider two more sets of data just like Table 2, except with regard to the target feature, G:

TABLE 4:

Case 1:	A	B	C	D	G
Case 2:	$\sim A$	B	C	D	G
Case 3:	A	$\sim B$	C	$\sim D$	G

TABLE 5:

Case 1:	A	B	C	D	$\sim G$
Case 2:	$\sim A$	B	C	D	$\sim G$
Case 3:	A	$\sim B$	C	$\sim D$	$\sim G$

Because G is present in all of the cases in Table 4, no candidates can be eliminated by the SCT. This result is trivial, however. Table 4 does not provide rigorous testing for a sufficient condition, because our attention is restricted to a range of cases that is too narrow. Nothing could possibly be eliminated as a sufficient condition as long as G is always present.

Similarly, G is absent in all of the cases in Table 5, so no candidates can be eliminated by the NCT. Still, because this data is so limited, its failure to eliminate candidates does not even begin to show that anything is a necessary condition.

For both rules, then, rigorous testing involves seeking out cases in which failing the test is a live possibility. For the SCT, this requires looking both at cases in which the candidates are present and also at cases in which the target is absent. For the NCT, rigorous testing requires looking both at cases in which the candidates are absent and also at cases in which the target is present. Without cases like these, passing the tests is rather like a person bragging that he has never struck out when, in fact, he has never come up to bat.

REACHING POSITIVE CONCLUSIONS

Suppose that we performed rigorous testing on candidate C, and it passed the SCT with flying colors. Can we now draw the positive conclusion that C is a sufficient condition? That depends on which kinds of candidates and cases have been considered. Since rigorous testing was passed, these three conditions are met:

1. We have not found any case in which the candidate, C, is present and the target, G, is absent.
2. We have tested some cases in which the candidate, C, is present.
3. We have tested some cases in which the target, G, is absent.

For it to be reasonable to reach a positive conclusion that C is sufficient for G, this further condition must also be met:

4. We have tested enough cases of the various kinds that are likely to include a case in which C is present and G is absent if there is any such case.

This new condition cannot be applied in the mechanical way that conditions (1)–(3) could be applied. To determine whether condition (4) is met, we need to rely on *background information* about how many cases are "enough" and about which kinds of cases "are likely to include a case in which C is present and G is absent, if there is any such case." For example, if we are trying to figure out whether our software is causing our computer to crash, we do not need to try the same kind of computer in different colors. What we need to try are different kinds of CPUs, hard drives, monitors, software, and so on, because we know that these are the kinds of factors that can affect performance. Background information like this is what tells us when we have tested enough cases of the right kinds.

Of course, our background assumptions might turn out to be wrong. Even if we have tested many variations of every factor that we think might be relevant, we still might be surprised and find a further case in which C and ~G are present. All that shows, however, is that our inference is defeasible, like all inductive arguments. Despite the possibility that future discoveries might undermine it, our inductive inference can still be strong if our background beliefs are justified and if we have looked long and hard without finding any case in which C is present and G is absent.

Similar rules apply in reverse to positive conclusions about necessary conditions. We have good reason to suppose that candidate C is a necessary condition for target G, if the following conditions are met:

1. We have not found any case in which the candidate, C, is absent and the target, G, is present.

2. We have tested some cases in which the candidate, C, is absent.

3. We have tested some cases in which the target, G, is present.

4. We have tested enough cases of the various kinds that are likely to include a case in which C is absent and G is present, if there is any such case.

As before, this argument is defeasible; but, if our background assumptions are justified, the fact that conditions 1–4 are all met can still provide a strong reason for the positive conclusion that C is a necessary condition for G.

The SCT and NCT themselves are still negative and deductive; but that does not make them better than the positive tests encapsulated in conditions (1)–(4). The negative SCT and NCT are of no use when we need to argue that some condition *is* sufficient or *is* necessary. Such positive conclusions can be reached only by applying something like condition (4), which will require relying on background information. These inductive arguments might not be as clear-cut or secure as the negative ones, but they can still be inductively strong under the right circumstances. That is all they claim to be.

APPLYING THESE METHODS TO FIND CAUSES

In stating the SCT and NCT and applying these tests to abstract patterns of conditions to eliminate candidates, our procedure was fairly mechanical. We cannot be so mechanical when we try to reach positive conclusions that certain conditions are necessary, sufficient, or both. Applying these rules to actual concrete situations introduces a number of further complications, especially when using our tests to determine causes.

NORMALITY. First, it is important to keep in mind that in our ordinary understanding of causal conditions, we usually take it for granted that the setting is normal. It is part of common knowledge that if you strike a match, then it will light. Thus, we consider striking a match sufficient to make it light. But if someone has filled the room with carbon dioxide, then the match will not light, no matter how it is struck. Here one may be inclined to say that, after all, striking a match is not sufficient to light it. We might try to be more careful and say that if a match is struck *and* the room is not filled with carbon dioxide, then it will light. But this new conditional overlooks other possibilities—for example, that the room has been filled with nitrogen, that the match has been fireproofed, that the wrong end of the match was struck, that the match has already been lit, and so forth. It now seems that the antecedent of our conditional will have to be endlessly long in order to spec-ify a true or genuine sufficient condition. In fact, however, we usually feel quite happy with saying that if you strike a match, then it will light. We sim-ply do not worry about the possibility that the room has been filled with car-bon dioxide, the match has been fireproofed, and so on. Normally we think that things are normal, and give up this assumption only when some good reason appears for doing so.

These reflections suggest the following *contextualized* restatement of our original definitions of sufficient conditions and necessary conditions:

> *F* is a sufficient condition for *G* if and only if, whenever *F* is present in a normal context, *G* is present there as well.

> *F* is a necessary condition for *G* if and only if, whenever *F* is absent from a normal context, *G* is absent from it as well.

What will count as a normal context will vary with the type and the aim of an investigation, but all investigations into causally sufficient conditions and causally necessary conditions take place against the background of many factors that are taken as fixed.

BACKGROUND ASSUMPTIONS. If we are going to subject a causal hypothe-sis to rigorous testing employing the SCT and the NCT, we have to seek out a wide range of cases in which it might possibly be refuted. In general, the wider the range of possible refuters the better. But some limit must be put on this activity, or else testing will get hopelessly bogged down. If we are testing a drug to see whether it will cure a disease, we should try it on a variety of people of various ages, medical histories, body types, and so on, but we will not check to see whether it works on people named Edmund or check to see whether it works on people who drive Volvos. Such factors, we want to say, are plainly irrelevant. But what makes them irrelevant? How do we distin-guish relevant from irrelevant considerations?

The answer to this question is that our reasoning about causes occurs within a framework of beliefs that we consider already established as true. This framework contains a great deal of what is called *common knowledge*— knowledge we expect almost every sane adult to possess. We all know, for example, that human beings cannot breathe underwater, cannot walk through walls, cannot be in two places at once, and so on. The stock of these commonplace beliefs is almost endless. Because they are commonplace beliefs, they tend not to be mentioned, yet they play an important role in distinguishing relevant factors from irrelevant ones. Furthermore, *specialized* knowledge contains its own principles that are largely taken for granted by specialists. Doctors, for example, know a great deal about the detailed structure of the human body, and this background knowledge constantly guides their thought in dealing with specific illnesses. Thus, accepted beliefs establish a framework in which new ideas are judged. We can call the beliefs that give our system of beliefs its basic structure *framework beliefs.* In general, we do not question these framework beliefs, and things that do not fit in with them are not taken seriously. For example, if someone claimed to discover that blood does not circulate, no doctor would take the time to refute the claim. To take this suggestion seriously would be to challenge our whole way of viewing human beings and many other organisms.

Not all beliefs have this central status in our system of beliefs. They can be abandoned or modified without seriously harming our basic beliefs about the world. Someone might mistakenly believe that Portland is the capital of Oregon. Having discovered that the capital is really Salem, that person will drop one belief and replace it with another. Normally this change in belief will have little effect on many other beliefs and probably no effect on framework beliefs. In contrast, if scientists came to doubt that the sun is larger than the Earth, most of their conception of the physical universe would have to change. This suggests that, in our system of beliefs, some beliefs matter more or carry more weight than others, and they are given up only under great pressure. Other beliefs can be given up with hardly a thought. Discovering that Salem, not Portland, is the capital of Oregon can normally be taken in stride; discovering that half the world's population is made up of invading aliens from another planet would profoundly change our way of looking at things.

Given this picture, we see that beliefs are not tested in isolation from other beliefs. Testing takes place within a system of beliefs that shapes the form the testing will take. The Austrian philosopher Ludwig Wittgenstein put the matter this way:

> 105. All testing, all confirmation and disconfirmation of a hypothesis takes place already within a system. And this system is not a more or less arbitrary and doubtful point of departure for all our arguments: no, it belongs to the essence of what we call an argument. The system is not so much the point of departure, as the element in which arguments have their life.[11]

[11]Ludwig Wittgenstein, *On Certainty,* trans. G. E. M. Anscombe (Oxford: Basil Blackwell, 1969).

We can now see how our belief system develops and grows. Things that have been learned in the past guide the search for new knowledge. They do this in two ways: We use the belief system to reject what we take to be false or irrelevant hypotheses, and we also use it to suggest interesting new hypotheses. New beliefs are added to old beliefs, and these, in turn, suggest further possible new beliefs. The more well-founded beliefs we have, the more we are able to discover further well-founded beliefs. Learning about the world is a bootstrap operation.

The situation, however, is more complicated than this. We not only increase our stock of beliefs, but sometimes we discover that some of our previously held beliefs are false. For example, we might learn to our astonishment that a close friend is a member of a terrorist organization. Such a discovery almost certainly would lead us to reconsider a great many beliefs we have about him. Occasionally even framework beliefs are called into question and then rejected. The replacement of the Earth-centered (geocentric) theory of the solar system of Ptolemy by the sun-centered (heliocentric) theory of Copernicus is one example of a revolutionary change;[12] the replacement of Newtonian physics by Einstein's relativistic physics is another. But such revolutions in thought are rare. Furthermore, such theories, as novel as they may be, leave most of the general framework beliefs untouched. If Einstein's theory (or any theory) entailed that human beings fly by flapping their ears, that would be enough reason for rejecting it. Even the most revolutionary changes in thought, when looked at from a distance, appear remarkably conservative of our *total* system of beliefs.

A DETAILED EXAMPLE. To get a clearer idea of the complex interplay between the rules we have been examining and the reliance on background information, it will be helpful to look in some detail at actual applications of these rules. For this purpose, we will examine an attempt to find the cause of a particular phenomenon, an outbreak of what came to be known as Legionnaires' disease. The example not only shows how causal reasoning relies on background assumptions, it has another interesting feature as well: In the process of discovering the cause of Legionnaires' disease, the investigators were forced to *abandon* what was previously taken to be a well-established causal generalization. In fact, until it was discarded, this false background principle gave them no end of trouble.

The following account of the outbreak of Legionnaires' disease and the subsequent difficulties in finding out what caused it is drawn from an article in *Scientific American*.[13]

---

[12]For the classic discussion of these two systems, see Galileo's *Dialogue Concerning the Two World Systems—Ptolemaic and Copernican,* which is excerpted in Chapter 16.

[13]These excerpts are drawn from David W. Fraser and Joseph E. McDade, "Legionellosis," *Scientific American,* October 1979, 82–99.

> The 58th convention of the American Legion's Pennsylvania Department was held at the Bellevue-Stratford Hotel in Philadelphia from July 21 through 24, 1976. . . . Between July 22 and August 3, 149 of the conventioneers developed what appeared to be the same puzzling illness, characterized by fever, coughing and pneumonia. This, however, was an unusual, explosive outbreak of pneumonia with no apparent cause. . . . Legionnaires' disease, as the illness was quickly named by the press, was to prove a formidable challenge to epidemiologists and laboratory investigators alike.

Notice that at this stage the researchers begin with the assumption that they are dealing with a single illness and not a collection of similar but different illnesses. That assumption could turn out to be wrong; but, if the symptoms of the various patients are sufficiently similar, this is a natural starting assumption. Another reasonable starting assumption is that this illness had a single causative agent. This assumption, too, could turn out to be false, though it did not. The assumption that they were dealing with a single disease with a single cause was at least a good simplifying assumption, one to be held onto until there was good reason to give it up. In any case, we now have a clear specification of our target feature, G: the occurrence of a carefully described illness that came to be known as Legionnaires' disease. The situation concerning it was puzzling because people had contracted a disease with symptoms much like those of pneumonia, yet they had not tested positive for any of the known agents that cause such diseases.
    The narrative continues as follows:

> The initial step in the investigation of any epidemic is to determine the character of the illness, who has become ill and just where and when. The next step is to find out what was unique about the people who became ill: where they were and what they did that was different from other people who stayed well. Knowing such things may indicate how the disease agent was spread and thereby suggest the identity of the agent and where it came from.

Part of this procedure involves a straightforward application of the NCT: Was there any interesting feature that was always present in the history of people who came down with the illness? Progress was made almost at once on this front:

> We quickly learned that the illness was not confined to Legionnaires. An additional 72 cases were discovered among people who had not been directly associated with the convention. They had one thing in common with the sick conventioneers: for one reason or another they had been in or near the Bellevue-Stratford Hotel.

Strictly speaking, of course, all these people who had contracted the disease had more than one thing in common. They were, for example, all alive at the time they were in Philadelphia, and being alive is, in fact, a necessary condition for getting Legionnaires' disease. But the researchers were not interested in this necessary condition because it is a normal background condition for the contraction of any disease. Furthermore, it did not provide a condition that distinguished those who contracted the disease from those who did not.

The overwhelming majority of people who were alive at the time did not contract Legionnaires' disease. Thus, the researchers were not interested in this necessary condition because it would fail so badly when tested as a sufficient condition. On the basis of common knowledge and specialized medical knowledge, a great many other conditions were also kept off the candidate list.

One prime candidate on the list was presence at the Bellevue-Stratford Hotel. The application of the NCT to this candidate was straightforward. Everyone who had contracted the disease had spent time in or near that hotel. Thus, presence at the Bellevue-Stratford could not be eliminated as a necessary condition of Legionnaires' disease.

The application of the SCT was more complicated, because not everyone who stayed at the Bellevue-Stratford contracted the disease. Other factors made a difference: "Older conventioneers had been affected at a higher rate than younger ones, men at three times the rate for women." Since some young women (among others) who were present at the Bellevue-Stratford did not get Legionnaires' disease, presence at that hotel could be eliminated as a sufficient condition of Legionnaires' disease. Nonetheless, it is part of medical background knowledge that susceptibility to disease often varies with age and gender. Given these differences, some people who spent time at the Bellevue-Stratford were at higher risk for contracting the disease than others. The investigation so far suggested that, for some people, being at the Bellevue-Stratford was connected with a sufficient condition for contracting Legionnaires' disease.

As soon as spending time at the Bellevue-Stratford became the focus of attention, other hypotheses naturally suggested themselves. Food poisoning was a reasonable suggestion, since it is part of medical knowledge that diseases are sometimes spread by food. It was put on the list of possible candidates, but failed. Investigators checked each local restaurant and each function where food and drink were served. Some of the people who ate in each place did not get Legionnaires' disease, so the food at these locations was eliminated by the SCT as a sufficient condition of Legionnaires' disease. These candidates were also eliminated by the NCT as necessary conditions because some people who did get Legionnaires' disease did not eat at each of these restaurants and functions. Thus, the food and drink could not be the cause.

Further investigation turned up another important clue to the cause of the illness.

> Certain observations suggested that the disease might have been spread through the air. Legionnaires who became ill had spent on the average about 60 percent more time in the lobby of the Bellevue-Stratford than those who remained well; the sick Legionnaires' had also spent more time on the sidewalk in front of the hotel than their unaffected fellow conventioneers. . . . It appeared, therefore, that the most likely mode of transmission was airborne.

Merely breathing air in the lobby of the Bellevue-Stratford Hotel still could not be a necessary or sufficient condition, but the investigators reasoned that something in the lobby air probably caused Legionnaires' disease, since the rate of the disease varied up or down in proportion to the time spent in the lobby (or near it on the sidewalk in front). This is an application of the method of concomitant variation, which will be discussed below.

Now that the focus was on the lobby air, the next step was to pinpoint a specific cause in that air. Again appealing to background medical knowledge, there seemed to be three main candidates for the airborne agents that could have caused the illness: "heavy metals, toxic organic substances, and infectious organisms." Examination of tissues taken from patients who had died from the disease revealed "no unusual levels of metallic or toxic organic substances that might be related to the epidemic," so this left an infectious organism as the remaining candidate. Once more we have an application of NCT. If the disease had been caused by heavy metals or toxic organic substances, then there would have been unusually high levels of these substances in the tissues of those who had contracted the disease. Because this was not so, these candidates were eliminated as necessary conditions of the disease.

Appealing to background knowledge once more, it seemed that a bacterium would be the most likely source of an airborne disease with the symptoms of Legionnaires' disease. But researchers had already made a routine check for bacteria that cause pneumonia-like diseases, and they had found none. For this reason, attention was directed to the possibility that some previously unknown organism had been responsible but had somehow escaped detection.

It turned out that an undetected and previously unknown bacterium *had* caused the illness, but it took more than four months to find this out. The difficulties encountered in this effort show another important fact about the reliance on a background assumption: Sometimes it turns out to be false. To simplify, the standard way to test for the presence of bacteria is to try to grow them in culture dishes—flat dishes containing nutrients that bacteria can live on. If, after a reasonable number of tries, a colony of a particular kind of bacterium does not appear, then it is concluded that the bacterium is not present. As it turned out, the bacterium that caused Legionnaires' disease would not grow in the cultures commonly used to detect the presence of bacteria. Thus, an important background assumption turned out to be false.

After a great deal of work, a suspicious bacterium was detected using a live-tissue culture rather than the standard synthetic culture. The task, then, was to show that this particular bacterium in fact caused the disease. Again to simplify, when people are infected by a particular organism, they often develop antibodies that are specifically aimed at this organism. In the case of Legionnaires' disease, these antibodies were easier to detect than the bacterium itself. They also remained in the patients' bodies after the infection had run its course. We thus have another chance to apply the NCT: If Legionnaires' disease was caused by this particular bacterium, then whenever the disease was present, this antibody should be present as well. The suspicious bacterium passed this test with flying colors and was named, appropriately enough, *Legionella pneumophila*. Because the investigators had worked so hard to test such a wide variety of candidates, they assumed that the disease must have some cause among the candidates that they checked. So, since only one candidate remained, they felt justified in reaching a positive conclusion that the bacterium was a necessary condition of Legionnaires' disease.

The story of the search for the cause of Legionnaires' disease brings out two important features of the use of inductive methods in the sciences. First, it involves a complicated interplay between what is already established and what is being tested. Confronted with a new problem, established principles can be used to suggest theoretically significant hypotheses to be tested. The tests then eliminate some hypotheses and leave others. If, at the end of the investigation, a survivor remains that fits in well with our previously established principles, then the stock of established principles is increased. The second thing that this example shows is that the inductive method is fallible. Without the background of established principles, the application of inductive principles like the NCT and the SCT would be undirected; yet sometimes these established principles let us down, for they can turn out to be false. The discovery of the false background principle that hindered the search for the cause of Legionnaires' disease led to important revisions in laboratory techniques. The discovery that certain fundamental background principles are false can lead to revolutionary changes in science. (See Chapter 16.)

CALLING THINGS CAUSES. After their research was finally completed, with the bacterium identified, described, and named, it was then said that *Legionella pneumophila* was the *cause* of Legionnaires' disease. What was meant by this? To simplify a bit, suppose *L. pneumophila* (as it is abbreviated) entered the bodies of *all* those who contracted the disease: Whenever the disease was present, *L. pneumophila* was present. Thus, *L. pneumophila* passes the NCT. We will further suppose, as is common in bacterial infections, that some people's immune systems were successful in combating *L. pneumophila,* and they never actually developed the disease. Thus, the presence of *L. pneumophila* would not pass the SCT. This suggests that we sometimes call something a cause if it passes the NCT, even if it does not pass the SCT.

But even if we sometimes consider necessary conditions to be causes, we certainly do not consider *all* necessary conditions to be causes. We have already noted that to get Legionnaires' disease, one has to be alive, yet no one thinks that being alive is the cause of Legionnaires' disease. To cite another example, this time one that is not silly, it might be that another necessary condition for developing Legionnaires' disease is that the person be in a run-down condition—healthy people might always be able to resist *L. pneumophila.* Do we then want to say that being in a run-down condition is the cause of Legionnaires' disease? As we have described the situation, almost certainly not, but we might want to say that it is an important *causal factor* or *causally relevant factor.*

Although the matter is far from clear, what we call *the* cause rather than simply *a* causal factor or causally relevant factor seems to depend on a number of considerations. We tend to reserve the expression "the cause" for *changes* that occur prior to the effect, and describe *permanent* or *standing* features of the context as "causal factors" instead. That is how we speak about Legionnaires' disease. Being exposed to *L. pneumophila*, which was a specific event that occurred before the onset of the disease, *caused it*. Being in a run-down condition, which was a feature that patients possessed for some time before they contracted the disease, was not called the cause, but instead called a causal factor.

It is not clear, however, that we always draw the distinction between what we call the cause and what we call a causal factor based on whether something is a prior event or a standing condition. For example, if we are trying to explain why certain people who came in contact with *L. pneumophila* contracted the disease whereas others did not, then we might say that the former group contracted the disease because they were in a run-down condition. Thus, by limiting our investigation only to those who came in contact with *L. pneumophila,* our perspective has changed. We want to know why some within that group contracted the disease and others did not. Citing the run-down condition of those who contracted the disease as the cause now seems entirely natural. These examples suggest that we call something *the* cause when it plays a particularly important role relative to the purposes of our investigation. Usually this will be an event or change taking place against the background of fixed necessary conditions; sometimes it will not.

Sometimes we call *sufficient* conditions causes. We say that short circuits cause fires because in many normal contexts, a short circuit is sufficient to cause a fire. Of course, short circuits are not necessary to cause a fire, because, in the same normal contexts, fires can be caused by a great many other things. With sufficient conditions, as with necessary conditions, we often draw a distinction between what we call the cause as opposed to what we call a causal factor, and we seem to draw it along similar lines. Speaking loosely, we might say that we sometimes call the *key* components of sufficient conditions *causes*. Then, holding background conditions fixed, we can use the SCT to evaluate such causal claims.

In sum, we can use the NCT to eliminate proposed necessary causal conditions. We can use the SCT to eliminate proposed sufficient causal conditions. Those candidates that survive these tests may be called causal conditions or causal factors if they fit in well with our system of other causal generalizations. Finally, some of these causal conditions or causal factors will be called causes if they play a key role in our causal investigations. Typically, though not always, we call something the cause of an event if it is a prior event or change that stands out against the background of fixed conditions.

CONCOMITANT VARIATION

The use of the sufficient condition test and the necessary condition test depends on certain features of the world being sometimes present and sometimes absent. Some features of the world, however, are always present to some degree. Because they are always present, the NCT will never eliminate them as possible necessary conditions of any event, and the SCT will never eliminate anything as a sufficient condition for them. Yet the *extent* or *degree* to which a feature exists in the world is often a significant phenomenon that demands causal explanation.

An example should make this clear. In recent years, a controversy has raged over the impact of acid rain on the environment of the northeastern United States and Canada. Part of the controversy involves the proper interpretation of the data that have been collected. The controversy has arisen for the following reason: The atmosphere always contains a certain amount of acid, much of it from natural sources. It is also known that an excess of acid in the environment can have severe effects on both plants and animals. Lakes are particularly vulnerable to the effects of acid rain. Finally, it is also acknowledged that industries, mostly in the Midwest, discharge large quantities of sulfur dioxide (SO_2) into the air, and this increases the acidity of water in the atmosphere. The question—and here the controversy begins—is whether the contribution of acid from these industries is the cause of the environmental damage downwind of them.

How can we settle such a dispute? The two rules we have introduced provide no immediate help, for, as we have seen, they provide a rigorous test of a causal hypothesis only when we can find contrasting cases with the presence or the absence of a given feature. The NCT provides a rigorous test for a necessary condition only if we can find cases in which the feature does not occur and then check to make sure that the target feature does not occur either. The SCT provides a rigorous test for a sufficient condition only when we can find cases in which the target phenomenon is absent and then check whether the candidate sufficient condition is absent as well. In this case, however, neither check applies, for there is always a certain amount of acid in the atmosphere, so it is not possible to check what happens when atmospheric acid is completely absent. Similarly, environmental damage, which is the target phenomenon under investigation, is so widespread in our modern industrial society that it is also hard to find a case in which it is completely absent.

So, if there is always acid in the atmosphere, and environmental damage always exists at least to some extent, how can we determine whether the SO_2 released into the atmosphere is *significantly* responsible for the environmental damage in the affected areas? Here we use what John Stuart Mill called the *Method of Concomitant Variation*. We ask whether the amount of environmental damage varies directly in proportion to the amount of SO_2 released into the environment. If environmental damage increases with the amount of SO_2 released into the environment and drops when the amount of SO_2 is lowered, this means that the level of SO_2 in the atmosphere is *positively correlated* with environmental damage. We would then have good reason to believe that lowering SO_2 emissions would lower the level of environmental damage, at least to some extent.

Arguments relying on the method of concomitant variation are difficult to evaluate, especially when there is no generally accepted background theory that makes sense of the concomitant variation. Some such variations are well understood. For example, most people know that the faster you drive, the more gasoline you consume. (Gasoline consumption varies *directly* with speed.) Why? There is a good theory here: It takes more energy to drive at a high speed than at a low speed, and this energy is derived from the gasoline consumed in the car's engine. Other correlations are less well understood. There seems to be a high correlation between how much a woman smokes during pregnancy and how happy her children are when they reach age 30. The correlation here is not nearly as good as the correlation between gasoline consumption and speed, for many people are very happy at age 30 even though their mothers smoked a lot during pregnancy, and many others are very unhappy at age 30 even though their mothers never smoked. Furthermore, no generally accepted background theory has been found to explain the correlation that does exist.

This reference to background theory is important, because two sets of phenomena can be correlated to a very high degree, even with no direct causal relationship between them. A favorite example that appears in many statistics texts is the discovered positive correlation in boys between foot size and quality of handwriting. It is hard to imagine a causal relation holding in either direction. Having big feet should not make you write better and, just as obviously, writing well should not give you big feet. The correct explanation is that both foot size and handwriting ability are positively correlated with age. Here a noncausal correlation between two phenomena (foot size and handwriting ability) is explained by a third common correlation (maturation) that *is* causal.

At times, it is possible to get causal correlations *backward*. For example, a few years ago, sports statisticians discovered a negative correlation between forward passes thrown and winning in football. That is, the more forward passes a team threw, the less chance it had of winning. This suggested that passing is not a good strategy, since the more you do it, the more likely you are to lose. Closer examination showed, however, that the causal relationship, in fact, went in the other direction. Toward the end of a game, losing teams tend to throw a great many passes in an effort to catch up. In other words, teams throw a lot of passes because they are losing, rather than the other way around.

Finally, some correlations seem inexplicable. For example, a strong positive correlation holds between the birth rate in Holland and the number of storks nesting in chimneys. There is, of course, a background theory that would explain this—storks bring babies—but that theory is not favored by modern science. For the lack of any better background theory, the phenomenon just seems weird.

So, given a strong correlation between phenomena of types *A* and *B*, four possibilities exist:

1. *A* is the cause of *B*.
2. *B* is the cause of *A*.
3. Some third thing is the cause of both.
4. The correlation is simply accidental.

Before we accept any one of these possibilities, we must have good reasons for preferring it over the other three.

EXERCISE XII

In each of the following examples a strong correlation, either negative or positive, holds between two sets of phenomena, *A* and *B*. Try to decide whether *A* is the cause of *B*, *B* is the cause of *A*, both are caused by some third factor, *C*, or the correlation is simply accidental. Explain your choice.

1. At one time there was a strong negative correlation between the number of mules in a state (*A*) and the salaries paid to professors at the state university (*B*). In other words, the more mules, the lower professional salaries.[14]

2. It has been claimed that there is a strong positive correlation between those students who take sex education courses (*A*) and those who contract venereal disease (*B*).

3. "Washington (UPI)—Rural Americans with locked doors, watchdogs or guns may face as much risk of burglary as neighbors who leave doors unlocked, a federally financed study says. The study, financed in part by a three-year $170,000 grant from the Law Enforcement Assistance Administration, was based on a survey of nearly 900 families in rural Ohio. Sixty percent of the rural residents surveyed regularly locked doors [*A*], but were burglarized more often than residents who left doors unlocked [*B*]."[15]

4. There is a high positive correlation between the number of fire engines in a particular borough in New York City (*A*) and the number of fires that occur there (*B*).[16]

[14]From Gregory A. Kimble, *How to Use (and Misuse) Statistics* (Englewood Cliffs, NJ: Prentice-Hall, 1978), 182.

[15]"Locked Doors No Bar to Crime, Study Says," *Santa Barbara* [California] *Newspress,* Wednesday, February 16, 1977. This title suggests that locking your doors will not increase safety. Is that a reasonable lesson to draw from this study?

[16]From Kimble, *How to Use (and Misuse) Statistics,* 182.

5. For a particular United States president, there is a negative correlation between the number of hairs on his head (*A*) and the population of China (*B*).

6. My son's height (*A*) increases along with the height of the tree outside my front door (*B*).

7. The speed of a car (*A*) is exactly the same as the speed of its shadow (*B*).

8. The length of a runner's ring finger minus the length of the runner's index finger (*A*) is correlated with the runner's speed in the 100-yard dash. (*B*)

DISCUSSION QUESTIONS

1. Now that it seems beyond doubt that smoking is dangerous to people's health, a new debate has arisen concerning the possible health hazards of smoke on nonsmokers. Collect statements pro and con on this issue and evaluate the strength of the inductive arguments on each side.

2. In *Twilight of the Idols*, Nietzsche claims that the following examples illustrate "the error of mistaking cause for consequence." Do you agree? Why or why not?

> Everyone knows the book of the celebrated Cornaro in which he recommends his meager diet as a recipe for a long and happy life—a virtuous one, too. . . . I do not doubt that hardly any book (the Bible rightly excepted) has done so much harm, has shortened so many lives, as this curiosity, which was so well meant. The reason: mistaking the consequence for the cause. The worthly Italian saw in his diet the *cause* of his long life; while the prerequisite of long life, an extraordinarily slow metabolism, a small consumption, was the cause of his meager diet. He was not free to eat much *or* little as he chose, his frugality was *not* an act of "free will": he became ill when he ate more. But if one is not a bony fellow of this sort one does not merely do well, one positively needs to eat *properly*. A scholar of *our day*, with his rapid consumption of nervous energy, would kill himself with Cornaro's regimen. . . .
>
> Long life, a plentiful posterity is *not* the reward of virtue, virtue itself is rather just that slowing down of the metabolism which also has, among other things, a long life, a plentiful posterity, in short *Cornarism,* as its outcome.—The Church and morality say: "A race, a people perishes through vice and luxury." My *restored* reason says: when a people is perishing, degenerating physiologically, vice and luxury (that is to say the necessity for stronger and stronger and more and more frequent stimulants, such as every exhausted nature is acquainted with) *follow* therefrom. A young man grows prematurely pale and faded. His friends say: this and that illness is to blame. I say: *that* he became ill, *that* he failed to resist the illness, was already the consequence of an impoverished life, an hereditary exhaustion. The newspaper reader says: this party will ruin itself if it makes errors like this. My *higher* politics says: a party which makes errors like this is already finished—it is no longer secure in its instincts. Every error, of whatever kind, is a consequence of degeneration of instinct, degeneration of will: one has thereby virtually defined the *bad*. Everything *good* is instinct—and consequently easy, necessary, free. Effort is an objection, the *god* is typically distinguished from the hero (in my language: *light* feet are the first attribute of divinity).[17]

[17]Friedrich Nietzsche, *Twilight of the Idols* and *The Anti-Christ*, trans. R. J. Hollingdale (1889; Harmondsworth: Penguin, 1968), 47–48.

STATISTICAL GENERALIZATION

To apply the method of concomitant variation to the issue of whether smoking causes lung cancer, we need to know the rates of smoking and the rates of lung cancer. In this case and many others like it, the crucial relationships do not hold universally, so we cannot apply the tests for necessary and sufficient conditions that were discussed above. How, then, can we determine those rates?

The answer lies in another common form of inductive reasoning, which is often called *statistical generalization*. In statistical generalizations, we cite characteristics of a sample of a population to support a claim about the character of the population as a whole. Opinion polls work this way. Suppose a candidate wants to know how popular she is with voters. Because it would be practically impossible to survey all voters, she takes a sample of voting opinion and then infers that the opinions of those sampled indicate the overall opinion of voters. Thus, if 60 percent of the voters sampled say that they will vote for her, she concludes that she will get more or less 60 percent of the vote in the actual election. As we shall see later, inferences of this kind often go wrong, even when made by experts, but the general pattern of this reasoning is quite clear: Statistical features of a sample are used to make statistical claims about the population as a whole.

Basically the same form of reasoning can be used to reach a universal conclusion. An example is the inductive inference discussed at the start of this chapter: All observed ravens are black, so all ravens are black. Again, we sample part of a population to draw a conclusion about the whole.

How do we assess such inferences? To begin to answer this question, we can consider a simple example of a statistical generalization. On various occasions, Harold has tried to use Canadian quarters in American telephones and found that they have not worked. From this he draws the conclusion that Canadian quarters do not work in American telephones. Harold's inductive reasoning looks like this:

> In the past, when I tried to use Canadian quarters in American telephones, they have not worked.
> ∴ Canadian quarters do not work in American telephones.

The force of the conclusion is that Canadian quarters *never* work in American telephones.

In evaluating this argument, what questions should we ask? We can start with a question that we should ask of any argument.

SHOULD WE ACCEPT THE PREMISES?

Perhaps Harold has a bad memory, has kept bad records, or is a poor observer. For some obscure reason, he may even be lying. It is important to ask this question explicitly, because fairly often the premises, when challenged, will not stand up to scrutiny.

If we decide that the premises are acceptable (that is, true and justified), then we can shift our attention to the relationship between the premises and the conclusion and ask how much support the premises give to the conclusion. One commonsense question is this: "How many times has Harold tried to use Canadian quarters in American telephones?" If the answer is "Once," then our confidence in his argument should drop to almost nothing. So, for statistical generalizations, it is always appropriate to ask about the size of the sample.

Is the Sample Large Enough?

One reason we should be suspicious of small samples is that they can be affected by runs of luck. Suppose Harold flips a Canadian quarter four times and it comes up heads each time. From this, he can hardly conclude that Canadian quarters always come up heads when flipped. He could not even reasonably conclude that *this* Canadian quarter would always come up heads when flipped. The reason for this is obvious enough: If you spend a lot of time flipping coins, runs of four heads in a row are not all that unlikely (the probability is actually one in sixteen), and therefore samples of this size can easily be distorted by chance. On the other hand, if Harold flipped the coin twenty times and it continued to come up heads, he would have strong grounds for saying that this coin, at least, will always come up heads. In fact, he would have strong grounds for thinking that he has a two-headed coin. Because an overly small sample can lead to erroneous conclusions, we need to make sure that our sample includes enough trials.

How many is enough? On the assumption, for the moment, that our sampling has been fair in all other respects, how many samples do we need to provide the basis for a strong inductive argument? This is not always an easy question to answer, and sometimes answering it demands subtle mathematical techniques. Suppose your company is selling 10 million computer chips to the Department of Defense, and you have guaranteed that no more than 0.2 percent of them will be defective. It would be prohibitively expensive to test all the chips, and testing only a dozen would hardly be enough to reasonably guarantee that the total shipment of chips meets the required specifications. Because testing chips is expensive, you want to test as few as possible; but because meeting the specifications is crucial, you want to test enough to guarantee that you have done so. Answering questions of this kind demands sophisticated statistical techniques beyond the scope of this text.

Sometimes, then, it is difficult to decide how many samples are needed to give reasonable support to inductive generalizations; yet many times it is obvious, without going into technical details, that the sample is too small. Drawing an inductive conclusion from a sample that is too small can lead to the fallacy of *hasty generalization*. It is surprising how common this fallacy is. We see a person two or three times and find him cheerful, and we immediately leap to the conclusion that he is a cheerful person. That is, from a few instances of cheerful behavior, we draw a general conclusion about his personality. When we meet him later and find him sad, morose, or grouchy, we then conclude that he has changed—thus swapping one hasty generalization for another.

This tendency toward hasty generalization was discussed more than 200 years ago by the philosopher David Hume, who saw that we have a strong tendency to "follow general rules which we rashly form to ourselves, and which are the source of what we properly call prejudice."[18] This tendency toward hasty generalization has been the subject of extensive psychological investigation. The cognitive psychologists Amos Tversky and Daniel Kahneman put the matter this way:

> We submit that people view a sample randomly drawn from a population as highly representative, that is, similar to the population in all essential characteristics. Consequently, they expect any two samples drawn from a particular population to be more similar to one another and to the population than sampling theory predicts, at least for small samples.[19]

To return to a previous example, we make our judgments of someone's personality on the basis of a very small sample of his or her behavior and expect this person to behave in similar ways in the future when we encounter further samples of behavior. We are surprised, and sometimes indignant, when the future behavior does not match our expectations.

By making our samples sufficiently large, we can guard against distortions due to "runs of luck," but even very large samples can give us a poor basis for a statistical generalization. Suppose that Harold has tried hundreds of times to use a Canadian quarter in an American telephone, and it has never worked. This will increase our confidence in his generalization, but size of sample alone is not a sufficient ground for a strong inductive argument. Suppose that Harold has tried the same coin in hundreds of different telephones, or tried a hundred different Canadian coins in the same telephone. In the first case, there might be something wrong with this particular coin; in the second case, there might be something wrong with this particular telephone. In neither case would he have good grounds for making the general claim that *no* Canadian quarters work in *any* American telephones. This leads us to the third question we should ask of any statistical generalization.

IS THE SAMPLE BIASED?

When the sample, however large, is not representative of the population, then it is said to be unfair or biased. Here we can speak of the fallacy of *biased sampling*.

---

[18]David Hume, *A Treatise of Human Nature*, 2d ed. (1739; Oxford: Oxford University Press, 1978), 146.

[19]Amos Tversky and Daniel Kahneman, "Belief in the Law of Small Numbers," *Psychological Bulletin* 76, no. 2 (1971), 105.

One of the most famous errors of biased sampling was committed by a magazine named the *Literary Digest*. Before the presidential election of 1936, this magazine sent out 10 million questionnaires asking which candidate the recipient would vote for: Franklin Roosevelt or Alf Landon. It received 2.5 million returns, and on the basis of the results, confidently predicted that Landon would win by a landslide: 56 percent for Landon to only 44 percent for Roosevelt. When the election results came in, Roosevelt had won by an even larger landslide in the opposite direction: 62 percent for Roosevelt to a mere 38 percent for Landon.

What went wrong? The sample was certainly large enough; in fact, by contemporary standards it was much larger than needed. It was the way the sample was selected, not its size, that caused the problem: The sample was randomly drawn from names in telephone books and from club membership lists. In 1936 there were only 11 million telephones in the United States, and many of the poor—especially the rural poor—did not have telephones. During the Great Depression there were more than 9 million unemployed in America; they were almost all poor and thus underrepresented on club membership lists. Finally, a large percentage of these underrepresented groups voted for Roosevelt, the Democratic candidate. As a result of these biases in its sampling, along with some others, the *Literary Digest* underestimated Roosevelt's percentage of the vote by a whopping 18 percent.

Looking back, it may be hard to believe that intelligent observers could have done such a ridiculously bad job of sampling opinion, but the story repeats itself, though rarely on the grand scale of the *Literary Digest* fiasco. In 1948, for example, the Gallup poll, which had correctly predicted Roosevelt's victory in 1936, predicted, as did other major polls, a clear victory for Thomas Dewey over Harry Truman. Confidence was so high in this prediction that the *Chicago Tribune* published a banner headline declaring that Dewey had won the election before the votes were actually counted.

What went wrong this time? The answer here is more subtle. The Gallup pollsters (and others) went to great pains to make sure that their sample was representative of the voting population. The interviewers were told to poll a certain number of people from particular social groups—rural poor, suburban middle class, urban middle class, ethnic minorities, and so on—so that the proportions of those interviewed matched, as closely as possible, the proportions of those likely to vote. (The *Literary Digest* went bankrupt after its incorrect prediction, so the pollsters were taking no chances.) Yet somehow bias crept into the sampling; the question was, how? One speculation was that a large percentage of those sampled did not tell the truth when they were interviewed; another was that a large number of people changed their minds at the last minute. So perhaps the data collected were not reliable. The explanation generally accepted was more subtle. Although Gallup's workers were told to interview specific numbers of people from particular classes (so many from the suburbs, for example), they were not instructed to choose people randomly from within each group. Without seriously thinking about it, they tended to go to "nicer" neighborhoods and interview "nicer" people.

Because of this, they biased the sample in the direction of their own (largely) middle-class preferences and, as a result, underrepresented constituencies that would give Truman his unexpected victory.

IS THE RESULT BIASED IN SOME OTHER WAY?

Because professionals using modern techniques can make bad statistical generalizations through biased sampling, it is not surprising that our every-day, informal inductive generalizations are often inaccurate. Sometimes we go astray because of small samples and biased samples. This happens, for example, when we form opinions about what people think or what people are like by asking only our friends. But bias can affect our reasoning in other ways as well.

One of the main sources of bias in everyday life is *prejudice*. Even if we sample a wide enough range of cases, we often reinterpret what we hear or see in light of some preconception. People who are prejudiced will find very little good and a great deal bad in those they despise, no matter how these people actually behave. In fact, most people are a mixture of good and bad qualities. By ignoring the former and dwelling on the latter, it is easy enough for a prejudiced person to confirm negative opinions. Similarly, stereotypes, which can be either positive or negative, often persist in the face of over-whelming counterevidence. Criticizing the beliefs common in Britain in his own day, David Hume remarked:

> An Irishman cannot have wit, and a Frenchman cannot have solidity; for which reason, though the conversation of the former in any instance be very agreeable, and of the latter very judicious, we have entertained such a prejudice against them, that they must be dunces and fops in spite of sense and reason.[20]

Although common stereotypes have changed somewhat since Hume's day, prejudice continues to distort the beliefs of many people in our own time.

Another common source of bias in sampling arises from phrasing ques-tions in ways that encourage certain answers while discouraging others. Even if a fair sample is asked a question, it is well known that the way a question is phrased can exert a significant influence on how people will answer it. Questions like the following are not intended to elicit information, but instead to push people's answers in one direction rather than another.

> Which do you favor: (a) preserving a citizen's constitutional right to bear arms or (b) leaving honest citizens defenseless against armed criminals?

> Which do you favor: (a) restricting the sale of assault weapons or (b) knuckling under to the demands of the well-financed gun lobby?

[20]Hume, *A Treatise of Human Nature*, 146–47.

In both cases, one alternative is made to sound attractive, the other unattractive. When questions of this sort are used, it is not surprising that different pollsters can come up with wildly different results.

SUMMARY

Now we can summarize and restate our questions with more accuracy. Confronted with inductive generalizations, there are four questions that we should routinely ask:

1. Are the premises acceptable?
2. Is the sample too small?
3. Is the sample biased?
4. Are the results affected by other sources of bias?

EXERCISE XIII

By asking the preceding questions, specify what, if anything, is wrong with the following statistical generalizations:

1. K-Mart asked all of their customers throughout the country whether they prefer K-Mart to Walmart, and 90 percent said they did, so 90 percent of all shoppers in the country prefer K-Mart.
2. A Swede stole my bicycle, so most Swedes are thieves.
3. I've never tried it before, but I just put a kiwi fruit in a tub of water. It floated. So most kiwi fruits float in water.
4. I have lots of friends. Most of them think that I would make a great president. So most Americans would probably agree.
5. In exit polls after people had just voted, most people told our candidate that they voted for her, so probably most people did vote for her.
6. Mary told me that all of her older children are geniuses, so her baby will probably be a genius, too.
7. When asked whether they would prefer a tax break or a bloated budget, almost everyone said that they wanted a tax break. So a tax break is overwhelmingly popular with the people.
8. When hundreds of convicted murderers in states without the death penalty were asked whether they would have committed the murder if the state had a death penalty, most of them said that they would not have done it. So most murders can be deterred by the death penalty.

EXERCISE XIV

Ann Landers caused a stir when she announced the results of a mail poll that asked her women readers to respond to the following question:

> Would you be content to be held and treated tenderly, and forget about "the act"?

Her readers were instructed to answer "Yes" or "No" and indicate whether they were over (or under) forty years of age. The result was that 72 percent of the respondents answered "Yes," and of those who answered "Yes," 40 percent indicated that they were under forty years of age.

What are we to make of these results? Ann Landers expressed surprise that so many of those who answered "Yes" came from the under-forty group. But for her, "the greatest revelation" was "what the poll says about men as lovers. Clearly, there is trouble in paradise" (*Ask Ann Landers*, January 14 and 15, 1985).

The poll, of course, did not employ scientific methods of sampling (nor did Ann Landers claim that it did), so it is important to look for sources of bias before drawing any conclusions from this poll. Discuss at least three possible sources of bias that could make the Landers sample unrepresentative of the opinions of the population of adult women in America.

STATISTICAL APPLICATIONS

In a statistical generalization, we draw inferences concerning a population from information concerning a sample of that population. If 60 percent of the population sampled said that they would vote for candidate X, we might draw the conclusion that roughly 60 percent of the population will vote for candidate X. With a *statistical application*,[21] we reason in the reverse direction: From information concerning a population, we draw a conclusion concerning a member or subset of that population. Here is an example:

> Ninety-seven percent of the Republicans in California voted for Bush.
> Marvin is a Republican from California.
>
> ∴ Marvin voted for Bush.

---

[21]Statistical applications are often called statistical syllogisms, but they should not be confused with categorical syllogism, as discussed in Chapter 7.

Such arguments have the following general form:

> X percent of Fs have the feature G.
> a is an F.
> ─────────────────────────
> ∴ a has the feature G.[22]

Obviously, when we evaluate the strength of a statistical application, the percentage of Fs that have the feature G will be important. As the figure approaches 100 percent, the argument gains strength. Thus, our original argument concerning Marvin is quite strong. We can also get strong statistical applications when the figure approaches 0 percent. The following is a strong inductive argument:

> Three percent of the socialists from California voted for Bush.
> Maureen is a socialist from California.
> ─────────────────────────
> ∴ Maureen did *not* vote for Bush.

Statistical applications of the kind considered here will be strong only if the figures are close to 100 percent or 0 percent. When the percentages are in the middle of this range, such statistical applications are weak.

A more interesting problem in evaluating the strength of a statistical application concerns the *relevance* of the premises to the conclusion. In the above schematic representation, F stands for what is called the *reference class*. In our first example, being a Republican from California is the reference class; in our second example, being a socialist from California is the reference class. A striking feature of statistical applications is that using different reference classes can yield incompatible results. To see this, consider the following example:

> Three percent of Kerry's relatives voted for Bush.
> Marvin is a relative of Kerry.
> ─────────────────────────
> ∴ Marvin did not vote for Bush.

We now have a statistical application that gives us strong support for the claim that Marvin did not vote for Bush. This is incompatible with our first statistical application, which gave strong support to the claim that he did. To overlook this conflict between arguments based on different reference classes would be a kind of fallacy. Which statistical application, if either,

---

[22] We can also have a *probabilistic* version of the statistical syllogism:

> Ninety-seven percent of the Republicans from California voted for Bush.
> Marvin is a Republican from California.
> ─────────────────────────
> ∴ There is a 97 percent chance that Marvin voted for Bush.

We will discuss arguments concerning probability in the next chapter.

should we trust? This will depend on which of the reference classes we take to be more relevant. Which counts more, political affiliation or family ties? That might be hard to say.

One way of dealing with competing statistical applications is to combine the reference classes. We could ask, for example, what percentage of Republicans from California who are relatives of Kerry voted for Bush? The result might come out this way:

> Forty-two percent of Republicans from California who were relatives of Kerry voted for Bush.
> Marvin is a Republican from California who is a relative of Kerry.
> _____
> ∴ Marvin voted for Bush.

This statistical application provides very weak support for its conclusion. Indeed, it supplies some weak support for the denial of its conclusion—that is, for the claim that Marvin did *not* vote for Bush.

This situation can be diagrammed with ellipses of varying sizes to represent the percentages of Californians and relatives of Kerry who do or do not vote for Bush. First, we draw an ellipse to represent Republicans from California and place a vertical line so that it cuts off roughly (very roughly!) ninety-seven percent of the area of that ellipse to represent the premise that ninety-seven percent of the Republicans from California voted for Bush:

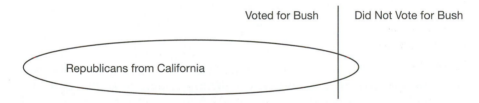

Next, we add a second ellipse to represent Kerry's relatives:

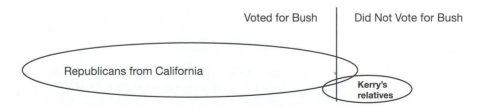

Only about three percent of the small ellipse is left of the line to represent the premise that three percent of Kerry's relatives voted for Bush. The area that lies within both ellipses represents the people who are both Republicans from California and also relatives of Kerry. About forty-two percent of that area is left of the line to represent the premise that forty-two percent of

Republicans from California who were relatives of Kerry voted for Bush. The whole diagram now shows how all of these premises can be true, even though they lead to conflicting conclusions.

This series of arguments illustrates in a clear way what we earlier called the defeasibility of inductive inferences: A strong inductive argument can be made weak by adding further information to the premises. Given that Marvin is a Republican from California, we seemed to have good reason to think that he voted for Bush. But when we added to this the additional piece of information that he was a relative of Kerry, the original argument lost most of its force. And new information could produce another reversal. Suppose we discover that Marvin, though a relative of Kerry, actively campaigned for Bush. Just about everyone who actively campaigns for a candidate votes for that candidate, so it seems that we again have good reason for thinking that Marvin voted for Bush.

It is clear, then, that the way we select our reference classes will affect the strength of a statistical application. The general idea is that we should define our reference classes in a way that brings all relevant evidence to bear on the subject. But this raises difficulties. It is not always obvious which factors are relevant and which are not. In our example, party affiliation is relevant to how people voted in the 2004 election; shoe size presumably is not. Whether gender is significant, and, if so, how significant, is a matter for further statistical research.

These difficulties concerning the proper way to fix reference classes reflect a feature of all inductive reasoning: To be successful, such reasoning must take place within a broader framework that helps determine which features are significant and which features are not. Without this framework, there would be no reason not to consider shoe size when trying to decide how someone will vote. This shows how statistical applications, like all of the other inductive arguments that we studied in this chapter, cannot work properly without appropriate background assumptions.

EXERCISE XV

Carry the story of Marvin two steps further, producing two more reversals in the strength of the statistical application with the conclusion that Marvin voted for Bush.

EXERCISE XVI

For each of the following statistical applications, identify the reference class, and then evaluate the strength of the argument in terms of the percentages or proportions cited and the relevance of the reference class.

1. Less than 1 percent of the people in the world voted for Bush.
   Gale is a person in the world.
   ∴ Gale did not vote for Bush.

2. Very few teams repeat as Super Bowl champions.
   New England was the last Super Bowl champion.
   ∴ New England will not repeat as Super Bowl champion.

3. A very high percentage of people in the Senate are men.
   Hilary Clinton is in the Senate.
   ∴ Hilary Clinton is a man.

4. Three percent of socialists with blue eyes voted for Bush.
   Maureen is a socialist with blue eyes.
   ∴ Maureen did not vote for Bush.

5. Ninety-eight percent of what John says is true.
   John said that his father is also named John.
   ∴ John's father is named John.

6. Ninety-eight percent of what John says is true.
   John said that the Giants are going to win.
   ∴ The Giants are going to win.

7. Half the time he doesn't know what he is doing.
   He is eating lunch.
   ∴ He does not know that he is eating lunch.

8. Most people do not understand quantum mechanics.
   My physics professor is a person.
   ∴ My physics professor probably does not understand quantum mechanics.

9. Almost all birds can fly.
   This penguin is a bird.
   ∴ This penguin can fly.

10. Most people who claim to be psychic are frauds.
    Mary claims to be psychic.
    ∴ Mary is a fraud.

DISCUSSION QUESTION

Although both in science and in daily life, we rely heavily on the methods of inductive reasoning, this kind of reasoning raises a number of perplexing problems. The most famous problem concerning the legitimacy of induction was formulated by the eighteenth-century philosopher David Hume, first in his *Treatise of Human Nature* and then later in his *Enquiry Concerning Human Understanding*. A simplified version of Hume's skeptical argument goes as follows: Our inductive generalizations seem to rest on the assumption that *unobserved* cases will follow the patterns that we discovered in *observed* cases. That is, our inductive generalizations seem to presuppose that nature operates uniformly: The way things are observed to behave here and now are accurate indicators of how things behave anywhere and at any time. But by what right can we assume that nature is uniform? Because this claim itself asserts a contingent matter of fact, it could only be established by inductive reasoning. But because all inductive reasoning presupposes the principle that nature is uniform, any inductive justification of this principle would seem to be circular. It seems, that we have no ultimate justification for our inductive reasoning at all. Is this a good argument or a bad one? Why?

10

TAKING CHANCES

This chapter offers an elementary discussion of probability and decision making. People make many common mistakes about probability, which are illustrated here. To help avoid these fallacies, we need to approach probability more carefully, so formal laws of probability are presented along with Bayes's theorem. *These tools are then used to explain the related notions of* expected monetary value *and* overall value, *which help us assess reasoning about choices involving* risk. Decisions under ignorance *pose separate problems, for which a number of rules have been proposed. Although these rules are useful in many situations, their limitations are also noted.*

SOME FALLACIES OF PROBABILITY

As we saw in Chapter 9 on inductive reasoning, many arguments do not pretend to reach their conclusions with certainty. They merely try to show that a conclusion is likely or probable. Judgments about probability also play a crucial role in many of our most important decisions. Mistakes about probability can then lead to disasters. Doctors lose patients' lives, stockbrokers lose clients' money, and coaches lose games because they overestimate or underestimate probabilities. Such mistakes are common and fall into several regular patterns. It is useful to understand these fallacies, so that we can learn to avoid them.

THE GAMBLER'S FALLACY

Casinos thrive partly because so many gamblers misunderstand probability. One mistake is so common that it has been named the *gambler's fallacy*. When people have a run of bad luck, they often increase their bets because they assume that they are due for a run of good luck to even things out. For example, gambling systems are sometimes based on this fallacious idea. People keep track of the numbers that come up on a roulette wheel, trying to discover a number that has not come up for a long time. They then pile their money on that number on the assumption that it is due. They usually end up losing a bundle.

These gamblers seem to base their reasoning on something called the *law of averages.* "In the long run," they assume, "things will even out (or average out)." Interpreted one way, this amounts to what mathematicians call the *law of large numbers,* and it is perfectly correct. For example, when flipping a coin, we expect it to come up heads half the time, so with ten flips, it should come up heads five times. But if we actually check this out, we discover that the number of times it comes up heads in ten flips varies significantly from this predicted value, sometimes coming up heads more than five times, sometimes coming up fewer. What the law of large numbers tells us is that the actual percentage of heads will tend to come closer to the theoretically predicted percentage of heads the more trials we make. If you flipped a coin a million times, it would be very surprising if the percentage of heads were more than 1 percent away from the predicted 50 percent.

When interpreted as the law of large numbers, the so-called law of averages contains an important truth, but it is often misinterpreted in a way that leads to the gambler's fallacy. Some people take the law of averages to imply that each possible outcome will occur the average number of times in each series of trials. To see that this is a fallacy, we can go back to flipping coins. Toss a coin until it comes up heads three times in a row. (This will take less time than you might imagine.) What is the probability that it will come up heads a fourth time? Put crudely, some people think that the probability of it coming up heads again must be very small, because it is unlikely that a fair coin will come up heads four times in a row, so a tails is needed *to even things out.* That is wrong. The chances of getting heads on any given toss is the same, regardless of what happened on previous tosses. Previous results cannot affect the probabilities on this new toss.

STRANGE THINGS HAPPEN

Another common mistake is to ignore improbable events. It is very unlikely that a fair coin will come up heads nineteen times in a row, so you might think it could never happen. You would be wrong. Of course, if you sat flipping a single coin, you might spend a very long time before you hit a sequence of nineteen consecutive heads, but there is a way of getting this result (with a little help from your friends) in a single afternoon. You start out with $6,000 worth of pennies and put them in a large truck. (Actually, the truck need not be very large.) Dump the coins out and then pick up all the coins that come up heads. Put them back in the truck and repeat the procedure nineteen times, always returning only those coins that come up heads to the truck. With tolerably good luck, on the nineteenth dump of the coins, you will get at least one coin that comes up heads again. Any such coin will have come up heads nineteen times in a row.

What is the point of this example? It is intended to show that we often attribute abilities or the lack of abilities to people when, in fact, their performances may be statistically insignificant. When people invest with stockbrokers, they tend to shift to a new broker when they lose money. When they hit on a broker who earns them money, they stay and praise this broker's abilities. In fact, some financial advisors seem to be better than others—they have a long history of sound financial advice—but the financial community is, in many ways, like the truckload of pennies we have just examined. There are many brokers giving all sorts of different advice and, by chance alone, some of them are bound to give good advice. Furthermore, some of them are bound to have runs of success, just as some of the pennies dumped from the truck will have long strings of coming up heads. Thus, in some cases, what appears to be brilliance in predicting stock prices may be nothing more than a run of statistically expected good luck.

The gambling casinos of the world are like the truck full of pennies as well. With roulette wheels spinning in a great many places over a great deal of time, startlingly long runs are bound to occur. For example, in 1918, black came up twenty-six consecutive times on a roulette wheel in Monte Carlo. The odds against this are staggering. But before we can decide what to make of this event, we would have to judge it in the context of the vast number of times that the game of roulette has been played.

HONORS EXERCISE

Students familiar with computer programming should not find it difficult to write a program that will simulate a Monte Carlo roulette wheel and keep track of long runs of black and long runs of red. On a Monte Carlo wheel, the odds of coming up black are $18/37$. The same odds hold for coming up red. Write such a program; run it for a day; then report back the longest runs.

HEURISTICS

In daily life, we often have to make decisions quickly without pausing to weigh evidence carefully. To deal with this overload of decisions, we commonly employ what cognitive psychologists call *informal judgmental heuristics*. Technically, a *heuristic* is a device that provides a general strategy for solving a problem or coming to a decision. (For example, a good heuristic for solving geometry problems is to start with the conclusion you are trying to reach and then work backward.) Recent research in cognitive psychology has shown, first, that human beings rely very heavily on heuristics and, second, that we often have too much confidence in them. The result is that our probability judgments often go very wrong, and sometimes our thinking gets utterly mixed up. In this regard, two heuristics are particularly instructive: the *representative heuristic* and the *availability heuristic*.

THE REPRESENTATIVE HEURISTIC. A simple example illustrates how errors can arise from the representative heuristic. Imagine that you are randomly dealt five-card hands from a standard deck. Which of the following two hands is more likely to come up?

Hand #1	Hand #2
Three of clubs	Ace of spades
Seven of diamonds	Ace of hearts
Nine of diamonds	Ace of clubs
Queen of hearts	Ace of diamonds
King of spades	King of spades

A surprisingly large number of people will automatically say that the second hand is much less likely than the first. Actually, if you think about it for a bit, it should be obvious that any two specific hands have exactly the same likelihood of being dealt in a fair game. Here people get confused because the first hand is unimpressive; and, because unimpressive hands come up all the time, it strikes us as a *representative* hand. In many card games, however, the second hand is very impressive—something worth talking about—and thus looks unrepresentative. Our reliance on representativeness blinds us to a simple and obvious point about probabilities: Any specific hand is as likely to occur as any other.

A set of experiments carried out by Tversky and Kahneman yielded an even more remarkable result.[1] Students were given the following description of a fictitious person named Linda:

Linda is 31 years old, single, outspoken and very bright. She majored in philosophy. As a student, she was deeply concerned with issues of discrimination and social justice, and also participated in anti-nuclear demonstrations.

The students were then asked to rank the following statements with respect to the probability that they were also true of Linda:

Linda is a teacher in elementary school.
Linda works in a bookstore and takes yoga classes.
Linda is active in the feminist movement.
Linda is a psychiatric social worker.
Linda is a member of the League of Women Voters.
Linda is a bank teller.
Linda is an insurance salesperson.
Linda is a bank teller and is active in the feminist movement.

Not surprisingly, the students thought that it was most likely that Linda was a feminist, and least likely that she was a bank teller. What was surprising was that 89 percent of the subjects in one experiment thought that it was more likely that Linda was both a bank teller and a feminist than that she

[1]Amos Tversky and Daniel Kahneman, "Extensional Versus Intuitive Reasoning: The Conjunction Fallacy in Probability Judgment," *Psychological Review* 90, no. 4 (October 1983), 297.

was simply a bank teller. Now, if you think about that for a moment, you will see that it cannot be right. The probability that two things are true can never be higher than the probability that just one of them is true, since that one is true whenever both are true. What creates confusion here seems to be something like this: Unreflectively, people think that the claim that Linda is both a bank teller and a feminist at least says something plausible about her, whereas the simple claim that she is a bank teller isn't plausible at all. But that is just bad reasoning. Here reliance on the representative heuristic doesn't merely give us an inaccurate estimate of a probability; it actually leads us into a logical blunder.

THE AVAILABILITY HEURISTIC.   Because sampling and taking surveys is costly, we often do it imaginatively, that is, in our heads. If you ask a baseball fan which team has the better batting average, Detroit or San Diego, that person might just remember, might go look it up, or might think about each team and try to decide which has the most good batters. The latter approach, needless to say, would be a risky business, but many baseball fans have remarkable knowledge of the batting averages of top hitters. Even with this knowledge, however, it is easy to go wrong. The players that naturally come to mind are the stars on each team. They are more *available* to our memory, and we are likely to make our judgment on the basis of them alone. Yet such a sample can easily be biased because *all* the batters contribute to the team average, not just the stars. The fact that the weak batters on one team are much better than the weak batters on the other can swing the balance.

Tversky and Kahneman conducted another experiment that shows how the availability heuristic can lead to incoherent results. Subjects were asked the following question:

> In four pages of a novel (about 2,000 words), how many words would you expect to find that have the form _ _ _ _ing (seven-letter words that end with "ing")? Indicate your best estimate by circling one of the values below:
>
> 1–2   3–4   5–7   8–10   11–15   16+

A second version of the question requested estimates for words of the form _ _ _ _ _n_. The median estimates were 13.4 for _ _ _ _ *ing* words and 4.7 for _ _ _ _ _n_ words. This answer is again logically incoherent. There must be at least as many _ _ _ _ _n_ words in the text as _ _ _ _ *ing* words, since every _ _ _ _ *ing* word is also an _ _ _ _ _n_ word. Why didn't the subjects think about this? The answer is that we rely on the availability heuristic, and it is easy to think of _ _ _ _ *ing* words; all sorts of verbs with "ing" endings pop into our minds at once. There is nothing similarly memorable about seven-letter words ending with "_n_". Thus relying on what naturally pops into our heads will often produce false, even incoherent, probability judgments.

The point of examining these heuristics and noting the logical errors that they produce is *not* to suggest that we should cease relying on them. First, there is a good chance that this would be psychologically impossible, because the use of such heuristics seems to be built into our psychological makeup. Second, over a wide range of standard cases, these heuristics give *quick* and largely *accurate* estimates. Difficulties typically arise in using these heuristics when the situation is *nonstandard,* that is, when the situation is complex or out of the ordinary.

To avoid such mistakes when making important judgments about probabilities, we need to ask, "Is the situation sufficiently standard to allow the use of informal judgmental heuristics?" Because this is a mouthful, we might simply ask, "Is this the sort of thing that people can figure out in their heads?" When the answer to that question is "No," as it often is, then we need to turn to more formal procedures for determining probabilities.

DISCUSSION QUESTION

In a remarkable study, Thomas Gilovich, Robert Vallone, and Amos Tversky found a striking instance of people's tendency to treat things as statistically significant when they are not.[2] In professional basketball, certain players have the reputation of being *streak shooters*. Streak shooters seem to score points in batches, then go cold and are not able to buy a basket. Stated more precisely, in streak shooting "the performance of a player during a particular period is significantly better than expected on the basis of the player's overall record" (pp. 295–6). To test whether streak shooting really exists, the authors made a detailed study of a year's shooting record for the players on the Philadelphia 76ers. This team included Andrew Toney, noted around the league as being a streak shooter. The authors found no evidence for streak shooting, not even for Andrew Toney. How would you go about deciding whether streak shooting exists or not? If, as Gilovich, Vallone, and Tversky have argued, belief in this phenomenon is a "cognitive illusion," why do so many people, including most professional athletes, believe that it does exist?

[2]Thomas Gilovich, Robert Vallone, and Amos Tversky, "The Hot Hand in Basketball: On the Misperception of Random Sequences," *Cognitive Psychology* 17 (1985), 295–314.

THE LANGUAGE OF PROBABILITY

The first step in figuring out probabilities is to adopt a more precise way of talking. Our common language includes various ways of expressing probabilities. The guarding terms discussed in Chapter 3 provide examples of informal ways of expressing probability commitments. Thus, someone might say that it is unlikely that the New England Patriots will win the Superbowl this year without saying *how* unlikely it is. We can also specify various degrees of probability. Looking out the window, we might say that there is a fifty-fifty chance of rain. More vividly, someone might have remarked that Ralph Nader does not have a snowball's chance in hell of ever winning a presidential election. In each case, the speaker is indicating the relative strength of the evidence for the occurrence or nonoccurrence of some event. To say that there is a fifty-fifty chance that it will rain indicates that we hold that the evidence is equally strong that it will rain rather than not rain. The metaphor in the third statement indicates that the person who uttered it believed that the probability of Nader winning a presidential election is essentially nonexistent.

We can make our probability claims more precise by using numbers. Sometimes we use percentages. For example, the weather bureau might say that there is a 75 percent chance of snow tomorrow. This can naturally be changed to a fraction: The probability is 3/4 that it will snow tomorrow. Finally, this fraction can be changed to a decimal expression: There is a 0.75 probability that it will snow tomorrow.

The probability scale has two endpoints: the absolute certainty that the event will occur and the absolute certainty that it will not occur. Because you cannot do better than absolute certainty, a probability can neither rise above 100 percent nor drop below 0 percent (neither above 1, nor below 0). (This should sound fairly obvious, but it is possible to become confused when combining percentages and fractions, as when Yogi Berra was supposed to have said that success is one-third talent and 75 percent hard work.) Of course, what we normally call *probability* claims usually fall between these two endpoints. For this reason, it sounds somewhat peculiar to say that there is a 100 percent chance of rain and just plain weird to say the chance of rain is 1 out of 1. Even so, these peculiar ways of speaking cause no procedural difficulties and rarely come up in practice.

A PRIORI **PROBABILITY**

When people make probability claims, we have a right to ask why they assign the probability they do. In the chapter on inductive reasoning, we saw how statistical procedures can be used for establishing probability claims. Here we will examine the so-called *a priori* approach to probabilities. A simple example will bring out the differences between these two approaches. We might wonder what the probability is of drawing an ace from a standard deck of fifty-two cards. Using the procedure discussed in the previous chapter, we could make a great many random draws from the deck (replacing the card each time) and then form a statistical generalization concerning the results. We would discover that an ace tends to come up roughly one-thirteenth of the time. From this we could draw the conclusion that the chance of drawing an ace is one in thirteen.

But we do not have to go to all this trouble. We can assume that each of the fifty-two cards has an equal chance of being selected. Given this assumption, an obvious line of reasoning runs as follows: There are four aces in a standard fifty-two-card deck, so the probability of selecting one randomly is four in fifty-two. That reduces to one chance in thirteen. Here the set of favorable outcomes is a subset of the total number of equally likely outcomes, and to compute the probability that the favorable outcome will occur, we merely divide the number of favorable outcomes by the total number of possible outcomes. This fraction gives us the probability that the event will occur on a random draw. Since all outcomes here are equally likely,

$$\text{Probability of drawing an ace} = \frac{\text{number of aces}}{\text{total number of cards}} = \frac{4}{52} = \frac{1}{13}$$

Notice that in coming to our conclusion that there is one chance in thirteen of randomly drawing an ace from a fifty-two-card deck, we simply used mathematical reasoning. This illustrates the *a priori* approach to probabilities. It is called the *a priori* approach because we arrive at the result simply by reasoning about the circumstances.

In calculating the probability of drawing an ace from a fifty-two-card deck, we took the ratio of favorable equally likely outcomes to total equally likely outcomes. Generally, then, the probability of a hypothesis *h*, symbolized "Pr(*h*)," when all outcomes are equally likely, is expressed as follows:

$$\text{Pr}(h) = \frac{\text{favorable outcomes}}{\text{total outcomes}}$$

We can illustrate this principle with a slightly more complicated example. What is the probability of throwing an eight on the cast of two dice? Here are all the equally likely ways in which two dice can turn up on a single cast:

Total 36

As indicated, five of the thirty-six possible outcomes produce an eight, so the probability of throwing an eight is 5/36.

Using the above chart, answer the following questions about the total on the throw of two dice:

1. What is the probability of throwing a five?
2. Which number has the highest probability of being thrown? What is its probability?
3. What is the probability of throwing an eleven?
4. What is the probability of throwing either a seven or an eleven?
5. Which is more likely: throwing either a five or an eight?
6. Which is more likely: throwing a five or an eight, or throwing a two or a seven?
7. What is the probability of throwing a ten or above?
8. What is the probability of throwing an even number?
9. What is the probability of throwing an odd number?
10. What is the probability of throwing a value from four to six?
11. What is the probability of throwing either a two or a twelve?
12. What is the probability of throwing a value from two to twelve?

SOME LAWS OF PROBABILITY

Suppose you have determined the probability that certain simple events will occur; how do you go about applying this to combinations of events? This is a complex question, and one that can be touched on only lightly in this text. There are, however, some simple rules of probability that are worth knowing because they can guide us in making choices when outcomes are uncertain.

By convention, events are assigned probabilities between 0 and 1 (inclusive). An event is going to either occur or not occur; that, at least, is certain (that is, it has a probability of 1). From this it is easy to see how to calculate the probability that the event will not occur given the probability that it will occur: We simply subtract the probability that it will occur from 1. This is our first rule:

RULE 1. The probability that an event will not occur is 1 minus the probability that it will occur. Symbolically:

$$\Pr(\text{not } h) = 1 - \Pr(h)$$

For example, the probability of drawing an ace from a standard deck is one in thirteen, so the probability of *not* drawing an ace is twelve in thirteen.

This makes sense because there are forty-eight out of fifty-two ways of not drawing an ace, and this reduces to twelve chances in thirteen.

RULE 2. Given two independent events, the probability of their both occurring is the product of their individual probabilities. Symbolically (where h_1 and h_2 are independent):

$$Pr(h_1 \text{ \& } h_2) = Pr(h_1) \times Pr(h_2)$$

Here the word "independent" needs explanation. Suppose you randomly draw a card from the deck, then put it back, shuffle, and draw again. In this case, the outcome of the first draw provides no information about the outcome of the second draw, so it is *independent* of it. What is the probability of drawing two aces in a row using this system? Using Rule 2, we see that the answer is $1/13 \times 1/13$, or 1 chance in 169.

The situation is different if we do *not* replace the card after the first draw. Rule 2 does not apply to this case because the two events are no longer independent. The chances of getting an ace on the first draw are still one in thirteen, but if an ace is drawn (and not returned to the pack), then there is one less ace in the deck, so the chances of drawing an ace on the next draw are reduced to three in fifty-one. Thus, the probability of drawing two consecutive aces (without returning the first draw to the deck) is $4/52 \times 3/51$, or 1 in 221, which is considerably lower than 1 in 169.

If we want to extend Rule 2 to cover cases in which the events are not independent, we will have to speak of the probability of one event occurring *given that another has occurred*. The probability that h_2 will occur given that h_1 has occurred is called the *conditional* probability of h_2 on h_1 and is usually symbolized thus: $Pr(h_2|h_1)$. This probability is calculated by considering only those cases where h_1 is true and then, *within that group*, dividing the number of cases where h_2 is true by the total number of cases in that group. Symbolically:

$$Pr(h_2|h_1) = \frac{\text{favorable outcomes where } h_1}{\text{total outcomes where } h_1} = \frac{\text{outcomes where } h_1 \text{ and } h_2}{\text{total outcomes where } h_1}$$

Using this notion of conditional probability, Rule 2 can be modified as follows to deal with cases in which events need not be independent:

RULE 2G. Given two events, the probability of their both occurring is the probability of the first occurring times the probability of the second occurring, given that the first has occurred. Symbolically:

$$Pr(h_1 \text{ \& } h_2) = Pr(h_1) \times Pr(h_2|h_1)$$

Notice that, in the event that h_1 and h_2 are independent, the probability of h_2 is not related to the occurrence of h_1, so the probability of h_2 on h_1 is simply the probability of h_2. Thus, Rule 2 is simply a special case of the more general Rule 2G.

We can extend these rules to cover more than two events. For example, with Rule 2, however many events we might consider, provided that they are independent of each other, the probability of all of them occurring is the product of each one of them occurring. For example, the chances of flipping a coin and having it come up heads is one chance in two. What are the chances of flipping a coin eight times and having it come up heads every time? The answer is:

$$1/2 \times 1/2 \times 1/2 \times 1/2 \times 1/2 \times 1/2 \times 1/2 \times 1/2$$

which equals 1 chance in 256.

Our next rule allows us to answer questions of the following kind: What are the chances of either an eight or a two coming up on a single throw of the dice? Going back to the chart, we saw that we could answer this question by counting the number of ways in which a two can come up (which is one) and adding this to the number of ways in which an eight can come up (which is five). We could then conclude that the chances of one or the other of them coming up is six chances in thirty-six, or 1/6. The principle involved in this calculation can be stated as follows:

RULE 3. The probability that at least one of two mutually exclusive events will occur is the sum of the probabilities that each of them will occur. Symbolically (where h_1 and h_2 are mutually exclusive):

$$Pr(h_1 \text{ or } h_2) = Pr(h_1) + Pr(h_2)$$

To say that events are *mutually exclusive* means that they cannot both occur. You cannot, for example, get both a ten and an eight on the same cast of two dice. You might, however, throw neither one of them.

When events are not mutually exclusive, the rule for calculating disjunctive probabilities becomes more complicated. Suppose, for example, that exactly half the class is female and exactly half the class is over nineteen and the age distribution is the same for females and males. What is the probability that a randomly selected student will be either a female or over nineteen? If we simply add the probabilities ($1/2 + 1/2 = 1$), we would get the result that we are certain to pick someone who is either female or over nineteen. But that answer is wrong, because a quarter of the class is male and not over nineteen, and one of them might have been randomly selected. The correct answer is that the chances are 3/4 of randomly selecting someone who is either female or over nineteen.

We can see that this is the correct answer by examining the following table:

	Over Nineteen	Not over Nineteen
Female	25%	25%
Male	25%	25%

It is easy to see that in 75 percent of the cases, a randomly selected student will be either female or over nineteen. The table also shows what went wrong with our initial calculation. The top row shows that 50 percent of the students are female. The left column shows that 50 percent of the students are over nineteen. But we cannot simply add these figures to get the probability of a randomly selected student being either female or over nineteen. Why not? Because that would double-count the females over nineteen. We would count them once in the top row and then again in the left column. To compensate for such double-counting, we need to subtract the students who are both female and over nineteen. The upper left figure shows that this is 25 percent. So the correct way to calculate the answer is $50\% + 50\% - 25\% = 75\%$.

This pattern is reflected in the general rule governing the calculation of disjunctive probabilities:

RULE 3G. The probability that at least one of two events will occur is the sum of the probabilities that each of them will occur, minus the probability that they will both occur. Symbolically:

$$\Pr(h_1 \text{ or } h_2) = \Pr(h_1) + \Pr(h_2) - \Pr(h_1 \& h_2)$$

If h_1 and h_2 are mutually exclusive, then $\Pr(h_1 \& h_2) = 0$, and Rule 3G reduces to Rule 3.

Before stating Rule 4, we can think about a particular example. What is the probability of tossing heads at least once in eight tosses of a coin? Here it is tempting to reason in the following way: There is a 50 percent chance of getting heads on the first toss and a 50 percent chance of getting heads on the second toss, so after two tosses it is already certain that we will toss heads at least once, and thus after eight tosses there should be a 400 percent chance. In other words, you cannot miss. There are two good reasons for thinking that this argument is fishy. First, probability can never exceed 100 percent; and second, there must be some chance, however small, that we could toss a coin eight times and not have it come up heads.

The best way to look at this question is to restate it so that the first two rules can be used. Instead of asking what the probability is that heads will come up at least once, we can ask what the probability is that it will *not* come up at least once. To say that heads will *not* come up even once is equivalent to saying that tails *will* come up eight times in a row. By Rule 2 we know how to compute that probability: It is 1/2 multiplied by itself eight times, and that, as we saw, is 1/256. Finally, by Rule 1 we know that the probability that this will not happen (that heads will come up at least once) is $1 - (1/256)$. In other words, the probability of tossing heads at least once in eight tosses is 255/256. That comes close to a certainty, but it is not quite a certainty.

We can generalize these results as follows:

RULE 4. The probability that an event will occur at least once in a series of independent trials is simply 1 minus the probability that it will *not* occur in that number of trials. Symbolically (where n is the number of independent trials):

The probability that h will occur at least once in n trials $= 1 - \text{Pr}(\text{not } h)^n$

Strictly speaking, Rule 4 is unnecessary since it can be derived from Rules 1 and 2, but it is important to know because it blocks a common misunderstanding about probabilities: People often think that something is a sure thing when it is not.

Another common confusion is between permutations and combinations. A *permutation* is a set of items whose order is specified. A *combination* is a set of items whose order is not specified. Imagine, for example, that three cards—the jack, queen, and king of spades—are face down in front of you. If you pick two of these cards in turn, there are three possible combinations: jack and queen, jack and king, and queen and king. In contrast, there are six possible permutations: jack then queen, queen then jack, jack then king, king then jack, queen then king, and king then queen.

Rule 2 is used to calculate probabilities of permutations—of conjunctions of events in a particular order. For example, if you flip a fair coin twice, what is the probability of its coming up heads and tails in *that* order (that is, heads on the first flip and tails on the second flip)? Since the flips are independent, Rule 2 tells us that the answer is $0.5 \times 0.5 = 0.25$. This answer is easily confirmed by counting the possible permuations (heads then heads, heads then tails, tails then heads, tails then tails). Only one of these four permutations (heads then tails) is a favorable outcome.

We need to calculate probabilities of combinations in a different way. For example, if you flip a fair coin twice, what is the probability of its landing heads and tails in *any* order? There are two ways for this to happen. The coin could come up either heads then tails or tails then heads. These alternatives are mutually exclusive, so the probability of this disjunction by Rule 3 is $0.25 + 0.25 = 0.5$. This is confirmed by two possibilities (heads then tails, tails then heads) out of four (heads then heads, heads then tails, tails then heads, tails then tails). Another way to calculate this probability is to realize that the first flip doesn't matter. Whatever you get on the first flip (heads or tails), you need the opposite on the second flip. You are certain to get either heads or tails on the first flip, so this probability is 1.0. Then, regardless of what happens on the first flip, the probability of getting the opposite on the second flip is 0.5. These results are independent, so the probability of their conjuction by Rule 2 is the product $1.0 \times 0.5 = 0.5$.

We can also use our rules to calculate probabilities of combinations without independence. Rule 2G tells us that the probability of drawing an ace, not putting this card back in the deck, and then drawing a king is

$4/52 \times 4/51 = 16/2,652$. But what is the probability of drawing an ace and a king *in any order*? It is the probability of drawing either an ace or a king and then drawing the other one given that you drew the first one. That probability by Rule 2G is $8/52 \times 4/51 = 32/2,652$. The difference between this result and the previous one, where the order was specified, shows why we need to determine whether we are dealing with permutations or combinations.

EXERCISE II

Use the rules of probability to calculate these probabilities:

1. What is the probability of rolling a one on one throw of a fair six-sided die?

2. What is the probability of *not* rolling a one on one throw of a fair six-sided die?

3. If you roll a one on your first throw of a fair six-sided die, what is the probability of rolling *another* one on a second throw of that die?

4. If you roll two fair six-sided dice one time, what are the chances that *both* of the dice will come up a one?

5. If you roll two fair six-sided dice one time, what are the chances that *one or the other* of the dice will come up a one?

6. If you roll two fair six-sided dice one time, what are the chances that *one and only one* of the dice will come up a one?

7. If you roll two fair six-sided dice one time, what are the chances that *at least one* of the dice will come up a one?

8. If you roll two fair six-sided dice one time, what are the chances that *at least one* of the dice will *not* come up a one?

9. If you roll six fair six-sided dice one time, what are the chances that *at least one* of the dice will come up a one?

10. If you roll six fair six-sided dice one time, what are the chances that *at least one* of the dice will *not* come up a one?

EXERCISE III

Compute the probability of making the following draws from a standard fifty-two-card deck:

1. Drawing either a seven or a five on a single draw.

2. Drawing neither a seven nor a five on a single draw.

3. Drawing a seven and then, without returning the first card to the deck, drawing a five on the next draw.

4. Same as 3, but the first card is returned to the deck and the deck is shuffled after the first draw.

5. Drawing at least one spade in a series of three consecutive draws, when the card drawn is not returned to the deck.

6. Drawing at least one spade in a series of four consecutive draws, when the card drawn is not returned to the deck.

7. Same as 6, but the card is returned to the deck after each draw and the deck is reshuffled.

8. Drawing a heart and a diamond in that order in two consecutive draws, when the first card is returned to the deck and the deck is shuffled after the first draw.

9. Drawing a heart and a diamond in any order in two consecutive draws, when the first card is returned to the deck and the deck is shuffled after the first draw.

10. Drawing a heart and a diamond in any order in two consecutive draws, when the first card is not returned to the deck after the first draw.

EXERCISE IV

Suppose there are two little lotteries in town, each of which sells exactly 100 tickets.

1. If each lottery has only one winning ticket, and you buy two tickets to the *same* lottery, what is the probability that you will have a winning ticket?

2. If each lottery has only one winning ticket, and you buy one ticket to each of the *two* lotteries, what is the probability that you will have at least one winning ticket?

3. If each lottery has only one winning ticket, and you buy one ticket to each of the two lotteries, what is the probability that you will have *two* winning tickets?

4. If each lottery has two winning tickets, and you buy one ticket to each of the two lotteries, what is the probability that you will have at least one winning ticket?

5. If each lottery has two winning tickets, and you buy two tickets to the same lottery, what is the probability that you will have two winning tickets?

6. If each lottery has two winning tickets, and you buy two tickets to the same lottery, what is the probability that you will have at least one winning ticket?

1. You are presented with two bags, one containing two ham sandwiches and the other containing a ham sandwich and a cheese sandwich. You reach in one bag and draw out a ham sandwich. What is the probability that the other sandwich in the bag is also a ham sandwich?

2. You are presented with three bags: two contain a chicken-fat sandwich and one contains a cheese sandwich. You are asked to guess which bag contains the cheese sandwich. You do so, and the bag you have selected is set aside. (You obviously have one chance in three of guessing correctly.) From the two remaining bags, one containing a chicken-fat sandwich is then removed. You are now given the opportunity to switch your selection to the remaining bag. Will such a switch increase, decrease, or leave unaffected your chances of correctly selecting the bag with the cheese sandwich in it?

DISCUSSION QUESTION

In a fair lottery with a million tickets, the probability that ticket #1 will lose is 0.999999, the probability that ticket #2 will lose is also 0.999999, and so on for each ticket. On this basis, you might seem justified in believing each premise in the following argument:

> Ticket #1 will lose.
> Ticket #2 will lose.
> Ticket #3 will lose.
> [and so on, until:]
> Ticket #1,000,000 will lose.
> There are only 1,000,000 tickets.
>
> ∴ Every ticket will lose.

This conclusion must be false, since the lottery is fair. But the conclusion follows from the premises, each of which seems justified. Does this argument justify us in believing its conclusion? Why or why not?

BAYES'S THEOREM

Although dice and cards provide nice, simple models for learning how to calculate probabilities, real life is usually more complicated. One particularly interesting and important form of problem arises often in medicine. Suppose that Wendy tests positive for colon cancer. The treatment for colon cancer is painful and dangerous, so, before subjecting Wendy to that treatment, her doctor wants to determine how likely it is that Wendy really has colon cancer. After all, no test is perfect. Regarding the test that was used on Wendy, previous studies have revealed the following probabilities:

The probability that a person in the general population has colon cancer is 0.3 percent (or 0.003).

If a person has colon cancer, then the probability that the test is positive is 90 percent (or 0.9).

If a person does not have colon cancer, then the probability that the test is positive is 3 percent (or 0.03).

On these assumptions, what is the probability that Wendy actually has colon cancer, given that she tested positive? Most people guess that this probability is fairly high. Even most trained physicians would say that Wendy probably has colon cancer.[3]

What is the correct answer? To calculate the probability that a person who tests positive actually has colon cancer, we need to divide the number of favorable outcomes by the number of total outcomes. The favorable outcomes include everyone who tests positive and really has colon cancer. (This outcome is not "favorable" to Wendy, so we will describe this group as *true positives*.) The total outcomes include everyone who tests positive. This includes the true positives plus the *false positives*, which are those who test positive but do not have colon cancer. Given the stipulated probabilities, in a normal population of 100,000 people, there will be 270 true positives (100,000 × 0.003 × 0.9) and 2,991 false positives ((100,000 − 300) × 0.03). Thus, the probability that Wendy has colon cancer is about 270/(270 + 2,991). That is only about 8.3 percent, when most people estimate above 50 percent!

Why do people, including doctors, overestimate these probabilities so badly? Part of the answer seems to be that they focus on the rate of true positives (90 percent) and forget that, because there are so many people without colon cancer (99.7 percent of the total population), even a small *rate* of false positives (3 percent) will yield a large *number* of false positives (2,991) that swamps the much smaller number of true positives (270). (When the question about probability was reformulated in terms of the number of people in each group, most doctors come up with the correct answer.) For whatever reason, people have a strong tendency to make mistakes in cases like these, so we need to be careful, especially when so much is at stake.

One way to calculate probabilities like these uses a famous theorem that was first presented by an English clergyman named Thomas Bayes (1702–61). A simple proof of this theorem applies the laws of probability from the preceding section. We want to figure out Pr(*h*|*e*), that is, the probability of the hypothesis *h* (e.g., Wendy has colon cancer), given the evidence *e* (e.g., Wendy tested postive for colon cancer). To get there, we start from Rule 2G:

1. $\Pr(e \& h) = \Pr(e) \times \Pr(h|e)$

---

[3]See *Calculated Risk: How to Know When Numbers Deceive You*, by Gerd Gigerenzer (New York: Simon & Schuster, 2003).

Dividing both sides by Pr(*e*) gives us:

2. $\Pr(h|e) = \dfrac{\Pr(e \And h)}{\Pr(e)}$

If two formulas are logically equivalent, they must have the same probability. We can establish by truth tables that "*e*" is logically equivalent to "(*e*&*h*) ∨ (*e*&~*h*)." (See Chapter 6.) Consequently, we may replace "*e*" in the denominator of (2) with "(*e*&*h*) ∨ (*e*&~*h*)" to get:

3. $\Pr(h|e) = \dfrac{\Pr(e \And h)}{\Pr((e \And h) \vee (e \And \sim h))}$

Since "*e*&*h*" and "*e*&~*h*" are mutually exclusive, we can apply Rule 3 to the denominator of (3) to get:

4. $\Pr(h|e) = \dfrac{\Pr(e \And h)}{\Pr(e \And h) + \Pr(e \And \sim h)}$

Finally, we apply Rule 2G to (4) and get:

(BT) $\Pr(h|e) = \dfrac{\Pr(h) \times \Pr(e|h)}{[\Pr(h) \times \Pr(e|h)] + [\Pr(\sim h) \times \Pr(e|\sim h)]}$

This is a simplified version of Bayes's theorem.

This theorem enables us to calculate the desired probability in our original example:

h = the patient has colon cancer

e = the patient tests positive for colon cancer

$\Pr(h) = 0.003$

$\Pr(\sim h) = 1 - \Pr(h) = 0.997$

$\Pr(e|h) = 0.9$

$\Pr(e|\sim h) = 0.03$

If we substitute these values into Bayes's theorem, we get:

(BT) $\Pr(h|e) = \dfrac{0.003 \times 0.9}{[0.003 \times 0.9] + [0.997 \times 0.03]} = $ about 0.083

In this way, we can calculate the conditional probability of the hypothesis given the evidence from its reverse, that is, from the conditional probability of the evidence given the hypothesis. That is what makes Bayes's theorem so useful.

Many people find a different method more intuitive. The first step is to set up a table. The two factors to be related are (1) whether the patient has colon cancer and (2) whether the patient tests positive for colon cancer. To chart all possible combinations of these two factors, we need a table like this:

	Colon Cancer	Not Colon Cancer	Total
Test Positive			
Do Not Test Positive			
Total			

Next we need to enter a population size in the lower right box. The probabilities will not be affected by the population size, but it is cleaner to pick a population that is large enough to get whole numbers when the population is multiplied by the given probabilities. To determine the right size population, add the number of places to the right of the decimal point in the two most specific probabilities, then pick a population of 10 to the power of that sum. In our example, the most specific probabilities are 0.003 and 0.03, and $3 + 2 = 5$, so we can enter 10^5:

	Colon Cancer	Not Colon Cancer	Total
Test Positive			
Do Not Test Positive			
Total			100,000

This population size represents the total number of people who are tested. We have no information about the ones who are not tested, so they cannot figure into our calculations.

The bottom row can now be filled in by dividing the total population into those who have colon cancer and those who do not have colon cancer. Just multiply the population size by the probability of colon cancer (Pr(h)) to get a number for the second box on the bottom row. This figure represents the total number of people with colon cancer in this population. Then subtract that product from the population size and put the remainder in the remaining box. This represents the total number of people without colon cancer in this population. Since these two groups exhaust the population, they must add up to the total population size. In our case, we were given that the probability that a person in the general population has colon cancer is 0.003. On this basis, we can fill in the bottom row of the table:

	Colon Cancer	Not Colon Cancer	Total
Test Positive			
Do Not Test Positive			
Total	300	99,700	100,000

Next, fill out the second column by dividing the total number of people *with* colon cancer into those who test positive and those who do not test positive. These numbers can be calculated with the given conditional probability of testing positive, given colon cancer (PR(e|h)). In our example, if a person has colon cancer, the probability that the test is positive is 0.9. Thus, 270 (0.9 × 300) of the people in the colon cancer column will test positive and the rest (300 − 270 = 30) will not, so we get these figures:

	Colon Cancer	Not Colon Cancer	Total
Test Positive	270		
Do Not Test Positive	30		
Total	300	99,700	100,000

Similarly, we can fill out the third column by dividing the total number of people *without* colon cancer into those who test positive and those who do not test positive. Here we use the conditional probability of a positive test, given that a person does not have colon cancer (PR(e|~h)). This probability was given as 0.03, and 0.03 × 99,700 = 2,991. This number means that, out of a normal population of 99,700 without colon cancer, 2,991 will test positive. Since the figures in this column must add up to a total of 99,700, the remaining figure is 99,700 − 2,991 = 96,709:

	Colon Cancer	Not Colon Cancer	Total
Test Positive	270	2,991	
Do Not Test Positive	30	96,709	
Total	300	99,700	100,000

Finally, we can fill out the fourth column by calculating total numbers of people who test positive or do not test positive. Simply add across the rows:

	Colon Cancer	Not Colon Cancer	Total
Test Positive	270	2,991	3,261
Do Not Test Positive	30	96,709	96,739
Total	300	99,700	100,000

Check your calculations by adding the right column: 3,261 + 96,739 = 100,000.

Now that our population is divided up, the solution is staring you in the face. This table shows us that, in a normal population of 100,000 tested people distributed according to the given probabilities, a total of 3,261 will test positive. Out of those, 270 will have colon cancer. Thus, the probability that the patient has colon cancer, given that this patient tested positive, is 270/3,261, which is about 0.083 or 8.3 percent, just as before.

You can also read off other conditional probabilities. If you want to know the conditional probability of *not* having colon cancer, given that your test did *not* come out positive, then you need to look at the row for those who do not test positive. The figure at the right of this row tells you that a total of 96,739 out of the total population do not test positive. The column under "Not Colon Cancer" then tells you that 96,709 of these do not have colon cancer. Thus, the conditional probability of *not* having colon cancer given your test did *not* come out positive is 96,709/96,739 or about 0.9997. That means that, if you test negative, the odds are extremely high that you do not have colon cancer.

EXERCISE VI

1. What would Wendy's chances of having colon cancer be if the other probabilities remained the same as in the original example, except that the probability that a person in the general population has colon cancer is only 0.1 percent (or 0.001)?

2. What would Wendy's chances of having colon cancer be if the other probabilities remained the same as in the original example, except that the probability that a person in the general population has colon cancer is 1 percent (0.001)?

3. What would Wendy's chances of having colon cancer be if the other probabilities remained the same as in the original example, except that the conditional probability that the test is positive, given that the patient has colon cancer, is only 50 percent (or 0.5)?

4. What would Wendy's chances of having colon cancer be if the other probabilities remained the same as in the original example, except that the conditional probability that the test is positive, given that the patient has colon cancer, is 99 percent (or 0.99)?

5. What would Wendy's chances of having colon cancer be if the other probabilities remained the same as in the original example, except that the conditional probability that the test is positive, given that the patient does not have colon cancer, is 1 percent (or 0.01)?

6. What would Wendy's chances of having colon cancer be if the other probabilities remained the same as in the original example, except that the conditional probability that the test is positive, given that the patient does not have colon cancer, is 10 percent (0.1)?

7. In your neighborhood, 20 percent of the houses have high levels of radon gas in their basements, so you ask an expert to test your basement. An inexpensive test comes out positive in 80 percent of the basements that actually have high levels of radon, but it also comes out positive in 10 percent of the basements that do not have high levels of radon. If this inexpensive test comes out positive in your basement, what is the probability that there is a high level of radon gas in your basement?

8. A more expensive test for radon is also more accurate. It comes out positive in 99 percent of the basements that actually have high levels of radon. It also tests positive in 2 percent of the basements that do not have high levels of radon. As in problem 7, 20 percent of the houses in your neighborhood have radon in their basement. If the expensive test comes out positive in your basement, what is the probability that there is a high level of radon gas in your basement?

9. Late last night a car ran into your neighbor and drove away. In your town there are 500 cars; 2 percent are Porsches. The only eyewitness to the hit and run says the car that hit your neighbor was a Porsche. Tested under similar conditions, the eyewitness mistakenly classifies cars of other makes as Porsches 10 percent of the time, and correctly classifies Porsches as such 80 percent of the time. What are the chances that the car that hit your neighbor was a Porsche?

10. Late last night a dog bit your neighbor. In your small town, there are 400 dogs; 95 percent of them are black labrador retrievers, the other 5 percent are pit bulls. The only eyewitness to the event, a veteran dog breeder, says that the dog who bit your neighbor was a pit bull. Tested under similar low-light conditions, the eyewitness mistakenly classifies black labs as pit bulls only 2 percent of the time, and correctly classifies pit bulls as pit bulls 90 percent of the time. What are the chances that the dog who bit your neighbor was a pit bull?

11. The probability that a student reads the assigned pages before a lecture is 80 percent (or 0.8). If a student does the assigned reading in advance, then the probability that the student will understand the lecture is 90 percent (or 0.9). If a student does not do the assigned reading in advance, then the probability that the student will understand the lecture is 10 percent (or 0.1). What is the probability that a student did the reading in advance, given that she understood the lecture? What is the probability that a student did not do the reading in advance, given that she did not understand the lecture?

12. The probability that a student reads the assigned pages before a lecture is 60 percent (or 0.6). If a student does the assigned reading in advance, then the probability that, when asked, the student will tell the professor that he did the reading is 100 percent (or 1.0). If a student does not do the assigned reading in advance, then the probability that, when asked, the student will tell the professor that he did the reading is 70 percent (or 0.7). What is the probability that a student did the reading in advance, given that, when asked, he told the professor that he did the reading? What is the probability that a student did not do the reading in advance, given that, when asked, he told the professor that he did not do the reading?

EXPECTED MONETARY VALUE

It is obvious that having some sense of probable outcomes is important for running our lives. If we hear that there is a 95 percent chance of rain, this usually provides a good enough reason to call off a picnic. But the exact relationship between probabilities and decisions is complex and often misunderstood.

The best way to illustrate these misunderstandings is to look at lotteries in which the numbers are fixed and clear. A $1 bet in a lottery might make you as much as $10 million. That sounds good. Why not take a shot at $10 million for only a dollar? Of course, there is not much chance of winning the lottery—say, only 1 chance in 20 million—and that sounds bad. Why throw $1 away on nothing? So we are pulled in two directions. What we want to know is just how good the bet is. Is it, for example, better or worse than a wager in some other lottery? To answer questions of this kind, we need to introduce the notion of *expected monetary value.*

The idea of expected monetary value takes into account three features that determine whether a bet is financially good or not: the probability of winning, the net amount you gain if you win, and the net amount you lose if you lose. Suppose that on a $1 ticket there is 1 chance in 20 million of winning the New York State Lottery, and you will get $10 million from the state if you do. First, it is worth noticing that, if the state pays you $10 million, your net gain on your $1 ticket is only $9,999,999. The state, after all, still has your original $1. So the *net gain* equals the payoff minus the cost of betting. This is not something that those who win huge lotteries worry about, but taking into account the cost of betting becomes important when this cost becomes high relative to the size of the payoff. There is nothing complicated about the net amount that you lose when you lose on a $1 ticket: it is $1.[4]

We can now compute the *expected monetary value* or *financial worth* of a bet in the following way:

Expected monetary value =

(the probability of winning $\times$ the net gain in money of winning) −

(the probability of losing times the net loss in money of losing)

In our example, a person who buys a $1 ticket in the lottery has 1 chance in 20 million of a net gain of $9,999,999 and 19,999,999 chances in 20 million of a net loss of a dollar. So the expected monetary value of this wager equals:

$(1/20,000,000 \times \$9,999,999) - (19,999,999/20,000,000 \times \$1)$

That comes out to −$0.50.

What does this mean? One way of looking at it is as follows: If you could somehow buy up all the lottery tickets and thus ensure that you would win, your $20 million investment would net you $10 million, or $0.50 on the

---

[4]If the lottery gave a consolation prize of a shiny new quarter to all losers, then the net loss would be only seventy-five cents. Since most lotteries do not give consolation prizes, the net loss equals the cost of playing such lotteries.

dollar—certainly a bad investment. Another way of looking at the situation is as follows: If you invested a great deal of money in the lottery over many millions of years, you could expect to win eventually, but, in the long run, you would be losing fifty cents on every ticket you bought. One last way of looking at the situation is this: You go down to your local drugstore and buy a *blank* lottery ticket for $0.50. Since it is blank, you have no chance of winning, with the result that you lose $0.50 every time you bet. Although almost no one looks at the matter in this way, this is, in effect, what you are doing *over the long run* when you buy lottery tickets.

We are now in a position to distinguish favorable and unfavorable expected monetary values. The expected monetary value is favorable when it is greater than zero. Changing our example, suppose the chances of hitting a $20 million payoff on a $1 bet are 1 in 10 million. In this case, the state still has the $1 you paid for the ticket, so your gain is actually $19,999,999. The expected monetary value is calculated as follows:

$$(1/10,000,000 \times \$19,999,999) - (9,999,999/10,000,000 \times \$1)$$

That comes to $1. So financially this is a good bet. For *in the long run* you will gain $1 for every $1 you bet in such a lottery.

The rule, then, has three parts: (1) If the expected monetary value of the bet is more than zero, then the expected monetary value is *favorable*. (2) If the expected monetary value of the bet is less than zero, then the expected monetary value is *unfavorable*. (3) If the expected monetary value of the bet is zero, then the bet is *neutral*—a waste of time as far as money is concerned.

EXERCISE VII

Compute the probability and the expected monetary value for the following bets. Each time, you lay down $1 to bet that a certain kind of card will be drawn from a standard fifty-two-card deck. If you win, you collect the amount indicated, so your net gain is $1 less. If you lose, of course, you lose your $1.

Example: Draw a seven of spades. Win: $26.
Probability of winning = 1/52
Expected value: $[1/52 \times \$(26 - 1)] - (51/52 \times \$1) = -\$0.50$

1. Draw a seven of spades or a seven of clubs. Win: $26.
2. Draw a seven of any suit. Win: $26.
3. Draw a face card (jack, queen, or king). Win: $4.
4. Do not draw a face card (jack, queen, or king). Win: $2.
5. On two consecutive draws (without returning the first card to the deck), draw a seven of spades, then a seven of clubs. Win: $1,989.
6. Same as in problem 3, but this time the card is returned to the deck and the deck is shuffled before the second draw. Win: $1,989.
7. On two consecutive draws (without returning the first card to the deck), do not draw a club. Win: $1.78.

8. Same as in problem 7, but this time the card is returned to the deck and the deck is shuffled before the second draw. Win: $1.78.

9. On four consecutive draws (without returning any cards to the deck), draw a seven of spades, then a seven of clubs, then a seven of hearts, then a seven of diamonds. Win: $1,000,001.

10. On four consecutive draws (without returning any cards to the deck), draw four sevens in any order. Win: $1,000,001.

EXERCISE VIII

Fogelin's Palace in Border, Nevada, offers the following unusual bet. If you win, then you make a 50 percent profit on your bet; if you lose, you take a 40 percent loss. That is, if you bet $1 and win, you get back $1.50; if you bet $1 and lose, you get back $0.60. The chances of winning are fifty-fifty. This sounds like a marvelous opportunity, but there is one hitch: to play, you must let your bet ride with its winnings, or losses, for four plays. For example, starting with $100, a four-bet sequence might look like this:

	Win	Win	Lose	Win
Total	$150	$225	$135	$202.50

At the end of this sequence, you can pick up $202.50, and thus make a $102.50 profit. It seems that Fogelin's Palace is a good place to gamble, but consider the following argument on the other side. Because the chances of winning are fifty-fifty, you will, on the average, win half the time. But notice what happens in such a case:

	Win	Lose	Lose	Win
Total	$150	$90	$54	$81

So, even though you have won half the time, you have come out $19 behind.

Surprisingly, it does not matter what order the wins and losses come in; if two are wins and two are losses, you come out behind. (You can check this.) So, because you are only going to win roughly half the time, and when you win half the time you actually lose money, it now seems to be a bad idea to gamble at Fogelin's Palace.

What should you do; gamble at Fogelin's Palace or not? Why?

EXPECTED OVERALL VALUE

Given that lotteries usually have an extremely unfavorable expected monetary value, why do millions of people invest billions of dollars in them each year? Part of the answer is that some people are stupid, superstitious, or both. People will sometimes reason, "Somebody has to win; why not me?" They can also convince themselves that their lucky day has come. But that is not the whole story, for most people who put down money on lottery tickets realize that the bet is a bad bet, but think that it is worth doing anyway. People fantasize about what they will do with the money if they win, and that is fun. Furthermore, if the bet is only $1, and the person making the bet is not desperately poor, losing is not going to hurt much. Even if the expected monetary value on the lottery ticket is the loss of fifty cents, this might strike someone as a reasonable price for the fun of thinking about winning. (After all, you accept a sure loss of $8 every time you pay $8 to see a movie.) So a bet that is bad from a purely monetary point of view might be acceptable when other factors are considered.

The reverse situation can also arise: A bet may be unreasonable, even though it has a positive expected monetary value. Suppose, for example, that you are allowed to participate in a lottery in which a $1 ticket gives you 1 chance in 10 million of getting a payoff of $20 million. Here, as noted above, the expected monetary value of a $1 bet is a profit of $1, so from the point of view of expected monetary value, it is a good bet. This makes it sound reasonable to bet in this lottery, and a small bet probably is reasonable. But under these circumstances, would it be reasonable for you to sell everything you owned to buy a lottery ticket? The answer to this is almost certainly no, for, even though the expected monetary value is positive, the odds of winning are still low, and the loss of your total resources would be personally catastrophic.

When we examine the effects that success or failure will have on a *particular* person relative to his or her own needs, resources, preferences, and so on, we are then examining what we shall call the *expected overall value* or *expected utility* of a choice. Considerations of this kind often force us to make adjustments in weighing the significance of costs and payoffs. In the examples we have just examined, the immediate catastrophic consequences of a loss outweigh the long-term gains one can expect from participating in the lottery.

Another factor that typically affects the expected overall value of a bet is the phenomenon known as the *diminishing marginal value* or *diminishing marginal utility* of a payoff as it gets larger. Diminishing marginal value is illustrated by the following example. Suppose someone offers to pay a debt by buying you a hamburger. Provided that the debt matches the cost of a hamburger and you feel like having one, you might go along with this. But suppose this person offers to pay off a debt ten times larger by buying you ten hamburgers? The chances are that you will reject the offer, for even though ten hamburgers *cost* ten times as much as one hamburger, they are not *worth* ten times as much to you. At some point you will get stuffed and not want any more. The notion of marginal value applies to money as well. If you are starving, $10 will mean a lot to you. You might be willing to work hard to get it. If you are wealthy, $10 more or less makes little difference; losing $10 might only be an annoyance.

Because of this phenomenon of diminishing marginal value, betting on lotteries is an even worse bet than most people suppose. A lottery with a payoff of $20 million sounds attractive, but it does not seem to be twenty times more attractive than a payoff of $1 million. So even if the expected monetary value of your $1 bet in a lottery is the loss of $0.50, the actual value to you is really something less than this, and so the bet is even worse than it seemed at first.

In general, then, when payoffs are large, the expected overall value of the payoff to someone is reduced because of the effects of diminishing marginal value. But not always. It is possible to think of exotic cases in which expected overall value increases with the size of the payoff. Suppose a witch told you that she would turn you into a toad if you did not give her $10 million by tomorrow. You believe her, because you know for a fact that she has turned others into toads. You have $1 to your name and you are given the opportunity to participate in the first lottery described above, where a $1 ticket gives you 1 chance in 20 million of hitting a $10 million payoff. We saw that the expected monetary value of that wager was an unfavorable minus $.50. But now consider the overall value of $1 to you if you are turned into a toad. Toads have no use for money, so to you, as a toad, the value of the dollar would drop to nothing. Thus, unless some other, more attractive alternatives are available, it would be reasonable to buy a lottery ticket, despite the unfavorable expected monetary value of the wager.

EXERCISE IX

1. Though the situation is somewhat far-fetched, suppose you are going to the drugstore to buy medicine for a friend who will die without it. You have only $10—exactly what the medicine costs. Outside the drugstore a young man is playing three-card monte, a simple game in which the dealer shows you three cards, turns them over, shifts them briefly from hand to hand, and then lays them out, face down, on the top of a box. You are supposed to identify a particular card (usually the ace of spades), and if you do, you are paid even money. You yourself are a magician and know the sleight-of-hand trick that fools most people, and you are sure that you can guess the card correctly nine times out of ten. First, what is the expected monetary value of a bet of $10? In this context, would it be reasonable to make this bet? Why or why not?

2. Provide an example of your own where a bet can be reasonable even though the expected monetary value is unfavorable, and another example where the bet is unreasonable even though the expected monetary value is favorable. Explain what makes these bets reasonable or unreasonable.

Consider the following game: You flip a coin continuously until you get tails once. If you get no heads (= tails on the first flip), then you are paid nothing. If you get one heads (= tails on the second flip), then you are paid $2. If you get two heads (= tails on the third flip), then you are paid $4. If you get three heads, then you are paid $8. And so on. The general rule is that, for any number n, if you get n heads, you are paid 2^n. What is the expected monetary value of this game? What would you pay to play this game? Why?

DECISIONS UNDER IGNORANCE

So far we have discussed choices where the outcomes of the various options are not certain, but we know their probabilities. Decisions of this kind are called *decisions under risk.* In other cases, however, we do not know the probabilities of various outcomes. Decisions of this kind are called *decisions under ignorance.* If we do not have any idea where the probabilities of various outcomes lie, the ignorance is complete. If we know that these probabilities lie within some general range, the ignorance is partial.

As an example of partial ignorance, suppose that, just after graduating from college, you are offered three jobs. First, the Exe Company offers you a salary of $20,000. Exe is well established and secure. The next offer comes from the Wye Company. Here the salary is $30,000, but Wye is a new company, so it is less secure. You think that this new company will probably do well, but you don't know how likely it is to last. It might go bankrupt, and then you will be left without a job. The final offer comes from the Zee Company, which is as stable as Exe and offers you a salary of $40,000 per year. These offers are summarized in the following table:

	Wye does not go bankrupt	Wye goes bankrupt
Take job at Exe	$20,000	$20,000
Take job at Wye	$30,000	0
Take job at Zee	$40,000	$40,000

Let's assume that other factors (such as benefits, vacations, location, interest, working conditions, bonuses, raises, and promotions) are all equally desirable in the three jobs. Which job should you take?

The answer is clear: Take the job from the Zee Company. This decision is easy because you end up better off regardless of whether or not Wye goes bankrupt, so it doesn't matter how likely Wye's bankruptcy is. Everyone agrees that you should choose any option that is best whatever happens. This is called the *rule of dominance.*

The problem with the rule of dominance is that it can't help you make choices when no option is better regardless of what happens. Suppose you discover that the letter from the Zee Company is a forgery—part of a cruel joke by your roommate. Now your only options are Exe and Wye. The job with Wye will be better if Wye does not go bankrupt, but the job with Exe will be better if Wye does go bankrupt. Neither job is better no matter what happens, so the rule of dominance does not apply.

To help you choose between Exe and Wye, you might look for a rational way to assign probabilities despite your ignorance of which assignments are correct. One approach of this kind uses the *rule of insufficient reason:* When you have no reason to think that any outcome is more likely than any other, assume that the outcomes are equally probable. This assumption enables us to calculate expected monetary value or utility, as in the preceding sections, and then we can choose the option with the highest expected utility. In our example, this rule of insufficient reason favors the job at Exe, because your expected income in that job is $20,000, whereas your expected income in the job at Wye is only $15,000 (= 0.5 × $30,000), assuming that the Wye company has as much chance of going bankrupt as of staying in business.

The problem with the rule of insufficient reason is that it may seem arbitrary to assume that unknown probabilities are equal. Often we suspect that the probabilities of various outcomes are not equal, even while we do not know what the probabilities are. Moreover, the rule of insufficient reason yields different results when the options are described differently. We can distinguish four possibilities: Wye goes bankrupt, stays the same size, Wye increases in size, and Wye decreases in size but stays in business. If we do not have any reason to see any of these outcomes as more likely than any other, then the rule of insufficient reason tells us to assign them equal probabilities. On that assumption, and if you will keep your job as long as Wye stays in business, then you have only one chance in four of losing your job; so your expected income in the job at Wye is now $22,500 (= 3/4 × $30,000). Thus, if we stick with the rule of insufficient reason, the expected value of the job at Wye and whether you should take that job seem to depend on how the options are divided. That seems crazy in this case.

Another approach tries to work without any assumptions about probability in cases of ignorance. Within this approach, several rules might be adopted. One possibility is the *maximax rule,* which tells you to choose the option whose best outcome is better than the best outcome of any other option. If you follow the maximax rule, you will accept the job with the Wye Company, because the best outcome of that job is a salary of $30,000 when this new company does not go bankrupt, and this is better than any outcome with the Exe Company. Optimists and risk-takers will favor this rule.

Other people are more pessimistic and tend to avoid risks. They will favor a rule more like the *maximin rule,* which says to choose the option whose worst outcome is better than the worst outcome of any other option. If you follow the maximin rule, you will accept the job with the Exe Company, because the worst outcome in that job is a steady salary of $20,000, whereas the worst outcome is unemployment if you accept the job with the Wye company.

Each of these rules works by focusing exclusively on part of your information and disregarding other things that you know. The maximax rule considers only the best outcomes for each option—the best-case scenario. The maximin rule pays attention to only the worst outcome for each option—the worst-case scenario. Because they ignore other outcomes, the maximax rule strikes many people as too risky (since it does not consider how much you could lose by taking a chance), and the maximin rule strikes many people as too conservative (since it does not consider how much you could have gained if you had taken a small risk).

Another problem is that the maximax and maximin rules do not take probabilities into account at all. This makes sense when you know nothing about the probabilities. But when some (even if limited) information about probabilities is available, then it seems better to use as much information as you have. Suppose, for example, that each of two options might lead to disaster, and you do not know *how* likely a disaster is after either option, but you do know that one option is *more* likely to lead to disaster than another. In such situations, some decision theorists argue that you should choose the option that minimizes the chance that any disaster will occur. This is called the *disaster avoidance* rule.

To illustrate this rule, consider a different kind of case:

> A forty-year-old man is diagnosed as having a rare disease and consults the world's leading expert on the disease. He is informed that the disease is almost certainly not fatal but often causes serious paralysis that leaves its victims bedridden for life. (In other cases it has no lasting effects.) The disease is so rare that the expert can offer only a vague estimate of the probability of paralysis: 20 to 60 percent. There is an experimental drug that, if administered now, would almost certainly cure the disease. However, it kills a significant but not accurately known percentage of those who take it. The expert guesses that the probability of the drug being fatal is less than 20 percent, and the patient thus assumes that he is definitely less likely to die if he takes the drug than he is to be paralyzed if he lets the disease run its course. The patient would regard bedridden life as preferable to death, but he considers both outcomes as totally disastrous compared to continuing his life in good health. Should he take the drug?[5]

Since the worst outcome is death, and this outcome will not occur unless he takes the drug, the maximin rule would tell him *not* to take the drug. In contrast, the disaster avoidance rule would tell him *to* take the drug, because both death and paralysis are disasters and taking the drug minimizes his chances that any disaster will occur. Thus, although the disaster avoidance rule opposes risk taking, it does so in a different way than the maximin rule.

We are left, then, with a plethora of rules: insufficient reason, dominance, maximax, maximin, and disaster avoidance. Others have been proposed as

[5]Gregory Kavka, "Deterrence, Utility, and Rational Choice," reprinted in *Moral Paradoxes of Nuclear Deterrence* (New York: Cambridge University Press, 1987), 65–66. Kavka uses this medical example to argue for his disaster avoidance rule and, by analogy, to defend the rationality of nuclear deterrence.

well. With all of these rules in the offing, it is natural to ask which is correct. Unfortunately, there is no consensus on this issue. Each rule applies and seems plausible in some cases but not in others. Many people conclude that each rule is appropriate to different kinds of situations. It is still not clear, however, which rule should govern decisions in which circumstances. The important problem of decision under ignorance remains unsolved.

DISCUSSION QUESTIONS

1. In the game of ignorance, you draw one card from a deck, but you do not know how many cards or which kinds of cards are in the deck. It might be a normal deck or it might contain only diamonds or only aces of spades or any other combination of cards. It costs nothing to play. If you bet that the card you draw will be a spade, and it is a spade, then you win $100. If you bet that the card you draw will not be a spade, and it is not a spade, then you win $90. You may make only one bet. Which bet would you make if you followed the maximax rule? The maximin rule? The disaster avoidance rule? The rule of insufficient reason? Which rule seems most plausible in this case? Which bet should you make? Why?

2. In which circumstances do you think it is appropriate to use the dominance rule? The rule of insufficient reason? The maximax rule? The maximin rule? The disaster avoidance rule? Why?

3. Suppose that you may choose either of two envelopes. You know that one envelope contains twice as much money as the other, but you do not know the amount of money in either envelope. Then you choose an envelope, open it, and see that it contains $100. Thus, the other envelope must contain either $50 or $200. At this point, you are given a choice: You may exchange your envelope for the other envelope. Should you switch envelopes, according to the rule of insufficient reason? Is this result plausible? Why or why not?

4. The idea discussed earlier—that in making decisions under conditions of uncertainty we should consider the prospective gains and losses together with relevant probabilities—was clearly stated in *The Port-Royal Logic*, an influential work published by the French writers Arnauld and Nicole in 1662. Speaking of the majority of humankind, these writers tell us that they

> fall into an illusion which is more deceptive in proportion as it appears to them to be reasonable; it is, that they regard only the greatness or importance of the advantage which they hope for, or of the disadvantage which they fear, without considering at all the probability which there is of that advantageous or disadvantageous event befalling. Thus, when they apprehend any great evil, as the loss of their livelihood or their fortune, they think it the part of prudence to neglect no precaution for preserving these; and if it is some great good, as the gain of a hundred thousand crowns, they think that they act wisely in seeking to obtain it, if the hazard is a small amount, however little likelihood there may be of a success.[6]

[6]This passage comes from the final chapter of *The Port-Royal Logic*, generally thought to be by Antoine Arnauld and Pierre Nicole, trans. Thomas Spencer Baynes (Edinburgh: Sutherland and Knox, 1851).

To correct this defect in reasoning, these authors suggest that "It is necessary to consider not only the good and evil in themselves, but also the probability of their happening and not happening." This is sound advice, for it will prevent us from taking excessive precautions against large evils that are hardly likely to occur and from squandering money (for example, in lotteries) seeking enormous gains that we have only a minute chance of obtaining.

These authors conclude their discussion with a striking remark concerning the reverse situation that obtains concerning *salvation.*

> It belongs to infinite things alone, as eternity and salvation, that they cannot be equalled by any temporal advantage; and thus we ought never to place them in the balance with any of the things of the world. This is why the smallest degree of facility for the attainment of salvation is of higher value than all the blessings of the world put together; and why the slightest peril of being lost is more serious than all temporal evils, considered simply as evils. (p. 369)

The authors conclude that we ought to spend all our efforts, however great, in an attempt to attain salvation.

This is obviously an argument concerning what we have called *expected overall value.* State it clearly and evaluate it.

5. The following article raises another interesting problem in dealing with eternity.[7] How would you answer it?

PLAYING GAMES WITH ETERNITY: THE DEVIL'S OFFER

By Edward J. Gracely

Suppose Ms C dies and goes to hell, or to a place that seems like hell. The devil approaches and offers to play a game of chance. If she wins, she can go to heaven. If she loses, she will stay in hell forever; there is no second chance to play the game. If Ms C plays today, she has a 1/2 chance of winning. Tomorrow the probability will be 2/3. Then 3/4, 4/5, 5/6, etc., with no end to the series. Thus every passing day increases her chances of winning. At what point should she play the game?

The answer is not obvious: after any given number of days spent waiting, it will still be possible to improve her chances by waiting yet another day. And any increase in the probability of winning a game with infinite stakes has an infinite utility. For example, if she waits a year, her probability of winning the game would be approximately .997268; if she waits one more day, the probability would increase to .997275, a difference of only .000007. Yet even .000007 multiplied by infinity is infinite.

On the other hand, it seems reasonable to suppose the cost of delaying for a day to be finite—a day's more suffering in hell. So the infinite expected benefit from a delay will always exceed the cost.

This logic might suggest that Ms C should wait forever, but clearly such a strategy would be self-defeating: why should she stay forever in a place in order to increase her chances of leaving it? So the question remains: what should Ms C do?

[7]Edward J. Gracely, "Playing Games with Eternity: The Devil's Offer," *Analysis* 48, no. 3 (1988), 113.

11

FALLACIES OF CLARITY

This chapter examines some of the main ways in which arguments can be defective or fallacious. The defects considered here arise when language is not used clearly enough for the context. The first kind of unclarity is vagueness. *Vagueness occurs when, in a given context, a term is used in a way that allows too many cases in which it is unclear whether or not the term applies. Vagueness underlies several common fallacies, including some* slippery-slope *arguments. The second kind of unclarity is* ambiguity. *Ambiguity occurs when it is unclear which meaning of a term is intended in a given context. Ambiguity leads to the fallacy of* equivocation, *which will be defined and illustrated. The chapter closes with a discussion of different kinds of definitions that can be useful in avoiding or responding to fallacies of clarity.*

WHAT IS A FALLACY?

When inferences are defective, they are called *fallacious*. When defective styles of reasoning get repeated over and over, because people often are fooled by them, then we have an argumentative *fallacy* that is worth flagging with a name. The number and variety of argumentative fallacies are limited only by the imagination. Consequently, there is little point in trying to construct a complete list of fallacies. What is crucial is to get a feel for the most common and most seductive kinds of fallacy. Once this is done, we should be able to recognize many other kinds as well.

USES OF UNCLARITY

In a good argument, a person states a conclusion clearly and then, with equal clarity, gives reasons for this conclusion. The arguments of everyday life often fall short of this standard. Usually, unclear language is a sign of unclear thought. There are times, however, when people are intentionally unclear. They might use unclarity for poetic effect or to leave details to be decided later. But often their goal is to confuse others. This is called *obfuscation*.

Before we look at the various ways in which language can be unclear, a word of caution is needed. There is no such thing as absolute clarity. Whether something is clear or not depends on the context in which it occurs. A botanist does not use common vocabulary in describing and classifying plants. At the same time, it would usually be foolish for a person to use botanical terms in describing the appearance of her back yard. Aristotle said it is the mark of an educated person not to expect more rigor than the subject matter will allow. Because clarity and rigor depend on context, it takes judgment and good sense to pitch an argument at the right level.

Non Sequitur   **by Wiley**

VAGUENESS

Perhaps the most common form of unclarity is *vagueness*. It arises when a concept applies along a continuum or a series of very small changes. The standard example is baldness. A person with a full head of hair is not bald. A person without a hair on his head is bald. In between, however, is a range of cases in which we cannot say definitely whether the person is bald or not. These are called *borderline cases.* Here we say something less definite, such as that this person is "going bald."

No Hair at All   Borderline Cases   Full Head of Hair

Bald   Not Bald

Notice that our inability to apply the concept of baldness in a borderline case is not due to ignorance of the number of hairs on the person's head. It will not help to count the number of hairs there. Even if we knew the exact number, we would still not be able to say whether the person was bald or not. The same is true of most adjectives that concern properties admitting of degrees—for example, "rich," "healthy," "tall," "wise," and "ruthless."

We can also encounter borderline cases that do not depend on differences of degree along a continuum. Vagueness can arise when a word refers to a group of things that are not united by a fixed common trait but, instead, are united by what Ludwig Wittgenstein called a system of *family resemblances:*

> 66. Consider for example the proceedings that we call "games." I mean board-games, card-games, ball-games, Olympic games, and so on. What is common to them all?—Don't say: "There must be something common, or they would not be called 'games' "—but look and see whether there is anything common to all.—For if you look at them you will not see something that is common to all, but similarities, relationships, and a whole series of them at that. To repeat: don't think, but look!—Look for example at board-games, with their multifarious relationships. Now pass to card-games; here you find many correspondences with the first group, but many common features drop out, and others appear. When we pass next to ball-games, much that is common is retained, but much is lost.—Are they all 'amusing'? Compare chess with noughts and crosses. Or is there always winning and losing, or competition between players? Think of [solitaire]. In ball games there is winning and losing; but when a child throws his ball at the wall and catches it again, this feature has disappeared. Look at the parts played by skill and luck; and at the difference between skill in chess and skill in tennis. Think now of games like ring-a-ring-a-roses; here is the element of amusement, but how many other characteristic features have disappeared! And we can go through the many, many other groups of games in the same way; can see how similarities crop up and disappear.
>
> And the result of this examination is: we see a complicated network of similarities overlapping and criss-crossing: sometimes overall similarities, sometimes similarities of detail.
>
> 67. I can think of no better expression to characterize these similarities than "family resemblances"; for the various resemblances between members of a family: build, features, colour of eyes, gait, temperament, etc. etc. overlap and criss-cross in the same way. . . .[1]

If Wittgenstein is right concerning family resemblance, then certain questions need not have determinate answers. People used to argue over whether abstract art is art at all. Abstract art is similar to traditional representational art in many ways, strikingly different in others. The question, then, is which takes precedence: the similarities or the differences? It may help us in making a decision if we were shown how abstract art emerged out of traditional, non-abstract art. This will give prominence to similarities. It will not, however, satisfy those who think that abstract art has departed too far from traditional art to count as art. This example shows that whether something falls under a family resemblance concept is a matter of degree, namely, the degree of similarity and difference. Here, however, we are dealing with multiple factors rather than with a single factor varying along a continuum. As a result, questions of this kind—"Is tossing a Frisbee a

---

[1]Ludwig Wittgenstein, *Philosophical Investigations,* trans. G.E.M. Anscombe (Oxford: Basil Blackwell, 1958).

game?" "Is abstract art art?" "Is a ballet dancer an athlete?"—may not admit of definitive answers.

For the most part, imprecision—the lack of sharply defined limits—causes little difficulty. In fact, this is a useful feature of our language, for suppose we *did* have to count the number of grains of salt between our fingers to determine whether or not we hold a *pinch* of salt. It would take a long time to follow a simple recipe that calls for a pinch of salt.

Yet difficulties can arise when borderline cases themselves are at issue. Suppose that a state passes a law forbidding all actions that offend a large number of people. There will be many cases that clearly fall under this law and many cases that clearly do not fall under it. There will also be many cases in which it will not be clear whether or not they fall under this law. Laws are sometimes declared unconstitutional for this very reason. Here we shall say that the law is vague. In calling the law vague, we are criticizing it. We are not simply noticing the existence of borderline cases, for there will usually be borderline cases no matter how careful we are. Instead, we are saying that there are *too many* borderline cases for this context. More precisely, we shall say that an expression in a given context is *vague* or is *used vaguely* if it leaves open too wide a range of borderline cases for the successful and legitimate use of that expression in that context.

Vagueness thus depends on context. To further illustrate this context dependence, consider the expression "light football player." There are, of course, borderline cases between those football players who are light and those who are not light. But on these grounds alone, we would not say that the expression is vague. It is usually a perfectly serviceable expression, and we can indicate borderline cases by saying such things as "Jones is a bit light for a football player." Suppose, however, that Ohio State and Cal Tech wish to have a game between their light football players. It is obvious that the previous understanding of what counts as being light is too vague for this new context. At Ohio State, anyone under 210 pounds is considered light. At Cal Tech, anyone over 150 pounds is considered heavy. What is needed, then, is a ruling, such as that anyone under 175 pounds will be considered a light-weight. This example illustrates a common problem and its solution. A term that works perfectly well in one area becomes vague when applied in some other (usually more specialized) area. This vagueness can then be removed by adopting more precise rules in the problematic area. Vagueness is resolved by definition.

EXERCISE I

For each of the following terms, give one case to which the term clearly applies, one case to which the term clearly does not apply, and one borderline case. Then try to explain why the borderline case is a borderline case.

Example: "Summer month" clearly applies to July; clearly does not apply to January; and June is a borderline case, because the summer solstice is June

21, and schools usually continue into June, but June, July, and August are, nonetheless, often described as the summer months in the northern hemisphere.

1. large animal
2. populous state
3. long book
4. old professor
5. popular singer
6. powerful person
7. difficult subject
8. late meeting
9. arriving late to a meeting

EXERCISE II

Each of the following sentences contains words or expressions that are potentially vague. Describe a context in which this vagueness might make a difference, and explain what difference it makes. Then reduce this vagueness by replacing the underlined expression with one that is more precise.

Example: Harold has a bad reputation.

Context: If Harold applies for a job as a bank security guard, then some but not all kinds of bad reputation are relevant. A reputation for doing bad construction work is irrelevant, but a reputation for dishonesty is relevant.

Replacement: Harold is a known thief.

1. Ross has a large income.
2. Cocaine is a dangerous drug.
3. Ruth is a clever woman.
4. Andre is a terrific tennis player.
5. Mark is not doing too well (after his operation).
6. Shaq's a big fellow.
7. Dan's grades are low.
8. Walter can't see well.
9. The earthquake was a disaster.

```
                    ┌─────────────────────────┐
                    │  DISCUSSION QUESTION     │
```

As we saw, Wittgenstein held that the things we call games are united by a complex system of varying degrees of family resemblances. What about tools? Are things we call "tools" also related to each other by a system of family resemblances? In answering this question, consider such things as hammers, wrenches, rulers, levels, nails, and rolls of tape. Are they all tools or are only some of them tools? Defend your answer.

HEAPS

The existence of borderline cases is essential to various styles of reasoning that have been identified and used since ancient times. One such argument was called the *argument from the heap* or the *sorites argument* (from the Greek word "soros," which means "heap"). The classic example was intended to show that it is impossible to produce a heap of sand by adding one grain at a time. As a variation on this, we will show that no one can become rich. The argument can be formulated as a long series like this:

(1) Someone with only one cent is not rich.
(2) If someone with only one cent is not rich, then someone with only two cents is not rich.
_____
∴ (3) Someone with only two cents is not rich.

(4) If someone with only two cents is not rich, then someone with only three cents is not rich.
_____
∴ (5) Someone with only three cents is not rich.

(6) If someone with only three cents is not rich, then someone with only four cents is not rich.
_____
∴ (7) Someone with only four cents is not rich.

[and so on, until:]
_____
∴ (199,999,999,999) Someone with only 100,000,000,000 cents is not rich.

The problem, of course, is that someone with 100,000,000,000 cents *is* rich. If someone denies this, we can keep on going. Or we can just sum up the whole argument like this:

(1*) Someone with only one cent is not rich.
(2*) For any number, n, if someone with only n cents is not rich, then someone with $n + 1$ cents is not rich.
_____
∴ (3*) Someone with any number of cents is not rich.

Premise (2*) is, of course, just a generalization of premises (2), (4), (6), and so on.

Despite its plausibility, everyone should agree that there is something wrong with these arguments. If we hand over enough pennies to Peter, previously poor Peter will become the richest person in the world. Another sign of a problem is that a parallel argument runs in the other direction: Someone with 100 billion cents is rich. For any number, n, if someone with n cents is rich, then someone with $n - 1$ cents is also rich. Therefore, someone with no cents at all is rich. This is absurd (since we are not talking about how rich one's life can be as long as one has friends).

We can see that these arguments turn on borderline cases in the following way: The argument would fail if we removed borderline cases by laying down a ruling (maybe for tax purposes) that anyone with a million dollars or more is rich and anyone with less than this is not rich. A person with $999,999.99 would then pass from not being rich to being rich when given a single penny, so premise (2*) would be false at that point under this ruling. Of course, we do not usually use the word "rich" with this much precision. We see some people as clearly rich and others as clearly not rich, but in between there is a fuzzy area where we are not prepared to say that people either are or are not rich. In this fuzzy area, as well as in the clear areas, a penny one way or the other will make no difference.

That is how the argument works, but exactly where does it go wrong? This question is not easy to answer and remains a subject of vigorous debate. Here is one way to view the problem: Consider a person who is 80 pounds overweight, where we would all agree that that person would pass from being fat to not being fat by losing over 100 pounds. If he or she lost an ounce a day for five years, this would be *equivalent* to losing just over 114 pounds. An argument from the heap denies that this person would ever cease to be fat. (So what is the point of dieting?) Anyone who accepted that conclusion, or (3*), would seem to claim that a series of insignificant changes *cannot* be equivalent to a significant change. Surely, this is wrong. Here we might be met with the reply that every change must occur at some particular time (and place), but there would be no particular day on which this person would pass from being fat to not being fat. The problem with this reply is that, with concepts like this, changes seem to occur gradually over long stretches of time without occurring at any single moment. Anyway, however or whenever it occurs, the change does occur. Some people do cease to be fat if they lose enough weight.

This tells us that conclusions of arguments from the heap, such as (3*), are false, so these arguments cannot be sound. Almost everyone agrees to that much. Moreover, if an appropriate starting point is chosen, then premises like (1) and (1*) will also be accepted as true by almost everyone. So the main debate focuses on premise (2*) and on whether the argument is valid. Some philosophers reject premise (2*) and claim that there is a precise point at which a person becomes rich, even though we don't know where that point is. Others try to avoid any sharp cutoff point by developing some kind of alternative logic. Still others just admit that the premises seem true, and the argument seems valid, but the conclusion seems false, so the argument creates a paradox to which they have no solution. These views become complicated and technical, so we will not discuss them here. Suffice it to say that almost everyone agrees that conclusions like (3*) and (199,999,999,999) are false, so arguments from the heap are unsound for one reason or another. That is why such arguments are labeled *fallacies*.

DISCUSSION QUESTION

Where exactly do *you* think arguments from the heap go wrong?

SLIPPERY SLOPES

Near cousins to arguments from the heap are *slippery-slope arguments*. Like arguments from the heap, slippery-slope arguments exploit borderline cases, but they reach different conclusions. Some slippery-slope arguments inch their way through the borderline area to show that there is *no significant difference* between things at opposite ends of a scale. Whereas the argument from the heap is used in an effort to show that nobody can really become or be bald, a slippery-slope argument could be trotted out to try to show that there is no *real* or *defensible* or *significant* or *important* difference between being bald and not being bald. The claim is not that no change occurs because the person who loses all his hair is still not bald, as in an argument from the heap. Instead, the slippery-slope argument claims that we should not classify people as either bald or not bald, because there is no significant difference between these classifications.

Whether a difference is real or defensible or significant or important depends on a variety of factors. In particular, what is significant for one purpose might not be significant for other purposes. Different concerns then yield different kinds of slippery-slope arguments. We will discuss three kinds, beginning with what can be called *conceptual* slippery-slope arguments, since they raise doubts about whether certain conceptual distinctions are coherent or useful.

CONCEPTUAL SLIPPERY-SLOPE ARGUMENTS

Conceptual slippery-slope arguments try to show that things at opposite ends of a continuum do not differ in any way that would be important enough to justify drawing a distinction in one's concepts or theories. As an example, consider the difference between living and nonliving things:

We all agree that a salt crystal is *not* alive. Yet a salt crystal is very similar to other more complex crystals, and these crystals are similar to certain

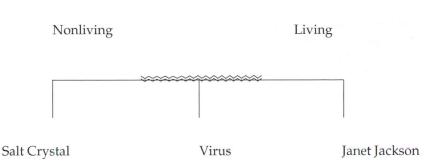

viruses. Still, a virus is on the borderline between living and nonliving things. A virus does not take nourishment and does not reproduce itself. Instead, a virus invades the reproductive mechanisms of cells, and these cells then produce the virus. As viruses become more complex, the differences between them and "higher" life forms become less obvious. Through a series of such small transitions, we finally reach a creature who is obviously alive: Janet Jackson. So far, we have merely described a series of gradual transitions along a *continuum*. We get a conceptual slippery-slope argument when we draw the following conclusion from these facts: There is no significant difference between living things and nonliving things.

To avoid this conclusion, we need to figure out where the argument goes wrong. Such arguments often seem to depend on the following principles:

1. We should not draw a distinction between things that are not significantly different.
2. If A is not significantly different from B, and B is not significantly different from C, then A is not significantly different from C.

This first principle is interesting, complicated, and at least *generally* true. We shall examine it more closely in a moment. The second principle is obviously false. As already noted, a series of insignificant differences can add up to a significant difference. Senator Everett Dirksen put the point well when he said, "A billion dollars here and a billion dollars there can add up to some real money." To the extent that conceptual slippery-slope arguments depend on this questionable assumption, they provide no more support for their conclusions than do arguments from the heap.

Unlike arguments from the heap, however, conceptual slippery-slope arguments do often lead people to accept their conclusions. Slippery-slope arguments have been used to deny the difference between sanity and insanity (some people are just a little weirder than others), between health and sickness (some people just feel a little better or die a little sooner than others), and between amateur and professional athletics (some athletes just get paid a little more or more directly than other athletes). When many small differences make a big difference, such conceptual slippery-slope arguments are fallacious.

This fallacy is seductive, because it is often hard to tell when many small differences *do* make a big difference. Here is a recent controversial example: Some humans have very dark skin. Others have very pale skin. As members of these different groups marry, their children's skin can have any intermediate shade of color. This smooth spectrum leads some people to deny that any differences among races will be important to developed theories in biology or even sociology. Their argument seems to be that the wealth of intermediate cases will make it difficult or impossible to formulate precise and exceptionless laws that apply to one racial group but not to others, so differences among races will play no important role in sciences that seek such laws. Critics respond that some scientific laws about races still might hold without exception even if skin color and other features do vary in tiny increments.

Whichever side one takes, this controversy shows that, even if there is a smooth spectrum between endpoints, this continuity is not enough *by itself* to show that there are no scientifically significant differences among races. That conclusion would need to be supported by more than just a conceptual slippery-slope argument. To show that certain concepts are useless for the purposes of a certain theory, one would need to add much more information, particularly about the purposes of that theory and its laws. That is what determines which differences are important in that particular area. Conceptual slippery-slope arguments might work in conjunction with such additional premises, but they cannot work alone.

EXERCISE III

Whenever we find one thing passing over into its opposite through a gradual series of borderline cases, we can construct (a) an argument from the heap and (b) a conceptual slippery-slope argument by using the following method: Find some increase that will not be large enough to carry us outside the borderline area. Then use the patterns of argument given above. Applying this method, formulate arguments for the following claims. Then explain what is wrong with these arguments.

1. a. There are no heaps.
   b. There is no difference between a heap and a single grain of sand.
2. a. Nobody is tall.
   b. There is no difference between being tall and being short.
3. a. Books do not exist.
   b. There is no difference between a book and a pamphlet.
4. a. Heat is not real.
   b. There is no difference between being hot and being cold.
5. a. Taxes are never high.
   b. There is no difference between high taxes and low taxes.
6. a. Science is an illusion.
   b. There is no difference between science and faith.

1. Do you think that differences among races have any role in developed theories in biology or sociology or any other science? Why or why not?

2. If animals evolve gradually from one species to another, does that show that there is no significant difference in biology between any species (say, horses and dogs)? Why or why not? Does it show that there is no important difference in moral theory between the rights of humans and the rights of animals in other species? Why or why not?

FAIRNESS SLIPPERY-SLOPE ARGUMENTS

When borderline cases form a continuum, even if the end points are clearly different, it is still often difficult to draw a line between cases or to justify drawing a line at one point rather than at a different point. Then, if someone classifies a case at one end of the continuum, an opponent can offer a challenge by asking the question "Where do you draw the line?"

Sometimes, even though a line is hard to draw, this challenge is out of place. If I say that Babe Ruth was a superstar, I will not be refuted if I cannot draw a sharp dividing line between athletes who are superstars and those who are not. There are some difficult borderline cases, but Babe Ruth is not one of them. Nor will we be impressed if someone tells us that the difference between Babe Ruth and the thousands of players who never made it to the major leagues is "*just* a matter of degree." What is usually wrong with this phrase is the emphasis on the word "just," which suggests that differences of degree do not count. Of course, it is a matter of degree, but the difference in degree is so great that it should be marked by a special word.

There are, however, occasions when a challenge to drawing a line is appropriate. For example, most schools and universities have grading systems that draw a fundamental distinction between passing grades and failing grades. Of course, a person who barely passes a course does not perform very differently from one who barely fails a course, yet they are treated very differently. Students who barely pass a course get credit for it; those who barely fail it do not. This, in turn, can lead to serious consequences in an academic career and even beyond. It is entirely reasonable to ask for a justification of a procedure that treats cases that are so similar in such strikingly different ways. We are not being tenderhearted; we are raising an issue of *fairness* or *justice*. It seems unfair to treat very similar cases in strikingly different ways.

The claim is not that there is no difference between passing and failing. That is why this argument is not a conceptual slippery-slope argument. The claim, instead, is that the differences that do exist (as little as one point out of a hundred on a test) do not make it fair to treat people so differently (credit versus no credit for the course). This unfairness does not follow merely from the scores forming a continuum, but the continuum does put pressure on us to show why small differences in scores do justify big differences in treatment.

Questions about the fairness of drawing a line often arise in the law. For example, given reasonable cause, the police generally do not have to obtain a warrant to search a motor vehicle, for the obvious reason that the vehicle might be driven away while the police go to a judge to obtain a warrant. On the other hand, with few exceptions, the police may not search a person's home without a search warrant. In the case of *California v. Carney*,[2] the U.S. Supreme Court had to rule on whether the police needed a warrant to search for marijuana in an "oversized van, fully mobile," parked in a downtown parking lot in San Diego. Because the van was a fully mobile vehicle, it seemed to fall under the first principle, but because it also served as its owner's home, it seemed to fall under the second. The difficulty, as the Court saw, was that there is a gray area between those things that clearly are motor vehicles and not homes (for example, motorcycles) and those things that clearly are homes and not motor vehicles (for example, apartments). Chief Justice Warren Burger wondered about a mobile home in a trailer park hooked up to utility lines with its wheels removed. Justice Sandra Day O'Connor asked whether a tent, because it is highly mobile, could also be searched without a warrant. As the discussion continued, houseboats (with or without motors or oars), covered wagons, and finally a house being moved from one place to another on a trailer truck came under examination. In the end, our highest court decided that the van in question was a vehicle and could be searched without first obtaining a warrant to do so. The court did not fully explain why it is fair to allow warrantless searches—and to send people to jail as a result—in cases of vans used as homes but not in other very similar cases.

Questions about where to draw a line often have even more important implications than in the case just examined. Consider the death penalty. Most societies have reserved the death penalty for those crimes they consider the most serious. But where should we draw the line between crimes punishable by death and crimes not punishable by death? Should the death penalty be given to murderers of prison guards? To rapists? To drug dealers? To drunk drivers who cause death? Wherever we draw the line, it seems to be an unavoidable consequence of the death penalty that similar cases will be treated in radically different ways. A defender of the death penalty can argue that it is not unfair to draw a line because, once the line is drawn, the public will have fair warning about which crimes are subject to the death penalty and which are not. It will then be up to each person to decide whether to risk his or her life by crossing this line. It remains a matter of debate, however, whether the law can be administered in a way that makes

---

[2]1471 U.S. 386 (1984). This case was reported by Linda Greenhouse, "Of Tents with Wheels and Houses with Oars," *New York Times*, May 15, 1985.

this argument plausible. If the laws themselves are administered in an arbitrary way, arguments of this kind lose their force.

The finality of death raises a profoundly difficult problem in another area, too: the legalization of abortion. There are some people who think abortion is never justified and ought to be declared totally illegal. There are others who think abortion does not need any justification at all and should be completely legalized. Between these extremes, there are many people who believe abortion is justified in certain circumstances but not in others (such as when abortion is the only way to save the life of the mother but not when it prevents only lesser harms to the mother). There are also those who think abortion should be allowed for a certain number of months of pregnancy, but not thereafter. People holding these middle positions face the problem of deciding where to draw a line, and this makes them subject to criticisms from holders of either extreme position.

This problem admits of no easy solution. Because every line we draw will seem arbitrary to some extent, a person who holds a middle position needs to argue that it is better to draw *some* line—even a somewhat arbitrary one—than to draw no line at all. The recognition that some line is needed, and why, can often help us locate the real issues. This is the first step toward a reasonable position.

Of course, this still does not tell us *where* to draw the line. A separate argument is needed to show that the line should be drawn at one point, or in one area, rather than another. In the law, such arguments often appeal to value judgments about the effects of drawing the line at one place rather than another. For example, it is more efficient to draw a line where it is easy to detect, and drawing the line at one place will provide greater protection for some values or some people than will drawing it at another place. Different values often favor drawing different lines, and sometimes such arguments are not available at all. Thus, in the end, it will be difficult to solve many of these profound and important problems.

DISCUSSION QUESTION

Is it unfair for teachers to fail students who get one point out of a hundred less than others students who pass? Why or why not? Would an alternative grading system be fairer?

CAUSAL SLIPPERY-SLOPE ARGUMENTS

One more kind of slippery slope argument is also common. In these arguments, the claim is made that, once a certain kind of event occurs, other similar events will also occur, and this will lead eventually to disaster. The most

Farcus

by David Waisglass
Gordon Coulthart

© 1992 Farcus Cartoons

WAISGLASS/COULTHART

**What began with a few pencils
and paper clips ...**

famous (or infamous) argument of this kind was used by the U.S. government to justify its intervention in Vietnam in the 1960s. It was claimed that, if the communists took over Vietnam, they would then take over Cambodia, the rest of Asia, and other continents, until they ruled the whole world. This was called the domino theory, since the fall of one country would make neighboring countries fall as well. Arguments of this kind are sometimes called *domino arguments.* Such arguments claim that one event, which might not seem bad by itself, would lead to other, more horrible events, so such arguments can also be called *parades of horrors.*

Causal slippery slopes can also slide into good results. After all, someone who wants communists to take over the world might use the above domino argument to show why the United States should *not* intervene in Vietnam. Such optimistic slippery-slope arguments are, however, much less common than parades of horrors, so we will limit our discussion to the pessimistic versions.

These arguments resemble other slippery-slope arguments in that they depend on a series of small changes. The domino argument does not, however, claim that there is no difference between the first step and later steps—

between Vietnam going communist and the rest of Asia going communist. Nor is there supposed to be anything unfair about letting Vietnam go communist without letting other countries also go communist. The point of a parade of horrors is that certain events will *cause* horrible effects because of their similarity or proximity to other events. Since the crucial claim is about causes and effects, these arguments will be called *causal slippery-slope arguments*.

We saw another example in Chapter 4. While arguing against an increase in the clerk hire allowance, Kyl says,

> The amount of increase does not appear large. I trust, however, there is no one among us who would suggest that the addition of a clerk would not entail allowances for another desk, another typewriter, more materials, and it is not beyond the realm of possibility that the next step would then be a request for additional office space, and ultimately new buildings.

Although this argument is heavily guarded, the basic claim is that increasing the clerk hire allowance is likely to lead to much larger expenditures that will break the budget. The argument can be represented more formally this way:

(1) If the clerk hire allowance is increased, other expenditures will also probably be increased.
(2) These other increases would be horrible.

∴ (3) The clerk hire allowance should not be increased.

Opponents can respond in several ways. One response is to deny that the supposedly horrible effects really are so horrible. One might argue, for example, that additional office space and new buildings would be useful. This response is often foreclosed by describing the effects in especially horrible terms.

A second possible response would be to deny that increasing the clerk hire allowance really would have the horrible effects that are claimed in the first premise. One might argue, for example, that the old offices already have adequate room for additional clerks.

Often the best response is a combination of these. One can admit that certain claimed effects would be horrible, but deny that these horrible effects really are likely. Then one can acknowledge that some more minor problems will ensue, but argue that these costs are outweighed by the benefits of the program.

To determine which, if any, of these responses is adequate, one must look closely at each particular argument and ask the following questions:

Are any of the claimed effects really very bad?

Are any of these effects really very likely?

Do these dangers outweigh all the benefits of what is being criticized?

If the answers to all these questions are "Yes," then the causal slippery-slope argument is strong. But if any of these questions receives a negative answer, then the causal slippery-slope argument is questionable on that basis.

EXERCISE IV

Classify each of the following arguments as either (H) an argument from the heap, (C) a conceptual slippery-slope argument, (F) a fairness slippery-slope argument, or (S) a causal slippery-slope argument. Explain why you classify each example as you do.

1. We have to take a stand against sex education in junior high schools. If we allow sex education in the eighth grade, then the seventh graders will want it, and then the sixth graders, and pretty soon we will be teaching sex education to our little kindergartners.

2. But, officer, you wouldn't arrest me if I drove only one inch left of the center of the lane. And if you wouldn't arrest me for driving at one place, it wouldn't be fair to arrest me for deviating just one inch further left. So you shouldn't arrest me for driving on the wrong side of the road.

3. If you try to smoke one cigarette a day, you will end up smoking two and then three and four and five, and so on, until you smoke two packs every day. So don't try even one.

4. People are found not guilty by reason of insanity when they cannot avoid breaking the law. But people who are brought up in certain deprived social circumstances are not much more able than the insane to avoid breaking the law. So it would be unjust to find them guilty.

5. People are called mentally ill when they do very strange things, but many so-called eccentrics do things that are just as strange. So there is no real difference between insanity and eccentricity.

6. If we let doctors kill dying patients who are in great pain, then they will kill other patients who are in less pain and patients who are only slightly disabled. Eventually, they will kill anyone who is not wanted by society.

7. A human egg one minute after fertilization is not very different from what it is one minute later, or one minute after that, and so on. Thus, there is really no difference between just-fertilized eggs and adult humans.

8. Since no moment in the continuum of development between an egg and a baby is especially significant, it is not fair to grant a right to life to a baby unless one grants the same right to every fertilized egg.

9. A woman should be allowed to get an abortion to prevent a 100 percent chance of death. But if a 100 percent chance of death justifies abortion, then it would not be fair to forbid abortion in order to prevent a 99 percent chance of death. And 1 percent cannot make a difference anywhere down the line. So abortion should be allowed in order to prevent *any* chance of death to a mother.

10. "If a man indulges himself in murder, very soon he comes to think little of robbing, and from robbing, he comes next to drinking, and Sabbath breaking, and from that to incivility and procrastination. Once begin upon this downward path, you never know where you are to stop. Many a man dated his ruin from some murder or other that perhaps he thought little of at the time."[3]

[3]Thomas de Quincey, "Second Paper on Murder, Considered as One of the Fine Arts," in *Miscellaneous Essays* (Boston: Ticknor, Reed, and Fields, 1864), 63. Thanks to Julia Driver for sharing this example.

EXERCISE V

For fun, construct your own examples of an argument from the heap, a conceptual slippery-slope argument, a fairness slippery-slope argument, and a causal slippery-slope argument.

EXERCISE VI

Explain the reasons, if any, for drawing a definite line in each of the following cases. Then further explain how this line can be drawn, if at all, in a reasonable way.

1. Minimum (or maximum?) age to drive a car
2. Minimum age to vote
3. Minimum age to enter (or be drafted into) the military
4. Minimum age to drink alcoholic beverages
5. Minimum age for election to the U.S. presidency
6. Maximum age before retirement becomes mandatory

EXERCISE VII

Determine whether each of the following arguments provides adequate support, or any support, for its conclusion. Explain why.

1. We shouldn't require eye tests for bus drivers, because perfect eyesight and blindness differ only in degrees between 20/20 and 20/2000.
2. I shouldn't get a speeding ticket for going fifty-six miles per hour, because my driving did not all of a sudden get more dangerous when I passed the speed limit of fifty-five.

3. Someone who arrives a second after a party starts is not late, and one second cannot make the difference to whether someone is late, so nobody is ever late to a party.

4. No student should ever be allowed to ask a question during a lecture, because once one student asks a question, then another one wants to ask a question, and pretty soon the teacher doesn't have any time left to lecture.

5. Pornography shouldn't be illegal, because you can't draw a line between pornography and erotic art.

6. Marijuana should be legal, because it is no more dangerous than alcohol or nicotine.

7. Marijuana should be illegal, because people who try marijuana are likely to go on to try hashish, and then snorting cocaine, and then freebasing cocaine or shooting heroin.

8. The government should not put any new restrictions on free trade, because once they place some restrictions, they will place more and more until foreign trade is so limited that our own economy will suffer.

9. The government should not remove any of the current barriers to free trade, because once they remove some barriers, this will hurt some local businesses. Then they will remove more barriers, which will hurt more local businesses, and so on, until our economy suffers greatly.

10. Governments should never bargain with any terrorist. Once they do, they will have to bargain with every other terrorist who comes along.

11. The United States should oppose military aggression wherever it happens, no matter how minor, because letting any aggression go unpunished will just encourage even more horrible forms of aggression and will eventually lead to war throughout the world.

12. When Kenneth Carr was chair of the Nuclear Regulatory Commission, he gave the following argument for extending the licenses of more nuclear power plants beyond the forty-year limit: "There's nothing that says that if they're safe when they're 39 years and 364 days old, then ipso facto they're unsafe the next day."[4]

13. "That human life is a continuum from generation to generation seems irrefutably logical. Therefore, if it is wrong to take life at one point on the continuum, then it is wrong to take it at any point. If it is wrong to take life at the mid-point, it is wrong to take it at the beginning or the end."[5]

14. If assault weapons are banned, Congress will ban handguns next, and then rifles. Eventually, hunters will not be able to hunt, and law-abiding citizens will have no way to defend themselves against criminals.

15. "To conclude that the Government may permit designated symbols to be used to communicate only a limited set of messages would be to enter a

[4]Quoted in the *New York Times*, June 24, 1991.

[5]From a letter written by then New Hampshire Senator Gordon Humphrey.

territory having no discernible or defensible boundaries. Could the Government, on this theory, prohibit the burning of state flags? Of copies of the Presidential seal? Of the Constitution? In evaluating these choices under the First Amendment, how would we decide which symbols were sufficiently special to warrant this unique status? To do so, we would be forced to consult our own political preferences, and to impose them on the citizenry, in the very way the First Amendment forbids us to do."[6]

[6]From Justice Brennan's majority opinion in *Texas v. Johnson* 109 S. Ct. 2533 (1989), questioning the constitutionality of laws against burning the U.S. flag.

DISCUSSION QUESTIONS

1. Explain and evaluate the following argument against restrictions on hate speech:

   > To attempt to craft free speech exceptions only for racist speech would create a significant risk of a slide down the proverbial "slippery slope." . . . Censorial consequences could result from many proposed or adopted university policies, including the Stanford code, which sanctions speech intended to "insult or stigmatize" on the basis of race or other prohibited grounds. For example, certain feminists suggest that all heterosexual sex is rape because heterosexual men are aggressors who operate in a cultural climate of pervasive sexism and violence against women. Aren't these feminists insulting or stigmatizing heterosexual men on the basis of their sex and sexual orientation? And how about a Holocaust survivor who blames all ("Aryan") Germans for their collaboration during World War II? Doesn't this insinuation insult and stigmatize on the basis of national and ethnic origin? And surely we can think of numerous other examples that would have to give us pause.[7]

2. Explain and evaluate the following response to critics of college restrictions on hate speech:

   > [Defenders of such restrictions] will ask whether an educational institution does not have the power . . . to enact reasonable regulations aimed at assuring equal personhood on campus. If one characterizes the issue this way, . . . a different set of slopes will look slippery. If we do not intervene to protect equality here, what will the next outrage be?[8]

3. What, if anything, is shown when slippery-slope arguments can be used on both sides of an issue?

[7]Nadine Strossen, "Regulating Racist Speech on Campus: A Modest Proposal?" *Duke Law Journal* (1990), 537–538. When she wrote this, Strossen was on the National Board of Directors of the American Civil Liberties Union.

[8]Richard Delgado, "Campus Antiracism Rules: Constitutional Narratives in Collison," *Northwestern University Law Review* 85 (1991), 346.

Frank and Ernest

MEETING TONIGHT-
HOW TO GET
MONEY OUT
OF POLITICS

IT'S EITHER A CAMPAIGN
REFORM RALLY OR
A LOBBYIST'S
WORKSHOP.

THAVES

AMBIGUITY

The idea of vagueness is based on a common feature of words in our language: Many of them leave open a range of borderline cases. The notion of *ambiguity* is also based on a common feature of our language: Words often have a number of different meanings. For example, the *New Merriam-Webster Pocket Dictionary* has the following entry under the word "cardinal":

> **cardinal** adj. 1: of basic importance; chief, main, primary,
>
> 2: of cardinal red color.
>
> n. 1: an ecclesiastical official of the Roman Catholic Church ranking next below the pope,
>
> 2: a bright red,
>
> 3: any of several American finches of which the male is bright red.

In the plural, "the Cardinals" is the name of an athletic team that inhabits St. Louis; "cardinal" also describes the numbers used in simple counting.

It is not likely that people would get confused about these very different meanings of the word "cardinal," but we might imagine a priest, a bird-watcher, and a baseball fan all hearing the remark "The cardinals are in town." The priest would prepare for a solemn occasion, the bird-watcher would get out binoculars, and the baseball fan would head for the stadium. In this context, the remark might be criticized as ambiguous. More precisely, we shall say that an expression in a given context is *ambiguous* or is used ambiguously if and only if it is misleading or potentially misleading because it is hard to tell which of a number of possible meanings is intended in that context.

Actually, the term "ambiguous" itself seems to be ambiguous. As defined above, an expression is used ambiguously only if it is obscure or unclear which meaning is intended. Using this definition, the word "bank" is *not* used ambiguously in the following sentence:

Joan deposited $500 in the bank and got a receipt.

Some writers, however, call an expression ambiguous simply if it admits of more than one interpretation, without adding that it is not possible to tell which meaning is intended. With this definition, the above sentence is ambiguous because it could mean that Joan placed $500 in a riverbank, and someone, for whatever reason, gave her a receipt for doing so. On this second definition of ambiguity, virtually every expression is ambiguous, because virtually every expression admits of more than one interpretation. On the first definition, only uses of expressions that are misleading or potentially misleading will be called ambiguous. In what follows, we will use the word "ambiguous" in accordance with the first definition. Ambiguity then depends on the context, because whether something is misleading also depends on context.

In everyday life, context usually settles which of a variety of meanings is appropriate. Yet sometimes genuine misunderstandings do arise. An American and a European discussing "football" may have different games in mind. The European is talking about what Americans call "soccer"; the American is talking about what Europeans call "American football." It is characteristic of the ambiguous use of a term that when it comes to light, we are likely to say something like, "Oh, you mean *that* kind of cardinal!" or "Oh, you were talking about *American* football!" This kind of misunderstanding can cause trouble. When it does, if we want to criticize the expression that creates the problem, we call it ambiguous.

Thus, "ambiguous" is both dependent on context and a term of criticism in much the same ways as "vague." But these kinds of unclarity differ in other ways. In a context where the use of a word is ambiguous, it is not clear which of two meanings to attach to a word. In a context where the use of a word is vague, we cannot attach *any* clear meaning to the use of a word.

So far we have talked about the ambiguity of individual terms or words. This is called *semantic ambiguity.* But sometimes we do not know which interpretation to give to a phrase or a sentence because its grammar or syntax admits of more than one interpretation. This is called *syntactic ambiguity* or *amphiboly.* Thus, if we talk about *the conquest of the Persians,* we might be referring either to the Persians' conquering someone or to someone's conquering the Persians. Sometimes the grammar of a sentence leaves open a great many possible interpretations. For example, consider the following sentence:

Only sons marry only daughters.

One thing this might mean is that a person who is a male only child will marry a person who is a female only child. Again, it might mean that sons are the only persons who marry daughters and do not marry anyone else. Other interpretations are possible as well.[9]

The process of rewriting a sentence so that one of its possible meanings becomes clear is called *disambiguating* the sentence. One way of disambiguating

[9]This example comes from Paul Benacerraf.

a sentence is to rewrite it as a whole, spelling things out in detail. That is how we disambiguated the sentence "Only sons marry only daughters." Another procedure is to continue the sentence in a way that supplies a context that forces one interpretation over others. Consider the sentence "Mary had a little lamb." Notice how the meaning changes completely under the following continuations:

1. Mary had a little lamb; it followed her to school.
2. Mary had a little lamb and then some broccoli.

Just in passing, it is not altogether obvious how we should describe the ambiguity in the sentence "Mary had a little lamb." The most obvious suggestion is that the word "had" is ambiguous, meaning "owned" on the first reading and "ate" on the second reading. Notice, however, that this also forces alternative readings for the expression "a little lamb." Presumably, it was a small, whole, live lamb that followed Mary to school, whereas it would have been a small amount of cooked lamb that she ate. So if we try to locate the ambiguity in particular words, we must say that not only the word "had" but also the word "lamb" are being used ambiguously. This is a reasonable approach, but another is available. In everyday speech, we often leave things out. Thus, instead of saying "Mary had a little *portion of meat derived from a* lamb *to eat*," we simply say "Mary had a little lamb," dropping out the italicized words on the assumption that they will be understood. In most contexts, such deletions cause no misunderstanding. But sometimes deletions are misunderstood, and this can produce ambiguity.

EXERCISE VIII

Show that each of the following sentences admits of at least two interpretations by (1) rewriting the sentence as a whole in two different ways and (2) expanding the sentence in two different ways to clarify the context:

Example: Kenneth let us down.

Rewriting: Kenneth lowered us.

                Kenneth disappointed us.

Expanding: Kenneth let us down with a rope.

                Kenneth let us down just when we needed him.

1. Barry Bonds (the baseball player) was safe at home.
2. I don't know what state Meredith is in.
3. Where did you get bitten?
4. The president sent her congratulations.
5. Visiting professors can be boring.
6. Wendy ran a marathon.
7. The meaning of the term "altering" is changing.

8. I don't want to get too close to him.

9. I often have my friends for dinner.

10. Slow Children Playing. (On a street sign.)

11. Save Soap and Waste Paper. (On a sign during World War II.)

12. In his will, he left $1,000 to his two sons, Jim and John.

13. There is some explanation for everything.

14. She is an Asian historian.

15. Nobody may be in the lounge this evening.

16. Nobody came to the concert at 8 P.M.

EXERCISE IX

Follow the same instructions for the following actual newspaper headlines.[10]

1. Milk Drinkers Turn to Powder

2. Anti-busing Rider Killed by Senate

3. Mrs. Gandhi Stoned in Rally in India

4. College Graduates Blind Senior Citizen

5. Jumping Bean Prices Affect the Poor

6. Tuna Biting off Washington Coast

7. Time for Football and Meatball Stew

8. Police Kill Man with Ax

9. Squad Helps Dog Bite Victim

10. Child Teaching Expert to Speak

11. Prostitutes Appeal to Pope

12. Legalized Outhouses Aired by Legislature

13. Survivor of Siamese Twins Joins Parents

14. Judge Permits Club to Continue Sex Bar

15. Teenage Prostitution Problem Is Mounting

16. Police Can't Stop Gambling

17. Caribbean Islands Drift to the Left

18. Greeks Fine Hookers

[10]Most of these examples come from Columbia Journalism Review, editors, *Squad Helps Dog Bite Victim and Other Flubs from the Nation's Press* (Garden City, NY: Doubleday, 1980).

Poetry, songs, and jokes often intentionally exploit multiple meanings for effect. Find examples in poems, songs, and jokes that you like. Are these examples of ambiguity on the above definition? Why or why not?

EQUIVOCATION

Ambiguity can cause a variety of problems for arguments. Often it produces hilarious or embarrassing side effects, and it is hard to get your arguments taken seriously if your listeners are giggling over an unintended double entendre in which one of the double meanings has risqué connotations. Ambiguity can also generate bad arguments that involve the *fallacy of equivocation*. An argument is said to commit this fallacy when it uses the same expression in different senses in different parts of the argument, and this ruins the argument. Here is a silly example:[11]

> Six is an odd number of legs for a horse.
> Odd numbers cannot be divided by two.
>
> ∴ Six cannot be divided by two.

Clearly, "odd" means "unusual" in the first premise, but it means "not even" in the second premise. Consequently, both premises are true, even though the conclusion is false, so the argument is not valid.

Let's consider another, more serious, example. In *Utilitarianism*, John Stuart Mill claims to "prove" that "happiness is a good" with the following argument:

> The only proof capable of being given that an object is visible is that people actually see it. The only proof that a sound is audible is that people hear it. In like manner the sole evidence it is possible to produce that anything is desirable is that people actually desire it. . . . [E]ach person, so far as he believes it to be attainable, desires his own happiness. This, however, being a fact, we have not only all the proof which the case admits of, but all which it is possible to require, that happiness is a good.[12]

Mill has sometimes been charged with committing a transparent fallacy in this passage. Specifically, the following argument is attributed to him:

> (1) If something is desired, then it is desirable.
> (2) If it is desirable, then it is good.
>
> ∴ (3) If something is desired, then it is good.

[11]We are indebted to Carl Wolf for this example.

[12]John Stuart Mill, *Utilitarianism* (1861; Indianapolis: Hackett, 1979), 34.

Mill never presents his argument in this form, and it may be uncharitable to attribute it to him. Still, whether it is Mill's way of arguing or not, it provides a good specimen of a fallacy of equivocation.

The objection to this argument is that the word "desirable" is used in different senses in the two premises. Specifically, in the first premise, it is used to mean "capable of being desired," whereas in the second premise, it is used to mean "worthy of being desired." If so, the argument really amounts to this:

> (1*) If something is desired, then it is capable of being desired.
> (2*) If something is worthy of being desired, then it is good.
>
> ∴ (3) If something is desired, then it is good.

This argument is clearly not valid. To make the charge of equivocation stick, however, it has to be shown that the argument is not valid when the meaning of the word "desirable" is used in the same sense in the two premises. This produces two cases to be examined:

> (1*) If something is desired, then it is capable of being desired.
> (2**) If something is capable of being desired, then it is good.
>
> ∴ (3)   If something is desired, then it is good.

We now have a valid argument, but the second premise is not true, for sometimes people are capable of desiring things that are not good. The second way of restoring validity takes the following form:

> (1**) If something is desired, then it is worthy of being desired.
> (2*) If something is worthy of being desired, then it is good.
>
> ∴ (3)   If something is desired, then it is good.

Again, we have a valid argument, but this time the first premise is false, since sometimes people do desire things that they should not desire. Thus, in both cases, altering the premises to produce a valid argument produces a false premise, so the argument cannot be sound.

This is a pattern that emerges when dealing with arguments that involve the fallacy of equivocation. When the premises are interpreted in a way that produces a valid argument, then at least one of the premises is false. When the premises are interpreted in a way that makes them true, then the argument is not valid. Here, then, is the strategy for dealing with arguments that may involve a fallacy of equivocation:

1. Distinguish the possible meanings of the potentially ambiguous expressions in the argument.

2. For each possible meaning, restate the argument so that each expression clearly has the same meaning in all of the premises and the conclusion.

3. Evaluate the resulting arguments separately.

EXERCISE XI

Each of the following arguments trades on an ambiguity. For each, locate the ambiguity by showing that one or more of the statements can be interpreted in different ways.

1. We shouldn't hire Peter, because our company has a policy against hiring drug users, and I saw Peter take aspirin, which is a drug.
2. Man is the only rational animal, and no woman is a man, so women are not rational.
3. My doctor has been practicing medicine for thirty years, and practice makes perfect, so my doctor must be nearly perfect.
4. "Our bread does have fiber, because it contains wood pulp." (The Federal Trade Commission actually ordered the Continental Baking Company to indicate in their advertising that this is the kind of fiber in their Fresh Horizons bread.)
5. Our cereal is all natural, for there is obviously nothing supernatural about it.
6. Ice cream is never all natural, since it never appears in nature without human intervention.
7. The apostles were twelve. Matthew was an apostle. Hence, Matthew was twelve. (Attributed to Bertrand Russell.)
8. I have a right to spend all my money on lottery tickets. Therefore, when I spend all my money on lottery tickets, I am doing the right thing.
9. Anyone who tries to violate a law, even if the attempt fails, should be punished. People who try to fly are trying to violate the law of gravity. So they should be punished. (This argument is reported to have been used in an actual legal case during the nineteenth century.)
10. You passed no one on the road; therefore, you walked faster than no one.
11. Everything must have some cause; therefore, something must be the cause of everything.
12. If I have only one friend, then I cannot say that I have any number of friends. So one is not any number.[13]

[13]This example comes from Timothy Duggan.

DISCUSSION QUESTIONS

1. Suppose a newspaper is criticized as a scandalous rumor monger, and its editor responds as follows. Does the editor's argument involve the fallacy of equivocation?

It's not wrong for newspapers to pass on rumors about sex scandals. Newspapers have a duty to print stories that are in the public interest, and the public clearly has a great interest in rumors about sex scandals, since, when newspapers print such stories, their circulation increases, and they receive a large number of letters.[14]

[14]This is a paraphrase of an actual argument given by a newspaper editor as reported by Deni Elliot.

2. In the following passage, Tom Hill, Jr. claims that a common argument against affirmative action commits a fallacy of equivocation. Do you agree that this argument equivocates? Why or why not?

> Some think that the injustice of all affirmative action programs is obvious or easily demonstrated. [One argument] goes this way: "Affirmative action, by definition, gives preferential treatment to minorities and women. This is discrimination in their favor and against non-minority males. All discrimination by public institutions is unjust, no matter whether it is the old kind or the newer 'reverse discrimination.' So all affirmative action programs in public institutions are unjust."
>
> This deceptively simple argument, of course, trades on an ambiguity. In one sense, to "discriminate" means to "make a distinction," to pay attention to a difference. In this evaluatively neutral sense, of course, affirmative action programs do discriminate. But public institutions must, and justifiably do, "discriminate" in this sense, for example, between citizens and noncitizens, freshmen and seniors, the talented and the retarded, and those who pay their bills and those who do not. Whether it is unjust to note and make use of a certain distinction in a given context depends upon many factors: the nature of the institution, the relevant rights of the parties involved, the purposes and effects of making that distinction, and so on.
>
> All this would be obvious except for the fact that the word "discrimination" is also used in a pejorative sense, meaning (roughly) "making use of a distinction in an unjust or illegitimate way." To discriminate in this sense is obviously wrong, but now it remains an open question whether the use of gender and race distinctions in affirmative action programs is really "discrimination" in this sense. The simplistic argument uses the evaluatively neutral sense of "discrimination" to show that affirmative action discriminates; it then shifts to the pejorative sense when it asserts that discrimination is always wrong. Although one may, in the end, *conclude* that all public use of racial and gender distinctions is unjust, to do so requires more of an *argument* than the simple one (just given) that merely exploits an ambiguity of the word "discrimination."[15]

3. Many people argue that homosexuality is immoral because it is unnatural. In the following reading,[16] Burton Leiser criticizes this argument for equivocating on five meanings of the term "natural." Does the argument really equivocate? Why or why not?

HOMOSEXUALITY AND NATURAL LAW

---■---

by Burton Leiser

When theologians and moralists speak of homosexuality, contraception, abortion, and other forms of human behavior as being unnatural and say that for that reason such behavior must be considered to be wrong, in what sense are they using the word *unnatural*? Are they saying that homosexual behavior and the use of contraceptives are [1] *contrary to the scientific laws of nature,* are they

---

[15]Thomas E. Hill, Jr., "The Message of Affirmative Action," in Hill, *Autonomy and Self-Respect* (New York: Cambridge University Press, 1991), 193–94.

[16]Burton Leiser, "Homosexuality and Natural Law," in Leiser, *Liberty, Justice and Morals,* 3d ed. (New York: Macmillan, 1986), 52–57.

saying that they are [2] *artificial* forms of behavior, or are they using the terms *natural* and *unnatural* in some third sense?

They cannot mean that homosexual behavior (to stick to the subject presently under discussion) violates the laws of nature in the first sense [including, for example, Boyle's law that the volume of a gas varies inversely with the pressure that is applied to it], for . . . in *that* sense it is impossible to violate the laws of nature. Those laws, being merely descriptive of what actually does happen, would have to *include* homosexual behavior if such behavior does actually take place. . . .

If those who say that homosexual behavior is unnatural are using the term *unnatural* in the second sense as artificial, it is difficult to understand their objection. That which is artificial is often far better than what is natural. . . . [Moreover,] homosexual behavior can hardly be considered unnatural in this sense. There is nothing artificial about such behavior. On the contrary, it is quite natural, in this sense, to those who engage in it. And, even if it were not, this is not in itself a ground for condemning it.

It would seem, then, that those who condemn homosexuality as an unnatural form of behavior must mean something else by the word *unnatural,* something not covered by either of the preceding definitions. A third possibility is this:

3. *Anything uncommon or abnormal is unnatural.* If this is what is meant by those who condemn homosexuality on the ground that it is unnatural, it is quite obvious that their condemnation cannot be accepted without further argument. The fact that a given form of behavior is uncommon provides no justification for condemning it. . . . Great artists, poets, musicians, and scientists are uncommon in this sense; but clearly the world is better off for having them, and it would be absurd to condemn them or their activities for their failure to be common and normal. If homosexual behavior is wrong, then, it must be for some reason other than its unnaturalness in this sense of the word.

4. *Any use of an organ or an instrument that is contrary to its principal purpose or function is unnatural.* Every organ and every instrument—perhaps even every creature—has a function to perform, one for which it is particularly designed. Any use of those instruments and organs that is consonant with their purposes is natural and proper, but any use that is inconsistent with their principal functions is unnatural and improper, and to that extent evil or harmful. Human teeth, for example, are admirably designed for their principal functions—biting and chewing the kinds of food suitable for human consumption. But they are not particularly well suited for prying the caps from beer bottles. If they are used for that purpose, they are likely to crack or break under the strain. . . .

What are the sex organs peculiarly suited to do? . . . Our sexual organs are uniquely adapted for procreation, but that is obviously not the only function for which they are adapted. Human beings may—and do—use those organs for a great many other purposes, and it is difficult to see why any *one* use should be considered to be the only proper one. The sex organs seem to be particularly well adapted to give their owners and others intense sensations of pleasure. Unless one believes that pleasure itself is bad, there seems to be little reason to believe that the use of the sex organs for the production of pleasure in oneself or in others is evil. In view of the peculiar design of these organs, with their great concentration of nerve endings, it would seem that they were designed (if they *were* designed) with that very goal in mind, and that their use for such purposes would be no more unnatural than their use for the purpose of procreation.

Nor should we overlook the fact that human sex organs may be and are used to express, in the deepest and most intimate way open to man, the love of one person for another. Even the most ardent opponents of "unfruitful" intercourse admit that sex does serve this function. They have accordingly conceded that a man and his wife may have intercourse even though she is pregnant, or past the age of child bearing, or in the infertile period of her menstrual cycle. . . .

To sum up, then, the proposition that any use of an organ that is contrary to its principal purpose or function is unnatural assumes that organs *have* a principal purpose or function, but this may be denied on the ground that the purpose or function of a given organ may vary according to the needs or desires of its owner. It may be denied on the ground that a given organ may have more than one principal purpose or function, and any attempt to call one use or another the only natural one seems to be arbitrary, if not question-begging. Also, the proposition suggests that what is unnatural is evil or depraved. This goes beyond the pure description of things, and enters into the problem of the evaluation of human behavior, which leads us to the fifth meaning of *natural.*

5. *That which is natural is good, and whatever is unnatural is bad.* . . . Clearly, [people who say this] cannot have intended merely to reduce the word *natural* to a synonym of *good, right,* and *proper,* and *unnatural* to a synonym of *evil, wrong, improper, corrupt,* and *depraved.* If that were all they had intended to do, . . . it would follow inevitably that whatever is good must be natural, and vice versa, by definition. This is certainly not what the opponents of homosexuality have been saying when they claim that homosexuality, being unnatural, is evil. For if it were, their claim would be quite empty. They would be saying merely that homosexuality, being evil, is evil—a redundancy that could as easily be reduced to the simpler assertion that homosexuality is evil. This assertion, however, is not an argument. . . . "Unnaturalness" and "wrongfulness" are not synonyms, then, but different concepts.

The problem with which we are wrestling is that we are unable to find a meaning for *unnatural* that enables us to arrive at the conclusion that homosexuality is unnatural or that if homosexuality is unnatural, it is therefore wrongful behavior. We have examined [five] common meanings of *natural* and *unnatural,* and have seen that none of them performs the task that it must perform if the advocates of this argument are to prevail. Without some more satisfactory explanation of the connection between the wrongfulness of homosexuality and its alleged unnaturalness, the argument [that homosexuality is wrong because it is unnatural] must be rejected.

DEFINITIONS

It is sometimes suggested that a great many disputes could be avoided if people simply took the precaution of defining their terms. To some extent this is true. People do sometimes seem to disagree just because they are using terms in different ways, even though they agree on the nonverbal issues.

Nonetheless, definitions will not solve all problems, and a mindless insistence on definitions can turn a serious discussion into a semantic quibble. If you insist on defining every term, you will never be satisfied, because every definition will introduce new terms to be defined. Furthermore, definitions themselves can be confusing or obfuscating as, for example, when an economist tells us:

I define "inflation" as too much money chasing too few goods.

Not only is this definition metaphorical and obscure, it also has a theory of the causes of inflation built into it.

To use definitions correctly, we must realize that they come in various forms and serve various purposes. There are at least five kinds of definitions that need to be distinguished:

1. *Lexical* or *dictionary definitions* are the most common kind of definition. We consult a dictionary when we are ignorant about the meaning of a word in a particular language. If you do not happen to know what the words "jejune," "ketone," or "Kreis" mean, then you can look these words up in an English, a scientific, and a German dictionary, respectively.

Except for an occasional diagram, dictionaries explain the meaning of a word by using other words that the reader presumably already understands. These explanations often run in a circle, such as when the *Oxford American Dictionary* defines "car" as "automobile" and "automobile" as "car." Circular definitions can still be useful, because if you know what one of the terms in the circle means, you can use that background knowledge plus the definition to figure out what the other terms mean.

The goal of dictionary definitions is to supply us with factual information about the standard meanings of words in a particular language. As dictionary definitions are, in effect, factual claims about how people in general actually use certain words, dictionary definitions can be either accurate or inaccurate. The *Oxford American Dictionary* defines one meaning of "fan" as "a device waved in the hand or operated mechanically to create a current of air." This is, strictly speaking, incorrect because a bellows also meets these conditions but is not a fan. Dictionary definitions can be criticized or defended on the basis of a speaker's sense of the language or, more formally, by empirical surveys of what speakers accept as appropriate or reject as inappropriate uses of the term.

2. *Disambiguating definitions* specify a sense in which a word or phrase is or might be being used by a particular speaker on a particular occasion. ("When I said that the banks were collapsing, I meant river banks, not financial institutions.") Disambiguating definitions can tell us which dictionary definition actually is intended in a particular context, or they can distinguish several meanings that might be intended. They can also be used to remove syntactic ambiguity or amphiboly. ("When I said that all of my friends are not students, I meant that not all of them are students, not that none of them are students.")

Whether the ambiguity is semantic or syntactic, the goal of a disambiguating definition is to capture what the speaker intended, so such definitions can be justified by asking the speaker what he or she meant. This is a different question than asking what a word means. Whereas dictionary definitions ask what words mean or how they are used by most speakers of the language, a disambiguating definition focuses on a particular speaker and asks which meaning that speaker intended on a particular occasion.

Such disambiguating definitions can be used in response to arguments that seem to commit the fallacy of equivocation. A critic can use disambiguating definitions to distinguish possible meanings and then ask, "Did you mean this or that?" The person who gave the argument can answer by picking one of these alternatives or by providing another disambiguating definition to specify what was meant. Speakers are sometimes not sure which meaning they intended, and then the critic needs to show that the argument cannot work if a single disambiguating definition is followed throughout. Whether one sides with the arguer or the critic, arguments that use terms ambiguously cannot be evaluated thoroughly without the help of disambiguating definitions.

3. *Stipulative definitions* are used to assign a meaning to a new (usually technical) term or to assign a new or special meaning to a familiar term. They have the following general form: "By such and such expression I (or we) will mean so and so." Thus, mathematicians introduced the new term "googol" to stand for the number expressed by 1 followed by 100 zeroes. Physicists use words like "charm," "color," and "strangeness" to stand for certain features of subatomic particles. Stipulative definitions do not report what a word means; they give a new word a meaning or an old word a new meaning.

Notice that if I say, "I stipulate that . . ." I thereby stipulate that . . . ; so such utterances are explicit performatives, and stipulation is a speech act. (See Chapter 1.) This explains why stipulative definitions cannot be false, since no performatives can be false. Stipulative definitions can, however, be criticized in other ways. They can be vague or ambiguous. They can be useless or confusing. Someone who stipulates a meaning for a term might go on to use the term with a different meaning (just as people sometimes fail to keep their promises). Still, stipulative definitions cannot be false by virtue of failing to correspond to the real meaning of a word, because they give that meaning to that word.

4. *Precising definitions* are used to resolve vagueness. They are used to draw a sharp (or sharper) boundary around the things to which a term refers, when this collection has a fuzzy or indeterminate boundary in ordinary usage. For example, it is not important for most purposes to decide how big a population center must be in order to count as a city rather than as a town. We can deal with the borderline cases by using such phrases as "very small city" or "quite a large town." It will not make much difference which phrase we use on most occasions. Yet it is not hard to imagine a situation in which it might make a difference whether a center of population is a city or not. As a city, it might be eligible for development funds that are not available to towns. Here a precising definition—a definition that draws a sharp boundary where none formerly existed—would be useful.

Precising definitions are, in effect, combinations of stipulative definitions and dictionary definitions. Like stipulative definitions, they involve a choice. One could define a city as any population center with more than 50,000 people, or one could decide to decrease the minimum to 30,000 people. Precising definitions are not completely arbitrary, however, because they usually should conform to the generally accepted meaning of a term. It would be unreasonable to define a city as any population center with more than seventeen people. Dictionary definitions, thus, set limits to precising definitions.

Precising definitions are also not arbitrary in another way: There can be good reasons to prefer one precising definition over another, when adopting the preferred definition will have better effects than the alternative. If development funds are to be distributed only to cities, then to define cities as having more than 50,000 people will deny those funds to smaller population centers with, say, 10,000 people. Consequently, we need some reason to resolve the vagueness of the term "city" in one way rather than another. In this case, the choice might be based on the amount of funds available for development. In a more dramatic example, a precising definition of "death" might be used to resolve controversial issues about euthanasia—about what doctors may or must do to patients who are near death—and then our choices between possible precising definitions might be based on our deepest value commitments. In any case, we need some argument to show that one precising definition is better than other alternatives.

Such arguments often leave some leeway. Even if one can justify defining cities as having a minimum of 50,000 people instead of 10,000, one's reason is not likely to justify a cutoff at 50,000 as opposed to 49,000. A different kind of defense would be needed if someone used a slippery-slope argument to show that it is unfair to provide development funds to one city with 50,000 people but to deny such funds to its neighbor with only 49,000 people. Against this kind of charge, the only way to defend a precising definition might be to show that some precising definition is needed, the cutoff should lie inside a certain general area, one's preferred definition does lie within that area, and no alternative is any better. Such responses might also apply to nearby alternatives, but they are still sometimes enough to support a precising definition. If responses like these are not available, then a precising definition can be criticized as unjustified.

5. *Systematic or theoretical definitions* are introduced to give a systematic order or structure to a subject matter. For example, in geometry, every term must be either a primitive (undefined) term or a term defined by means of these primitive terms. Thus, if we take points and distances as primitives, we can define a straight line as the shortest distance between two points. Then, assuming some more concepts, we can define a triangle as a closed figure with exactly three straight lines as sides. By a series of such definitions, the terms in geometry are placed in systematic relationships with one another.

In a similar way, we might try to represent family relationships using only the primitive notions of parent, male, and female. We could then construct definitions of the following kind:

> "*A* is the brother of *B*." = "*A* and *B* have the same parents and *A* is male."

> "*A* is *B*'s grandmother." = "*A* is a parent of a parent of *B* and *A* is female."[17]

Things become more complicated when we try to define such notions as "second cousin once removed" or "stepfather." Yet, by extending some basic definitions from simple to more complicated cases, all family relationships can be given a systematic presentation.

Formulating systematic definitions for family relationships is relatively easy, but similar activities in science, mathematics, and other fields can demand genius. It often takes deep insight into a subject to see which concepts are genuinely fundamental and which are secondary and derivative. When Sir Isaac Newton defined force in terms of mass and acceleration, he was not simply stating how he proposed to use certain words; he was introducing a fundamental conceptual relationship that improved our understanding of the physical world.

Such theoretical definitions can be evaluated on the basis of whether they really do help us formulate better theories and understand the world. Evaluating theoretical definitions often requires a great deal of empirical

---

[17]Notice that in these definitions an individual word is not defined in isolation. Instead, a whole sentence containing the word is replaced by another whole sentence in which the defined word does not appear. Definitions of this kind are called "contextual definitions" because a context containing the word is the unit of definition. Dictionary, disambiguating, stipulative, and precising definitions can also be presented in this contextual form.

investigation. When water was defined as H_2O,[18] this made it possible to formulate more precise laws about how water interacted with other chemicals. Other alternatives were available. Whereas molecules count as H_2O, and hence as water, even if they contain unusual isotopes of hydrogen and oxygen, chemists could define water so that it would have to contain only the most common isotopes of hydrogen and oxygen. Why don't they? Because they discovered that differences among isotopes generally do not affect how molecules of H_2O react with other chemicals. As a result, the simplest and most useful generalizations about the properties of water can be formulated in terms of H_2O without regard to certain isotopes of hydrogen and oxygen. This illustrates one way in which choosing one theoretical definition over another can lead to a better theory.

Definitions can play important roles in the presentation of arguments, but demands for definitions can also hinder the progress of an argument. In the middle of discussions people often ask for definitions or even state, usually with an air of triumph, that everything depends on the way you define your terms. We saw in the opening chapter that definitions are not always needed, and most issues do not turn on the way in which words are defined. When asked for a definition, it is appropriate to reply: "What sort of definition do you want, and why do you want it?" Of course, if you are using a word in a way that departs from customary usage, or using it in some special way of your own, or using a word that is too vague for the given context, or using a word in an ambiguous way, then the request for a definition is perfectly in order. In such cases, the demand for a definition represents an important move within the argument rather than a distraction from it.

EXERCISE XII

Look up lexical or dictionary definitions for the following words. (For fun, you might try to guess the meanings of these words before you look them up, as in the game "Balderdash.")

1. jejune
2. ketone
3. fluvial
4. xebec
5. plangent

[18]If you doubt that the identity "Water is H_2O" is used as a definition, just consider how you would react to someone who claims to have discovered some water that is *not* H_2O. We would dismiss this person as linguistically confused, as the discovered stuff cannot properly be called "water" if it is not H_2O.

EXERCISE XIII

1. Give a stipulative definition for the word "klurg."
2. Stipulate a word to stand for the chunks of ice that form under car fenders in winter.
3. Describe something that does not have a common name, for which it would be useful to stipulate a name. Explain how the name would be useful.

EXERCISE XIV

Give precising definitions for the following words. In each case, supply a context that gives your precising definition a point.

1. book
2. alcoholic beverage
3. crime
4. warm
5. fast

EXERCISE XV

Give disambiguating definitions for the following words. In each case, supply a context in which your definition might be needed to avoid confusion.

1. run
2. pen
3. game
4. painting
5. fast

EXERCISE XVI

Using the notions of parents, male, and female as basic, give systematic definitions of the following family relationships:

1. *A* and *B* are sisters.
2. *A* and *B* are siblings.
3. *A* is *B*'s half-brother.
4. *A* is *B*'s niece.
5. *A* is *B*'s cousin.

The definition of "sexual relations" was crucial to the issue of whether President Bill Clinton committed perjury. Find and distinguish the various definitions of "sexual relations" at play in the following selection from President Clinton's testimony before the independent counsel, Kenneth Starr, on August 17, 1998.[19] In your opinion, does either President Clinton or the lawyers who are questioning him use definitions improperly? Why or why not?

Q: (BY MR. BITTMAN): Mr. President, were you physically intimate with Monica Lewinsky? . . .

A: (BY PRESIDENT CLINTON): When I was alone with Ms. Lewinsky on certain occasions in early 1996 and once in early 1997, I engaged in conduct that was wrong. These encounters did not consist of sexual intercourse. They did not constitute sexual relations as I understood that term to be defined at my January 17th, 1998 deposition. . . .

Q: Let us then move to the definition that was provided you during your deposition. We will have that marked as Grand Jury Exhibit WJC-2. . . .

> [Definition of Sexual Relations] For the purposes of this deposition, a person engages in "sexual relations" when the person knowingly engages in or causes—(1) contact with the genitalia, anus, groin, breast, inner thigh, or buttocks of any person with an intent to arouse or gratify the sexual desire of any person; (2) contact between any part of the person's body or an object and the genitals or anus of another person; or (3) contact between the genitals or anus of the person and any part of another person's body. "Contact" means intentional touching, either directly or through clothing.

Q: This is an exact copy, Mr. President, of the exhibit that was provided you during that deposition. And I'm sure you remember from the deposition that paragraph (1) of the definition remained in effect. Judge Wright ruled that that was to be the guiding defintion, and that paragraphs (2) and (3) were stricken. . . .

Did you understand the words in the first portion of the exhibit, Mr. President, that is, "for the purposes of this deposition, a person engages in 'sexual relations' when the person knowingly engages in or causes"? Did you understand, do you understand the words there in that phrase?

A: Yes. . . . My understanding of this definition is it covers contact by the person being deposed with the enumerated areas, if the contact is done with an intent to arouse or gratify. That's my understanding of the definition. . . .

Q: I suppose, since you have now read portions of the transcript again, that you were reminded that you did not ask for any clarification of the terms. Is that correct? Of the definition?

A: No, sir. I thought it was a rather—when I read it, I thought it was a rather strange definition. But it was the one the Judge decided on and I was bound by it. So, I took it. . . .

[19]Reprinted in Kenneth Starr, *Appendices to the Referral . . . by the Office of the Independent Counsel . . .* (House Document 105-311) (Washington, DC: U.S. Government Printing Office, 1998), 393, 460–1, 464, 466, 469–70, 472–4, 509–10, 571–2, 601–2.

Q: And you remember that Ms. Lewinsky's affidavit said that she had had no sexual relationship with you. Do you remember that?

A: I do.

Q: And do you remember in the deposition that Mr. Bennett asked you about that. This is at the end of the—towards the end of the deposition. And you indicated, he asked you whether the statement that Ms. Lewinsky made in her affidavit was—

A: Truthful.

Q: —true. And you indicated that it was absolutely correct.

A: I did. . . . I believe at the time that she filled out this affidavit, if she believed that the definition of sexual relationship was two people having intercourse, then this is accurate. And I believe that is the definition that most ordinary Americans would give it. If you said Jane and Harry have a sexual relationship, and you're not talking about people being drawn into a lawsuit and being given definitions, and then a great effort to trick them in some way, but you are just talking about people in ordinary conversations, I'll bet the grand jurors, if they were talking about two people they know, and said they have a sexual relationship, they meant they were sleeping together; they meant they were having intercourse together. So, I'm not at all sure that this affidavit is not true and was not true in Ms. Lewinsky's mind at the time she swore it out. . . .

Q: (BY MR. WISENBERG): Mr. President, I want to, before I go into a new subject area, briefly go over something you were talking about with Mr. Bittman. The statement of your attorney, Mr. Bennett, at the Paula Jones deposition, "Counsel is fully aware . . . that Ms. Lewinsky has filed, has an affidavit which they are in possession of saying that there is absolutely no sex of any kind in any manner, shape or form, with President Clinton." That statement is made by your attorney in front of Judge Susan Webber Wright, correct?

A: That's correct.

Q: That statement is a completely false statement. Whether or not Mr. Bennett knew of your relationship with Ms. Lewinsky, the statement that there was "no sex of any kind in any manner, shape or form, with President Clinton," was an utterly false statement. Is that correct?

A: It depends on what the meaning of the word "is" is. If the—if he—if "is" means is and never has been, that is not—that is one thing. If it means there is none, that was a completely true statement. . . .

Q: I just want to make sure I understand, Mr. President. Do you mean today that because you were not engaging in sexual activity with Ms. Lewinsky during the deposition that the statement of Mr. Bennett might be literally true?

A: No, sir. I mean that at the time of the deposition, it had been—that was well beyond any point of improper contact between me and Ms. Lewinsky. So that anyone generally speaking in the present tense, saying there is not an improper relationship, would be telling the truth if that person said there was not, in the present tense; the present tense encompassing many months. That's what I meant by that. . . .

Q: If Monica Lewinsky has stated that her affidavit that she didn't have a sexual relationship with you is, in fact, a lie, I take it you disagree with that?

A: No. I told you before what I thought the issue was there. I think the issue is how do you define sexual relationship. And there was no definition imposed on her at the time she executed the affidavit. Therefore, she was free to give it any reasonable meaning. . . .

Q: Well, the grand jury would like to know, Mr. President, why it is that you think that oral sex performed on you does not fall within the definition of sexual relations as used in your deposition.

A: Because that is—if the deponent is the person who has oral sex performed on him, then the contact is with—not with anything on that list, but with the lips of another person. It seems to be self-evident that that's what it is. And I thought it was curious. . . .

12

FALLACIES OF RELEVANCE AND VACUITY

*T*his chapter will consider two more kinds of defects in arguments. Fallacies of relevance *arise when a premise, true or not, is not adequately related to the conclusion.
Such irrelevance comes in endless varieties, but we will focus on two of the most
common forms:* arguments ad hominem *and* appeals to authority. *Arguments of
these kinds are not always fallacious, so we will discuss various factors that determine when such arguments are defective and when they are not. The other group of
fallacies includes* fallacies of vacuity. *These arise when an argument doesn't get
anywhere, either because its premises already somehow depend on the conclusion or
because its conclusion is empty.* Circular arguments *and arguments that* beg the
question *fall into this category. So do positions that make themselves immune to
criticism by being* self-sealing.

FALLACIES OF RELEVANCE

In a good argument, we present statements that are true in order to offer support for some conclusion. One way to depart from this ideal is to state things
that are true themselves, but have no bearing on the truth of the conclusion.

We might wonder why irrelevant remarks can have any influence at all.
The answer is that we generally assume that a person's remarks are relevant,
for this is one of the conditions for smooth and successful conversation (as
Grice pointed out in his rule of Relevance, discussed in Chapter 1). That it is
possible to exploit people by violating this natural assumption is shown in
the following passage from *The Catcher in the Rye.*

> The new elevator boy was sort of on the stupid side. I told him, in this very
> casual voice, to take me up the Dicksteins'. . . .
>
> He had the elevator doors all shut and all, and was all set to take me up, and
> then he turned around and said, "They ain't in. They're at a party on the four-
> teenth floor."
>
> "That's all right," I said. "I'm supposed to wait for them. I'm their nephew."
>
> He gave me this sort of stupid, suspicious look. "You better wait in the lobby,
> fella," he said.

"I'd like to—I really would," I said. "But I have a bad leg. I have to hold it in a certain position. I think I'd better sit down in the chair outside their door."

He didn't know what the hell I was talking about, so all he said was "oh" and took me up. Not bad, boy. It's funny. All you have to do is say something nobody understands and they'll do practically anything you want them to.[1]

It is clear what is going on here. When you offer something as a reason, it is conversationally implied that there is some connection between it and the thing you are arguing for. In most cases, the connection is obvious, and there is no need to spell it out. In other cases, the connection is not obvious, but in the spirit of cooperation others are willing to assume that the connection exists. In the present case, there seems to be no connection between having a bad leg and sitting in one particular chair. Why, then, does the elevator operator not challenge this statement? Part of the reason is that it is not easy to challenge what people say; among other things, it is not polite. But politeness does not seem to hold the elevator operator back; instead, he does not want to appear stupid. The person who offers a reason conversationally implies a connection, and we do not like to admit that we fail to see this connection. This combination of generosity and fear of looking stupid leads us to accept all sorts of irrelevant statements as reasons.

Fallacies of relevance are surprisingly common in everyday life. The best strategy for dealing with them is simply to cross out all irrelevant claims and then see what is left. Sometimes nothing is left. On the other hand, we should not be heavy-handed in making charges of irrelevance. Sometimes the occurrence of irrelevance is innocent; good arguments often contain irrelevant asides. More important, relevance is often secured by way of a conversational implication, so we really have to know what is going on in a given context to decide whether a remark is relevant or not. We can illustrate this last point by examining two kinds of arguments that often involve fallacies of irrelevance: *arguments ad hominem* and *appeals to authority*.

AD HOMINEM ARGUMENTS

Literally, an argument ad hominem is an argument directed against a person who is arguing for a claim rather than against that person's claim or argument. On the face of it, this seems to involve irrelevance, for the character or social position or status of a person should have nothing to do with the truth of what that person says or with the soundness or strength of that person's arguments. Many ad hominem fallacies cite personal characteristics that obviously have nothing to do with the matter at hand. Even when protesters dress shabbily, their clothing shows nothing about the legitimacy of their protest. A speaker's ethnic background, race, sex, sexual orientation, physical appearance, and bathing habits almost never give us any good reason to challenge the truth of what that person says or the soundness of his or her

---

[1]J. D. Salinger, *The Catcher in the Rye* (New York: Bantam Books, 1951), 157–58.

argument. Ad hominem fallacies very often deal in such irrelevant matters. They are often introduced just to distract us from the real point at issue.

In some unusual cases, however, a speaker's character or position *is* a reason to doubt the truth of what he says. Suppose that Lucy is suspected of committing murder, but Louie testifies that he was with her at the time of the murder. Then the prosecution shows that Louie provided a similar alibi for an accused murderer at ten trials in the past year, and every time he was found to have lied in exchange for money. Louie never testifies without being paid, he says whatever he is paid to say, and people do not hire him if they have any better defense. This background about Louie provides some reason to believe that what Louie said was false—that he was not with Lucy at the time of the murder. Lucy still might not have committed the murder, but we can't take Louie's word for it. Ad hominem arguments like this can be called *deniers*, since they deny the truth of what is said or the strength or soundness of an argument. Although most ad hominem deniers are fallacious, the case of Louie shows that some are not.

A different kind of ad hominem argument questions a person's right to make a claim or present an argument. Imagine that the Senate is debating tax rates. During one session, Tad stands up and argues for a reduction in taxes. Tad can be criticized if he is not a senator, because then he lacks the status that confers the right to speak in this setting. Even outside of any formal institution, if a neighbor tells someone that she ought to take her children to a certain church, the mother might respond, "You are in no position to tell me what to do, you busybody" or just "Mind your own business." Arguments like this can be called *silencers*, because the revoke the right to speak without necessarily denying the truth of what is said.

A third variety of ad hominem argument is more subtle. Consider the following exchange:

> **Norm:** The cold war is over, and bad relations between Cuba and the United States hurt both countries, so it is time for the United States to develop normal relations with Cuba.
>
> **Cliff:** Yeah, so you can make a bundle importing cigars from those commies.

Cliff's reply is an attack on the motives of Norm and not on the truth of what Norm said. Nor is Cliff denying that Norm has a right to speak. Yet the remark is not without some relevance—it is not off the wall. In a conversational exchange, we rely on the integrity of the person who is speaking, and when we have reasons to believe that the person's integrity is questionable, we sometimes say so. This is the significance of Cliff's remark. Cliff points to a fact that gives some reason for us not to trust Norm's integrity in a discussion of the United States' relations with Cuba.

Cliff's attack might or might not be justified. If the only reason why Norm favors normal relations between the United States and Cuba is that this would enable Norm to make more money, then Cliff's ad hominem attack is well founded. But if Norm's real reason for saying what he does is that he honestly believes that normal relations would be beneficial both to the United States and to Cuba, then Norm's position does not depend on any lack of integrity. In that case, Cliff's attack is not well founded, even if it so happens that Norm would profit from normal relations.

Whether justified or not, ad hominem arguments of this third variety can be called *dismissers,* because they dismiss the speaker as untrustworthy and unreliable. Their point is not to deny the truth of the claim or the speaker's right to say it. Instead, a dismisser is supposed to show why the fact that this speaker supports a claim is not a good reason to believe that claim (or to deny it, for that matter).

These three kinds of ad hominem arguments all start from premises about the person's character or status. That's what makes them ad hominem arguments. They differ in their conclusions: Deniers conclude that a claim is untrue or that an argument is unsound or weak. Silencers conclude that someone lacks the right to speak in a certain context. Dismissers conclude that someone is untrustworthy or unreliable. Each can be either justified or unjustified, so there are six kinds that can be diagrammed like this, using examples mentioned above:

Ad Hominem Arguments	Justified	Not Justified
Deniers	Louie, the hired perjurer	Shabby protesters
Silencers	Tad if he is not a senator	Tad if he is a senator
Dismissers	Cliff's reply if Norm lacks integrity	Cliff's reply if Norm does not lack integrity

What logicians usually call ad hominem fallacies are unjustified deniers. Even when the premises of such an argument are true, they are irrelevant to the conclusion. That makes them fallacies of relevance. Once you get used to spotting ad hominem fallacies, they seem common and obvious.

When assessing an ad hominem argument, the first step is to determine whether its conclusion is about someone's right to speak, about someone's reliability, or about the truth, soundness, or strength of what is claimed. The second step is to determine whether its premises provide adequate justification for its conclusion. This will enable you to place the argument in the above table. These steps will often not be easy or obvious. Although perjurers for hire almost always lie, most people exhibit some middling degree of reliability. When people are known for passing on rumors without checking their truth, this might be a reason to doubt what they say when they pass on yet another rumor (even if it is not a reason to believe that what they say is false). In assessing what they say, it would be best to look for additional evidence. If none is available, then we need to ask how often their testimony is true on matters of this kind. Only by careful inspection of individual cases can we determine the strength of such ad hominem arguments.

Another tricky case occurs when someone is accused of inconsistency over time. If your neighbor says that the best time to prune roses is in the autumn, but then the next spring she tells you that the spring is the best time to prune roses, this inconsistency would give you some reason to doubt her expertise as a gardener. Maybe over the winter she got new information that changed her mind, but her reliability is in question until you have some explanation of why she would say different things at different times. If she wavers between contrary positions, no more than half of her views can be correct, so you have reason to ask your neighbor, "Why should I trust you?"

What she is saying now still might be correct. Maybe she made a mistake but has since learned the truth. Moreover, if she gave an argument for her claim (such as that pruned roses grow back more quickly in the spring, and the best time to prune roses is when they grow back more quickly), then that argument still might be sound. The soundness of her current argument and the truth of her current claim do not depend on what she said last fall. For this reason, it is normally a fallacy to reject someone's view or argument on the basis of an inconsistency with their views at other times. Their current position needs to be assessed as they stand now. (Whether we want political leaders whose views blow with the wind is, of course, another issue.)

A different kind of inconsistency occurs in the traditional fallacy called *tu quoque*, a Latin term that means "you are another." When a parent tells a child to quit smoking, the child might respond, "Look who's talking. You've been smoking for years. If it's so bad, why don't you stop?" The force of this charge might be just that the parent is hypocritical or that one has no right to criticize others for doing something that one does oneself. If that is the point, then the child's response is a silencer. This attack might or might not be justified. In any case, the parent's smoking does not give any reason at all to conclude that smoking is not bad. To use a *tu quoque* argument to reach *that* conclusion would be an unjustified denier (and an ad hominem fallacy). Even hypocrites can make true claims and give good arguments. Thus, to show that someone's claims and arguments are defective, one normally needs to look at those claims and arguments themselves, not at the behavior of the speaker.

Instead of citing past beliefs or acts of a speaker, some ad hominem arguments aim at the source or origin of the speaker's belief. When its origin is irrelevant to the truth of a claim, such arguments commit what is called the *genetic fallacy*. Whole movements are sometimes accused of genetic fallacies. Marxists often reject opposing views because those views arose under capitalism. Freudians sometimes dismiss critics on the basis of how those critics were raised as children. Usually, the same kind of argument is available to their opponents as well. Critics of Freud sometimes cite his childhood and training to explain away his views. The fact that genetic arguments can be used just as well for contrary conclusions suggests that they do not really support either side.

The problem with genetic arguments is that lots of good ideas have questionable origins. Much mathematics originated within Pythagorean cults. Gravity and much of chemical theory were first discussed by alchemists who were trying to turn lead into gold. The structure of the benzene ring is reported to have come to Kekule von Stradonitz in a dream about a snake biting its tail. Early religions were close to magic and were used by rich and powerful leaders to control their subordinates. In all of these cases, the origin of the ideas cannot be used to refute those views or the arguments for them. Learning the genesis of an idea can help improve one's understanding of its content and of the process of scientific discovery. Origins sometimes indicate where to look for evidence or for objections. Still, to evaluate an idea or an argument, one should focus on that idea or argument, not on its origin.

EXERCISE I

For each of the following arguments, indicate whether it involves (1) an ad hominem denier against a speaker's claim or argument, (2) an ad hominem silencer against a person's right to speak, (3) an ad hominem dismisser against someone's trustworthiness, or (4) none of these. Explain your answer. Be sure to focus on what is explicitly said and not on what might be conversationally implied in each example.

> Example: Sure, Sara says she saw me cheat in the game, but Sara's stupid, so you shouldn't pay any attention to her.

> Answer: This is an ad hominem dismisser, since the point is that Sara is unreliable. The speaker does not deny what Sara says or that she has a right to say it.

1. Sure, Sadie says she saw me cheat, but it was very dark, and her vision is horrible, so she must have seen something else and thought it was me cheating.

2. Sure, Sam says he saw me cheat, but the only reason he says it is that he wants to win the game. He's a real jerk.

3. Sure, Steve says she saw me cheat, but he wasn't even playing the game. It's not his place to accuse those of us who were playing.

4. Sure, Sybill says she saw me cheat, but I didn't even take the exam, so I couldn't have cheated on it.

5. Sure, Sally says she saw me cheat, but she accuses everyone, and she's almost always wrong, so you should know that she is wrong this time, too.

EXERCISE II

Explain the point of each of the following remarks. Indicate whether each remark involves an ad hominem silencer, dismissal, denier, or none of these. Then say whether the argument provides an adequate justification for its conclusion, and why.

1. I've heard all the reasons why you think smoking is bad, but you're still smoking yourself, so you're not being consistent. I doubt that your advice is sincere if you don't follow it yourself.

2. The American Tobacco Company has argued for years that smoking is not really unhealthy, but what would you expect the company to say? It would take the same position regardless of any evidence, so I can't trust them.

3. The main opposition to tax reductions comes from people who depend on government programs funded by taxes, so they can hardly be impartial, but only those who are impartial should be allowed to speak on such a crucial issue for our whole country.

4. The main support for tax reductions comes from people who pay taxes, so their views can't be a reliable indicator of what the best policy is.

5. Very few citizens have studied the entire tax code, and nobody understands the effect of taxes on the economy, so we have little reason to believe them when they say that present tax policies will destroy the economy.

6. The Joint Chiefs of Staff argue that the U.S. government needs to increase its military budget, but an opponent responds, "Well, of course, *they* will want as much money as they can get for their departments. They always ask for more money even though most of the time they don't really need it. So this time, again, they probably don't need it."

7. After Congress passes a military draft during a war, an opponent says, "If members of Congress were eligible for the draft, they would not vote for it. So we must not really need a draft."

8. Of course, the party in power is opposed to term limits. That's just because they want to stay in power.

9. An economist cites recent trends in sales of raw materials as evidence of an upturn in the economy, and then a critic, who doubts the economist's prediction, responds, "If you're so smart, why ain't you rich?"

10. As a criticism of pro-choice activists, Ronald Reagan said, "I've noticed that everybody who is for abortion has already been born."

11. Attacking male opponents of abortion, a feminist claims, "Most opponents of abortion are men."

12. When a member of a fraternity argued for co-ed houses in place of fraternities, a critic responded, "When he quits his fraternity in protest and joins a co-ed house, then he will earn the right to criticize us."

13. When Fred argues at a fraternity meeting that his house should admit women, another member announces, "Let me remind you all that Fred held exactly the opposite position last year."

14. Almost everyone who thinks that drugs are harmless has taken drugs, so we can't trust their views.

15. Let he who is without sin among you cast the first stone. (John 8:7)

DISCUSSION QUESTIONS

1. In a heated discussion, people will sometimes ask an opponent, "Why are you being so defensive?" This is obviously a rhetorical question. What is the point of this question? Does it implicitly involve an ad hominem fallacy?

2. In the biblical story of Job, Job is described as a person who "was blameless and upright, one who feared God and turned away from evil" (Job 1:1). Satan challenges God to allow him to subject Job to the worst calamities to see if Job's faith will remain unchanged. After the most extreme misfortunes, Job finally cries out and asks why he should be made to suffer so (Job 38:1–4):

   > Then the Lord answered Job out of the whirlwind:
   >
   > Who is this that darkens counsel by words without knowledge?
   >
   > Gird up your loins like a man.
   >
   > I will question you, and you shall declare to me.
   >
   > Where were you when I laid the foundation of the earth?
   >
   > Tell me, if you have understanding.

   Does God's response to Job involve an ad hominem silencer, dismisser, or denier? Is it justified? Why or why not?

3. Nietzsche is often accused of committing the genetic fallacy when he uses speculation about the origin of Christian moral beliefs as part of his critique of what he called slave morality. In your opinion, does Nietzsche commit a genetic fallacy in the following passage? Why or why not? Can the origin of a moral belief ever show that that moral belief is false or unjustified or indefensible? Why or why not?

   > Let us articulate this new demand: we need a critique of moral values, the value of these values themselves must first be called into question—and for that there is needed a knowldge of the conditions and circumstances in which they grew, under which they evolved and changed, . . . a knowledge of a kind that has never yet existed or even been desired. One has taken the value of these "values" as given, as factual, as beyond all question; one has hitherto never doubted or hesitated in the slightest degree in supposing "the good man" to be of greater value than "the evil man," of greater value in the sense of furthering the advancement and prosperity of man in general (the future of man included). But what if the reverse were true? What if a symptom of regression were inherent in the "good," likewise a danger, a seduction, a poison, a narcotic, through which the present was possibly living at the expense of the future? Perhaps more comfortably, less dangerously, but at the same time in a meaner style, more basely?—So that precisely morality would be to blame if the highest power and splendor actually possible to the type man was never in fact attained? So that precisely morality was the danger of dangers?[2]

[2]Friedrich Nietzsche, *On the Genealogy of Morals*, trans. Walter Kaufmann, in *Basic Writings of Nietzsche* (New York: Random House, 1968), 456. Nietzsche goes on to argue that (slave) morality is the danger of dangers, so the reader is supposed to answer the rhetorical questions at the end of the passage in the affirmative.

APPEALS TO AUTHORITY

Often in the midst of an argument, we cite an authority to back up what we say. As we saw in Chapter 3, this is a standard way of offering assurances. In citing an authority, instead of giving reasons for what we say, we indicate that someone (the authority cited) could give them.

Although logicians sometimes speak of the *fallacy* of appealing to authorities, we should notice in the first place that there is often nothing wrong with citing authorities or experts to support what we say. An authority is a person or institution with a privileged position concerning certain information. Through training, a doctor is an expert on certain diseases. A person who works in the Department of Agriculture can be an expert on America's soybean production. Someone who grew up in the swamps might be an expert on trapping muskrats. Because some people stand in a better position to know things than others, there is nothing wrong with citing them as authorities. In fact, an appeal to experts and authorities is essential if we are to make up our minds on subjects outside our own range of competence.

At the same time, appeals to authority can be abused, and there are some obvious questions we should ask whenever such an appeal is made. Most obviously, we should always ask whether the person cited is, in fact, an authority in the area under discussion. If the answer to this question is "No," then we are dealing with a *fallacy of relevance.* For example, being a movie star does not qualify a person to speak on the merits of a particular brand of toothpaste. Endorsements by athletes of hair creams, deodorants, beer, and automobiles are in the same boat. Of course, we have to be careful in making this charge. It is possible that certain athletes make systematic studies of deodorants before giving one deodorant their endorsement. But it is not likely.

Most people realize that athletes, movie stars, and the like are featured in advertisements primarily to attract attention and not because they are experts concerning the products they are endorsing. It is more surprising how often the wrong authorities are brought in to judge serious matters. To cite one example, Uri Geller had little difficulty convincing a group of distinguished British scientists that he possessed psychic powers. In particular, he was able to convince them that he could bend spoons by mental powers alone. In contrast, James Randi, a professional magician, had little difficulty detecting and duplicating the tricks that bamboozled the scientific observers. The remarkable feature of this case was not that a group of scientists could be fooled by a magician, but rather that these scientists assumed that they had the expertise necessary to decide whether a paranormal phenomenon had taken place or not. After all, the most obvious explanation of Geller's feats was that he had somehow cheated. To test this possibility, what was needed was not a scientist with impeccable scholarly credentials, but a magician who could do the same tricks himself and therefore knew what to look for.[3]

[3]For an entertaining and instructive account of this case, see James Randi, *The Magic of Uri Geller* (New York: Ballantine Books, 1975).

It is, of course, difficult to decide whether someone is an expert in a field when you yourself are not, but certain clues will help you make this decision. If the supposed authority claims to have knowledge of things that he or she could not possibly possess (for example, about private conversations the person could not have heard), then you have little reason to trust other things that person has to say. You know that he or she has no qualms about making things up. Furthermore, it is often possible to spot-check certain claims in order to make sure that they are correct. It may take one expert to determine another, but it often takes little more than good common sense and an unwillingness to be fooled to detect a fraud.

Even in those cases in which it is clear that the person cited is an expert in the field, we can still ask whether the question is of the kind that can now be settled by an appeal to experts. It is important to raise this question, because sometimes the best experts simply get things wrong. For example, in 1932 Albert Einstein, who was surely an expert in the field, declared, "There is not the slightest indication that [nuclear] energy will ever be obtainable. It would mean that the atom would have to be shattered at will." Just a year later, the atom was, in fact, split. Even so, a leading British physicist, Ernest Lord Rutherford, insisted that the splitting of the atom would not lead to the development of nuclear power, saying, "The energy produced by the atom is a very poor kind of thing. Anyone who expects a source of power from the transformation of these atoms is talking moonshine."[4] Given the knowledge available at the time, both Einstein and Rutherford may have been justified in their claims, but their assertions were, after all, more speculations than scientifically supported statements of fact. The lesson to be learned from this is that the best experts are sometimes fallible, and become more fallible when they go beyond established facts in their discipline to speculate about the future.

Although the next question may seem obvious, we often forget to ask whether the authority has been cited correctly. When a person cites an authority, he or she is making a factual claim that so-and-so holds some particular view. Sometimes the claim is false. Here is an example:

According to medical authorities, the rash from poison ivy is contagious when it is oozing.

If someone told you this, you would probably believe it. In fact, the citation is incorrect. According to medical authorities, the rash from poison ivy is never contagious. Yet many people hold that it is contagious, and they think

[4]Both quotations are from Christopher Cerf and Victor Navasky, *The Experts Speak* (New York: Pantheon Books, 1984), 215. This work contains a marvelous collection of false and sometimes just plain stupid things that have been claimed by experts. One notable example is the remark made by the Union general John B. Sedgwick just before being fatally shot in the head by a Confederate marksman: "They couldn't hit an elephant at this dist—"(135).

that they have medical opinion on their side. It is hard to deal with people who cite authorities incorrectly, for we do not carry an almanac or encyclopedia around with us. Yet, again, it is a good idea to spot-check appeals to authority, for, short of lying, people often twist authorities to support their own opinions.

It is also worth asking whether the authority cited can be trusted to tell the truth. To put this more bluntly, we should ask whether a particular authority has any good reason to lie or misrepresent facts. Presumably, the officials who know most about food production in China will be the heads of the various agricultural bureaus. But it would be utterly naive to take their reports at face value. Inadequate agricultural production has been a standing embarrassment of the Chinese economy. As a consequence, there is pressure at every level to make things look as good as possible. Even if the state officials were inclined to tell the truth, which is a charitable assumption, the information they receive is probably not very accurate.

Experts also lie because it can bring fame and professional advancement. Science, sometimes at the highest level, has been embarrassed by problems of the falsification and misrepresentation of data. Consider the case of Sir Cyril Burt. Burt's research concerned the inheritance of intelligence. More specifically, he wanted to show that there is a significant correlation between the IQs of parents and their children. The difficulty was to find a way to screen out other influences—for example, that of home environment. To overcome this, Burt undertook a systematic study of identical twins who had been separated at birth and raised in various social settings. His study revealed a very high correlation between the IQs of these twins, and that gave strong reason to believe that IQ, to some significant extent, depends on heredity rather than environment. Unfortunately, Burt's data, or at least a significantly large portion of it, were cooked—that is, made up.

It is interesting that Burt's bogus research could go unchallenged for so long. It is also interesting how he was finally unmasked. First, to many his results seemed too good to be true. He claimed to have found more than fifty identical twins who had been separated at birth and raised in contrasting environments. Given the rarity of such creatures, that is a very large number to have found. Second, the correlations he claimed to find were extremely high—indeed, much higher than those usually found in research in this area. Both of these facts raised suspicions. Stephen Jay Gould describes Burt's final undoing as follows:

> Princeton psychologist Leon Kamin first noted that, while Burt had increased his sample of twins from fewer than twenty to more than fifty in a series of publications, the average correlation between pairs for IQ remained unchanged to the third decimal place—a statistical situation so unlikely that it matches the vernacular definition of impossible. Then, in 1976, Oliver Gillie, medical correspondent of the London *Sunday Times*, elevated the charge from inexcusable carelessness to conscious fakery. Gillie discovered, among many other things, that Burt's two "collaborators" . . . the women who supposedly collected and processed his data,

either never existed at all, or at least could not have been in contact with Burt while he wrote the papers bearing their names.[5]

Outright fraud of this kind, especially by someone so highly placed, is admittedly uncommon. Yet it does occur, and it provides a good reason for being suspicious of authorities, especially when their results have not been given independent confirmation.

One last question we can ask is why the appeal to authority is being made at all. To cite an authority is to give assurances. As we noticed earlier, people usually give assurances to strengthen weak points in their arguments. It is surprising how often we can see what is wrong with an argument just by noticing where it is backed by appeals to authority. Beyond this, we should be suspicious of arguments that rely on too many authorities. (We might call this the fallacy of excessive footnotes.) Good arguments tend to stand on their own.

To go back to the beginning, in our complicated and specialized world, reliance on experts and authorities is unavoidable. Yet we can still be critical of appeals to authority by asking these questions:

1. Is the cited authority in fact an authority in the area under discussion?
2. Is this the kind of question that can now be settled by expert opinion?
3. Has the authority been cited correctly?
4. Can the cited authority be trusted to tell the truth?
5. Why is an appeal to authority being made at all?

If the answers to 1–4 are "Yes," then the appeal to authority is probably justified. Still, even the best appeal to authority is an inductive argument, and even the best authorities make mistakes, so the conclusion of any appeal to authority might turn out to be false. We can reduce errors by appealing to better authorities, but no authority can guarantee the truth.

EXERCISE III

Answer the five questions in the text about each of the following appeals to authority, and then decide whether each appeal to authority is legitimate or fallacious.

1. The surgeon general says that smoking is hazardous to your health, so it is.
2. The surgeon general says that abortion is immoral, so it is.
3. Michael Jordan says that Air Jordan sneakers are springier, so they must be springier.
4. This must be a great movie, because the billboard says that *Time* magazine called it "terrific."

[5]Stephen Jay Gould, *The Mismeasure of Man* (New York: W. W. Norton, 1981), 235.

5. My friend Joe says that this new movie is hilarious, so it must be worth watching.

6. Ben and Jerry's ice cream must be the best, because Fat Fred eats more ice cream than anyone else I know, and he says that Ben and Jerry's is the best.

7. But Dad, I *did* leave the party by midnight, just like you told me to. Just ask Anna or Lars or Katie or Greg or Sara or Carol or Ann. Even the parking attendant, Jeff, saw me leave. And I also saw Nick and Hannah and Andrew and Linnea in the parking lot, so they will also tell you that I am telling the truth. Please, Dad, believe me!

8. There must be life on other planets, because many great scientists are looking for it, so they must think it is there.

9. Lefty Lopez must be the best pitcher of the year, because he won the Cy Young Award (awarded by the Baseball Writers Association to the best pitcher of the year).

10. Vanna must be the most beautiful woman in America, because she won the Miss America contest.

11. There were 250,000 protesters at the rally, because organizers gave that figure.

12. There were 25,000 protesters at the rally, because its opponents said so.

13. True Christians ought to give away all their money, because the Bible says, "Blessed are the poor."

MORE FALLACIES OF RELEVANCE

Questions like those used to evaluate appeals to authority can also be used to assess some other common styles of reasoning that are often accused of being fallacious. Here is one example:

> The American people are convinced that, if we get involved in North Korea, we will be stuck there for a long time. So we shouldn't invade in the first place.

This argument, of course, depends on suppressed premises. On one reconstruction, the argument is that, because Americans fear getting stuck in North Korea, they oppose American involvement, and a democratic government should not do what the people oppose, so we should not get involved in North Korea. The argument also seems to suggest another reason why America should not get involved—namely, that if we do, our troops will be stuck in North Korea. The only reason given for believing this is that lots of American people believe it. So the argument seems to be that, because so many Americans believe it, it must be true.

Such an argument is not an appeal to authority, since no person is claimed to be an authority or an expert. Instead, the argument is an *appeal to popular opinion.* When the popular opinion is supposed to have been shared for a long time, the argument can be called an *appeal to tradition.* Such arguments assume that, when many people agree on some issue, they are likely to be right. This assumption is often incorrect. An opinion might be shared by many people just because they all learned it from a common source, such as television or some prominent politicians. Then the shared opinion is not reliable unless its source is reliable. Of course, the shared opinion *might* be true; America might get stuck in North Korea if it does get involved. But the argument for this conclusion is still fallacious, because the mere fact that an opinion is widely held is not enough to show that the opinion is true.

Although such appeals to popular opinion are often fallacious, there are also some areas where popular opinion is evidence of truth. If most people think that a book is entertaining and easy to understand, then it is entertaining and easy to understand. If most people think that the sky looks blue, this is evidence that the sky does look blue. Thus, not all appeals to popular opinion are defective or fallacious.

To determine whether or not a particular appeal to popular opinion is fallacious, we need to ask questions that are much like the questions we asked about appeals to authority. These include:

1. Is this opinion actually widely held?
2. Is this the kind of area where popular opinion is likely to be right?
3. Why is an appeal to popular opinion being made at all?

Even when superficial examination reveals that an appeal to popular opinion is fallacious, such arguments still seem to convince many people. This might be because many people want to agree with others so that they will be popular and will not have to think for themselves.

Other appeals are not to beliefs, but instead to emotions. One common form of appeal to emotion is an *appeal to pity.* Defense lawyers often dwell on the sad circumstances in which a defendant grew up or on how badly the defendant's family will be hurt if the defendant goes to prison. Such an appeal to pity might show that the defendant should not receive the maximum sentence. But when such an appeal to pity is used to argue that the defendant is not guilty or should not be found guilty, then the argument is almost always fallacious.

Appeals to emotion can also be positive. Many advertisements work by linking a product to positive feelings. Everyone knows that a car does not become better just because it is displayed in beautiful scenery, but it is amazing how much the scenery in advertisements can affect people's inclinations to buy a certain car. Similarly, advocates of a treaty or government program often paint pictures of how wonderful life will be if the treaty or program works out well. Such appeals to emotion might provide some reason to adopt their plan, but these arguments can be very misleading if it is unlikely that everything will work out so well and if serious dangers will arise when something goes wrong. Thus, even when emotional reactions are relevant to some extent, one must be careful not to let them cloud the other side of the issue.

EXERCISE IV

For each of the following arguments, indicate whether it is an appeal to popular opinion, an appeal to tradition, or an appeal to emotion. (The argument might fit into more than one of these categories. If so, explain why.) Then determine whether it is fallacious, and why.

1. For centuries throughout Europe, women were burned for being witches, so there must have been lots of witches.

2. "Polls show an overwhelming majority of the American people want a lot less immigration or even an immigration moratorium. . . . These are persistent results over time. Most of the people cannot be wrong all of the time!"[6]

3. There must be life on other planets, because most people think there is. Just read a few tabloids.

4. Most people who live in the United States think that it is the greatest country ever, so it must be.

5. There are more Buddhists than followers of any other religion, so there must be more truth in Buddhism.

6. Incest must be immoral, because people all over the world for many centuries have seen it as immoral.

7. The Golden Rule is accepted in almost every system of ethics both in the past and in the present, so there is probably something to it.

8. Chris must not be guilty, because twelve jurors, who saw all the evidence, agreed on a verdict of not guilty.

[6]From an advertisement placed by FAIR (Federation for American Immigration Reform), *Atlantic Monthly* (June 1995), 67.

ADVANCED SECTION: A COMMON FORM FOR FALLACIES OF RELEVANCE

There are so many different fallacies of relevance that one might wonder whether anything important is common to them all. Such fallacies arise when the premises are not adequately related to the conclusion. But to say that is not to say much, until we get a better idea of when the relation between premises and conclusion is adequate.

One illuminating approach to this issue treats the kinds of arguments that are subject to fallacies of relevance as statistical applications.[7] As explained in Chapter 9, statistical applications take the following form:

X percent of Fs are G.
a is an F.

∴ a is G (or is probably G).

[7]This approach to fallacies of relevance was, to our knowledge, first used by Merrilee Salmon in *Introduction to Logic and Critical Thinking* (San Diego: Harcourt Brace Jovanovich, 1984). Our discussion is greatly indebted to her work.

Different fallacies of relevance share this form but replace the variables "*F*" and "*G*" with different values.

In ad hominem deniers, "*F*" refers to a kind of person, and "*G*" refers simply to being false. More fully spelled out, ad hominem deniers look like this:

> A high percentage of what is said by people of this kind in
>   circumstances of this kind about topics of this kind is false.
> This statement was made by a person of this kind in circumstances
>   of this kind about a topic of this kind.
> ———————————————————————————————
> ∴ This statement is (probably) false.

Arguments with this form, like other statistical applications, can be strong or weak. The argument is strong if the group of people really is unreliable in the way that the first premise claims. This is the case when "people of this kind" refers to perjurers for hire, as in the example of Louie in the section on ad hominem arguments. If, however, "people of this kind" refers to a speaker's sex, race, religion, and so on, then the first premise will usually not be true, because people in these groups are no more likely than others to believe or say things that are false. Only prejudice could lead anyone to accept such a premise. That explains why such ad hominem arguments are fallacies. A similar analysis applies to other genetic fallacies.

Appeals to authority share the same form but reach the opposite conclusion, because "*G*" refers to being true, instead of to being false. Here is a familiar example that was discussed above:

> A high percentage of what is said by the surgeon general in his official
>   capacity about the medical effects of activities is true.
> The statement that smoking is hazardous to your health was made by
>   the surgeon general in his official capacity.
> ———————————————————————————————
> ∴ The statement that smoking is hazardous to your health is (probably)
>   true.

As we saw, different kinds of authorities get it right different percentages of the time on different topics. That is why the first premise needs to refer to the kind of authority, to the circumstances, and also to the topic. When the authority is properly qualified, such arguments can be strong, even though, like all statistical syllogisms, they are inductive, deductively invalid, and hence defeasible.

Fallacious appeals to authorities can now be seen as instances of common mistakes about reference classes that often weaken statistical applications, as we saw in Chapter 9. Recall Uri Geller's claim to be able to bend spoons with his mind, discussed in the section on appeals to authority. When the scientists were convinced by Geller's demonstration, Geller's followers applied the generalization that most of what scientists believe about physical objects (such as spoons) is true. However, they overlooked a narrower reference class. Much of what scientists believe in response to magic tricks is not true.

This new claim (about scientists' beliefs in response to magic) includes more of the relevant information than did the original premise (about scientists' beliefs in general). That is why the original argument is weak and fallacious.

Many fallacies of relevance can be analyzed as statistical applications that commit mistakes of kinds that are also common for other statistical applications: They depend on false premises or overly general reference classes. This analysis reveals what is common to these fallacies of relevance. It also explains what we need to look out for in order to avoid such fallacies. Specifically, we need to make sure that the premises are true when the reference class is properly specified.

EXERCISE V

Reconstruct the arguments in Exercises II, III, and IV as statistical applications in standard form.

FALLACIES OF VACUITY

Arguments are fallacious when they don't go anywhere. This happens in two main ways. Sometimes an argument begins by assuming its conclusion or some independent reason for its conclusion, so the argument makes no real progress beyond its own assumptions. In other cases, the argument's conclusion is empty, so the argument has nowhere in particular to go. Both kinds of argument are vacuous, so we call them *fallacies of vacuity.*

CIRCULAR REASONING

One purpose of arguments is to establish the truth of a claim to someone who doubts it. In a typical situation, one person, A, makes a claim; another person, B, raises objections to it; then A tries to find arguments that respond to the objections and justify the original statement. Schematically:

A asserts that p is true.

B raises objections x, y, and z against it.

A then offers reasons to overcome these objections.

What must A's responses be like to meet B's objections? To start with the simplest case, A cannot meet B's challenge simply by repeating the original assertion. If someone is maintaining that arms races inevitably lead to war, it will not help to offer as a justification for this the very claim that is in dispute—that arms races inevitably lead to war. The argument would look like this:

Arms races inevitably lead to war.
_____
∴ Arms races inevitably lead to war.

This argument is, of course, *valid*, since the premise cannot be true without the conclusion being true as well. Furthermore, if the premise is true, then the argument is also *sound*. All the same, the argument has no force in this conversational setting because any objection that B has to the conclusion is straight off an objection to the premise, since they are identical.

Unfortunately, people usually do not make it so easy to tell when they reason in a circle. Often, circular reasoning is disguised by restating the conclusion in different words. Someone might argue that arms races inevitably lead to war, since countries always eventually start fighting each other after they have built up their supplies of weapons in an attempt to gain more firepower than their adversaries. This premise means the same as the conclusion, because an arms race is just a competition in which countries build up their supplies of weapons to accumulate more than their adversaries; so this reasoning is still circular. Another way to hide circular reasoning is to put forward a statement first as a conclusion to be proved, and then only much later—after several subarguments or tangents—use the same statement as a premise in its own behalf. Although this trick is often hard to detect in a long and complex argument, such reasoning is still indirectly circular if any premise in a chain of arguments repeats or restates the eventual conclusion. Thus, we have *circular reasoning* if and only if one of the premises that is used directly or indirectly to support a conclusion is equivalent to the conclusion itself.

BEGGING THE QUESTION

Reasoning in a circle is normally bad reasoning, but it is not easy to say exactly what is bad about it. The problem with circular reasoning becomes clearer when we notice that the same defect is shared by arguments that are not circular. Instead of arguing, "Arms races inevitably lead to war, so they do," we could avoid circularity by adding a few words to get this new argument:

> If arms races don't inevitably lead to war, then I'm a monkey's uncle.
> I'm not a monkey's uncle.
>
> ∴ Arms races inevitably lead to war.

This argument is not circular, because neither premise repeats the conclusion. It is also valid and might even be sound. Still, it is no good as an argument for the same reason as "Arms races inevitably lead to war, so they do." The problem lies in its first premise. The consequent of the first premise ("I'm a monkey's uncle") is obviously false, so that first premise is false unless its antecedent ("Arms races don't inevitably lead to war") is false. But that means that the conclusion must be true in order for the first premise to be true. Thus, one could not have any reason to believe the first premise if one did not already have the very same reason to believe the conclusion. One's reason to believe the premise depends on one's prior belief in the conclusion or on one's reason to believe the conclusion. In short, one has no independent reason for the premise.

This is a problem if the conclusion is disputed and the argument is being used to get someone who rejects the conclusion to change his or her mind and accept it. Anyone who rejects the conclusion will simply reject the premise. For the argument to show someone that he or she ought to accept the conclusion, the arguer would need an independent reason to believe the premise. But then that independent reason does all of the real work, and the argument as stated does nothing to establish the conclusion. It is, in a word, vacuous.

The point is not just that an opponent would deny the premise. If that were enough to make an argument fail, then arguments would almost never succeed. The point is instead that, when an opponent objects to a premise, the arguer cannot show that the opponent has reason to accept that premise simply by asserting what the opponent denies. Bare assertion and reassertion do nothing to overcome objections. To show that the opponent has reason to accept the premise and, hence, the conclusion, the arguer needs some independent evidence for the premise. Because there needs to be—but cannot be—an independent reason for the premise "If arms races don't inevitably lead to war, then I'm a monkey's uncle," the argument with this premise must beg the question in any normal context.

More generally, we can say that an argument *begs the question* in a context if and only if (1) it depends on a premise that is not supported by any reason that is independent of the conclusion, and (2) there is a need for such an independent reason. In these circumstances, we can also say that the premise begs the question.

The need for an independent justification arises from the context and the purpose for which the argument is being used. A premise *needs* support from an independent reason, for example, when it is in dispute or subject to objection and the arguer's goal is to give an audience some reason to accept the premise and, on that basis, to accept the conclusion. That such a need for an independent reason exists but is not satisfied explains why the argument can be criticized by saying that it commits the fallacy of begging the question.

This fallacy is often very hard to detect, both because it is affected by the context and also because there are many ways to hide the fact that a premise depends on the conclusion. Consequently, people often use arguments that beg the question when they have nothing better to say, especially on a controversial issue. It is common, for example, to hear an argument something like the following:

> It's always wrong to murder human beings.
> <u>Capital punishment involves murdering human beings.</u>
>
> ∴ Capital punishment is wrong.

Here the first premise is true by definition, since calling something murder implies that it is a wrongful killing. The second premise is, however, question-begging, for calling capital punishment murder assumes the point at issue, that is, that capital punishment is wrong. As a result, anyone who objects to the conclusion would or should raise exactly the same objections to the second premise, and one could not give any adequate reason for the second premise without first arguing for the conclusion.

More subtly than this, opponents of abortion typically refer to the human fetus as an unborn baby or simply as a baby. It may seem a matter of indifference how the fetus is referred to, but this is not true. One of the central points in the debate over abortion is whether the fetus has the status of a person and thus has the rights that any person has. It is generally acknowledged in our society that babies are persons and therefore have the rights of persons. By referring to the fetus as an unborn baby (or simply as a baby), a point that demands argument is taken for granted, without argument. That counts as begging the question. Of course, many opponents of abortion argue for the claim that a human fetus has the moral status of a person and thus do not beg this central question in the debate. Still, if they give no such independent argument, then they do beg the question.

Similarly, if someone argues for the pro-choice position simply on the grounds that a woman has a right to control the destiny of her own body, this also begs an important question, because it takes for granted the claim that the fetus is part of a woman's body, not an independent being with rights of its own. Of course, defenders of the pro-choice position need not beg the question in this way, but they often do. Whether a particular argument or premise is question-begging will depend on whether there is a need for an independent reason, which in turn depends on the context in which the argument is given. One way for an argument to beg the question is for it to rely, either explicitly or implicitly, on an unsupported premise that is a matter of dispute in the particular argumentative context. Thus, referring to a human fetus as a baby will be question-begging in contexts in which the moral status of the fetus is at issue, but it may not be question-begging when this is not an issue.

Because begging the question depends in this way on context, we should be careful before charging opponents with begging the question. Some people charge every opponent with begging the question, almost like a knee-jerk reaction. However, even if an opponent uses a premise that you reject, this does not yet show that the argument begs the question, since your opponent might have plenty of independent evidence for the premise. Before you accuse people of begging the question, you should ask them to give you their reasons for the disputed premise. If they can come up with an independent reason, then they did not beg the question, and you might learn something from them. However, if they do not have any independent reason for the premise, then they did indeed beg the question.

EXERCISE VI

For each of the following arguments, does it involve circular reasoning? Does it beg the question in any context? If so, in which contexts? Explain your answers.

1. A student of mine told me that I am her favorite professor, and I know that she is telling the truth, because no student would lie to her favorite professor.

2. Intoxicating beverages should be banned, because they can make people drunk.

3. Capitalism is the only correct economic system, because without it free enterprise would be impossible.

4. Free trade is good for the country, because it brings all the advantages of an unimpeded flow of goods between countries.

5. Gun-control laws are wrong, because they violate the citizen's right to bear arms.

6. When *B* applies for a job from *A:*

   A: How can we know that you are trustworthy?

   B: Mr. Davidson will write me a recommendation.

   A: But why should we trust him?

   B: I assure you that he is honest.

7. The Bible is the inerrant word of God, because God speaks only the truth, and repeatedly in the Bible God tells us that the Bible consists of his words.

8. We have to accept change, because without change there is no progress.

9. Premarital sex is wrong, because premarital sex is fornication, and fornication is a sin.

10. The drinking age should be lowered to eighteen, because eighteen-year-olds are mature enough to drink.

11. We should never give security clearances to homosexuals, because they can be blackmailed into revealing classified information. They are subject to blackmail, because we will revoke their security clearances if we find out they are gay.

12. People with suicidal tendencies are insane, because they want to kill themselves.

13. Jeffrey can't really be insane, because he says he is.

DISCUSSION QUESTIONS (ADVANCED)

1. Explanations are often presented in the form of arguments, and sometimes these arguments seem circular. Here is one example:

   Tom: Why are so many people moving out of Claremont this year?

   Sue: Because its economy is going down so fast.

   Tom: But why is its economy going down so fast?

   Sue: Because so many people are moving out of town.

   Does Sue argue in a circle? If so, does this show that her explanations beg the question? Are they defective in some other way?
   Next consider a second dialogue:

   Amy: Why is Jarred going down on the seesaw right now?

   John: Because Jeremiah is going up on the other side of the seesaw.

   Amy: But why is Jeremiah going up right now?

   John: Because Jarred is going down.

   Does John argue in a circle? If so, does this make his explanations question-begging? Are they defective in some other way? More generally, when, if ever, can circular arguments provide good explanations?

2. Explain John Stuart Mill's argument in the following passage. Do you agree? Why or why not?

   It must be granted that in every syllogism, considered as an argument to prove the conclusion, there is a *petitio principii* [a begging of the question]. When we say,

   > All men are mortal.
   > Socrates is a man.
   >
   > ∴ Socrates is mortal;

   it is unanswerably urged by the adversaries of the syllogistic theory that the proposition, "Socrates is mortal," is presupposed in the more general assumption, "All men are mortal"; that we cannot be assured of the mortality of all men unless we are already certain of the mortality of every individual man. . . . That, in short, no reasoning from generals to particulars can, as such, prove anything, since from a general principle we cannot infer any particulars but those which the principle itself assumes as known.[8]

3. In response to some philosophers who denied the existence of objects in the external world, G. E. Moore held up his hands and argued roughly like this: "Here is one hand. Here is another. Therefore, there are (at least two) objects in the external world."[9] Does this argument beg the question? Why or why not?

[8]John Stuart Mill, *A System of Logic* (London; 1843), book 2, chapter 3, section 2.

[9]G. E. Moore, "Proof of an External World," in Moore, *Philosophical Papers* (London: Allen and Unwin, 1959), 127–50.

4. Suppose Andrea asks, "How many days are there in November?" In response, Cummings says, "Let's see. How does that mnemonic go? Oh yeah: Thirty days has September, April, June, and November. So November has thirty days." Is this argument circular? Does it beg the question? Why or why not?

5. Does the following argument beg the question in any contexts? If so, in which contexts? Why?

Some arguments beg the question.

∴ Some arguments beg the question.[10]

[10]This example comes from Roy Sorensen, "Unbeggable Questions," *Analysis* 56 (January 1966), 51.

SELF-SEALERS

It is characteristic of certain positions that no evidence can *possibly* refute them. This may seem to be a wonderful feature for a position to have. In fact, however, it *usually* makes the position useless. We can start with a silly example. A Perfect Sage claims to be able to predict the future in detail. The Perfect Sage's predictions take the following form:

Two weeks from today at 4:37 you are going to be doing *exactly* what you will be doing.

Of course, whatever you are doing at that time will be exactly what you are doing, so this prediction cannot possibly be wrong. But this is only because it does not tell us anything in particular about the future. *Whatever* happens, the prediction is going to be true, and this is just what is wrong with it. The prediction is *empty* or *vacuous*.

People do not, of course, go around making predictions of this kind, but they do sometimes hold positions that are empty or vacuous in much the same way. A clairvoyant claims to be able to predict the future, but every time a prediction fails, she says that this just proves that someone set up bad vibrations that interfered with her visions. So if the prediction turns out to be true, she claims that this shows her clairvoyance; if it turns out to be false, she cites this as evidence of interference. No matter what happens, then, the clairvoyant's claim to be clairvoyant cannot be refuted. Her claim to clairvoyance is as empty and vacuous as the Perfect Sage's prediction.

Positions that are set up in this way so that nothing can possibly refute them we will call *self-sealers*.[11] A self-sealing position is one that is so constructed that no evidence can possibly be brought against it no matter what happens. This shows its vacuity, and it is precisely for this reason that we reject it.

People do not usually hold self-sealing positions in a blatant way; they tend to back into them. A person who holds that the American economy is controlled by an international Jewish conspiracy will point out people of Jewish extraction (or with Jewish names) who occupy important positions in financial institutions. This at least counts as evidence, though very weak evidence. And there seems to be much stronger evidence on the other side: There are a great many people in these institutions who are not Jews. To counter this claim, the person now argues that many of these other people are secretly Jews or are tools of the Jewish conspiracy. The Jews have allowed some non-Jews to hold important positions in order to conceal their conspiracy. What evidence is there for this? Well, none really, but that only helps prove how clever the Jewish conspiracy is. At this point, the position has become self-sealing, for all evidence cited against the existence of the conspiracy will be converted into evidence for its cleverness.

Self-sealing arguments are hard to deal with, because people who use them will often shift their ground. A person will begin by holding a significant position that implies that facts are one way rather than another, but under the pressure of criticism will self-seal the position so that no evidence can possibly count against it. That is, the person will slide back and forth between two positions—one that is not self-sealed, and so is significant but subject to refutation, and another that is self-sealed, and so is not subject to criticism but is also not significant. The charge that is leveled against a theory that vacillates in this way is that it is either *vacuous* or *false*. It is vacuous if self-sealing, false if not.

One way of challenging a self-sealing position is to ask what possible fact could prove it wrong. This is a good question to ask, but it can be misunderstood and met with the triumphant reply: "Nothing can prove my position wrong, because it is right." A better way to show the insignificance of a self-sealing theory is to put the challenge in a different form: "If your position has any significance, it should tell us that certain things will occur whereas certain other things will not occur. If it cannot do this, it really tells us nothing at all; so please make some specific predictions, and we will see how they come out."

Ideologies and worldviews tend to be self-sealing. The Marxist ideology sometimes has this quality. If you fail to see the truth of the Marxist ideology, that just shows that your social consciousness has not been raised. The very fact that you reject the Marxist ideology shows that you are not yet capable of understanding it and that you are in need of reeducation. This is perfect self-sealing. Sometimes psychoanalytic theory gets involved in this same kind of self-sealing. People who vigorously disagree with certain psychoanalytic claims can be accused of repressing these facts. If a boy denies that he

---

[11]We owe this phrase to Ted Honderich. He owes it, directly or indirectly, to Leon Lipson.

wants to murder his father and sleep with his mother, this itself can be taken as evidence of the strength of these desires and of his unwillingness to acknowledge them. If this kind of reasoning gets out of hand, then psychoanalytic theory also becomes self-sealing and empty. Freud was aware of this danger and warned against it.

So far, we have seen two ways in which an argument can be self-sealing: (1) It can invent an ad hoc or arbitrary way of dismissing every possible criticism. The clairvoyant can always point to interfering conditions without going to the trouble of saying what they are. The anti-Semite can always cite Jewish cleverness to explain away counterevidence. We might call this self-sealing *by universal discounting.* (2) A theory can also counter criticism by attacking its critics. Critics of Marxism are charged with having a decadent bourgeois consciousness that blinds them to the facts of class conflict. The critic's response to psychoanalytic theory is analyzed (and then dismissed) as repression, a reaction formation, or something similar. Here self-sealing is achieved through an ad hominem fallacy. We might call this self-sealing *by going upstairs,* because the theorist is looking down on the critic.

Yet another form of self-sealing is this: (3) Words are used in such a way that a position becomes true *by definition.* For example, a person makes the strong claim that all human actions are selfish. This is an interesting remark, but it seems to be false, for it is easy to think of cases in which people have acted in self-sacrificing ways. To counter these obvious objections, the argument takes the following turn: When a person acts in a self-sacrificing way, what that person *wants* to do is help another even at her own expense. This is her desire or her motive, and that is what she acts to fulfill. So the action is selfish after all, because the person is acting to achieve what she wants. This is a self-sealing move, for it will not help to cite any behavior—even heroic self-destructive behavior—as counterevidence. If a person desires to do something even if it involves the sacrifice of her life, then she acts to fulfill her desire, and the act is again called selfish.

It is not hard to see what has happened in this case. The arguer has chosen to use the word "selfish" in a new and peculiar way: A person is said to act selfishly if she acts to do what she desires to do. This is not what we usually mean by this word. We ordinarily say that a person acts selfishly if she is too much concerned with her own interests at the expense of the interests of others. On this standard use of the word "selfish," there are any number of counterexamples to the claim that all human actions are selfish. But these counterexamples do not apply when the word "selfish" is used in a new way, where "acting selfishly" comes close to meaning just "acting." The point is that under this new meaning of "selfish," it becomes empty (or almost empty) to say that all human actions are selfish. We are thus back to a familiar situation. Under one interpretation (the ordinary interpretation), the claim that all human actions are selfish is interesting but false. Under another interpretation (an extraordinary interpretation), the claim is true but vacuous. The position gets all its *apparent* interest and plausibility from a rapid two-step back and forth between these positions.

Self-sealing arguments are not easy to handle, for they change their form under pressure. The best strategy is to begin by charging a person who uses such an argument with saying something trivial, vacuous, or boring. If, to meet this charge, he or she says something quite specific and important, then argument can proceed along normal lines. But it is not always easy to get down to brass tacks in this way. This becomes clear if you examine an argument between a Marxist and an anti-Marxist, between a psychoanalyst and a critic of psychoanalysis, or between individuals with different religious views. Their positions are often sealed against objections from each other, and then their arguments are almost always at cross-purposes.

Although we have emphasized how large-scale ideologies can become self-sealing, small-scale claims in everyday life are also often sealed against any possible refutation. In fact, a number of common words are used to this end. If someone says, "All true conservatives support school prayer," and a critic points out a conservative who opposes school prayer, then the original claim might be defended by saying, "He is not *truly* (or *really*) a conservative." If this response is trotted out in every case, it turns out that the original claim does not exclude anything. Similarly, the claim that "some students need to work harder than others, but if any student works hard enough, he or she will get good grades" can be protected simply by declaring that any student who works hard but does not get good grades does not work hard *enough*. Finally, someone who says, "If you think it over thoroughly, you will agree with me" can dismiss anyone who disagrees simply by denying that he thought it over *thoroughly*. Of course, these terms—"true," "real," "thorough(ly)," and "enough"—do not always make positions self-sealing. Nonetheless, these and other common terms are often used to seal positions against any possible criticism. When these terms are used in these ways, the resulting positions are empty and can be criticized in the same ways as self-sealing ideologies.

DISCUSSION QUESTIONS

1. Antony Flew wrote:

   Someone tells us that God loves us as a father loves his children. We are reassured. But then we see a child dying of inoperable cancer of the throat. His earthly father is driven frantic in his efforts to help, but his Heavenly Father shows no obvious sign of concern. Some qualification is made—God's love is "not merely human love" or it is "an inscrutable love," perhaps—and we realize that such offerings are quite compatible with the truth of the assertion that "God loves us as a father (but, of course . . .)." We are reassured again. But then perhaps we ask: what is this assurance of God's (appropriately qualified) love worth, what is this apparent guarantee really a guarantee against? Just what would have to happen not merely (morally and wrongly) to tempt us but also (logically and rightly) to entitle us to say "God does not love us" or even "God does not exist"?[12]

How would you answer Flew's question? If the answer to Flew's question were that nothing could entitle us to say this, as Flew suggests, would this show that religious positions like this are self-sealing? That they are empty? Why or why not?

2. During the nineteenth century, evidence mounted that apparently showed that the Earth had existed for millions, perhaps hundreds of millions, of years. This seemed to contradict the account given in Genesis that holds that the Earth was created less than 10,000 years ago. In response to this challenge, Philip Henry Gosse, an English theist, replied roughly as follows: In creating Adam and Eve, God would endow them with navels, and thus it would seem that they had been born in the normal way, and thus also seem that they had existed for a number of years before they were created by God. Beyond this, their hair, fingernails, bones, and so on would all show evidence of growth, again giving evidence of previous existence. The same would be true of the trees that surrounded them in the Garden of Eden, which would have rings. Furthermore, the sediment in the rivers should suggest that they had flowed for very many years in the past. In sum, although the Earth was created fairly recently, God would have created it in a way that would make it appear that it had existed for many more years, perhaps millions of years in the past. Thus, the actual creation of the Earth less than 10,000 years ago is compatible with scientific evidence that suggests that it is much older than this. Evaluate this line of reasoning.

3. Some creationist critics of Darwin's theory of natural selection argue as follows:

Natural selection is a tautologous concept (circular reasoning) because it simply requires the fittest organisms to leave the most offspring and at the same time it identifies the fittest organisms as those that leave the most offspring. Thus natural selection seemingly does not provide a testable explanation of how mutation would produce more fit organisms.[13]

Does this argument show that Darwin's theory is self-sealing? How could defenders of natural selection best respond?

4. Freud claims that, no matter how much they deny it, all women at least unconsciously want to have penises. Could there be any evidence that this claim is false? If so, what kind of evidence, and how could Freud best respond? If not, what does this show about Freud's claim?

[12]Antony Flew, "Theology and Falsification," in *New Essays in Philosophical Theology*, ed. A. Flew and A. MacIntyre (New York: Macmillan, 1955), 98–99.

[13]Duane T. Gish, Richard B. Bliss, and Wendell R. Bird, "Summary of Scientific Evidence for Creation," *Impact* nos. 95–96 (May/June 1981).

5. Christina Hoff Sommers wrote:

The women currently manning—womanning—the feminist ramparts do not take well to criticism. How could they? As they see it, they are dealing with a massive epidemic of male atrocity and a constituency of benighted women who have yet to comprehend the seriousness of their predicament. Hence, male critics must be "sexist" and "reactionary," and female critics "traitors," "collaborators," or "backlashers." This kind of reaction has had a powerful inhibiting effect. It has alienated and silenced women and men alike.[14]

Do you agree? Why or why not? If feminists are guilty of what Sommers claims, does this make their positions self-sealing? Does it make their positions empty?

[14]Christina Hoff Sommers, *Who Stole Feminism? How Women Have Betrayed Women* (New York: Simon and Schuster, 1994), 18.

13

USES OF ARGUMENTS

It is common to assume that the only function of arguments is to justify a disputed claim. This chapter will attempt to correct this one-sided view of arguments. In many cases, the primary purpose of giving an argument is not to establish some truth but is instead to refute another argument or claim. Arguments can also systematize and simplify a theory by revealing interconnections among its terms and claims. Another important use of arguments is to explain why something is true after everybody agrees that it is true. When explanations of conduct are intended to put that conduct in a better light, they serve as excuses, which can also be formulated as arguments. As we shall see, these different uses of argument have distinctive criteria of adequacy, since arguments can be evaluated according to how well they serve the purposes for which they are used.

JUSTIFICATIONS

One of the most prominent uses of arguments is to justify a disputed claim. For example, if I claim that September 11, 2001, was a Tuesday, and you deny this or simply express some doubt, then we might look for a calendar. But suppose we don't have a calendar for 2001. Luckily, we do find a calendar for 2002. Now I can justify my claim to you by presenting this sound argument: The calendar shows that September 11 was on Wednesday in 2002; 2002 was not a leap year, since 2002 is not divisible by four; non-leap years have 365 days, which is 1 more day than 52 weeks; so September 11 must have been on Tuesday in 2001. You should now be convinced.

What have I done? My utterance of this argument has the *effect* of changing your mind, that is, getting you to believe my conclusion. Of course, I might also be able to change your mind by hypnotizing you. But normally I do not want to use hypnosis. I also do not want to change your mind by manufacturing a fake calendar for 2002 with the wrong dates. Such tricks would not satisfy my goals fully. This shows that changing your mind is not all that I am trying to accomplish. What else do I want? My additional aim is to show you that you *should* change your mind, and why. I want to give you a *good reason* to change your mind. I want my argument not only to make you believe my conclusion but also to make you *justified* in believing my conclusion.

The above example is typical of one kind of justification, but there are other patterns. Suppose that I share your doubts about which day of the week it was on September 11, 2001. Then I might use the same argument to justify my belief as well as yours. Indeed, you don't even need to be present. If I am all alone, and I just want to figure out which day of the week it was on September 11, 2001, then I might think in terms of this same argument. Here the goal is not to convince anybody else, but the argument is still used to find a good reason to believe the conclusion.

In cases like these, we can say that the argument is used for *impersonal normative justification*. The justification is normative because the goal is to find a reason that is a good reason. It is impersonal because what is sought is a reason that is or should be accepted as a good reason by everyone capable of grasping this argument. The purpose is to show that there *is* a reason to believe the conclusion, regardless of who *has* a reason to believe it. Other arguments, in contrast, are aimed at specific people, and the goal is to show that those particular people are committed to the conclusion or have a reason to believe the conclusion. Such individualized uses of arguments seek what can be called *personal justification*.

There should be nothing surprising about different people having different reasons. I might climb a mountain to appreciate the view at the top, whereas you climb it to get exercise, and your friend climbs it to be able to talk to you while you climb it. Different people can have different reasons for the same action. Similarly, different people can have different reasons to believe the same conclusion. Suppose that someone is murdered in the ballroom with a revolver. I might have good reason to believe that Miss Peacock did not commit the murder, because I saw her in the library at the time the murder was committed. You might not trust me when I tell you that I saw her, but you still might have good reason to believe that she is innocent, because you believe that Colonel Mustard did it alone. Even if I doubt that Colonel Mustard did it, we still each have our own reasons to agree that Miss Peacock is innocent.

When different people with different beliefs are involved, we need to ask who is supposed to accept the reason that is given in an argument. A speaker might give an argument to show a listener that the speaker has a reason to believe something, even though the speaker knows that the audience does not and need not accept that reason. Suppose that you are an atheist, but I am a fundamentalist Christian, and you ask me why I believe that Jesus rose from the dead. I might respond that the Bible says that Jesus rose from the dead, and what the Bible says must be true, so Jesus rose from the dead. This argument tells you what *my* reasons are for believing what I believe, even if *you* do not accept those reasons. My argument can be used to show you that I have reasons and what my reasons are, regardless of whether those reasons are good ones and whether you believe that they are.

The reverse can also happen. A speaker might give an argument to show a listener that the listener has a reason to believe something, even though the speaker does not accept that reason. Suppose that you often throw loud parties late into the night right next to my bedroom. I want to convince you to stop or at least quiet down. Fortunately, you think that every citizen ought to obey the law. I disagree, for I am an anarchist bent on undermining all governments and laws. Still, I want to get a good night's sleep before the protest tomorrow, so I might argue that it is illegal to make that much noise so late, and you ought to obey the law, so you ought to stop throwing such loud parties. This argument can show *you* that you are committed to its conclusion, even if *I* believe that its premises are false.

Of course, whether I succeed in showing my audience that they have a reason to believe my conclusion depends on who my audience is. My argument won't work against loud neighbors who don't care about the law. Consequently, we need to know who the audience is and what they believe in order to be able to show them what reason they have to believe a conclusion.

In all of these cases, arguments are used to show that someone has a reason to believe the conclusion of the argument. That is why all of these uses can be seen as providing different kinds of justification. The differences become crucial when we try to evaluate such arguments. If my goal is to show you that you have a reason to believe something, then I can be criticized for using a premise that you reject. Your beliefs are no basis for criticism, however, if all I want is to show my own reasons for believing the conclusion. Thus, to evaluate an argument properly, we often need to determine not only whether the argument is being used to justify a belief but also which kind of justification is sought and who the audience is.

DISCUSSION QUESTION

Is it always illegitimate to try to convince someone else to believe something on the basis of a premise that you yourself reject? Why or why not? Consider a variety of cases.

REFUTATIONS

Arguments are also sometimes used to refute other arguments. To *refute* an argument is to show that it is no good. Some writers, however, have incorrectly used the term "refute" to mean something much weaker. They say such things as that Bill Clinton refuted the charges brought against him by those attempting to impeach him, meaning nothing more by this than that he rejected them or replied to them. This, however, is not what the word "refute" means. To refute the charges brought against him, Clinton would have to *give reason to believe* that these charges were erroneous. Refuting a charge requires giving an adequate argument against it. This takes a lot more work than simply rejecting it.

Nonetheless, it is also important to remember that we can refute an argument without proving that its conclusion is false. A refutation of an argument is sufficient if it raises objections that cannot be answered. Consequently, the patterns of successful refutations mirror the criteria for a good argument, because the point of a refutation is to show that one of these criteria has not been met. Refutations, then, take four main forms: (1) We can argue that some of the premises are dubious or even false; (2) we can argue that the conclusion of the argument leads to absurd results; (3) we can show that the conclusion does not follow from the premises;[1] and (4) we can show that the argument begs the question. This last charge was discussed in Chapter 12, so here we will focus on the first three methods of refutation.

COUNTEREXAMPLES

The first main way to attack an argument is to challenge one of its premises. We can argue that there is no good reason to accept a particular premise as true, asking, for example, "How do you know that?" If there is no way to justify a premise, then the argument fails to justify its conclusion. More strongly, we can argue that the premise is actually false. In this second case, we refute an argument by refuting one of its premises.

One common way to refute a premise by showing that it is false is by producing a counterexample. Counterexamples are typically aimed at universal claims. This is true because a *single* contrary instance will show that a universal claim is false. If someone claims that *all* snakes lay eggs, then pointing out that rattlesnakes bear their young alive is sufficient to refute this universal claim. If the person retreats to the weaker claim that *most* snakes lay eggs, the guarding term makes it much harder to refute the claim. A single example of a snake that bears its young alive is not enough to refute this claim; we would have to show that a majority of snakes do not lay eggs. Here, instead of trying to refute the statement, we may ask the person to produce his *argument* in behalf of it. We can then attack this argument. Finally, if the person retreats to the very weak claim that at least *some* snakes lay eggs, then this statement becomes very difficult to refute. Even if it were false (which it is not), to show this we would have to check every fool snake and establish that it does not lay eggs. So, as a rough-and-ready rule, we can say that the stronger a statement is, the more subject it is to refutation; the weaker it is, the less subject it is to refutation.

---

[1]To refute an inductive argument, it is not enough to show that the argument is not valid, because inductive arguments are not intended to be valid. Instead, you need to show that the argument is weak by inductive standards. We discussed inductive arguments and their standards in Chapter 9. We will focus on deductive arguments in this chapter.

When a universal claim is refuted by a single case, that case is a *counterexample*. The pattern of reasoning is perfectly simple: To refute a claim that *everything* of a certain kind has a certain feature, we need find only *one* thing of that kind lacking that feature. In response to a counterexample, many people just repeat the misleading saying, "That's the exception that proves the rule." What most people do not realize is that "proves" originally meant "tests," so all this saying means is that an apparent exception can be used to test a rule or a universal claim. When the exception is a true counterexample, the universal claim fails the test.

There are only two ways to defend a universal claim against a purported counterexample. Because the universal claim says that all things of a certain kind have a certain feature, (1) one can deny that the apparent counterexample really is a thing of that kind, or (2) one can deny that the supposed counterexample really lacks that feature. For example, a defender of the claim that all snakes lay eggs might deny (1) that rattlesnakes are snakes, or (2) that rattlesnakes bear their young alive. Neither of these responses is plausible in this case. That is what makes this counterexample *decisive*.

Other counterexamples are not decisive. Indeed, some purported counterexamples miss their targets entirely. If a person claims that all snakes except rattlesnakes lay eggs, someone might respond with another counterexample: male snakes. This counterexample does not really refute the intended claim, since that claim was meant to be about the methods by which female snakes of various species give birth when they do give birth.

When a counterexample can be answered with a simple clarification or modification that does not affect the basic force of the original claim, it is a *shallow* counterexample. A *deep* counterexample is one that requires the original claim to be modified in more important or interesting ways. Shallow counterexamples can sometimes be fun as jokes, but they are usually not much help in refuting arguments, since basically the same argument can be resurrected in a slightly different form. Indeed, people who give too many shallow counterexamples can be annoying. If you really want to understand a subject matter, you should look for counterexamples that are deep.

Deep and decisive counterexamples are not always easy to think up. Some people are much better at it than others. Socrates was a genius in this respect. He wandered through the streets of ancient Athens questioning various people, often important political figures, challenging them to explain what they meant by various terms such as "justice," "knowledge," "courage," "friendship," and "piety." As narrated by Plato, these exchanges fall into a standard pattern: Socrates asks for a definition of some important notion; after some skirmishing, a definition is offered; Socrates immediately finds a counterexample to this definition; the definition is then changed or replaced by another; once more Socrates produces a counterexample; and so on. With effortless ease, Socrates seemed able to produce counterexamples to any definition or any principle that others offered. There is no better introduction to the art of giving counterexamples than a specimen of the Socratic method.

Theaetetus was a brilliant young man, gifted in mathematics. In the dialogue that bears his name, Theaetetus and Socrates try (unsuccessfully) to arrive at a correct definition of "knowledge." They notice an important difference between knowledge and mere belief: It is possible for someone to *believe* something that is false, but it is not possible for someone to *know* something that is false. This leads Theaetetus to suggest a simple definition of knowledge: Knowledge equals true belief. This proposed definition is refuted in the following exchange:

SOCRATES: [There is] a whole profession to prove that true belief is not knowledge.

THEAETETUS: How so? What profession?

SOCRATES: The profession of those paragons of intellect known as orators and lawyers. There you have men who use their skill to produce conviction, not by instruction, but by making people believe whatever they want them to believe. You can hardly imagine teachers so clever as to be able, in the short time allowed by the clock, to instruct their hearers thoroughly in the true facts of a case of robbery or other violence which those hearers had not witnessed.

THEAETETUS: No, I cannot imagine that; but they can convince them.

SOCRATES: And by convincing you mean making them believe something.

THEAETETUS: Of course.

SOCRATES: And when a jury is rightly convinced of facts which can be known only by an eye-witness, then, judging by hearsay and accepting a true belief, they are judging without knowledge, although, if they find the right verdict, their conviction is correct?

THEAETETUS: Certainly.

SOCRATES: But if true belief and knowledge were the same thing, the best of jurymen could never have a correct belief without knowledge. It now appears that they must be different things.[2]

One thing to notice about this discussion is that Theaetetus does not dig in his heels and insist that the ignorant members of the jury do know that the person is innocent provided only that they believe it and it is true. Faced with the counterexample, he retreats at once. Why is this? Why not stay with the definition and reject the counterexample as false? The answer is that for many concepts, there is general agreement about their application to particular cases, even if there is no general agreement about a correct definition. To take an extreme example, everyone agrees that Hitler was a dictator (even Hitler), and no one supposes that Thomas Jefferson was a dictator (even his enemies). So any definition of "dictator" must be wrong if it implies that Hitler was not a dictator or that Thomas Jefferson was a dictator. Of course, people do disagree about borderline cases, so there might be no perfectly exact definition of "dictator." Nonetheless, any definition that does not square with the clear cases can be refuted by citing one of these clear cases as a counterexample.

Ethics is an area where arguments often turn on counterexamples. Consider the traditional moral precept "Do unto others as you would have them do unto you." This principle captures an important moral insight, but, if taken quite literally, it is also subject to counterexamples. Jones, a sadomasochist, enjoys beating other people. When asked whether he would like to be treated in that way, he replies, "Yes." It is obvious that the Golden Rule was not intended to approve of Jones's behavior. The task, then, is to reformulate this rule to avoid this counterexample. That is not as easy as it might seem.

No discussion of counterexamples is complete without a mention of the Morgenbesser retort. Though the exact story is now shrouded in the mists of time, it has come down to us from the 1950s in the following form: In a lecture, a British philosopher remarked that he knew of many languages in which a double negative means an affirmative, but not one language in which a double affirmative means a negative. From the back of the room came Morgenbesser's retort: "Yeah, yeah."

EXERCISE I

Find a counterexample to each of the following claims, if possible.

> Example: *Claim:* "Sugar" is the only word in which an *s* is pronounced *sh.*
> *Counterexample:* Oh, sure.

1. No prime number is even.
2. Three points always determine a plane.
3. Balloons that are filled with helium always rise in the air.
4. All mammals bear their young live.
5. You can never get too much of a good thing.
6. What you don't know can't hurt you.
7. You can't be too careful.
8. You should never look a gift horse in the mouth.
9. It is always wrong to tell a lie.
10. You should never ask someone else to do something that you are not willing to do yourself.
11. If lots of people do something, then it must not be wrong for me to do it.
12. If it would be horrible for everyone to do something, then it would be morally wrong for anyone to do it.
13. If it would not be horrible for everyone to do something, then it would not be morally wrong for anyone to do it.
14. Wherever you use the word "nearly," you could use the word "almost" instead, without affecting the truth or the good sense of what you have said.

EXERCISE II

There cannot possibly be any counterexamples to the following claims. Explain why.

1. There is life on the moon.
2. Killing is usually wrong.
3. Any short person is a person.
4. Every horse is an animal.
5. $2 + 2 = 4$.
6. Everything with a size has a shape.
7. Everything that is green has a shape.
8. There's no way to turn a right-hand glove around to get a left-hand glove.

DISCUSSION QUESTIONS

1. Could there be any counterexample to the claim that no ball is both red all over and green all over at the same time? Why or why not?
2. How can the Golden Rule best be reformulated to avoid the above counterexample of the sadomasochist? Can you think of any counterexamples to this reformulation of the Golden Rule?
3. Is the Morgenbesser retort a shallow counterexample or a deep counterexample? Why?
4. When theologians claim that God can do anything, atheists sometimes respond that God cannot make a stone that is so large that God cannot lift it, or that God cannot make a circle with four sides. Are these really counterexamples to the theologians' claim? Why or why not?
5. Suppose there are only two balls in a bag, and someone claims, "Most of the balls in the bag are red." Does a single black ball in the bag refute this claim? Is it a counterexample to this claim? Does this show that counterexamples can refute some claims that are not universal?
6. When people today respond to counterexamples by saying, "That's the exception that proves the rule," they usually do not mean, "That's the exception that tests the rule," which was its original meaning. What do they mean?
7. St. Augustine tells us that he was captivated by astrology until his conversion to Christianity. He then abandoned it, he says, for the following reason:

> I turned my attention to the case of twins, who are generally born within a short time of each other. Whatever significance in the natural order the astrologers may attribute to this interval of time, it is too short to be appreciated by human observation and no allowance can be made for it in the charts which an astrologer has to consult in order to cast a true horoscope. His predictions, then, will not be true, because he would have consulted the same charts for both Esau and Jacob and would have made the

same predictions for each of them, whereas it is a fact that the same things did not happen to them both. Therefore, either he would have been wrong in his predictions or, if his forecast was correct, he would not have predicted the same future for each. And yet he would have consulted the same chart in each case. This proves that if he had foretold the truth, it would have been by luck, not by skill.[3]

Exactly which claim by astrologers is St. Augustine trying to refute? Is his counterexample deep? Is it decisive? Why or why not?

8. Could twins also be used to show that IQ is not completely determined by genes? If so, how? If not, why not?

[3]St. Augustine, *Confessions*, trans. R. S. Pine-Coffin (Harmondsworth, England: Penguin Books, 1961), 142.

REDUCTIO AD ABSURDUM

Particular counterexamples can normally be used to refute claims only if those claims are universal, so how can we refute claims that are not universal? One method is to show that the claim to be refuted implies something that is ridiculous or absurd in ways that are independent of any particular counterexample. This mode of refutation is called a *reductio ad absurdum*, which means a reduction to absurdity. Reductios, as they are called for short, can refute many different kinds of propositions. They are sometimes directed at a premise in an argument, but they are also used to refute a conclusion. This method of refutation will not show exactly *what* is wrong with the argument for that conclusion, but it will show that *something* is wrong with the argument, because it cannot be sound if its conclusion is false. That might be enough in some situations.

For example, suppose someone argues that because there is a tallest mountain and a heaviest human, there must also be a largest integer. We might respond by arguing as follows: Suppose there is a largest integer. Call it N. Since N is an integer, $N + 1$ is also an integer. Moreover, $N + 1$ is larger than N. But it is absurd to think that any integer is larger than the largest integer. Therefore, our supposition—that there is a largest integer—must be false.

In this mathematical example a contradiction is derived, but absurdity also comes in other forms. Suppose a neighbor tells a parent, "The local public schools are so bad that you ought to send your kids to private school," and the parent responds, "Do you think I'm rich?" The point of this rhetorical question is that it is absurd to think that the parent is rich, presumably because of her lifestyle or house, which the neighbor can easily see. Without being rich, the parent cannot afford a private school, so the neighbor's advice is useless.

Often the absurdity is derived indirectly. A wonderful example occurred in the English parliamentary debate on capital punishment. One member of

Parliament was defending the death penalty on the grounds that the alterna-tive—life in prison—was much more cruel than death. This claim was met with the following reply: On this view, those found guilty of first-degree murder ought to be given life in prison, and the death penalty should be given to those who commit some lesser offense. The first speaker could respond in several ways, because this reductio depends on background assumptions that the first speaker could question. First, he might deny that the most severe crime should receive the most severe penalty possible. If the first speaker sees life in prison as too cruel to be inflicted on anyone, then he might call for the abolition of life imprisonment and keep the death penalty as the most severe punishment. Alternatively, the first speaker could claim that, even though the death penalty is less severe than life in prison, it is still fitting in some other way for the most severe crime, first-degree murder. Finally, of course, the first speaker could simply *accept* the supposedly absurd result and apply life imprisonment to first-degree murder, while using the death penalty for lesser crimes. In fact, however, the first speaker was unwilling to accept any of these alternatives. He simply tried a rhetori-cal trick and got caught.

These reductios are fairly good, but other reductios fail for a variety of reasons. To succeed in refuting a claim, reductio ad absurdum argument must meet two main requirements. First, the result must really be *absurd*. Often opponents try to reduce a view to absurdity but really only draw out implications of the view that are not absurd at all. For example, in a famous debate in which Thomas Huxley defended a theory of evolution, Bishop Wilberforce asked Huxley whether he had descended from apes on his mother's side or on his father's side of the family. This question was intended to draw laughter from the crowd, and it did, partly because they and Wilberforce thought that any answer to the question would be absurd. Nonetheless, Huxley could respond that he had descended from apes on both sides of his family. Because that response was not really absurd—regardless of how absurd it seemed to Wilberforce—the bishop's attempt did not really refute Huxley's claim.

In other cases, one cannot deny that a certain result really would be absurd, but the reductio still fails because the claim to be refuted does not really *imply* that absurdity. For example, opponents sometimes say that the theory of evolution implies that animals are constantly evolving, so they cannot be divided into separate species. This would be absurd, because it is easy to observe distinct species. The theory of evolution, however, does not really imply this absurdity, so this reductio fails to refute that theory. It fails to meet the second requirement for successful reductios, which is that the claim to be refuted must actually imply the absurdity.

Finally, it is important to notice that reductios can be deep or shallow in much the same way as counterexamples. Sometimes a claim really does imply a result that is absurd, but it can be modified in some minor way so as to avoid the absurd result. For example, if a fan says, "Tiger Woods is better than any golfer ever," someone might respond that Woods is himself a golfer, so this claim implies that Woods is better than himself, which is absurd. Of course, the fan meant to say, "Woods is better than any *other* golfer ever," so this reductio is shallow. The reductio does refute the original form of the claim, but the main force of the claim is restored by the minor modification. A reductio ad absurdum is deep only if it reveals that a claim implies an absurd result that cannot be avoided without modifying the claim in essential respects or giving it up entirely.

In sum, then, a reductio ad absurdum argument tries to show that one claim, X, is false because it implies another claim, Y, that is absurd. To evaluate such an argument, the following questions should be asked:

1. Is Y really absurd?
2. Does X really imply Y?
3. Can X be modified in some minor way so that it no longer implies Y?

If either of the first two questions is answered in the negative, then the reductio fails; if the third question receives an affirmative answer, then the reductio is shallow. Otherwise, the reductio ad absurdum argument is both successful and deep.

EXERCISE III

Evaluate the following reductio ad absurdum arguments by asking the above three questions.

1. CLAIM TO BE REFUTED: Even the worst enemies can become friends.

   REDUCTIO: If people are enemies, they are not friends. If they do become friends, then they are not enemies. So it's absurd to think that enemies can be friends.

2. CLAIM TO BE REFUTED: This ball is both red and green all over.

   REDUCTIO: If it is red, it reflects light within a certain range of wavelengths. If it is green, it reflects light within a different range of wavelengths. These ranges do not overlap, so it is absurd to think that anything can reflect both kinds of light. Thus, a ball cannot be both red and green.

3. CLAIM TO BE REFUTED: Most children in Lake Wobegon are above average (in intelligence).

   REDUCTIO: If so, the average (intelligence) would really be higher than it is; and then it would not be true that most children in Lake Wobegon are above the real average (intelligence).

4. ARGUMENT TO BE REFUTED: Your brain is mostly empty space, because the subatomic particles in it are very far apart.

   REDUCTIO: That's absurd, because my brain is solid, and it works pretty well.

5. CLAIM TO BE REFUTED: Some things are inconceivable.

   REDUCTIO: Consider something that is inconceivable. Since you are considering it, you are conceiving it. But then it is conceivable as well as inconceivable. That is absurd. So nothing is inconceivable.

Spell out a reductio ad absurdum argument to refute each of the following claims. If no such reductio is possible, explain why.

1. Some sisters are nephews.
2. Some fathers were never children.
3. Most students scored better than the median grade on the last test.
4. Almost everyone in this class is exceptional.
5. There is an exception to every universal claim.
6. I know that I do not know anything.
7. Some morally wrong actions are morally permitted.
8. There is a male barber in this town who shaves all and only the men in this town who do not shave themselves. (Hint: does he shave himself?)
9. God exists outside of time, and we will meet him someday.
10. Most of the sentences in this exercise are true.

The legal case of *Plessy v. Ferguson* 163 U.S. 537 (1896), excerpted in Chapter 14, questioned a law requiring racial segregation in railroad cars. Opponents of the law gave the following reductio argument:

> The same argument that will justify the state legislature in requiring railways to provide separate accommodations for the two races will also authorize them to require separate cars to be provided for people whose hair is of a certain color, or who are aliens, or who belong to certain nationalities, or to enact laws requiring colored people to walk upon one side of the street, and white people upon the other, or requiring white men's houses to be painted white, and colored men's black, or their vehicles or business signs to be of different colors, upon the theory that one side of the street is as good as the other, or that a house or vehicle of one color is as good as one of another color.

How do defenders of segregation respond to this argument? Is their response adequate? Is any response adequate? Why or why not?

ATTACKING STRAW MEN

Very often when trying to refute either by counterexample or by reductio, people move too quickly. The general rule is this: Before trying to refute someone's claim, it is important to make sure that you understand his or her position. If you misunderstand what your opponent is claiming, but you go ahead and attack a specific claim anyway, then the claim you attack will not be the claim that your opponent made. You might even fail to refute any position that anyone ever really held. This is called the fallacy of *attacking a straw man*.

Sometimes people attack a straw man intentionally. They mischaracterize their opponents' position on purpose to make their opponents look silly by associating their opponents with a position that is silly. An example comes from Rush Limbaugh, who wrote:

> Liberals tell kids in schools all over America that the best way to protect them-selves from AIDS is to wear condoms while engaging in sexual intercourse. It's a lie. They are imposing a death sentence on kids. The failure rate for condoms is around 17 percent. They're teaching kids to play Russian roulette.[4]

This argument is aimed at a position that almost no liberals hold. Everyone who works in this area recognizes that abstinence is more effective than con-dom use, and teachers—no matter how liberal—usually tell this to students and believe that this should be told to students, even if condoms are also dis-cussed. Moreover, most liberals do not advocate that school-age kids engage in sexual intercourse, even if they do advocate that kids use condoms *if* they engage in sexual intercourse. Thus, it mischaracterizes liberals to say that they are "teaching kids to play Russian roulette."

The fallacy of attacking a straw man can also arise from an honest mis-take. Some people get so wrapped up in their own arguments that they for-get the view against which they are arguing. The opponent can also be partly to blame. If someone states her position obscurely, it might not be clear whether the speaker would go so far as to make a certain claim. Then some-one might attack that further claim, honestly believing that the speaker had adopted it. Alternatively, a critic might refute that further claim simply to make the speaker clarify her position by explicitly saying that that is not what she meant to say. In such ways, it might be useful to refute a position that the speaker does not really hold, even though, of course, doing so does not refute any position that the speaker actually does hold.

EXERCISE V

Do the following arguments attack a straw man? Why or why not?

1. Anyone who thinks that the United States should not have sent troops to Iraq must think that the suffering Saddam Hussein inflicted on his own citizens doesn't matter much.

2. Anyone who thinks the United States should have sent troops to Iraq must think that they will only be there for a short time.

3. Humans could not have been created in the image of God, because God is not a physical being, and only physical beings can have images.

4. Atheists think that God does not exist, so everything is permitted. But even atheists must admit that I would not be permitted to kill them! So atheism is nonsense.

5. The theory of evolution says that humans are not different from apes, but humans are clearly smarter than apes, so the theory of evolution must be wrong.

---

[4]Limbaugh, *See, I Told You So* (New York: Pocket Books, 1993), 222. There are also problems with Limbaugh's claim that condoms have a 17 percent failure rate (whatever that means).

Find three more examples of attacking straw men in your local newspaper.

REFUTATION BY PARALLEL REASONING

Even if its premises and conclusion cannot be refuted by any counterexample or reductio, a deductive argument can also be refuted by showing that it is invalid. We know that an argument is not valid if it starts from true premises and leads to a false conclusion. Often, however, we cannot point this out to refute an argument, because the truth or falsity of the conclusion is the very thing at issue. When this problem arises, a typical device is to point out that by arguing in the same way, or a similar way, we can reach a conclusion that is unsatisfactory.

Here is a simple example:

> Mᴀᴛᴛʜᴇᴡ: If I had a higher salary, I could buy more things; so, if everyone had higher salaries, everyone could buy more things.
>
> Kɪʀsᴛʏ: That's just like arguing that, if one person stands up at a ball game, he will get a better view; so, if everyone stands up, everyone will get a better view.

At first sight, it may not be obvious whether Matthew's style of reasoning is valid or not. Kirsty's response shows that Matthew's argument is invalid by providing an instance in which the same style of reasoning takes us from something true to something that is obviously false, because, if everyone stands up at a ball game, only the tallest people will be able to see better. Kirsty's response also shows *why* Matthew's argument is invalid: Just as one person's ability to see can be affected by other people standing up, because this raises the height that is necessary to see, so one person's ability to buy can be affected by other people having more money, if this raises prices and thereby raises the amount of money that is necessary to buy things.

Refuting an argument by showing that it is *just like* another argument that is obviously no good is a common device in everyday discussions. Here's another example:

> Cᴀʀʏ: Most of the people in this class are college students. Most college students study hard. Therefore, most of the people in this class study hard.
>
> Dᴀᴠɪᴅ: That's just like arguing that most whales live in the sea, and most animals that live in the sea are fish, so most whales are fish.

At first sight, it might not be clear how the second argument could show anything about the first argument. What do whales have to do with students? The point, however, is simply that the two arguments share a basic form. Thus, if the second argument is not valid by virtue of that form, then the first is also not valid by virtue of that same form. The second argument is obviously not valid, since its premises are true but its conclusion is false. This shows that the first argument is not valid, at least by virtue of this shared form. Even though the first argument still might be valid on some other basis, a defender of it at least owes an alternative account of its validity. Often there will be none.

Of course, not every refutation of this kind is so simple or so successful. To understand the criteria that must be met for such a refutation to work, it will be useful to consider a more complex example that reveals some of the ways to respond to a charge of "That's just like arguing . . ." The example concerns proposed legal restrictions on gun ownership. The National Rifle Association (NRA) feared that these restrictions would lead to a total ban on guns, which they opposed, so they widely distributed a bumper sticker that read:

(1) If guns are outlawed, only outlaws will have guns.

The point, presumably, was that most people would add the suppressed premise:

(2) It would be bad if only outlaws had guns,

and reach the conclusion:

(3) Therefore, guns should not be outlawed.

This argument is not completely clear, partly because it is not clear who counts as an "outlaw." Some critics poke fun at this bumper sticker because (1) seems true by definition if outlaws include anyone who breaks any law, because anyone with a gun breaks a law if guns are outlawed. But what the NRA probably means by "outlaws" are people who commit violent crimes, such as robbery and murder. It is not strictly true that these will be the only people with guns if guns are outlawed, since police and some present gun owners would keep their guns. Nonetheless, these exceptions do not touch the NRA's main claim, which is that law-abiding people who would give up their guns if guns were outlawed would then not have guns to defend themselves against violent criminals.

How can an opponent try to refute this argument? There are several possibilities, but what defenders of gun control in fact did was distribute other bumper stickers. One of them read:

(1*) If gum is outlawed, only outlaws will have gum.

The main point might be just to parody the NRA bumper sticker, but, if we take it more seriously, (1*) also suggests an application of the method of refutation by parallel reasoning. The parallel argument would continue like this:

(2*) It would be bad if only outlaws had gum.

(3*) Therefore, gum should not be outlawed.

This conclusion, however, is not obviously false. Indeed, it seems true: People should be allowed to chew gum. Moreover, (2*) seems false, because nothing particularly bad would happen if only outlaws chewed gum. For these reasons, this bumper sticker cannot really refute the original argument. This failure illustrates two general tests: A refutation by parallel reasoning works only if the conclusion of the parallel argument really is unacceptable and only if the premises of the parallel argument really are true.

But opponents of the NRA did not stop there. They distributed a third bumper sticker:

(1**) If guns are outlawed, only outlaws will shoot their children by mistake.

The argument behind this new bumper sticker is again not clear. If it is a straightforward instance of refutation by parallel reasoning, then the parallel argument would add, "It would be bad if only outlaws shot their children by mistake" and conclude, "Guns should not be outlawed." But that is the very conclusion the NRA wants to reach; so this newest argument could not refute the original one. Nonetheless, a different argument might lie behind this third bumper sticker. The point seems to be that gun owners sometimes shoot their children by mistake, and we can minimize such tragedies by reducing the number of gun owners through laws against guns. The argument then runs something like this:

(1**) If guns are outlawed, only outlaws will shoot their children by mistake.

(2**) It would be good if outlaws were the only ones who shot their children by mistake.

(3**) Therefore, guns should be outlawed.

This conclusion would seem false to the NRA, and this argument might also seem to suggest that the same form of reasoning could lead to opposite conclusions: (3) and (3**). Moreover, (2**) seems true. This premise does not say that it is good for outlaws to shoot their children by mistake. Instead, it says that it would be good if nobody else shot their children by mistake. So far, so good. Notice, however, that this latest argument, (1**)–(3**), does not really have the same form as the original argument, (1)–(3), because (2**) and (3**) are about what is good and what ought to be law, whereas (2) and (3) are about what is bad and what ought not to be law.

The next question is whether this disanalogy is *important*. If not, the latest bumper sticker still might refute the original one. The NRA, however, might argue that this difference *is* important. The fact that a law has bad effects overall *does* show that the law should not be passed, whereas the fact that a law would have good effects overall is *not* enough to show that the law should be passed, since the law still might violate individual rights that cannot be overridden by good effects on others. This claim is controversial, but, if it can be defended, then this parallel argument, (1**)–(3**), fails to show that the original argument, (1)–(3), is invalid. More generally, then, a refutation by parallel reasoning works only if the two arguments really do have relevantly similar structures—that is, only if one argument really is *just like* the other in relevant respects.

In sum, the method of refutation by parallel reasoning can be used to show that an argument is invalid by presenting another argument with essentially the same form in which the inference takes us from obvious truths to an obvious falsehood. In response to such an attack, a defender of the original argument has three main options. The defender might (1) deny that the conclusion of the parallel argument is false, (2) deny that the premises of the parallel argument are true, or (3) deny that the supposedly parallel argument really has essentially the same form. If any of these responses is justified, then the attempt to refute the original argument by parallel reasoning fails.

Admittedly, this procedure is not precise. There will sometimes be disputes about whether the premises of the parallel argument really are true, or clearly true, and whether the conclusion of the parallel argument really is false, or clearly false. Moreover, we have given no general explanation of the notion that two arguments have the *same basic form*. Some forms of argument were discussed in Chapters 6–8, but they are only part of the story. Yet it remains a fact that people can often see that two arguments have the same essential form and, through seeing this, decide that an argument presented to them is invalid. This ability is the basis of sound logical judgment. It is also the basis of wit. It is at best mildly funny to say that if God had wanted us to fly, he would have given us wings. You have to be fairly clever to reply at once, "If God had wanted us to stay on the ground, he would have given us roots."

EXERCISE VI

In each of the following examples, does the parallel argument succeed in refuting the original argument? Why or why not? Consider the three possible responses listed above. If the original argument is refuted, is there some simple way to fix it so that it cannot be refuted in this way? If so, how? (You might try to add a premise whose analogue would be false in the parallel argument.)

1. **CHRIS:** The United States is wealthy, so its citizens are wealthy as well.

   PAT: That's just like arguing that a building is expensive, so the nails in its walls are expensive as well.

2. **CHAUVINIST:** Since women are the only people who can bear children, they should bear children.

   FEMINIST: That's like arguing that, if I am the only person who can wiggle my own ears, then I should wiggle my own ears.

3. **NEWT:** Orphanages are fine places, as the movie *Boys Town* shows.

   CRITIC: That's just like saying that Oz is a fine place, as *The Wizard of Oz* shows.

4. **Scientist:** My initial steps toward human cloning, no matter how controversial, are important because they bring the debate out into the public.

   Opponent: That's just like arguing that we should start a fire in a house in order to bring the debate about getting a new fire engine out into the public.[5]

5. **A Young Child at 6:00 a.m.:** It's morning. Morning is the time to wake up. So it's time to wake up.

   The Child's Sleepy Parent: That's just like arguing that it's daytime, and daytime is the time to eat lunch, so it's time to eat lunch.

6. **Mark:** You shouldn't walk on that grass, because if everybody did that, the grass would die.

   Bob: That's just like arguing that I shouldn't go to this movie right now, because if everybody did that, the theater would be packed like a can of sardines.

7. **Thomas:** Everything in the world has a cause, so the world itself must have a cause.

   Tony: That's just like arguing that everyone in this class has a mother, so the class itself must have a mother.

8. **Hawk:** Nuclear deterrence must work, because we have never had a nuclear exchange as long as we have maintained nuclear deterrence.

   Dove: That's just like arguing that hanging garlic by the front door must keep thieves away, because I put garlic there and my house has never been robbed.

9. **Liberal:** We ought to provide condoms for high school students, because they are going to have sex anyway.

   Limbaugh: That's just like arguing that we should provide high school students with guns, because they are going to use them anyway.[6]

10. **King:** "In your statement you asserted that our actions, even though peaceful, must be condemned because they precipitate violence. But can this assertion be logically made? Isn't this like condemning the robbed man because his possession of money precipitated the evil act of robbery?"[7]

11. **A:** He owns a red car, so he owns a car.

    B: That's just like arguing that he owns a toy duck, so he owns a duck.

12. **A:** He is holding a baby girl, so he is holding a baby.

    B: That's just like arguing that he sees a fire truck, so he sees a fire.

[5]Paraphrased from an interview on National Public Radio.

[6]Paraphrased from Rush Limbaugh, *See, I Told You So* (New York: Pocket Books, 1993), 222.

[7]Martin Luther King, Jr., "Letter from Birmingham Jail," http://almaz.com/nobel/peace/MLK-jail.html, paragraph 21.

EXERCISE VII

For each of the following arguments, find another argument with the same basic form in which the premise or premises are clearly true and the conclusion is clearly false.

1. If tea is dangerous, so is coffee. Tea isn't dangerous. So coffee isn't either.

2. If it were about to rain, it would be cloudy. It is cloudy. So it's about to rain.

3. Fred had either ice cream or cake for dessert. He had cake. So he must not have had ice cream.

4. You cannot pass laws against dangerous drugs, because there is no way of drawing a sharp line between dangerous and nondangerous drugs.

5. If you have never written a novel, then you are in no position to make judgments about novels. So don't presume to criticize mine.

6. Women are the natural persons to raise children, because they are the ones who give birth to them.

7. There's nothing wrong with smoking, since the longer you smoke, the longer you live.

8. If one has nothing to hide, one should not be afraid of being investigated. So no one should object to being investigated.

9. Radicals should not be granted freedom of speech, because they deny this freedom to others.

10. In nature, a species is more likely to survive when its weak members die out, so we should let the weak in our society die out.

11. Buses use more gas than cars, so the city cannot reduce gas consumption by providing more buses.

12. Boxing can't be very bad, since so many people like it.

13. This war is just, for to say otherwise in public would be to aid our enemies.

14. If you don't buy the most expensive shoes, you buy cheap ones. You don't want cheap shoes. So you should buy the most expensive shoes.

15. I'd rather be smart than strong, so I am going to quit exercising and spend all day in the library.

16. You don't want to be this murderer's next victim, so you had better convict her and send her to prison where she can't hurt you.

17. If it weren't for America, these refugees would have nowhere to go; so they should adopt the American way of life and give up their old culture.

18. You can't be right, because, if the answer were that obvious, someone would have thought of it before.

DISCUSSION QUESTIONS

Using the standards discussed above, assess the following attempts to refute by parallel reasoning:

1. Gaunilo's reply to Anselm in Chapter 17, p. 549.
2. Searle's reply to Turing in Chapter 18, pp. 590–95.

SYSTEM AND SIMPLICITY

We often use arguments to justify our claims and refute other claims when we disagree with people about what is true or when we are not sure ourselves about whether a claim is true. Arguments can also be useful in other ways even when everyone is sure that a certain claim is true. Nobody denies the Pythagorean theorem in Euclidean geometry, which says that the square of the hypotenuse of a right triangle is equal to the sum of the squares of the other two sides. Despite this agreement, however, geometry students are taught how to prove this theorem again. Even when one proof is accepted, geometers might look for another proof that is simpler in that it uses fewer steps or depends on fewer assumptions. Why? If everyone already accepts the theorem as proved, what is accomplished by proving it again, even if in a new way? The answer is not completely clear, but at least one purpose is to display or discover connections among various claims within geometry. When the Pythagorean theorem is proved from axioms, the proof shows that those axioms are sufficient conditions for the truth of the theorem. When a larger group of theorems is proved from the axioms, the overall theory becomes more systematic in that more of its parts are connected.

Why do geometers want the simplest proof? One reason is that simpler proofs are usually easier to follow, so a simpler proof will increase our understanding of the theorem and of why it is true. Moreover, a simpler proof reveals what is necessary to make the theorem true. If theorem T can be derived only by assuming axioms A, B, and C, then all three axioms seem to be part of what makes the theorem true, and it seems that the theorem would not be true if any of these axioms were not true. But if someone comes up with a proof that uses only axioms A and B, but not axiom C, then this new proof or argument shows that axiom C is not needed to make theorem T true, and that T would still be a theorem even if axiom C had to be given up. In such ways, a geometric proof can increase our understanding of a theorem and of a whole theory, even if there was never any doubt about the truth of the theorem.

This use of arguments is best known in mathematics, but it is also common in other areas. Some biologists, for example, have tried to derive the theory of evolution from a small set of axioms. Economists sometimes do the same for their theories. Moral philosophers also often try to derive their moral beliefs from a small set of basic principles. One example is Immanuel Kant. Kant recognized that most people believe that killing, hurting, lying, and breaking promises are morally wrong except in unusual circumstances. In his moral theory, Kant tried to derive these common moral beliefs from his categorical imperative, which (in one version) says: Do not treat people as means only. What did Kant hope to gain by this derivation? Kant held that common people who had never heard of his categorical imperative could be fully justified in believing that it is usually morally wrong to lie. Thus, the argument from the categorical imperative was not intended to justify this common moral belief. Instead, it was supposed to show how this claim is related to other common moral beliefs and to other areas of ethics. It does so by revealing a feature that is shared by all of the acts that are morally wrong—namely, they all involve using other people as means only. Kant's derivation was also supposed to help us understand what makes these acts morally wrong. Kant's categorical imperative is controversial, so it is not clear that it really does increase our understanding of morality. Nonetheless, the point here is simply that arguments deriving common moral beliefs from the categorical imperative or some other basic ethical principle aim at increasing our understanding of morality. This use of arguments is distinct from both justification and refutation.

EXPLANATIONS

Another important use of arguments is to provide explanations. Explanations answer questions about how or why something happened. We explain how a mongoose got out of his cage by pointing to a hole he dug under the fence. We explain why Smith was acquitted by saying that he got off on a technicality. The purpose of explanations is not to prove that something happened, but to make sense of things.

An example will bring out the difference between justification and explanation. One person claims that a school's flagpole is thirty-five feet tall, and someone else asks her to justify this claim. In response, she might produce a receipt from the Allegiance Flagpole Company acknowledging payment for a flagpole thirty-five feet in height. Alternatively, she may put a stick straight up into the ground, measure the stick's length and its shadow's length, then measure the length of the flagpole's shadow, and calculate the length of the flagpole. Neither of these justifications, however, will answer a different question: *Why* is the flagpole thirty-five feet tall? This new question could be answered in all sorts of ways, depending on context: The school could not afford a taller one. It struck the committee as about the right height for the location. That was the only size flagpole in stock. There is a state law limiting flagpoles to thirty-five feet. And so on. These answers help us understand why the flagpole is thirty-five feet tall. They explain its height.

Sometimes simply filling in the details of a story provides an explanation. For example, we can explain how a two-year-old girl foiled a bank robbery by saying that the robber tripped over her while fleeing from the bank. Here we have made sense out of an unusual event by putting it in the context of a plausible *narrative*. It is unusual for a two-year-old girl to foil a bank robbery, but there is nothing unusual about a person tripping over a child when running recklessly at full speed in a crowded area.

Although the narrative is probably the most common form of explanation in everyday life, we also often use arguments to give explanations. We can explain a certain event by deriving it from established principles and accepted facts. This derivation has the following form:

> General principles or laws
> A statement of initial conditions
> _____
> ∴ A statement of the phenomenon to be explained

By "initial conditions" we mean those facts in the context that, together with appropriate general principles and laws, allow us to derive the result that the event to be explained occurs.

This sounds quite abstract, but one example should clarify the basic idea. Suppose we put an ice cube into a glass and then fill the glass with water to the brim. The ice will stick out above the surface of the water. What will happen when the ice cube melts? Will the water overflow? Will it remain at the same level? Will it go down? Here we are asking for a *prediction*, and it will, of course, make sense to ask a person to *justify* whatever prediction he or she makes.

Stumped by this question, we let the ice cube melt to see what happens. We observe that the water level remains unchanged. After a few experiments, we convince ourselves that this result always occurs. We now have a new question: *Why* does this occur? We want an explanation of this phenomenon.

The explanation turns upon the law of buoyancy, which says:

> An object in water is buoyed up by a force equal to the weight of the water it displaces.

This law implies that, if we put an object in water, it will continue to sink until it displaces a volume of water whose weight is equal to its own weight (or else the object hits the bottom of the container). With this in mind, go back to the original problem. An ice cube is itself simply water in a solid state. Thus, when it melts, it will exactly fill in the volume of water it displaced, so the water level will remain unchanged.

We can now see how this explanation conforms to the argumentative pattern mentioned above:

General principles or laws	(Primarily the law of buoyancy)
Initial conditions	(An ice cube floating in a glass of water filled to the brim)
_____	
∴ Phenomenon explained	(The level of the water remaining unchanged after the ice cube melts)

This explanation is fairly good. People with only a slight understanding of science can follow it and see why the water level remains unchanged. We should also notice that it is not a *complete* explanation, because certain things are simply taken for granted—for example, that things do not change weight when they pass from a solid to a liquid state. To put the explanation into perfect argumentative form, this assumption and many others would have to be stated explicitly. This is never done in everyday life and is only rarely done in the most exact sciences.

Here is an example of an explanation that is less technical.[8] Houses in Indonesia sometimes have their electrical outlets in the middle of the wall rather than at floor level. Why? A beginning of an explanation is that flooding is a danger in The Netherlands. Citing this fact does not help much, however, unless one remembers that Indonesia was formerly a Dutch colony. Even remembering this leaves gaps in the explanation. We can understand why the Dutch might put their electrical outlets above floor level in The Netherlands. It is safer in a country where flooding is a danger. Is flooding, then, a similar danger in Indonesia? Apparently not. So why did the Dutch continue this practice in Indonesia? To answer this question, we must cite another broad principle: Colonial settlers tend to preserve their home customs, practices, and styles. In this particular case, the Dutch continued to build Dutch-style houses with the electrical outlets where (for them) they are normally placed—that is, in the middle of the wall rather than at floor level.

Even though this is not a scientific explanation, it shares many features of the scientific explanation examined previously. First, we have a curious fact: the location of electrical outlets in some houses in Indonesia. By way of explanation, certain important facts are cited:

> Indonesia was a Dutch colony.
>
> Flooding is a danger in The Netherlands.
>
> And so on.

These facts are then woven together by certain general principles:

> Where flooding is a danger, it is safer to put electrical outlets above floor level.
>
> People tend to do what is safer.
>
> Colonial settlers tend to preserve their home practices even when the practical significance of those practices is diminished.
>
> And so on.

Taken together, these facts and principles make sense of an anomalous fact—that is, they explain it.

Is this explanation any good? Explanations are satisfactory for *practical* purposes if they remove bewilderment or surprise. An explanation is

---

[8]This example comes from Alan Ross Anderson.

satisfactory if it tells us *how* or *why* something happened in a way that is relevant to the concerns of a particular context. Our examples of explanations do seem to accomplish that much. Still, some explanations are better than others. In Chapter 9, we presented some criteria for evaluating explanations, but it might seem that even the best explanations are not very useful because they take so much for granted. In explaining why the water level remains the same when the ice cube melts, we cited the law of buoyancy. Now, why should that law be true? What explains *it*? To explain the law of buoyancy, we would have to derive it from other laws that are more general and, perhaps, more intelligible. In fact, this has been done. Archimedes simultaneously proved and explained the law of buoyancy by deriving it from the laws of the lever. How about the laws of the lever? Can they be proved and explained by deriving them from still higher and more comprehensive laws? Perhaps. Yet reasons give out, and sooner or later explanation (like justification) comes to an end. It is the task of science and all rational inquiry to move that boundary further and further back. But even when there is more to explain, that does not show that a partial explanation is totally useless. As we have seen, explanations can be useful even when they are incomplete, and even though they are not used to justify any disputed claim. Explanation is, thus, a separate use of arguments.

EXERCISE VIII

Write a brief argument to explain each of the following. Indicate what facts and what general principles are employed in your explanations. (Do not forget those principles that may seem too obvious to mention.)

1. Why a lighter-than-air balloon rises.
2. Why there is an infield fly rule in baseball.
3. Why there is an international date line.
4. Why there are more psychoanalysts in New York City than in any other city or, for that matter, in most countries in the world.
5. Why average temperatures tend to be higher closer to the equator.
6. Why there are usually more college freshmen who plan to go to medical school than there are seniors who still plan to go to medical school.
7. Why almost no textbooks are more than eighteen inches high.
8. Why most cars have four tires (instead of more or fewer).
9. Why paintings by Van Gogh cost so much.
10. Why wages go up when unemployment goes down.[9]

[9]This claim is often disputed, but see D. Blanchflower and Andrew Oswald, *The Wage Curve* (Cambridge: MIT Press, 1994).

EXCUSES

Sometimes we are charged with acting in an improper or particularly stupid way. There are various ways in which we can defend ourselves against such a charge. (1) We can deny that we performed the action in question. Such a *disclaimer* might offer what is called an *alibi* intended to show that we were not in a position to perform the action with which we are charged. If we admit performing the action, we still have two more options. (2) We can try to *justify* the action—that is, show why it was not improper or stupid but was the right thing to do because we had an adequate reason to do it. (3) We can admit that we performed the action and also admit that it was improper or stupid, and then offer an *excuse* intended to show why we were not fully responsible for what we did.

The following exchanges between *A* and *B* illustrate these different kinds of defense.

> **A:** Why did you shove Harold into the gulch?
>
> **B:** I didn't shove him into the gulch. I was on the other side of town, as Gina will testify.

Here Gina provides an *alibi*, on the basis of which *B* *disclaims* (or denies performing) the action.

> **A:** Why did you shove Harold into the gulch?
>
> **B:** He was about to be shot by an assassin.

Here *B* admits that he did shove Harold into the gulch. His response is supposed to *justify* *B*'s action by showing that it was the right thing to do. To accomplish this, all *B* does is cite the single fact that an assassin was about to shoot Harold, but this justification also depends on some general principles that are so obvious that we simply take them for granted. For example, we assume that saving a person's life is, in general, a good thing; that a person in a gulch is less likely to be struck by a bullet than a person standing in plain view; and that the amount of harm that might come from falling into a gulch is much less than the harm that would be caused by being struck by a bullet. Against the background of these principles and others, *B*'s remark explains his otherwise inexplicable conduct by showing that it was *justified*.

Notice what happens when we change the example in the following way:

> **A:** Why did you shove Harold into the gulch?
>
> **B:** I mistakenly thought that he was about to be shot.

B's remark here explains why he acted as he did; it helps us understand his behavior. But this remark no longer justifies (or at least no longer fully justifies) his conduct, since he does not claim that what he did was the right thing to do. He thought it was the right thing to do at the time, but now he admits that he was mistaken. Here we would say that *B* is offering an excuse for what he did. An *excuse* is a special kind of explanation, specifically, an explanation of human behavior intended to put it in a better light by reducing the agent's responsibility. It will often happen that even the best possible light will involve the admission of some wrongdoing. In the third dialogue, *B* admits to having made a mistake. In some contexts this might be a serious admission, but in the present context *B* does better by admitting that he was stupid, rather than acknowledging that he shoved poor Harold into the gulch as an act of sheer malice.

Even if *B* admits that he maliciously pushed Harold into the gulch, he may offer a weaker kind of excuse that cites *mitigating circumstances:*

A: Why did you shove Harold into the gulch?

B: He had been bugging me all afternoon, and I lost my temper.

You are not supposed to push people into gulches just because they have been bugging you, so *B*'s response does not justify his conduct. Yet it does provide a *partial* excuse, and thus makes it seem less vicious than if *B* had pushed Harold into the gulch with no provocation whatsoever.

We evaluate excuses in much the same way that we evaluate other explanations. An excuse will involve statements of fact, and these may be either true or false. We can also challenge the background principles employed in the excuse. We will not be impressed by someone who tells us that he ran seven stoplights so that he would not be late for a movie. The desire to see the start of a movie does not excuse such dangerous behavior, both because the danger to others is far greater than the expected gain for the driver and also because the driver should have left earlier. Finally, as with other explanations, the facts together with the background principles should make sense of the excused behavior and help us understand why it occurred.

To evaluate an excuse, we can ask the following questions:

1. Broadly speaking, what are the facts?
2. With what is the person being charged?
3. What lesser wrong will the person settle for instead?
4. How does the excuse answer the more serious charge?

In our third dialogue, (1) *B* shoved Harold into a gulch. (2) On the face of it, this looks like an attempt to injure Harold. (3) *B* is willing to admit that he made a mistake of fact. (4) Given this admission, his action was not malicious because it can be seen as a laudable, if flawed, attempt to save Harold from death or serious injury. These answers show that this excuse works fairly well, but other excuses will be found to be much more dubious when we look at them carefully in light of these questions.

EXERCISE IX

Determine whether each of the following is being offered as a disclaimer, a justification, or an excuse. Is each adequate for its intended use?

1. People with an IQ of 40 should not be given the death penalty, because they are not capable of understanding the consequences of their actions.
2. I had a very good reason to steal the drug: My wife would have died without it.
3. Alice shouldn't be kept after school with the rest of the class. She can't be the one who threw the eraser, because she was in the bathroom.
4. I had to give him the money. He would have killed me if I didn't.
5. I just couldn't stop myself. When I saw the money lying on the ground, I had to take it. Then I just couldn't bring myself to turn it in. You would have done the same thing.
6. I lied to you in order to keep the party a surprise. Surprise parties are lots of fun. Besides, I had promised not to tell.
7. I dropped the baby because I was startled by a lightning flash nearby.
8. I didn't know it was a closed-book exam. That's the only reason why I used my book. I never would have looked at it if I had known.

EXERCISE X

Imagine that you are writing a letter home asking for money. In the closing paragraph, you feel called on to offer some excuse for not having written home for two months. Write such an excuse (not just an apology) in a perfectly natural way, and then analyze it, using the questions given above.

EXERCISE XI

In William Shakespeare's *Much Ado about Nothing*, Benedick, after previously denouncing women and marriage in the strongest terms, is trapped into falling in love with Beatrice. In the following passage he attempts to explain his sudden turnabout.

> I may chance have some odd quirks and remnants of wit broken on me because I have railed so long against marriage. But doth not the appetite alter? A man loves the meat in his youth that he cannot endure in his age. Shall quips and sentences and these paper bullets of the brain awe a man from the career of his humor? No, the world must be peopled. When I said I would die a bachelor, I did not think I should live till I were married.

Using the four questions given above, analyze the excuse given in the last sentence.

EXERCISE XII

Find an example of a public official offering an excuse for something he or she has done. Analyze its structure using the above four questions.

DISCUSSION QUESTIONS

1. Refuting an argument does not always require showing its conclusion to be false. Why not?

2. It is sometimes said that science tells us *how* things happen but does not tell us *why* they happen. In what ways is this contention right, and in what ways is it wrong?

3. When a claim is made that someone's conduct is *inexcusable,* what precisely is being asserted? How does it differ from calling the conduct simply bad or even very bad?

4. Taken literally, "Excuse me" is a request. For what?

AREAS OF
ARGUMENTATION

14

LEGAL REASONING

Particular subject matters sometimes give rise to special kinds of arguments and special standards of strength. Law is a prime example, for legal systems have their own procedures and authorities. Legal decisions are often based on statutes, constitutions, and precedents that are peculiar to a particular legal system. These sources of law are often vague, and they can conflict, so they need to be interpreted. This chapter will discuss legal interpretation and legal reasoning in general. The general forms of legal arguments will then be illustrated by looking in more detail at the law of discrimination and affirmative action.

Legal decisions have concrete effects on people's lives. In criminal cases, judges can deprive people of their freedom or even their lives. In civil cases, judges often take away large sums of money, the custody of children, and so on. Constitutional decisions can affect the basic rights of all citizens, even those who have never been in a courtroom. These decisions are made because certain legal arguments are accepted and others are rejected.

Unfortunately, it is sometimes difficult to find any good reason for a legal decision. Crucial facts might not be known, and the law is sometimes unclear or inconsistent. Some cases "fall between the cracks," so no law seems to apply. Human beings have a remarkable ability to produce weird cases that would tax the wisdom of Solomon.

Even in the toughest cases, judges and juries must reach *some* decision. Outside the law, we can often just let matters ride—we can postpone a decision until further facts are established, or even declare that the issues are too vague to admit of any decision. This is rarely an option in a legal case. If *A* sues *B*, either *A* or *B* must win. The judge cannot say, "This case is too tough for me. I'm not going to rule on it." Throwing the case out of court amounts to ruling in favor of the defendant. A decision must be made, usually in a relatively short period of time.

These pressures have led lawyers and judges to develop many ingenious ways to argue. Lawyers cite statutes, precedents, and historical contexts. They claim the authority of common sense and science, and they cite scholarly articles, even some by philosophers. They deploy metaphors and rhetorical devices—almost anything to convince the judge or jury to decide in favor of their clients. The variety of these arguments makes legal reasoning complex and also fascinating.

Despite this variety, some rough generalizations can be made: A decision in a legal case usually depends on (1) questions of fact and (2) questions of law.

COMPONENTS OF LEGAL REASONING

QUESTIONS OF FACT

A *criminal law* prohibits a certain kind of behavior and assigns a punishment to those who violate it. When a person is accused of violating this law, a trial is held to determine whether *in fact* he or she has done so. The judge instructs the jury on the law bearing on the case. If the members of the jury then decide that the accused has violated the law, they find him or her guilty, and the judge usually hands down the punishment stated in the statute.

In a *civil* suit, one party sues another, say, for breach of contract. Because states have laws governing contracts, once more a trial is held to decide whether *in fact* there was a contract (instead of some other speech act) and whether *in fact* it was breached. If a breach of contract is found, the judge or jury awards damages as the law specifies.

Although questions of fact arise in all cases, criminal and civil cases do differ in *the burden of proof*—in who is required to establish the facts and to what degree of certainty. In a criminal procedure, the prosecution must establish its case *beyond a reasonable doubt.* In a civil case, the burden of proof is less. Generally, the case is won by the party who shows that the *preponderance* of evidence favors his or her side of the case. Although this is a bit too simple, it is sometimes said that if the scales tip ever so slightly in favor of *A* rather than *B,* then *A* wins the case.

The only way to carry the burden of proof is to present *evidence.* This evidence can contain conflicts and unclarities, which make it hard to prove the facts. Sometimes the facts are so complex that they simply cannot be proved one way or the other, and sometimes the distinction between facts and law is not so clear.

These problems arise often in cases that raise larger social issues. For example, in the case of *Brown v. Board of Education* (excerpted below), the Supreme Court answered the question of law by saying "the opportunity of an education . . . is a right which must be available to all on equal terms." The Court next asked: "Does segregation of children in public schools solely on the basis of race . . . deprive the children of the minority group of equal educational opportunities?" This question was presented as a question of fact. The Court answered in the affirmative and tried to justify its answer by citing various psychological studies of the performance of minority children from segregated schools. This answer would be accepted by most people today, but the studies used as proof were controversial and inconclusive, so the Court had to decide whether studies of this kind were reliable enough to serve as evidence in this case. Moreover, the answer to the above question also depends on what counts as "equal educational opportunities" for the purposes of the law. For example, the studies cited by the Court found that segregated schools "affect the motivation of a child to learn," but these factual studies could not determine whether lowered *motivation* to learn counts as lowered *opportunity* to learn. The Court had to decide this issue because it in effect determines what the law is—what it prohibits and what it allows. Thus, what was presented as a question of fact turned out to be at least partly a question of law. In such cases, it is not clear where law ends and facts begin.

QUESTIONS OF LAW

Even after the facts are determined, no decision can be reached without determining what the law is. The law varies from place to place and from time to time, so we have to know what the law is at the right time and place. This is determined mainly by looking at the legal institutions that actually exist. In our legal system, there are three main sources of the law: statutes, the Constitution, and precedents.

STATUTES.   Roughly, statutes are general rules of law passed by legislatures. Statutes are made at various levels (federal, state, and local), and they cover various subjects, including crimes as well as property, contracts, and other areas of civil law. There are also statutes governing the procedures and kinds of evidence that can be presented in court.

When a general statute is applied to a particular case, the legal argument is often primarily deductive. For example, Sally drove ninety-five miles per hour in front of Hanover High School at 4 P.M. on a school day. It is illegal to drive over fifteen m.p.h. in front of any school at 4 P.M. on a school day. Therefore, Sally's driving was illegal. Of course, there are lots of suppressed premises, such as that ninety-five m.p.h. is over fifteen m.p.h. Other assumptions are trickier: Sally might not be found guilty if she had an excuse or justification, such as that a terrorist held a gun to her head. Still, it is often obvious that Sally had no excuse or justification. If we add this claim as a premise, then, with a little fiddling, the legal argument against Sally can be made deductively sound.

Such simple cases are common, but they are also boring. Things get much more difficult and interesting when a statute is *vague,* so that it is not clear whether the statute applies to the case at issue. Then the statute must be *interpreted.* We need some way to tell more precisely what the law prohibits and what it allows.

The first step in interpreting a statute is to look carefully at the *words* in the statute and their literal *meanings.* But the courts must often look beyond the mere words of the statute. This need arises when the words are unclear and when they lead to absurd results. For example, suppose a city council passes an ordinance requiring zoos to provide clean, dry cages for all mammals. This works fine until one zoo puts a whale in its aquarium. The whale would be in trouble if the courts stuck to the words of the ordinance. Fortunately, the courts can also consider the *intentions* of the legislators, which can be gleaned from their debates about the law. Of course, the city council might not have thought at all about whales, or they might have thought that whales are fish instead of mammals. Thus, if their intentions are what the legislators consciously had in mind, then we also need to consider the deeper, more general *purpose* of the legislators—the goal they were trying to reach or the moral outlook they were trying to express. This purpose is revealed by the wider historical context and by other laws made by the same legislature. In our example, the purpose of the statute was obviously to provide a healthy environment for mammals in zoos. This purpose is best served by interpreting the ordinance so that it does not require dry cages for whales.

In addition to words, intentions, and purposes, *moral beliefs* are often used to interpret statutes. Judges often argue that a statute should be interpreted one way by claiming that any other interpretation would lead to some kind of practical difficulty or moral unfairness. Such arguments are effective when everyone agrees about what is immoral or unfair, but judges often depend on more controversial moral beliefs. Critics claim that judges should not use their own moral views in this way, but there is no doubt that judges do in fact reason from such moral premises.

It should be clear that none of these methods of interpretation is mechanical, and none guarantees a single best interpretation of every statute. Part of the legal controversy is often over which factors can or should be used to argue for an interpretation. When all is said and done, legal reasoning from statutes is often far from the straightforward deduction that it appears to be in simple cases.

THE CONSTITUTION. Even when a statute has been interpreted, it is sometimes not clear whether the statute is *valid*—whether it has any legal force. This is determined by the Constitution. The Constitution occupies a special place in the legal system of the United States. If any statute conflicts with the Constitution, including its amendments, that statute has no legal force. Generally it is not the role of courts to enact laws, but the courts do have the power to strike down laws if they conflict with provisions in our Constitution.

It is easy to imagine clear cases of laws that violate constitutional provisions. If the state of Kansas began printing its own money, that would plainly violate the constitutional provision that reserves this right to the federal government. But, typically, those constitutional questions that reach the courts are not clear-cut. Even more so than statutes, provisions in the Constitution are very general and sometimes vague. This vagueness serves a purpose: The framers of the Constitution recognized that they could not foresee every eventuality, so they wanted to allow future courts to interpret the

Constitution as cases arose. But the vagueness of the Constitution also creates problems. Interpretations can often conflict and fuel controversy. As with statutes, arguments for and against interpretations of the Constitution usually refer to the words of the Constitution, the intentions and purposes of the framers of the Constitution, the effects of adopting an interpretation, moral beliefs, and so on. Such arguments are often inconclusive. The Supreme Court is then the final arbiter on questions of constitutionality.

PRECEDENTS.   The United States legal system is not only a constitutional system; it is also partly a system of common law. This means that lawyers and judges often cite precedents in arguments for present decisions. A *precedent* is simply a past case or decision that is supposed to be similar to the present case.

The practice of citing precedents might seem strange at first sight. Why should one case provide any reason for a decision in a different case? The answer is that the cases resemble each other in important respects. Of course, when there is an important enough difference between the cases, they should be *distinguished,* and then the precedent provides no argument in the present case. But, when there is no important enough difference, like cases should be treated alike. If similar precedents were not followed, the legal system would lack continuity, and this would make it unfair and ineffective. Of course, past decisions that were mistaken or immoral should not be continued. That is why precedents can be *overturned.* Nonetheless, our legal system assumes that, if there is no adequate reason to overturn a precedent or to distinguish the precedent from the present case, then the precedent provides some reason to decide the present case in the same way as the precedent. This general doctrine of precedent is often called *stare decisis*—to adhere to previous decisions.

Precedents are used for many different purposes. When a statute is vague, precedents are often used to argue for one interpretation over another. When no statute applies directly, precedents are often used to argue about what the law is. Precedents can also be used in arguments for general questions of fact, or simply as sources of persuasive rhetoric.

The form of arguments from precedents also varies. Often a judge or lawyer merely quotes part of the opinion in the precedent and treats that quotation as an authoritative pronouncement of the law. Arguments from precedents are then similar to arguments from legislative statutes, and there often arises a similar need to interpret the judicial pronouncement in the precedent. In other precedents, the judge chooses to make the decision without explicitly formulating any general rule of law. The precedent can still be used to argue for future decisions by emphasizing analogies and discounting differences between the precedent and the present case.

One example occurs in the case of *Plessy v. Ferguson* (1896) (excerpted below). Louisiana passed a statute that required blacks and whites to use "separate but equal" cars in trains. Plessy refused to comply, and he claimed that the Louisiana law violated the Fourteenth Amendment to the

Constitution, which forbids states to deprive anyone of "the equal protection of the laws."

In his argument for this claim, Plessy cited the precedent of *Yick Wo v. Hopkins* 118 U.S. 356 (1886). That case was about an ordinance in San Francisco that required a permit from the Board of Supervisors for any public laundry not operated in a brick or stone building. On its face, this ordinance was supposed simply to prevent fires. In practice, however, the Board of Supervisors granted permits to all but one of the non-Chinese applicants and denied permits to all the Chinese applicants. Because of this practice, Yick Wo claimed that the ordinance violated the equal protection clause. The Supreme Court agreed and declared the ordinance unconstitutional, at least insofar as it gave the city power to grant and refuse permits "without regard to the competency of the persons applying, or the propriety of the places selected for the carrying on of business."

The argument from a precedent to a decision in a present case is often presented as an argument from *analogy*.[1] In this form, the argument emphasizes similarities between the cases, and then concludes that the decision in the present case should be the same as in the precedent. Plessy's argument then appears to run something like this:

(1) The ordinance in *Yick Wo* was declared unconstitutional.
(2) The ordinance in *Yick Wo* is similar to the statute in *Plessy* in several respects.

∴ (3) The statute in *Plessy* also ought to be declared unconstitutional.

This argument is not very good as it stands, so we need to add some suppressed premises.

The first step is to construct a list of the respects in which the cases are similar. That is not always so easy. When we are evaluating someone else's argument, we can focus on the similarities that he or she mentions. But when we are constructing our own legal arguments, we have to be more creative; we have to formulate the respects in which the cases are supposed to be similar. Some similarities do not matter: It is clearly irrelevant that the laws in *Yick Wo* and *Plessy* both contain more than ten words or that both apply to large cities. This much is assumed by both sides in the case, and legal reasoning would be impossible without assuming that many such similarities are irrelevant. Likewise, not all differences matter: It is not important, even if true, that Yick Wo was married and over fifty years old, but Plessy was not. To discount or distinguish the precedent, one must show that some difference between *Yick Wo* and *Plessy* is important enough to justify reaching different decisions in these cases. The central question, then, asks which factors—similarities and differences—do matter. In general, the answer is that a factor is relevant when it is needed to justify the decision in the prece-

---

[1]For an elegant discussion of the role of analogical reasoning in the law, see Edward Levi, *An Introduction to Legal Reasoning* (Chicago: University of Chicago Press, 1963).

dent. These factors are often called the *ratio decidendi*—the reason for the decision.

Incorporating the doctrine of precedents as a suppressed premise, the argument from *Yick Wo* to *Plessy* can now be reconstructed as follows:

(1) The ordinance in *Yick Wo* was declared unconstitutional.

(2) The ordinance in *Yick Wo* is similar to the statute in *Plessy* in several respects (*A, B, C, D,* and so on).

(3) These are the features that justified declaring the ordinance in *Yick Wo* unconstitutional.

(4) There are no important enough differences between *Yick Wo* and *Plessy* to justify distinguishing the precedent.

(5) *Yick Wo* ought not to be overturned.

(6) If a precedent is similar to a present case in the respects that justified the decision in the precedent, and if the precedent ought not to be either overturned or distinguished, then the present case ought to be decided in the same way as the precedent.

∴ (7) The statute in *Plessy* ought to be declared unconstitutional.

This argument is now valid, but this does not get us very far. We still need to know whether its premises are true.

Clearly, the crucial question is this: How do we determine which features of the precedent are needed to justify that decision? What we need to do is to extract a general rule of law that provides the best justification for the precedent decision.

The most obvious way to argue that a certain feature is important is to look at the written opinion in the precedent and see what the Court said—more specifically, what reasons it gave for its decision. In *Yick Wo*, the Court wrote:

> whatever may have been the intent of the ordinances as adopted, . . . though the law itself be fair on its face and impartial in appearance, yet, if it is applied and administered by public authority with an evil eye and an unequal hand, so as practically to make unjust and illegal discriminations between persons in similar circumstances, material to their rights, the denial of equal justice is still within the prohibition of the Constitution.

Here the Court explicitly announces that the intent of the ordinance and its appearance (for example, whether the ordinance explicitly mentions race or ethnic background) did *not* matter to their decision. The Court also declares that it *did* matter that the ordinance in practice creates inequalities in rights. Such official pronouncements by a court have considerable force for future courts in legal arguments.

Another way to determine which factors matter is to apply the necessary condition test or the sufficient condition test from Chapter 9 to a group of precedents. These tests had to be passed by each side in the *Plessy* case. Plessy claimed that a sufficient condition of unconstitutionality is that a law has a discriminatory *effect* on the rights of a particular racial or ethnic group.

This claim would fail the sufficient condition test if there were any precedent still in force in which a law was found to have a discriminatory effect but the law was not found unconstitutional. Because there was no such precedent, the sufficient condition test does not exclude Plessy's claim that discriminatory effect is sufficient by itself to make a law unconstitutional.

On the other side, the Court claimed that discriminatory effect is not sufficient, because discriminatory *motive* is a necessary condition for a law to be unconstitutional under the equal protection clause. For this claim to pass the necessary condition test, there must have been no precedent still in force in which a law was held unconstitutional under the equal protection clause but the Court did not find any discriminatory motive. Plessy claimed that *Yick Wo* was such a case, but the Court responded that, even if those who passed the ordinance had no discriminatory motive, the administration of the ordinance in *Yick Wo* "was held to be a covert attempt on the part of the municipality to make an arbitrary and unjust discrimination against the Chinese race." If so, the necessary condition test does not rule out the Court's claim that discriminatory motive is necessary for unconstitutionality in this case.

This disagreement reveals the limits on the tests of necessary conditions and sufficient conditions. These tests are useful when there is a rich body of coherent precedents. But when there are not enough precedents of the right kinds, and when the precedents are not coherent, the necessary condition test and the sufficient condition test cannot be used to rule out conflicting interpretations of the precedents.

When the actual precedents are not enough, judges sometimes refer to *hypothetical cases.* In *Plessy,* a judge might imagine a law with discriminatory effect but no discriminatory motive. If the judge can show why this law should be found unconstitutional, this would suggest that a discriminatory motive is not really necessary for a violation of the equal protection clause. This takes some imagination, and it also requires judges to apply their moral beliefs about which laws should be allowed. Some critics deny that moral arguments should have any legal force, because they are so controversial. Nonetheless, there is no doubt that judges often do in fact assume such moral beliefs in arguments from precedents.

A final point to remember is that arguments from precedents are usually inconclusive, like other inductive arguments. (See Chapter 9.) One reason is that more precedents might be found, and these new precedents might conflict with the precedents in the original argument. Another reason is that any precedent can be overturned. Precedents are not supposed to be overturned unless they are very badly mistaken or immoral, but this is always a possibility. Nonetheless, even though arguments from precedents always might be refuted in such ways, precedents can still provide reasons for legal decisions.

So far we have looked at arguments from precedents as ways to determine what is necessary or sufficient to violate the law. Even after this is determined, the law still must be applied to the facts in the present case. In

Plessy, the Court held that there was no intent to discriminate, because the statute in *Plessy* was "reasonable" and "enacted in good faith for the promotion of the public good and not for the annoyance or oppression of a particular class." This claim is highly questionable. In his famous dissent, Justice Harlan denies it when he writes:

> Everyone knows that the statute in question had its origin in the purpose, not so much to exclude white persons from railroad cars occupied by blacks, as to exclude colored people from coaches occupied by or assigned to white persons. . . . No one would be so wanting in candor as to assert the contrary.

If Harlan is right, the Court's argument has a false premise, so the statute in *Plessy* should have been found unconstitutional even if the Court was right about what was necessary to find a law unconstitutional.

We can summarize this discussion by listing various ways in which arguments from precedents can fail:

1. The precedent and the present case might not *truly* resemble each other in the ways that the argument claims.
2. The respects in which the cases resemble each other might not be *important* enough to justify the same decision in the present case.
3. The precedent and the present case might also differ from each other in important respects that justify *distinguishing* the precedent.
4. The precedent might be mistaken or immoral enough to be *overturned*.
5. There might be other, stronger precedents that *conflict* with the precedent in the argument.

Whenever you evaluate or present any argument from a precedent, you need to ask whether the argument fails in any of these ways.

DISCUSSION QUESTIONS

Analyze and evaluate the legal reasoning from precedents and statutes in the following opinion. If you were a justice on the Court, how much in damages would you award to the Peevyhouses?

1. $29,000 (the cost of fulfilling the contract)
2. $25,000 (the amount sued for)
3. $5000 (the amount awarded by the trial jury)
4. $300 (the diminution in the value of the property due to the failure to fulfill the contract)

PEEVYHOUSE V. GARLAND COAL & MINING CO.

■

(Supreme Court of Oklahoma, 382 P. 2d 109, 1962)

Justice Jackson [with whom Justices Welch, Davison, Halley, and Johnson concur]:

. . . Briefly stated, the facts are as follows: plaintiffs [Willie and Lucille Peevy-house] owned a farm containing coal deposits, and in November, 1954, leased the premises to defendant [Garland Coal & Mining Company] for a period of five years for coal mining purposes. A "strip-mining" operation was contemplated in which the coal would be taken from pits on the surface of the ground, instead of from underground mine shafts. In addition to the usual covenants found in a coal mining lease, defendant specifically agreed to perform certain restorative and remedial work at the end of the lease period. It is unnecessary to set out the details of the work to be done, other than to say that it would involve the moving of many thousands of cubic yards of dirt, at a cost estimated by expert witnesses at about $29,000.00. However, plaintiffs sued for only $25,000.00.

During the trial, it was stipulated that all covenants and agreements in the contract had been fully carried out by both parties, except the remedial work above; defendant conceded that this work had not been done. . . . [The jury] returned a verdict for plaintiffs for $5,000.00—only a fraction of the "cost of performance," *but more than the total value of the farm even after the remedial work is done.*

On appeal, the issue is sharply drawn. Plaintiffs contend that the true measure of damages in this case is what it will cost plaintiffs to obtain performance of the work that was not done because of defendant's default. Defendant argues that the measure of damages is the cost of performance "limited, however, to the total difference in the market value before and after the work was performed."

Plaintiffs rely on *Groves v. John Wunder Co.* . . . In that case, the Minnesota court, in a substantially similar situation, adopted the "cost of performance" rule as opposed to the "value" rule. The result was to authorize a jury to give plaintiff damages in the amount of $60,000, where the real estate concerned would have been worth only $12,160, even if the work contracted for had been done.

It may be observed that *Groves v. John Wunder Co.* . . . is the only case which has come to our attention in which the cost of performance rule has been followed under circumstances where the cost of performance greatly exceeded the diminution in value resulting from the breach of contract. Incidentally, it appears that this case was decided by a plurality rather than a majority of the members of the court.

Defendant relies principally upon *Sandy Valley & E. R. Co. v. Hughes* . . . ; *Bigham v. Wabash-Pittsburg Terminal Ry. Co.* . . . ; and *Sweeney v. Lewis Const. Co.* . . . These were all cases in which, under similar circumstances, the appellate courts followed the "value" rule instead of the "cost of performance" rule.

The explanation may be found in the fact that the situations presented are artificial ones. It is highly unlikely that the ordinary property owner would agree to pay $29,000 (or its equivalent) for the construction of "improvements" upon his property that would increase its value only about ($300) three hundred dollars. The result is that we are called upon to apply principles of law theoretically based upon reason and reality to a situation which is basically unreasonable and unrealistic.

In *Groves v. John Wunder Co.* . . . , the Minnesota court apparently considered the contract involved to be analogous to a building and construction contract, and cited authority for the proposition that the cost of performance or completion of the building as contracted is ordinarily the measure of damages in actions for damages for the breach of such a contract.

In an annotation following the Minnesota case . . . , the annotator places the three cases relied on by defendant (*Sandy Valley, Bigham* and *Sweeney*) under the classification of cases involving "grading and excavation contracts."

We do not think either analogy is strictly applicable to the case now before us. The primary purpose of the lease contract between plaintiffs and defendant was neither "building and construction" nor "grading and excavation." It was merely to accomplish the economical recovery and marketing of coal from the premises, to the profit of all parties. The special provisions of the lease contract pertaining to remedial work were incidental to the main object involved.

Even in the case of contracts that are unquestionably building and construction contracts, the authorities are not in agreement as to the factors to be considered in determining whether the cost of performance rule or the value rule should be applied. The American Law Institute's Restatement of the Law, Contracts, . . . submits the proposition that the cost of performance is the proper measure of damages "if this is possible and does not involve *unreasonable economic waste*"; and that the diminution in value caused by the breach is the proper measure "if construction and completion in accordance with the contract would involve *unreasonable economic waste*" [emphasis supplied]. In an explanatory comment immediately following the text, the Restatement makes it clear that the "economic waste" referred to consists of the destruction of a substantially completed building or other structure. Of course no such destruction is involved in the case now before us.

. . . 23 O.S. [Oklahoma statutes] 1961 §§96 and 97 provide as follows:

> §96 . . . Notwithstanding the provisions of this chapter, no person can recover a greater amount in damages for the breach of an obligation, than he would have gained by the full performance thereof on both sides. . . .

> §97 . . . Damages must, in all cases, be reasonable, and where an obligation of any kind appears to create a right to unconscionable and grossly oppressive damages, contrary to substantial justice, no more than reasonable damages can be recovered.

Although it is true that the above sections of the statute are applied most often in tort cases [involving a private or civil wrong or injury other than the breach of a contract], they are by their own terms, and the decisions of this court, also applicable in actions for damages for breach of contract. It would seem that they are peculiarly applicable here where, under the "cost of performance" rule, plaintiffs might recover an amount about nine times the total value of their farm. Such would seem to be "unconscionable and grossly oppressive damages, contrary to substantial justice" within the meaning of the statute. Also, it can hardly be denied that if plaintiffs here are permitted to recover under the "cost of performance" rule, they will receive a greater benefit from the breach than could be gained from full performance, contrary to the provisions of Sec. 96.

An analogy may be drawn between the cited sections and the provisions of 15 O.S. 1961 §§ 214 and 215. These sections tend to render void any provisions of a contract which attempt to fix the amount of stipulated damages to be paid in case of a breach, except where it is impracticable or extremely difficult to determine the actual damages. This results in spite of the agreement of the parties, and the obvious and well known rationale is that insofar as they exceed the actual damages suffered, the stipulated damages amount to a penalty or forfeiture which the law does not favor.

23 O.S. 1961 §§ 96 and 97 have the same effect in the case now before us. *In spite of the agreement of the parties,* these sections limit the damages recoverable to a reasonable amount not "contrary to substantial justice"; they prevent plaintiffs from recovering a "greater amount in damages for the breach of an obligation" than they would have "gained by the full performance thereof."

We therefore hold that where, in a coal mining lease, lessee agrees to perform certain remedial work on the premises concerned at the end of the lease period, and thereafter the contract is fully performed by both parties except that the remedial work is not done, the measure of damages in an action by lessor against lessee for damages for breach of contract is ordinarily the reasonable cost of performance of the work; however, where the contract provision breached was merely incidental to the main purpose in view, and where the economic benefit which would result to lessor by full performance of the work is grossly disproportionate to the cost of performance, the damages which lessor may recover are limited to the diminution in value resulting to the premises because of the non-performance.

We believe the above holding is in conformity with the intention of the Legislature as expressed in the statutes mentioned, and in harmony with the better-reasoned cases from the other jurisdictions where analogous fact situations have been considered. It should be noted that the rule as stated does not interfere with the property owner's right to "do what he will with his own" . . . , or his right, if he chooses, to contract for "improvements" which will actually have the effect of reducing his property's value. Where such result is in fact contemplated by the parties, and is a main or principal purpose of those contracting, it would seem that the measure of damages for breach would ordinarily be the cost of performance.

We are of the opinion that the judgment of the trial court for plaintiffs should be, and it is hereby, modified and reduced to the sum of $300.00, and as so modified it is affirmed.

Justice Irwin (dissenting) [along with Chief Justice Williams,
Vice Chief Justice Blackbird, and Justice Berry]:

In the instant action defendant has made no attempt to even substantially perform. The contract in question is not immoral, is not tainted with fraud, and was not entered into through mistake or accident and is not contrary to public policy. It is clear and unambiguous and the parties understood the terms thereof, and the approximate cost of fulfilling the obligations could have been approximately ascertained. There are no conditions existing now which could not have been reasonably anticipated when the contract was negotiated and executed. The defendant could have performed the contract if it desired. It has accepted and reaped the benefits of its contract and now urges that plaintiffs' benefits under the contract be denied. If plaintiffs' benefits are denied, such benefits would inure to the direct benefit of the defendant.

Therefore, in my opinion, the plaintiffs were entitled to specific performance of the contract and since defendant has failed to perform, the proper measure of damages should be the cost of performance. Any other measure of damage would be holding for naught the express provisions of the contract; would be taking from the plaintiffs the benefits of the contract and placing those benefits in defendant which has failed to perform its obligations; would be granting benefits to defendant without a resulting obligation; and would be completely rescinding the solemn obligation of the contract for the benefit of the defendant to the detriment of the plaintiffs by making an entirely new contract for the parties.

I therefore respectfully dissent to the opinion promulgated by a majority of my associates.

THE LAW OF DISCRIMINATION

These general methods of legal reasoning can be seen at work in a particular area of constitutional law—the law of discrimination. To understand the cases in this area, some background will be helpful.

The provision of the Constitution that governs discrimination is the equal protection clause of the Fourteenth Amendment. It provides as follows:

> No state shall make or enforce any law which shall . . . deny to any person within its jurisdiction the equal protection of the laws.

The clearest thing about this clause is that it is not clear. Whatever it means, it cannot mean that laws cannot ever treat people unequally. Criminal laws treat those who commit crimes quite differently from those who do not. The general idea behind the clause seems to be that like cases should be treated in like ways. Put negatively, the clause prohibits unequal treatment when there is no significant difference. This, however, is still both general and vague, for we need principles that determine what sorts of likenesses matter and what kinds of differences are significant.

Going back to the historical context in which the Fourteenth Amendment was adopted, we know that it was *intended* to prohibit unequal treatment on the basis of "race, color, or previous condition of servitude" (a phrase that occurs in the companion Fifteenth Amendment on voting rights). More specifically, it was one of those constitutional provisions intended to protect the newly emancipated slaves. This was the primary *purpose* of these provisions, but the *language* is more general, giving like protection to all citizens of the United States.

After the Fourteenth Amendment was adopted, many questions arose concerning its interpretation and application. The amendment explicitly refers only to state laws, but the state does many things besides pass laws, so the courts had to determine what counts as a *state action.* In a series of cases, the amendment was interpreted to mean that only positive actions of the state fell under the amendment. Thus, when thugs broke up a black political rally, with the police standing by doing nothing to protect the demonstrators, the Supreme Court ruled that this was not a violation of the equal protection clause because the state itself had not participated in the action (*U.S. v. Cruikshank,* 1875). On this view, the state was forbidden to aid discrimination, but it was not required to protect anyone against it.

Another issue that arose concerned what the state has to do to justify treating people differently. Here the courts decided that it was not their business to examine the details of legislation to make sure that the laws were as equitable as possible. The task of making laws, they held, falls to legislatures, and the courts gave legislatures wide latitude in formulating these laws. Flagrant violations of the equal protection clause could lead to the decision that the law was unconstitutional, but only if the law failed what became known as the *rational-relation test.* This test required only that the unequal treatment of individuals be reasonably likely to achieve some legitimate end.

A final issue was whether the Fourteenth Amendment protected only the civil rights of citizens or also rights of other kinds. In *Strauder v. West Virginia* (1880), a law that made blacks ineligible for jury duty was struck down on the grounds that the equal protection clause prohibits discrimination in areas of civil rights. In *Yick Wo v. Hopkins* (1886), the Court applied the equal protection clause to discrimination in areas of economic rights. *Yick Wo* also established that the equal protection clause protects not only blacks but also other groups (such as Chinese) and that laws that do not explicitly mention racial or ethnic groups can violate the equal protection clause if they are applied unequally in practice.

In 1896, the Supreme Court decided the case of *Plessy v. Ferguson,* about a Louisiana statute enforcing racial segregation in public transportation. This was clearly a state action, and the Court continued to apply the rational-relation test. The main issues were whether the equal protection clause extends to social rights, whether the segregation law served any reasonable purpose, and whether the separate facilities were truly equal. The Court held that the segregation statute did not violate the equal protection clause so long as the facilities were equal. This became known as the *separate-but-equal doctrine.*

PLESSY V. FERGUSON

◾

(163 U.S. 537, 1896)

Mr. Justice Brown delivered the opinion of the Court:

This case turns upon the constitutionality of an act of the general assembly of the State of Louisiana, passed in 1890, providing for separate railway carriages for the white and colored races. . . . The information filed in the criminal district court charged in substance that Plessy, being a passenger between two stations within the state of Louisiana, was assigned by officers of the company to the coach used for the race to which he belonged, but he insisted upon going into a coach used by the race to which he did not belong. . . .

The constitutionality of this act is attacked upon the ground that it conflicts [with the 14th Amendment]. . . . The object of the amendment was undoubtedly to enforce the absolute equality of the two races before the law, but in the nature of things it could not have been intended to abolish distinctions based upon color, or to enforce social, as distinguished from political, equality, or a commingling of the two races upon terms unsatisfactory to either. Laws permitting, and even requiring, their separation in places where they are liable to be brought into contact do not necessarily imply the inferiority of either race to the other, and have been generally, if not universally, recognized as within the competency of the state legislatures in the exercise of their police power. The most common instance of this is connected with the establishment of separate schools for white and colored children, which have been held to be a valid exercise of the legislative power even by courts of states where the political rights of the colored race have been longest and most earnestly enforced. . . .

It is . . . suggested by the learned counsel for the plaintiff in error that the same argument that will justify the state legislature in requiring railways to provide separate accommodations for the two races will also authorize them to require separate cars to be provided for people whose hair is of a certain color, or who are aliens, or who belong to certain nationalities, or to enact laws requiring colored people to walk upon one side of the street, and white people upon the other, or requiring white men's houses to be painted white, and colored men's black, or their vehicles or business signs to be of different colors, upon the theory that one side of the street is as good as the other, or that a house or vehicle of one color is as good as one of another color. The reply to all this is that every exercise of the police power must be reasonable, and extend only to such laws as are enacted in good faith for the promotion of the public good, and not for the annoyance or oppression of a particular class. Thus in *Yick Wo v. Hopkins* it was held by this court that a municipal ordinance of the city of San Francisco to regulate the carrying on of public laundries within the limits of the municipality violated the provisions of the Constitution of the United States if it conferred upon the municipal authorities arbitrary power, at their own will, and without regard to discretion, in the legal sense of the term, to give or withhold consent as to persons or places, without regard to the competency of the persons applying, or the propriety of the places selected for the carrying on of the business. It was held to be a covert attempt on the part of the municipality to make an arbitrary and unjust discrimination against the Chinese race. While this was the case of a municipal ordinance, a like principle has been held to apply to acts of a state legislature passed in the exercise of the police power.

So far, then, as a conflict with the 14th Amendment is concerned, the case reduces itself to the question whether the statute of Louisiana is a reasonable regulation, and with respect to this there must necessarily be a large discretion on the part of the legislature. In determining the question of reasonableness it is at liberty to act with reference to the established usages, customs, and traditions of the people, and with a view to the promotion of their comfort, and the preservation of the public peace and good order. Gauged by this standard, we cannot say that a law which authorizes or even requires the separation of the two races in public conveyances is unreasonable or more obnoxious to the 14th Amendment than the acts of Congress requiring separate schools for colored children in the District of Columbia, the constitutionality of which does not seem to have been questioned, or the corresponding acts of state legislatures.

We consider the underlying fallacy of the plaintiff's argument to consist in the assumption that the enforced separation of the two races stamps the colored race with a badge of inferiority. If this be so, it is not by reason of anything found in the act, but solely because the colored race chooses to put that construction upon it. . . .

FROM *PLESSY* TO *BROWN*

As soon as *Plessy* was decided, Southern and some border states rapidly passed a whole series of segregation laws. These were subsequently upheld by the courts on the precedent of *Plessy* and its separate-but-equal doctrine. The result was the introduction of a system of racial segregation throughout much of the country.

The doctrine of the rational-relation test remained basically unchanged until the 1940s. During World War II, the Supreme Court had to decide whether it was constitutional to relocate Japanese[n] Americans away from Pacific ports. In *Korematsu v. United States*, 323 U.S. 214 at 216 (1944), the Court announced that

> all legal restrictions which curtail the rights of a single racial group are immediately suspect. That is not to say that all such restrictions are unconstitutional. It is to say that the courts must subject them to the most rigid scrutiny.

It is ironic that the Court did not strike down the Japanese relocation orders, but these cases established a new interpretation of equal protection that eventually greatly increased the power of the courts to strike down discriminatory laws.

On this new interpretation of the equal protection clause, most laws still need to pass only the rational-relation test, but there are two features of a law that serve as *triggers* of strict scrutiny. A law must pass *strict scrutiny* if the law either restricts a *fundamental right* or employs a *suspect classification*. Fundamental rights concern such things as the right to vote or the right to procreate. A classification is suspect if it concerns race, religion, national origin, and so on. Under the new interpretation of the equal protection clause, states could still pass laws restricting fundamental rights, and these laws could still employ suspect classifications, but, when they did so, a heavy burden of proof fell on them. To justify such a law, the state had to show that (1) the legislation serves a *legitimate* and *compelling* state interest, and that (2) it does so in the *least intrusive* way possible (or, as later courts put it, the legislation must be "narrowly tailored" to fit the interest). This is the *strict-scrutiny test.*

It should be clear that the rational-relation test is easy to meet, whereas the test of strict scrutiny is nearly impossible to satisfy. It is not hard to show that a piece of legislation has some chance of serving some legitimate goal— that is the rational-relation test. It is difficult to show that the purpose of a law is compelling—that is, of overwhelming importance; and it is even more difficult to show that the stated purpose cannot be achieved by any less intrusive means. Thus, in adopting this new test, the Court no longer showed great deference to state legislatures, as it did in *Plessy,* when it applied the rational-relation test. Instead, the heaviest burden was shifted to the states in areas that involved what the Court declared to be suspect classifications or fundamental rights.

This new test is implicit in the decision of *Brown v. Board of Education* (1954), which declared segregation in public schools unconstitutional. The *Brown* opinion does not directly mention strict scrutiny, but this test looms in the background. Segregation clearly involves a suspect classification, but the Court emphasizes that "the opportunity of an education . . . is a *right* which must be available to all on equal terms" (emphasis added). The next step is to argue that segregated schools violate this right by their very nature, even if all "tangible" factors are equal. This violation of a fundamental right triggers strict scrutiny, and the *Brown* opinion then simply assumes that segregation in education will fail this test. Separate but equal is thus found unconstitutional, at least in education, and *Plessy* is in effect overturned.

BROWN V. BOARD OF EDUCATION

(347 U.S. 483, 1954)

Mr. Chief Justice Warren delivered the opinion of the Court:

These cases come to us from the States of Kansas, South Carolina, Virginia, and Delaware. They are premised on different facts and different local conditions, but a common legal question justifies their consideration together in this consolidated opinion.

In each of the cases, minors of the Negro race, through their legal representatives, seek the aid of the courts in obtaining admission to the public schools of their community on a nonsegregated basis. In each instance, they had been denied admission to schools attended by white children under laws requiring or permitting segregation according to race. This segregation was alleged to deprive the plaintiffs of the equal protection of the laws under the Fourteenth Amendment. In each of the cases other than the Delaware case, a three-judge federal district court denied relief to the plaintiffs on the so-called "separate but equal" doctrine announced by this Court in *Plessy v. Ferguson.* Under that doctrine, equality of treatment is accorded when the races are provided substantially equal facilities, even though these facilities be separate. In the Delaware case, the Supreme Court of Delaware adhered to that doctrine, but ordered that the plaintiffs be admitted to the white schools because of their superiority to the Negro schools.

The plaintiffs contend that segregated public schools are not "equal" and cannot be made "equal," and that hence they are deprived of the equal protection of the laws. Because of the obvious importance of the question presented, the Court took jurisdiction. Argument was heard in the 1952 Term, and reargument was heard this Term on certain questions propounded by the Court.

Reargument was largely devoted to the circumstances surrounding the adoption of the Fourteenth Amendment in 1868. It covered exhaustively consideration of the Amendment in Congress, ratification by the states, then existing practices in racial segregation, and the views of proponents and opponents of the Amendment. This discussion and our own investigation convince us that, although these sources cast some light, it is not enough to resolve the problem with which we are faced. At best, they are inconclusive. The most avid proponents of the post-War Amendments undoubtedly intended them to remove all legal distinctions among "all persons born or naturalized in the United States." Their opponents, just as certainly, were antagonistic to both the letter and the spirit of the Amendments and wished them to have the most limited effect. What others in Congress and the state legislatures had in mind cannot be determined with any degree of certainty.

An additional reason for the inconclusive nature of the Amendment's history, with respect to segregated schools, is the status of public education at that time. In the South, the movement toward free common schools, supported by general taxation, had not yet taken hold. Education of white children was largely in the hands of private groups. Education of Negroes was almost nonexistent, and practically all of the race were illiterate. In fact, any education of Negroes was forbidden by law in some states. Today, in contrast, many Negroes have achieved outstanding success in the arts and sciences as well as in the business and professional world. It is true that public school education at the time of the Amendment had advanced further in the North, but the effect of the Amendment on northern states was generally ignored in the congressional debates. Even in the North, the conditions of public education did not approximate those existing today. The curriculum was usually rudimentary; ungraded schools were common in rural areas; the school term was but three months a year in many states; and compulsory school attendance was virtually unknown. As a consequence, it is not surprising that there should be so little in the history of the Fourteenth Amendment relating to its intended effect on public education.

In the first cases in this Court construing the Fourteenth Amendment, decided shortly after its adoption, the Court interpreted it as proscribing all state-imposed discriminations against the Negro race. The doctrine of "separate but equal" did not make its appearance in this Court until 1896 in the case of *Plessy v. Ferguson* involving not education but transportation. American courts have since labored with the doctrine for over half a century. In this Court, there have been six cases involving the "separate but equal" doctrine in the field of public education. In *Cumming v. County Board of Education* and *Gong Lum v. Rice* the validity of the doctrine itself was not challenged. In more recent cases, all on the graduate school level, inequality was found in that specific benefits enjoyed by white students were denied to Negro students of the same educational qualifications. In none of these cases was it necessary to re-examine the doctrine to grant relief to the Negro plaintiff. And in *Sweatt v. Painter* the Court expressly reserved decision on the question whether *Plessy v. Ferguson* should be held inapplicable to public education.

In the instant cases, that question is directly presented. Here, unlike *Sweatt v. Painter,* there are findings below that the Negro and white schools involved have been equalized, or are being equalized, with respect to buildings, curricula, qualifications and salaries of teachers, and other "tangible" factors. Our decision, therefore, cannot turn on merely a comparison of these tangible factors in the Negro and white schools involved in each of the cases. We must look instead to the effect of segregation itself on public education.

In approaching this problem, we cannot turn the clock back to 1868 when the Amendment was adopted, or even to 1896 when *Plessy v. Ferguson* was written. We must consider public education in the light of its full development and its present place in American life throughout the Nation. Only in this way can it be determined if segregation in public school deprives these plaintiffs of the equal protection of the laws.

Today, education is perhaps the most important function of state and local governments. Compulsory school attendance laws and the great expenditures for education both demonstrate our recognition of the importance of education to our democratic society. It is required in the performance of our most basic public responsibilities, even service in the armed forces. It is the very foundation of good citizenship. Today it is a principal instrument in awakening the child to cultural values, in preparing him for later professional training, and in helping him to adjust normally to his environment. In these days, it is doubtful that any child may reasonably be expected to succeed in life if he is denied the opportunity of an education. Such an opportunity, where the state has undertaken to provide it, is a right which must be made available to all on equal terms.

We come then to the question presented: Does segregation of children in public schools solely on the basis of race, even though the physical facilities and other "tangible" factors may be equal, deprive the children of the minority group of equal educational opportunities? We believe that it does.

In *Sweatt v. Painter*, in finding that a segregated law school for Negroes could not provide them equal educational opportunities, this Court relied in large part on "those qualities which are incapable of objective measurement but which make for greatness in a law school." In *McLaurin v. Oklahoma State Regents* the Court, in requiring that a Negro admitted to a white graduate school be treated like all other students, again resorted to intangible considerations: " . . . his ability to study, to engage in discussions and exchange views with other students, and, in general, to learn his profession." Such considerations apply with added force to children in grade and high schools. To separate them from others of similar age and qualifications solely because of their race generates a feeling of inferiority as to their status in the community that may affect their hearts and minds in a way unlikely ever to be undone. The effect of this separation on their educational opportunities was well stated by a finding in the Kansas case by a court which nevertheless felt compelled to rule against the Negro plaintiffs:

> Segregation of white and colored children in public schools has a detrimental effect upon the colored children. The impact is greater when it has the sanction of the law; for the policy of separating the races is usually interpreted as denoting the inferiority of the Negro group. A sense of inferiority affects the motivation of a child to learn. Segregation with the sanction of law, therefore, has a tendency to [retard] the education and mental development of Negro children and to deprive them of some of the benefits they would receive in a racial[ly] integrated school system.

Whatever may have been the extent of psychological knowledge at the time of *Plessy v. Ferguson*, this finding is amply supported by modern authority. Any language in *Plessy v. Ferguson* contrary to this finding is rejected.

We conclude that in the field of public education the doctrine of "separate but equal" has no place. Separate educational facilities are inherently unequal. Therefore, we hold that the plaintiffs and others similarly situated for whom the actions have been brought are, by reason of the segregation complained of, deprived of the equal protection of the laws guaranteed by the Fourteenth Amendment. . . .

DISCUSSION QUESTIONS

1. Can *Brown* be used as a precedent to argue against the constitutionality of racial segregation in *public transportation*? Why or why not? Be sure to consider the similarities and differences between education and transportation.

2. Can *Brown* be used as a precedent to argue against the constitutionality of segregation by *gender* in public schools (for example, in sports)? Why or why not? Be sure to consider the similarities and differences between gender and race, and whether gender should be a suspect classification for the purposes of the strict[n] scrutiny test.

3. What should count as a state action? Apply your views to the case of *Moose Lodge v. Irvis* (407 U.S. 163, 1972), where Pennsylvania granted a liquor license to a private club that refused to serve blacks, but some blacks complained that they were deprived because only a limited number of liquor licenses were available.

FROM *BROWN* TO *BAKKE*

After *Brown*, the Supreme Court struck down segregation in many other areas—transportation, parks, libraries, and so on—as well as laws against racial intermarriage (though not until 1967). Another string of decisions required states to use busing as a means to end segregation in school systems. The Court also required some employers to hire or promote minimum percentages of minorities to overcome the effects of illegal discrimination in employment.

In response to these court decisions, some schools and companies voluntarily took steps to overcome what they saw as the effects of past discrimination. These steps required them to use racial classifications, and that raised the issue of reverse discrimination. Part of the issue was about what to call such programs. Their opponents label them "reverse discrimination," but their defenders refer to them as "affirmative action." Both names involve evaluation, so neither should be used without an argument. A more neutral description is "preferential treatment," so we will tend to use this term.

The classic case in this area is *Regents of the University of California v. Bakke* (1978) (hereafter, *Bakke*). The basic situation was that the medical school of the University of California at Davis had very few minority students, so they created a special admissions program that gave preferential treatment to minorities who were disadvantaged. Bakke, who was not a member of any of the specified minorities, applied to the school but was rejected even though he had higher scores on admissions tests than some minority members who were admitted under the special admissions program.

Bakke claimed that Davis's special admissions program violated the equal protection clause of the U.S. Constitution, the California Constitution, and Title VI of the Civil Rights Act of 1964, which provides: "No person in the United States shall, on the ground of race, color, or national origin, be excluded from participation in, be denied the benefits of, or be subjected to discrimination under any program or activity receiving Federal financial assistance." The Supreme Court was thus asked to rule on four main issues:

1. Did the Davis special[n] admissions program violate the equal protection clause of the Constitution?

2. Does reference to race without judicial findings of particular past discrimination violate this constitutional guarantee?

3. Did the Davis special[n] admissions program violate Title VI of the Civil Rights Act?

4. Should Davis be required to admit Bakke into its medical school?

The decision of the Supreme Court on these issues is so complicated that it takes a scorecard to follow it:

Question Ruled On	Brennan, Marshall, Blackmun, and White	Powell	Burger, Stewart, Stevens, and Rehnquist	The majority
1	No	Yes	No decision	No decision
2	No	No	No decision	No
3	No	Yes	Yes	Yes
4	No	Yes	Yes	Yes

Because the justices split into two groups of four, the remaining justice, Powell, determined the majority on most issues. Powell, however, was the only justice who argued that the Davis program was unconstitutional. Four others (Brennan, Marshall, Blackmun, and White) dissented. The remaining four (Burger, Stevens, Stewart, and Rehnquist) chose not to address this constitutional issue because they had already ruled out the Davis program under Title VI. Since a majority did not join Powell in his opinion, the Court did *not* explicitly declare the Davis program unconstitutional. But the Davis program was held to violate Title VI, and Davis was ordered to admit Bakke, because Burger, Stevens, Stewart, and Rehnquist did join Powell on these issues. Despite Davis's loss, the Court took the opposite position on the second issue. Powell argued that it was not always unconstitutional for the state to refer to race, and he created a majority when he was joined by Brennan, Marshall, Blackmun, and White. Thus, each group of justices got part of what it wanted.

The constitutional issues are raised most directly in the opinions of Powell and Brennan (excerpted below). These opinions differ not only in their conclusions but also in their interpretations of the equal protection clause. Powell argued that the Davis program and any consideration of race must be subjected to the test of strict scrutiny. He held that the Davis program did not meet the high standards of this test, but some other consideration of race might.

In contrast, Brennan argued for a new interpretation of the equal protection clause. On this new interpretation, strict scrutiny would still be applied to most racial classifications, but, when certain conditions were met, the courts would apply a less exacting test—often called *middle-level scrutiny*.

The test of middle-level scrutiny requires the state to show that (1) the state action serves a *legitimate, articulated,* and *important* state interest; (2) it does not *stigmatize* or inflict any pervasive injury on those who are excluded; and (3) it bears a *substantial* relation to the purpose, and there is no *significantly* less intrusive means to serve the purpose. Brennan argued that this more lenient test should be applied when the state uses a racial classification to serve a *benign, remedial purpose.* The purpose of a racial classification is benign when it was not adopted out of any discriminatory motive, and it is remedial if the state used the racial classification because the state found that, without the racial classification, an underprivileged group would suffer harm or differential impact because of past discrimination in society at large.

The conditions under which to apply middle-level scrutiny are the heart of the controversy. Powell criticized Brennan's conditions on the grounds that the notion of stigma is too vague and that it is not groups but individuals who are protected by the equal[n] protection clause. Brennan responded by distinguishing stigma from other harms and by emphasizing the importance of groups. Powell also argued that some kinds of preferential treatment (which use *goals,* as in the Harvard admissions program) are less intrusive than other kinds of preferential treatment (which use *quotas,* as in the Davis program). Brennan responded that this difference is not significant, because both kinds of preferential treatment produce the same result for those who are excluded.

REGENTS OF THE UNIVERSITY OF CALIFORNIA V. BAKKE

(438 U.S. 268, 1978)

Summary by the Reporter of Decisions:

The Medical School of the University of California at Davis (hereinafter Davis) had two admissions programs for the entering class of 100 students— the regular admissions program and the special admissions program. Under the regular procedure, candidates whose overall undergraduate grade point average fell below 2.5 on a scale of 4.0 were summarily rejected. About one out of six applicants was then given an interview, following which he was rated on a scale of 1 to 100 by each of the committee members (five in 1973 and six in 1974), his rating being based on the interviewers' summaries, his overall grade point average, his science courses grade point average, and his Medical College Admissions Test (MCAT) scores, letters of recommendation, extracurricular activities, and other biographical data, all of which resulted in a total "benchmark score." The full admissions committee then made offers of admission on the basis of their review of the applicant's file and his score, considering and acting upon applications as they were received. The committee chairman was responsible for placing names on the waiting list and had discretion to include persons with "special skills." A separate committee, a majority of whom were members of minority groups, operated the special admissions program. The 1973 and 1974 application forms, respectively, asked candidates whether they wished to be considered as "economically and/or educationally disadvantaged" applicants and members of a "minority group" (blacks, Chicanos, Asians, American Indians). If an applicant of a minority group was found to be "disadvantaged," he would be rated in a manner similar to the one employed by the general admissions committee. Special candidates, however, did not have to meet the 2.5 grade point cut-off and were not ranked against candidates in the general admissions process. About one-fifth of the special applicants were invited for interviews in 1973 and 1974, following which they were given benchmark scores, and the top choices were then given to the general admissions committee, which could reject special candidates for failure to meet course requirements or other specific deficiencies. The special committee continued to recommend candidates until 16 special admission selections had been made. During a four-year period 63 minority students were admitted to Davis under the special program and 44 under the general program. No disadvantaged whites were admitted under the special program, though many applied.

Respondent, a white male, applied to Davis in 1973 and 1974, in both years being considered only under the general admissions program. Though he had a 468 out of 500 score in 1973, he was rejected since no general applicants with scores less than 470 were being accepted after respondent's application, which was filed late in the year, had been processed and completed. At that time four special admission slots were still unfilled. In 1974 respondent applied early, and though he had a total score of 549 out of 600, he was again rejected. In neither year was his name placed on the discretionary waiting list. In both years special applicants were admitted with significantly lower scores than respondent's. After his second rejection, respondent filed this action in state court for mandatory injunctive and declaratory relief to compel his admission to Davis, alleging that the special admissions program operated to exclude him on the basis of his race in violation of the Equal Protection Clause of the Fourteenth Amendment, a provision of the California Constitution, and §601 of Title VI of the Civil Rights Act of 1964. . . .

Excerpts from Justice Powell's opinion:

III

Racial and ethnic classifications . . . are subject to stringent examination without regard to . . . additional characteristics. We declared as much in the first cases explicitly to recognize racial distinctions as suspect: ". . . [A]ll legal restrictions which curtail the rights of a single racial group are immediately suspect. That is not to say that all such restrictions are unconstitutional. It is to say that courts must subject them to the most rigid scrutiny" (*Korematsu*, 323 U.S. 214 at 216 [1944]). The Court has never questioned the validity of those pronouncements. . . .

Petitioner urges us to adopt for the first time a more restrictive view of the Equal Protection Clause and hold that discrimination against members of the white "majority" cannot be suspect if its purpose can be characterized as "benign." The clock of our liberties, however, cannot be turned back to 1868. It is far too late to argue that the guarantee of equal protection to *all* persons permits the recognition of special wards entitled to a degree of protection greater than that accorded others.

Moreover, there are serious problems of justice connected with the idea of preference itself. First, it may not always be clear that a so-called preference is in fact benign. Courts may be asked to validate burdens imposed upon individual members of particular groups in order to advance the group's general interest. . . . Nothing in the Constitution supports the notion that individuals may be asked to suffer otherwise impermissible burdens in order to enhance the societal standing of their ethnic groups. Second, preferential programs may only reinforce common stereotypes holding that certain groups are unable to achieve success without special protection based on a factor having no relationship to individual worth. . . . Third, there is a measure of inequity in forcing innocent persons in respondent's position to bear the burdens of redressing grievances not of their making.

Petitioner contends that on several occasions this Court has approved preferential classifications without applying the most exacting scrutiny. Most of the cases upon which petitioner relies are drawn from three areas: school desegregation, employment discrimination, and sex discrimination. Each of the cases cited presented a situation materially different from the facts of this case. . . . [W]e have never approved preferential classifications in the absence of proven constitutional or statutory violations. . . . When a classification denies an individual opportunities or benefits enjoyed by others solely because of his race or ethnic background, it must be regarded as suspect. . . .

IV

We have held that in "order to justify the use of a suspect classification, a State must show that its purpose or interest is both constitutionally permissible and substantial, and that its use of the classification is 'necessary . . . to the accomplishment' of its purpose or the safeguarding of its interest." The special admissions program purports to serve the purposes of: (i) "reducing the historic deficit of traditionally disfavored minorities in medical schools and the medical profession"; (ii) countering the effects of societal discrimination; (iii) increasing the number of physicians who will practice in communities currently underserved; and (iv) obtaining the educational benefits that flow from an ethnically diverse student body. It is necessary to decide which, if any, of these purposes is substantial enough to support the use of a suspect classification. . . .

If petitioner's purpose is to assure within its student body some specified percentage of a particular group merely because of its race or ethnic origin, such a preferential purpose must be rejected not as insubstantial but as facially invalid. Preferring members of any one group for no reason other than race or ethnic origin is discrimination for its own sake. This the Constitution forbids. . . .

The State certainly has a legitimate and substantial interest in ameliorating, or eliminating where feasible, the disabling effects of identified discrimination. The line of school desegregation cases, commencing with *Brown,* attests to the importance of this state goal and the commitment of the judiciary to affirm all lawful means toward its attainment. In the school cases, the States were required by court order to redress the wrongs worked by specific instances of racial discrimination. That goal was far more focused than the remedying of the effects of "societal discrimination," an amorphous concept of injury that may be ageless in its reach into the past.

We have never approved a classification that aids persons perceived as members of relatively victimized groups at the expense of other innocent individuals in the absence of judicial, legislative or administrative findings of constitutional or statutory violations. . . . After such findings have been made, the governmental interest in preferring members of the injured groups at the expense of others is substantial, since the legal rights of the victims must be vindicated. . . . Without such findings of constitutional or statutory violations, it cannot be said that the government has any greater interest in helping one individual than in refraining from harming another. Thus, the government has no compelling justification for inflicting such harm.

Petitioner does not purport to have made, and is in no position to make, such findings. Its broad mission is education, not the formulation of any legislative policy or the adjudication of particular claims of illegality. . . . Hence, the purpose of helping certain groups whom the faculty of the Davis Medical School perceived as victims of "societal discrimination" does not justify a classification that imposes disadvantages upon persons like respondent, who bear no responsibility for whatever harm the beneficiaries of the special admissions program are thought to have suffered.

Petitioner identifies, as another purpose of its program, improving the delivery of health care services to communities currently underserved. It may be assumed that in some situations a State's interest in facilitating the health care of its citizens is sufficiently compelling to support the use of a suspect classification. But there is virtually no evidence in the record indicating that petitioner's special admissions program is either needed or geared to promote that goal. The court below addressed this failure of proof: "The University concedes it cannot assure that minority doctors who entered under the program, all of whom express an 'interest' in participating in a disadvantaged community, will actually do so. . . . " [Thus the petitioner] simply has not carried its burden of demonstrating that it must prefer members of particular ethnic groups over all other individuals in order to promote better health care delivery to deprived citizens. Indeed, petitioner has not shown that its preferential classification is likely to have any significant effect on the problem. . . .

The fourth goal asserted by petitioner is the attainment of a diverse student body. This clearly is a constitutionally permissible goal for an institution of higher education. Academic freedom, though not a specifically enumerated constitutional right, long has been viewed as a special concern of the First Amendment. The freedom of a university to make its own judgments as to education includes the selection of its student body. . . . Thus, in arguing that its universities must be accorded the right to select those students who will contribute the most to the "robust exchange of ideas," petitioner invokes a countervailing constitutional interest, that of the First Amendment. In this light, petitioner must be viewed as seeking to achieve a goal that is of paramount importance in the fulfillment of its mission. . . .

It may be assumed that the reservation of a specified number of seats in each class for individuals from the preferred ethnic groups would contribute to the attainment of considerable ethnic diversity in the student body. But petitioner's argument that this is the only effective means of serving the interest of diversity is seriously flawed. In a most fundamental sense the argument misconceives the nature of the state interest that would justify consideration of race or ethnic background. It is not an interest in simple ethnic diversity, in which a specific percentage of the student body is in effect guaranteed to be members of selected ethnic groups, with the remaining percentage an undifferentiated aggregation of students. The diversity that furthers a compelling state interest encompasses a far broader array of qualifications and characteristics of which racial or ethnic origin is but a single though important element. Petitioner's special admissions program, focused *solely* on ethnic diversity, would hinder rather than further attainment of genuine diversity.

The experience of other university admissions programs, which take race into account in achieving the educational diversity valued by the First Amendment, demonstrates that the assignment of a fixed number of places to a minority group is not a necessary means toward that end. An illuminating example is found in the Harvard College program:

> In recent years Harvard College has expanded the concept of diversity to include students from disadvantaged economic, racial and ethnic groups. Harvard College now recruits not only Californians or Louisianans but also blacks and Chicanos and other minority students.
>
> In practice, this new definition of diversity has meant that race has been a factor in some admission decisions. When the Committee on Admissions reviews the large middle group of applicants who are 'admissible' and deemed capable of doing good work in their courses, the race of an applicant may tip the balance in his favor just as geographic origin or a life spent on a farm may tip the balance in other candidates' cases. A farm boy from Idaho can bring something to Harvard College that a Bostonian cannot offer. Similarly, a black student can usually bring something that a white person cannot offer. . . .
>
> In Harvard College admissions the Committee has not set target-quotas for the number of blacks, or of musicians, football players, physicists or Californians to be admitted in a given year. . . . But that awareness [of the necessity of including

more than a token number of black students] does not mean that the Committee sets the minimum number of blacks or of people from west of the Mississippi who are to be admitted. It means only that in choosing among thousands of applicants who are not only 'admissible' academically but have other strong qualities, the Committee, with a number of criteria in mind, pays some attention to distribution among many types and categories of students. (Brief for Columbia University, Harvard University, Stanford University, and the University of Pennsylvania, as *Amici Curiae*, App. 2, 3.)

In such an admissions program, race or ethnic background may be deemed a "plus" in a particular applicant's file, yet it does not insulate the individual from comparison with all other candidates for the available seats. The file of a particular black applicant may be examined for his potential contribution to diversity without the factor of race being decisive when compared, for example, with that of an applicant identified as an Italian-American if the latter is thought to exhibit qualities more likely to promote beneficial educational pluralism. Such qualities could include exceptional personal talents, unique work or service experience, leadership potential, maturity, demonstrated compassion, a history of overcoming disadvantage, ability to communicate with the poor, or other qualifications deemed important. In short, an admissions program operated in this way is flexible enough to consider all pertinent elements of diversity in light of the particular qualifications of each applicant, and to place them on the same footing for consideration, although not necessarily according them the same weight. Indeed, the weight attributed to a particular quality may vary from year to year depending upon the "mix" both of the student body and the applicants for the incoming class.

This kind of program treats each applicant as an individual in the admissions process. The applicant who loses out on the last available seat to another candidate receiving a "plus" on the basis of ethnic background will not have been foreclosed from all consideration for that seat simply because he was not the right color or had the wrong surname. It would mean only that his combined qualifications, which may have included similar nonobjective factors, did not outweigh those of the other applicant. His qualifications would have been weighed fairly and competitively, and he would have no basis to complain of unequal treatment under the Fourteenth Amendment.

It has been suggested that an admissions program which considers race only as one factor is simply a subtle and more sophisticated—but no less effective—means of according racial preference than the Davis program. A facial intent to discriminate, however, is evident in petitioner's preference program and not denied in this case. No such facial infirmity exists in an admissions program where race or ethnic background is simply one element—to be weighed fairly against other elements—in the selections process. "A boundary line," as Mr. Justice Frankfurter remarked in another connection, "is none the worse for being narrow." And a Court would not assume that a university, professing to employ a facially nondiscriminatory admissions policy, would operate it as a cover for the functional equivalent of a quota system. In short, good faith would be presumed in the absence of a showing to the contrary in the manner permitted by our cases.

In summary, it is evident that the Davis special admissions program involves the use of an explicit racial classification never before countenanced by this Court. It tells applicants who are not Negro, Asian, or "Chicano" that they are totally excluded from a specific percentage of the seats in an entering class. No matter how strong their qualifications, quantitative and extracurricular, including their own potential for contribution to educational diversity, they are never afforded the chance to compete with applicants from the preferred groups for the special admission seats. At the same time, the preferred applicants have the opportunity to compete for every seat in the class.

The fatal flaw in petitioner's preferential program is its disregard of individual rights as guaranteed by the Fourteenth Amendment. Such rights are not absolute. But when a State's distribution of benefits or imposition of burdens hinges on the color of a person's skin or ancestry, that individual is entitled to a demonstration that the challenged classification is necessary to promote a substantial state interest. Petitioner has failed to carry this burden. For this reason, that portion of the California court's judgment holding petitioner's special admissions program invalid under the Fourteenth Amendment must be affirmed.

Excerpts from Justice Brennan's opinion:

. . . Unquestionably we have held that a government practice or statute which restricts "fundamental rights" or which contains "suspect classifications" is to be subjected to "strict scrutiny" and can be justified only if it furthers a compelling government purpose and, even then, only if no less restrictive alternative is available. . . . But no fundamental right is involved here. . . . Nor do whites as a class have any of the "traditional indicia of suspectness: the class is not saddled with such disabilities, or subjected to such a history of purposeful unequal treatment, or relegated to such a position of political powerlessness as to command extraordinary protection from the majoritarian political process."

[The] fact that this case does not fit neatly into our prior analytic framework for race cases does not mean that it should be analyzed by applying the very loose rational-basis standard of review that is the very least that is always applied in equal protection cases.

. . . [B]ecause of the significant risk that racial classifications established for ostensibly benign purposes can be misused, causing effects not unlike those created by invidious classifications, it is inappropriate to inquire only whether there is any conceivable basis that might sustain such a classification. Instead, to justify such a classification an important and articulated purpose for its use must be shown. In addition, any statute must be stricken that stigmatizes any group or that singles out those least well represented in the political process to bear the brunt of a benign program. Thus our review under the Fourteenth Amendment should be strict—not "'strict' in theory and fatal in fact," because it is stigma that causes fatality—but strict and searching nonetheless. . . .

Davis' articulated purpose of remedying the effects of past societal discrimination is, under our cases, sufficiently important to justify the use of race-conscious admissions programs where there is a sound basis for concluding that minority underrepresentation is substantial and chronic, and that the handicap of past discrimination is impeding access of minorities to the medical school. . . .

Certainly, on the basis of the undisputed factual submissions before this Court, Davis had a sound basis for believing that the problem of underrepresentation of minorities was substantial and chronic and that the problem was attributable to handicaps imposed on minority applicants by past and present racial discrimination. Until at least 1973, the practice of medicine in this country was, in fact, if not in law, largely the prerogative of whites. In 1950, for example, while Negroes comprised 10% of the total population, Negro physicians constituted only 2.2% of the total number of physicians. The overwhelming majority of these, moreover, were educated in two predominantly Negro medical schools, Howard and Meharry. By 1970, the gap between the proportion of Negores in medicine and their proportion in the population had widened: The number of Negroes employed in medicine remained frozen at 2.2% while the Negro population had increased to 11.1%. The number of Negro admittees to predominantly white medical schools, moreover, had declined in absolute numbers during the years 1955 to 1964.

Moreover, Davis had a very good reason to believe that the national pattern of underrepresentation of minorities in medicine would be perpetuated if it retained a single admissions standard. For example, the entering classes in 1968 and 1969, the years in which such a standard was used, included only one Chicano and two Negroes out of 100 admittees. Nor is there any relief from this pattern of underrepresentation in the statistics for the regular admissions program in later years.

Davis clearly could conclude that the serious and persistent underrepresentation of minorities in medicine depicted by these statistics is the result of handicaps under which minority applicants labor as a consequence of a background of deliberate, purposeful discrimination against minorities in education and in society generally, as well as in the medical profession. . . .

The second prong of our test—whether the Davis program stigmatizes any discrete group or individual and whether race is reasonably used in light of the program's objectives—is clearly satisfied by the Davis program.

It is not even claimed that Davis' program in any way operates to stigmatize or single out any discrete and insular, or even any identifiable, nonminority group. Nor will harm comparable to that imposed upon racial minorities by exclusion or separation on grounds of race be the likely result of the program. It does not, for example, establish an exclusive preserve for minority students apart from and exclusive of whites. Rather, its purpose is to overcome the effects of segregation by bringing the races together. True, whites are excluded from participation in the special admissions program, but this fact only operates to reduce the number of whites to be admitted in the regular admissions program in order to permit admission of a reasonable percentage—less than their proportion of the California population—of otherwise underrepresented qualified minority applicants.

Nor was Bakke in any sense stamped as inferior by the Medical School's rejection of him. . . . Unlike discrimination against racial minorities, the use of racial preferences for remedial purposes does not inflict a pervasive injury upon individual whites in the sense that wherever they go or whatever they do there is a significant likelihood that they will be treated as second-class citizens because of their color. This distinction does not mean that the exclusion of a white resulting from the preferential use of race is not sufficiently serious to require justification; but it does mean that the injury inflicted by such a policy is not distinguishable from disadvantages caused by a wide range of government actions, none of which has ever been thought impermissible for that reason alone.

In addition, there is simply no evidence that the Davis program discriminates intentionally or unintentionally against any minority group which it purports to benefit. The program does not establish a quota in the invidious sense of a ceiling on the number of minority applicants to be admitted. Nor can the program reasonably be regarded as stigmatizing the program's beneficiaries or their race as inferior. The Davis program does not simply advance less qualified applicants; rather, it compensates applicants, whom it is uncontested are fully qualified to study medicine, for educational disadvantage which it was reasonable to conclude was a product of state-fostered discrimination. Once admitted, these students must satisfy the same degree requirements as regularly admitted students; they are taught by the same faculty in the same classes; and their performance is evaluated by the same standards by which regularly admitted students are judged. Under these circumstances, their performance and degrees must be regarded equally with the regularly admitted students with whom they compete for standing. Since minority graduates cannot justifiably be regarded as less well qualified than non-minority graduates by virtue of the special admissions program, there is no reasonable basis to conclude that minority graduates at schools using such programs would be stigmatized as inferior by the existence of such programs. . . .

Finally, Davis' special admissions program cannot be said to violate the Constitution simply because it has set aside a predetermined number of places for qualified minority applicants rather than using minority status as a positive factor to be considered in evaluating the applications of disadvantaged minority applicants. For purposes of constitutional adjudication, there is no difference between the two approaches. In any admissions program which accords special consideration to disadvantaged racial minorities, a determination of the degree of preference to be given is unavoidable, and any given preference that results in the exclusion of a white candidate is no more or less constitutionally acceptable than a program such as that at Davis. Furthermore, the extent of the preference inevitably depends on how many minority applicants the particular school is seeking to admit in any particular year so long as the number of qualified minority applicants exceeds that number. There is no sensible, and certainly no constitutional, distinction between, for example, adding a set number of points to the admissions rating of disadvantaged minority applicants as an expression of the preference with the expectation that this will result in the admission of an approximately determined number of qualified minority applicants and setting a fixed number of places for such applicants as was done here.

Accordingly, we would reverse the judgment of the Supreme Court of California holding the Medical School's special admissions program unconstitutional and directing respondent's admission, as well as that portion of the judgment enjoining the Medical School from according any consideration to race in the admissions process.

DISCUSSION QUESTIONS

1. The middle level of scrutiny that Justice Brennan favors in *Bakke* was used previously in gender[n] discrimination cases. These precedents, however, should be distinguished from the Davis program, according to Justice Powell. Assess Powell's arguments for this claim in the following selection from his *Bakke* opinion:

   Gender-based distinctions are less likely to create the analytical and practical problems present in preferential programs premised on racial or ethnic criteria. With respect to gender there are only two possible classifications. The incidence of the burdens imposed by preferential classifications is clear. There are no rival groups who can claim that they, too, are entitled to preferential treatment. Classwide questions as to the group suffering previous injury and groups which fairly can be burdened are relatively manageable for reviewing courts. . . . The resolution of these same questions in the context of racial and ethnic preferences presents far more complex and intractable problems than gender-based classifications. More importantly, the perception of racial classifications as inherently odious stems from a lengthy and tragic history that gender-based classifications do not share. In sum, the Court has never viewed such classifications as inherently suspect or as comparable to racial or ethnic classifications for the purpose of equal-protection analysis.

2. *Fullilove v. Klutznik*, 448 U.S. 448 (1980), concerned a congressional spending program that required at least 10 percent of the federal funds granted for local public works projects be used to procure services or supplies from businesses owned and controlled by members of minority groups. Assume the *Bakke* case as a precedent and argue for or against the constitutionality of this program. Could any consideration of race in awarding government funds be constitutional, according to the reasoning in *Bakke*? Be sure to consider any significant differences between employment and education.

FROM *BAKKE* TO *GRUTTER* AND *GRATZ*

The legal story of affirmative action gets very complicated after the *Bakke* decision. Because of the split within the Court, it was not clear which parts, if any, of Powell's opinion had force as precedent. It was also not clear which kinds of programs were close enough to the Harvard program that Powell endorsed; and it was not clear how to extend Powell's emphasis on diversity in education to other areas, such as employment and government contracts. As a result, some affirmative action programs were struck down and others were upheld while commentators scrambled to explain the underlying pattern and rationale for the Court's decisions.

The year after Bakke, in *United Steelworkers of America v. Weber*, 445 U.S. 193 (1979), the Supreme Court upheld a preferential[n] treatment quota in employment. Later, in *Richmond v. J. A. Croson Co.*, 488 U.S. 469 (1989), the Court struck down a local program that set aside a specified percentage of municipal contracts for minority-controlled firms. Then, in *Metro Broadcasting v. FCC*, 497 U.S. 547 (1990), the Court allowed a Federal Communications Commission "distress sale" policy that permitted a broadcaster whose license or renewal application has been designated for a revocation hearing to sell the license to a buyer if, but only if, that buyer is at least 50 percent minority-owned. Of course, the majority opinions gave reasons for each decision, but dissents were common and fierce, and it was hard to see how the pieces of the puzzle fit together.

The law was somewhat clearer in college admissions. As Justice O'Connor put it, "Since this Court's splintered decision in *Bakke*, Justice Powell's opinion announcing the judgment of the Court has served as the touchstone for constitutional analysis of race-conscious admissions policies. Public and private universities across the Nation have modeled their own admissions programs on Justice Powell's views on permissible race-conscious policies." Still, there was great uncertainty about exactly which kinds of admissions programs were allowed by Powell's reasoning in *Bakke*. Some critics also held that the precedent of *Bakke* should be overturned or disregarded, and the Court should hold, instead, that all race-conscious programs are unconstitutional.

This issue came to a head in 2003, when the Court considered two very different kinds of admissions programs practiced at the University of Michigan under its President, Lee Bollinger (hence the names of the cases below). Michigan's Law School admissions program was very much like the Harvard program that Powell endorsed, so that program was upheld. The admissions program at Michigan's undergraduate College of Literature, Science, and the Arts, in contrast, gave a specific number of points to all applicants in underrepresented minority groups. Critics claimed that this program amounted to a "quota" more like the Davis Medical School admissions program that Powell had struck down in *Bakke*, and the Court struck it down. The differences between these programs thus define the line between what is and is not permitted in college admissions today.

GRUTTER V. BOLLINGER

■

(539 U.S. 306, 2003)

Syllabus:

The University of Michigan Law School (Law School), one of the Nation's top law schools, follows an official admissions policy that seeks to achieve student body diversity through compliance with *Regents of Univ. of Cal. v. Bakke.* Focusing on students' academic ability coupled with a flexible assessment of their talents, experiences, and potential, the policy requires admissions officials to evaluate each applicant based on all the information available in the file, including a personal statement, letters of recommendation, an essay describing how the applicant will contribute to Law School life and diversity, and the applicant's undergraduate grade point average (GPA) and Law School Admissions Test (LSAT) score. Additionally, officials must look beyond grades and scores to so-called "soft variables," such as recommenders' enthusiasm, the quality of the undergraduate institution and the applicant's essay, and the areas and difficulty of undergraduate course selection. The policy does not define diversity solely in terms of racial and ethnic status and does not restrict the types of diversity contributions eligible for "substantial weight," but it does reaffirm the Law School's commitment to diversity with special reference to the inclusion of African-American, Hispanic, and Native-American students, who otherwise might not be represented in the student body in meaningful numbers. By enrolling a "critical mass" of underrepresented minority students, the policy seeks to ensure their ability to contribute to the Law School's character and to the legal profession.

When the Law School denied admission to petitioner Grutter, a white Michigan resident with a 3.8 GPA and 161 LSAT score, she filed this suit, alleging that respondents had discriminated against her on the basis of race in violation of the Fourteenth Amendment, Title VI of the Civil Rights Act of 1964, and 42 U.S.C. § 1981; that she was rejected because the Law School uses race as a "predominant" factor, giving applicants belonging to certain minority groups a significantly greater chance of admission than students with similar credentials from disfavored racial groups; and that respondents had no compelling interest to justify that use of race. . . .

*Justice O'Connor delivered the opinion of the Court, in which
Justices Stevens, Souter, Ginsburg, and Breyer joined:*

II

. . . We have held that all racial classifications imposed by government "must be analyzed by a reviewing court under strict scrutiny." This means that such classifications are constitutional only if they are narrowly tailored to further compelling governmental interests. . . .

III

A

With these principles in mind, we turn to the question whether the Law School's use of race is justified by a compelling state interest. Before this Court, as they have throughout this litigation, respondents assert only one justification for their use of race in the admissions process: obtaining "the educational benefits that flow from a diverse student body." . . .

The Law School's educational judgment that such diversity is essential to its educational mission is one to which we defer. The Law School's assessment that diversity will, in fact, yield educational benefits is substantiated by respondents and their amici. Our scrutiny of the interest asserted by the Law School is no less strict for taking into account complex educational judgments in an area that lies primarily within the expertise of the university. Our holding today is in keeping with our tradition of giving a degree of deference to a university's academic decisions, within constitutionally prescribed limits. . . .

As part of its goal of "assembling a class that is both exceptionally academically qualified and broadly diverse," the Law School seeks to "enroll a 'critical mass' of minority students." The Law School's interest is not simply "to assure within its student body some specified percentage of a particular group merely because of its race or ethnic origin." That would amount to outright racial balancing, which is patently unconstitutional. Rather, the Law School's concept of critical mass is defined by reference to the educational benefits that diversity is designed to produce.

These benefits are substantial. As the District Court emphasized, the Law School's admissions policy promotes "cross-racial understanding," helps to break down racial stereotypes, and "enables [students] to better understand persons of different races." These benefits are "important and laudable," because "classroom discussion is livelier, more spirited, and simply more enlightening and interesting" when the students have "the greatest possible variety of backgrounds." . . .

Moreover, universities, and in particular, law schools, represent the training ground for a large number of our Nation's leaders. . . . In order to cultivate a set of leaders with legitimacy in the eyes of the citizenry, it is necessary that the path to leadership be visibly open to talented and qualified individuals of every race and ethnicity. All members of our heterogeneous society must have confidence in the openness and integrity of the educational institutions that provide this training. . . .

B

Even in the limited circumstance when drawing racial distinctions is permissible to further a compelling state interest, government is still "constrained in how it may pursue that end: [T]he means chosen to accomplish the [government's] asserted purpose must be specifically and narrowly framed to accomplish that purpose." The purpose of the narrow tailoring requirement is to ensure that "the means chosen 'fit' . . . the compelling goal so closely that there is little or no possibility that the motive for the classification was illegitimate racial prejudice or stereotype." . . .

To be narrowly tailored, a race-conscious admissions program cannot use a quota system. . . . We are satisfied that the Law School's admissions program, like the Harvard plan described by Justice Powell, does not operate as a quota. Properly understood, a "quota" is a program in which a certain fixed number or proportion of opportunities are "reserved exclusively for certain minority groups." . . . The Law School's goal of attaining a critical mass of underrepresented minority students does not transform its program into a quota. As the Harvard plan described by Justice Powell recognized, there is of course "some relationship between numbers and achieving the benefits to be derived from a diverse student body, and between numbers and providing a reasonable environment for those students admitted." . . . Nor, as Justice Kennedy posits, does the Law School's consultation of the "daily reports," which keep track of the racial and ethnic composition of the class (as well as of residency and gender), "suggest[ ] there was no further attempt at individual review save for race itself" during the final stages of the admissions process. To the contrary, the Law School's admissions officers testified without contradiction that they never gave race any more or less weight based on the information contained in these reports. Moreover, . . . the number of African-American, Latino, and Native-American students in each class at the Law School varied from 13.5 to 20.1 percent, a range inconsistent with a quota.

That a race-conscious admissions program does not operate as a quota does not, by itself, satisfy the requirement of individualized consideration. When using race as a "plus" factor in university admissions, a university's admissions program must remain flexible enough to ensure that each applicant is evaluated as an individual and not in a way that makes an applicant's race or ethnicity the defining feature of his or her application. The importance of this individualized consideration in the context of a race-conscious admissions program is paramount. Here, the Law School engages in a highly individualized, holistic review of each applicant's file, giving serious consideration to all the ways an applicant might contribute to a diverse educational environment. The Law School affords this individualized consideration to applicants of all races. There is no policy, either de jure or de facto, of automatic acceptance or rejection based on any single "soft" variable. Unlike the program at issue in *Gratz v. Bollinger* [see below], the Law School awards no mechanical, predetermined diversity "bonuses" based on race or ethnicity. . . . .

What is more, the Law School actually gives substantial weight to diversity factors besides race. The Law School frequently accepts nonminority applicants with grades and test scores lower than underrepresented minority applicants (and other nonminority applicants) who are rejected. This shows that the Law School seriously weighs many other diversity factors besides race that can make a real and dispositive difference for nonminority applicants as well. By this flexible approach, the Law School sufficiently takes into account, in practice as well as in theory, a wide variety of characteristics besides race and ethnicity that contribute to a diverse student body. . . .

Petitioner and the United States argue that the Law School's plan is not narrowly tailored because race-neutral means exist to obtain the educational benefits of student body diversity that the Law School seeks. We disagree. Narrow tailoring does not require exhaustion of every conceivable race-neutral alternative. Nor does it require a university to choose between maintaining a reputation for excellence or fulfilling a commitment to provide educational opportunities to members of all racial groups. Narrow tailoring does, however, require serious, good faith consideration of workable race-neutral alternatives that will achieve the diversity the university seeks.

We agree with the Court of Appeals that the Law School sufficiently considered workable race-neutral alternatives. The District Court took the Law School to task for failing to consider race-neutral alternatives such as "using a lottery system" or "decreasing the emphasis for all applicants on undergraduate GPA and LSAT scores." But these alternatives would require a dramatic sacrifice of diversity, the academic quality of all admitted students, or both. . . . The United States advocates "percentage plans," recently adopted by public undergraduate institutions in Texas, Florida, and California to guarantee admission to all students above a certain class-rank threshold in every high school in the State. The United States does not, however, explain how such plans could work for graduate and professional schools. Moreover, even assuming such plans are race-neutral, they may preclude the university from conducting the individualized assessments necessary to assemble a student body that is not just racially diverse, but diverse along all the qualities valued by the university. We are satisfied that the Law School adequately considered race-neutral alternatives currently capable of producing a critical mass without forcing the Law School to abandon the academic selectivity that is the cornerstone of its educational mission. . . .

We take the Law School at its word that it would "like nothing better than to find a race-neutral admissions formula" and will terminate its race-conscious admissions program as soon as practicable. It has been 25 years since Justice Powell first approved the use of race to further an interest in student body diversity in the context of public higher education. Since that time, the number of minority applicants with high grades and test scores has indeed increased. We expect that 25 years from now, the use of racial preferences will no longer be necessary to further the interest approved today.

IV

In summary, the Equal Protection Clause does not prohibit the Law School's narrowly tailored use of race in admissions decisions to further a compelling interest in obtaining the educational benefits that flow from a diverse student body. Consequently, petitioner's statutory claims based on Title VI and 42 USC § 1981 also fail.

*Chief Justice Rehnquist, with whom
Justices Scalia, Kennedy, and Thomas join, dissenting:*

I do not believe . . . that the University of Michigan Law School's means are narrowly tailored to the interest it asserts. The Law School claims it must take the steps it does to achieve a "'critical mass'" of underrepresented minority students. But its actual program bears no relation to this asserted goal. . . .

From 1995 through 2000, the Law School admitted between 1,130 and 1,310 students. Of those, between 13 and 19 were Native American, between 91 and 108 were African-Americans, and between 47 and 56 were Hispanic. If the Law School is admitting between 91 and 108 African-Americans in order to achieve "critical mass," thereby preventing African-American students from feeling "isolated or like spokespersons for their race," one would think that a number of the same order of magnitude would be necessary to accomplish the same purpose for Hispanics and Native Americans. . . .

Only when the "critical mass" label is discarded does a likely explanation for these numbers emerge. . . . [F]rom 1995 through 2000 the percentage of admitted applicants who were members of these minority groups closely tracked the percentage of individuals in the school's applicant pool who were from the same groups . . . The tight correlation between the percentage of applicants and admittees of a given race, therefore, must result from careful race based planning by the Law School. . . . The Law School has offered no explanation for its actual admissions practices and, unexplained, we are bound to conclude that the Law School has managed its admissions program, not to achieve a "critical mass," but to extend offers of admission to members of selected minority groups in proportion to their statistical representation in the applicant pool. But this is precisely the type of racial balancing that the Court itself calls "patently unconstitutional."

*Justice Thomas, with whom Justice Scalia joins as to Parts I–VII,
concurring in part and dissenting in part:*

II

The Law School adamantly disclaims any race-neutral alternative that would reduce "academic selectivity," which would in turn "require the Law School to become a very different institution, and to sacrifice a core part of its educational mission." In other words, the Law School seeks to improve marginally the education it offers without sacrificing too much of its exclusivity and elite status.

The proffered interest that the majority vindicates today, then, is not simply "diversity." Instead the Court upholds the use of racial discrimination as a tool to advance the Law School's interest in offering a marginally superior education while maintaining an elite institution. Unless each constituent part of this state interest is of pressing public necessity, the Law School's use of race is unconstitutional. I find each of them to fall far short of this standard.

III

... Under the proper standard, there is no pressing public necessity in maintaining a public law school at all and, it follows, certainly not an elite law school. Likewise, marginal improvements in legal education do not qualify as a compelling state interest.

VI

The absence of any articulated legal principle supporting the majority's principal holding suggests another rationale. I believe what lies beneath the Court's decision today are the benighted notions that one can tell when racial discrimination benefits (rather than hurts) minority groups, and that racial discrimination is necessary to remedy general societal ills. ...

I must contest the notion that the Law School's discrimination benefits those admitted as a result of it. ... [N]owhere in any of the filings in this Court is any evidence that the purported "beneficiaries" of this racial discrimination prove themselves by performing at (or even near) the same level as those students who receive no preferences. ... The Law School tantalizes unprepared students with the promise of a University of Michigan degree and all of the opportunities that it offers. These overmatched students take the bait, only to find that they cannot succeed in the cauldron of competition. ... While these students may graduate with law degrees, there is no evidence that they have received a qualitatively better legal education (or become better lawyers) than if they had gone to a less "elite" law school for which they were better prepared. ...

Beyond the harm the Law School's racial discrimination visits upon its test subjects, no social science has disproved the notion that this discrimination "engenders attitudes of superiority or, alternatively, provoke[s] resentment among those who believe that they have been wronged by the government's use of race." "These programs stamp minorities with a badge of inferiority and may cause them to develop dependencies or to adopt an attitude that they are 'entitled' to preferences."

It is uncontested that each year, the Law School admits a handful of blacks who would be admitted in the absence of racial discrimination. Who can differentiate between those who belong and those who do not? The majority of blacks are admitted to the Law School because of discrimination, and because of this policy all are tarred as undeserving. This problem of stigma does not depend on determinacy as to whether those stigmatized are actually the "beneficiaries" of racial discrimination. When blacks take positions in the highest places of government, industry, or academia, it is an open question today whether their skin color played a part in their advancement. ...

DISCUSSION QUESTIONS

1. Reconstruct Justice O'Connor's main argument in the selection from her majority opinion in *Grutter*.

2. Reconstruct Chief Justice Rehnquist's main arguments in the selection from his dissenting opinion in *Grutter*. How could Justice O'Connor best respond? Is this response adequate? Why or why not?

3. What is Justice Thomas's point in the selections from Sections II–III of his dissenting opinion in *Grutter*? How could Justice O'Connor best respond? Is this response adequate? Why or why not?

4. What is Justice Thomas's point in the selections from Section VI of his dissenting opinion in *Grutter*? How could Justice O'Connor best respond? Is this response adequate? Why or why not?

5. How would you have decided the *Grutter* case? Why?

GRATZ V. BOLLINGER

(539 U.S. 244, 2003)

Syllabus:

Petitioners Gratz and Hamacher, both of whom are Michigan residents and Caucasian, applied for admission to the University of Michigan's (University) College of Literature, Science, and the Arts (LSA) in 1995 and 1997, respectively. Although the LSA considered Gratz to be well qualified and Hamacher to be within the qualified range, both were denied early admission and were ultimately denied admission. [The] University's Office of Undergraduate Admissions (OUA) . . . considers a number of factors in making admissions decisions, including high school grades, standardized test scores, high school quality, curriculum strength, geography, alumni relationships, leadership, and race. During all relevant periods, the University has considered African-Americans, Hispanics, and Native Americans to be "underrepresented minorities," and it is undisputed that the University admits virtually every qualified applicant from these groups. The current guidelines use a selection method under which every applicant from an underrepresented racial or ethnic minority group is automatically awarded 20 points of the 100 needed to guarantee admission. . . .

Chief Justice Rehnquist delivered the opinion of the Court, in which Justices O'Connor, Scalia, Kennedy, and Thomas joined:

We granted certiorari in this case to decide whether "the University of Michigan's use of racial preferences in undergraduate admissions violates the Equal Protection Clause of the Fourteenth Amendment, Title VI of the Civil

Rights Act of 1964 . . . , or 42 USC § 1981. . . ." Because we find that the manner in which the University considers the race of applicants in its undergraduate admissions guidelines violates these constitutional and statutory provisions, we reverse that portion of the District Court's decision upholding the guidelines.

II

B

. . . It is by now well established that "all racial classifications reviewable under the Equal Protection Clause must be strictly scrutinized." . . . To withstand our strict scrutiny analysis, respondents must demonstrate that the University's use of race in its current admission program employs "narrowly tailored measures that further compelling governmental interests." . . . We find that the University's policy, which automatically distributes 20 points, or one-fifth of the points needed to guarantee admission, to every single "underrepresented minority" applicant solely because of race, is not narrowly tailored to achieve the interest in educational diversity that respondents claim justifies their program.

In *Bakke,* Justice Powell . . . explained . . . that in his view it would be permissible for a university to employ an admissions program in which "race or ethnic background may be deemed a 'plus' in a particular applicant's file." . . . Justice Powell's opinion in *Bakke* emphasized the importance of considering each particular applicant as an individual, assessing all of the qualities that individual possesses, and in turn, evaluating that individual's ability to contribute to the unique setting of higher education. The admissions program Justice Powell described, however, did not contemplate that any single characteristic automatically ensured a specific and identifiable contribution to a university's diversity. . . . Instead, under the approach Justice Powell described, each characteristic of a particular applicant was to be considered in assessing the applicant's entire application.

The current LSA policy does not provide such individualized consideration. The LSA's policy automatically distributes 20 points to every single applicant from an "underrepresented minority" group, as defined by the University. The only consideration that accompanies this distribution of points is a factual review of an application to determine whether an individual is a member of one of these minority groups. Moreover, unlike Justice Powell's example, where the race of a "particular black applicant" could be considered without being decisive, the LSA's automatic distribution of 20 points has the effect of making "the factor of race . . . decisive" for virtually every minimally qualified underrepresented minority applicant.

Also instructive in our consideration of the LSA's system is the example provided in the description of the Harvard College Admissions Program, which Justice Powell both discussed in, and attached to, his opinion in Bakke. The example was included to "illustrate the kind of significance attached to race" under the Harvard College program. It provided as follows:

> The Admissions Committee, with only a few places left to fill, might find itself forced to choose between A, the child of a successful black physician in an academic community with promise of superior academic performance, and B, a black who grew up in an inner-city ghetto of semi-literate parents whose academic achievement was lower but who had demonstrated energy and leadership as well as an apparently abiding interest in black power. If a good number of black students much like A but few like B had already been admitted, the Committee might prefer B; and vice versa. If C, a white student with extraordinary artistic talent, were also seeking one of the remaining places, his unique quality might give him an edge over both A and B. Thus, the critical criteria are often individual qualities or experience *not dependent upon race but sometimes associated with it.* (emphasis added)

This example further demonstrates the problematic nature of the LSA's admissions system. Even if student C's "extraordinary artistic talent" rivaled that of Monet or Picasso, the applicant would receive, at most, five points under the LSA's system. At the same time, every single underrepresented minority applicant, including students A and B, would automatically receive 20 points for submitting an application. Clearly, the LSA's system does not offer applicants the individualized selection process described in Harvard's example. Instead of considering how the differing backgrounds, experiences, and characteristics of students A, B, and C might benefit the University, admissions counselors reviewing LSA applications would simply award both A and B 20 points because their applications indicate that they are African-American, and student C would receive up to 5 points for his "extraordinary talent."

Respondents emphasize the fact that the LSA has created the possibility of an applicant's file being flagged for individualized consideration by the ARC. We think that the flagging program only emphasizes the flaws of the University's system as a whole when compared to that described by Justice Powell. Again, students A, B, and C illustrate the point. First, student A would never be flagged. This is because, as the University has conceded, the effect of automatically awarding 20 points is that virtually every qualified underrepresented minority applicant is admitted. Student A, an applicant "with promise of superior academic performance," would certainly fit this description. Thus, the result of the automatic distribution of 20 points is that the University would never consider student A's individual background, experiences, and characteristics to assess his individual "potential contribution to diversity." Instead, every applicant like student A would simply be admitted.

It is possible that students B and C would be flagged and considered as individuals. This assumes that student B was not already admitted because of the automatic 20-point distribution, and that student C could muster at least 70 additional points. But the fact that the "review committee can look at the applications individually and ignore the points," once an application is flagged is of little comfort under our strict scrutiny analysis. The record does not reveal precisely how many applications are flagged for this individualized consideration, but it is undisputed that such consideration is the exception and not the rule in the operation of the LSA's admissions program. Additionally, this individualized review is only provided after admissions counselors automatically distribute the University's version of a "plus" that makes race a decisive factor for virtually every minimally qualified underrepresented minority applicant.

Respondents contend that "the volume of applications and the presentation of applicant information make it impractical for [LSA] to use the . . . admissions system" upheld by the Court today in *Grutter.* But the fact that the implementation of a program capable of providing individualized consideration might present administrative challenges does not render constitutional an otherwise problematic system. Nothing in Justice Powell's opinion in *Bakke* signaled that a university may employ whatever means it desires to achieve the stated goal of diversity without regard to the limits imposed by our strict scrutiny analysis.

We conclude, therefore, that because the University's use of race in its current freshman admissions policy is not narrowly tailored to achieve respondents' asserted compelling interest in diversity, the admissions policy violates the Equal Protection Clause of the Fourteenth Amendment. . . .

Justice Souter, with whom Justice Ginsburg joins as to Part II, dissenting:

II

The record does not describe a system with a quota like the one struck down in *Bakke*, which "insulated" all nonminority candidates from competition from certain seats. . . . The plan here, in contrast, lets all applicants compete for all places and values an applicant's offering for any place not only on grounds of race, but on grades, test scores, strength of high school, quality of course of study, residence, alumni relationships, leadership, personal character, socioeconomic disadvantage, athletic ability, and quality of a personal essay. A nonminority applicant who scores highly in these other categories can readily garner a selection index exceeding that of a minority applicant who gets the 20-point bonus.

Subject to one qualification to be taken up below, this scheme of considering, through the selection index system, all of the characteristics that the college thinks relevant to student diversity for every one of the student places to be filled fits Justice Powell's description of a constitutionally acceptable program: one that considers "all pertinent elements of diversity in light of the particular qualifications of each applicant" and places each element "on the same footing for consideration, although not necessarily according them the same weight." In the Court's own words, "each characteristic of a particular applicant [is] considered in assessing the applicant's entire application." An unsuccessful nonminority applicant cannot complain that he was rejected "simply because he was not the right color"; an applicant who is rejected because "his combined qualifications . . . did not outweigh those of the other applicant" has been given an opportunity to compete with all other applicants.

The one qualification to this description of the admissions process is that membership in an underrepresented minority is given a weight of 20 points on the 150-point scale. On the face of things, however, this assignment of specific points does not set race apart from all other weighted considerations. Nonminority students may receive 20 points for athletic ability, socioeconomic disadvantage, attendance at a socioeconomically disadvantaged or predominantly minority high school, or at the Provost's discretion; they may also receive 10 points for being residents of Michigan, 6 for residence in an underrepresented Michigan county, 5 for leadership and service, and so on.

The Court nonetheless finds fault with a scheme that "automatically" distributes 20 points to minority applicants because "the only consideration that accompanies this distribution of points is a factual review of an application to determine whether an individual is a member of one of these minority groups." The objection goes to the use of points to quantify and compare characteristics, or to the number of points awarded due to race, but on either reading the objection is mistaken.

The very nature of a college's permissible practice of awarding value to racial diversity means that race must be considered in a way that increases some applicants' chances for admission. Since college admission is not left entirely to inarticulate intuition, it is hard to see what is inappropriate in assigning some stated value to a relevant characteristic, whether it be reasoning ability, writing style, running speed, or minority race. Justice Powell's plus factors necessarily are assigned some values. The college simply does by a numbered scale what the [Michigan] law school accomplishes in its "holistic review,"; the distinction does not imply that applicants to the undergraduate college are denied individualized consideration or a fair chance to compete on the basis of all the various merits their applications may disclose.

Nor is it possible to say that the 20 points convert race into a decisive factor comparable to reserving minority places as in *Bakke*. Of course we can conceive of a point system in which the "plus" factor given to minority applicants would be so extreme as to guarantee every minority applicant a higher rank than every nonminority applicant in the university's admissions system. But petitioners do not have a convincing argument that the freshman admissions system operates this way. The present record obviously shows that nonminority applicants may achieve higher selection point totals than minority applicants owing to characteristics other than race, and the fact that the university admits "virtually every qualified underrepresented minority applicant," may reflect nothing more than the likelihood that very few qualified minority applicants apply, as well as the possibility that self-selection results in a strong minority applicant pool. It suffices for me, as it did for the District Court, that there are no Bakke-like set-asides and that consideration of an applicant's whole spectrum of ability is no more ruled out by giving 20 points for race than by giving the same points for athletic ability or socioeconomic disadvantage. . . .

In contrast to the college's forthrightness in saying just what plus factor it gives for membership in an underrepresented minority, it is worth considering the character of one alternative thrown up as preferable, because supposedly not based on race. Drawing on admissions systems used at public universities in California, Florida, and Texas, the United States contends that Michigan could get student diversity in satisfaction of its compelling interest by guaranteeing admission to a fixed percentage of the top students from each high school in Michigan.

While there is nothing unconstitutional about such a practice, it nonetheless suffers from a serious disadvantage.* It is the disadvantage of deliberate obfuscation. The "percentage plans" are just as race conscious as the point scheme (and fairly so), but they get their racially diverse results without saying directly what they are doing or why they are doing it. In contrast, Michigan states its purpose directly and, if this were a doubtful case for me, I would be tempted to give Michigan an extra point of its own for its frankness. Equal protection cannot become an exercise in which the winners are the ones who hide the ball.

DISCUSSION QUESTIONS

1. Describe the main differences among the following admissions programs. Which of these differences are relevant to the constitutionality of these programs, in your opinion?

   a. The admissions program at Davis Medical School

   b. The admissions program at Harvard College

   c. The admissions program at Michigan Law School

   d. The admissions program at Michigan's College of Literature, Science, and the Arts

   e. The percentage plan used in California, Florida, and Texas

   f. A lottery among all qualified candidates

2. In your opinion, would the admissions program at Michigan's College of Literature, Science, and the Arts be unconstitutional if, instead of 20 points, it awarded only 5 points to members of underrepresented minority groups? What if it awarded 50 points? Does the number of points matter at all? Why or why not?

3. Much of the debate between Justices Rehnquist and Souter in *Gratz* concerns whether applicants receive "individualized consideration." What exactly does this mean? Why is it important in this context?

---

*Of course it might be pointless in the State of Michigan, where minorities are a much smaller fraction of the population than in California, Florida, or Texas.

4. What are the implications of *Grutter* and *Gratz* for admissions policies in private colleges and universities? For preferential treatment in hiring? In government contracts?

5. Find out what kinds of preferential treatment programs exist in your own school or town, and then argue either that these programs are constitutional or that they are not.

BURDEN OF PROOF

A remarkable feature of the line of cases from *Plessy* through *Brown* to *Bakke*, *Grutter,* and *Gratz* is the extent to which interpretations of the equal protection clause turn on the matter of *burden of proof.* Under the rational-relation test that governed *Plessy,* the state bears a light burden when it is asked to show that its actions do not conflict with the equal[n] protection clause. In contrast, the strict-scrutiny test that governed *Brown,* and that Powell applied in *Bakke,* places a very heavy burden on the state to justify any use of suspect classification or any interference with fundamental rights. The middle-level test advocated by Brennan in *Bakke* is an effort to lighten the burden of strict scrutiny so as to permit legislation that explicitly tries to aid those who have been disadvantaged by past discrimination.

It may seem peculiar that an important legal decision can turn on such a technical and procedural matter as burden of proof. But the question of burden of proof often plays a decisive role in a legal decision, so it is worth knowing something about it.

The two basic questions concerning burden of proof are (1) *who* bears this burden and (2) how *heavy* is the burden. In our system of criminal justice, the rules governing burden of proof are fairly straightforward. The state has the burden of establishing the guilt of the accused. The defendant has no obligation to establish his or her innocence. That is what is meant by saying that the defendant is *innocent until proven guilty.* The burden of proof is also very heavy on the state in criminal procedures, for it must show *beyond a reasonable doubt* that the accused is guilty. If the prosecution shows only that it is more likely than not that the accused has committed a crime, then the jury should vote for acquittal.

Turning to civil law, there is no simple way of explaining burden of proof. Very roughly, the plaintiff (the one who brings the suit) has an initial burden to establish a *prima facie* case—that is, a case that is strong enough that it needs to be rebutted—on behalf of his or her complaint. The burden then shifts to the respondent (the one against whom the suit is being brought) to answer these claims. The burden may then shift back and forth depending on the nature of the procedure. Provided that both sides have met their legally required burdens of proof, the case is then decided on the basis of the *preponderance of evidence*; that is, the judge or jury decides which side has made the stronger case.

Burden of proof is primarily a legal notion, but it is sometimes used, often loosely, outside the law. The notion of burden of proof is needed within the law because law cases are adversarial and the Court has to come to a decision. Outside the law, people have a general burden to *have* good reasons for what they say. That is the second part of Grice's rule of Quality. More specifically, people have a burden to be able to *present* some reasons when they make accusations or statements that run counter to common opinion.

The important thing to see is that you cannot establish the truth of something through an appeal to the burden of proof. The following argument is perfectly weird:

> There is life in other parts of the universe, because you can't prove otherwise.

Of course, no one can prove that there is *not* life elsewhere in the universe, but this has no tendency to show that there *is*. Attempts to prove the truth of something through appeals to burden of proof—often called arguments from ignorance—are another example of a fallacy of *relevance*. (See Chapter 12.)

Nonetheless, the importance of burden of proof in the law does give force to another kind of argument. In a criminal case, the following argument would be perfectly fine:

> The defendant ought to be found not guilty, because the prosecution has not proven beyond a reasonable doubt that she is guilty.

This argument would also be a fallacy of relevance if the burden of proof were not so important. But the relevant burden of proof makes this argument strong in a court of law. Who bears the burden of proof and how heavy the burden is determine which legal arguments work. Consider the following argument:

> This law uses a suspect classification, and the state has not shown that it serves any compelling purpose, so the law is unconstitutional.

This argument is strong if the strict-scrutiny interpretation is accepted (assuming the premises are true). But this argument fails if a weaker burden of proof is required, as in the middle-level scrutiny interpretation. When one chooses between interpretations of equal protection and between different burdens of proof, one also chooses which arguments will have force in courts of law. This is another example of a general phenomenon that has been stressed throughout this book—that background assumptions can determine whether an argument is any good.

DISCUSSION QUESTION

Try to formulate general rules governing who has the burden of proof when people disagree. Be sure to consider a variety of areas, such as science, religion, philosophy, morality, and personal life.

MORAL REASONING

Many acts—such as lying to a friend—are not illegal, but they still seem immoral. Thus, even if such an act is legally permitted, this does not show that it is morally permitted. That is a separate issue, and it is one that many people care deeply about, because they want to do what is moral and avoid doing what is immoral. But how can we show that an act is moral or immoral? One kind of argument will not do. We can often show that an act is illegal by citing official pronouncements by judges and legislators, such as precedents and statutes. In contrast, morality is not decided by any official. There are no authoritative books in which we can look up whether a certain act is immoral without asking whether that book is correct. This affects the nature of moral arguments and the criteria for evaluating them. We cannot appeal to any documents or officials to justify our moral beliefs, so moral beliefs must be based on something else. The kinds of arguments that can be used to justify moral beliefs will be the topic of this chapter.

MORAL DISAGREEMENTS

People often disagree on moral questions. When these disagreements arise, it is often difficult—and sometimes impossible—to resolve them. At times these disagreements turn on questions of fact. If one person thinks that an action will have a particular consequence, and another thinks that it will not, they might well disagree on the moral worth of that action. For example, those who have defended the United States' decision to drop atomic bombs on Japan have often claimed that it was the only way to end the war quickly without creating a great number of casualties on both sides. Many critics of this decision have denied this factual claim.

Moral disagreements can also arise from disagreements about moral principles. To many people, it is immoral to have sex outside marriage. To others, it is immoral to interfere with such acts.

Despite such disagreements, it is surprising how much agreement there is on general moral principles. In our society, most people accept a great many moral principles as a matter of course. If a policy has no other consequence but to produce widespread misery, it is rejected out of hand. We share a conception of justice that includes, among other things, equality of opportunity and equality before the law. Most people also have a conception of human dignity: A human being is not a thing to be used and disposed of for personal advantage.

With all this agreement, how does moral disagreement arise at all? One answer is that in certain circumstances, our moral principles *conflict* with one another, and people are inclined to resolve these conflicts in different ways. People often agree on principles about welfare, justice, and human dignity, and yet, by weighing these principles differently or seeing the situation in a different light, they arrive at opposing moral conclusions.

Another kind of moral disagreement concerns the *range* or *scope* of moral principles. Even if everyone agrees that death and suffering are bad, they often disagree about *whose* death and suffering count. With few exceptions, it is thought to be wrong to inflict death and suffering on human beings. Most people have a similar attitude toward their pet dogs or cats. Some, however, go further and claim that it is also immoral to kill any animals—including cows, chickens, and fish—just to produce tasty food for humans.

The hardest problems combine issues of *range* with *conflicts of principles*. It is a disagreement of this complex kind that we will focus on in this chapter. The problem is abortion. The main issues are (1) whether fetuses lie within the range of a standard moral principle against killing, and (2) how to resolve conflicts between the principles that protect fetuses and other principles concerning, for example, human welfare and a woman's control over her body.

THE PROBLEM OF ABORTION

When faced with a moral problem, it often seems clear what the problem is, but this assumption can be mistaken. Sometimes a problem is formulated so vaguely that there is no way even to begin to solve it. People can argue for hours or even years without realizing that they are really talking about different things.

To clarify a moral problem, the first step is to specify precisely what is being judged—which action or kind of action is at issue. In the problem of abortion, the first step is to specify exactly what counts as an abortion. It is common to define abortion as the termination of a pregnancy. This includes spontaneous abortions or miscarriages, but these raise no moral problems because they are not the result of human action. Furthermore, the moral problem of abortion arises only when the death of the fetus is an expected consequence of terminating the pregnancy. To focus on these problematic cases, from now on we will take "abortion" to mean the intentional termination of a pregnancy with the expected consequence that the fetus dies as a result.

After the class of actions is picked out, we need to determine what is being asked about this class of actions—what kind of moral judgment is at stake. It is one thing to ask whether abortion is *morally wrong,* and another thing to ask whether abortion *should be illegal.* These are both moral questions (because the second asks what the law should be and not what it is), but they can be answered differently. It is not uncommon for people to claim that abortion is morally wrong but should not be made illegal, because it is a matter of personal, not public, morality. (See the passage by Mario Cuomo in Exercise II of Chapter 4.) It is also important to distinguish the question of whether abortion is or is not morally *wrong* from the separate question of whether abortion is or is not *good.* People who deny that abortion is morally wrong do not hold that abortion is a positive good. They do not, for example, recommend that people get pregnant so that they can have abortions. So, from now on, we will focus on the issue of the moral wrongness of abortion.

THE "PRO-LIFE" ARGUMENT

We can begin to understand this problem if we reconstruct the main argument against abortion, using the method discussed in Chapter 5. Most opponents of abortion call themselves "pro-life" and base their position on an appeal to a moral principle involving the "right to life." Of course, most opponents of abortion are not opposed to killing weeds, germs, or even fish. What they have in mind, then, is probably a principle such as this:

> It is always morally wrong to kill a human being.

This principle by itself does not rule out abortion. To reach this conclusion, we need further premises of the following kind:

> Abortion involves killing a human fetus.

> A human fetus is a human being.

With these premises, the anti-abortion argument will have the following form:

> (1) It is always morally wrong to kill a human being.
> (2) Abortion involves killing a human fetus.
> (3) A human fetus is a human being.
>
> ∴ (4) Abortion is morally wrong.

This argument is valid and reasonably charitable, so we have completed the first stage of reconstruction.

We next ask if the premises of this argument are true. The second premise is not controversial, given our definition of abortion; but the third premise raises many problems. Much of the debate concerning abortion turns on the question of whether a fetus is a human being. We will examine this question later on. For now, we will assume for the sake of argument that a fetus is a human being. That leaves only the first premise.

Some people—for example, strong pacifists—accept premise (1), but most people who adopt strong anti-abortion positions do not. This comes out in the following way. Many of those who oppose abortion are in favor of the death penalty for certain crimes. Therefore, they do not accept the general principle that it is always wrong to take a human life. What they need, then, is a principle that allows taking a human life in some instances but not in others. In an effort to achieve this, those who oppose abortion could reformulate the first premise in these words:

(1*) It is always morally wrong to kill an *innocent* human being.

Here the word "innocent" allows an exception for the death penalty being imposed on those who are found guilty of certain crimes. Of course, if we simply stick this premise into the previous argument, the result is invalid:

(1*) It is always morally wrong to kill an innocent human being.
(2) Abortion involves killing a human fetus.
(3) A human fetus is a human being.

∴ (4) Abortion is wrong.

To make it valid, we need to add a new premise, so that the whole argument looks like this:

(1*) It is always morally wrong to kill an innocent human being.
(2) Abortion involves killing a human fetus.
(3) A human fetus is a human being.
(4*) A human fetus is innocent.

∴ (5) Abortion is morally wrong.

Even stated this way, however, the first premise seems to admit of counterexamples. If someone's life is threatened by a madman, it is generally thought that the person has the right to use whatever means are necessary against the madman to prevent being killed. This may include killing the madman, even though the insane are usually thought to be morally innocent of their deeds. If so, the moral principle must be modified again, and then we get something like this:

(1**) It is always morally wrong to kill an innocent human being *except in self-defense.*

It is still possible to find difficulties with this principle that will lead some to add further modifications or clarifications. Children, for example, are often the innocent victims of bombing raids, yet the raids are often thought to be justified, because these deaths are not intended, even though they are foreseeable. At this point it is common to modify the principle again by including a reference to intentions. We shall not, however, pursue this complex line of reasoning here.[1]

---

[1] For a discussion of this approach, and for a model of how to argue about a moral principle, see Philippa Foot, "The Problem of Abortion and the Doctrine of Double Effect," in Foot, *Virtues and Vices and Other Essays in Moral Philosophy* (Berkeley: University of California Press, 1978), 19–32.

We have arrived, then, at a principle that seems to make sense out of a position that is against abortion but in favor of the death penalty and self-defense. With these modifications included, the argument now looks like this:

(1**) It is always morally wrong to kill an innocent human being except in self-defense.
(2) Abortion involves killing a human fetus.
(3) A human fetus is a human being.
(4*) A human fetus is innocent.

∴ (5) Abortion is always morally wrong.

Again, however, by making the premises more plausible, we created a new problem: The argument is invalid as it stands, since the qualification "except in self-defense" is missing from the conclusion. The proper conclusion of the argument should be:

(5*) Abortion is always morally wrong except in self-defense.

Rewriting the conclusion in this way has an important consequence: The argument no longer leads to a conclusion that abortion is *always* wrong. This qualified conclusion could permit abortion in those cases in which it is needed to defend the life of the pregnant woman who bears the fetus. In fact, this is the position that many people who are generally opposed to abortion adopt: Abortion is wrong except in those cases in which it is necessary to save the life of the mother. Although this does not lay down an absolute pro-hibition, it is still a strong anti-abortion position, since it would condone abortion in only a few exceptional cases.

"PRO-CHOICE" RESPONSES

We can now examine the way in which those who adopt the liberal or "pro-choice" position will respond to the conservative or "pro-life" argument as it has just been spelled out. The second premise should not be a subject for controversy, given our definition of abortion. Nor does it seem likely that the fourth premise will be attacked on the ground that the fetus is not innocent. How could a fetus be guilty of anything?

This leaves three strategies for the liberal: (1) Further modify the moral principle in the first premise to allow more exceptions. (2) Deny the third premise—that the fetus is a human being. (3) Oppose this conservative argu-ment with a different argument based on a different moral principle.

FURTHER MODIFICATIONS.   Even if it is agreed that abortion is justified when it saves the mother's life, we still need to ask whether this is the only exception or whether abortion is justified in other cases as well. Many pro-life conservatives admit that abortion is also justified when the pregnancy results from rape or incest. It is not easy to see how to modify the moral principle against killing to allow an exception in cases of rape and incest, so this exception is controversial. We will return to this issue later. But even if exceptions are made both for life-threatening pregnancies and for pregnancies due to rape and incest, the range of morally permissible abortions will still be very small.

Pro-choice liberals can, however, argue for a wider range of morally permissible abortions by extending the self-defense exception. It can be argued that a woman has a right to defend not only her life but also her physical and psychological well-being. Liberals can also argue that the exception of rape shows that abortion is allowed when the woman is not responsible for her pregnancy, and this might include cases in which the woman tried to prevent pregnancy by using contraceptives. Granting exceptions of this kind does not provide the basis for an absolute right to an abortion, but it does move things away from a "pro-life" position in the direction of a "pro-choice" position.

THE STATUS OF THE FETUS.   So far we have assumed for the sake of argument that a human fetus is a human being. But pro-choice liberals often deny this premise. It may seem hard to deny that a human fetus is human. After all, it is not an aardvark. Liberals, however, claim that the real issue is not about biological species. The real issue is whether a human fetus is covered by the moral principle against killing, and whether it is protected to the same extent as an adult human. Anything that is protected to this extent is said to have a "right to life" and will be called a "person." The issue, then, is whether a human fetus is a person. If a fetus *is* a person, the burden of proof is on those who defend abortion to show why the moral principle against killing should be set aside or modified. If a fetus is *not* a person, this moral principle cannot show that there is anything wrong with abortion for any reason—with what is called "abortion on demand."

Any argument that a fetus either is a person or is not a person must proceed from some idea of which properties make something a person—which properties warrant the protection of moral principles. To argue that a fetus is not a person, pro-choice liberals need to find some feature that fetuses lack and that is necessary for personhood. In response, pro-life conservatives need to find some feature that fetuses have and that is sufficient for personhood.

Many conditions of personhood have been suggested. This list is not complete:

Genetic code (which determines biological species)

Ensoulment (when a soul enters the body)

Brain activity (first detected around eight weeks)

Sentience (capacity to feel pain and pleasure)

Viability (when the fetus can survive outside the womb)

Rationality (and other related capacities)

Pro-life conservatives usually emphasize tests such as genetic code, which is formed at conception, or ensoulment, which is supposed to occur at or shortly after conception. In contrast, pro-choice liberals usually employ tests such as viability, which is reached during the second trimester, or rationality, which comes sometime after birth (depending on what counts as rationality—ability to choose and plan, self-consciousness, and so on). Thus, the personhood of fetuses during the first trimester is usually asserted by conservatives and denied by liberals on this issue.

How can we determine whether a feature is necessary or sufficient for personhood? We can start by rejecting any test of personhood that leads to *implausible* results. Pro-life conservatives argue that rationality is not necessary for personhood, because, whatever rationality is, newborn babies and severely retarded adults are not rational, but it is still morally wrong to kill them. Other tests of personhood are ruled out because they do not seem *important* enough. Pro-choice liberals argue that a certain genetic code is not sufficient to make something a person, because there is no reason to favor one genetic code over another except that it later produces other important features, such as rationality. It is also common to rule out a test of personhood if we cannot *know* when the test is passed. For example, many people reject ensoulment as a criterion of personhood, because they see no way to tell when, if ever, a fetus has a soul. And tests of personhood are also often rejected if they depend on factors that are *extraneous*. Conservatives often argue that viability cannot be a test of personhood, because the point when a fetus can survive outside the womb depends on what technology happens to be available to doctors at the time.

In addition to features that fetuses have when they are fetuses, they also seem to have the *potential* to develop many more, including rationality. Opponents of abortion often use this premise to argue that fetuses are persons and have a right to life. The first problem with this argument is that it seems to assume that something has a right if it has the potential to come to have that right. But this is clearly too strong. A three-year-old child does not have the right to vote even though it has the potential to develop into someone who will have the right to vote. Furthermore, the notion of potential is not clear. If the fetus has the potential, why do the egg and sperm not have it? This does not refute potentiality as a test of personhood, but much more must be done to show what potentiality is and why it is sufficient to make something a person even before the potential is realized.

All these positions on personhood are controversial, and many people feel uncertain about which is the correct one. A major issue in many moral problems is how to deal with uncertainties such as this. One reaction is a position called "gradualism."[2] We have assumed so far that the fetus either has a full right to life or has no right to life at all, but rights sometimes come in varying strengths. Gradualists claim that a fetus slowly develops a right to

---

[2]Gradualism is discussed in more detail in Joel Feinberg, "Abortion," in *Matters of Life and Death,* 2d ed., ed. Tom Regan (New York: Random House, 1986), 256–93.

life which is at first very weak. As pregnancy progresses, this right gets stronger, so it takes more to justify abortion. Late abortions still might be permitted, but only in extreme circumstances. This position is still vague, but it is attractive to some people who want to avoid placing too much emphasis on any single point in fetal development.

Uncertainty is also exploited in other ways. We discussed slippery-slope arguments already in Chapter 11. Another way to exploit uncertainty is to put the burden on the other side to produce a reason for drawing a line at some point. For example, Ronald Reagan said, "Anyone who doesn't feel sure whether we are talking about a second human life should clearly give life the benefit of the doubt." However, the same kind of argument is also available to defenders of abortion: Since we are not sure whether the fetus is a person, but we are sure that the pregnant woman has rights over her body, we should give the benefit of the doubt to the pregnant woman. We should always suspect that there is something wrong with an argument that can be used equally well in opposing directions.

CONFLICTING PRINCIPLES.   A third kind of pro-choice response is to invoke another principle, which conflicts with the pro-life principle against killing. Pro-choice liberals often emphasize two such principles: one about the rights of the pregnant woman to control her own body and another about overall human welfare. We will focus for now on human welfare.

Defenders of abortion often argue that abortion can sometimes be justified in terms of the welfare of the woman who bears the fetus, or in terms of the welfare of the family into which it will be born, or even in terms of the welfare of the child itself (if it were to be born with a severe disability or into an impoverished situation). This argument, when spelled out, looks like this:

(1) An action that best increases overall human welfare is not morally wrong.
(2) Abortion is sometimes the best way of increasing overall human welfare.

∴ (3) Abortion is sometimes not morally wrong.

What are we to say about this argument? It seems valid in form, so we can turn to the premises themselves and ask whether they are acceptable. The first (and leading) premise of the argument is subject to two immediate criticisms. First, it is vague. Probably what a person who uses this kind of argument has in mind by speaking of human welfare is a certain level of material and psychological well-being. Of course, this is still vague, but it is clear enough to make the premise a target of the second, more important, criticism. Although maximizing human welfare may, in general, be a good thing, it is not the only relevant consideration in deciding how to act. For example, it might be true that our society would be much more prosperous on the whole if 10 percent of the population were designated slaves who would do all the menial work. Yet even if a society could be made generally happy in this way, most people would reject such a system on the grounds that it is unfair to the slave class. (See the discussion of counterexamples in Chapter 13.) For reasons of this kind, most people would modify premise (1) in the following way:

(1*) An action that best increases human welfare is not morally wrong, provided that it is not unfair.

But if the first premise is modified in this way, then the entire argument must be restated to reflect this revision. It will now look like this:

(1*) An action that best increases human welfare is not morally wrong, provided that it is not unfair.
(2*) Abortion is sometimes an action that best increases human welfare.

∴ (3*) Abortion is sometimes not morally wrong, provided that it is not unfair.

It should be obvious how opponents of abortion will reply to this argument. They will maintain that abortion almost always involves unfairness—namely, to the fetus—so abortion is still wrong in almost all cases, as the pro-life argument claimed. Once more we have encountered a standard situation: Given a strong premise (premise 1), it is possible to derive a particular conclusion, but this strong premise is subject to criticism and therefore must be modified. When the premise is modified, it no longer supports the original conclusion that the person presenting the argument wishes to establish.

The argument does not stop here. A defender of abortion might reply in a number of ways. Some theory of fairness might be developed to argue that many abortions are not unfair to the fetus, because the fetus has no right to use the pregnant woman's body. (See Thomson, below.) The burden of the argument may shift to the question of whether or not a human fetus is a person and therefore possessed of a right to fair treatment. It might also be argued that questions of human welfare are sometimes more important than issues of fairness. During war and some emergencies, for example, members of a certain segment of the population are called on to risk their lives for the good of the whole in ways that might seem unfair to them.

When the argument is put on this new basis, the question becomes this: Are there circumstances in which matters of welfare become so urgent that the rights of the fetus (assuming the fetus has rights) are overridden? The obvious case in which this might happen is when the life of the bearer of the fetus is plainly threatened. For many conservatives on abortion, abortion is permitted in such cases. Some who hold a pro-choice position will maintain that severe psychological, financial, or personal losses to the pregnant woman may also take precedence over the life of the fetus. Furthermore, if not aborted, many fetuses would live in very deprived circumstances, and some would not develop very far or live very long, because they have deadly diseases, such as Tay-Sachs. How severe must these losses, deprivations, and diseases be? From our previous discussion of slippery-slope arguments in Chapter 11, we know that we should not expect any sharp lines here. Indeed, people will tend to be spread out in their opinions along a continuum ranging from a belief in complete prohibition to no prohibition.

ANALOGICAL REASONING IN ETHICS

Using the method for reconstructing arguments, we now have a fairly clear idea of the main options on the abortion issue. But understanding the structure of the debate—though essential for dealing with it intelligently—does not settle it. If the reasons on all sides are fully spelled out and disagreement remains, what is to be done?

At this stage, those who do not simply turn to abuse often appeal to *analogical arguments*. The point of an analogical argument is to reach a conclusion in a controversial case by comparing it to a similar situation in which it is clearer what is right or wrong. In fact, a great deal of ethical reasoning uses such analogies. We have already seen one simple analogy between an abortion to save the life of the mother and self-defense against an insane person. To get a better idea of how analogical reasoning works in ethics, we will concentrate on a more complex analogy, which raises the issue of whether abortion is morally permissible in cases of pregnancy due to rape.

A classic analogical argument is given by Judith Jarvis Thomson in "A Defense of Abortion" (reprinted below). Thomson grants for the sake of argument that a fetus is a person. Then she tells the following story:

> You wake up in the morning and find yourself back to back in bed with an unconscious violinist. A famous unconscious violinist. He has been found to have a fatal kidney ailment, and the Society of Music Lovers has canvassed all the available medical records and found that you alone have the right blood type to help. They have therefore kidnapped you, and last night the violinist's circulatory system was plugged into yours, so that your kidneys can be used to extract poisons from his blood as well as your own. The director of the hospital now tells you, "Look, we're sorry the Society of Music Lovers did this to you—we would never have permitted it if we had known. But still, they did it, and the violinist now is plugged into you. To unplug you would be to kill him. But never mind, it's only for nine months. By then he will have recovered from his ailment, and can safely be unplugged from you."

Thomson claims that it is not wrong for you to unplug yourself from the violinist in this situation, and most people seem to agree with her judgment in this case. By analogy, abortion after rape is not wrong either.

The basic assumption of this analogical argument is that we should not make different moral judgments in cases that do not differ. More positively:

> (1) If two actions are similar in all morally relevant respects, and if one of the acts is not morally wrong, then the other act is also not morally wrong.

Now we can apply this principle to Thomson's story:

> (2) It is not morally wrong for you to unplug the violinist in Thomson's example.
> (3) To unplug the violinist and to abort a pregnancy due to rape are similar in all morally relevant respects.
>
> ∴ (4) It is not morally wrong for a woman to abort a pregnancy due to rape.

This argument is valid, so, following the normal procedure, we can ask whether the premises are true. The first premise seems plausible, and it is accepted in most moral theories. Most people also accept the second premise. Consequently, the discussion usually focuses on the third premise—on the similarities and differences between Thomson's story and abortion in a pregnancy due to rape.

First, consider these similarities between Thomson's story and abortion after rape:

1. Both the fetus and the violinist are on or near the Earth.
2. Kidnapping is immoral and illegal, like rape.
3. The hospital stay lasts nine months, like pregnancy.
4. The violinist is innocent and a human being, like the fetus (given our present assumption).
5. Unplugging the violinist is supposed to be killing, like an abortion.

Now here are some differences between the situations:

6. The fetus cannot play the violin, but the violinist can.
7. The person who is plugged into the violinist might not be female.
8. The person who is plugged into the violinist cannot leave the hospital room, but pregnant women can still move around, even if they have some difficulty.
9. Abortion involves killing, but unplugging the violinist is merely refusing to save.

It is obvious that some of the similarities and differences are *not* relevant. It does not matter whether killing occurs near the Earth. Killing is usually wrong, even on the starship *Enterprise*. It is also accepted that differences in musical talent and in sex cannot justify killing. The other similarities and differences on our list *do* seem important. They each concern harm and responsibility, matters that must be considered in reaching a moral judgment about these actions. The force of Thomson's analogical argument is that the very features that lead us to conclude that it would not be wrong to unplug the violinist are also found in the case of pregnancy due to rape. Furthermore, there are no relevant differences that are important enough to override the significance of these similarities. These considerations, if correct, provide a reason for treating the two cases in the same way. If we agree, as Thomson thinks we will, that it is not wrong to unplug the violinist, then we have a reason to conclude that abortion after rape is not wrong either.

Responses to Thomson's argument have largely turned on emphasizing the differences between the two situations. Many critics claim that Thomson's argument fails because abortion involves *killing*, whereas unplugging does not. If you stay plugged to the violinist, this will save the violinist, so to unplug yourself is to *fail to save* the violinist. But critics deny that to unplug yourself from the violinist is the same as to *kill* the violinist, or to take the violinist's life. They argue that there is a crucial difference between killing and failing to save, because a negative duty not to kill is much stronger than any positive duty to save another person's life.

To determine whether unplugging the violinist is more like acts of killing or more like other acts of refusing to save, we might consider more analogies. Thomson also introduces additional analogies that seem more like abortions in which the pregnancy is not due to rape. In the end, our sense of which features seem most important will determine how we evaluate all such analogical arguments. The analogies bring certain features to our attention, but we have to decide which features are important, and how important they are.

WEIGHING FACTORS

Our discussion has brought us to the following point: Disagreements concerning abortion in general cannot be reduced to a yes-no dispute. Most opponents of abortion acknowledge that abortion is permissible in some (though very few) cases. Most defenders of abortion admit that there are some (though not restrictively many) limitations on when abortion is permissible. Where people place themselves on this continuum does not depend on any simple acceptance of one argument over another, but instead on the weight they give certain factors. To what extent does a fetus have rights? The pro-life position we examined earlier grants the fetus a full (or close to full) right to life. The pro-choice position usually grants few or no rights to the fetus. In what areas do questions of welfare override certain individual rights? The conservative in this matter usually restricts this to those cases in which the very life of the mother is plainly threatened. As the position on abortion becomes more liberal, the more extensive becomes the range of cases in which the rights, if any, of the fetus are set aside in favor of the rights of the bearer of the fetus. Where a particular person strikes this balance is not only a function of basic moral beliefs but also a function of different weights assigned to them.

How can one deal with such bedrock disagreements? The first thing to see is that logic alone will not settle them. Starting from a certain conception of persons, it is possible to argue coherently for a pro-choice view on abortion; starting from another point of view, it is possible to argue coherently for a pro-life view on abortion. The next important thing to see is that it is possible to *understand* an opposing view—that is, get a genuine feeling for its inner workings—even if you disagree with it completely. Logical analysis might show that particular arguments are unsound or have unnoticed and unwanted implications. This might force clarification and modification. But the most important service that logical analysis can perform is to lay bare the fundamental principles that lie beneath surface disagreements. Analysis will sometimes show that these disagreements are fundamental and perhaps irreconcilable. Dealing with such irreconcilable differences in a humane way is one of the fundamental tasks of a society dedicated to freedom and a wide range of civil liberties.

DISCUSSION QUESTIONS

1. Reconstruct and evaluate the arguments against abortion that are stated or suggested in the following short passages from Ronald Reagan, *Abortion and the Conscience of the Nation* (Thomas Nelson: New York, 1984). Be sure to specify the exact conclusion and spell out important suppressed premises. How would an opponent best respond to each argument?

   a. "We cannot diminish the value of one category of human life—the unborn—without diminishing the value of all human life" (18).

   b. "I have often said that when we talk about abortion, we are talking about two lives—the life of the mother and the life of the unborn child. Why else do we call a pregnant woman a mother?" (21).

   c. "I have also said that anyone who doesn't feel sure whether we are talking about a second human life should surely give life the benefit of the doubt. If you don't know whether a body is alive or dead, you would never bury it. I think this consideration itself should be enough for all of us to insist on protecting the unborn" (21).

   d. "Medical practice confirms at every step the correctness of these moral sensibilities. Modern medicine treats the unborn child as a patient. Medical pioneers have made great breakthroughs in treating the unborn—for genetic problems, vitamin deficiencies, irregular heart rhythms, and other medical conditions" (21–22).

   e. "I am convinced that Americans do not want to play God with the value of human life. It is not for us to decide who is worthy to live and who is not" (30).

   f. "Malcolm Muggeridge, the English writer, goes right to the heart of the matter: 'Either life is always and in all circumstances sacred, or intrinsically of no account; it is inconceivable that it should be in some cases the one and in some the other'" (34).

2. Reconstruct and evaluate the arguments in defense of abortion that are stated or suggested in the following short passages from Mary Gordon, "A Moral Choice," *Atlantic Monthly*, April 1990, 78–84. Be sure to specify the exact conclusion and spell out important suppressed premises. How would an opponent best respond to each argument?

a. "Common sense, experience, and linguistic usage point clearly to the fact that we habitually consider, for example, a seven-week-old fetus to be different from a seven-month-old one. . . . We have different language for the experience of the involuntary expulsion of the fetus from the womb depending upon the point of gestation at which the expulsion occurs. If it occurs early in the pregnancy, we call it a miscarriage; if late, we call it a stillbirth" (80).

b. "Our ritual and religious practices underscore the fact that we make distinctions among fetuses. If a woman took the bloody matter—indistinguishable from a heavy period—of an early miscarriage and insisted upon putting it in a tiny coffin and marking its grave, we would have serious concerns about her mental health. By the same token, we would feel squeamish about flushing a seven-month-old fetus down the toilet—something we would normally do with an early miscarriage. There are no prayers for the matter of a miscarriage, nor do we feel there should be. Even a Catholic priest would not baptize the issue of an early miscarriage" (80).

c. "We must make decisions on abortion based on an understanding of how people really do live. We must be able to say that poverty is worse than not being poor, that having dignified and meaningful work is better than working in conditions of degradation, that raising a child one loves and has desired is better than raising a child in resentment and rage, that it is better for a twelve-year-old not to endure the trauma of having a child when she is herself a child" (81–82).

d. "It is possible for a woman to have a sexual life unriddled by fear only if she can be confident that she need not pay for a failure of technology or judgment (and who among us has never once been swept away in the heat of a sexual moment?) by taking upon herself the crushing burden of unchosen motherhood" (82).

e. "There are some undeniable bad consequences of a woman's being forced to bear a child against her will. First is the trauma of going through a pregnancy and giving birth to a child who is not desired, a trauma more long-lasting than that experienced by some (only some) women who experience an early abortion. The grief of giving up a child at its birth—and at nine months it is a child one has felt move inside one's body—is underestimated both by anti-choice partisans and by those for whom access to adoptable children is important. This grief should not be forced on any woman—or, indeed, encouraged by public policy" (84).

f. "We must be realistic about the impact on society of millions of unwanted children in an overpopulated world" (84).

g. "Making abortion illegal will result in the deaths of women, as it has always done. Is our historical memory so short that none of us remember aunts, sisters, friends, or mothers who were killed or rendered sterile by septic abortions? . . . Can anyone genuinely say that it would be a moral good for us as a society to return to those conditions?" (84).

WHY ABORTION IS IMMORAL[3]

■

by Don Marquis

The view that abortion is, with rare exceptions, seriously immoral has received little support in the recent philosophical literature. No doubt most philosophers affiliated with secular institutions of higher education believe that the anti-abortion position is either a symptom of irrational religious dogma or a conclusion generated by seriously confused philosophical argument. The purpose of this essay is to undermine this general belief. This essay sets out an argument that purports to show, as well as any argument in ethics can show, that abortion is, except possibly in rare cases, seriously immoral, that it is in the same moral category as killing an innocent adult human being.

The argument is based on a major assumption. Many of the most insightful and careful writers on the ethics of abortion—such as Joel Feinberg, Michael Tooley, Mary Anne Warren, H. Tristram Engelhardt, Jr., L. W. Sumner, John T. Noonan, Jr., and Philip Devine*—believe that whether or not abortion is morally permissible stands or falls on whether or not a fetus is the sort of being whose life it is seriously wrong to end. The argument of this essay will assume, but not argue, that they are correct.

Also, this essay will neglect issues of great importance to a complete ethics of abortion. Some anti-abortionists will allow that certain abortions, such as abortion before implantation or abortion when the life of a woman is threatened by a pregnancy or abortion after rape, may be morally permissible. This essay will not explore the casuistry of these hard cases. The purpose of this essay is to develop a general argument for the claim that the overwhelming majority of deliberate abortions are seriously immoral. . . .

II.

. . . we can start from the following unproblematic assumption concerning our own case: it is wrong to kill *us*. Why is it wrong? Some answers can be easily eliminated. It might be said that what makes killing us wrong is that a killing brutalizes the one who kills. But the brutalization consists of being inured to the performance of an act that is hideously immoral; hence, the brutalization does not explain the immorality. It might be said that what

---

[3]*The Journal of Philosophy*, vol. 86, no. 4 (April 1989), 183–202.

*Feinberg, "Abortion," in *Matters of Life and Death: New Introductory Essays in Moral Philosophy*, Tom Regan, ed. (New York: Random House, 1986), 256–293; Tooley, "Abortion and Infanticide," *Philosophy and Public Affairs*, II, 1 (1972): 37–65, Tooley, *Abortion and Infanticide* (New York: Oxford, 1984); Warren, "On the Moral and Legal Status of Abortion," *The Monist*, LVII, 1 (1973): 43–61; Engelhardt, "The Ontology of Abortion," *Ethics*, LXXXIV, 3 (1974): 217–234; Sumner, *Abortion and Moral Theory* (Princeton: University Press, 1981); Noonan, "An Almost Absolute Value in History," in *The Morality of Abortion: Legal and Historical Perspectives*, Noonan, ed. (Cambridge: Harvard, 1970); and Devine, *The Ethics of Homicide* (Ithaca: Cornell, 1978).

makes killing us wrong is the great loss others would experience due to our absence. Although such hubris is understandable, such an explanation does not account for the wrongness of killing hermits, or those whose lives are relatively independent and whose friends find it easy to make new friends.

A more obvious answer is better. What primarily makes killing wrong is neither its effect on the murderer nor its effect on the victim's friends and relatives, but its effect on the victim. The loss of one's life is one of the greatest losses one can suffer. The loss of one's life deprives one of all the experiences, activities, projects, and enjoyments that would otherwise have constituted one's future. Therefore, killing someone is wrong, primarily because the killing inflicts (one of) the greatest possible losses on the victim. To describe this as the loss of life can be misleading, however. The change in my biological state does not by itself make killing me wrong. The effect of the loss of my biological life is the loss to me of all those activities, projects, experiences, and enjoyments which would otherwise have constituted my future personal life. These activities, projects, experiences, and enjoyments are either valuable for their own sakes or are means to something else that is valuable for its own sake. Some parts of my future are not valued by me now, but will come to be valued by me as I grow older and as my values and capacities change. When I am killed, I am deprived both of what I now value which would have been part of my future personal life, but also what I would come to value. Therefore, when I die, I am deprived of all of the value of my future. Inflicting this loss on me is ultimately what makes killing me wrong. This being the case, it would seem that what makes killing *any* adult human being prima facie seriously wrong is the loss of his or her future.*

How should this rudimentary theory of the wrongness of killing be evaluated? It cannot be faulted for deriving an "ought" from an "is," for it does not. The analysis assumes that killing me (or you, reader) is prima facie seriously wrong. The point of the analysis is to establish which natural property ultimately explains the wrongness of the killing, given that it is wrong. A natural property will ultimately explain the wrongness of killing, only if (1) the explanation fits with our intuitions about the matter and (2) there is no other natural property that provides the basis for a better explanation of the wrongness of killing. This analysis rests on the intuition that what makes killing a particular human or animal wrong is what it does to that particular human or animal. What makes killing wrong is some natural effect or other of the killing. Some would deny this. For instance, a divine-command theorist in ethics would deny it. Surely this denial is, however, one of those features of divine-command theory which renders it so implausible.

The claim that what makes killing wrong is the loss of the victim's future is directly supported by two considerations. In the first place, this theory explains why we regard killing as one of the worst of crimes. Killing is espe-

*I have been most influenced on this matter by Jonathan Glover, *Causing Death and Saving Lives* (New York: Penguin, 1977), ch. 3; and Robert Young, "What Is So Wrong with Killing People?" *Philosophy*, I.IV, 210 (1979): 515–528.

cially wrong, because it deprives the victim of more than perhaps any other crime. In the second place, people with AIDS or cancer who know they are dying believe, of course, that dying is a very bad thing for them. They believe that the loss of a future to them that they would otherwise have experienced is what makes their premature death a very bad thing for them. A better theory of the wrongness of killing would require a different natural property associated with killing which better fits with the attitudes of the dying. What could it be?

The view that what makes killing wrong is the loss to the victim of the value of the victim's future gains additional support when some of its implications are examined. In the first place, it is incompatible with the view that it is wrong to kill only beings who are biologically human. It is possible that there exists a different species from another planet whose members have a future like ours. Since having a future like that is what makes killing someone wrong, this theory entails that it would be wrong to kill members of such a species. Hence, this theory is opposed to the claim that only life that is biologically human has great moral worth, a claim which many anti-abortionists have seemed to adopt. This opposition, which this theory has in common with personhood theories, seems to be a merit of the theory.

In the second place, the claim that the loss of one's future is the wrong-making feature of one's being killed entails the possibility that the futures of some actual nonhuman mammals on our own planet are sufficiently like ours that it is seriously wrong to kill them also. Whether some animals do have the same right to life as human beings depends on adding to the account of the wrongness of killing some additional account of just what it is about my future or the futures of other adult human beings which makes it wrong to kill us. No such additional account will be offered in this essay. Undoubtedly, the provision of such an account would be a very difficult matter. Undoubtedly, any such account would be quite controversial. Hence, it surely should not reflect badly on this sketch of an elementary theory of the wrongness of killing that it is indeterminate with respect to some very difficult issues regarding animal rights.

In the third place, the claim that the loss of one's future is the wrong-making feature of one's being killed does not entail, as sanctity of human life theories do, that active euthanasia is wrong. Persons who are severely and incurably ill, who face a future of pain and despair, and who wish to die will not have suffered a loss if they are killed. It is, strictly speaking, the value of a human's future which makes killing wrong in this theory. This being so, killing does not necessarily wrong some persons who are sick and dying. Of course, there may be other reasons for a prohibition of active euthanasia, but that is another matter. Sanctity-of-human-life theories seem to hold that active euthanasia is seriously wrong even in an individual case where there seems to be good reason for it independently of public policy considerations. This consequence is more implausible, and it is a plus for the claim that the loss of a future of value is what makes killing wrong that it does not share this consequence.

In the fourth place, the account of the wrongness of killing defended in this essay does straightforwardly entail that it is prima facie seriously wrong to kill children and infants, for we do presume that they have futures of value. Since we do believe that it is wrong to kill defenseless little babies, it is important that a theory of the wrongness of killing easily account for this. Personhood theories of the wrongness of killing, on the other hand, cannot straightforwardly account for the wrongness of killing infants and young children.* Hence, such theories must add special ad hoc accounts of the wrongness of killing the young. The plausibility of such ad hoc theories seems to be a function of how desperately one wants such theories to work. The claim that the primary wrong-making feature of a killing is the loss to the victim of the value of its future accounts for the wrongness of killing young children and infants directly; it makes the wrongness of such acts as obvious as we actually think it is. This is a further merit of this theory. Accordingly, it seems that this value of a future-like-ours theory of the wrongness of killing shares strengths of both sanctity-of-life and personhood accounts while avoiding weaknesses of both. In addition, it meshes with a central intuition concerning what makes killing wrong.

The claim that the primary wrong-making feature of a killing is the loss to the victim of the value of its future has obvious consequences for the ethics of abortion. The future of a standard fetus includes a set of experiences, projects, activities, and such which are identical with the futures of adult human beings and are identical with the futures of young children. Since the reason that is sufficient to explain why it is wrong to kill human beings after the time of birth is a reason that also applies to fetuses, it follows that abortion is prima facie seriously morally wrong.

This argument does not rely on the invalid inference that, since it is wrong to kill persons, it is wrong to kill potential persons also. The category that is morally central to this analysis is the category of having a valuable future like ours; it is not the category of personhood. The argument to the conclusion that abortion is prima facie seriously morally wrong proceeded independently of the notion of person or potential person or any equivalent. Someone may wish to start with this analysis in terms of the value of a human future, conclude that abortion is, except perhaps in rare circumstances, seriously morally wrong, infer that fetuses have the right to life, and then call fetuses "persons" as a result of their having the right to life. Clearly, in this case, the category of person is being used to state the *conclusion* of the analysis rather than to generate the argument of the analysis. . . .

Of course, this value of a future-like-ours *argument*, if sound, shows only that abortion is prima facie wrong, not that it is wrong in any and all circumstances. Since the loss of the future to a standard fetus, if killed, is, however, at least as great a loss as the loss of the future to a standard adult human being who is killed, abortion, like ordinary killing, could be justified only by the most compelling reasons. The loss of one's life is almost the greatest mis-

*Feinberg, Tooley, Warren, and Engelhardt have all dealt with this problem.

fortune that can happen to one. Presumably abortion could be justified in some circumstances, only if the loss consequent on failing to abort would be at least as great. Accordingly, morally permissible abortions will be rare indeed unless, perhaps, they occur so early in pregnancy that a fetus is not yet definitely an individual. Hence, this argument should be taken as showing that abortion is presumptively very seriously wrong, where the presumption is very strong—as strong as the presumption that killing another adult human being is wrong.

III.

How complete an account of the wrongness of killing does the value of a future-like-ours account have to be in order that the wrongness of abortion is a consequence? This account does not have to be an account of the necessary conditions for the wrongness of killing. Some persons in nursing homes may lack valuable human futures, yet it may be wrong to kill them for other reasons. Furthermore, this account does not obviously have to be the sole reason killing is wrong where the victim did have a valuable future. This analysis claims only that, for any killing where the victim did have a valuable future like ours, having that future by itself is sufficient to create the strong presumption that the killing is seriously wrong.

One way to overturn the value of a future-like-ours argument would be to find some account of the wrongness of killing which is at least as intelligible and which has different implications for the ethics of abortion. Two rival accounts possess at least some degree of plausibility. One account is based on the obvious fact that people value the experience of living and wish for that valuable experience to continue. Therefore, it might be said, what makes killing wrong is the discontinuation of that experience for the victim. Let us call this the *discontinuation account*.* Another rival account is based upon the obvious fact that people strongly desire to continue to live. This suggests that what makes killing us so wrong is that it interferes with the fulfillment of a strong and fundamental desire, the fulfillment of which is necessary for the fulfillment of any other desires we might have. Let us call this the *desire account*.†

Consider first the desire account as a rival account of the ethics of killing which would provide the basis for rejecting the anti-abortion position. Such an account will have to be stronger than the value of a future-like-ours account of the wrongness of abortion if it is to do the job expected of it. To entail the wrongness of abortion, the value of a future-like-ours account has only to provide a sufficient, but not a necessary, condition for the wrongness of killing. The desire account, on the other hand, must provide us also with a necessary condition for the wrongness of killing in order to generate a

---

*I am indebted to Jack Bricke for raising this objection.

†Presumably a preference utilitarian would press such an objection. Tooley once suggested that his account has such a theoretical underpinning. See his "Abortion and Infanticide," pp. 44–5.

pro-choice conclusion on abortion. The reason for this is that presumably the argument from the desire account moves from the claim that what makes killing wrong is interference with a very strong desire to the claim that abortion is not wrong because the fetus lacks a strong desire to live. Obviously, this inference fails if someone's having the desire to live is not a necessary condition of its being wrong to kill that individual.

One problem with the desire account is that we do regard it as seriously wrong to kill persons who have little desire to live or who have no desire to live or, indeed, have a desire not to live. We believe it is seriously wrong to kill the unconscious, the sleeping, those who are tired of life, and those who are suicidal. The value-of-a-human-future account renders standard morality intelligible in these cases; these cases appear to be incompatible with the desire account.

The desire account is subject to a deeper difficulty. We desire life, because we value the goods of this life. The goodness of life is not secondary to our desire for it. If this were not so, the pain of one's own premature death could be done away with merely by an appropriate alteration in the configuration of one's desires. This is absurd. Hence, it would seem that it is the loss of the goods of one's future, not the interference with the fulfillment of a strong desire to live, which accounts ultimately for the wrongness of killing.

It is worth noting that, if the desire account is modified so that it does not provide a necessary, but only a sufficient, condition for the wrongness of killing, the desire account is compatible with the value of a future-like-ours account. The combined accounts will yield an anti-abortion ethic. This suggests that one can retain what is intuitively plausible about the desire account without a challenge to the basic argument of this paper.

It is also worth noting that, if future desires have moral force in a modified desire account of the wrongness of killing, one can find support for an anti-abortion ethic even in the absence of a value of a future-like-ours account. If one decides that a morally relevant property, the possession of which is sufficient to make it wrong to kill some individual, is the desire at some future time to live—one might decide to justify one's refusal to kill suicidal teenagers on these grounds, for example—then, since typical fetuses will have the desire in the future to live, it is wrong to kill typical fetuses. Accordingly, it does not seem that a desire account of the wrongness of killing can provide a justification of a pro-choice ethic of abortion which is nearly as adequate as the value of a human-future justification of an anti-abortion ethic.

The discontinuation account looks more promising as an account of the wrongness of killing. It seems just as intelligible as the value of a future-like-ours account, but it does not justify an anti-abortion position. Obviously, if it is the continuation of one's activities, experiences, and projects, the loss of which makes killing wrong, then it is not wrong to kill fetuses for that reason, for fetuses do not have experiences, activities, and projects to be continued or discontinued. Accordingly, the discontinuation account does not have the anti-abortion consequences that the value of a future-like-ours account has. Yet, it seems as intelligible as the value of a future-like-ours account, for when we think of what would be wrong with our being killed, it does seem as if it is the discontinuation of what makes our lives worthwhile which makes killing us wrong.

Is the discontinuation account just as good an account as the value of a future-like-ours account? The discontinuation account will not be adequate at all, if it does not refer to the *value* of the experience that may be discontinued. One does not want the discontinuation account to make it wrong to kill a patient who begs for death and who is in severe pain that cannot be relieved short of killing. (I leave open the question of whether it is wrong for other reasons.) Accordingly, the discontinuation account must be more than a bare discontinuation account. It must make some reference to the positive value of the patient's experiences. But, by the same token, the value of a future-like-ours account cannot be a bare future account either. Just having a future surely does not itself rule out killing the above patient. This account must make some reference to the value of the patient's future experiences and projects also. Hence, both accounts involve the value of experiences, projects, and activities. So far we still have symmetry between the accounts.

The symmetry fades, however, when we focus on the time period of the value of the experiences, etc., which has moral consequences. Although both accounts leave open the possibility that the patient in our example may be killed, this possibility is left open only in virtue of the utterly bleak future for the patient. It makes no difference whether the patient's immediate past contains intolerable pain, or consists in being in a coma (which we can imagine is a situation of indifference), or consists in a life of value. If the patient's future is a future of value, we want our account to make it wrong to kill the patient. If the patient's future is intolerable, whatever his or her immediate past, we want our account to allow killing the patient. Obviously, then, it is the value of that patient's future which is doing the work in rendering the morality of killing the patient intelligible.

This being the case, it seems clear that whether one has immediate past experiences or not does no work in the explanation of what makes killing wrong. The addition the discontinuation account makes to the value-of-a-human-future account is otiose. Its addition to the value-of-a-future account plays no role at all in rendering intelligible the wrongness of killing. Therefore, it can be discarded with the discontinuation account of which it is a part.

IV.

The analysis of the previous section suggests that alternative general accounts of the wrongness of killing are either inadequate or unsuccessful in getting around the anti-abortion consequences of the value of a future-like-ours argument. A different strategy for avoiding these anti-abortion consequences involves limiting the scope of the value-of-a-future argument. More precisely, the strategy involves arguing that fetuses lack a property that is essential for the value-of-a-future argument (or for any anti-abortion argument) to apply to them.

One move of this sort is based upon the claim that a necessary condition of one's future being valuable is that one values it. Value implies a valuer. Given this one might argue that, since fetuses cannot value their futures, their futures are not valuable to them. Hence, it does not seriously wrong them deliberately to end their lives.

This move fails, however, because of some ambiguities. Let us assume that something cannot be of value unless it is valued by someone. This does not entail that my life is of no value unless it is valued by me. I may think, in a period of despair, that my future is of no worth whatsoever, but I may be wrong because others rightly see value—even great value—in it. Furthermore, my future can be valuable to me even if I do not value it. This is the case when a young person attempts suicide, but is rescued and goes on to significant human achievements. Such young people's futures are ultimately valuable to them, even though such futures do not seem to be valuable to them at the moment of attempted suicide. A fetus's future can be valuable to it in the same way. Accordingly, this attempt to limit the anti-abortion argument fails.

Another similar attempt to reject the anti-abortion position is based on Tooley's claim that an entity cannot possess the right to life unless it has the capacity to desire its continued existence. It follows that, since fetuses lack the conceptual capacity to desire to continue to live, they lack the right to life. Accordingly, Tooley concludes that abortion cannot be seriously prima facie wrong (*op. cit.*, pp. 46–7).

What could be the evidence for Tooley's basic claim? Tooley once argued that individuals have a prima facie right to what they desire and that the lack of the capacity to desire something undercuts the basis of one's right to it (*op. cit.*, pp. 44–5). This argument plainly will not succeed in the context of the analysis of this essay, however, since the point here is to establish the fetus's right to life on other grounds. Tooley's argument assumes that the right to life cannot be established in general on some basis other than the desire for life. This position was considered and rejected in the preceding section of this paper.

One might attempt to defend Tooley's basic claim on the grounds that, because a fetus cannot apprehend continued life as a benefit, its continued life cannot be a benefit or cannot be something it has a right to or cannot be something that is in its interest. This might be defended in terms of the general proposition that, if an individual is literally incapable of caring about or taking an interest in some X, then one does not have a right to X or X is not a benefit or X is not something that is in one's interest.*

---

*Donald VanDeVeer seems to think this is self-evident. See his "Whither Baby Doe?" in *Matters of Life and Death*, p. 233.

Each member of this family of claims seems to be open to objections. As John C. Stevens* has pointed out, one may have a right to be treated with a certain medical procedure (because of a health insurance policy one has purchased), even though one cannot conceive of the nature of the procedure. And, as Tooley himself has pointed out, persons who have been indoctrinated, or drugged, or rendered temporarily unconscious may be literally incapable of caring about or taking an interest in something that is in their interest or is something to which they have a right, or is something that benefits them. Hence, the Tooley claim that would restrict the scope of the value of a future-like-ours argument is undermined by counterexamples.† . . .

V.

In this essay, it has been argued that the correct ethic of the wrongness of killing can be extended to fetal life and used to show that there is a strong presumption that any abortion is morally impermissible. If the ethic of killing adopted here entails, however, that contraception is also seriously immoral, then there would appear to be a difficulty with the analysis of this essay.

But this analysis does not entail that contraception is wrong. Of course, contraception prevents the actualization of a possible future of value. Hence, it follows from the claim that futures of value should be maximized that contraception is prima facie immoral. This obligation to maximize does not exist, however; furthermore, nothing in the ethics of killing in this paper entails that it does. The ethics of killing in this essay would entail that contraception is wrong only if something were denied a human future of value by contraception. Nothing at all is denied such a future by contraception, however.

Candidates for a subject of harm by contraception fall into four categories: (1) some sperm or other, (2) some ovum or other, (3) a sperm and an ovum separately, and (4) a sperm and an ovum together. Assigning the harm to some sperm is utterly arbitrary, for no reason can be given for making a sperm the subject of harm rather than an ovum. Assigning the harm to some ovum is utterly arbitrary, for no reason can be given for making an ovum the subject of harm rather than a sperm. One might attempt to avoid these problems by insisting that contraception deprives both the sperm and the ovum separately of a valuable future like ours. On this alternative, too many futures are lost. Contraception was supposed to be wrong, because it deprived us of one future of value, not two. One might attempt to avoid this problem by holding that contraception deprives the combination of sperm and ovum of a valuable future like ours. But here the definite article misleads.

*Must the Bearer of a Right Have the Concept of That to Which He Has a Right?" *Ethics*, XCV, 1 (1984): 68–74.

†See Tooley again in "Abortion and Infanticide," pp. 47–49.

At the time of contraception, there are hundreds of millions of sperm, one (released) ovum and millions of possible combinations of all of these. There is no actual combination at all. Is the subject of the loss to be a merely possible combination? Which one? This alternative does not yield an actual subject of harm either. Accordingly, the immorality of contraception is not entailed by the loss of a future-like-ours argument simply because there is no nonarbitrarily identifiable subject of the loss in the case of contraception.

VI.

The purpose of this essay has been to set out an argument for the serious presumptive wrongness of abortion subject to the assumption that the moral permissibility of abortion stands or falls on the moral status of the fetus.

Since a fetus possesses a property, the possession of which in adult human beings is sufficient to make killing an adult human being wrong, abortion is wrong. This way of dealing with the problem of abortion seems superior to other approaches to the ethics of abortion, because it rests on an ethics of killing which is close to self-evident, because the crucial morally relevant property clearly applies to fetuses, and because the argument avoids the usual equivocations on "human life," "human being," or "person." The argument rests neither on religious claims nor on Papal dogma. It is not subject to the objection of "speciesism." Its soundness is compatible with the moral permissibility of euthanasia and contraception. It deals with our intuitions concerning young children.

Finally, this analysis can be viewed as resolving a standard problem—indeed, *the* standard problem—concerning the ethics of abortion. Clearly, it is wrong to kill adult human beings. Clearly, it is not wrong to end the life of some arbitrarily chosen single human cell. Fetuses seem to be like arbitrarily chosen human cells in some respects and like adult humans in other respects. The problem of the ethics of abortion is the problem of determining the fetal property that settles this moral controversy. The thesis of this essay is that the problem of the ethics of abortion, so understood, is solvable.

DISCUSSION QUESTIONS

1. Marquis's argument against abortion can be seen as an inference to the best explanation of why it is morally wrong to kill normal adult human beings. What does Marquis take to be the best explanation of this? Why does he think it is better than the alternatives? Can you give an even better explanation that accounts for the cases that Marquis discusses?

2. Is Marquis's argument different in important ways from traditional arguments based on the premise that a fetus is a person or a potential person? Why or why not?

A DEFENSE OF ABORTION[4],[*]

■

by Judith Jarvis Thomson

. . . Opponents of abortion commonly spend most of their time establishing that the fetus is a person, and hardly any time explaining the step from there to the impermissibility of abortion. Perhaps they think the step too simple and obvious to require much comment. Or perhaps instead they are simply being economical in argument. Many of those who defend abortion rely on the premise that the fetus is not a person, but only a bit of tissue that will become a person at birth; and why pay out more arguments than you have to? Whatever the explanation, I suggest that the step they take is neither easy nor obvious, that it calls for closer examination than it is commonly given, and that when we do give it this closer examination we shall feel inclined to reject it.

I propose, then, that we grant that the fetus is a person from the moment of conception. How does the argument go from here? Something like this, I take it. Every person has a right to life. So the fetus has a right to life. No doubt the mother has a right to decide what shall happen in and to her body; everyone would grant that. But surely a person's right to life is stronger and more stringent than the mother's right to decide what happens in and to her body, and so outweighs it. So the fetus may not be killed; an abortion may not be performed.

It sounds plausible. But now let me ask you to imagine this. You wake up in the morning and find yourself back to back in bed with an unconscious violinist. A famous unconscious violinist. He has been found to have a fatal kidney ailment, and the Society of Music Lovers has canvassed all the available medical records and found that you alone have the right blood type to help. They have therefore kidnapped you, and last night the violinist's circulatory system was plugged into yours, so that your kidneys can be used to extract poisons from his blood as well as your own. The director of the hospital now tells you, "Look, we're sorry the Society of Music Lovers did this to you—we would never have permitted it if we had known. But still, they did it, and the violinist now is plugged into you. To unplug you would be to kill him. But never mind, it's only for nine months. By then he will have recovered from his ailment, and can safely be unplugged from you." Is it morally incumbent on you to accede to this situation? No doubt it would be very nice of you if you did, a great kindness. But do you *have* to accede to it? What if it were not nine months, but nine years? Or longer still? What if the director of the hospital says, "Tough luck, I agree, but you've now got to stay in bed, with the violinist plugged into you, for the rest of your life. Because

[4]*Philosophy and Public Affairs* 1, no. 1 (Fall 1971), 47–66.

[*]I am very much indebted to James Thomson for discussion, criticism, and many helpful suggestions.

remember this. All persons have a right to life, and violinists are persons. Granted you have a right to decide what happens in and to your body, but a person's right to life outweighs your right to decide what happens in and to your body. So you cannot ever be unplugged from him." I imagine you would regard this as outrageous, which suggests that something really is wrong with that plausible-sounding argument I mentioned a moment ago.

In this case, of course, you were kidnapped; you didn't volunteer for the operation that plugged the violinist into your kidneys. Can those who oppose abortion on the ground I mentioned make an exception for a pregnancy due to rape? Certainly. They can say that persons have a right to life only if they didn't come into existence because of rape; or they can say that all persons have a right to life, but that some have less of a right to life than others, in particular, that those who came into existence because of rape have less. But these statements have a rather unpleasant sound. Surely the question of whether you have a right to life at all, or how much of it you have, shouldn't turn on the question of whether or not you are the product of a rape. And in fact the people who oppose abortion on the ground I mentioned do not make this distinction, and hence do not make an exception in the case of rape.

Nor do they make an exception for a case in which the mother had to spend the nine months of her pregnancy in bed. They would agree that would be a great pity, and hard on the mother; but all the same all persons have a right to life, the fetus is a person, and so on. I suspect, in fact, that they would not make an exception for a case in which, miraculously enough, the pregnancy went on for nine years or even the rest of the mother's life.

Some won't even make an exception for a case in which continuation of the pregnancy is likely to shorten the mother's life; they regard abortion as impermissible even to save the mother's life. Such cases are nowadays very rare, and many opponents of abortion do not accept this extreme view. All the same, it is a good place to begin: a number of points of interest come out in respect to it.

1. Let us call the view that abortion is impermissible even to save the mother's life "the extreme view." I want to suggest first that it does not issue from the argument I mentioned earlier without the addition of some fairly powerful premises. Suppose a woman has become pregnant, and now learns that she has a cardiac condition such that she will die if she carries the baby to term. What may be done for her? The fetus, being a person, has a right to life, but as the mother is a person too, so has she a right to life. Presumably they have an equal right to life. How is it supposed to come out that an abortion may not be performed? If mother and child have an equal right to life, shouldn't we perhaps flip a coin? Or should we add to the mother's right to life her right to decide what happens in and to her body which everybody seems to be ready to grant—the sum of her rights now outweighing the fetus's right to life?

The most familiar argument here is the following. We are told that performing the abortion would be directly killing* the child, whereas doing nothing would not be killing the mother, but only letting her die. Moreover, in killing the child, one would be killing an innocent person, for the child has committed no crime, and is not aiming at his mother's death. And then there are a variety of ways in which this might be continued. (1) But as directly killing an innocent person is always and absolutely impermissible, an abortion may not be performed. Or, (2) as directly killing an innocent person is murder, and murder is always and absolutely impermissible, an abortion may not be performed.† Or, (3) as one's duty to refrain from directly killing an innocent person is more stringent than one's duty to keep a person from dying, an abortion may not be performed. Or, (4) if one's only options are directly killing an innocent person or letting a person die, one must prefer letting the person die, and thus an abortion may not be performed.‡

Some people seem to have thought that these are not further premises which must be added if the conclusion is to be reached; but that they follow from the very fact that an innocent person has a right to life.§ But this seems to me to be a mistake, and perhaps the simplest way to show this is to bring out that while we must certainly grant that innocent persons have a right to life, the theses in (1) through (4) are all false. Take (2), for example. If directly killing an innocent person is murder, and thus is impermissible, then the mother's directly killing the innocent person inside her is murder, and thus is impermissible. But it cannot seriously be thought to be murder if the

---

*The term "direct" in the arguments I refer to is a technical one. Roughly what is meant by "direct killing" is either killing as an end by itself, or killing as a means to some end, for example, the end of saving someone else's life. See [the following] note for an example of its use.

†Cf. *Encyclical Letter of Pope Pius XI on Christian Marriage*, St. Paul Editions (Boston, n.d.), p. 32: "however much we may pity the mother whose health and even life is gravely imperiled in the performance of the duty allotted to her by nature, nevertheless what could ever be a sufficient reason for excusing in any way the direct murder of the innocent? This is precisely what we are dealing with here." Noonan (*The Morality of Abortion*, p. 43) reads this as follows: "What cause can ever avail to excuse in any way the direct killing of the innocent? For it is a question of that."

‡The thesis in (4) is in an interesting way weaker than those in (1), (2), and (3): they rule out abortion even in cases in which both mother *and* child will die if the abortion is not performed. By contrast, one who held the view expressed in (4) could consistently say that one needn't prefer letting two persons die to killing one.

§Cf. the following passage from Pius XII, *Address to the Italian Catholic Society of Midwives*: "The baby in the maternal breast has the right to life immediately from God—Hence there is no man, no human authority, no science, no medical, eugenic, social, economic or moral 'indication' which can establish or grant a valid juridical ground for a direct deliberate disposition of an innocent human life, that is a disposition which looks to its destruction either as an end or as a means to another end perhaps in itself not illicit. The baby, still not born, is a man in the same degree and for the same reason as the mother" (quoted in Noonan, *The Morality of Abortion*, p. 45).

mother performs an abortion on herself to save her life. It cannot seriously be said that she *must* refrain, that she *must* sit passively by and wait for her death. Let us look again at the case of you and the violinist. There you are, in bed with the violinist, and the director of the hospital says to you, "It's all most distressing, and I deeply sympathize, but you see this is putting an additional strain on your kidneys, and you'll be dead within the month. But you *have* to stay where you are all the same. Because unplugging you would be directly killing an innocent violinist, and that's murder, and that's impermissible." If anything in the world is true, it is that you do not commit murder, you do not do what is impermissible, if you reach around to your back and unplug yourself from that violinist to save your life.

The main focus of attention in writings on abortion has been on what a third party may or may not do in answer to a request from a woman for an abortion. This is in a way understandable. Things being as they are, there isn't much a woman can safely do to abort herself. So the question asked is what a third party may do, and what the mother may do, if it is mentioned at all, is deduced, almost as an afterthought, from what it is concluded that third parties may do. But it seems to me that to treat the matter in this way is to refuse to grant to the mother that very status of person which is so firmly insisted on for the fetus. For we cannot simply read off what a person may do from what a third party may do. Suppose you find yourself trapped in a tiny house with a growing child. I mean a very tiny house, and a rapidly growing child—you are already up against the wall of the house and in a few minutes you'll be crushed to death. The child on the other hand won't be crushed to death; if nothing is done to stop him from growing he'll be hurt, but in the end he'll simply burst open the house and walk out a free man. Now I could well understand it if a bystander were to say, "There's nothing we can do for you. We cannot choose between your life and his, we cannot be the ones to decide who is to live, we cannot intervene." But it cannot be concluded that you too can do nothing, that you cannot attack it to save your life. However innocent the child may be, you do not have to wait passively while it crushes you to death. Perhaps a pregnant woman is vaguely felt to have the status of house, to which we don't allow the right of self-defense. But if the woman houses the child, it should be remembered that she is a person who houses it.

I should perhaps stop to say explicitly that I am not claiming that people have a right to do anything whatever to save their lives. I think, rather, that there are drastic limits to the right of self-defense. If someone threatens you with death unless you torture someone else to death, I think you have not the right, even to save your life, to do so. But the case under consideration here is very different. In our case there are only two people involved, one whose life is threatened, and one who threatens it. Both are innocent: the one who is threatened is not threatened because of any fault, the one who threatens does not threaten because of any fault. For this reason we may feel that we bystanders cannot intervene. But the person threatened can.

In sum, a woman surely can defend her life against the threat to it posed by the unborn child, even if doing so involves its death. And this shows not merely that the theses in (1) through (4) are false; it shows also that the extreme view of abortion is false, and so we need not canvass any other possible ways of arriving at it from the argument I mentioned at the outset.

2. The extreme view could of course be weakened to say that while abortion is permissible to save the mother's life, it may not be performed by a third party, but only by the mother herself. But this cannot be right either. For what we have to keep in mind is that the mother and the unborn child are not like two tenants in a small house which has, by an unfortunate mistake, been rented to both: the mother *owns* the house. The fact that she does adds to the offensiveness of deducing that the mother can do nothing from the supposition that third parties can do nothing. But it does more than this: it casts a bright light on the supposition that third parties can do nothing. Certainly it lets us see that a third party who says "I cannot choose between you" is fooling himself if he thinks this is impartiality. If Jones has found and fastened on a certain coat, which he needs to keep him from freezing, but which Smith also needs to keep him from freezing, then it is not impartiality that says "I cannot choose between you" when Smith owns the coat. Women have said again and again "This is *my* body!" and they have reason to feel angry, reason to feel that it has been like shouting into the wind. Smith, after all, is hardly likely to bless us if we say to him, "Of course it's your coat; anybody would grant that it is. But no one may choose between you and Jones who is to have it."

We should really ask what it is that says "no one may choose" in the face of the fact that the body that houses the child is the mother's body. It may be simply a failure to appreciate this fact. But it may be something more interesting, namely the sense that one has a right to refuse to lay hands on people, even where it would be just and fair to do so, even where justice seems to require that somebody do so. Thus justice might call for somebody to get Smith's coat back from Jones, and yet you have a right to refuse to be the one to lay hands on Jones, a right to refuse to do physical violence to him. This, I think, must be granted. But then what should be said is not "no one may choose," but only "*I* cannot choose," and indeed not even this, but "*I* will not *act*," leaving it open that somebody else can or should, and in particular that anyone in a position of authority, with the job of securing people's rights, both can and should. So this is no difficulty. I have not been arguing that any given third party must accede to the mother's request that he perform an abortion to save her life, but only that he may.

I suppose that in some views of human life the mother's body is only on loan to her, the loan not being one which gives her any prior claim to it. One who held this view might well think it impartiality to say "I cannot choose." But I shall simply ignore this possibility. My own view is that if a human being has any just, prior claim to anything at all, he has a just, prior claim to his own body. And perhaps this needn't be argued for here anyway, since, as

I mentioned, the arguments against abortion we are looking at do grant that the woman has a right to decide what happens in and to her body.

But although they do grant it, I have tried to show that they do not take seriously what is done in granting it. I suggest the same thing will reappear even more clearly when we turn away from cases in which the mother's life is at stake, and attend, as I propose we now do, to the vastly more common cases in which a woman wants an abortion for some less weighty reason than preserving her own life.

3. Where the mother's life is not at stake, the argument I mentioned at the outset seems to have a much stronger pull. "Everyone has a right to life, so the unborn person has a right to life." And isn't the child's right to life weightier than anything other than the mother's own right to life, which she might put forward as grounds for an abortion?

This argument treats the right to life as if it were unproblematic. It is not, and this seems to me to be precisely the source of the mistake.

For we should now, at long last, ask what it comes to, to have a right to life. In some views having a right to life includes having a right to be given at least the bare minimum one needs for continued life. But suppose that what in fact is the bare minimum a man needs for continued life is something he has no right at all to be given? If I am sick unto death, and the only thing that will save my life is the touch of Henry Fonda's cool hand on my fevered brow, then all the same, I have no right to be given the touch of Henry Fonda's cool hand on my fevered brow. It would be frightfully nice of him to fly in from the West Coast to provide it. It would be less nice, though no doubt well meant, if my friends flew out to the West Coast and carried Henry Fonda back with them. But I have no right at all against anybody that he should do this for me. Or again, to return to the story I told earlier, the fact that for continued life that violinist needs the continued use of your kidneys does not establish that he has a right to be given the continued use of your kidneys. He certainly has no right against *you* that you should give him con-tinued use of your kidneys. For nobody has any right to use your kidneys unless you give him such a right; and nobody has the right against you that you shall give him this right—if you do allow him to go on using your kid-neys, this is a kindness on your part, and not something he can claim from you as his due. Nor has he any right against anybody else that *they* should give him continued use of your kidneys. Certainly he had no right against the Society of Music Lovers that they should plug him into you in the first place. And if you now start to unplug yourself, having learned that you will otherwise have to spend nine years in bed with him, there is nobody in the world who must try to prevent you, in order to see to it that he is given something he has a right to be given.

Some people are rather stricter about the right to life. In their view, it does not include the right to be given anything, but amounts to, and only to, the right not to be killed by anybody. But here a related difficulty arises. If every-body is to refrain from killing that violinist, then everybody must refrain from doing a great many different sorts of things. Everybody must refrain from slitting his throat, everybody must refrain from shooting him—and everybody must refrain from unplugging you from him. But does he have a right against everybody that they shall refrain from unplugging you from him? To refrain from doing this is to allow him to continue to use your kidneys. It could be argued that he has a right against us that we should allow him to continue to use your kidneys. That is, while he had no right against us that we should give him the use of your kidneys, it might be argued that he anyway has a right against us that we shall not now intervene and deprive him of the use of your kidneys. I shall come back to third-party interventions later. But certainly the violinist has no right against you that *you* shall allow him to continue to use your kidneys. As I said, if you do allow him to use them, it is a kindness on your part, and not something you owe him.

The difficulty I point to here is not peculiar to the right to life. It reappears in connection with all the other natural rights; and it is something which an adequate account of rights must deal with. For present purposes it is enough just to draw attention to it. But I would stress that I am not arguing that people do not have a right to life—quite to the contrary, it seems to me that the primary control we must place on the acceptability of an account of rights is that it should turn out in that account to be a truth that all persons have a right to life. I am arguing only that having a right to life does not guarantee having either a right to be given the use of or a right to be allowed continued use of another person's body—even if one needs it for life itself. So the right to life will not serve the opponents of abortion in the very simple and clear way in which they seem to have thought it would.

4. There is another way to bring out the difficulty. In the most ordinary sort of case, to deprive someone of what he has a right to is to treat him unjustly. Suppose a boy and his small brother are jointly given a box of chocolates for Christmas. If the older boy takes the box and refuses to give his brother any of the chocolates, he is unjust to him, for the brother has been given a right to half of them. But suppose that, having learned that otherwise it means nine years in bed with that violinist, you unplug yourself from him. You surely are not being unjust to him, for you gave him no right to use your kidneys, and no one else can have given him any such right. But we have to notice that in unplugging yourself, you are killing him; and violinists, like everybody else, have a right to life, and thus in the view we were considering just now, the right not to be killed. So here you do what he supposedly has a right you shall not do, but you do not act unjustly to him in doing it.

The emendation which may be made at this point is this: the right to life consists not in the right not to be killed, but rather in the right not to be killed unjustly. This runs a risk of circularity, but never mind: it would enable us to square the fact that the violinist has a right to life with the fact that you do not act unjustly toward him in unplugging yourself, thereby killing him. For if you do not kill him unjustly, you do not violate his right to life, and so it is no wonder you do him no injustice.

But if this emendation is accepted, the gap in the argument against abortion stares us plainly in the face: it is by no means enough to show that the fetus is a person, and to remind us that all persons have a right to life—we need to be shown also that killing the fetus violates its right to life, i.e., that abortion is unjust killing. And is it?

I suppose we may take it as a datum that in a case of pregnancy due to rape the mother has not given the unborn person a right to the use of her body for food and shelter. Indeed, in what pregnancy could it be supposed that the mother has given the unborn person such a right? It is not as if there were unborn persons drifting about the world, to whom a woman who wants a child says, "I invite you in."

But it might be argued that there are other ways one can have acquired a right to the use of another person's body than by having been invited to use it by that person. Suppose a woman voluntarily indulges in intercourse, knowing of the chance it will issue in pregnancy, and then she does become pregnant; is she not in part responsible for the presence, in fact the very existence of the unborn person inside her? No doubt she did not invite it in. But doesn't her partial responsibility for its being there itself give it a right to the use of her body?* It so, then her aborting it would be more like the boy's taking away the chocolates, and less like your unplugging yourself from the violinist—doing so would be depriving it of what it does have a right to, and thus would be doing it an injustice.

And then, too, it might be asked whether or not she can kill it even to save her own life: If she voluntarily called it into existence, how can she now kill it, even in self-defense?

The first thing to be said about this is that it is something new. Opponents of abortion have been so concerned to make out the independence of the fetus, in order to establish that it has a right to life, just as the mother does, that they have tended to overlook the possible support they might gain from making out that the fetus is *dependent* on the mother, in order to establish that she has a special kind of responsibility for it, a responsibility that gives it rights against her which are not possessed by an independent person—such as an ailing violinist who is a stranger to her.

On the other hand, this argument would give the unborn person a right to its mother's body only if her pregnancy resulted from a voluntary act, undertaken in full knowledge of the chance a pregnancy might result from it. It would leave out entirely the unborn person whose existence is due to rape. Pending the availability of some further argument, then, we would be left with the conclusion that unborn persons whose existence is due to rape have no right to the use of their mothers' bodies, and thus that aborting them is not depriving them of anything they have a right to and hence is not unjust killing.

And we should also notice that it is not at all plain that this argument really does go even as far as it purports to. For there are cases and cases, and

*The need for a discussion of this argument was brought home to me by members of the Society for Ethical and Legal Philosophy, to whom this paper was originally presented.

the details make a difference. If the room is stuffy, and I therefore open a window to air it, and a burglar climbs in, it would be absurd to say, "Ah, now he can stay, she's given him a right to the use of her house—for she is partially responsible for his presence there, having voluntarily done what enabled him to get in, in full knowledge that there are such things as burglars, and that burglars burgle." It would be still more absurd to say this if I had had bars installed outside my windows, precisely to prevent burglars from getting in, and a burglar got in only because of a defect in the bars. It remains equally absurd if we imagine it is not a burglar who climbs in, but an innocent person who blunders or falls in. Again, suppose it were like this: people-seeds drift about in the air like pollen, and if you open your windows, one may drift in and take root in your carpets or upholstery. You don't want children, so you fix up your windows with fine mesh screens, the very best you can buy. As can happen, however, and on very, very rare occasions does happen, one of the screens is defective; and a seed drifts in and takes root. Does the person-plant who now develops have a right to the use of your house? Surely not—despite the fact that you voluntarily opened your windows, you knowingly kept carpets and upholstered furniture, and you knew that screens were sometimes defective. Someone may argue that you are responsible for its rooting, that it does have a right to your house, because after all you *could* have lived out your life with bare floors and furniture, or with sealed windows and doors. But this won't do—for by the same token anyone can avoid a pregnancy due to rape by having a hysterectomy, or anyway by never leaving home without a (reliable!) army.

It seems to me that the argument we are looking at can establish at most that there are *some* cases in which the unborn person has a right to the use of its mother's body, and therefore *some* cases in which abortion is unjust killing. There is room for much discussion and argument as to precisely which, if any. But I think we should side-step this issue and leave it open, for at any rate the argument certainly does not establish that all abortion is unjust killing.

5. There is room for yet another argument here, however. We surely must all grant that there may be cases in which it would be morally indecent to detach a person from your body at the cost of his life. Suppose you learn that what the violinist needs is not nine years of your life, but only one hour: all you need do to save his life is to spend one hour in that bed with him. Suppose also that letting him use your kidneys for that one hour would not affect your health in the slightest. Admittedly you were kidnapped. Admittedly you did not give anyone permission to plug him into you. Nevertheless it seems to me plain you *ought* to allow him to use your kidneys for that hour—it would be indecent to refuse.

Again, suppose pregnancy lasted only an hour, and constituted no threat to life or health. And suppose that a woman becomes pregnant as a result of rape. Admittedly she did not voluntarily do anything to bring about the existence of a child. Admittedly she did nothing at all which would give the unborn person a right to the use of her body. All the same it might well be said, as in the newly emended violinist story, that she *ought* to allow it to remain for that hour-that it would be indecent in her to refuse. . . .

So my own view is that even though you ought to let the violinist use your kidneys for the one hour he needs, we should not conclude that he has a right to do so—we should say that if you refuse, you are, like [a] boy who owns all the chocolates and will give none away, self-centered and callous, indecent in fact, but not unjust. And similarly, that even supposing a case in which a woman pregnant due to rape ought to allow the unborn person to use her body for the hour he needs, we should not conclude that he has a right to do so; we should conclude that she is self-centered, callous, indecent, but not unjust, if she refuses. The complaints are no less grave; they are just different. However, there is no need to insist on this point. If anyone does wish to deduce "he has a right" from "you ought," then all the same he must surely grant that there are cases in which it is not morally required of you that you allow that violinist to use your kidneys, and in which he does not have a right to use them, and in which you do not do him an injustice if you refuse. And so also for mother and unborn child. Except in such cases as the unborn person has a right to demand it—and we were leaving open the possibility that there may be such cases—nobody is morally *required* to make large sacrifices, of health, of all other interests and concerns, of all other duties and commitments, for nine years, or even for nine months, in order to keep another person alive.

6. We have in fact to distinguish between two kinds of Samaritan: the Good Samaritan and what we might call the Minimally Decent Samaritan. The story of the Good Samaritan, you will remember, goes like this:

> A certain man went down from Jerusalem to Jericho, and fell among thieves, which stripped him of his raiment, and wounded him, and departed, leaving him half dead.
>
> And by chance there came down a certain priest that way; and when he saw him, he passed by on the other side.
>
> And likewise a Levite, when he was at the place, came and looked on him, and passed by on the other side.
>
> But a certain Samaritan, as he journeyed, came where he was and when he saw him he had compassion on him.
>
> And went to him, and bound up his wounds, pouring in oil and wine, and set him on his own beast, and brought him to an inn, and took care of him.
>
> And on the morrow, when he departed, he took out two pence, and gave them to the host, and said unto him, "Take care of him: and whatsoever thou spendest more, when I come again, I will repay thee." (Luke 10:30–35)

The Good Samaritan went out of his way, at some cost to himself, to help one in need of it. We are not told what the options were, that is, whether or not the priest and the Levite could have helped by doing less than the Good Samaritan did, but assuming they could have, then the fact they did nothing at all shows they were not even Minimally Decent Samaritans, not because they were not Samaritans, but because they were not even minimally decent.

These things are a matter of degree, of course, but there is a difference, and it comes out perhaps most clearly in the story of Kitty Genovese, who, as you will remember, was murdered while thirty-eight people watched or listened, and did nothing at all to help her. A Good Samaritan would have rushed out to give direct assistance against the murderer. Or perhaps we had better allow that it would have been a Splendid Samaritan who did this, on the ground that it would have involved a risk of death for himself. But the thirty-eight not only did not do this, they did not even trouble to pick up a phone to call the police. Minimally Decent Samaritanism would call for doing at least that, and their not having done it was monstrous.

After telling the story of the Good Samaritan, Jesus said "Go, and do thou likewise." Perhaps he meant that we are morally required to act as the Good Samaritan did. Perhaps he was urging people to do more than is morally required of them. At all events it seems plain that it was not morally required of any of the thirty-eight that he rush out to give direct assistance at the risk of his own life, and that it is not morally required of anyone that he give long stretches of his life—nine years or nine months—to sustaining the life of a person who has no special right (we were leaving open the possibility of this) to demand it.

Indeed, with one rather striking class of exceptions, no one in any country in the world is *legally* required to do anywhere near as much as this for anyone else. The class of exceptions is obvious. My main concern here is not the state of the law in respect to abortion, but it is worth drawing attention to the fact that in no state in this country is any man compelled by law to be even a Minimally Decent Samaritan to any person; there is no law under which charges could be brought against the thirty-eight who stood by while Kitty Genovese died. By contrast, in most states in this country women are compelled by law to be not merely Minimally Decent Samaritans, but Good Samaritans to unborn persons inside them. This doesn't by itself settle anything one way or the other, because it may well be argued that there should be laws in this country—as there are in many European countries—compelling at least Minimally Decent Samaritanism.* But it does show that there is a gross injustice in the existing state of the law. And it shows also that the groups currently working against liberalization of abortion laws, in fact working toward having it declared unconstitutional for a state to permit abortion, had better start working for the adoption of Good Samaritan laws generally, or earn the charge that they are acting in bad faith.

I should think, myself, that Minimally Decent Samaritan laws would be one thing, Good Samaritan laws quite another, and in fact highly improper. But we are not here concerned with the law. What we should ask is not whether anybody should be compelled by law to be a Good Samaritan, but whether we must accede to a situation in which somebody is being

---

*For a discussion of the difficulties involved, and a survey of the European experience with such laws, see *The Good Samaritan and the Law,* ed. James M. Ratcliffe (New York, 1966).

compelled—by nature, perhaps—to be a Good Samaritan. We have, in other words, to look now at third-party interventions. I have been arguing that no person is morally required to make large sacrifices to sustain the life of another who has no right to demand them, and this even where the sacrifices do not include life itself; we are not morally required to be Good Samaritans or anyway Very Good Samaritans to one another. But what if a man cannot extricate himself from such a situation? What if he appeals to us to extricate him? It seems to me plain that there are cases in which we can, cases in which a Good Samaritan would extricate him. There you are, you were kidnapped, and nine years in bed with that violinist lie ahead of you. You have your own life to lead. You are sorry, but you simply cannot see giving up so much of your life to the sustaining of his. You cannot extricate yourself, and ask us to do so. I should have thought that—in light of his having no right to the use of your body—it was obvious that we do not have to accede to your being forced to give up so much. We can do what you ask. There is no injustice to the violinist in our doing so.

7. Following the lead of the opponents of abortion, I have throughout been speaking of the fetus merely as a person, and what I have been asking is whether or not the argument we began with, which proceeds only from the fetus being a person, really does establish its conclusion. I have argued that it does not.

But of course there are arguments and arguments, and it may be said that I have simply fastened on the wrong one. It may be said that what is important is not merely the fact that the fetus is a person, but that it is a person for whom the woman has a special kind of responsibility issuing from the fact that she is its mother. And it might be argued that all my analogies are therefore irrelevant—for you do not have that special kind of responsibility for that violinist, Henry Fonda does not have that special kind of responsibility for me. And our attention might be drawn to the fact that men and women both *are* compelled by law to provide support for their children.

I have in effect dealt (briefly) with this argument in section 4 above; but a (still briefer) recapitulation now may be in order. Surely we do not have any such "special responsibility" for a person unless we have assumed it, explicitly or implicitly. If a set of parents do not try to prevent pregnancy, do not obtain an abortion, and then at the time of birth of the child do not put it out for adoption, but rather take it home with them, then they have assumed responsibility for it, they have given it rights, and they cannot *now* withdraw support from it at the cost of its life because they now find it difficult to go on providing for it. But if they have taken all reasonable precautions against having a child, they do not simply by virtue of their biological relationship to the child who comes into existence have a special responsibility for it. They may wish to assume responsibility for it, or they may not wish to. And I am suggesting that if assuming responsibility for it would require large sacrifices, then they may refuse. A Good Samaritan would not refuse—or anyway, a Splendid Samaritan, if the sacrifices that had to be made were enormous. But then so would a Good Samaritan assume responsibility for that violinist; so would Henry Fonda, if he is a Good Samaritan, fly in from the West Coast and assume responsibility for me.

8. My argument will be found unsatisfactory on two counts by many of those who want to regard abortion as morally permissible. First, while I do argue that abortion is not impermissible, I do not argue that it is always permissible. There may well be cases in which carrying the child to term requires only Minimally Decent Samaritanism of the mother, and this is a standard we must not fall below. I am inclined to think it a merit of my account precisely that it does *not* give a general yes or a general no. It allows for and supports our sense that, for example, a sick and desperately frightened fourteen-year-old schoolgirl, pregnant due to rape, may *of course* choose abortion, and that any law which rules this out is an insane law. And it also allows for and supports our sense that in other cases resort to abortion is even positively indecent. It would be indecent in the woman to request an abortion, and indecent in a doctor to perform it, if she is in her seventh month, and wants the abortion just to avoid the nuisance of postponing a trip abroad. The very fact that the arguments I have been drawing attention to treat all cases of abortion, or even all cases of abortion in which the mother's life is not at stake, as morally on a par ought to have made them suspect at the outset.

Secondly, while I am arguing for the permissibility of abortion in some cases, I am not arguing for the right to secure the death of the unborn child. It is easy to confuse these two things in that up to a certain point in the life of the fetus it is not able to survive outside the mother's body; hence removing it from her body guarantees its death. But they are importantly different. I have argued that you are not morally required to spend nine months in bed, sustaining the life of that violinist; but to say this is by no means to say that if, when you unplug yourself, there is a miracle and he survives, you then have a right to turn around and slit his throat. You may detach yourself even if this costs him his life; you have no right to be guaranteed his death by some other means, if unplugging yourself does not kill him. There are some people who will feel dissatisfied by this feature of my argument. A woman may be utterly devastated by the thought of a child, a bit of herself, put out for adoption and never seen or heard of again. She may therefore want not merely that the child be detached from her, but more, that it die. Some opponents of abortion are inclined to regard this as beneath contempt—thereby showing insensitivity to what is surely a powerful source of despair. All the same, I agree that the desire for the child's death is not one which anybody may gratify, should it turn out to be possible to detach the child alive.

At this place, however, it should be remembered that we have only been pretending throughout that the fetus is a human being from the moment of conception. A very early abortion is surely not the killing of a person, and so is not dealt with by anything I have said here.

1. Exactly what is Thomson trying to show with her examples of the burglar and the people-seeds? Reconstruct and evaluate these arguments from analogy. Remember to say which similarities and differences are important, and why.

2. Thomson distinguishes what is morally indecent from what is morally wrong. Explain her distinction. Are any acts morally indecent but not morally wrong? If so, give examples. If not, why not? Does Thomson deny that abortion is morally indecent? If so, does she argue for this denial?

3. Determine whether you think abortion is morally wrong in the following cases:

    a. Where the mother is in danger of dying if she does not have an abortion.

    b. Where the pregnancy is due to rape.

    c. Where contraception was used, but it failed.

    d. Where the fetus has a disease that usually causes death within a year or two.

    e. Where the fetus has a disease that usually causes severe mental retardation.

    f. Where the pregnant woman is mentally or physically unable to be a good mother.

    g. Where the mother will suffer severe personal losses if the pregnancy continues.

Now try to formulate principles and analogies to justify your positions in these controversial cases.

4. Which underlying principles, if any, could protect human lives with only a few exceptions, yet allow us to take lives of:

    a. Contract killers sentenced to capital punishment

    b. Humans who are in irreversible comas

    c. Ourselves in suicide

    d. Children who live next to munitions factories that are bombed in a war

    e. Animals for food, clothing, and entertainment

5. Describe a moral problem that you have faced in your personal life, and apply the methods of moral reasoning that you have learned in this chapter.

16

SCIENTIFIC REASONING

The products of science are all around us. We depend on science when we drive cars, listen to compact discs, and cook food in microwaves. Still, few people understand how science operates. To some, the scientific enterprise seems to consist of nothing more than amassing huge quantities of data to prove or disprove some hypothesis. There is more to science than that. Scientists also seek theories that are profound and far-reaching, or even elegant and beautiful, as is shown by how scientists themselves speak about their theories. The goal of scientific theory is not just to list and describe but to make sense of nature, explain it, make it more intelligible. To choose among conflicting scientific theories, we have to decide which theory makes the most sense and provides the best explanations. This chapter will bring out this complex nature of science by discussing the scientific enterprise in general and then focusing on a particular debate about the existence and nature of biological evolution.

STANDARD SCIENCE

The beginning of science lies in observation. When we look at the world around us, we see that many things happen. Apples fall off trees, the leaves of some trees change color in the autumn, the tides come in and go out, chickens lay eggs, and so on. One job of scientists is to describe and classify what happens and what exists. But scientists also wonder *why* some things happen rather than others. Maple trees change color in the fall, and spruce trees do not, but why? Chickens lay eggs, and monkeys do not, but why? A sphere of wood floats in water, and a gold sphere does not, but why? And why does gold float when pressed into the shape of a boat? These questions ask for *explanations.*

To provide an explanation, scientists often give arguments of the kind discussed in Chapter 13. The event to be explained is derived from a general principle plus a statement of initial conditions or particular facts. For example, given the general principle that a solid sphere floats in water if and only if it is less dense than water, and also given the particular facts that wood is less dense than water, whereas gold is more dense than water, we can explain why a wooden sphere floats in water and a gold sphere does not.

Scientists often seek *deeper* explanations by asking why certain general principles themselves are true. The principle that a sphere floats in water only when it is less dense than water can be explained as an instance of the more general principle that *anything* floats only when it displaces more than its own weight in water. This broader principle not only explains why a wooden sphere floats in water but also why a piece of gold will float when molded into the form of a boat. This broader principle is in turn explained by deriving it from even more basic principles about gravity and the mutual repulsion of molecules. A larger scientific theory is thus used to explain not only why particular things happen but also why certain general principles hold.

Of course, scientists often put forward conflicting theories, so we need some way to test which theory is correct. One simple method is to use the theory to make *predictions*. Since an explanation depends on principles that are general, these principles have implications beyond the particular phenomenon that they were originally intended to explain. The theory thus predicts what will happen in circumstances that the scientist has not yet observed. We can then test the theory by seeing whether these predictions hold true. For example, we can make spheres out of a wide variety of materials, calculate their densities, and then see which ones float. If any sphere floats that is denser than water, then we have to give up our principle that a sphere floats in water *only if* it is less dense than water. (This is an application of the necessary[n] condition test, discussed in Chapter 9.) If we find a sphere that is less dense than water but does not float, then we have to give up the principle that a sphere floats *if* it is less dense than water. (This is an application of the sufficient[n] condition test, discussed in Chapter 9.)

These methods help us rule out certain scientific principles, but the fact that a principle implies true predictions does not, by itself, prove that the principle is true. That argument would commit something like the fallacy of affirming the consequent (see Exercise XVIII in Chapter 6). Nonetheless, we can still say that a theory is *confirmed* if it yields true predictions, and it is confirmed more strongly if it yields more, more varied, and more unexpected true predictions.

Scientific method is actually much more complex than this simple example suggests. This becomes apparent when we encounter *anomalies*. Suppose we have confirmed and explained the principle that a sphere floats in water if and only if it is less dense than water. Suppose also that another principle is well confirmed: A substance gets smaller and more dense as it gets colder. Taken together, these principles predict that a sphere of ice should sink in water. Ice is colder than water, so, according to the second principle, ice should be more dense than water, and that, given the first principle, means that it should not float in water. Of course, our prediction is wrong, since spheres of ice do float in water. What do we do now? The obvious solution is to modify the principle that a substance gets smaller and more dense as it gets colder. This holds for most substances, but not for water. Water expands and thus gets less dense as it freezes.

We could have tried another solution. We could have denied the other principle: that a sphere floats in water if and only if it is less dense than water. Why do scientists not do this? One reason is that we have independent evidence that water expands when it freezes. That is why jars of water burst when they are left in a freezer. Another reason is that we could not give up this principle alone, because it follows from more basic principles about gravity and the mutual repulsion of molecules. Thus, many other areas of science would be affected if we gave up the principle that a sphere floats in water if and only if it is less dense than water. That all these other scientific theories are not only well confirmed but useful is what makes scientists give up one principle rather than another when an anomaly arises.

At this point we might seek an even deeper explanation and ask why water expands when it freezes. In fact, to this day, nobody seems to have a fully adequate explanation of this common phenomenon. There are various theories but no agreement about how to explain the expansion of water. It has something to do with the way in which liquid water crystallizes to form ice, but nobody is quite sure why water crystallizes in that way. Does this show that certain phenomena are beyond scientific understanding? Probably not. But it does suggest that science may never be complete. More questions arise as science progresses, and there may always be questions that remain unanswered. As scientists discover and explain more and more phenomena and see connections among principles in different areas, every new step gives rise to more questions that need to be answered. That is one way in which science makes progress.

CONFLICTING SCIENTIFIC INTERPRETATIONS

Another type of scientific development is more radical—knowledge is not simply extended, but instead one scientific framework is replaced (or largely replaced) by another. In biology, the germ theory of disease and the theory of evolution through natural selection are examples of such revolutionary developments. Einstein's theory of relativity and the rise of quantum mechanics were also revolutionary developments in physics. Indeed, every branch of science has undergone at least one such revolutionary change during the past few centuries.

There are some important differences between scientific progress within a framework and the replacement of one framework by another.[1] In the first place, such changes in framework usually meet with strong resistance. A new conceptual framework will be unfamiliar and hard to understand and may even seem absurd or unintelligible. Even today, for example, the thought that the Earth is spinning on its axis and revolving around the sun

---

[1]Thomas Kuhn gives prominence to this difference in his important work, *The Structure of Scientific Revolutions*, 2d ed. (Chicago: University of Chicago Press, 1970).

seems completely counter to our commonsense view of the world. Also, arguments on behalf of a new framework will be very different from arguments that occur *within* a framework. Disputes over conceptual frameworks cannot be settled by a straightforward appeal to facts. The long debate between Albert Einstein and Niels Bohr concerning quantum theory did not turn on matters of fact but on their interpretation. Einstein could not accept the indeterminacy involved in the quantum theory's interpretation of the world, and he worked until the end of his life to find some alternative to it. At present, almost no scientist shares Einstein's reservations.

The following selection illustrates a clash between two such scientific frameworks in astronomy. The interlocutors are Salviati, Sagredo, and Simplicio. Salviati represents the Copernican system; Simplicio, the Ptolemaic system; Sagredo acts as a moderator, forcing the others to clarify and defend their positions on whether the Earth moves. In attacking the Copernican system, Simplicio lists various arguments from Aristotle that are supposed to show that the Earth does not move. In Aristotle's view, every object has a natural place and motion. The natural motion of heavy objects is towards the center of the Earth, whose nature is to sit still and receive them. That is supposed to explain why unsupported heavy objects fall straight down. Salviati replies that observations of falling objects do not show that the Ptolemaic system is correct and the Copernican system incorrect, since these observations can be explained in either world system. More generally, Salviati argues that no terrestrial phenomenon—that is, no phenomenon observable on the Earth—can be cited to show that one of these systems is true and the other false. For that matter, no celestial phenomena will settle this issue either, because both world systems provide interpretations of the motions of heavenly bodies. That proponents of each of these systems can agree on particular facts, yet disagree profoundly on their correct interpretation, shows that we are dealing with a conflict between general frameworks, or general world systems. Arguments of this kind are quite different from those that take place within a given scientific framework.

DIALOGUE CONCERNING THE TWO WORLD SYSTEMS—PTOLEMAIC AND COPERNICAN[2]

by Galileo Galilei

SALVIATI: Aristotle says, then, that a most certain proof of the earth's being motionless is that things projected perpendicularly upward are seen to return by the same line to the same place from which they were thrown, even though the movement is extremely high. This, he argues,

[2]From *Dialogue Concerning the Two World Systems—Ptolemaic and Copernican,* trans. Stillman Drake (Berkeley: University of California Press, 1953), 139–49.

could not happen if the earth moved, since in the time during which the projectile is moving upward and then downward it is separated from the earth, and the place from which the projectile began its motion would go a long way toward the east, thanks to the revolving of the earth, and the falling projectile would strike the earth that distance away from the place in question. Thus we can accommodate here the argument of the cannon ball as well as the other argument, used by Aristotle and Ptolemy, of seeing heavy bodies falling from great heights along a straight line perpendicular to the surface of the earth. Now, in order to begin to untie these knots, I ask Simplicio by what means he would prove that freely falling bodies go along straight and perpendicular lines directed toward the center, should anyone refuse to grant this to Aristotle and Ptolemy.

SIMPLICIO: By means of the senses, which assure us that the tower is straight and perpendicular, and which show us that a falling stone goes along grazing it, without deviating a hairsbreadth to one side or the other, and strikes at the foot of the tower exactly under the place from which it was dropped.

SALV: But if it happened that the earth rotated, and consequently carried along the tower, and if the falling stone were seen to graze the side of the tower just the same, what would its motion then have to be?

SIMP: In that case one would have to say "its motions," for there would be one with which it went from top to bottom, and another one needed for following the path of the tower.

SALV: The motion would then be a compound of two motions: the one with which it measures the tower, and the other with which it follows it. From this compounding it would follow that the rock would no longer describe that simple straight perpendicular line, but a slanting one, and perhaps not straight.

SIMP: I don't know about its not being straight, but I understand well enough that it would have to be slanting, and different from the straight perpendicular line it would describe with the earth motionless.

SALV: Hence just from seeing the falling stone graze the tower, you could not say for sure that it described a straight and perpendicular line, unless you first assumed the earth to stand still.

SIMP: Exactly so; for if the earth were moving, the motion of the stone would be slanting and not perpendicular.

SALV: Then here, clear and evident, is the paralogism [fallacy] of Aristotle and of Ptolemy, discovered by you yourself. They take as known that which is intended to be proved.

SIMP: In what way? It looks to me like a syllogism in proper form, and not a *petitio principii* [a begging of the question].

SALV: In this way: Does he not, in his proof, take the conclusion as unknown?

Simp: Unknown, for otherwise it would be superfluous to prove it.

Salv: And the middle term; does he not require that to be known?

Simp: Of course; [otherwise it would be an attempt to prove what is unknown by something else that is unknown.]

Salv: Our conclusion, which is unknown and is to be proved; is this not the motionlessness of the earth?

Simp: That is what it is.

Simp: Is not the middle term, which must be known, the straight and perpendicular fall of the stone?

Simp: That is the middle term.

Salv: But wasn't it concluded a little while ago that we could not have any knowledge of this fall being straight and perpendicular unless it was first known that the earth stood still? Therefore in your syllogism, the certainty of the middle term is drawn from the uncertainty of the conclusion. Thus you see how, and how badly, it is a paralogism.

Sagredo: On behalf of Simplicio I should like, if possible, to defend Aristotle, or at least to be better persuaded as to the force of your deduction. You say that seeing the stone graze the tower is not enough to assure us that the motion of the rock is perpendicular (and this is the middle term of the syllogism) unless one assumes the earth to stand still (which is the conclusion to be proved). For if the tower moved along with the earth and the rock grazed it, the motion of the rock would be slanting, and not perpendicular. But I reply that if the tower were moving, it would be impossible for the rock to fall grazing it; therefore, from the scraping fall is inferred the stability of the earth.

Simp: So it is. For to expect the rock to go grazing the tower if that were carried along by the earth would be requiring the rock to have two natural motions; that is, a straight one toward the center, and a circular one about the center, which is impossible.

Salv: So Aristotle's defense consists in its being impossible, or at least in his having considered it impossible, that the rock might move with a motion mixed of straight and circular. For if he had not held it to be impossible that the stone might move both toward and around the center at the same time, he would have understood how it could happen that the falling rock might go grazing the tower whether that was moving or was standing still, and consequently he would have been able to perceive that this grazing could imply nothing as to the motion or rest of the earth.

Nevertheless this does not excuse Aristotle, not only because if he did have this idea he ought to have said so, it being such an important point in the argument, but also, and more so, because it cannot be said either that such an effect is impossible or that Aristotle considered it impossible. The former cannot be said because, as I shall shortly prove to you, this is not only possible but necessary; and the latter cannot be said either, because Aristotle himself admits that fire moves naturally upward in a straight line and also turns in the diurnal motion which is imparted by the sky to all the element of fire and to the greater part of the air. Therefore if he saw no impossibility in the mixing of straight-upward with circular motion, as communicated to fire and to the air up as far as the moon's orbit, no more should he deem this impossible with regard to the rock's straight-downward motion and the circular motion natural to the entire globe of the earth, of which the rock is a part.

Simp: It does not look that way to me at all. If the element of fire goes around together with the air, this is a very easy and even a necessary thing for a particle of fire, which, rising high from the earth, receives that very motion in passing through the moving air, being so tenuous and light a body and so easily moved. But it is quite incredible that a very heavy rock or a cannon ball which is dropped without restraint should let itself be budged by the air or by anything else. Besides which, there is the very appropriate experiment of the stone dropped from the top of the mast of a ship, which falls to the foot of the mast when the ship is standing still, but falls as far from that same point when the ship is sailing as the ship is perceived to have advanced during the time of the fall, this being several yards when the ship's course is rapid. . . .

Salv: Tell me, Simplicio: Do you feel convinced that the experiment on the ship squares so well with our purpose that one may reasonably believe that whatever is seen to occur there must also take place on the terrestrial globe?

Simp: So far, yes; . . .

Salv: Rather, I hope that you will stick to it, and firmly insist that the result on the earth must correspond to that on the ship, so that when the latter is perceived to be prejudicial to your case you will not be tempted to change your mind.

You say, then, that since when the ship stands still the rock falls to the foot of the mast, and when the ship is in motion it falls apart from there, then conversely, from the falling of the rock at the foot it is inferred that the ship stands still, and from its falling away it may be deduced that the ship is moving. And since what happens on the ship must likewise happen on the land, from the falling of the rock at the foot of the tower one necessarily infers the immobility of the terrestrial globe. Is that your argument?

Simp: That is exactly it, briefly stated, which makes it easy to understand.

Salv: Now tell me: If the stone dropped from the top of the mast when the ship was sailing rapidly fell in exactly the same place on the ship to which it fell when the ship was standing still, what use could you make of this falling with regard to determining whether the vessel stood still or moved?

Simp: Absolutely none; just as by the beating of the pulse, for instance, you cannot know whether a person is asleep or awake, since the pulse beats in the same manner in sleeping as in waking.

Salv: Very good. Now, have you ever made this experiment of the ship?

Simp: I have never made it, but I certainly believe that the authorities who adduced it had carefully observed it. Besides, the cause of the difference is so exactly known that there is no room for doubt.

Salv: You yourself are sufficient evidence that those authorities may have offered it without having performed it, for you take it as certain without having done it, and commit yourself to the good faith of their dictum. Similarly it not only may be, but must be that they did the same thing too—I mean, put faith in their predecessors, right on back without ever arriving at anyone who had performed it. For anyone who does will find that the experiment shows exactly the opposite of what is written: that is, it will show that the stone always falls in the same place on the ship: whether the ship is standing still or moving with any speed you please. Therefore, the same cause holding good on the earth as on the ship, nothing can be inferred about the earth's motion or rest from the stone falling always perpendicularly to the foot of the tower. . . .

EVOLUTION

The Darwinian revolution in biology challenged—and continues to challenge—many common assumptions about the nature of science and the nature of man. As a result, Darwin's views on evolution and natural selection encountered vehement opposition right from the start.

These conflicts attracted public attention—a rarity for debates in philosophy of science—in 1981 when the State of Arkansas adopted Act 590 mandating a "balanced treatment for Creation-Science and Evolution-Science." Opponents charged that this bill was unconstitutional on the grounds that it violated the U.S. Constitution's First Amendment prohibition on "the establishment of religion." Early in 1982 the U.S. District Court in *McLean v. Arkansas* ruled that Act 590 violated the First Amendment. It was therefore struck down as unconstitutional.

McLean v. Arkansas could have been argued on a number of grounds. One possible position is that explicit religious instruction does not violate the Constitution. Those defending the Arkansas bill did not, however, adopt this approach. Instead, they argued that creation-science is a genuine *scientific* alternative to the theory of evolution through natural selection. As such, it can be presented and evaluated in the same manner that any scientific theory is presented and evaluated. Thus, defenders of instruction in creation-science deny that teaching this subject matter amounts to introducing religious instruction into public education. The opponents of teaching creation-science in public schools argue that creation-science is not a science, and therefore has no place in a science curriculum. They further argue that it has no place in any other part of a public school curriculum, because its purposes are clearly religious and thus violate the First Amendment's principle of separation of church and state.

Henry M. Morris has been a vigorous defender of the view that creationism should be taught as a *scientific* alternative to Darwin's theory of evolution. The following excerpts from his writings argue that evolution is not scientific and that creationism is. Morris's views are then criticized by the late Stephen J. Gould, a prominent biologist. While discussing this particular case study, Morris and Gould provide simple examples of scientific reasoning—good or bad. They also raise more general issues about the nature of religion, the nature of science, and the relation between religion and science. These issues remain alive today as creationists and their followers continue their attempts to restrict the teaching of evolution and to introduce the teaching of creationism in public schools.

THE SCIENTIFIC CASE AGAINST EVOLUTION: A SUMMARY[3]

by Henry M. Morris

PART I

Belief in evolution is a remarkable phenomenon. It is a belief passionately defended by the scientific establishment, despite the lack of any observable scientific evidence for macroevolution (that is, evolution from one distinct kind of organism into another). This odd situation is briefly documented here by citing recent statements from leading evolutionists admitting their lack of proof. These statements inadvertently show that evolution on any significant scale does not occur at present, and never happened in the past.

EVOLUTION IS NOT HAPPENING NOW

First of all, the lack of a case for evolution is clear from the fact that no one has ever seen it happen. If it were a real process, evolution should still be occurring, and there should be many "transitional" forms that we could observe. What we see instead, of course, is an array of distinct "kinds" of plants and animals with many varieties *within* each kind, but with very clear

[3]*Acts and Facts, ICR's Monthly Newsletter,* Impact no. 330 (December 2000) and 331 (January 2001). Online edition http://www.icr.org/pubs/imp/index.html.

and apparently unbridgeable gaps between the kinds. That is, for example, there are many varieties of dogs and many varieties of cats, but no "dats" or "cogs." Such variation is often called microevolution, and these minor horizontal (or downward) changes occur fairly often, but such changes are not true "vertical" evolution.

Evolutionary geneticists have often experimented on fruit flies and other rapidly reproducing species to induce mutational changes hoping they would lead to new and better species, but these have all failed to accomplish their goal. No truly new species has ever been produced, let alone a new "basic kind."

A current leading evolutionist, Jeffrey Schwartz, professor of anthropology at the University of Pittsburgh, has recently acknowledged that:

> . . . it was and still is the case that, with the exception of Dobzhansky's claim about a new species of fruit fly, the formation of a new species, by any mechanism, has never been observed.*

The scientific method traditionally has required experimental observation and replication. The fact that macroevolution (as distinct from microevolution) has never been observed would seem to exclude it from the domain of true science. Even Ernst Mayr, the dean of living evolutionists, longtime professor of biology at Harvard, who has alleged that evolution is a "simple fact," nevertheless agrees that it is an "historical science" for which "laws and experiments are inappropriate techniques"† by which to explain it. One can never actually *see* evolution in action.

EVOLUTION NEVER HAPPENED IN THE PAST

Evolutionists commonly answer the above criticism by claiming that evolution goes too slowly for us to see it happening today. They used to claim that the real evidence for evolution was in the fossil record of the past, but the fact is that the billions of known fossils do not include a single unequivocal transitional form with transitional structures in the process of evolving.

> Given that evolution, according to Darwin, was in a continual state of motion . . . it followed logically that the fossil record should be rife with examples of transitional forms leading from the less to the more evolved.‡

Even those who believe in rapid evolution recognize that a considerable number of generations would be required for one distinct "kind" to evolve into another more complex kind. There ought, therefore, to be a considerable number of true transitional structures preserved in the fossils (after all, there are billions of nontransitional structures there!). But (with the exception of a

---

*Jeffrey H. Schwartz, *Sudden Origins* (New York: John Wiley, 1999), p. 300.

†Ernst Mayr, "Darwin's Influence on Modern Thought," *Scientific American* (vol. 283, July 2000), p. 83.

‡Jeffrey H. Schwartz, op. cit., p. 89.

few very doubtful creatures such as the controversial feathered dinosaurs and the alleged walking whales) they are not there.

> Instead of filling in the gaps in the fossil record with so-called missing links, most paleontologists found themselves facing a situation in which there were only gaps in the fossil record, with no evidence of transformational intermediates between documented fossil species.*

The entire history of evolution from the evolution of life from non-life to the evolution of vertebrates from invertebrates to the evolution of man from the ape is strikingly devoid of intermediates: the links are all missing in the fossil record, just as they are in the present world.

With respect to the origin of life, a leading researcher in this field, Leslie Orgel, has said after noting that neither proteins nor nucleic acids could have arisen without the other, concludes

> And so, at first glance, one might have to conclude that life could never, in fact, have originated by chemical means.†

Being committed to total evolution as he is, Dr. Orgel cannot accept any such conclusion as that. Therefore, he speculates that RNA may have come first, but then he still has to admit that:

> The precise events giving rise to the RNA world remain unclear . . . investigators have proposed many hypotheses, but evidence in favor of each of them is fragmentary at best.‡

Translation: "There is no known way by which life could have arisen naturalistically." Unfortunately, two generations of students have been taught that Stanley Miller's famous experiment on a gaseous mixture, practically *proved* the naturalistic origin of life. But not so!

> Miller put the whole thing in a ball, gave it an electric charge, and waited. He found that amino acids and other fundamental complex molecules were accumulating at the bottom of the apparatus. His discovery gave a huge boost to the scientific investigation of the origin of life. Indeed, for some time it seemed like creation of life in a test tube was within reach of experimental science. Unfortunately, such experiments have not progressed much further than the original prototype, leaving us with a sour aftertaste from the primordial soup.§

Neither is there any clue as to how the one-celled organisms of the primordial world could have evolved into the vast array of complex multi-celled invertebrates of the Cambrian period. Even dogmatic evolutionist Gould admits that:

*Ibid.

†Leslie E. Orgel, "The Origin of Life on the Earth," *Scientific American* (vol. 27 1, October 1994), p. 78.

‡Ibid, p. 83.

§Massimo Pigliucci, "Where Do We Come From?" *Skeptical Inquirer* (vol. 23, September/October 1999), p. 24.

The Cambrian explosion was the most remarkable and puzzling event in the history of life.*

Equally puzzling, however, is how some invertebrate creature in the ancient ocean, with all its "hard parts" on the outside, managed to evolve into the first vertebrate—that is, the first fish—with its hard parts all on the inside.

Yet the transition from spineless invertebrates to the first backboned fishes is still shrouded in mystery, and many theories abound.†

Other gaps are abundant, with no real transitional series anywhere. A very bitter opponent of creation science, paleontologist Niles Eldredge, has acknowledged that there is little, if any, evidence of evolutionary transitions in the fossil record. Instead, things remain the same!

It is a simple ineluctable truth that virtually all members of a biota remain basically stable, with minor fluctuations, throughout their durations. . . .‡

So how do evolutionists arrive at their evolutionary trees from fossils of organisms which didn't change during their durations?

Fossil discoveries can muddle over attempts to construct simple evolutionary trees—fossils from key periods are often not intermediates, but rather hodge podges of defining features of many different groups . . . Generally, it seems that major groups are not assembled in a simple linear or progressive manner—new features are often "cut and pasted" on different groups at different times.§

As far as ape/human intermediates are concerned, the same is true, although anthropologists have been eagerly searching for them for many years. Many have been proposed, but each has been rejected in turn.

All that paleoanthropologists have to show for more than 100 years of digging are remains from fewer than 2000 of our ancestors. They have used this assortment of jawbones, teeth and fossilized scraps, together with molecular evidence from living species, to piece together a line of human descent going back 5 to 8 million years to the time when humans and chimpanzees diverged from a common ancestor.¶

Anthropologists supplemented their extremely fragmentary fossil evidence with DNA and other types of molecular genetic evidence from living animals to try to work out an evolutionary scenario that will fit. But this genetic evidence really doesn't help much either, for it contradicts the fossil evidence.

*Stephen Jay Gould, "The Evolution of Life," chapter I in *Evolution: Facts and Fallacies*. ed. by J. William Schopf (San Diego, CA: Academic Press, 1999), p. 9.

†J. O. Long, *The Rise of Fishes* (Baltimore: John Hopkins University Press, 1995), p. 30.

‡Niles Eldredge, *The Pattern of Evolution* (New York: W. H. Freeman and Co., 1998), p. 157.

§Neil Shubin, "Evolutionary Cut and Paste," *Nature* (vol. 349, July 2, 1998), p. 12.

¶Colin Tudge, "Human Origins Revisited," *New Scientist* (vol. 146, May 20, 1995), p. 24.

The overall effect is that molecular phylogenetics is by no means as straightforward as its pioneers believed. . . . The Byzantine dynamics of genome change has many other consequences for molecular phylogenetics, including the fact that different genes tell different stories.*

Summarizing the genetic data from humans, another author concludes, rather pessimistically:

Even with DNA sequence data, we have no direct access to the processes of evolution, so objective reconstruction of the vanished past can be achieved only by creative imagination.†

Since there is no real scientific evidence that evolution is occurring at present or ever occurred in the past, it is reasonable to conclude that evolution is not a fact of science, as many claim. In fact, it is not even science at all, but an arbitrary system built upon faith in universal naturalism.

Part II

We have noted from the statements of leading evolutionary scientists that no true vertical evolution from one kind of organism to a more complex kind has ever been observed in all human history.

Similar admissions from evolutionists have acknowledged that no examples of such evolutionary transitions have yet been documented in any of the billions of fossilized remains from the supposed geological ages of the past.

Actually, these negative evidences against evolution are, at the same time, strong positive evidences for special creation. They are, in fact, specific predictions based on the creation model of origins.

Creationists would obviously predict ubiquitous gaps between created kinds, though with many varieties capable of arising within each kind, in order to enable each basic kind to cope with changing environments without becoming extinct. Creationists also would anticipate that any "vertical changes" in organized complexity would be downward, since the Creator (by definition) would create things correctly to begin with. Thus, arguments and evidences against evolution are, at the same time, positive evidences for creation.

The Equivocal Evidence from Genetics

Nevertheless, because of the lack of any direct evidence for evolution, evolutionists are increasingly turning to dubious circumstantial evidences, such as similarities in DNA or other biochemical components of organisms as their "proof" that evolution is a scientific fact. A number of evolutionists have

---

*Roger Lewin, "Family Feud," *New Scientist* (vol. 157, January 24, 1998), p. 39.

†N. A. Takahata, "Genetic Perspective on the Origin and History of Humans," *Annual Review of Ecology and Systematics* (vol. 26, 1995), p. 343.

even argued that DNA itself is evidence for evolution, since it is common to all organisms. More often is the argument used that similar DNA structures in two different organisms prove common evolutionary ancestry.

Neither argument is valid. There is no reason whatever why the Creator could not or would not use the same type of genetic code based on DNA for all His created life forms. This is evidence for intelligent design and creation, not evolution.

The most frequently cited example of DNA commonality is the human/chimpanzee "similarity," noting that chimpanzees have more than 90% of their DNA the same as humans. This is hardly surprising, however, considering the many physiological resemblances between people and chimpanzees. Why shouldn't they have similar DNA structures in comparison, say, to the DNA differences between men and spiders?

Similarities—whether of DNA, anatomy, embryonic development, or anything else—are better explained in terms of creation by a common Designer than by evolutionary relationship. The great differences between organisms are of greater significance than the similarities, and evolutionism has no explanation for these if they all are assumed to have had the same ancestor. How could these great gaps between kinds ever arise at all, by any natural process?

The apparently small differences between human and chimpanzee DNA obviously produce very great differences in their respective anatomies, intelligence, etc. The superficial similarities between all apes and human beings are nothing compared to the differences in any practical or observable sense.

Nevertheless, evolutionists, having largely become disenchanted with the fossil record as a witness for evolution because of the ubiquitous gaps where there should be transitions, recently have been promoting DNA and other genetic evidence as proof of evolution. However, this is often inconsistent with, not only the fossil record, but also with the comparative morphology of the creatures. Commenting on a few of the numerous anomalous results in the genetic story, Dr. Roger Lewin summarizes the situation thus, as noted in Part I of this series:

> The overall effect is that molecular phylogenetics is by no means as straightforward as its pioneers believed. . . . The Byzantine dynamics of genome change has many other consequences for molecular phylogenetics, including the fact that different genes tell different stories.[*]

Lewin mentions just a few typical contradictions yielded by this type of evidence in relation to more traditional Darwinian "proofs."

> The elephant shrew, consigned by traditional analysis to the order insectivores . . . is in fact more closely related to . . . the true elephant. Cows are more closely related to dolphins than they are to horses. The duck-billed platypus . . . is on equal evolutionary footing with . . . kangaroos and koalas.[†]

[*]Roger Lewin, "Family Feud," *New Scientist* (vol. 157, January 24, 1998), p. 39.

[†]Ibid., p. 36

There are many even more bizarre comparisons yielded by this approach.

The abundance of so-called "junk DNA" in the genetic code also has been offered as a special type of evidence for evolution, especially those genes which they think have experienced mutations, sometimes called "pseudo-genes."* However, evidence is accumulating rapidly today that these supposedly useless genes do actually perform useful functions.

Enough genes have already been uncovered in the genetic midden to show that what was once thought to be waste is definitely being transmitted into scientific code.† It is thus wrong to decide that junk DNA, even the so-called "pseudogenes," have no function. That is merely an admission of ignorance and an object for fruitful research. Like the so-called "vestigial organs" in man, once considered as evidence of evolution but now all known to have specific uses, so the junk DNA and pseudogenes most probably are specifically useful to the organism, whether or not those uses have yet been discovered by scientists.

At the very best this type of evidence is strictly circumstantial and can be explained just as well in terms of primeval creation supplemented in some cases by later deterioration, just as expected in the creation model.

The real issue is, as noted before, whether there is any observable evidence that evolution is occurring now or has ever occurred in the past. As we have seen, even evolutionists have to acknowledge that this type of *real* scientific evidence for evolution does not exist.

A good question to face is: *Why* are all *observable* evolutionary changes either horizontal and trivial (so-called microevolution) or downward toward deterioration and extinction? The answer seems to be found in the universally applicable laws of the science of thermodynamics.

EVOLUTION IS IMPOSSIBLE

The main scientific reason why there is no evidence for evolution in either the present or the past (except in the creative imagination of evolutionary scientists) is because one of the most fundamental laws of nature precludes it. The law of increasing entropy—also known as the second law of thermodynamics—stipulates that all systems in the real world tend to go "downhill," as it were, toward disorganization and decreased complexity.

This law of entropy is, by any measure, one of the most universal, best-proved laws of nature. It applies not only in physical and chemical systems, but also in biological and geological systems—in fact *all* systems, without exception.

> No exception to the second law of thermodynamics has ever been found—not even a tiny one. Like conservation of energy (the "first law"), the existence of a

*Rachel Nowak, "Mining Treasures from 'Junk DNA,'" *Science* (vol. 263, February 4, 1994), p. 608.

†Ibid.

law so precise and so independent of details of models must have a logical foundation that is independent of the fact that matter is composed of interacting particles.*

The author of this quote is referring primarily to physics, but he does point out that the second law is "independent of details of models." Besides, practically all evolutionary biologists are reductionists—that is, they insist that there are no "vitalist" forces in living systems, and that *all* biological processes are explicable in terms of physics and chemistry. That being the case, biological processes also must operate in accordance with the laws of thermodynamics, and practically all biologists acknowledge this.

Evolutionists commonly insist, however, that evolution is a fact anyhow, and that the conflict is resolved by noting that the earth is an "open system," with the incoming energy from the sun able to sustain evolution throughout the geological ages in spite of the natural tendency of all systems to deteriorate toward disorganization. That is how an evolutionary entomologist has dismissed W. A. Dembski's impressive recent book, *Intelligent Design*. This scientist defends what he thinks is "natural processes' ability to increase complexity" by noting what he calls a "flaw" in "the arguments against evolution based on the second law of thermodynamics." And what is this flaw?

> Although the overall amount of disorder in a closed system cannot decrease, local order within a larger system can increase even without the actions of an intelligent agent.[†]

This naive response to the entropy law is typical of evolutionary dissimulation. While it is true that local order can increase in an open system if certain conditions are met, the fact is that evolution does not meet those conditions. Simply saying that the earth is open to the energy from the sun says nothing about *how* that raw solar heat is converted into increased complexity in any system, open or closed.

The fact is that the best known and most fundamental equation of thermodynamics says that the influx of heat into an *open* system will *increase* the entropy of that system, not decrease it. All known cases of decreased entropy (or increased organization) in open systems involve a guiding program of some sort and one or more energy conversion mechanisms.

Evolution has neither of these. Mutations are not "organizing" mechanisms, but disorganizing (in accord with the second law). They are commonly harmful, sometimes neutral, never beneficial (at least as far as observed mutations are concerned). Natural selection cannot generate order, but can only "sieve out" the disorganizing mutations presented to it, thereby

---

*E. H. Lieb and Jakob Yngvason, "A Fresh Look at Entropy and the Second Law of Thermodynamics," *Physics Today* (vol. 53, April 2000), p. 32.

[†]Norman A. Johnson, "Design Flaw," *American Scientist* (vol. 88, May/June 2000), p. 274.

conserving the existing order, but never generating new order. In principle, it may be barely conceivable that evolution could occur in open systems, in spite of the *tendency* of all systems to disintegrate sooner or later. But no one yet has been able to show that it actually *has* the ability to overcome this universal tendency, and that is the basic reason why there is still no *bona fide* proof of evolution, past or present.

From the statements of evolutionists themselves, therefore, we have learned that there is no real *scientific evidence* for real evolution. The only observable evidence is that of very limited horizontal (or downward) changes within strict limits. Evolution never occurred in the past, is not occurring at present, and could never happen at all.

DISCUSSION QUESTIONS

1. Morris distinguishes microevolution or horizontal evolution from macroevolution or vertical evolution. What is supposed to be the difference? Is this difference important to his position? Why or why not?

2. Morris emphasizes that "no one has ever seen it [macroevolution] happen." Is this true? Does it matter? Do any other legitimate sciences postulate processes that no one has ever seen happen?

3. Morris claims that fewer transitional forms have been found than would be expected if gradual evolution had occurred. Explain his point. How could defenders of evolution best respond?

4. Morris argues that similarities in DNA among species do not support evolution. What does explain such similarities, according to Morris? Which explanation is better? Why?

5. Morris writes, "arguments and evidences against evolution are, at the same time, positive evidences for creation." Why does he say this? Do you agree? Why or why not?

6. What is "junk DNA"? Why has this "been offered as a special type of evidence for evolution"? How does Morris respond to this evidence? Is his response adequate? Why or why not?

7. Morris cites the second law of thermodynamics as precluding evolution. What is this law? Why is it supposed to rule out evolution, according to Morris? Do you agree? Why or why not?

8. In his closing paragraph, Morris says both that there is no scientific evidence for evolution and that evolution could never happen. Does one of these claims imply the other? Why or why not?

EVOLUTION AS FACT AND THEORY[4]

■

by Stephen Jay Gould

Kirtley Mather, who died last year at age eighty-nine, was a pillar of both science and the Christian religion in America and one of my dearest friends. The difference of half a century in our ages evaporated before our common interests. The most curious thing we shared was a battle we each fought at the same age. For Kirtley had gone to Tennessee with Clarence Darrow to testify for evolution at the Scopes trial of 1925. When I think that we are enmeshed again in the same struggle for one of the best documented, most compelling and exciting concepts in all of science, I don't know whether to laugh or cry.

According to idealized principles of scientific discourse, the arousal of dormant issues should reflect fresh data that give renewed life to abandoned notions. Those outside the current debate may therefore be excused for suspecting that creationists have come up with something new, or that evolutionists have generated some serious internal trouble. But nothing has changed; the creationists have not a single new fact or argument. Darrow and Bryan were at least more entertaining than we lesser antagonists today. The rise of creationism is politics, pure and simple; it represents one issue (and by no means the major concern) of the resurgent evangelical right. Arguments that seemed kooky just a decade ago have reentered the mainstream.

CREATIONISM IS NOT SCIENCE

The basic attack of the creationists falls apart on two general counts before we even reach the supposed factual details of their complaints against evolution. First, they play upon a vernacular misunderstanding of the word "theory" to convey the false impression that we evolutionists are covering up the rotten core of our edifice. Second, they misuse a popular philosophy of science to argue that they are behaving scientifically in attacking evolution. Yet the same philosophy demonstrates that their own belief is not science, and that "scientific creationism" is therefore meaningless and self-contradictory, a superb example of what Orwell called "newspeak."

In the American vernacular, "theory" often means "imperfect fact"—part of a hierarchy of confidence running downhill from fact to theory to hypothesis to guess. Thus the power of the creationist argument: Evolution is "only" a theory, and intense debate now rages about many aspects of the theory. If evolution is less than a fact, and scientists can't even make up their minds about the theory, then what confidence can we have in it? Indeed,

[4]*Discover Magazine*, 2, 5 (May 1981), pp. 34–37. Reprinted in *Hen's Teeth and Horse's Toes* (New York: Norton, 1994), 253–62.

President Reagan echoed this argument before an evangelical group in Dallas when he said (in what I devoutly hope was campaign rhetoric): "Well, it is a theory. It is a scientific theory only, and it has in recent years been challenged in the world of science—that is, not believed in the scientific community to be as infallible as it once was."

Well, evolution is a theory. It is also a fact. And facts and theories are different things, not rungs in a hierarchy of increasing certainty. Facts are the world's data. Theories are structures of ideas that explain and interpret facts. Facts do not go away when scientists debate rival theories to explain them. Einstein's theory of gravitation replaced Newton's, but apples did not suspend themselves in mid-air pending the outcome. And human beings evolved from apelike ancestors whether they did so by Darwin's proposed mechanism or by some other, yet to be discovered.

Moreover, "fact" does not mean "absolute certainty." The final proofs of logic and mathematics flow deductively from stated premises and achieve certainty only because they are *not* about the empirical world. Evolutionists make no claim for perpetual truth, though creationists often do (and then attack us for a style of argument that they themselves favor). In science, "fact" can only mean "confirmed to such a degree that it would be perverse to withhold provisional assent." I suppose that apples might start to rise tomorrow, but the possibility does not merit equal time in physics classrooms.

Evolutionists have been clear about this distinction between fact and theory from the very beginning, if only because we have always acknowledged how far we are from completely understanding the mechanisms (theory) by which evolution (fact) occurred. Darwin continually emphasized the difference between his two great and separate accomplishments: establishing the fact of evolution, and proposing a theory—natural selection—to explain the mechanism of evolution. He wrote in *The Descent of Man*: "I had two distinct objects in view; firstly, to show that species had not been separately created, and secondly, that natural selection had been the chief agent of change. . . . Hence if I have erred in . . . having exaggerated its [natural selection's] power. . . . I have at least, as I hope, done good service in aiding to overthrow the dogma of separate creations."

Thus Darwin acknowledged the provisional nature of natural selection while affirming the fact of evolution. The fruitful theoretical debate that Darwin initiated has never ceased. From the 1940s through the 1960s, Darwin's own theory of natural selection did achieve a temporary hegemony that it never enjoyed in his lifetime. But renewed debate characterizes our decade, and, while no biologist questions the importance of natural selection, many now doubt its ubiquity. In particular, many evolutionists argue that substantial amounts of genetic change may not be subject to natural selection and may spread through populations at random. Others are challenging Darwin's linking of natural selection with gradual, imperceptible change through all intermediary degrees; they are arguing that most evolutionary events may occur far more rapidly than Darwin envisioned.

Scientists regard debates on fundamental issues of theory as a sign of intellectual health and a source of excitement. Science is—and how else can I say it?—most fun when it plays with interesting ideas, examines their implications, and recognizes that old information may be explained in surprisingly new ways. Evolutionary theory is now enjoying this uncommon vigor. Yet amidst all this turmoil no biologist has been led to doubt the fact that evolution occurred; we are debating how it happened. We are all trying to explain the same thing: the tree of evolutionary descent linking all organisms by ties of genealogy. Creationists pervert and caricature this debate, by conveniently neglecting the common conviction that underlies it, and by falsely suggesting that we now doubt the very phenomenon we are struggling to understand.

Using another invalid argument, creationists claim that "the dogma of separate creations," as Darwin characterized it a century ago, is a scientific theory meriting equal time with evolution in high school biology curricula. But a prevailing viewpoint among philosophers of science belies this creationist argument. Philosopher Karl Popper has argued for decades that the primary criterion of science is the falsifiability of its theories. We can never prove absolutely, but we can falsify. A set of ideas that cannot, in principle, be falsified is not science.

The entire creationist argument involves little more than a rhetorical attempt to falsify evolution by presenting supposed contradictions among its supporters. Their brand of creationism, they claim, is, "scientific" because it follows the Popperian model in trying to demolish evolution. Yet Popper's argument must apply in both directions. One does not become a scientist by the simple act of trying to falsify another scientific system; one has to present an alternative system that also meets Popper's criterion—it too must be falsifiable in principle.

"Scientific creationism" is a self-contradictory, nonsense phrase precisely because it cannot be falsified. I can envision observations and experiments that would disprove any evolutionary theory I know, but I cannot imagine what potential data could lead creationists to abandon their beliefs. Unbeatable systems are dogma, not science. Lest I seem harsh or rhetorical, I quote creationism's leading intellectual, Duane Gish, Ph.D., from his recent (1978) book *Evolution? The Fossils Say No!* "By creation we mean the bringing into being by a supernatural Creator of the basic kinds of plants and animals by the process of sudden, or fiat, creation. We do not know how the Creator created, what processes He used, *for He used processes which are not now operating anywhere in the natural universe* [Gish's italics]. This is why we refer to creation as special creation. We cannot discover by scientific investigations anything about the creative processes used by the Creator." Pray tell, Dr. Gish, in the light of your last sentence, what then is "scientific" creationism?

THE FACT OF EVOLUTION

Our confidence that evolution occurred centers upon three general arguments. First, we have abundant, direct, observational evidence of evolution in action, from both the field and the laboratory. It ranges from countless experiments on change in nearly everything about fruit flies subjected to artificial selection in the laboratory to the famous British moths that turned black when industrial soot darkened the trees upon which they rest. (The moths gain protection from sharp-sighted bird predators by blending into the background.) Creationists do not deny these observations; how could they? Creationists have tightened their act. They now argue that God only created "basic kinds," and allowed for limited evolutionary meandering within them. Thus toy poodles and Great Danes come from the dog kind and moths can change color, but nature cannot convert a dog to a cat or a monkey to a man.

The second and third arguments for evolution—the case for major changes—do not involve direct observation of evolution in action. They rest upon inference, but are no less secure for that reason. Major evolutionary change requires too much time for direct observation on the scale of recorded human history. All historical sciences rest upon inference, and evolution is no different from geology, cosmology, or human history in this respect. In principle, we cannot observe processes that operated in the past. We must infer them from results that still survive: living and fossil organisms for evolution, documents and artifacts of human history, strata and topography for geology.

The second argument—that the imperfection of nature reveals evolution—strikes many people as ironic, for they feel that evolution should be most elegantly displayed in the nearly perfect adaptation expressed by some organisms—the chamber of a gull's wing, or butterflies that cannot be seen in ground litter because they mimic leaves so precisely. But perfection could be imposed by a wise creator or evolved by natural selection. Perfection covers the tracks of past history. And past history—the evidence of descent—is our mark of evolution.

Evolution lies exposed in the *imperfections* that record a history of descent. Why should a rat run, a bat fly, a porpoise swim, and I type this essay with structures built of the same bones unless we all inherited them from a common ancestor? An engineer, starting from scratch, could design better limbs in each case. Why should all the large native mammals of Australia be marsupials, unless they descended from a common ancestor isolated on this island continent? Marsupials are not "better," or ideally suited for Australia; many have been wiped out by placental mammals imported by man from other continents. This principle of imperfection extends to all historical sciences. When we recognize the etymology of September, October, November, and December (seventh, eighth, ninth, and tenth, from the Latin), we know that two additional items (January and February) must have been added to an original calendar of ten months.

The third argument is more direct: Transitions are often found in the fossil record. Preserved transitions are not common—and should not be, according to our understanding of evolution (see next section)—but they are not entirely wanting, as creationists often claim. The lower jaw of reptiles contains several bones, that of mammals only one. The non-mammalian jawbones are reduced, step by step, in mammalian ancestors until they become tiny nubbins located at the back of the jaw. The "hammer" and "anvil" bones of the mammalian ear are descendants of these nubbins. How could such a transition be accomplished? the creationists ask. Surely a bone is either entirely in the jaw or in the ear. Yet paleontologists have discovered two transitional lineages or therapsids (the so-called mammal-like reptiles) with a double jaw joint—one composed of the old quadrate and articular bones (soon to become the hammer and anvil), the other of the squamosal and dentary bones (as in modern mammals). For that matter, what better transitional form could we desire than the oldest human, *Australopithecus afarensis*, with its apelike palate, its human upright stance, and a cranial capacity larger than any ape's of the same body size but a full 1,000 cubic centimeters below ours? If God made each of the half dozen human species discovered in ancient rocks, why did he create in an unbroken temporal sequence of progressively more modern features—increasing cranial capacity, reduced face and teeth, larger body size? Did he create to mimic evolution and test our faith thereby?

AN EXAMPLE OF CREATIONIST ARGUMENT

Faced with these facts of evolution and the philosophical bankruptcy of their own position, creationists rely upon distortion and innuendo to buttress their rhetorical claim. If I sound sharp or bitter, indeed I am—for I have become a major target of these practices.

I count myself among the evolutionists who argue for a jerky, or episodic, rather than a smoothly gradual, pace of change. In 1972 my colleague Niles Eldredge and I developed the theory of punctuated equilibrium. We argued that two outstanding facts of the fossil record—geologically "sudden" origin of new species and failure to change thereafter (stasis)—reflect the predictions of evolutionary theory, not the imperfections of the fossil record. In most theories, small isolated populations are the source of new species, and the process of speciation takes thousands or tens of thousands of years. This amount of time, so long when measured against our lives, is a geological microsecond. It represents much less than 1 per cent of the average life span for a fossil invertebrate species—more than 10 million years. Large, widespread, and well-established species, on the other hand, are not expected to change very much. We believe that the inertia of large populations explains the stasis of most fossil species over millions of years.

We proposed the theory of punctuated equilibrium largely to provide a different explanation for pervasive trends in the fossil record. Trends, we argued, cannot be attributed to gradual transformation within lineages, but must arise from the differential success of certain kinds of species. A trend, we argued, is more like climbing a flight of stairs (punctuations and stasis) than rolling up an inclined plane.

Since we proposed punctuated equilibria to explain trends, it is infuriating to be quoted again and again by creationists—whether through design or stupidity, I do not know—as admitting that the fossil record includes no transitional forms. Transitional forms are generally lacking at the species level, but are abundant between larger groups. The evolution from reptiles to mammals, as mentioned earlier, is well documented. Yet a pamphlet entitled "Harvard Scientists Agree Evolution Is a Hoax" states: "The facts of punctuated equilibrium which Gould and Eldredge . . . are forcing Darwinists to swallow fit the picture that Bryan insisted on, and which God has revealed to us in the Bible."

Continuing the distortion, several creationists have equated the theory of punctuated equilibrium with a caricature of the beliefs of Richard Goldschmidt, a great early geneticist. Goldschmidt argued, in a famous book published in 1940, that new groups can arise at once through major mutations. He referred to these suddenly transformed creatures as "hopeful monsters." (I am attracted to some aspects of the non-caricatured version, but Goldschmidt's theory still has nothing to do with punctuated equilibrium.) Creationist Luther Sunderland talks of the "punctuated equilibrium hopeful monster theory" and tells his hopeful readers that "it amounts to tacit admission that anti-evolutionists are correct in asserting there is no fossil evidence supporting the theory that all life is connected to a common ancestor." Duane Gish writes, "According to Goldschmidt and now apparently according to Gould, a reptile laid an egg from which the first bird, feathers and all, was produced." Any evolutionist who believed such nonsense would rightly be laughed off the intellectual stage; yet the only theory that could ever envision such a scenario for the evolution of birds is creationism—God acts in the egg.

Conclusion

I am both angry at and amused by the creationists; but mostly I am deeply sad. Sad for many reasons. Sad because so many people who respond to creationist appeals are troubled for the right reason, but venting their anger at the wrong target. It is true that scientists have often been dogmatic and elitist. It is true that we have often allowed the white-coated, advertising image to represent us—"Scientists say that Brand X cures bunions ten times faster than . . ." We have not fought it adequately because we derive benefits from appearing as a new priesthood. It is also true that faceless bureaucratic state power intrudes more and more into our lives and removes choices that should belong to individuals and communities. I can understand that requiring that evolution be taught in the schools might be seen as one more insult on all these grounds. But the culprit is not, and cannot be, evolution or any other fact of the natural world. Identify and fight your legitimate enemies by all means, but we are not among them.

I am sad because the practical result of this brouhaha will not be expanded coverage to include creationism (that would also make me sad), but the reduction or excision of evolution from high school curricula. Evolution is one of the half dozen "great ideas" developed by science. It speaks to the profound issues of genealogy that fascinate all of us—the "roots" phenomenon writ large. Where did we come from? Where did life arise? How did it develop? How are organisms related? It forces us to think, ponder, and wonder. Shall we deprive millions of this knowledge and once again teach biology as a set of dull and unconnected facts, without the thread that weaves diverse material into a supple unity?

But most of all I am saddened by a trend I am just beginning to discern among my colleagues. I sense that some now wish to mute the healthy debate about theory that has brought new life to evolutionary biology. It provides grist for creationist mills, they say, even if only by distortion. Perhaps we should lie low and rally round the flag of strict Darwinism, at least for the moment—a kind of old-time religion on our part.

But we should borrow another metaphor and recognize that we too have to tread a straight and narrow path, surrounded by roads to perdition. For if we ever begin to suppress our search to understand nature, to quench our own intellectual excitement in a misguided effort to present a united front where it does not and should not exist, then we are truly lost.

DISCUSSION QUESTIONS

1. Gould distinguishes facts from theories. What is supposed to be the difference? Is this difference important to his position? Why or why not?

2. Gould argues that creationism is not scientific, because it is not falsifiable in principle. Is this a good test of science? Does evolution pass this test? Why or why not? (See Chapter 12 on self-sealers.)

3. Gould cites "abundant, direct, observational evidence of evolution in action." What exactly is this evidence? How does Morris respond? Is his response adequate? Why or why not?

4. Gould claims that "the imperfection of nature" is evidence of evolution. What is his point here? How could Morris best respond? Is this response adequate? Why or why not?

5. Gould's third argument is based on discovered transitional forms. Explain this argument. How could Morris best respond? Is this response adequate? Why or why not?

6. What is the theory of punctuated equilibrium? Do debates between this theory and standard Darwinian theory lend any support to creationism? Why or why not?

7. More recent allies of creationism argue for "intelligent design." This view has been championed by Michael Behe and William Dembski, among others. In the following passage, Dembski uses an analogy from Behe to argue that certain structures could not have evolved. Explain and evaluate their argument:

In *Darwin's Black Box* (1996), Behe presents a powerful argument for actual design in the cell. Central to his argument is his notion of irreducible complexity. A system is irreducibly complex if it consists of several interrelated parts so that removing even one part completely destroys the system's function. As an example of irreducible complexity Behe offers the standard mousetrap. A mousetrap consists of a platform, a hammer, a spring, a catch, and a holding bar. Remove any one of these five components, and it is impossible to construct a functional mousetrap.

Irreducible complexity needs to be contrasted with cumulative complexity. A system is cumulatively complex if the components of the system can be arranged sequentially so that the successive removal of components never leads to the complete loss of function. An example of a cumulatively complex system is a city. It is possible successively to remove people and services from a city until one is down to a tiny village—all without losing the sense of community, the city's "function."

From this characterization of cumulative complexity, it is clear that the Darwinian mechanism of natural selection and random mutation can readily account for cumulative complexity. Darwin's account of how organisms gradually become more complex as favorable adaptations accumulate is the flip side of the city in our example from which people and services are removed. In both cases, the simpler and more complex versions both work, only less or more effectively,

But can the Darwinian mechanism account for irreducible complexity? Certainly, if selection acts with reference to a goal, it can produce irreducible complexity. Take Behe's mousetrap. Given the goal of constructing a mousetrap, one can specify a goal-directed selection process that in turn selects a platform, a hammer, a spring, a catch, and a holding bar, and at the end puts all these components together to form a functional mousetrap. Given a pre-specified goal, selection has no difficulty producing irreducibly complex systems.

But the selection operating in biology is Darwinian natural selection. And by definition this form of selection operates without goals, has neither plan nor purpose, and is wholly undirected. The great appeal of Darwin's selection mechanism was, after all, that it would eliminate teleology from biology. Yet by making selection an undirected process, Darwin drastically reduced the type of complexity biological systems could manifest. Henceforth biological systems could manifest only cumulative complexity, not irreducible complexity.

As Behe explains in *Darwin's Black Box:* "An irreducibly complex system cannot be produced ... by slight, successive modifications of a precursor system, because any precursor to an irreducibly complex system that is missing a part is by definition nonfunctional. ... Since natural selection can only choose systems that are already working, then if a biological system cannot be produced gradually it would have to arise as an integrated unit, in one fell swoop, for natural selection to have anything to act on."

For an irreducibly complex system, function is attained only when all components of the system are in place simultaneously. It follows that natural selection, if it is going to produce an irreducibly complex system, has to produce it all at once or not at all. This would not be a problem if the systems in question were simple. But they're not. The irreducibly complex biochemical systems Behe considers are protein machines consisting of numerous distinct proteins, each indispensable for function. ... The irreducible complexity of such biochemical systems cannot be explained by the Darwinian mechanism, nor indeed by any naturalistic evolutionary mechanism proposed to date.[5]

[5]From William A. Dembski, "Science and Design," *First Things*, 86 (October 1, 1998).

8. The argument from Behe and Dembski (in the previous question) is criticized in the following quotation from a review by H. Allen Orr. Explain and evaluate this response:

> Behe's claim was refuted—and in at least two ways. Both showed how irreducibly complex systems could be reached via gradual, Darwinian paths. Dembski calls the first path "scaffolding." At each step, a part gets added that improves a structure's function. At some point, however, a substructure might appear that no longer needs the remaining parts. These useless parts could then fall away. The key point is that the substructure we're left with might be irreducibly complex. Remove any part now and all hell breaks loose. The second path was one that I championed. Dembski calls it "incremental indispensability." Here's the argument: "An irreducibly complex system can be built gradually by adding parts that, while initially just advantageous, become—because of later changes—essential. The logic is very simple. Some part (A) initially does some job (and not very well, perhaps). Another part (B) later gets added because it helps A. This new part isn't essential, it merely improves things. But later on, A (or something else) may change in such a way that B now becomes indispensable. This process continues as further parts get folded into the system. And at the end of the day, many parts may all be required." Dembski more or less concedes that the above paths show that irreducibly complex machines can be built via Darwinism.[6]

9. In your opinion, should creationism be taught in public high schools alongside evolution and natural selection as part of the science curriculum? Why or why not?

[6]H. Allen Orr, Book Review of *No Free Lunch*, by William Dembski, in *Boston Review* (March 28, 2004).

17

RELIGIOUS REASONING

Religion is central to the lives of many people across the world. They attend religious ceremonies and pray or meditate, sometimes several times a day. Even when they are not engaged in explicitly religious practices, religion also affects believers' views in morality, politics, and even science. (See Chapter 16.) Critics of religion disdain these influences and claim that religions depend on false or unjustified beliefs, especially the belief that God exists. Both sides of this debate present ingenious arguments, which will be explored in this chapter.

What is religion? That's not an easy question to answer. Religions are varied and complex. They include rituals, communities, institutions, texts, and beliefs. You cannot understand religion as a whole by looking merely at religious *beliefs*. Moreover, religious beliefs cover many topics, from the afterlife and the meaning of life to creation and miracles. You also cannot understand religion by considering only beliefs *about God*. Nonetheless, since belief in God is so central to so many religions, it is crucial to ask whether God exists.

Who or what is God? Different religions include different beliefs about God or gods. Nonetheless, the dominant traditions in the western world—Judaism, Christianity, and Islam—all derive from Abraham and share certain central beliefs about God. In traditional views, God is a person with the three "omnis": omnipotent (or all-powerful), omniscient (or all-knowing), and omnibenevolent (or all-good). Some theologians add that God is omnipresent (or equally present at all spaces and times), but many see God as eternal or existing outside of all time and space. Nonetheless, God is supposed to be active in time, such as when He causes miracles or answers prayers. Not all Jews, Christians, and Moslems share all of these claims about God, but they are accepted by traditional theologians.

People who believe in such a God are called *theists*. People who deny such a God (or any other god) are called *atheists*. Many people accept neither belief and claim that we cannot know whether God exists. They are called *agnostics*.

The readings in this chapter represent all three positions. They also illustrate most of the different kinds of arguments that were studied in Part I of this book. Anselm attempts a *reductio ad absurdum* of atheism, and Gaunilo responds with a refutation by parallel reasoning. (Compare Chapter 13.) Aquinas presents a deductive argument for God, whereas Mackie provides a deductive argument against God. (Compare Chapters 6–8.) Paley uses an argument from analogy, whereas Betty and Cordell discuss an inference to the best explanation, as does Rowe on the other side. (Compare Chapter 9.) Pascal invokes principles of probability and decision making under uncertainty. (Compare Chapter 10.) Flew accuses theists of a fallacy of vacuity. (Compare Chapter 12.) Our earlier discussions thus equip us to understand the arguments on both sides of this important issue.

In the final selection, Clifford raises the issue of whether religious belief may legitimately be based on faith alone apart from any reasons at all. He argues that it is wrong to believe anything on insufficient evidence. This principle has been used to support agnosticism, on the assumption that none of the arguments for or against God is sufficient.

GOD TRULY EXISTS[1]

■

by St. Anselm

Well then, Lord, You who give understanding to faith, grant me that I may understand, as much as You see fit, that You exist as we believe You to exist, and that You are what we believe You to be. Now we believe that You are something than which nothing greater can be thought. Or can it be that a thing of such a nature does not exist, since "the Fool has said in his heart, there is no God" [Ps. xiii. I, lii. I]? But surely, when this same Fool hears what I am speaking about, namely, "something-than-which-nothing-greater-can-be-thought," he understands what he hears, and what he understands is in his mind, even if he does not understand that it actually exists. For it is one thing for an object to exist in the mind, and another thing to understand that an object actually exists. Thus, when a painter plans beforehand what he is going to execute, he has [the picture] in his mind, but he does not yet think that it actually exists because he has not yet executed it. However, when he has actually painted it, then he both has it in his mind and understands that it exists because he has now made it. Even the Fool, then, is forced to agree that something-than-which-nothing-greater-can-be-thought exists in the mind, since he understands this when he hears it, and whatever is understood is in the mind. And surely that-than-which-a-greater-cannot-be-thought cannot exist in the mind alone. For if it exists solely in the mind even, it can be thought to exist in reality also, which is greater. If then that-than-which-a-greater-cannot-be-thought exists in the mind alone, this same

[1]From *St. Anselm's Proslogion with a Reply on Behalf of the Fool by Gaunilo and the Author's Reply to Gaunilo*, trans. M. J. Charlesworth (Oxford: Clarendon Press, 1965). The selection from Gaunilo in the following discussion question comes from this same source.

that-than-which-a-greater-*cannot*-be-thought is that-than-which-a-greater-*can*-be-thought. But this is obviously impossible. Therefore there is absolutely no doubt that something-than-which-a-greater-cannot-be-thought exists both in the mind and in reality.

DISCUSSION QUESTIONS

1. Anselm's ontological argument has puzzled philosophers for centuries. Carefully reconstruct the argument, making sure to spell out any suppressed premises. Is the argument both valid and sound? Why or why not?

2. The most famous objection to Anselm's argument is by Gaunilo in the following passage. He uses the method of parallel reasoning (see Chapter 13) to show that Anselm's form of argument leads to an absurd conclusion. Explain and assess this attempted refutation. How could Anselm best respond? Is this response adequate? Why or why not?

A REPLY TO THE FOREGOING BY A CERTAIN WRITER ON BEHALF OF THE FOOL

■

by Gaunilo

. . . they say that there is in the ocean somewhere an island which, because of the difficulty (or rather the impossibility) of finding that which does not exist, some have called the "Lost Island." And the story goes that it is blessed with all manner of priceless riches and delights in abundance, much more even than the Happy Isles, and, having no owner or inhabitant, it is superior everywhere in abundance of riches to all those other lands that men inhabit. Now, if anyone tell me that it is like this, I shall easily understand what is said, since nothing is difficult about it. But if he should then go on to say, as though it were a logical consequence of this: You cannot any more doubt that this island that is more excellent than all other lands truly exists somewhere in reality than you can doubt that it is in your mind; and since it is more excellent to exist not only in the mind alone but also in reality, therefore it must needs be that it exists. For if it did not exist, any other land existing in reality would be more excellent than it, and so this island, already conceived by you to be more excellent than others, will not be more excellent. If, I say, someone wishes thus to persuade me that this island really exists beyond all doubt, I should either think that he was joking, or I should find it hard to decide which of us I ought to judge the bigger fool—I, if I agreed with him, or he, if he thought that he had proved the existence of this island with any certainty, unless he had first convinced me that its very excellence exists in my mind precisely as a thing existing truly and indubitably and not just as something unreal or doubtfully real.

WHETHER GOD EXISTS?[2]

by St. Thomas Aquinas

Objection 1. It seems that God does not exist; because if one of two contraries be infinite, the other would be altogether destroyed. But the name *God* means that he is infinite goodness. If, therefore, God existed, there would be no evil discoverable; but there is evil in the world. Therefore, God does not exist.

Objection 2. Further, it is superfluous to suppose that what can be accounted for by a few principles has been produced by many. But it seems that everything we can see in the world can be accounted for by other principles, supposing God did not exist. For all natural things can be reduced to one principle, which is nature; and all voluntary things can be reduced to one principle, which is human reason, or will. Therefore there is no need to suppose God's existence.

On the contrary, It is said in the person of God: *I am who am* (Exod. iii, 14).

I answer that, The existence of God can be proved in five ways:

The first and more manifest way is the argument from motion. It is certain, and evident to our senses, that in the world some things are in motion. Now whatever is in motion is put in motion by another, for nothing can be in motion except it is in potentiality to that towards which it is in motion; whereas a thing moves inasmuch as it is in act. For motion is nothing else than the reduction of something from potentiality to actuality. But nothing can be reduced from potentiality to actuality, except by something in a state of actuality. Thus that which is actually hot, as fire, makes wood, which is potentially hot to be actually hot, and thereby moves and changes it. Now it is not possible that the same thing should be at once in actuality and potentiality in the same respect, but only in different respects. For what is actually hot cannot simultaneously be potentially hot; but it is simultaneously potentially cold. It is therefore impossible that in the same respect and in the same way a thing should be both mover and moved, i.e. that it should move itself. Therefore, whatever is in motion must be put in motion by another. If that by which it is put in motion be itself put in motion, then this also must needs be put in motion by another, and that by another again. But this cannot go on to infinity, because then there would be no first mover, and, consequently, no other mover; seeing that subsequent movers move only inasmuch as they are put in motion by the first mover; as the staff moves only because it is put in motion by the hand. Therefore it is necessary to arrive at a first mover, put in motion by no other; and this everyone understands to be God.

The second way is from the nature of the efficient cause. In the world of sense we find there is an order of efficient causes. There is no case known

---

[2] *The Summa Theologica of St. Thomas Aquinas*, Part I, Question 2, Article 3, Second and Revised Edition, 1920, trans. Fathers of the English Dominican Province. Online edition © 2002 by Kevin Knight, http://www.newadvent.org/summa/100203.htm.

(neither is it, indeed, possible) in which a thing is found to be the efficient cause of itself; for so it would be prior to itself, which is impossible. Now in efficient causes it is not possible to go on to infinity, because in all efficient causes following in order, the first is the cause of the intermediate cause, and the intermediate is the cause of the ultimate cause, whether the intermediate cause be several, or only one. Now to take away the cause is to take away the effect. Therefore, if there be no first cause among efficient causes, there will be no ultimate, nor any intermediate cause. But if in efficient causes it is possible to go on to infinity, there will be no first efficient cause, neither will there be an ultimate effect, nor any intermediate efficient causes; all of which is plainly false. Therefore it is necessary to admit a first efficient cause, to which everyone gives the name of God.

The third way is taken from possibility and necessity, and runs thus. We find in nature things that are possible to be and not to be, since they are found to be generated, and to corrupt, and consequently, they are possible to be and not to be. But it is impossible for these always to exist, for that which is possible not to be at some time is not. Therefore, if everything is possible not to be, then at one time there could have been nothing in existence. Now if this were true, even now there would be nothing in existence, because that which does not exist only begins to exist by something already existing. Therefore, if at one time nothing was in existence, it would have been impossible for anything to have begun to exist; and thus even now nothing would be in existence—which is absurd. Therefore, not all beings are merely possible, but there must exist something the existence of which is necessary. But every necessary thing either has its necessity caused by another, or not. Now it is impossible to go on to infinity in necessary things which have their necessity caused by another, as has been already proved in regard to efficient causes. Therefore we cannot but postulate the existence of some being having of itself its own necessity, and not receiving it from another, but rather causing in others their necessity. This all men speak of as God.

The fourth way is taken from the gradation to be found in things. Among beings there are some more and some less good, true, noble and the like. But "more" and "less" are predicated of different things, according as they resemble in their different ways something which is the maximum, as a thing is said to be hotter according as it more nearly resembles that which is hottest; so that there is something which is truest, something best, something noblest and, consequently, something which is uttermost being; for those things that are greatest in truth are greatest in being, as it is written in [Aristotle's] Metaph. ii. Now the maximum in any genus is the cause of all in that genus; as fire, which is the maximum heat, is the cause of all hot things. Therefore there must also be something which is to all beings the cause of their being, goodness, and every other perfection; and this we call God.

The fifth way is taken from the governance of the world. We see that things which lack intelligence, such as natural bodies, act for an end, and this is evident from their acting always, or nearly always, in the same way, so as to obtain the best result. Hence it is plain that not fortuitously, but designedly, do they achieve their end. Now whatever lacks intelligence cannot move towards an end, unless it be directed by some being endowed with knowledge and intelligence; as the arrow is shot to its mark by the archer. Therefore some intelligent being exists by whom all natural things are directed to their end; and this being we call God.

DISCUSSION QUESTIONS

1. Reconstruct and evaluate each of Aquinas's five proofs in standard form. Make sure to spell out any suppressed premises and specify the exact conclusion of each argument.

2. In the following passage, J. L. Mackie criticizes Aquinas's second proof of God's existence. Explain and evaluate Mackie's objection. How could Aquinas best respond? Is this response adequate? Why or why not?

> Unfortunately this argument is unsound. Although in a *finite* ordered series of causes the intermediate (or the earliest intermediate) is caused by the first item, this would not be so if there were an infinite series. In an infinite series, every item is caused by an earlier item. The way in which the first item is "removed" if we go from a finite to an infinite series does not entail the removal of the later items. In fact, Aquinas (both here and in the first way) has simply begged the question against an infinite regress of causes. . . .[3]

3. Mackie presents a separate objection in the following passage. Explain and evaluate this criticism. How could Aquinas best respond? Is this response adequate? Why or why not?

> The greatest weakness of this otherwise attractive argument is that some reason is required for making God the one exception to the supposed need for something else to depend on: why should God, rather than anything else, be taken as the only satisfactory termination of the regress [of causes]?[4]

[3]J. L. Mackie, "The Regress of Causes" in *The Miracle of Theism* (Oxford: Oxford University Press, 1982), 90.

[4]Ibid, 92.

THE WATCH AND THE WATCHMAKER[5]

by William Paley

ONE

In crossing a heath, suppose I pitched my foot against a stone and were asked how the stone came to be there, I might possibly answer that for anything I knew to the contrary it had lain there forever; nor would it, perhaps,

[5]*Natural Theology* (New York: G. F. Hopkins and Sons, 1836).

be very easy to show the absurdity of this answer. But suppose I had found a watch upon the ground, and it should be inquired how the watch happened to be in that place, I should hardly think of the answer which I had before given, that for anything I knew the watch might have always been there. Yet why should not this answer serve for the watch as well as for the stone? Why is it not as admissible in the second case as in the first? For this reason, and for no other, namely, that when we come to inspect the watch, we perceive— what we could not discover in the stone—that its several parts are framed and put together for a purpose, e.g., that they are so formed and adjusted as to produce motion, and that motion so regulated as to point out the hour of the day; that if the different parts had been differently shaped from what they are, of a different size from what they are, or placed after any other manner or in any other order than that in which they are placed, either no motion at all would have been carried on in the machine, or none which would have answered the use that is now served by it. . . . This mechanism being observed—it requires indeed an examination of the instrument, and perhaps some previous knowledge of the subject, to perceive and under- stand it; but being once, as we have said, observed and understood—the inference we think is inevitable, that the watch must have had a maker—that there must have existed, at some time and at some place or other, an artificer or artificers who formed it for the purpose which we find it actually to answer, who comprehended its construction and designed its use.

I. Nor would it, I apprehend, weaken the conclusion, that we had never seen a watch made—that we had never known an artist capable of making one—that we were altogether incapable of executing such a piece of work- manship ourselves, or of understanding in what manner it was performed; all this being no more than what is true of some exquisite remains of ancient art, of some lost arts, and, to the generality of mankind, of the more curious productions of modern manufacture. Does one man in a million know how oval frames are turned? Ignorance of this kind exalts our opinion of the unseen and unknown, but raises no doubt in our minds of the existence and agency of such an artist, at some former time and in some place or other. Nor can I perceive that it varies at all the inference, whether the question arise concerning a human agent or concerning an agent of a different species, or an agent possessing in some respects a different nature.

II. Neither, secondly, would it invalidate our conclusion, that the watch sometimes went wrong or that it seldom went exactly right. The purpose of the machinery, the design, and the designer might be evident, and in the case supposed, would be evident, in whatever way we accounted for the irregu- larity of the movement, or whether we could account for it or not. It is not necessary that a machine be perfect in order to show with what design it was made: still less necessary, where the only question is whether it were made with any design at all. . . .

VIII. Neither, lastly, would our observer be driven out of his conclusion or from his confidence in its truth by being told that he knew nothing at all about the matter. He knows enough for his argument; he knows the utility of the end; he knows the subserviency and adaptation of the means to the end. These points being known, his ignorance of other points, his doubts concerning other points affect not the certainty of his reasoning. The consciousness of knowing little need not beget a distrust of that which he does know.

Two

Suppose, in the next place, that the person who found the watch should after some time discover that, in addition to all the properties which he had hitherto observed in it, it possessed the unexpected property of producing in the course of its movement another watch like itself—the thing is conceivable; that it contained within it a mechanism, a system of parts—a mold, for instance, or a complex adjustment of lathes, files, and other tools—evidently and separately calculated for this purpose; let us inquire what effect ought such a discovery to have upon his former conclusion.

I. The first effect would be to increase his admiration of the contrivance, and his conviction of the consummate skill of the contriver. Whether he regarded the object of the contrivance, the distinct apparatus, the intricate, yet in many parts intelligible mechanism by which it was carried on, he would perceive in this new observation nothing but an additional reason for doing what he had already done—for referring the construction of the watch to design and to supreme art. . . .

IV. Nor is anything gained by running the difficulty farther back, that is, by supposing the watch before us to have been produced from another watch, that from a former, and so on indefinitely. Our going back ever so far brings us no nearer to the least degree of satisfaction upon the subject. Contrivance is still unaccounted for. We still want a contriver. . . .

Three

. . . [E]very indication of contrivance, every manifestation of design, which existed in the watch, exists in the works of nature; with the difference, on the side of nature, of being greater and more, and that in a degree which exceeds all computation. I mean that the contrivances of nature surpass the contrivances of art, in the complexity, subtlety, and curiosity of the mechanism; and still more, if possible, do they go beyond them in number and variety; yet in a multitude of cases, are not less evidently mechanical, not less evidently contrivances, not less evidently accommodated to their end, or suited to their office, than are the most perfect productions of human ingenuity.

I know no better method of introducing so large a subject, than that of comparing a single thing with a single thing: an eye, for example, with a telescope. As far as the examination of the instrument goes, there is precisely the same proof that the eye was made for vision, as there is that the telescope was made for assisting it. They are made upon the same principles; both being adjusted to the laws by which the transmission and refraction of rays of light are regulated. I speak not of the origin of the laws themselves; but such laws being fixed, the construction in both cases is adapted to them. . . .

To some it may appear a difference sufficient to destroy all similitude between the eye and the telescope, that the one is a perceiving organ, the other an unperceiving instrument. The fact is that they are both instruments. And as to the mechanism, at least as to mechanism being employed, and even as to the kind of it, this circumstance varies not the analogy at all. . . . The end is the same; the means are the same. The purpose in both is alike; the contrivance for accomplishing that purpose is in both alike. The lenses of the telescopes, and the humors of the eye, bear a complete resemblance to one another, in their figure, their position, and in their power over the rays of light, viz. in bringing each pencil to a point at the right distance from the lens; namely, in the eye, at the exact place where the membrane is spread to receive it. How is it possible, under circumstances of such close affinity, and under the operation of equal evidence, to exclude contrivance from the one; yet to acknowledge the proof of contrivance having been employed, as the plainest and clearest of all propositions, in the other? . . .

FIVE

Every observation which was made in our first chapter concerning the watch may be repeated with strict propriety concerning the eye, concerning animals, concerning plants, concerning, indeed, all the organized parts of the works of nature. As,

I. When we are inquiring simply after the *existence* of an intelligent Creator, imperfection, inaccuracy, liability to disorder, occasional irregularities may subsist in a considerable degree without inducing any doubt into the question; just as a watch may frequently go wrong, seldom perhaps exactly right, may be faulty in some parts, defective in some, without the smallest ground of suspicion from thence arising that it was not a watch, not made, or not made for the purpose ascribed to it. When faults are pointed out, and when a question is started concerning the skill of the artist or dexterity with which the work is executed, then, indeed, in order to defend these qualities from accusation, we must be able either to expose some intractableness and imperfection in the materials or point out some invincible difficulty in the execution, into which imperfection and difficulty the matter of complaint may be resolved; or, if we cannot do this, we must adduce such specimens of consummate art and contrivance proceeding from the same hand as may convince the inquirer of the existence, in the case before him, of impediments like those which we have mentioned, although, what from the nature of the case is very likely to happen, they be unknown and unperceived by him. This we must do in order to vindicate the artist's skill, or at least the perfection of it; as we must also judge of his intention and of the provisions employed in fulfilling that intention, not from an instance in which they fail but from the great plurality of instances in which they succeed. But, after all, these are different questions from the question of the artist's existence; or, which is the same, whether the thing before us be a work of art or not; and the questions ought always to be kept separate in the mind. So likewise it is in the works of nature. Irregularities and imperfections are of little or no weight in the consideration when that consideration relates simply to the existence of a Creator. . . .

Six

Were there no example in the world of contrivance except that of the *eye*, it would be alone sufficient to support the conclusion, which we draw from it, as to the necessity of an intelligent Creator. . . . The proof is not a conclusion that lies at the end of a chain of reasoning, of which chain each instance of contrivance is only a link, and of which, if one link fail, the whole fails; but it is an argument separately supplied by every separate example. An error in stating an example affects only that example. The argument is cumulative in the fullest sense of that term. The eye proves it without the ear; the ear without the eye. The proof in each example is complete; for when the design of the part and the conduciveness of its structure to that design is shown, the mind may set itself at rest; no further consideration can detract anything from the force of the example.

DISCUSSION QUESTIONS

1. Reconstruct and evaluate Paley's teleological argument. Is it an argument from analogy, an inference to the best explanation, both, or neither?

2. In the following selection, biologist Stephen Jay Gould suggests how Charles Darwin's theory of evolution as discussed in his book on orchids might undermine Paley's argument from design. Explain and evaluate Gould's objection. How could Paley best respond? Is this response adequate? Why or why not?

> Darwin begins his orchid book with an important evolutionary premise: continued self-fertilization is a poor strategy for long-term survival, since offspring carry only the genes of their single parent and populations do not maintain enough variation for evolutionary flexibility in the face of environmental change. Thus, plants bearing flowers with both male and female parts usually evolve mechanisms to ensure cross-pollination. Orchids have formed an alliance with insects. They have evolved an astonishing variety of "contrivances" to attract insects, guarantee that sticky pollen adheres to the visitor, and ensure that the attached pollen comes in contact with female parts of the next orchid visited by the insect.
>
> Darwin's book is a compendium of these contrivances, the botanical equivalent of a bestiary. And like the medieval bestiaries, it is designed to instruct. The message is paradoxical but profound. Orchids manufacture their intricate devices from the common components of ordinary flowers, parts usually fitted for very different functions. If God had designed a beautiful machine to reflect his wisdom and power, surely he would not have used a collection of parts generally fashioned for other purposes. Orchids were not made by an ideal engineer; they are jury-rigged from a limited set of available components. Thus, they must have evolved from ordinary flowers.

> Thus, the paradox, and the common theme of this trilogy of essays: Our text-books like to illustrate evolution with examples of optimal design—nearly perfect mimicry of a dead leaf by a butterfly or of a poisonous species by a palatable rela-tive. But ideal design is a lousy argument for evolution, for it mimics the postu-lated action of an omnipotent creator. Odd arrangements and funny solutions are the proof of evolution—paths that a sensible God would never tread but that a natural process, constrained by history, follows perforce.[6]
>
> [6]From *The Panda's Thumb: More Reflections in Natural History* by Stephen Jay Gould (New York: Norton, 1980). Compare also the reading from Gould in Chapter 16.

THE ANTHROPIC TELEOLOGICAL ARGUMENT[7]

by L. Stafford Betty and Bruce Cordell

We will consider . . . arguments for the existence of a cosmic orderer . . . based on the Big Bang and the anthropic principle.

The Big Bang. The first of these, the argument based on the Big Bang, is in many ways the most impressive. But it does not lend itself to mathematical analysis, and hence to a probability calculus (with odds computed for or against the argument), as readily as the other [argument]. Thus, we will treat it first and regard it as the weakest, i.e., the most "intuitive" of the argu-ments.

Most scientists and philosophers stop well short of reasoning backward from the cosmos as it exists today to the necessary existence of an ultimate mind and will behind the primeval explosion. But at least one, Hannes Alfven, concluded that the Big Bang "necessarily presupposes a divine cre-ation," while another, the British physicist Edmund Whitaker, maintained that there "is no ground for supposing that matter and energy existed before [the Big Bang] and was suddenly galvanized into action. . . . It is simpler to postulate creation *ex nihilo*—Divine will constituting Nature from nothing-ness." Whatever one's particular view of the ultimate cause of the Big Bang, it is certainly the case that a universe with a beginning in time—anywhere from thirteen to twenty billion years ago, according to latest estimates—is more likely to arouse speculation about a Creator than a steady-state, appar-ently beginningless universe of infinite duration.

This is reasonable because the Big Bang refers, according to latest refine-ments of the theory, to a time when matter-energy arose out of a condition which is mysterious to us, and will probably always be. Even if the Big Bang is the result of a "zero-point fluctuation," as some physicists have recently speculated, it would be necessary to ask what caused this fluctuation. At best this theory only moves back the unexplainable one step; the order, immensity,

[7]*International Philosophic Quarterly* 27, no. 4 (December 1987). Citations omitted.

complexity, and beauty of our present universe remains anchored in an irresistible surd.

At this point we must ask ourselves what is easier to imagine and thus to believe: that the cosmos' entire history should have arisen from this self-creating and self-explaining surd; or that a pre-existing mind and power of vast magnitude should have created the ingredients of the universe and triggered it at the Big Bang? This second alternative seems to us somewhat more likely. It is certainly no more preposterous. . . .

The Anthropic Principle. . . . According to Dewey Schwartzenburg, the anthropic principle (*anthropos*, Greek for "man") boils down to this: ". . . if the universe were in fact different in any significant way from the way it is, we wouldn't be here to wonder why it is the way it is." B. J. Carr and M. J. Rees, whose 1979 article in *Nature* is perhaps the most impressive scientific statement of the principle yet to appear, explain that the "possibility of life as we know it evolving in the Universe depends on the values of a few basic physical constants—and is in some respects remarkably sensitive to their numerical values."

What are those constants? Physicists speak of "coupling constants," but these in turn depend on such basic constants as the charge of the proton, the mass of the proton, the speed of light, the gravitational constant G in Newton's law of universal gravitation, and Planck's constant, h, which allows us to determine a quantum of energy emitted by an electron radiating at a particular frequency. In mathematical notation, h is equal to 6.625×10^{-34} J. sec, and "Big G," the gravitational constant, is equal to 6.67×10^{-11} newton-m²/kg².

What is remarkable—and it is this that forms the basis of the anthropic principle—is that if, for instance, Planck's constant had a different value, say 6.626×10^{-33} instead of 10^{-34}, the whole universe would be different from the way it is. More importantly, intelligent life could not have evolved in a substantially altered universe. For example, if gravity were significantly stronger than it is, stars would exhaust their hydrogen fuels much faster, and humanoid life (as we know it) could not appear in a universe where stars "died young." Or if the "strong force," which binds the nuclei of atoms together, were stronger, helium nuclei would dominate the universe, and no hydrogen would be left over; without hydrogen there would be no water, and without water there could not be life as we know it. This list of examples could go on indefinitely. The point is that, as far as we can tell, intelligent humanoid life could have evolved in only one narrowly select set of universes: the set including the universe we find ourselves in, a universe whose physical processes are governed by the precise basic constants that it possesses. Corwin states the case well:

> Life as we conceive it demands severe constraints on the initial conditions of the universe. Life and consciousness are not only the direct result of the initial conditions, but could only have resulted from a narrow range of initial conditions (i.e., the constants had to be precisely as they are). It is not that changes in the initial conditions would have changed the character of life, but rather that any significant change in the initial conditions would have ruled out the possibility of life

evolving later . . . the universe would have evolved as a life-less, unconscious entity.

It is no wonder that today a few scientists who are aware of the anthropic principle are asking the question, "Does all this mean that cosmology has come to the point of having to postulate a 'Creator'?" The answer would seem, at first glance, to be Yes. For how else can we explain all these "coincidences"? Let us use an analogy: Imagine nine jars, each containing ten slips of paper with one number from 0 to 9, one number to a slip, with each number represented, placed side by side. Suppose now that a mechanical device drew at random one slip from each jar, and that the numbers drawn in sequence happened to correspond *exactly* to your nine-numbered Social Security Number. What are the chances of a random drawing giving such a result? They are exactly one in a billion. Now suppose, unlike a legitimate, genuinely random lottery drawing, there was no special reason dictating that the drawing had to be random, even though the mechanical device *suggested* randomness. If your number were drawn, would it not be far more reasonable to assume that the drawing was *not* random, that it was instead being superintended by some intelligence behind the scenes who was in some way invisibly manipulating the mechanical device? Would it not, in other words, be reasonable to conclude that the drawing was fixed—fixed in your favor?

Don N. Page of the Institute for Advanced Study in Princeton, N.J., recently calculated the odds against the formation of our universe, and the figure was a good deal more than one in a billion. His exact computation was in fact one in $10,000,000,000^{124}$, a number so large that to call it "astronomical" would be to engage in a wild understatement. But are the odds *against a Cosmic Designer* so high? If we must make a forced choice between an unintelligent random process and an invisible Intelligence behind the scenes, as it appears we must, and if, furthermore, the chance against a random process accounting for the precise values of the basic constants of physics is well in excess of a billion to one, then a designer may be considered highly probable. In other words, the anthropic principle looks as if it might succeed, after careful analysis, in making highly probable the existence of a universal designer-creator. . . .

DISCUSSION QUESTIONS

1. Reconstruct and evaluate Betty and Cordell's arguments, making sure to spell out any suppressed premises and specify their exact conclusions.
2. In the following passage, B. J. Carr and M. J. Rees mention three possible objections to Betty and Cordell's anthropic argument. Explain their criticisms. Can any of these replies undermine the force of Betty and Cordell's argument? Why or why not?

From a physical point of view, the anthropic "explanation" of the various coincidences in nature is unsatisfactory, in three respects. First, it is entirely *post hoc*: it has not yet been used to predict any feature of the Universe . . . Second, the principle is based on what may be an unduly anthropocentric conception of an observer. The arguments invoked here assume that life requires elements heavier than hydrogen and helium, water, galaxies, and special types of stars and planets. It is conceivable that some form of dynamic disequilibrium is perhaps the only prerequisite that we can demand with real conviction. Third, the anthropic principle does not explain the exact values of the various coupling constants and mass-ratios, only their order of magnitudes. With enough anthropic conditions, one may be able to be more precise about the constants of nature, but the present situation is unsatisfactory.[8]

[8]B. J. Carr and M. J. Rees, "The Anthropic Principle and the Structure of the Physical World," *Nature* 278, 12 (April 1979), 612.

THE WAGER[9]

■

by Blaise Pascal

Let us now speak according to natural lights.

If there is a God, He is infinitely incomprehensible, since, having neither parts nor limits, He has no affinity to us. We are then incapable of knowing either what He is or if He is. This being so, who will dare to undertake the decision of the question? Not we, who have no affinity to Him.

Who then will blame Christians for not being able to give a reason for their belief, since they profess a religion for which they cannot give a reason? They declare, in expounding it to the world, that it is a foolishness, *stultitiam*; and then you complain that they do not prove it! If they proved it, they would not keep their word; it is in lacking proofs that they are not lacking in sense. "Yes, but although this excuses those who offer it as such, and takes away from them the blame of putting it forward without reason, it does not excuse those who receive it." Let us then examine this point, and say, "God is, or He is not." But to which side shall we incline? Reason can decide nothing here. There is an infinite chaos which separated us. A game is being played at the extremity of this infinite distance where heads or tails will turn up. What will you wager? According to reason, you can do neither the one thing nor the other; according to reason, you can defend neither of the propositions.

Do not then reprove for error those who have made a choice; for you know nothing about it. "No, but I blame them for having made, not this choice, but a choice; for again both he who chooses heads and he who chooses tails are equally at fault, they are both in the wrong. The true course is not to wager at all."

[9]From *Pensées and the Provincial Letters*, trans. W. F. Trotter (New York: Modern Library, 1941).

Yes; but you must wager. It is not optional. You are embarked. Which will you choose then? Let us see. Since you must choose, let us see which interests you least. You have two things to lose, the true and the good; and two things to stake, your reason and your will, your knowledge and your happiness; and your nature has two things to shun, error and misery. Your reason is no more shocked in choosing one rather than the other, since you must of necessity choose. This is one point settled. But your happiness? Let us weigh the gain and the loss in wagering that God is. Let us estimate these two chances. If you gain, you gain all; if you lose, you lose nothing. Wager, then, without hesitation that He is.—"That is very fine. Yes, I must wager; but I may perhaps wager too much."—Let us see. Since there is an equal risk of gain and of loss, if you had only to gain two lives, instead of one, you might still wager. But if there were three lives to gain, you would have to play (since you are under the necessity of playing), and you would be imprudent, when you are forced to play, not to chance your life to gain three at a game where there is an equal risk of loss and gain. But there is an eternity of life and happiness. And this being so, if there were an infinity of chances, of which one only would be for you, you would still be right in wagering one to win two, and you would act stupidly, being obliged to play, by refusing to stake one life against three at a game in which out of an infinity of chances there is one for you, if there were an infinity of an infinitely happy life to gain. But there is here an infinity of an infinitely happy life to gain, a chance of gain against a finite number of chances of loss, and what you stake is finite. It is all divided; wherever the infinite is and there is not an infinity of chances of loss against that of gain, there is no time to hesitate, you must give all. And thus, when one is forced to play, he must renounce reason to preserve his life, rather than risk it for infinite gain, as likely to happen as the loss of nothingness.

For it is no use to say it is uncertain if we will gain, and it is certain that we risk, and that the infinite distance between the *certainty* of what is staked and the *uncertainty* of what will be gained, equals the finite good which is certainly staked against the uncertain infinite. It is not so, as every player stakes a certainty to gain an uncertainty, and yet he stakes a finite certainty to gain a finite uncertainty, without transgressing against reason. There is not an infinite distance between the certainty staked and the uncertainty of the gain; that is untrue. In truth, there is an infinity between the certainty of gain and the certainty of loss. But the uncertainty of the gain is proportioned to the certainty of the stake according to the proportion of the chances of gain and loss. Hence it comes that, if there are as many risks on one side as on the other, the course is to play even, and then the certainty of the stake is equal to the uncertainty of the gain, so far is it from fact that there is an infinite distance between them. And so our proposition is of infinite force, when there is the finite to stake in a game where there are equal risks of gain and of loss, and the infinite to gain. This is demonstrable: and if men are capable of any truths, this is one.

"I confess it, I admit it. But, still, is there no means of seeing the faces of the cards?"—Yes, Scripture and the rest, etc. "Yes, but I have my hands tied and my mouth closed; I am forced to wager, and am not free. I am not released, and am so made that I cannot believe. What, then, would you have me do?"

True. But at least learn your inability to believe, since reason brings you to this, and yet you cannot believe. Endeavour then to convince yourself, not by increase of proofs of God, but by the abatement of your passions. You would like to attain faith, and do not know the way; you would like to cure yourself of unbelief, and ask the remedy for it. Learn of those who have been bound like you, and who now stake all their possessions. These are people who know the way which you would follow, and who are cured of an ill of which you would be cured. Follow the way by which they began; by acting as if they believed, taking the holy water, having masses said, etc. Even this will naturally make you believe, and deaden your acuteness.—"But this is what I am afraid of."—And why? What have you to lose?

But to show you that this leads you there, it is this which will lessen the passions, which are your stumbling-blocks.

The end of this discourse.—Now, what harm will befall you in taking this side? You will be faithful, honest, humble, grateful, generous, a sincere friend, truthful. Certainly you will not have those poisonous pleasures, glory and luxury; but will you not have others? I will tell you that you will thereby gain in this life, and that, at each step you take on this road, you will see so great certainty of gain, so much nothingness in what you risk, that you will at last recognize that you have wagered for something certain and infinite, for which you have given nothing.

DISCUSSION QUESTIONS

1. Reconstruct and evaluate Pascal's argument, making sure to spell out any suppressed premises and specify the exact conclusion.

2. In "The Will to Believe," William James writes, "We feel that a faith in masses and holy water adopted willfully after such a mechanical calculation would lack the inner soul of faith's reality; and if we were ourselves in the place of the Deity, we should probably take particular pleasure in cutting off believers of this pattern from their infinite reward."[10] What is James's point? Do you agree? If so, do you think it refutes Pascal's argument? Why or why not?

3. Pascal begins with the assumption that "We are then incapable of knowing either what He is or if He is." What exactly does he mean? Is this assumption necessary for Pascal's argument? Would his argument work just as well if there were a strong argument for the existence of God? If there were a strong argument against the existence of God?

4. In the following passage, James Cargile uses parallel reasoning to refute Pascal's argument. Explain Cargile's point. How could Pascal best respond? Is this response adequate? Why or why not?

[10]From *The Will to Believe and Other Essays in Popular Philosophy,* by William James (New York: Longmans, Green & Co., 1897), 6.

Either (a) there is a god who will send only religious people to heaven or (b) there is not. To be religious is to wager for (a). To fail to be religious is to wager for (b). We can't settle the question whether (a) or (b) is the case, at least not at present. But (a) is clearly vastly better than (b). With (a), infinite bliss is *guaranteed*, while with (b) we are still in the miserable human condition of facing death with no assurance as to what lies beyond. So (a) is clearly the best wager. . . .

This argument just presented is formally similar to the following: Either (a) there is a god who will send you to heaven only if you commit a painful ritual suicide within an hour of first reading this, or (b) there is not. We cannot settle the question whether (a) or (b) is the case or it is at least not settled yet. But (a) is vastly preferable to (b), since in situation (a) infinite bliss is *guaranteed*, while in (b) we are left in the miserable human condition. So we should wager for (a) by performing ritual suicide.

It might be objected that we can be sure that there is not a god who will send us to heaven only if we commit suicide but we can't be sure that there is not a god who will send us to heaven only if we are religious. However, a sceptic would demand proof of this. . . .[11]

[11]"Pascal's Wager," *Philosophy* 41 (1966), 254.

EVIL AND OMNIPOTENCE[12]

■

by J. L. Mackie

The traditional arguments for the existence of God have been fairly thoroughly criticized by philosophers. But the theologian can, if he wishes, accept this criticism. He can admit that no rational proof of God's existence is possible. And he can still retain all that is essential to his position, by holding that God's existence is known in some other, nonrational way. I think, however, that a more telling criticism can be made by way of the traditional problem of evil. Here it can be shown, not that religious beliefs lack rational support, but that they are positively irrational, that the several parts of the essential theological doctrine are inconsistent with one another, so that the theologian can maintain his position as a whole only by a much more extreme rejection of reason than in the former case. He must now be prepared to believe, not merely what cannot be proved, but what can be *disproved* from other beliefs that he also holds.

The problem of evil, in the sense in which I shall be using the phrase, is a problem only for someone who believes that there is a God who is both omnipotent and wholly good. And it is a logical problem, the problem of clarifying and reconciling a number of beliefs: it is not a scientific problem that might be solved by further observations, or a practical problem that might be solved by a decision or an action. These points are obvious; I mention

[12]*Mind* LXIV, No. 254 (1955).

them only because they are sometimes ignored by theologians, who some-times parry a statement of the problem with such remarks as "Well, can you solve the problem yourself?" or "This is a mystery which may be revealed to us later" or "Evil is something to be faced and overcome, not to be merely discussed."

In its simplest form the problem is this: God is omnipotent; God is wholly good; and yet evil exists. There seems to be some contradiction between these three propositions, so that if any two of them were true the third would be false. But at the same time all three are essential parts of most theological positions: the theologian, it seems, at once *must* adhere and *cannot consistently* adhere to all three. (The problem does not arise only for theists, but I shall discuss it in the form in which it presents itself for ordinary theism.)

However, the contradiction does not arise immediately; to show it we need some additional premises, or perhaps some quasi-logical rules connecting the terms "good," "evil," and "omnipotent." These additional principles are that good is opposed to evil, in such a way that a good thing always eliminates evil as far as it can, and that there are no limits to what an omnipotent thing can do. From these it follows that a good omnipotent thing eliminates evil completely, and then the propositions that a good omnipotent thing exists, and that evil exists, are incompatible. . . .

DISCUSSION QUESTIONS

1. Reconstruct and evaluate Mackie's argument, making sure to spell out any suppressed premises and specify the exact conclusion.

2. One common response to Mackie's argument is that an all-good, all-power-ful God might give humans free will, knowing that humans will some-times cause evil. Is this "free will" response adequate to justify God in allowing the evils that humans cause? What about evils that are not caused by humans? Why or why not?

THE EVIDENTIAL PROBLEM OF EVIL[13]

■

by William Rowe

. . . In developing the argument for atheism based on the existence of evil, it will be useful to focus on some particular evil that our world contains in considerable abundance. Intense human and animal suffering, for example, occurs daily and in great plentitude in our world. Such intense suffering is a clear case of evil. Of course, if the intense suffering leads to some greater good, a good we could not have obtained without undergoing the suffering in question, we might conclude that the suffering is justified, but it remains

---

[13]From "The Problem of Evil and Some Varieties of Atheism," *American Philosophical Quarterly* 16 (1979), 335–41. Notes omitted.

an evil nevertheless. For we must not confuse the intense suffering in and of itself with the good things to which it sometimes leads or of which it may be a necessary part. Intense human or animal suffering is in itself bad, an evil, even though it may sometimes be justified by virtue of being a part of, or leading to, some good which is unobtainable without it. What is evil in itself may sometimes be good as a means because it leads to something that is good in itself. In such a case, while remaining an evil in itself, the intense human or animal suffering is, nevertheless, an evil which someone might be morally justified in permitting.

Taking human and animal suffering as a clear instance of evil which occurs with great frequency in our world, the argument for atheism based on evil can be stated as follows:

(1) There exist instances of intense suffering which an omnipotent, omniscient being could have prevented without thereby losing some greater good or permitting some evil equally bad or worse.

(2) An omniscient, wholly good being would prevent the occurrence of any intense suffering it could, unless it could not do so without thereby losing some greater good or permitting some evil equally bad or worse.

(3) There does not exist an omnipotent, omniscient, wholly good being.

What are we to say about this argument for atheism, an argument based on the profusion of one sort of evil in our world? The argument is valid; therefore, if we have rational grounds for accepting its premises, to that extent we have rational grounds for accepting atheism. Do we, however, have rational grounds for accepting the premises of this argument?

Let's begin with the second premise. Let s_1 be an instance of intense human or animal suffering which an omniscient, wholly good being could prevent. We will also suppose that things are such that s_1 will occur unless prevented by the omniscient, wholly good (OG) being. We might be interested in determining what would be a *sufficient* condition of OG failing to prevent s_1. But, for our purpose here, we need only try to state a necessary condition for OG failing to prevent s_1. That condition, so it seems to me, is this:

Either (i) there is some greater good, G, such that G is obtainable by OG only if OG permits s_1,

or (ii) there is some greater good, G, such that G is obtainable by OG only if OG permits either s_1 or some evil equally bad or worse,

or (iii) s_1 is such that it is preventable by OG only if OG permits some evil equally bad or worse.

It is important to recognize that (iii) is not included in (i). For losing a good greater than s_1 is not the same as permitting an evil greater than s_1. And this because the *absence* of a good state of affairs need not itself be an evil state of affairs. It is also important to recognize that s_1 might be such that it is preventable by OG *without* losing G (so condition (i) is not satisfied) but also such that if OG did prevent it, G would be lost *unless* OG permitted some evil equal or worse than s_1. If this were so, it does not seem correct to require that OG prevent s_1. Thus, condition (ii) takes into account an important possibility not encompassed in condition (i).

Is it true that if an omniscient, wholly good being permits the occurrence of some intense suffering it could have prevented, then either (i) or (ii) or (iii) attains? It seems to me that it is true. But if it is true then so is premise (2) of the argument for atheism. For that premise merely states in more compact form what we have suggested must be true if an omniscient, wholly good being fails to prevent some intense suffering it could prevent. Premise (2) says that an omniscient, wholly good being would prevent the occurrence of any intense suffering it could, unless it could not do so without thereby losing some greater good or permitting some evil equally bad or worse. This premise (or something not too distant from it) is, I think, held in common by many atheists and nontheists. Of course, there may be disagreement about whether something is good, and whether, if it is good, one would be morally justified in permitting some intense suffering to occur in order to obtain it. Someone might hold, for example, that no good is great enough to justify permitting an innocent child to suffer terribly. Again, someone might hold that the mere fact that a given good outweighs some suffering and would be lost if the suffering were prevented, is not a morally sufficient reason for permitting the suffering. But to hold either of these views is not to deny (2). For (2) claims only that *if* an omniscient, wholly good being permits intense suffering *then* either there is some greater good that would have been lost, or some equally bad or worse evil that would have occurred, had the intense suffering been prevented. (2) does not purport to describe what might be a *sufficient* condition for an omniscient, wholly good being to permit intense suffering, only what is a *necessary* condition. So stated, (2) seems to express a belief that accords with our basic moral principles, principles shared by both theists and nontheists. If we are to fault the argument for atheism, therefore, it seems we must find some fault with its first premise.

Suppose in some distant forest lightning strikes a dead tree, resulting in a forest fire. In the fire a fawn is trapped, horribly burned, and lies in terrible agony for several days before death relieves its suffering. So far as we can see, the fawn's intense suffering is pointless. For there does not appear to be any greater good such that the prevention of the fawn's suffering would require either the loss of that good or the occurrence of an evil equally bad or worse. Nor does there seem to be any equally bad or worse evil so connected to the fawn's suffering that it would have had to occur had the fawn's suffering been prevented. Could an omnipotent, omniscient being have prevented the fawn's apparently pointless suffering? The answer is obvious, as even the theist will insist. An omnipotent, omniscient being could have easily prevented the fawn from being horribly burned, or, given the burning, could have spared the fawn the intense suffering by quickly ending its life, rather than allowing the fawn to lie in terrible agony for several days. Since the fawn's intense suffering was preventable and, so far as we can see, pointless, doesn't it appear that premise (1) of the argument is true, that there do exist instances of intense suffering which an omnipotent, omniscient being could have prevented without thereby losing some greater good or permitting some evil equally bad or worse?

It must be acknowledged that the case of the fawn's apparently pointless suffering does not *prove* that (1) is true. For even though we cannot see how the fawn's suffering is required to obtain some greater good (or to prevent equally bad or worse evil), it hardly follows that it is not so required. After all, we are often surprised by how things we thought to be unconnected turn out to be intimately connected. Perhaps, for all we know, there is some familiar good outweighing the fawn's suffering to which that suffering is connected in a way we do not see. Furthermore, there may well be unfamiliar goods, goods we haven't dreamed of, to which the fawn's suffering is inextricably connected. Indeed, it would seem to require something like omniscience on our part before we could lay claim to *knowing* that there is no greater good connected to the fawn's suffering in such a manner that an omnipotent, omniscient being could not have achieved that good without permitting that suffering or some evil equally bad or worse. So the case of the fawn's suffering surely does not enable us to *establish* the truth of (1).

The truth is that we are not in a position to prove that (1) is true. We cannot know with certainty that instances of suffering of the sort described in (1) do occur in our world. But it is one thing to *know* or *prove* that (1) is true and quite another thing to have *rational grounds* for believing (1) to be true. We are often in the position where in the light of our experience and knowledge it is rational to believe that a certain statement is true, even though we are not in a position to prove or to know with certainty that the statement is true. In the light of our past experience and knowledge it is, for example, very reasonable to believe that neither Goldwater nor McGovern will ever be elected President, but we are scarcely in the position of knowing with certainty that neither will ever be elected President. So, too, with (1), although we cannot know with certainty that it is true, it perhaps can be rationally supported, shown to be a rational belief.

Consider again the case of the fawn's suffering. Is it reasonable to believe that there is some greater good so intimately connected to that suffering that even an omnipotent, omniscient being could not have obtained that good without permitting that suffering or some evil at least as bad? It certainly does not appear reasonable to believe this. Nor does it seem reasonable to believe that there is some evil at least as bad as the fawn's suffering such that an omnipotent being simply could not have prevented it without permitting the fawn's suffering. But even if it should somehow be reasonable to believe either of these things of the fawn's suffering, we must then ask whether it is reasonable to believe either of these things of *all* the instances of seemingly pointless human and animal suffering that occur daily in our world. And surely the answer to this more general question must be no. It seems quite unlikely that *all* the instances of intense suffering occurring daily in our world are intimately related to the occurrence of greater goods or the prevention of evils at least as bad; and even more unlikely, should they somehow all be so related, that an omnipotent, omniscient being could not have achieved at least some of those goods (or prevented some of those evils) without permitting the instances of intense suffering that are supposedly related to them. In the light of our experience and knowledge of the variety and scale of human and animal suffering in our world, the idea that none of this suffering could have been prevented by an omnipotent being without thereby losing a greater good or permitting an evil at least as bad seems an extraordinarily absurd idea, quite beyond our belief. It seems then that although we cannot *prove* that (1) is true, it is, nevertheless, altogether *reasonable* to believe that (1) is true, that (1) is a *rational* belief.

Returning now to our argument for atheism, we've seen that the second premise expresses a basic belief common to many theists and nontheists. We've also seen that our experience and knowledge of the variety and profusion of suffering in our world provides *rational support* for the first premise. Seeing that the conclusion, "There does not exist an omnipotent, omniscient, wholly good being" follows from these two premises, it does seem that we have *rational support* for atheism, that it is reasonable for us to believe that the theistic God does not exist. . . .

DISCUSSION QUESTIONS

1. Reconstruct and evaluate Rowe's argument, making sure to spell out any suppressed premises and define crucial terms.

2. In what ways does the argument from evil that Rowe presents differ from that presented by Mackie? Are these differences important?

3. Rowe admits that he cannot prove his first premise. Does this admission destroy the force of his argument? Why or why not?

4. Could the value of free will justify God in allowing the fawn to suffer in Rowe's example? Why or why not? If not, could any other "greater good" justify this suffering? If so, what?

5. John Hick offers the following justification of the existence of moral and natural evil in the world. Explain and evaluate Hick's theodicy. How could Rowe best respond?

> In a world devoid of both dangers to be avoided and rewards to be won we may assume that there would have been virtually no development of the human intellect and imagination. . . . The fact of an objective world within which one has to learn to live, on penalty of pain or death, is also a basic development of one's moral nature. For it is because the world is one in which men and women can suffer harm by violence, disease, accident, starvation, etc.—that our actions affecting one another have moral significance. . . . Thus the hypothesis of a divine purpose in which finite persons are created at an epistemic distance from God, in order that they may gradually become children of God through their own moral and

> spiritual choices, requires that their environment, instead of being a pain-free and stress-free paradise, be broadly the kind of world which we find ourselves to be a part.[14]
>
> 6. What is the best response that a theist could give to Rowe's argument? Is this response adequate? Why or why not?
>
> [14]"Soul-Making Theodicy," in *Encountering Evil,* ed. Stephen T. Davis (Louisville, KY: John Knox Press, 1981).

THEOLOGY AND FALSIFICATION[15]

by Anthony Flew

Let us begin with a parable. It is a parable developed from a tale told by John Wisdom in his haunting and revelatory article, "Gods."* Once upon a time two explorers came upon a clearing in the jungle. In the clearing were growing many flowers and many weeds. One explorer says, "Some gardener must tend this plot." The other disagrees, "There is no gardener." So they pitch their tents and set a watch. No gardener is ever seen. "But perhaps he is an invisible gardener." So they set up a barbed-wire fence. They electrify it. They patrol with bloodhounds. (For they remember how H. G. Wells's "Invisible Man" could be both smelt and touched though he could not be seen.) But no shrieks ever suggest that some intruder has received a shock. No movements of the wire ever betray an invisible climber. The bloodhounds never give cry. Yet still the Believer is not convinced. "But there is a gardener, invisible, intangible, insensible to electric shocks, a gardener who has no scent and makes no sound, a gardener who comes secretly to look after the garden which he loves." At last the Sceptic despairs, "But what remains of your original assertion? Just how does what you call an invisible, intangible, eternally elusive gardener differ from an imaginary gardener or even from no gardener at all?"

In this parable we can see how what starts as an assertion, that something exists or that there is some analogy between certain complexes of phenomena, may be reduced step by step to an altogether different status, to an expression perhaps of a "picture preference." The Sceptic says there is no gardener. The Believer says there is a gardener (but invisible, etc.). One man talks about sexual behavior. Another man prefers to talk of Aphrodite (but knows that there is not really a superhuman person additional to, and somehow responsible for, all sexual phenomena). The process of qualification may be checked at any point before the original assertion is completely withdrawn

[15]*New Essays in Philosophical Theology,* ed. Anthony Flew and Alasdair MacIntyre (New York: Simon and Schuster, 1955).

Proceedings of the Aristotelian Society (1944–45). . . .

and something of that first assertion will remain (tautology). Mr. Wells's invisible man could not, admittedly, be seen, but in all other respects he was a man like the rest of us. But though the process of qualification may be, and of course usually is, checked in time, it is not always judiciously so halted. Someone may dissipate his assertion completely without noticing that he has done so. A fine brash hypothesis may thus be killed by inches, the death by a thousand qualifications.

And in this, it seems to me, lies the peculiar danger, the endemic evil, of theological utterance. Take such utterances as "God has a plan," "God created the world," "God loves us as a father loves his children." They look at first sight very much like assertions, vast cosmological assertions. (Merely remarking parenthetically that those who intend or interpret such utterances as crypto-commands, expressions of wishes, disguised ejaculations, concealed ethics, or as anything else but assertions, are unlikely to succeed in making them either properly orthodox or practically effective.) Now to assert that such and such is the case is necessarily equivalent to denying that such and such is not the case. Suppose then that we are in doubt as to what someone who gives vent to an utterance is asserting, or suppose that, more radically, we are sceptical as to whether he is really asserting anything at all, one way of trying to understand (or perhaps it will be to expose) his utterance is to attempt to find what he would regard as counting against, or as being incompatible with, its truth. For if the utterance is an assertion, it will necessarily be equivalent to a denial of the negation that assertion. And anything which would count against the assertion or which would induce the speaker to withdraw it and to admit that it had been mistaken, must be part of (or the whole of) the meaning of the negation of that assertion. And to know the meaning of the negation of an assertion is, near as makes no matter, to know the meaning of that assertion. And if there is nothing which a putative assertion denies, then there is nothing which it asserts either: and so it is not really an assertion. When the Sceptic in the parable asked the Believer, "Just how does what you call an invisible, intangible eternally elusive gardener differ from an imaginary gardener or even from no gardener at all?" he was suggesting that the Believer's earlier statement had been so eroded by qualification that it was no longer an assertion at all.

Now it often seems to people who are not religious as if there was no conceivable event or series of events the occurrence of which would be admitted by sophisticated religious people to be a sufficient reason for conceding "There wasn't a God after all" or "God does not really love us then." Someone tells us that God loves us as a father loves his children. We are reassured. But then we see a child dying of inoperable cancer of the throat. His earthly father is driven frantic in his efforts to help, but his Heavenly Father reveals no obvious sign of concern. Some qualification is made—God's love is "not merely a human love" or it is "an inscrutable love," perhaps—and we realize that sufferings are quite compatible with the truth of the assertion that, "God loves us as a father (but of course, . . .)." We are reassured again. But then perhaps we ask: what is this assurance of God's (appropriately qualified) love worth, what is this apparent guarantee really a guarantee against? Just what would have to happen not merely (morally and wrongly) to tempt but also (logically and rightly) to entitle us to say "God does not love us" or even "God does not exist"? I therefore put to [theists] the simple, central questions, "What would have to occur or to have occurred to constitute for you a disproof of the love of, or of the existence of, God?"

DISCUSSION QUESTIONS

1. Reconstruct and evaluate Flew's argument, making sure to spell out any important suppressed premises and specify the exact conclusion.
2. Flew takes religious utterances like "God loves us as a father loves his children" as assertions. What is the alternative? Why does Flew see them as assertions? Is this important to his argument? (See Chapter 1 on the speech act of assertion.)
3. Flew claims that an assertion must be falsifiable in order to have a definite content. Is this claim defensible in all cases? What implications does it have for other areas (such as science, ethics, or poetry)? Is this principle itself an assertion? Could anything falsify it? (Compare Chapter 12 on self-sealers.)
4. In the following passage, Basil Mitchell responds to Flew with another parable. Explain and evaluate Mitchell's point. How could Flew best respond?

> The theologian surely would not deny that the fact of pain counts against the assertion that God loves men. This very incompatibility generates the most intractable of theological problems—the problem of evil. So the theologian does recognize the fact of pain as counting against Christian doctrine. But it is true that he will not allow it—or anything—to count decisively against it; for he is committed by his faith to trust in God. His attitude is not that of the detached observer, but of the believer.
>
> Perhaps this can be brought out by yet another parable. In time of war in an occupied country, a member of the resistance meets one night a stranger who deeply impresses him. They spend that night together in conversation. The Stranger tells the partisan that he himself is on the side of the resistance—indeed that he is in command of it, and urges the partisan to have faith in him no matter what happens. The partisan is utterly convinced at that meeting of the Stranger's sincerity and constancy and undertakes to trust him.
>
> They never meet in conditions of intimacy again. But sometimes the Stranger is seen helping members of the resistance, and the partisan is grateful and says to his friends, "He is on our side."
>
> Sometimes he is seen in the uniform of the police handing over patriots to the occupying power. On these occasions his friends murmur against him: but the partisan still says, "He is on our side." He still believes that, in spite of appearances, the Stranger did not deceive him. Sometimes he asks the Stranger for help and receives it. He is then thankful. Sometimes he asks and does not receive it. Then he says, "The Stranger knows best." Sometimes his friends, in exasperation, say "Well, what would he have to do for you to admit that you were wrong and that he is not on our side?" But the partisan refuses to answer. He will not consent to put the Stranger to the test. And sometimes his friends complain, "Well, if that's what you mean by his being on our side, the sooner he goes over to the other side the better."

> The partisan of the parable does not allow anything to count decisively against the proposition "The Stranger is on our side." This is because he has committed himself to trust the Stranger. But he of course recognizes that the Stranger's ambiguous behaviour does count against what he believes about him. It is precisely this situation which constitutes the trial of his faith.[16]

[16]*New Essays in Philosophical Theology*, ed. Anthony Flew and Alasdair MacIntyre (New York: Simon and Schuster, 1955), 103–4.

DIVINE OMNISCIENCE AND VOLUNTARY ACTION[17]

by Nelson Pike

Last Saturday afternoon, Jones mowed his lawn. Assuming that God exists and is (essentially) omniscient in the sense outlined above, it follows that (let us say) eighty years prior to last Saturday afternoon, God knew (and thus believed) that Jones would mow his lawn at that time. But from this it follows, I think, that at the time of action (last Saturday afternoon) Jones was not *able*—that is, it was not *within Jones's power*—to refrain from mowing his lawn. If at the time of action, Jones had been able to refrain from mowing his lawn, then (the most obvious conclusion would seem to be) at the time of action, Jones was able to do something which would have brought it about that God held a false belief eighty years earlier. But God cannot in anything be mistaken. It is not possible that some belief of His was false. Thus, last Saturday afternoon, Jones was not able to do something which would have brought it about that God held a false belief eighty years ago. To suppose that it was would be to suppose that, at the time of action, Jones was able to do something having a conceptually incoherent description, namely something that would have brought it about that one of God's beliefs was false. Hence, given that God believed eighty years ago that Jones would mow his lawn on Saturday, if we are to assign Jones the power on Saturday to refrain from mowing his lawn, this power must not be described as the power to do something that would have rendered one of God's beliefs false. How then should we describe it vis-à-vis God and His belief? So far as I can see, there are only two other alternatives. First, we might try describing it as the power to do something that would have brought it about that God believed otherwise than He did eighty years ago; or, secondly, we might try describing it as the power to do something that would have brought it about that God (who, by hypothesis, existed eighty years earlier) did not exist eighty years earlier—that is, as the power to do something that would have brought it about that any person who believed eighty years ago that Jones would mow his lawn on Saturday (one of whom was, by hypothesis, God) held a false belief, and thus was not God. But again, neither of these latter can be accepted. Last Saturday afternoon, Jones was not able to do something that would have brought it about that God believed otherwise than He did eighty years ago. Even if we suppose (as was suggested by Calvin) that eighty years ago God knew Jones would mow his lawn on Saturday in the sense that He "saw" Jones mowing his lawn as if this action were occurring before Him, the fact remains that God knew (and thus believed) eighty years prior to Saturday that Jones would mow his lawn. And if God held such a belief eighty years prior to Saturday, Jones did not have the power on Saturday to do something that would have made it the case that God did not hold this belief eighty years earlier. No action performed at a given time can alter the fact that a given person held a certain belief at a time prior to the time in question. This last seems to be an a priori truth. For similar reasons, the last of the above alternatives must also be rejected. On the assumption that God existed eighty years prior to Saturday, Jones on Saturday was not able to do something that would have brought it about that God did not exist eighty years prior to that time. No action performed at a given time can alter the fact that a certain person existed at a time prior to the time in question. This, too, seems to me to be an a priori truth. But if these observations are correct, then, given that Jones mowed his lawn on Saturday, and given that God exists and is (essentially) omniscient, it seems to follow that at the time of action, Jones did not have the power to refrain from mowing his lawn. The upshot of these reflections would appear to be that Jones's mowing his lawn last Saturday cannot be counted as a voluntary action. Although I do not have an analysis of what it is for an action to be *voluntary*, it seems to me that a situation in which it would be wrong to assign Jones the *ability* or *power* to do *other* than he did would be a situation in which it would also be wrong to speak of his action as voluntary. As a general remark, if God exists and is (essentially) omniscient in the sense specified above, no human action is voluntary.

DISCUSSION QUESTIONS

1. Reconstruct and evaluate Pike's argument, making sure to spell out any suppressed premises.
2. Does Pike's argument show that a traditional God cannot exist? Why or why not?
3. Does Pike's argument undermine the "free will" defense to the problem of evil? Why or why not?
4. Would it matter to Pike's argument if God existed outside of time? Why or why not?

THE ETHICS OF BELIEF[18]

■

by William Clifford

. . . A shipowner was about to send to sea an emigrant ship. He knew that she was old, and not over-well built at the first; that she had seen many seas and climes, and often had needed repairs. Doubts had been suggested to him that possibly she was not seaworthy. These doubts preyed upon his mind, and made him unhappy; he thought that perhaps he ought to have her thoroughly overhauled and refitted, even though this should put him to great expense. Before the ship sailed, however, he succeeded in overcoming these melancholy reflections. He said to himself that she had gone safely through so many voyages and weathered so many storms that it was idle to suppose she would not come safely home from this trip also. He would put his trust in Providence, which could hardly fail to protect all these unhappy families that were leaving their fatherland to seek for better times elsewhere. He would dismiss from his mind all ungenerous suspicions about the honesty of builders and contractors. In such ways he acquired a sincere and comfortable conviction that his vessel was thoroughly safe and seaworthy; he watched her departure with a light heart, and benevolent wishes for the success of the exiles in their strange new home that was to be; and he got his insurance money when she went down in mid-ocean and told no tales.

What shall we say of him? Surely this, that he was verily guilty of the death of those men. It is admitted that he did sincerely believe in the soundness of his ship; but the sincerity of his conviction can in no wise help him, because *he had no right to believe on such evidence as was before him*. He had acquired his belief not by honestly earning it in patient investigation, but by stifling his doubts. And although in the end he may have felt so sure about it that he could not think otherwise, yet inasmuch as he had knowingly and willingly worked himself into that frame of mind, he must be held responsible for it.

Let us alter the case a little, and suppose that the ship was not unsound after all; that she made her voyage safely, and many others after it. Will that diminish the guilt of her owner? Not one jot. When an action is once done, it is right or wrong forever; no accidental failure of its good or evil fruits can possibly alter that. The man would not have been innocent, he would only have been not found out. The question of right or wrong has to do with the origin of his belief, not the matter of it; not what it was, but how he got it, not whether it turned out to be true or false, but whether he had a right to believe on such evidence as was before him. . . .

It may be said, however, that in [this case] it is not the belief which is judged to be wrong, but the action following upon it. The shipowner might say, "I am perfectly certain that my ship is sound, but still I feel it my duty to have her examined, before trusting the lives of so many people to her." . . .

---

[18]*Lectures and Essays* (New York: Macmillan, 1974). Originally published in 1879.

In the first place, let us admit that, so far as it goes, this view of the case is right and necessary; right, because even when a man's belief is so fixed that he cannot think otherwise, he still has a choice in regard to the action suggested by it, and so cannot escape the duty of investigating on the ground of the strength of his convictions; and necessary, because those who are not yet capable of controlling their feelings and thoughts must have a plain rule dealing with overt acts.

But this being premised as necessary, it becomes clear that it is not sufficient, and that our previous judgment is required to supplement it. For it is not possible so to sever the belief from the action it suggests as to condemn the one without condemning the other. . . . If a belief is not realized immediately in open deeds, it is stored up for the guidance of the future. It goes to make a part of that aggregate of beliefs which is the link between sensation and action at every moment of all our lives, and which is so organized and compacted together that no part of it can be isolated from the rest, but every new addition modifies the structure of the whole. No real belief, however trifling and fragmentary it may seem, is ever truly insignificant; it prepares us to receive more of its like, confirms those which resembled it before, and weakens others; and so gradually it lays a stealthy train in our inmost thoughts, which may some day explode into overt action, and leave its stamp upon our character for ever.

And no one man's belief is in any case a private matter which concerns himself alone. . . . [F]orasmuch as no belief held by one man, however seemingly trivial the belief, and however obscure the believer, is ever actually insignificant or without its effect on the fate of mankind, we have no choice but to extend our judgment to all cases of belief whatever. . . .

It is not only the leader of men, statesman, philosopher, or poet, that owes this bounden duty to mankind. Every rustic who delivers in the village alehouse his slow, infrequent sentences, may help to kill or keep alive the fatal superstitions which clog his race. Every hard-worked wife of an artisan may transmit to her children beliefs which shall knit society together, or rend it in pieces. No simplicity of mind, no obscurity of station, can escape the universal duty of questioning all that we believe. . . .

Every time we let ourselves believe for unworthy reasons, we weaken our powers of self-control, of doubting, of judicially and fairly weighing evidence. We all suffer severely enough from the maintenance and support of false beliefs and the fatally wrong actions which they lead to, and the evil born when one such belief is entertained is great and wide. But a greater and wider evil arises when the credulous character is maintained and supported, when a habit of believing for unworthy reasons is fostered and made permanent. . . . Habitual want of care about what I believe leads to habitual want of care in others about the truth of what is told to me. Men speak the truth to one another when each reveres the truth in his own mind and in the other's mind; but how shall my friend revere the truth in my mind when I myself am careless about it, when I believe things because I want to believe them, and because they are comforting and pleasant? Will he not learn to cry,

"Peace," to me, when there is no peace? By such a course I shall surround myself with a thick atmosphere of falsehood and fraud, and in that I must live. It may matter little to me, in my cloud-castle of sweet illusions and darling lies; but it matters much to Man that I have made my neighbours ready to deceive. The credulous man is father to the liar and the cheat; he lives in the bosom of this his family, and it is no marvel if he should become even as they are. So closely are our duties knit together, that whoso shall keep the whole law, and yet offend in one point, he is guilty of all.

To sum up: it is wrong always, everywhere, and for anyone, to believe anything upon insufficient evidence. . . .

DISCUSSION QUESTIONS

1. Reconstruct Clifford's argument for his final sentence. Do you agree? Why or why not?

2. Agnostics sometimes use Clifford's principle to argue against religious beliefs. Present this argument as forcefully as you can. Then assess the strength of this argument for agnosticism.

3. Can Clifford's principle be used to argue for atheism? Against atheism? Why or why not?

4. In the following passage, William James responds to Clifford's argument. Explain and evaluate James's response. How could Clifford best respond?

> Believe truth! Shun error!—these, we see, are two materially different laws; and by choosing between them we may end by coloring differently our whole intellectual life. We may regard the chase for truth as paramount, and the avoidance of error as secondary; or we may, on the other hand, treat the avoidance of error as more imperative, and let truth take its chance. Clifford . . . exhorts us to the latter course. Believe nothing, he tells us, keep your mind in suspense forever, rather than by closing it on insufficient evidence incur the awful risk of believing lies. You, on the other hand, may think that the risk of being in error is a very small matter when compared with the blessings of real knowledge, and be ready to be duped many times in your investigation rather than postpone indefinitely the chance of guessing true. I myself find it impossible to go with Clifford. We must remember that these feelings of our duty about either truth or error are in any case only expressions of our passional life. Biologically considered, our minds are as ready to grind out falsehood as veracity, and he who says, "Better go without belief forever than believe a lie!" merely shows his own preponderant private horror of becoming a dupe. He may be critical of many of his desires and fears, but this fear he slavishly obeys. He cannot imagine any one questioning its binding force. For my own part, I have also a horror of being duped; but I can believe that worse things than being duped may happen to a man in this world: so Clifford's exhortation has to my ears a thoroughly fantastic sound. It is like a general informing his soldiers that it is better to keep out of battle forever than to risk a single wound. Not so are victories either over enemies or over nature gained. Our errors are surely not such awfully solemn things. In a world where we are so certain to incur them in spite of all our caution, a certain lightness of heart seems healthier than this excessive nervousness on their behalf.[19]

[19]"The Will to Believe," in *The Will to Believe and Other Essays in Popular Philosophy* (New York: Longmans, Green & Co., 1897), 18–19.

18

PHILOSOPHICAL REASONING

It is not easy to explain the character of philosophical reasoning. Indeed, the nature of philosophical reasoning is itself a philosophical problem. We can, however, acquire some sense of it by comparing philosophical reasoning with reasoning as it occurs in daily life. In the opening chapters of this book, we noticed that, in everyday discussions, much is taken for granted and left unsaid. In general, there is no need to state points that are already a matter of agreement. In contrast, philosophers usually try to make underlying assumptions explicit and then subject them to critical examination. Still, even for the philosopher, something must trigger an interest in underlying assumptions. This usually arises when the advance of knowledge creates fundamental conflicts within the system of hitherto accepted assumptions. Thus, much that counts as modern philosophy is an attempt to come to terms with the relationship between modern science and the traditional conception of humankind's place in the universe. This chapter explores one such conflict arising from advances in computer theory.

In recent years, the rise of computer technology has generated a conflict with traditional concepts about human beings. Traditionally, humans have cited the capacity to think as the feature that sets them apart from and, of course, above all other creatures. Humans have been defined as rational animals. But we now live in an age in which computers seem able to perform tasks that, had a human being performed them, would certainly count as thinking. Not only can computers perform complex calculations very rapidly, they can also play an excellent game of chess. Do machines think? The question seems forced on us, and it is more than a semantic quibble. In deciding it, we are also reevaluating the status of an aspect of humanity that has long been considered its unique or distinctive feature. Once we decide whether machines can think, the next question is whether human beings are not themselves merely thinking machines.

The two essays presented in this chapter address such questions. The writer of the first essay, A. M. Turing, is one of the geniuses of the twentieth century. He not only developed much of the mathematics that underlies modern computer theory but also helped give computers their first remarkable application: the cracking of the German secret codes during World War II. In this essay, Turing considers whether machines can or cannot think. The brilliance of the essay does not depend on the answer he gives to the question, but rather on his attempt to formulate it in a way that would allow reasonable debate to take place concerning it. For this reason, Turing's essay has been considered a classic work on the subject for more than fifty years. In the second essay, John Searle presents and defends an analogy intended to refute not only Turing's argument but also any other claim that machines could ever think solely by virtue of having the right formal program.

COMPUTING MACHINERY AND INTELLIGENCE[1]

by A. M. Turing

1. THE IMITATION GAME

I propose to consider the question "Can machines think?" This should begin with definitions of the meaning of the terms "machine" and "think." The definitions might be framed so as to reflect so far as possible the normal use of the words, but this attitude is dangerous. If the meaning of the words "machine" and "think" are to be found by examining how they are commonly used, it is difficult to escape the conclusion that the meaning and the answer to the question, "Can machines think?" is to be sought in a statistical survey such as a Gallup poll. But this is absurd. Instead of attempting such a definition I shall replace the question by another, which is closely related to it and is expressed in relatively unambiguous words.

The new form of the problem can be described in terms of a game which we call the "imitation game." It is played with three people, a man (A), a woman (B), and an interrogator (C) who may be of either sex. The interrogator stays in a room apart from the other two. The object of the game for the interrogator is to determine which of the other two is the man and which is the woman. He knows them by labels X and Y, and at the end of the game he says either "X is A and Y is B" or "X is B and Y is A." The interrogator is allowed to put questions to A and B thus:

C: Will X please tell me the length of his or her hair?

Now suppose X is actually A, then A must answer. It is A's object in the game to try to cause C to make the wrong identification. His answer might therefore be

"My hair is shingled, and the longest strands are about nine inches long."

[1]*Mind*, vol. LIX, No. 236 (1950), 433–60.

In order that tones of voice may not help the interrogator the answers should be written, or better still, typewritten. The ideal arrangement is to have a teleprinter communicating between the two rooms. Alternatively the question and answers can be repeated by an intermediary. The object of the game for the third player (B) is to help the interrogator. The best strategy for her is probably to give truthful answers. She can add such things as "I am the woman, don't listen to him!" to her answers, but it will avail nothing as the man can make similar remarks.

We now ask the question, "What will happen when a machine takes the part of A in this game?" Will the interrogator decide wrongly as often when the game is played like this as he does when the game is played between a man and a woman? These questions replace our original, "Can machines think?"

2. CRITIQUE OF THE NEW PROBLEM

As well as asking, "What is the answer to this new form of the question," one may ask, "Is this new question a worthy one to investigate?" This latter question we investigate without further ado, thereby cutting short an infinite regress.

The new problem has the advantage of drawing a fairly sharp line between the physical and the intellectual capacities of a man. No engineer or chemist claims to be able to produce a material which is indistinguishable from the human skin. It is possible that at some time this might be done, but even supposing this invention available we should feel there was little point in trying to make a "thinking machine" more human by dressing it up in such artificial flesh. The form in which we have set the problem reflects this fact in the condition which prevents the interrogator from seeing or touching the other competitors, or hearing their voices. Some other advantages of the proposed criterion may be shown up by specimen questions and answers. Thus:

Q: Please write me a sonnet on the subject of the Forth Bridge.

A: Count me out on this one. I never could write poetry.

Q: Add 34957 to 70764.

A: (Pause about 30 seconds and then give as answer) 105621.

Q: Do you play chess?

A: Yes.

Q: I have K at my K1, and no other pieces. You have only K at K6 and R at R1. It is your move. What do you play?

A: (After a pause of 15 seconds) R–R8 mate.

The question and answer method seems to be suitable for introducing almost any one of the fields of human endeavor that we wish to include. We do not wish to penalize the machine for its inability to shine in beauty competitions, nor to penalize a man for losing in a race against an airplane. The conditions of our game make these disabilities irrelevant. The "witnesses" can brag, if they consider it advisable, as much as they please about their charms, strength or heroism, but the interrogator cannot demand practical demonstrations.

The game may perhaps be criticized on the ground that the odds are weighted too heavily against the machine. If the man were to try and pretend to be the machine, he would clearly make a very poor showing. He would be given away at once by slowness and inaccuracy in arithmetic. May not machines carry out something which ought to be described as thinking but which is very different from what a man does? This objection is a very strong one, but at least we can say that if, nevertheless, a machine can be constructed to play the imitation game satisfactorily, we need not be troubled by this objection.

It might be urged that when playing the "imitation game" the best strategy for the machine may possibly be something other than imitation of the behavior of a man. This may be, but I think it is unlikely that there is any great effect of this kind. In any case there is no intention to investigate here the theory of the game, and it will be assumed that the best strategy is to try to provide answers that would naturally be given by a man.

3. THE MACHINES CONCERNED IN THE GAME

The question which we put in §1 will not be quite definite until we have specified what we mean by the word "machine." It is natural that we should wish to permit every kind of engineering technique to be used in our machines. We also wish to allow the possibility that an engineer or team of engineers may construct a machine which works, but whose manner of operation cannot be satisfactorily described by its constructors because they have applied a method which is largely experimental. Finally, we wish to exclude from the machines men born in the usual manner. It is difficult to frame the definitions so as to satisfy these three conditions. One might for instance insist that the team of engineers should be all of one sex, but this would not really be satisfactory, for it is probably possible to rear a complete individual from a single cell of the skin (say) of a man. To do so would be a feat of biological technique deserving of the very highest praise, but we would not be inclined to regard it as a case of "constructing a thinking machine." This prompts us to abandon the requirement that every kind of technique should be permitted. We are the more ready to do so in view of the fact that the present interest in "thinking machines" has been aroused by a particular kind of machine, usually called an "electronic computer" or "digital computer." Following this suggestion we only permit digital computers to take part in our game.

This restriction appears at first sight to be a very drastic one. I shall attempt to show that it is not so in reality. . . . The digital computers considered [here] are classified among the "discrete state machines." These are the machines which move by sudden jumps or clicks from one quite definite state to another. . . . [A] special property of digital computers [is] that they can mimic any discrete state machine. [This property] is described by saying that they are *universal* machines. The existence of machines with this property has the important consequence that, considerations of speed apart, it is unnecessary to design various new machines to do various computing processes. They can all be done with one digital computer, suitably programmed for each case. It will be seen that as a consequence of this all digital computers are in a sense equivalent. . . .

It was suggested tentatively that the question, "Can machines think?" should be replaced by "Are there imaginable digital computers which would do well in the imitation game?" If we wish we can make this superficially more general and ask "Are there discrete state machines which would do well?" But in view of the universality property we see that either of these questions is equivalent to this, "Let us fix our attention on one particular digital computer C. Is it true that by modifying this computer to have an adequate storage, suitably increasing its speed of action, and providing it with an appropriate program, C can be made to play satisfactorily the part of A in the imitation game, the part of B being taken by a man?" . . .

6. CONTRARY VIEWS ON THE MAIN QUESTION

We may now consider the ground to have been cleared and we are ready to proceed to the debate on our question, "Can machines think?" and the variant of it quoted at the end of the last section. We cannot altogether abandon the original form of the problem, for opinions will differ as to the appropriateness of the substitution and we must at least listen to what has to be said in this connection.

It will simplify matters for the reader if I explain first my own beliefs in the matter. Consider first the more accurate form of the question. I believe that in about fifty years' time it will be possible to program computers, with a storage capacity of about 10^9, to make them play the imitation game so well that an average interrogator will not have more than 70 per cent chance of making the right identification after five minutes of questioning. The original question, "Can machines think?" I believe to be too meaningless to deserve discussion. Nevertheless I believe that at the end of the century the use of words and general educated opinion will have altered so much that one will be able to speak of machines thinking without expecting to be contradicted. I believe further that no useful purpose is served by concealing these beliefs. The popular view that scientists proceed inexorably from well-established fact to well-established fact, never being influenced by any unproved conjecture, is quite mistaken. Provided it is made clear which are proved facts and which are conjectures, no harm can result. Conjectures are of great importance since they suggest useful lines of research.

I now proceed to consider opinions opposed to my own.

(1) *The Theological Objection.* Thinking is a function of man's immortal soul. God has given an immortal soul to every man and woman, but not to any other animal or to machines. Hence no animal or machine can think.

I am unable to accept any part of this, but will attempt to reply in theological terms. I should find the argument more convincing if animals were classed with men, for there is a greater difference, to my mind, between the typical animate and the inanimate than there is between man and the other animals. The arbitrary character of the orthodox view becomes clearer if we consider how it might appear to a member of some other religious community. How do Christians regard the Moslem view that women have no souls? But let us leave this point aside and return to the main argument. It appears to me that the argument quoted above implies a serious restriction of the omnipotence of the Almighty. It is admitted that there are certain things that He cannot do such as making one equal to two, but should we not believe that He has freedom to confer a soul on an elephant if He sees fit? We might expect that He would only exercise this power in conjunction with a mutation which provided the elephant with an appropriately improved brain to minister to the needs of this soul. An argument of exactly similar form may be made for the case of machines. It may seem different because it is more difficult to "swallow." But this really only means that we think it would be less likely that He would consider the circumstances suitable for conferring a soul. The circumstances in question are discussed in the rest of this paper. In attempting to construct such machines we should not be irreverently usurping His power of creating souls, any more than we are in the procreation of children: rather we are, in either case, instruments of His will providing mansions for the souls that He creates.

However, this is mere speculation. I am not very impressed with theological arguments whatever they may be used to support. Such arguments have often been found unsatisfactory in the past. In the time of Galileo it was argued that the texts, "And the sun stood still . . . and hasted not to go down about a whole day" (Joshua x. 13) and "He laid the foundations of the earth, that it should not move at any time" (Psalm cv. 5) were an adequate refutation of the Copernican theory. With our present knowledge such an argument appears futile. When that knowledge was not available it made a quite different impression.

(2) *The "Heads in the Sand" Objection.* "The consequences of machines thinking would be too dreadful. Let us hope and believe that they cannot do so."

This argument is seldom expressed quite so openly as in the form above. But it affects most of us who think about it at all. We like to believe that Man is in some subtle way superior to the rest of creation. It is best if he can be shown to be *necessarily* superior, for then there is no danger of him losing his commanding position. The popularity of the theological argument is clearly connected with this feeling. It is likely to be quite strong in intellectual people, since they value the power of thinking more highly than others, and are more inclined to base their belief in the superiority of Man on this power.

I do not think that this argument is sufficiently substantial to require refutation. Consolation would be more appropriate: perhaps this should be sought in the transmigration of souls.

(3) *The Mathematical Objection.* There are a number of results of mathematical logic which can be used to show that there are limitations to the powers of discrete state machines. The best known of these results is known as Gödel's theorem, and shows that in any sufficiently powerful logical system statements can be formulated which can neither be proved nor disproved within the system, unless possibly the system itself is inconsistent. . . . This is the mathematical result: it is argued that it proves a disability of machines to which the human intellect is not subject.

The short answer to this argument is that although it is established that there are limitations to the powers of any particular machine, it has only been stated, without any sort of proof, that no such limitations apply to the human intellect. But I do not think this view can be dismissed quite so lightly. Whenever one of these machines is asked the appropriate critical question, and gives a definite answer, we know that this answer must be wrong, and this gives us a certain feeling of superiority. Is this feeling illusory? It is no doubt quite genuine, but I do not think too much importance should be attached to it. We too often give wrong answers to questions ourselves to be justified in being very pleased at such evidence of fallibility on the part of the machines. Further, our superiority can only be felt on such an occasion in relation to the one machine over which we have scored our petty triumph. There would be no question of triumphing simultaneously over *all* machines. In short, then, there might be men cleverer than any given machine, but then again there might be other machines cleverer again, and so on.

Those who hold to the mathematical argument would, I think, mostly be willing to accept the imitation game as a basis for discussion. Those who believe in the two previous objections would probably not be interested in any criteria.

(4) *The Argument from Consciousness.* This argument is very well expressed in Professor Jefferson's Lister Oration for 1949, from which I quote, "Not until a machine can write a sonnet or compose a concerto because of thoughts and emotions felt, and not by the chance fall of symbols, could we agree that machine equals brain—that is, not only write it but know that it had written it. No mechanism could feel (and not merely artificially signal, an easy contrivance) pleasure at its successes, grief when its values fuse, be warmed by flattery, be made miserable by its mistakes, be charmed by sex, be angry or depressed when it cannot get what it wants."

This argument appears to be a denial of the validity of our test. According to the most extreme form of this view the only way by which one could be sure that a machine thinks is to *be* the machine and to feel oneself thinking. One could then describe these feelings to the world, but of course no one would be justified in taking any notice. Likewise according to this view the only way to know that a *man* thinks is to be that particular man. It is in fact the solipsist point of view [which claims that only oneself exists]. It may be the most logical view to hold but it makes communication of ideas difficult. A is liable to believe "A thinks but B does not" while B believes "B thinks but A does not." Instead of arguing continually over this point it is usual to have the polite convention that everyone thinks.

I am sure that Professor Jefferson does not wish to adopt the extreme and solipsist point of view. Probably he would be quite willing to accept the imitation game as a test. The game (with the player B omitted) is frequently used in practice under the name of *viva voce* to discover whether someone really understands something or has "learned it parrot fashion." Let us listen in to a part of such a *viva voce*:

> INTERROGATOR: In the first line of your sonnet which reads "Shall I compare thee to a summer's day," would not "a spring day" do as well or better?
>
> WITNESS: It wouldn't scan.
>
> INTERROGATOR: How about "a winter's day." That would scan all right.
>
> WITNESS: Yes, but nobody wants to be compared to a winter's day.
>
> INTERROGATOR: Would you say Mr. Pickwick reminded you of Christmas?
>
> WITNESS: In a way.
>
> INTERROGATOR: Yet Christmas is a winter's day, and I do not think Mr. Pickwick would mind the comparison.
>
> WITNESS: I don't think you're serious. By a winter's day one means a typical winter's day, rather than a special one like Christmas.

And so on. What would Professor Jefferson say if the sonnet-writing machine was able to answer like this in the *viva voce*? I do not know whether he would regard the machine as "merely artificially signaling" these answers, but if the answers were as satisfactory and sustained as in the above passage I do not think he would describe it as "an easy contrivance." This phrase is, I think, intended to cover such devices as the inclusion in the machine of a record of someone reading a sonnet, with appropriate switching to turn it on from time to time. In short then, I think that most of those who support the argument from consciousness could be persuaded to abandon it rather than be forced into the solipsist position. They will then probably be willing to accept our test.

I do not wish to give the impression that I think there is no mystery about consciousness. There is, for instance, something of a paradox connected with any attempt to localize it. But I do not think these mysteries necessarily need to be solved before we can answer the question with which we are concerned in this paper.

(5) *Arguments from Various Disabilities*. These arguments take the form, "I grant you that you can make machines do all the things you have mentioned but you will never be able to make one to do X." Numerous features X are suggested in this connection. I offer a selection:

Be kind, resourceful, beautiful, friendly, have initiative, have a sense of humor, tell right from wrong, make mistakes, fall in love, enjoy strawberries and cream, make someone fall in love with it, learn from experience, use words properly, be the subject of its own thought, have as much diversity of behavior as a man, do something really new.

No support is usually offered for these statements. I believe they are mostly founded on the principle of scientific induction. A man has seen thousands of machines in his lifetime. From what he sees of them he draws a number of general conclusions. They are ugly, each is designed for a very limited purpose, when required for a minutely different purpose they are useless, the variety of behavior of any one of them is very small, etc., etc. Naturally he concludes that these are necessary properties of machines in general. Many of these limitations are associated with the very small storage capacity of most machines. (I am assuming that the idea of storage capacity is extended in some way to cover machines other than discrete state machines. The exact definition does not matter as no mathematical accuracy is claimed in the present discussion.) A few years ago, when very little had been heard of digital computers, it was possible to elicit much incredulity concerning them, if one mentioned their properties without describing their construction. That was presumably due to a similar application of the principle of scientific induction. These applications of the principle are of course largely unconscious. When a burned child fears the fire and shows that he fears it by avoiding it, I should say that he was applying scientific induction. (I could of course also describe his behavior in many other ways.) The works and customs of mankind do not seem to be very suitable material to which to apply scientific induction. A very large part of space-time must be investigated if reliable results are to be obtained. Otherwise we may (as most English children do) decide that everybody speaks English, and that it is silly to learn French.

There are, however, special remarks to be made about many of the disabilities that have been mentioned. The inability to enjoy strawberries and cream may have struck the reader as frivolous. Possibly a machine might be made to enjoy this delicious dish, but any attempt to make one do so would be idiotic. What is important about this disability is that it contributes to some of the other disabilities, e.g., to the difficulty of the same kind of friendliness occurring between man and machine as between white man and white man, or between black man and black man.

The claim that "machines cannot make mistakes" seems a curious one. One is tempted to retort, "Are they any the worse for that?" But let us adopt a more sympathetic attitude, and try to see what is really meant. I think this criticism can be explained in terms of the imitation game. It is claimed that the interrogator could distinguish the machine from the man simply by setting them a number of problems in arithmetic. The machine would be unmasked because of its deadly accuracy. The reply to this is simple. The machine (programmed for playing the game) would not attempt to give the *right* answers to the arithmetic problems. It would deliberately introduce mistakes in a manner calculated to confuse the interrogator. . . .

The claim that a machine cannot be the subject of its own thought can of course only be answered if it can be shown that the machine has *some* thought with *some* subject matter. Nevertheless, "the subject matter of a machine's operations" does seem to mean something, at least to the people who deal with it. If, for instance, the machine was trying to find a solution of the equation $x^2 - 40x - 11 = 0$ one would be tempted to describe this equation as part of the machine's subject matter at that moment. In this sort of sense a machine undoubtedly can be its own subject matter. It may be used to help in making up its own programs, or to predict the effect of alterations in its own structure. By observing the results of its own behavior it can modify its own programs so as to achieve some purpose more effectively. These are possibilities of the near future, rather than Utopian dreams.

The criticism that a machine cannot have much diversity of behavior is just a way of saying that it cannot have much storage capacity. Until fairly recently a storage capacity of even a thousand digits was very rare.

The criticisms that we are considering here are often disguised forms of the argument from consciousness. Usually if one maintains that a machine *can* do one of these things, and describes the kind of method that the machine could use, one will not make much of an impression. It is thought that the method (whatever it may be, for it must be mechanical) is really rather base. Compare the parenthesis in Jefferson's statement quoted above.

(6) *Lady Lovelace's Objection.* Our most detailed information of Babbage's Analytical Engine [a digital computer planned in the 1830s] comes from a memoir by Lady Lovelace. In it she states, "The Analytical Engine has no pretensions to *originate* anything. It can do *whatever we know how to order it* to perform" (her italics). This statement is quoted by Hartree who adds: "This does not imply that it may not be possible to construct electronic equipment which will 'think for itself,' or in which, in biological terms, one could set up a conditioned reflex, which would serve as a basis for 'learning.' Whether this is possible in principle or not is a stimulating and exciting question, suggested by some of these recent developments. But it did not seem that the machines constructed or projected at the time had this property."

I am in thorough agreement with Hartree over this. It will be noticed that he does not assert that the machines in question had not got the property, but rather that the evidence available to Lady Lovelace did not encourage her to believe that they had it. It is quite possible that the machines in question had in a sense got this property. For suppose that some discrete state machine has the property. The Analytical Engine was a universal digital computer, so that, if its storage capacity and speed were adequate, it could by suitable programming be made to mimic the machine in question. Probably this argument did not occur to the Countess or to Babbage. In any case there was no obligation on them to claim all that could be claimed. . . .

A variant of Lady Lovelace's objection states that a machine can "never do anything really new." This may be parried for a moment with the saw, "There is nothing new under the sun." Who can be certain that "original work" that he has done was not simply the growth of the seed planted in him by teaching, or the effect of following well-known general principles. A better variant of the objection says that a machine can never "take us by surprise." This statement is a more direct challenge and can be met directly. Machines take me by surprise with great frequency. This is largely because I do not do sufficient calculation to decide what to expect them to do, or rather because, although I do a calculation, I do it in a hurried, slipshod fashion, taking risks. Perhaps I say to myself, "I suppose the voltage here ought to be the same as there: anyway let's assume it is." Naturally I am often wrong, and the result is a surprise for me, for by the time the experiment is done these assumptions have been forgotten. These admissions lay me open to lectures on the subject of my vicious ways, but do not throw any doubt on my credibility when I testify to the surprises I experience.

I do not expect this reply to silence my critic. He will probably say that such surprises are due to some creative mental act on my part, and reflect no credit on the machine. This leads us back to the argument from consciousness, and far from the idea of surprise. It is a line of argument we must consider closed, but it is perhaps worth remarking that the appreciation of something as surprising requires as much of a "creative mental act" whether the surprising event originates from a man, a book, a machine or anything else.

The view that machines cannot give rise to surprises is due, I believe, to a fallacy to which philosophers and mathematicians are particularly subject. This is the assumption that as soon as a fact is presented to a mind all consequences of that fact spring into the mind simultaneously with it. It is a very useful assumption under many circumstances, but one too easily forgets that it is false. A natural consequence of doing so is that one then assumes that there is no virtue in the mere working out of consequences from data and general principles.

(7) *Argument from Continuity in the Nervous System.* The nervous system is certainly not a discrete state machine. A small error in the information about the size of a nervous impulse impinging on a neuron, may make a large difference to the size of the outgoing impulse. It may be argued that, this being so, one cannot expect to be able to mimic the behavior of the nervous system with a discrete state system.

It is true that a discrete state machine must be different from a continuous machine. But if we adhere to the conditions of the imitation game, the interrogator will not be able to take any advantage of this difference. The situation can be made clearer if we consider some other simpler continuous machine. A differential analyzer will do very well. (A differential analyzer is a certain kind of machine not of the discrete state type used for some kinds of calculation.) Some of these provide their answers in a typed form, and so are suitable for taking part in the game. It would not be possible for a digital computer to predict exactly what answers the differential analyzer would give to a problem, but it would be quite capable of giving the right sort of answer. For instance, if asked to give the value of *pi* (actually about 3.1416) it would be reasonable to choose at random between the values 3.12, 3.13, 3.14,

3.15, 3.16 with the probabilities of 0.05, 0.15, 0.55, 0.19, 0.06 (say). Under these circumstances it would be very difficult for the interrogator to distinguish the differential analyzer from the digital computer.

(8) *The Argument from Informality of Behavior.* It is not possible to produce a set of rules purporting to describe what a man should do in every conceivable set of circumstances. One might for instance have a rule that one is to stop when one sees a red traffic light, and to go if one sees a green one, but what if by some fault both appear together? One may perhaps decide that it is safest to stop. But some further difficulty may well arise from this decision later. To attempt to provide rules of conduct to cover every eventuality, even those arising from traffic lights, appears to be impossible. With all this I agree.

From this it is argued that we cannot be machines. I shall try to reproduce the argument, but I fear I shall hardly do it justice. It seems to run something like this. "If each man had a definite set of rules of conduct by which he regulated his life he would be no better than a machine. But there are no such rules, so men cannot be machines." The undistributed middle is glaring. I do not think the argument is ever put quite like this, but I believe this is the argument used nevertheless. There may however be a certain confusion between "rules of conduct" and "laws of behavior" to cloud the issue. By "rules of conduct" I mean precepts such as "Stop if you see red lights," on which one can act, and of which one can be conscious. By "laws of behavior" I mean laws of nature as applied to a man's body such as "if you pinch him he will squeak." If we substitute "laws of behavior which regulate his life" for "laws of conduct by which he regulates his life" in the argument quoted the undistributed middle is no longer insuperable. For we believe that it is not only true that being regulated by laws of behavior implies being some sort of machine (though not necessarily a discrete state machine), but that conversely being such a machine implies being regulated by such laws. However, we cannot so easily convince ourselves of the absence of complete laws of behavior as of complete rules of conduct. The only way we know of for finding such laws is scientific observation, and we certainly know of no circumstances under which we could say, "We have searched enough. There are no such laws." . . .

7. LEARNING MACHINES

The reader will have anticipated that I have no very convincing arguments of a positive nature to support my views. If I had, I should not have taken such pains to point out the fallacies in contrary views. Such evidence as I have I shall now give. . . .

The only really satisfactory support that can be given for the view expressed at the beginning of §6, will be that provided by waiting for the end of the century and then doing the experiment described. But what can we say in the meantime? What steps should be taken now if the experiment is to be successful? . . .

Instead of trying to produce a programme to simulate the adult mind, why not rather try to produce one which simulates the child's? If this were then subjected to an appropriate course of education, one would obtain the adult brain. Presumably the child brain is something like a notebook as one buys it from the stationer's. Rather little mechanism and lots of blank sheets. (Mechanism and writing are from our point of view almost synonymous.) Our hope is that there is so little mechanism in the child brain that something like it can be easily programmed. The amount of work in the education we can assume, as a first approximation, to be much the same as for the human child. . . .

We normally associate punishments and rewards with the teaching process. Some simple child machines can be constructed or programmed on this sort of principle. The machine has to be so constructed that the events which shortly preceded the occurrence of a punishment signal are unlikely to be repeated, whereas a reward signal increased the probability of repetition of the events which led up to it. These definitions do not presuppose any feelings on the part of the machine. . . .

We may hope that machines will eventually compete with men in all purely intellectual fields. But which are the best ones to start with? Even this is a difficult decision. Many people think that a very abstract activity, like the playing of chess, would be best. It can also be maintained that it is best to provide the machine with the best sense organs that money can buy, and then teach it to understand and speak English. This process could follow the normal teaching of a child. Things would be pointed out and named, etc. Again I do not know what the right answer is, but I think both approaches should be tried.

We can only see a short distance ahead, but we can see plenty there that needs to be done.

DISCUSSION QUESTIONS

1. Why does Turing replace the question "Can machines think?" with the question "Can any machine ever win the imitation game?" Must anyone who answers "Yes" to the first question also answer "Yes" to the second question? Must anyone who answers "No" to the first question also answer "No" to the second question? Is Turing's replacement fair to his opponents? Why or why not?

2. Turing predicted that by 2000, average interrogators would be fooled 70 percent of the time by machines after playing the imitation game for five minutes. We are now beyond 2000, but no machine is even close to this degree of success. Thus, Turing's prediction seems false (and not even close to true). Does this show that Turing's main argument is fallacious? Why or why not?

3. Turing claims that Jefferson's argument from consciousness lands him in solipsism. Reconstruct and evaluate this reductio ad absurdum refutation. How could Jefferson best reply? Is this reply adequate? Why or why not?

4. One variant of Lady Lovelace's objection claims that machines are programmed, so they "never do anything really new." Turing responds by arguing that machines can "take us by surprise." Is this response adequate? Why or why not? What does it mean to do something "really new"? Is there any sense in which humans do things that are really new but machines cannot? How can you tell?

5. Some compact disc players are of such high quality that it is sometimes impossible to distinguish the sound of the disc player from the sound of a live human voice. Would the Turing test show that such compact disc players can sing? Why or why not?

THE MYTH OF THE COMPUTER[2]

■

by John R. Searle

[A] theory, which is fairly widely held in cognitive science, can be summarized in three propositions.

1. *Mind as Program.* What we call minds are simply very complex digital computer programs. Mental states are simply computer states and mental processes are computational processes. Any system whatever that had the right program, with the right input and output, would have to have mental states and processes in the same literal sense that you and I do, because that is all there is to mental states and processes, that is all that you and I have. The programs in question are "self-updating" or "self-designing" "systems of representations."

2. *The Irrelevance of the Neurophysiology of the Brain.* In the study of the mind actual biological facts about actual human and animal brains are irrelevant because the mind is an "abstract sort of thing" and human brains just happen to be among the indefinitely large number of kinds of computers that can have minds. Our minds happen to be embodied in our brains, but there is no essential connection between the mind and the brain. Any other computer with the right program would also have a mind. . . .

3. *The Turing Test as the Criterion of the Mental.* The conclusive proof of the presence of mental states and capacities is the ability of a system to pass the Turing test, the test devised by Alan Turing and described in

---

[2] *The New York Review of Books* (April 29, 1982), 3. Searle is here reviewing Hofstadter and Dennett, *The Mind's I.* We removed references to that particular book, since Searle's argument is much more general.

his article in this book. If a system can convince a computer expert that it has mental states then it really has those mental states. If, for example, a machine could "converse" with a native Chinese speaker in such a way as to convince the speaker that it understood Chinese then it would literally understand Chinese. . . .

We might call this collection of theses "strong artificial intelligence" (strong AI).* These theses are certainly not obviously true and they are seldom explicitly stated and defended.

Let us inquire first into how plausible it is to suppose that specific biochemical powers of the brain are really irrelevant to the mind. . . . [I]f you consider specific mental states and processes—being thirsty, wanting to go to the bathroom, worrying about your income tax, trying to solve math puzzles, feeling depressed, recalling the French word for "butterfly"—then it seems at least a little odd to think that the brain is so irrelevant.

Take thirst, where we actually know a little about how it works. Kidney secretions of renin synthesize a substance called angiotensin. This substance goes into the hypothalamus and triggers a series of neuron firings. As far as we know these neuron firings are a very large part of the cause of thirst. Now obviously there is more to be said, for example, about the relations of the hypothalamic responses to the rest of the brain, about other things going on in the hypothalamus, and about the possible distinctions between the *feeling* of thirst and the *urge* to drink. Let us suppose we have filled out the story with the rest of the biochemical causal account of thirst.

Now the theses of the mind as program and the irrelevance of the brain would tell us that what matters about this story is not the specific biochemical properties of the angiotensin or the hypothalamus but only the formal computer programs that the whole sequence instantiates. Well, let's try that out as a hypothesis and see how it works. A computer can simulate the formal properties of the sequence of chemical and electrical phenomena in the production of thirst just as much as it can simulate the formal properties of anything else—we can simulate thirst just as we can simulate hurricanes, rainstorms, five-alarm fires, internal combustion engines, photosynthesis, lactation, or the flow of currency in a depressed economy. But no one in his right mind thinks that a computer simulation of a five-alarm fire will burn down the neighborhood, or that a computer simulation of an internal combustion engine will power a car or that computer simulations of lactation and photosynthesis will produce milk and sugar. To my amazement, however, I have found that a large number of people suppose that computer simulations of mental phenomena, whether at the level of brain processes or not, literally produce mental phenomena.

---

*"Strong" to distinguish the position from "weak" or "cautious" AI, which holds that the computer is simply a very useful tool in the study of the mind, not that the appropriately programmed computer literally has a mind.

Again, let's try it out. Let's program our favorite PDP-10 computer with the formal program that simulates thirst. We can even program it to point out at the end "Boy, am I thirsty!" or "Won't someone please give me a drink?" etc. Now would anyone suppose that we thereby have even the slightest reason to suppose that the computer is literally thirsty? Or that any simulation of any other mental phenomena, such as understanding stories, feeling depressed, or worrying about itemized deductions, must therefore produce the real thing? The answer, alas, is that a large number of people are committed to an ideology that requires them to believe just that. So let us carry the story a step further.

The PDP-10 is powered by electricity and perhaps its electrical properties can reproduce some of the actual causal powers of the electrochemical features of the brain in producing mental states. We certainly couldn't rule out that eventuality a priori. But remember: the thesis of strong AI is that the mind is "independent of *any* particular embodiment" because the mind is just a program and the program can be run on a computer made of anything whatever provided it is stable enough and complex enough to carry the program. The actual physical computer could be an ant colony . . . , a collection of beer cans, streams of toilet paper with small stones placed on the squares, men sitting on high stools with green eye shades—anything you like.

So let us imagine our thirst-simulating program running on a computer made entirely of old beer cans, millions (or billions) of old beer cans that are rigged up to levers and powered by windmills. We can imagine that the program simulates the neuron firings at the synapses by having beer cans bang into each other, thus achieving a strict correspondence between neuron firings and beer-can bangings. And at the end of the sequence a beer can pops up on which is written "I am thirsty." Now, to repeat the question, does anyone suppose that this Rube Goldberg apparatus is literally thirsty in the sense in which you and I are?

Notice that the thesis of [strong AI] is not that *for all we know* the collection of beer cans might be thirsty but rather that if it has the right program with the right input and output it *must* be thirsty (or understand Proust or worry about its income tax or have any other mental state) because that is all the mind is, a certain kind of computer program, and any computer made of anything at all running the right program would have to have the appropriate mental states.

I believe that everything we have learned about human and animal biology suggests that what we call "mental" phenomena are as much a part of our biological natural history as any other biological phenomena, as much a part of biology as digestion, lactation, or the secretion of bile. Much of the implausibility of the strong AI thesis derives from its resolute opposition to biology; the mind is not a concrete biological phenomenon but "an abstract sort of thing."

Still, in calling attention to the implausibility of supposing that the specific causal powers of brains are irrelevant to minds I have not yet fully exposed the preposterousness of the strong AI position, so let us press on and examine a bit more closely the thesis of mind as program.

Digital computer programs by definition consist of sets of purely formal operations on formally specified symbols. The ideal computer does such things as print a 0 on the tape, move one square to the left, erase a 1, move back to the right, etc. It is common to describe this as "symbol manipulation" or . . . the whole system as a "self-updating representational system"; but these terms are at least a bit misleading since as far as the computer is concerned the symbols don't *symbolize* anything or *represent* anything. They are just formal counters.

The computer attaches no meaning, interpretation, or content to the formal symbols; and qua computer it couldn't, because if we tried to give the computer an interpretation of its symbols we could only give it more uninterpreted symbols. The interpretation of the symbols is entirely up to the programmers and users of the computer. For example, on my pocket calculator if I print "$3 \times 3 =$," the calculator will print "9" but it has no idea that "3" means 3 or that "9" means 9 or that anything means anything. We might put this point by saying that the computer has a syntax but no semantics. The computer manipulates formal symbols but attaches no meaning to them, and this simple observation will enable us to refute the thesis of mind as program.

Suppose that we write a computer program to simulate the understanding of Chinese so that, for example, if the computer is asked questions in Chinese the program enables it to give answers in Chinese; if asked to summarize stories in Chinese it can give such summaries; if asked questions about the stories it has been given it will answer such questions.

Now suppose that I, who understand no Chinese at all and can't even distinguish Chinese symbols from some other kinds of symbols, am locked in a room with a number of cardboard boxes full of Chinese symbols. Suppose that I am given a book of rules in English that instruct me how to match these Chinese symbols with each other. The rules say such things as that the "squiggle-squiggle" sign is to be followed by the "squoggle-squoggle" sign. Suppose that people outside the room pass in more Chinese symbols and that following the instructions in the book I pass Chinese symbols back to them. Suppose that unknown to me the people who pass me the symbols call them "questions" and the book of instructions that I work from they call "the program"; the symbols I give back to them they call "answers to the questions" and me they call "the computer." Suppose that after a while the programmers get so good at writing the programs and I get so good at manipulating the symbols that my answers are indistinguishable from those of native Chinese speakers. I can pass the Turing test for understanding Chinese. But all the same I still don't understand a word of Chinese and neither does any other digital computer because all the computer has is what I have: a formal program that attaches no meaning, interpretation, or content to any of the symbols.

What this simple program shows is that no formal program by itself is sufficient for understanding, because it would always be possible in principle for an agent to go through the steps in the program and still not have the relevant understanding. And what works for Chinese would also work for other mental phenomena. I could, for example, go through the steps of the thirst-simulating program without feeling thirsty. The argument also, *en passant*, refutes the Turing test because it shows that a system, namely me, could pass the Turing test without having the appropriate mental states.* . . .

The details of how the brain works are immensely complicated and largely unknown, but some of the general principles of the relations between brain functioning and computer programs can be stated quite simply. First, we know that brain processes cause mental phenomena. Mental states are caused by and realized in the structure of the brain. From this it follows that any system that produced mental states would have to have powers equivalent to those of the brain. Such a system might use a different chemistry, but whatever its chemistry it would have to be able to cause what the brain causes. We know from the Chinese room argument that digital computer programs by themselves are never sufficient to produce mental states. Now since brains do produce minds, and since programs by themselves can't produce minds, it follows that the way the brain does it can't be by simply instantiating a computer program. (Everything, by the way, instantiates some program or other, and brains are no exception. So in that trivial sense brains, like everything else, are digital computers.) And it also follows that if you wanted to build a machine to produce mental states, a thinking machine, you couldn't do it solely in virtue of the fact that your machine ran a certain kind of computer program. The thinking machine couldn't work solely in virtue of being a digital computer but would have to duplicate the specific causal powers of the brain.

A lot of the nonsense talked about computers nowadays stems from their relative rarity and hence mystery. As computers and robots become more common, as common as telephones, washing machines, and forklift trucks, it seems likely that this aura will disappear and people will take computers for what they are, namely useful machines. In the meantime one has to try to avoid certain recurring mistakes that keep cropping up in . . . current discussions.

The first is the idea that somehow computer achievements pose some sort of threat or challenge to human beings. But the fact, for example, that a calculator can outperform even the best mathematician is no more significant or threatening than the fact that a steam shovel can outperform the best human digger. (An oddity of artificial intelligence, by the way, is the slowness of the programmers in devising a program that can beat the very best chess players. From the point of view of games theory, chess is a trivial game since each side has perfect information about the other's position and possible moves, and one had to assume that computer programs will soon be able to outperform any human chess player.)

---

*The "Chinese room argument" is stated in detail in my article "Minds, Brains, and Programs," . . . [which] originally appeared in *The Behavioral and Brain Sciences*, Vol. 3 (Cambridge University Press, 1980), along with twenty-seven responses and a reply to the responses.

A second fallacy is the idea that there might be some special human experience beyond computer simulation because of its special humanity. We are sometimes told that computers couldn't simulate feeling depressed or falling in love or having a sense of humor. But as far as simulation is concerned you can program your computer to print out "I am depressed," "I love Sally," or "Ha, ha," as easily as you can program it to print out "$3 \times 3 = 9$." The real mistake is to suppose that simulation is duplication, and that mistake is the same regardless of what mental states we are talking about.

A third mistake, basic to all the others, is the idea that if a computer can simulate having a certain mental state then we have the same grounds for supposing it really has that mental state as we have for supposing that human beings have that state. But we know from the Chinese room argument as well as from biology that this simple-minded behaviorism of the Turing test is mistaken.

Until computers and robots become as common as cars and until people are able to program and use them as easily as they now drive cars we are likely to continue to suffer from a certain mythological conception of digital computers. . . .

DISCUSSION QUESTIONS

1. Reconstruct and evaluate Searle's Chinese room argument in the form of an argument from analogy. Be sure to state his conclusion as precisely as you can.

2. Is Searle's analogy undermined by the fact that computers are much faster than any person in a Chinese room? Why or why not?

3. Could any future developments of more sophisticated computers (such as computers that can reprogram themselves) undermine Searle's argument? Why or why not?

4. Could any future discoveries about how the brain works (such as that brains work just like computers) undermine Searle's argument? Why or why not?

5. Searle admits that, in a "trivial sense brains, like everything else, are digital computers." Does this admission weaken his argument? Why or why not?

6. Some defenders of strong AI respond that, even if the person in the Chinese room does not understand Chinese, the system consisting of the person, room, and manual together does understand Chinese. Is this "systems reply" plausible? Why or why not?

7. Some opponents reply that Searle's Chinese room would have understanding if it had arms and legs so that it could move around as well as a television camera so that it could perceive its environment. Is this "robot reply" plausible? Why or why not?

8. Some critics charge that, given Searle's requirements, we cannot know whether other people have minds, because we cannot see whether they mean anything by the symbols they put out. Is Searle really committed to such a skeptical view? Why or why not?

9. Suppose that a friend of yours for many years is seriously injured in an accident and the doctors discover that she is made from wires, transistors, and so on. Would this be sufficient to show that your "friend" never really thought or felt anything? Why or why not?

10. Suppose that you are seriously injured in an accident and the doctors discover that *you* are made from wires, transistors, and so on. Would this convince you that you had never really thought or felt anything? If your answer to this question is different from your answer to the previous question, explain why.

11. Searle predicts that, "As computers and robots become more common, . . . people will take computers for what they are, namely useful machines." Do you agree? Why or why not?

CREDITS

This page constitutes an extension of the copyright page. We have made every effort to trace the ownership of all copyrighted material and to secure permission from copyright holders. In the event of any question arising as to the use of any material, we will be pleased to make the necessary corrections in future printings. Thanks are due to the following authors, publishers, and agents for permission to use the material indicated.

Chapter 1. 7: The Far Side by Gary Larson © 1994 FarWorks, Inc. All Rights Reserved. Used with permission. **21:** The Far Side by Gary Larson © 1996 FarWorks, Inc. All Rights Reserved. Used with permission.

Chapter 2. 32: Garfield © 1999 Paws, Inc. Reprinted with permission of Universal Press Syndicate. All rights reserved. **40:** Farcus reprinted by permission of LaughingStock Licensing Inc. **42:** Robin Lakoff, *Language and Woman's Place* (New York: Harper & Row, 1975), 23–25. Used by permission of the author.

Chapter 4. 77: *Dartmouth*: Letter to the Editor. "Greeks Should be Co-Ed" by Andrew Beebe, September 23, 1992. Used by permission of Andrew Beebe. **79:** Mario Cuomo, "Religious Belief and Public Morality: A Catholic Governor's Perspective," *Notre Dame Journal of Law, Ethics, and Public Policy*, Vol. 1 (1984), pp. 13–31. **83:** Andrew Sullivan, "Dead End—Cuomo's Abortion Contortion," *The New Republic*, May 6, 1991. Copyright © 1991 *The New Republic*. Reprinted with permission. **86:** From Equal Exchange. Advertisement. Copyright © 1997, 1998, 1999. Used by permission of Equal Exchange, Inc. **87:** © Land's End, Inc. Used with permission. **88:** John Russell, "Is Eakins our Greatest Painter?" *New York Times*, June 6, 1982, pp. 1, 31. Copyright © 1982 by The New York Times Co. Reprinted by permission. **88:** Robert Redford, "A Piece of 'God's Handiwork'," *Washington Post*, November 25, 1997, p. A19. Used by permission. **90:** Martin Esslin, "Beyond the Wasteland: What American TV Can Learn from the BBC," *Boston Review* vol. 7, no. 5, October 1982, pp. 13–19. **92:** Paul Davies, "Life (and Death) on Mars," *New York Times*, January 15, 2004, p. A33. Copyright © 2004 by The New York Times Co. Reprinted by permission. **93:** Paul Goodman, "A Proposal to Abolish Grading," from *Compulsory Miseducation and the Community of Schools* by Paul Goodman, copyright © 1962, 1964 by Paul Goodman. Used by permission of Random House, Inc. **95:** Charlie Buttrey, "Three Fallacies about Gun Rights," *Valley News*, August 29, 2001. Reprinted by permission of Charlie Buttrey.

Chapter 5. 126: Stanley Smith, "A Mere Matter of Deduction," from *Five-Minute Whodunits*. Copyright © 1997 by Stanley Smith. Reprinted with permission of Sterling Publishing Co., Inc., NY, NY. **127:** Stanley Smith, "Murder in a London Flat," from *Five-Minute Whodunits*. Copyright © 1997 by Stanley Smith. Reprinted with permission of Sterling Publishing Co., Inc., NY, NY. **128:** Stanley Smith, "A Theft at the Art Museum," from *Five-Minute Whodunits*. Copyright © 1997 by Stanley Smith. Reprinted with permission of Sterling Publishing Co., Inc., NY, NY. **128:** Stanley Smith, "Trivia and Significa," from *Five-Minute Whodunits*. Copyright © 1997 by Stanley Smith. Reprinted with permission of Sterling Publishing Co., Inc., NY, NY.

Chapter 6. 155: Farcus reprinted by permission of LaughingStock Licensing Inc.

Chapter 9. 269: Michael Downey, "A Gnawing Question is Answered," *Toronto Star*, October 10, 1999. Reprinted by permission of the author. **285:** David W. Fraser and Joseph McDade, "Legionellosis," *Scientific American*, October 1979. Reprinted by permission of Scientific American. **294:** Freidrich Nietzsche, *Twilight of the Idols: Or, How to Philosophize with a Hammer* and *The Anti-Christ*, trans. by R.J. Hollingdale (Penguin Classics, 1968). Copyright © 1968 R.J. Hollindale. Reprinted by permission of Penguin Group.

Chapter 11. 340: Non Sequitur reprinted by permission of Universal Press Syndicate. **352:** Farcus reprinted by permission of LaughingStock Licensing Inc. **358:** Frank and Ernest copyright © 2000 by Tom Thaves. Reprinted by permission. **365:** Burton Leiser, "Homosexuality and Natural Law," pp. 52–57 in *Liberty, Justice, and Morals: Contemporary Value Conflicts*, 3rd ed. Copyright © 1986. Reprinted by permission of Pearson Education, Inc., Upper Saddle River, NJ.

Chapter 15. 497: Don Marquis, "Why Abortion Is Immoral," *The Journal of Philosophy*, vol. 86, no. 4 (April 1989), pp. 183–202. Reprinted by permission. **507:** Judith Jarvis Thomson, "A Defense of Abortion," *Philosophy and Public Affairs* 1, no. 1 (Fall 1971), pp. 47–66.